W9-BVJ-080

THE
GANG
INTERVENTION
HANDBOOK

Arnold P. Goldstein
C. Ronald Huff
Editors

Research Press • 2612 North Mattis Avenue • Champaign, Illinois 61821

Advisory Editor, Frederick H. Kanfer

To Susan S., with special affection and deep admiration

—A. P. G.

To Pat, my wife and best friend for the past 25 years

—C. R. H.

Contents

Figures and Tables

FIGURES

TABLES

Preface

In recent years, youth gangs in the United States have grown in number, location, age span of membership, diversity of cultural origin, complexity of structure, degree of drug involvement, and, especially, level of violence. In companion with these several structural and behavior changes, the nature of the gang intervention process has changed also. Particularly in response to concerns about drugs and violence, older detached worker and social infusion approaches have been increasingly replaced by interventions dominated by the criminal justice system—suppression, deterrence, and incarceration. Yet gangs and gang-associated problems continue to grow, largely unabated. We believe it is time for another intervention strategy to prevail.

Gangs may involve older and younger youths; core and fringe members; males and females; Caucasians, African Americans, Latinos, Asians, and others; very, moderately, and mildly aggressive youths; those who are and who are not selling and/or using drugs; youths with or without family and community encouragement to join a neighborhood gang; youths who joined volitionally or hesitantly or under coercion. To respond to such great diversity with a single intervention strategy, *any* single strategy, seems both naive and foolish. Instead, we join Spergel and Curry (see chapter 12) and others who more appropriately have called for a *comprehensive* gang intervention strategy, a strategy tactically implemented by judiciously and prescriptively offering different youths different interventions and intervention combinations as a function of the several demographic, structural, and behavioral youth and gang qualities just noted. The present book seeks to provide the concrete means by which such a strategy may be carried out.

The chapters that follow provide a state-of-the-art description of gang intervention programming today and more than a peek at what it might consist of tomorrow. Part I, Introduction, sets the stage. Patterns of ganging and gang intervention in the United States are described, as are efforts to date of a preventive nature.

In large measure, to this point in our society's efforts to confront gang problems, interventions employed have originated within such professional fields as social work, sociology, criminology, and criminal justice. We feel the potential value of psychology-based interventions has been comparatively ignored. Part II, Psychological Interventions, seeks to correct this omission. Most of the psychological interventions thus described optimally target individual gang youths or youths at risk for gang involvement.

Part III, Contextual Interventions, broadens the target. The chapters included here acknowledge that not only gang youths themselves but also the several contexts in which they function must be the focus of intervention efforts. Thus, home, school, employment, and community-level approaches are both described and evaluated.

Because illegal and antisocial behaviors do constitute a significant portion of gang youth behavior, criminal justice interventions—police, prosecutorial, correctional—must also be a significant part of a comprehensive intervention strategic mix. Part IV includes chapters devoted to these types of intervention. Yes, we strongly believe they have been and are being overused in the United States today. No, they cannot be eliminated. We prefer a *balanced* approach that provides protection from those posing a "clear and present danger" while emphasizing prevention and intervention as the most productive long-term approaches.

For many gang youths, comprehensive programming in its optimal form would, therefore, include meaningful participation in several types of interventions —psychological, contextual, or criminal justice. In conducting all such interventions, it is absolutely essential that interveners deal with gang youths in a manner fully responsive to the diverse cultural meanings of gang membership and participation. It is also necessary that we address the macrolevel social and economic forces that make youths susceptible to gangs and crime—poverty, the growth of the urban underclass, racism, and the failure of our social, economic, and political institutions to cope with the reality that the illegitimate opportunities available to our young people are often more compelling and realistically attainable than the legitimate opportunities we would like them to pursue. Both cultural sensitivity and the public policy requisites of the gang intervention process are addressed in Part V, Special Intervention Parameters.

It is our hope that this book's detailed articulation of gang intervention programming will provide a menu from which to select those interventions most likely to assist any given youth or gang to move away from antisocial life-styles toward attitudes, behaviors, and commitments that are both prosocial and personally satisfying.

PART I

Introduction

CHAPTER 1

Gangs in the United States

C. Ronald Huff

INTRODUCTION

The phrase *gangs in the United States* used to refer primarily to gangs in New York, Chicago, and Los Angeles. That is no longer the case. Although gangs have existed in the United States since the late 19th century (Asbury, 1927), the recent proliferation of gangs in cities from the East Coast to Hawaii has received increasing attention from the mass media and from scholarly researchers. Gang research in the United States dates back to Thrasher's (1927) classic work, and seven decades later the most recent "new wave" of gangs is being chronicled by such researchers as Klein and Maxson (1989); Klein, Maxson, and Cunningham (1991); Hagedorn (1987, 1988); Vigil (1988); Vigil and Yun (1990); Taylor (1990a, 1990b); Chin (1986, 1990a, 1990b); Fagan (1989, 1990); Moore (1978, 1985); Campbell (1984, 1990); Jankowski (1991); and Huff (1989, 1990).

Who are these new gangs? How new are they? Who joins them and why? What functions do they fulfill? How much diffusion has occurred? How have gangs evolved? What linkages, if any, are there between gangs and drugs? These are some of the important questions being discussed nationally by policymakers, researchers, and the public. We will explore these and other issues as we survey the changing landscape of gangs in the United States, examine the diffusion of youth gangs throughout the nation, and set the stage for our discussion of the need for appropriate, culturally sensitive policies and programs that address both prevention and intervention.

Media accounts of gangs and gang-related crime often fail to distinguish among different types of groups, or collectivities, with distinctive dynamics, values, member characteristics, and organizational structures. In addition to youth gangs, these groups include motorcycle gangs, prison gangs, drug gangs, hate groups such as the neo-Nazi "skinheads," and even satanic/ritualistic/occult groups. It is not our intention to survey all of these very different types of groups. Instead, we will focus on youth gangs.

DEVELOPMENTAL AND DEFINITIONAL ISSUES

One of the classic questions posed about gangs has always been, How does one tell the difference between a group and a gang? Although no single definition of *gang* has ever received approval by consensus, historic events have now obliged us to confront a second question even as we continue to wrestle with the old one. The new question forced upon us is, How does one tell the difference between a gang and organized crime? The lines between the two have blurred in the past few years as gang behavior has changed and as new criminal organizations have arisen, often composed either of immigrant groups or of hard-core, sophisticated, highly lethal street gangs that are often making significant profits via drug sales and that may sometimes approximate what Carl Taylor (1990a, 1990b) calls "corporate gangs." *Youth gangs* or *street gangs* used to denote primarily groups of adolescent males involved in delinquent activity (mostly gang fights and turf battles with each other) as part of their everyday lives. That is no longer the case. The new gangs increasingly include young adults and are involved in more violent and sophisticated crimes. Likewise, *organized crime* used to refer to adult-run criminal enterprises that were sophisticated, well organized, and businesslike—attributes that may now also characterize certain activities of some youth gangs, though perhaps to a lesser extent.

To illustrate how blurred the definitional distinctions have become, consider the example of the Jamaican posses, which import and distribute drugs without relying on any "middlemen." Although these posses are frequently discussed in the same context as youth gangs, they are more like organized crime groups because they are made up of adults and control such business activities as importation and distribution. Moreover, their agenda appears to be more heavily focused on the drug business. Youth gang members, in contrast, may be involved in drug distribution either on their own (without direct gang involvement) or as one among many gang activities, both economic and noneconomic.

Horowitz (1990) has suggested that we should not prematurely narrow our definition of gang but should keep it pluralistic and dynamic, recognizing (a) that there is little likelihood of consensus anyway, (b) that we have discovered—and are still discovering—many differences among gangs, and (c) that the sources of our data significantly influence our respective definitions. To clarify our own view, we offer the following descriptions of two ideal-typical organizational types, recognizing that the lines between them may blur increasingly and that redefinition may be required.

Youth gang: A collectivity consisting primarily of adolescents and young adults who (a) interact frequently with one another; (b) are frequently and deliberately involved in illegal activities; (c) share a common collective identity that is usually, but not always, expressed through a gang name; and (d) typically express that identity by adopting certain symbols and/or claiming control over certain "turf" (persons, places, things, and/or economic markets).

Organized crime group: A collectivity consisting primarily of adults who (a) interact frequently with one another; (b) are frequently and deliberately involved in illegal activities directed toward economic gain, primarily through the provision of illegal goods and services; and (c) generally have better defined leadership and organizational structure than does the youth gang.

These definitions draw several principal distinctions. First, the composition of the membership tends to differ significantly, with youth gangs consisting primarily of adolescents and young adults, whereas organized crime groups are composed primarily of adults. The economic activities also differ: The organized crime group concentrates almost exclusively on economic gain through the provision of illegal goods and services—an *organizational* (collective) activity that is closely tied to the purpose of the group's existence. By way of contrast, drug sales by youth gang members tend to involve *individuals* (perhaps many of them) rather than the entire gang and commonly represent only one of many activities, legal and illegal, in which the gang and its members are involved. Such illegal economic activities are generally not central to the gang's reason for existence. Instead, given that gang members typically come from the urban underclass, these activities may represent a way of addressing members' economic needs—one kind of need among many that the gang exists to serve.

Terms such as *street gangs* or *drug gangs* seem to be variants of these two definitions, but they need qualification. If the term *drug gang* has a use, it may be to describe a gang that is currently specializing in drug selling but that consists primarily of adolescents and young adults who are not controlling the importation of the drug or its associated marketplace. Otherwise, the group would be indistinguishable from our organized crime group. Likewise, the term *street gang* seems to imply a locus of operation rather than distinguishing activities. We assume that, in general, street gangs are virtually the same as youth gangs as we define them, though often with a somewhat older mix of gang members.

Finally, we recognize that some people object to the inclusion of crime in a functional definition of gangs because "that is what we are trying to explain." We reject this argument and do not find it tautological to include the element of crime in our definition. Scholars have disagreed over this point for a long time, just as there has been disagreement over whether we ought to rely so heavily on legislatures for our definition of crime (an intentional act that violates the criminal code without an acceptable defense or justification). Nonetheless, just as we prefer to characterize as deviance (not crime) behavior that violates social norms but not criminal laws, we prefer to characterize as groups those collectivities whose behavior does not violate the law and as deviant groups (not gangs) those collectivities whose behavior violates social norms but not criminal laws. To extend the term *gang* to groups that do not commit crime would blur the distinction so that the term *youth gang*, for example, would become virtually synonymous with *youth group*, thus losing its meaning for criminologists, law enforcement agencies (which do not generally consider it their business to become involved with groups unless they commit crimes), and policymakers concerned with understanding and controlling crime and delinquency.

In analyzing youth gangs, it is important to acknowledge that it is normal and healthy for adolescents to want to be with their peers. In fact, adolescents who are loners often tend to be maladjusted. Because adolescents go to dances together, party together, shop together (and, in many cases, shop*lift* together), it should not be surprising that some of them join together in one type of social group known as a gang. Group experience, then, is a familiar and normative phenomenon in adolescent subculture, and gangs represent an extreme manifestation of that age-typical emphasis on being together and belonging to something.

Gangs are certainly not unique to the United States. In fact, most societies seem to have a term that corresponds, at least loosely, to our own term *gang*. Whether it is the *chimpira* of Japan, the *raggare* of Sweden, the Dutch *nozem*, the Italian *vitelloni*, the *stilyagi* of the USSR, the Yugoslavian *tapkaroschi*, or their counterparts in many other nations, there is usually some way of designating youth gangs. Many of these nations and cultures also distinguish between gangs and organized crime along the lines discussed earlier (for example, Japan has both *chimpira* and organized crime [*Yakuza*]). Each of these nations also has its own youth culture within which youth gangs must be viewed.

Although gang research (see, for example, Campbell, 1984, 1990) indicates that there are some true female gangs, as well as many female gang "groupies" (females whose gang connection is largely a by-product of their "belonging" to male gang members, a connection that both genders value),[1] the vast majority of gang members in the United States are males. More specifically, they are 14- to 24-year-old males, though the age range is typically from about 10 to over 30. Given this age range, we prefer the term *youth gang* because it encompasses both adolescents and young adults. In many cities, the average age of gang members who are arrested is in the early 20s, so it is accurate to say that these gangs represent a mix of teens and young adults. The predominance of young males in gangs may be attributable, at least in part, to the fact that many gang members come from female-headed households with no male adult role model present in the home and, often, no acceptable adult male role model involved in the youth's life.

The proportion of such female-headed families in the United States has grown dramatically in recent years. For example, among African American families, the proportion that is female headed rose from approximately 18 percent in 1940 to more than 40 percent by the 1980s. Moreover, approximately half of all African American families with children under 18 are now female headed (Wilson, 1987). This fact has direct implications for youth gang membership. The young males' unmet need for "male bonding" is all too readily met by local youth gangs. A need that could just as well be met in a positive, prosocial manner all too often is met through socialization into a gang, with its attendant exposure to delinquent or criminal value systems.

Though many gang members do come from intact nuclear families (Jankowski, 1991), the gang can serve as a surrogate extended family for adolescents who do not see their own families as meeting their needs for belonging, nurturance, and acceptance. Some contemporary youth gangs have even been known to accompany a member to the local cemetery and grieve with him on the anniversary of a family member's death, an action that we have always seen as a private, family function. Rather than viewing gangs as simply young criminals, then, we must (without romanticizing them) understand that gangs often respond to some of their members' important needs—such as support in grief, male bonding, and protection from rival gangs—though frequently in a socially and legally unacceptable manner. In fact, if we are to make progress in controlling gang-related crime, we must learn from the gangs. That is, we must analyze the sociological, psychological, and economic functions of gangs and see how gangs meet individual needs that we, as a society, are not sufficiently meeting. We shall revisit this issue in our discussion of policy and intervention in chapter 17.

THE NEW GANGS: DIFFUSION, DIVERSITY, AND DRUGS

Because Los Angeles, New York, and Chicago are our nation's largest media centers, there has been a tendency to identify gangs with those cities in particular. Whether it was Chicago's Vice Lords and Black Gangster Disciples or the Crips and the Bloods of Los Angeles, each of the past four decades has witnessed some prototype supergang (or rival supergangs) that has drawn national media attention. Recently, that focus has shifted westward, with Los Angeles supplanting New York City as the nation's media capital and, coincidentally, as its gang capital as well: Law enforcement agencies currently estimate more than 100,000 Crips and Bloods in greater Los Angeles alone and count as gang related more than 500 homicides annually.[2]

Popular culture, embodied in films, novels, rap songs, and plays, also reflects this shift. Portrayals of gangs and gang activities have evolved from the classic *West Side Story* and *The Warriors* (both dealing with New York City gangs) to *Colors* (Dennis Hopper's film about Los Angeles's Crips and Bloods) to the more recent (1991) films, *New Jack City* and *Boyz N the Hood*. The debuts of the latter three films were associated with gang-related violence inside and outside movie theaters across the nation, primarily because rival gangs and "wannabes" (marginal gang associates attempting to impress the hard-core members) were attracted to these films and found themselves on the same turf at the same time.

Gangs have evolved from the classic street-corner, neighborhood, turf-oriented gangs like that chronicled in Whyte's (1943) classic study of an Italian slum neighborhood in Boston to contemporary gangs that may claim as turf their girlfriends, designated shopping malls, and local skating rinks. Schools, which used to be a sort of neutral zone largely immune from gang warfare, are now the scene of gang battles and recruiting wars. Students passing through school corridors may be intimidated by gang members who claim to control the school. They may be coerced into joining a gang, beaten if they are perceived to belong to a rival gang, or, at the very least, have their lunch money extorted for protection from harm.

Furthermore, recent research suggests that one unintended consequence of court-ordered busing, initiated to redress racial segregation, has been the presence of rival gangs in the same schools (Hagedorn, 1988; Huff, 1989). Rather than neighborhood gangs that are reflected in neighborhood schools, we now see gang members from certain parts of the city who are bused across town to schools where they encounter rivals from whom they need protection.[3] Schools were never organized to deal with this situation, and many of them are struggling with new safety and security issues. (See chapters 7 and 8 for more detailed discussion of the schools.)

Another evolutionary development has been gang migration (actually gang member migration, as it is individual gang members, and not entire gangs, who are migrating). In 1986, popular wisdom had it that Los Angeles gangs, especially the Crips, were migrating across the United States and setting up franchises to distribute drugs. Research on Ohio gangs, however, gave reason for skepticism about this claim: From 1986 to 1988, every identified Ohio gang leader who had moved to Ohio from Los Angeles, Chicago, or Detroit was in Ohio because his parent(s) had moved there (Huff, 1989). In any case, several of these youths had been involved in gangs in Los Angeles, Chicago, or Detroit, and their experience made it relatively easy for them to start gangs in Ohio and to assume leadership roles in their new gangs.

During the period from 1986 to 1988, field research never produced any evidence of a continuing, direct connection between the new Ohio gangs and the cities of origin of their respective leaders. There were no Ohio "chapters" of Los Angeles gangs, for example, despite persistent rumors to the contrary.[4] This finding (Huff, 1989) confirmed the results of studies in other locations that were "non-core" gang cities, such as Evanston, Illinois (Rosenbaum & Grant, 1983), and Milwaukee (Hagedorn, 1987). Field research in these cities invalidated local rumors by demonstrating that the local gangs consisted of local youths, although in both cities—as in Ohio—gang graffiti and other gang symbols were decidedly influenced by Chicago gang graffiti and symbols.

The past several years, however, have seen a surge in gang migration. By 1989, members of Los Angeles gangs had been identified by law enforcement agencies in cities throughout the nation.[5] Many of these gang members have been involved in drug trafficking (U. S. Department of Justice, 1989). In Ohio, for example, Los Angeles gang members have been arrested in cities as small as Hamilton, Lorain, and Canton (and they were not in Canton to visit the pro football hall of fame!). In addition, drug trafficking involving Detroit gangs in Ohio has impacted on so many cities and towns along the Interstate 75 corridor (Detroit-Cincinnati) that the freeway has become known in some circles as " 'Caine Lane" (referring to cocaine). Moreover, Jamaican posses, which we classify as organized crime groups rather than as youth gangs, have begun operating in both Cleveland[6] and Columbus, primarily via a drug pipeline that originates in Jamaica and uses New York as a transshipment point to distribute drugs to Ohio and other markets.

Undeniably, gang member migration has increased markedly in the past 5 years. Why? On the basis of field research on gangs, interviews with fellow gang researchers and with Los Angeles and other law enforcement officials, and information from the Drug Enforcement Administration, there appear to be at least three important reasons:

1. Competition for drug turf has been less intense in the nation's smaller cities than in Los Angeles (where the competition has sometimes been on a block-by-block basis) or in Detroit.

2. There is greater potential profit to be made in the smaller cities: One "rock" of crack cocaine sells for as little as 3 to 5 dollars in Los Angeles or Detroit but will bring from 15 to 25 dollars in smaller Midwestern cities.

3. Because the crack cocaine problem is relatively recent in smaller cities, there has been less intensive law enforcement pressure on the drug trafficking networks. This, however, is changing rapidly as smaller cities recognize the extent of their drug problems and step up their law enforcement efforts.

Carl Taylor (1990b) relates gang member migration to an entrepreneurial spirit: "When young Detroiters invade the state of Ohio, they are in pursuit of the American dream. That dream may appear distorted to middle-class or working-class America, yet it is truly the spirit of American entrepreneurship" (p. 115). How do incoming gang members who are trafficking in drugs get a foothold in the local community? Typically, they base themselves with a local contact with whom they live and work (in the contact's home or, often, in a local motel or hotel) or else they use one of at least three other strategies we have identified and named:

1. *Double Down, or the Rock Game.* These are variants of the same strategy. The new trafficker either (a) offers a local person twice as much supply as he is accustomed to getting for a given dollar investment or (b) gives the person 10 rocks of crack cocaine to sell, with the incentive that the person need only pay the supplier for, say, 8 rocks, keeping the remaining profit for himself. Obviously, an entrepreneurially minded amateur might be enticed by such a nest egg, especially if he is unemployed and wants to accumulate money faster than he can with a fast-food restaurant job. The similarity between such strategies to hook drug *dealers* and strategies used to hook drug *users* is quite clear. In both cases, these generous introductory offers don't last very long!

2. *The Welfare Mother Scam.* This strategy involves approaching a mother receiving public assistance and offering to pay her rent and/or supply her with drugs in exchange for the use of her house. She may not even be told the purpose for which the house is to be used. In many such cases, a time comes when the gang member/trafficker stops paying the rent. A not uncommon scenario is for the woman to protest and demand that the agreement be kept, at which point she or her children may be assaulted or even killed. At the very least, the woman and her children end up feeling like prisoners in their own home. Some women, hooked on drugs, have even agreed to exchange sex for drugs. (In Los Angeles they are cynically called "rock stars" or "hubba whores" by those who use and abuse them.)

3. *Scare 'Em Off.* One strategy to discourage competitors for drug turf is to intimidate them into submission with brutal beatings, heinous murders, mutilations, and other incidents of dramatic violence designed to shock

competitors and enemies. This strategy has especially been associated with Jamaican posses, but it is used by youth gangs, drug gangs, and organized crime groups in connection with drug trafficking and the acquisition and protection of drug markets.

It would be misleading to imply that all gangs or all gang members are involved in drug distribution. That is not the case. In one of the best studies of the connection between gangs and drugs, researcher Jeffrey Fagan (1990) reached the following conclusion:

> Although gangs may be distinct social networks that are involved in substance use and crime, there appears to be diversity among gang members and gangs in their participation in these behaviors. Both gang and nongang youths are involved in serious delinquency and substance use, although perhaps fewer nongang youths participate in these behaviors and do so less often. (p. 210)

Earlier, Fagan (1989) identified four distinct types of gangs, one of which (the "organization gang") manifests extensive involvement in crime, drug use, and drug sales. This type of gang, which claimed the allegiance of 28 percent of Fagan's sample of gang members, demonstrates the linkage between gangs and drug-related crime.

Just as it would be misleading to imply that all gang members are involved in drug trafficking, it would be inaccurate to imply that drug trafficking in the United States depends primarily on gangs. In a recent study of Los Angeles, the city where that connection has been implied most often, Klein et al. (1991) found that, although many gang members were involved in crack distribution, trafficking in that drug was not primarily a street gang phenomenon. Nonetheless, gang members are extensively involved in drug trafficking. As James F. Short (1990) has observed in comparing the new wave of gangs with previous gangs in the United States, "much has changed today, largely for the worse. . . . There are more, and more lethal, guns available. Drug abuse and trafficking have become more widespread, contributing to the devastation of community life" (pp. 227–228).

Other empirical data support the gangs-drugs connection.[7] For example, Spergel (1991) found that of 276 gang members on probation in San Diego County, 75 percent had at some time been convicted of drug offenses. Similarly, Hagedorn (1991), in following up on the status of the 37 founding members of Milwaukee's three African American gangs, discovered that fully 59 percent of them had "graduated" from the gang into drug posses or small drug trafficking businesses during the preceding 5 years, whereas only 19 percent were working in full-time jobs. The drug market, perceived as a lucrative equal opportunity employer, does not discriminate against gang members, even though they may be dropouts and members of racial minority groups. The most common scenario appears to involve *individual* gang members in drug distribution networks that are neither gang controlled nor organized gang activities. Rather than wearing their colors, an act that often facilitated identification by law enforcement authorities and school personnel, individuals now tend to act more covertly and are less readily identifiable.

Violence over drug turf is no longer confined to the streets and barrios of Los Angeles or to Chicago's Cabrini Green or Robert Taylor Homes housing projects. The destabilizing drug economies in the cities (and even regional drug economies, associated with source cities dominating each region) spark violent conflicts pitting locals against Los Angeles Crips or Bloods; Jamaican posses; Detroit's Young Boys, Incorporated; the Miami Boys; the GI (Gary, Indiana) Boys; or other regional or local variants. Drug markets that were formerly regulated and controlled, largely by organized crime families, have now become deregulated through the incarceration, death, or retirement of many of these key organized crime figures. Given extensive demand for drugs, new suppliers have begun to fill the vacuum created by the demise of the organized crime figures. It appears that gang members are playing an important role in this development, even though they do not dominate or control the drug markets.

A CLOSER LOOK AT THE NEW GANGS

According to the U. S. Senate (1986) Governmental Affairs Committee's Permanent Subcommittee on Investigations and the U. S. General Accounting Office (1990), five "nontraditional criminal groups" are now posing significant challenges to our society and its efforts to control crime and drugs. These five groups consist of Colombian drug traffickers, Jamaican posses, Chinese gangs, Vietnamese gangs, and Los Angeles street gangs. The absence of a national agenda, the problems of outdated investigative techniques and cultural barriers, and the lack of cooperation and coordination among agencies were cited as major impediments to success in controlling the criminal activities of these groups (U. S. General Accounting Office, 1990). We would add that the scarcity of sound research has also hindered our understanding and our ability to develop appropriate policies and effective intervention strategies.

Three of the five nontraditional criminal groups—Los Angeles street gangs, Chinese gangs, and Vietnamese gangs—fall within the focus of this chapter. Each deserves a closer look to highlight its unique aspects as well as its commonalities with other gangs in the United States.

Los Angeles Street Gangs

At present, the two most notorious gang names in the United States are the Crips and the Bloods (aka Pirus). They are important not only because of their size, their violence, and their involvement in drug distribution but also because members of these gangs have been showing up in nearly every part of the nation in the past 5 years. What began as a Los Angeles problem has quickly evolved into a nationwide problem impacting scores of cities from coast to coast.

A profile of the Crips and the Bloods can be drawn from scholarly research, mass media accounts, law enforcement reports, and personal interviews conducted with law enforcement and investigative personnel over the past 5 years. Both the Crips and the Bloods began as primarily African American and Hispanic local (south Los Angeles) street gangs around 1969. The Crips were first; then the Bloods developed to provide protection against the Crips. In contrast with the image portrayed in the movie *Colors* (reasonably accurate at that time), there is little loyalty now within these gangs. Crips will kill other Crips and Bloods will kill other Bloods if there is drug profit at stake, for example. There can be nearly as much variance and conflict between different "sets" of the same gang as there is between rival gangs.

Members of these gangs generally range in age from the mid-teens to the mid-30s. Whereas the Crips and the Bloods have existed for 23 years, some other gangs in the United States (most notably the Hispanic gangs of Los Angeles) have been around for most of the past century, so there are multigenerational gang families and a broad range of membership, or at least loose affiliation. The Crips and the Bloods do not have centralized leadership but instead are organized into numerous sets (individual "gangs within gangs") usually based on (a) age and sophistication and/or (b) geographic location: For instance, "Junior Crips" refers to an age-graded set; "Hoover Crips" and "Rollin' 60s Crips" refer to Los Angeles street names or neighborhoods.

Although terms for gang strata vary around the country, most of the Los Angeles gangs have at least three major groupings, roughly corresponding to (a) leaders (often these are the OGs or Original Gangsters), (b) hard-cores, and (c) wannabes (who want to be hard-core gang members). Leaders and hard-core members are fully committed to the gang, including its delinquent and criminal activities. They have generally been with the gang for a considerable time and are somewhat older and more sophisticated. They would *never* associate with other gangs. The marginal associates, or wannabes, on the other hand, are not fully committed to the gang or to gang life and its agenda. They are usually experimenting with gangs and might even be seen in the company of rival gangs at different times. They are trying it out to see if they like it and if they fit in.

Gangs such as the Crips and the Bloods also have distinctive clothing and symbols that designate their affiliations. Children have been murdered simply because they were wearing the wrong color hat, handkerchief, or shoelaces (red for Bloods, blue or black for Crips) and were mistaken for the enemy. Increasingly, the clothing of choice includes expensive warm-up or jogging suits (for example, L. A. Dodger blue or Oakland Raiders black for Crips; Cincinnati Reds red for Bloods). In fact, the symbolic meaning of clothing can be as subtle as British Knights clothing, worn for the "BK" logo on this line of merchandise. The BK logo is a fashionable way to advertise that one is a Blood Killer (a loyal Crip who will kill or has killed Bloods) in a gangland that is not that far removed from Hollywood and the chic shops of Rodeo Drive. Expensive clothing, 150 dollar sneakers, beepers, and flashy cars imply that one is "rollin' " (making money by dealing drugs), whether or not that is actually the case.[8]

Los Angeles gangs also use graffiti distinctive in both content and form to mark their turf,[9] celebrate their perceived dominance of that area, and sometimes put down rival gangs (for example, by crossing out the rival gang's name, writing over it, or writing the rival name upside down). Such put-downs are frequently the immediate precipitants of violent assaults ("paybacks"). Los Angeles, for example, has been recording an average of 500 to 700 gang-related homicides per year, and even though the Los Angeles Police Department and Sheriff's Department's definition of *gang-related* is much broader than, for example, Chicago's (Maxson & Klein, 1990), there is unquestionably a great deal of gang-related violence in the Los Angeles metropolitan area. Moreover, about half of the victims of gang-related homicides in Los Angeles continue to be innocent citizens, including many children.

Chinese Gangs

We are only now beginning to acquire systematic knowledge about Chinese street gangs and Chinese organized crime. Before 1965, crime rates in Chinese subcommunities were, with rare exceptions, quite low (Beach, 1932; MacGill, 1938), and delinquency was unusual as well (Sung, 1977). One of the main reasons for these low rates of crime and delinquency was the fact that, before 1965, there were few Chinese adolescents living in the United States owing to the Chinese Exclusion Act of 1882 and the National Origins Act of 1924 (Fessler, 1983; Sung, 1979).

According to Kwong (1987) and Takagi and Platt (1978), 1965 was the watershed year in Chinese immigration because of the passage of that year's Immigration and Naturalization Act. This legislation established immigration priorities and granted China preferred nation status. Chinese immigration to the United States has grown dramatically in the intervening 25 years, with significant impact on Chinese subcommunities, whose families, district associations, and social agencies were not prepared to help the large number of immigrants adjust to their new communities (Chin, 1977; Huang & Pilisuk, 1977). Crime increased significantly, and Chinese gangs developed in San Francisco, Los Angeles, Boston, Toronto, Vancouver, and New York City. Although by some estimates there are fewer than 2,000 Chinese gang members in the United States, they have been involved in some very serious gang violence and heroin trafficking (Daly, 1983; U. S. Senate, 1986).

Most of our knowledge about Chinese gangs is based on the work of five scholars: Miller (1975); Loo (1976); Robinson and Joe (1980); and, especially, Ko-lin Chin (1986, 1990a, 1990b), whose research provides the basis for this discussion. We know that Chinese gangs are predominantly male (girls hang around with the males and may carry guns for them, but they are not admitted to membership). Most gang members are in their late teens or early 20s, with known ages ranging from 13 to 37. In the 1960s and 1970s most gang members were from Hong Kong, but since the late 1970s, members have also come from China and have included Vietnam-born Chinese as well. Some newly established Chinese gangs have even included Korean youths. All known members to date have been of Asian origin. Other than one Taiwanese gang, all speak Cantonese as the dialect of choice.

The typical Chinese gang includes about 20 to 50 hard-core members, along with some inactives and marginals. Current estimates indicate that New York City has about nine active Chinese gangs, with 200 to 400 total members. Most Chinese gangs have one or two leaders, except for the Ghost Shadows, who have four or five *tai lou* (big brothers) at the top. Next in the hierarchy are the lieutenants or associate leaders. They are in charge of the rank-and-file street soldiers (*ma jai*, or little horses), who control neighborhood turf and commit extortion, robbery, and street violence. The leaders also serve as liaison with the elders of the local *tongs* (community associations), and they receive payment from these elders or from the local gambling houses. Leaders rarely participate in street violence, but they do give orders, provide ammunition, and pay rewards for contract hits that are carried out by "shooters" at the street soldier level.

Initially, most Chinese gang members joined their gangs voluntarily, and they experienced a great deal of camaraderie. The past 15 years, however, have seen a large increase in the use of intimidation and coercion, including assault, in the recruitment of new members. Those targeted for recruitment are often lonely and vulnerable youths who are dropouts, speak little English, appear to have a lot of time on their hands, and seem to have few if any job prospects. A youth who decides to join a Chinese gang goes through an initiation ceremony in which he takes oaths, burns yellow paper, and drinks wine mixed with blood before the altar of General Kwan (a hero of the secret societies known as Triads)[10] and in the presence of the leaders.

A Chinese gang typically has two or more cliques that dislike and distrust each other. Intragang tension and conflict are common, erupting, for example, when one clique perceives that there has been an inequitable distribution of criminal profits. Leaders within gangs constantly plot to have one another killed, and a Chinese gang leader is in fact more likely to be killed by his own associates than by a rival gang (Chin, 1990a). Tong elders also sometimes provoke intragang conflict, which serves to keep the gangs divided rather than united and thus ensures that they will not acquire enough power to challenge the tong's status.

Finally, Chin (1990a) has identified seven unique characteristics that distinguish Chinese gangs from other ethnic gangs:

1. A close association with powerful community organizations

2. Investment in legitimate businesses and a considerable time commitment to business activities

3. National or international networks

4. Heavy influence from Chinese secret societies and the Triads

5. Immediate involvement in serious crime

6. Control of large amounts of money, with monetary profit as the main goal

7. Systematic victimization of local businesses

Vietnamese Gangs

Because of their more recent development in the United States, less is known about Vietnamese gangs than about the others. Our profile of these gangs is based primarily on the research of Vigil and Yun (1990) on Vietnamese gangs in southern California, where nearly half of the country's Vietnamese population lives. We know that the Vietnamese youth gangs, like the Vietnamese communities from which they come, developed in the wake of the immigration following the end of the Vietnam War. Although the initial Vietnamese refugees were relatively well educated, highly urbanized, young, and of high socioeconomic status, the subsequent migration of the "boat people" brought to the United States a large number of poorer, less educated, less urbanized, less employable Vietnamese who were much less prepared to adapt to American society (Bach & Bach, 1980; Grant, 1979; Marsh, 1980; Nguyen & Henkin, 1982; Skinner, 1980).

Whereas the average Asian American household income in 1980 was approximately 22,000 dollars per year (above the national average), the average annual income for Vietnamese households in Los Angeles County was approximately 9,000 dollars in the late 1980s (Larson, 1988). Many Vietnamese immigrants, like their Mexican counterparts, are unfamiliar with their legal rights and work for as little as a dollar an hour in illegal "sweatshops" in the garment industry. Cutbacks in federal assistance and the escalating cost of living in California have combined to create severe economic constraints for these Vietnamese immigrants, who are frequently attracted to the underground economy as a means of survival.

Certain Vietnamese cultural beliefs and traditions have made this population especially vulnerable to exploitation by youth gangs. For example, it is common for Vietnamese to shun banks and keep cash and gold bars in their homes (Berkman, 1984). In addition, they are frequently alienated from law enforcement officials because of their experiences in Southeast Asia, and they often refuse to either report crimes or cooperate in police investigations, fearing reprisals and believing that the police cannot adequately protect them. This, of course, leaves them quite vulnerable to extortion. There is also a significant cultural gap between the Vietnamese and the local police, who only recently have begun recruiting officers who can speak Vietnamese (Morganthau, Contreras, Lam, & Sandza, 1982).

The Vietnamese gangs appear to include primarily youths in their mid- to late teens and early 20s. These youths often refer to themselves as boys, as compared with older Vietnamese involved in organized crime groups such as the Frogmen, the Paratroopers, and the Black Eels. Gang members are often several years older than their officially reported ages; Vietnamese parents commonly underreport their children's ages by several years so that they can enroll in lower grades in school to compensate for their lack of proficiency in English. This practice, however, has led to great embarrassment for many Vietnamese youths, who have often been taunted and ridiculed at school for being in class with younger children.

Such ridicule at school, along with academic failure, lack of acceptance in the community, culture conflict, and racism, creates a great deal of anger and frustration in these youths, who also find it difficult to acquire the material goods touted in the mass media. These several factors appear to heighten their suscepti-bility to gang involvement. A gang can offer a surrogate family, money, recreation, and a sense of autonomy.

Gang members often acquire money via car theft and robbery and, later on, extortion. Vigil and Yun (1990) report that by intimidating other Vietnamese in their own homes, gang members can usually get about 15,000 to 20,000 dollars per residence. Such residential robberies of fellow countrymen may seem para-doxical given the ethnic pride found among the Vietnamese, but Vietnamese gang members prefer to target Vietnamese rather than whites or other ethnic groups who "know a lot of law and don't keep cash [within their homes]" (Vigil & Yun, 1990, p. 158).

The Vietnamese gangs tend to be very pragmatic, not only in their selection of victims but also in their avoidance of visible gang symbols, violent conflict over neighborhood turf ("That's stupid"), and drug dealing (deemed unnecessary because of the ease of residential robbery and undesirable because of high start-up costs). Vigil and Yun (1990) also report that Vietnamese gangs are extremely fluid, claiming no turf, having little or no differentiation of roles within the gang, and allowing members to drift into and out of the gang and even into other gangs. They are also fluid in terms of travel, with informants reporting that they had traveled to many states, committing robberies along the way and sharing one motel room (15 to 20 persons of both genders) rather than renting multiple rooms and thus arousing suspicion (Vigil & Yun, 1990).

Finally, the cautions voiced earlier concerning the need to distinguish between youth gangs and organized crime groups apply to Asian gangs. The media often confuse Vietnamese youth gangs with Asian organized crime groups when in fact there are dramatic differences between the two types of organizations. Specifically, (a) although some individual Vietnamese youth gang members have ties to indi-viduals involved in Asian organized crime groups, those ties are distant and indi-vidualized, not gang related; and (b) Asian organized crime groups have much better defined organizational structure and leadership than do the loosely knit Viet-namese youth gangs (Vigil & Yun, 1990).

GANGS IN THE UNITED STATES: THE CHALLENGE

This overview of the development, diffusion, and diversity of gangs in the United States; the functions they serve for their members; their dynamics; and their complex connection to the nation's drug markets illuminates the challenge ad-dressed by the remainder of this book. That challenge is to generate a comprehen-sive, multidisciplinary knowledge base for the development of effective, culturally sensitive policies and programs that address both prevention and intervention.

The following chapters will address the challenge posed by gangs from a broad, multidisciplinary perspective. Proposed responses range from individual, microlevel interventions to macrolevel social policy treating gangs as a symptom of more basic, underlying, causally prior social and economic forces affecting children and families in our society. We believe that a balanced approach will be required—one that addresses both prevention and intervention, both sticks and carrots, both individuals and groups, both the public and private sectors, both federal and state or local resources, and both the legal and illegal opportunities available to our young people.

NOTES

[1] Although the great majority of female gangs in the United States have been closely linked to male gangs and have often taken their names from those gangs (e.g., the Dynamite Devils and the Dynamite Devil Dolls in Cleveland), a new trend appears to be developing, especially on the East and West Coasts, toward truly autonomous female gangs. This should not be surprising, as greater autonomy for females is an expected result of the women's movement and is manifested in many other ways in our society.

[2] But see Maxson and Klein (1990) for an analysis of Los Angeles's definition of gang-related homicide as compared with Chicago's. The less restrictive Los Angeles definition has a significant impact on the classification of homicides as gang related.

[3] Large-scale, citywide busing has also created other crime-related problems. For example, in many school districts the busing proved so time consuming that the homeroom (attendance) period was moved from first period to second, or even third, period. Some students, bused from other parts of the city and arriving early, have committed multiple breaking-and-entering crimes in the school neighborhood. However, the perpetrator had a perfect alibi by the time attendance was taken, having reported to school in time to be counted as present. Follow-up investigation by law enforcement in such a case is hampered because the offender does not even live in the area of the crime.

[4] For example, the leader of Columbus's largest gang (Crips) in the mid-1980s lived part of the year in Los Angeles with one parent and the rest of the year in Columbus with his other parent. Having become involved in a Los Angeles Crips gang, he recruited a following in Columbus and decided to name his gang Crips as well. However, there was no direct connection, organizationally, between the two gangs. The name simply reflected a name and a tradition familiar to the leader.

[5] Law enforcement authorities in Los Angeles have created an extensive computerized data base containing information about Los Angeles gang members. Other law enforcement agencies around the nation may access this data base when they have questions concerning suspects who they believe may be Los Angeles gang members.

[6] The problem in Cleveland has been great enough that the Cleveland Police Department established a Caribbean Crime Task Force in addition to a gang unit.

[7] A great deal more research is needed on this issue because the relationship between gang involvement and drug trafficking appears quite complicated. Our own assessment is that, although the relationship is certainly not linear, gang members have substantial involvement in drug trafficking networks in many parts of the nation.

[8] There have been many instances in which apparent gang members were actually engaging in a practice known as "false-flagging" (trying to pass as gang members when they were not). Likewise, youths have emulated others who appeared to be "rollin'" (making money by selling drugs). For example, there have been many reports in Cleveland of young males carrying beepers and speaking with a Jamaican accent. Upon further inquiry, it inevitably turns out that these young men are lifelong Cleveland residents and the closest they have come to Jamaica is listening to reggae music!

[9] There are many similarities between the turf-marking behavior of gangs and the territory-marking behavior of certain animals, such as wolves. In addition, the stratification dynamics and competitive behavior of many gangs are quite similar to the dominance and deference rituals of wolves and other animals. Finally, the methods that gang members use to select victims on the street are not unlike those that predators use to select the weakest prey. Although humans are much more complex, ethological research often suggests important similarities between the behavior of humans and that of animals lower in the phylogenetic system of classification. Understanding Darwin also helps in understanding certain aspects of the gang's behavior, especially male dominance and deference rituals and the predatory victimization of "the weak" on the streets.

[10] According to Chin (1990a), Triad refers to a triangle of heaven, earth, and man. Secret Triad societies were formed three centuries ago as vehicles for patriotic Chinese to fight against the oppressive Ch'ing dynasty. In 1912, the Ch'ing government collapsed, and the Republic of China was formed. Since that time, some of these societies have been involved in crime.

REFERENCES

Asbury, H. (1927). *The gangs of New York*. New York: Knopf.

Bach, R. L., & Bach, J. B. (1980). Employment patterns of Southeast Asian refugees. *Monthly Labor Review, 103,* 31–38.

Beach, W. G. (1932). *Oriental crime in California*. Stanford, CA: Stanford University Press.

Berkman, L. (1984, September 30). Banks catering to Asians facing a culture gap. *Los Angeles Times.*

Campbell, A. (1984). *The girls in the gang: A report from New York City*. Oxford: Blackwell.

Campbell, A. (1990). Female participation in gangs. In C. R. Huff (Ed.), *Gangs in America*. Newbury Park, CA: Sage.

Chin, K. (1986). *Chinese Triad societies, tongs, organized crime, and street gangs in Asia and the United States*. Unpublished doctoral dissertation, University of Pennsylvania, Philadelphia.

Chin, K. (1990a). Chinese gangs and extortion. In C. R. Huff (Ed.), *Gangs in America*. Newbury Park, CA: Sage.

Chin, K. (1990b). *Chinese subculture and criminality: Non-traditional crime groups in America*. Westport, CT: Greenwood.

Chin, R. (1977). New York Chinatown today: Community in crisis. *Amerasia Journal, 1*(1), 1–32.

Daly, M. (1983, February). The war for Chinatown. *New York Magazine*, pp. 31–38.

Fagan, J. (1989). The social organization of drug use and drug dealing among urban gangs. *Criminology, 27*, 633–669.

Fagan, J. (1990). Social processes of delinquency and drug use among urban gangs. In C. R. Huff (Ed.), *Gangs in America*. Newbury Park, CA: Sage.

Fessler, L. W. (Ed.). (1983). *Chinese in America: Stereotyped past, changing present*. New York: Vantage.

Grant, B. (1979). *The boat people*. Sydney, Australia: Penguin.

Hagedorn, J. M. (1987). *Final report: Milwaukee Gang Research Project*. Milwaukee: University of Wisconsin—Milwaukee.

Hagedorn, J. M. (1988). *People and folks: Gangs, crime and the underclass in a rustbelt city*. Chicago: Lake View.

Hagedorn, J. M. (1991). *Gangs, neighborhoods, and public policy*. Unpublished manuscript.

Horowitz, R. (1990). Sociological perspectives on gangs: Conflicting definitions and concepts. In C. R. Huff (Ed.), *Gangs in America*. Newbury Park, CA: Sage.

Huang, K., & Pilisuk, M. (1977). At the threshold of the Golden Gate: Special problems of a neglected minority. *American Journal of Orthopsychiatry, 47*, 701–713.

Huff, C. R. (1989). Youth gangs and public policy. *Crime and Delinquency, 35*, 524–537.

Huff, C. R. (Ed.). (1990). *Gangs in America*. Newbury Park, CA: Sage.

Jankowski, M. S. (1991). *Islands in the street: Gangs and American urban society*. Berkeley, CA: University of California Press.

Klein, M. W., & Maxson, C. L. (1989). Street gang violence. In N. A. Weiner & M. E. Wolfgang (Eds.), *Violent crime, violent criminals*. Newbury Park, CA: Sage.

Klein, M. W., Maxson, C. L., & Cunningham, L. C. (1991). "Crack," street gangs, and violence. *Criminology, 29*, 623–650.

Kwong, P. (1987). *The new Chinatown*. New York: Hill & Wang.

Larson, D. (1988, October 23). Honor thy parents. *Los Angeles Times*.

Loo, C. K. (1976). *The emergence of San Francisco Chinese juvenile gangs from the 1950s to the present*. Unpublished master's thesis, San Jose State University, San Jose, CA.

MacGill, H. G. (1938). The Oriental delinquent in the Vancouver juvenile court. *Sociology and Social Research, 12*, 428–438.

Marsh, R. E. (1980). Socioeconomic status of Indochinese refugees in the United States: Progress and problems. *Social Security Bulletin, 43*, 11–12.

Maxson, C. L., & Klein, M. W. (1990). Street gang violence: Twice as great, or half as great? In C. R. Huff (Ed.), *Gangs in America*. Newbury Park, CA: Sage.

Miller, W. B. (1975). *Violence by youth gangs and youth groups as a crime problem in major American cities*. Report to the National Institute for Juvenile Justice and Delinquency Prevention.

Moore, J. W. (1978). *Homeboys: Gangs, drugs, and prison in the barrios of Los Angeles*. Philadelphia: Temple University Press.

Moore, J. W. (1985). Isolation and stigmatization in the development of an underclass: The case of Chicano gangs in East Los Angeles. *Social Problems, 33*(1), 1–10.

Morganthau, T., Contreras, J., Lam, H., & Sandza, R. (1982, August 2). Vietnamese gangs in California. *Newsweek.*

Nguyen, L. T., & Henkin, A. B. (1982). Vietnamese refugees in the United States: Adaptation and transitional status. *Journal of Ethnic Studies, 9*(4), 101–116.

Robinson, N., & Joe, D. (1980). Gangs in Chinatown. *McGill Journal of Education, 15,* 149–162.

Rosenbaum, D. P., & Grant, J. A. (1983). *Gang and youth problems in Evanston: Research findings and policy options.* Evanston, IL: Northwestern University, Center for Urban Affairs and Policy Research.

Short, J. F. (1990). New wine in old bottles? Change and continuity in American gangs. In C. R. Huff (Ed.), *Gangs in America.* Newbury Park, CA: Sage.

Skinner, K. (1980). Vietnamese in America: Diversity in adaptation. *California Sociologist, 3*(2), 103–124.

Spergel, I. A. (1991). *Youth gangs: Problem and response.* Washington, DC: United States Department of Justice, Office of Juvenile Justice and Delinquency Prevention.

Sung, B. L. (1977). *Gangs in New York's Chinatown* (Monograph No. 6). New York: City College of New York, Department of Asian Studies.

Sung, B. L. (1979). *Transplanted Chinese children.* New York: City College of New York, Department of Asian Studies.

Takagi, P., & Platt, T. (1978). Behind the gilded ghetto. *Crime and Social Justice, 9,* 2–25.

Taylor, C. S. (1990a). *Dangerous society.* East Lansing, MI: Michigan State University Press.

Taylor, C. S. (1990b). Gang imperialism. In C. R. Huff (Ed.), *Gangs in America.* Newbury Park, CA: Sage.

Thrasher, F. M. (1927). *The gang: A study of 1,313 gangs in Chicago.* University of Chicago Press.

U. S. Department of Justice, Office of Juvenile Justice and Delinquency Prevention. (1989). *Communitywide responses crucial for dealing with youth gangs.* Washington, DC: Author.

U. S. General Accounting Office. (1990). *Nontraditional organized crime: Law enforcement perspectives on five criminal groups.* Washington, DC: Author.

U. S. Senate. (1986). *Emerging criminal groups* (Hearings before the Permanent Subcommittee on Investigations of the Committee on Governmental Affairs). Washington, DC: U. S. Government Printing Office.

Vigil, J. D. (1988). *Barrio gangs.* Austin, TX: University of Texas Press.

Vigil, J. D., & Yun, S. C. (1990). Vietnamese youth gangs in southern California. In C. R. Huff (Ed.), *Gangs in America.* Newbury Park, CA: Sage.

Whyte, W. F. (1943). *Street corner society: The social structure of an Italian slum.* Chicago: University of Chicago Press.

Wilson, W. J. (1987). *The truly disadvantaged: The inner city, the underclass, and public policy.* University of Chicago Press.

CHAPTER 2

Gang Intervention:
A Historical Review

Arnold P. Goldstein

Juvenile gangs in the early decades of the 20th century, though at times involved in vandalism, fighting, theft, or other antisocial or delinquent acts, purportedly had an almost adventurously playful, benign quality (Furfey, 1926; Puffer, 1912; Sheldon, 1949). Or at least such a quaint perception seems to be the case from the highly violent gang perspective of the 1990s. Thrasher (1927/1963) observed during that earlier period:

> The quest for new experience seems to be particularly insistent in the adolescent, who finds in the gang the desired escape from, or compensation for, monotony. The gang actively promotes such highly agreeable activities as rough-house, movement and change, games and gambling, predatory activities, seeing thrillers in the movies, sports, imaginative play, roaming and roving, exploration, and camping and hiking. (p. 68)

Though Thrasher and others, anticipating the era of opportunities provision—the primary solution to ganging promoted in the 1960s and 1970s—urged social intervention in such "underlying conditions as inadequate family life, poverty, deteriorating neighborhoods, and ineffective religion, education, and recreation" (Thrasher, 1927/1963, p. 339), relatively little such intervention was systematically provided. Police intervention was sometimes necessary, but more generally the relatively low number of youth gangs in the United States, and the low level of both gang criminality and, especially, violence during these early years yielded but minor concern for formulating gang-oriented strategies and procedures for effective intervention.

As the century progressed and the negative societal conditions apparently generative of youth gang formation grew, so too did both the absolute number of gangs and their predatory and conflict-causing quality. Their junior, subsidiary, or ancillary role vis-à-vis adult criminal gangs during the depression years was, by midcentury, increasingly supplanted by juvenile gang initiated theft, vandalism, and fighting. The latter, though paling in comparison with the considerably more virulent gang violence of today, nevertheless aroused sufficient community concern that the search for effective means for intervention became especially active, eventually crystallizing in the widespread use of what came to be known as detached work programs.

DETACHED WORK PROGRAMS

Two of the major figures in gang intervention programming and evaluation during the past several decades, Irving Spergel of the University of Chicago and Malcolm Klein of the University of Southern California, have made important contributions to the origination and implementation of the detached work approach. Their respective views defining its nature and substance are of interest. According to Spergel (1965):

> The practice variously labeled detached work, street club, gang work, area work, extension youth work, corner work, etc., is the systematic effort of an agency worker, through social work or treatment techniques within the neighborhood context, to help a group of young people who are described as delinquent or partially delinquent to achieve a conventional adaptation. (p. 22)

> The assumption of youth agencies was that youth gangs were viable or adaptive and could be re-directed. Counseling and group activities could be useful in persuading youth gang members to give up unlawful behavior. The small gang group or subgroup was to be the center of attention of the street worker. (p. 145)

Klein (1971) defines this approach further:

> Detached work programs are grounded in one basic proposition: Because gang members do not ordinarily respond well to standard agency walls, it is necessary to take the programs to the gangs. Around this simple base of a worker reaching out to his client, other programmatic thrusts then take form—club meetings, sports activities, tutoring and remedial reading projects, leadership training, family counseling, casework, employment training, job finding, and so on. In addition, a community organization component is often built into the program. . . . The primary change mechanism is the rapport established between worker and gang members. (p. 46)

Detached work programs grew from a historical context reaching back to the mid-19th century, in which, as Brace (1872; cited in Bremmer, 1976) reported, charity and church groups—as well as Boy Scouts, Boys Clubs, YMCAs and settlement houses—sought to establish relationships with and programs for urban youths in trouble or at risk. Thrasher (1927/1963) spoke of similar efforts, and the Chicago Area Projects of the 1930s (Kobrin, 1959) provided much of the procedural prototype for the youth outreach, detached work programs that emerged in force in the 1950s and 1960s. And blossom they did. In the fertile context of the social action movements of the midcentury United States, many cities developed and put such programming in place. Their goals were diverse and ambitious. The New York City Youth Board (1960), with one of the major early programs (The Street Club Project), aspired to provide

> group work and recreation services to youngsters previously unable
> to use the traditional, existing facilities; the opportunity to make
> referrals of gang members for necessary treatment . . . the provision
> of assistance and guidance in the vocational area; and . . . the edu-
> cation of the community to the fact that . . . members of fighting
> gangs can be redirected into constructive, positive paths. (p. 7)

At a more general level, this and many of the detached work programs that soon followed also held as their broad goals the reduction of antisocial behavior; friendlier relations with other street gangs; increased participation of a democratic nature within the gang; increased responsibility for self-direction among individual gang members, as well as their improved social and personal adjustment; and better relations with the community of which the gang was a part.

As the movement evolved, most detached work programs came to the position that their central aspiration was values transformation, a rechanneling of the youths' beliefs and attitudes—and consequently, it was hoped, their behavior—in less antisocial and more prosocial directions. Some programs incorporated components of opportunities provision (Maxson & Klein, 1983), which years later was to supplant values transformation as the major thrust of gang intervention programming. Others, responding to the many intrapersonal, gang, and community forces that serve to maintain antisocial behavior, aspired to a considerably more modest goal—that detached work efforts would "hold the line with the individual delinquent . . . until normal processes of maturation take over" (Spergel, 1965, p. 43). As the use of detached work programs continued, and implementors developed a further sense of what such efforts might and might not appropriately aspire to accomplish, goal planning became both more refined and more complex. Spergel (1965), for example, described the purposes of detached work programming with delinquent gangs as fourfold:

1. *Control.* The first goal is to saturate an area with detached work services, offering them to all of the gangs in conflict in the area. In addition to the services and their consequences, such saturation yields surveillance and control opportunities that may themselves be conflict reducing.

2. *Treatment.* To the degree that the antisocial behavior of delinquent gang members is viewed as a result, at least in part, of psychological disturbance, successful counseling or therapeutic intervention becomes an appropriate

goal for the detached worker. In the 1950s and 1960s, such intervention was based largely on psychoanalytic notions and was often operationalized by expressive/cathartic interactions aimed at anxiety reduction and the development of more effective personal controls.

3. *Opportunities provision.* This class of program goals responds to the limited access to and use of educational, employment, and recreational resources often characteristic of delinquent gang youths. Programming, in this view, ought to aspire to develop and make available such resources, as well as to aid youths in making use of them.

4. *Value change.* Via a variety of means, this goal seeks a reorientation or rechanneling of values from antisocial to prosocial both in the youths and in the adults and organizations within the community, whose norms may be supportive of delinquent, criminal behavior and beliefs.

As observed earlier, several detached work programs were initiated across the United States—in New York City, Boston, Chicago, Los Angeles, San Francisco, El Paso, and elsewhere. Spergel (1965) has provided the following comprehensive and more or less sequential organization of their collective implementation procedures.

1. *Introduction.* Via self-introduction or introduction by a previous worker or a member of the community, worker and gang meet. The youths' initial response will be a function in part of whether they perceive the worker as a police-like control figure; as a social agency worker, perhaps welfare worker; or accurately, for the role(s) the worker intends to enact. And, if the worker is perceived accurately, youth response may vary according to whether having a worker is seen as status enhancing (the gang is bad enough to need one) or status diminishing (the gang prefers to avoid the delinquent label).

2. *Observation and orientation.* This is the structuring stage of the youth-worker relationship. The worker, capitalizing on one major advantage of being detached from agency to street, begins to observe the target youths in their natural, neighborhood contexts. As opportunities arise or can be created, by word and deed the worker begins to orient both the youths and their significant others (parents, community figures, etc.) to his or her intended and possible roles and functions.

3. *Meeting group tests.* Gang members test and retest the worker. Such testing may include displays of suspicion, ostracism, verbal abuse, and even physical aggression. Spergel (1965) comments:

> Testing takes many forms. For example, at first the
> youngsters may deliberately fabricate stories of fights
> or planned criminal activities, requests for help with jobs
> or problems at school. They are interested mainly in the

> way [the worker] responds to hypothetical situations. . . .
> The worker is also tested in a very personal way. The
> group wants to know why he is a street worker and what
> his personal ambitions are. . . . The group wants to know
> how far they can push him and in what way they can make
> him angry. (pp. 76–77)

4. *Assisting the group to solve a problem.* The initial testing ends, and the
   worker-youth relationship may be said to have been established, suggests
   Spergel (1965), when the worker assists the group in dealing successfully with
   a problem the group sees as significant: "Helping to solve a problem may be as
   simple as teaching the members how to shoot a basket, how to conduct a
   dance, or helping youngsters transfer from one school to another" (p. 79).

5. *Dealing with a sense of deprivation.* An early and often continuing task
   for the worker is helping ameliorate the youths' sense of estrangement
   from their community, perhaps their families, and from others who play
   a significant role in their lives. Gang youths often pessimistically fear
   further deprivation, including eventual loss of the worker. The emotional
   climate such a sense may create can substantially influence both the tone
   of worker-youth interactions and the likelihood of positive outcomes.

6. *Setting appropriate standards.* The overriding purpose of detached work
   programs, it will be recalled, is to assist gang youths in developing prosocial values and behavior and in relinquishing antisocial norms and actions. The behavior and perceived values of significant adults with whom
   the youths interact loom large in this challenging, revisionary effort:

   > The worker who is warm and friendly, who has gained the
   > respect and admiration of group members, may be used as
   > a role model. His behavior, attitudes, and beliefs may be-
   > come their standards. . . . [C]hanges in certain patterns of
   > behavior occur in a generalized, nonplanned way, because
   > of the worker's positive relationship with the members.
   > (Spergel, 1965, p. 84)

7. *Decision making.* In the belief that it both increases a sense of satisfaction
   in the youths and encourages conventional behavior, a democratic decision-
   making process is strongly promoted by the worker. As a component of
   this effort, the worker urges maximum group responsibility in the control of its own acting out behavior.

8. *Advice and normative controls.* These are straightforward instructional
   communications from worker to youth. On occasion, these communications
   may go beyond mere advice and admonitions regarding the consequences
   of planned delinquent behavior to address the value of conformity to
   more conventional norms and actions.

9. *Compelling conformity to conventional standards.* Under extreme circumstances, such as when the worker or someone else is under direct threat of violence, the worker may have to compel behavioral compliance through his or her own actions, with the aid of other staff, or with the assistance of the police.

10. *Other worker-initiated procedures.* Depending upon an almost limitless array of variables involving gang members, significant others, and environmental behaviors and events, the detached worker may be called upon to implement an exceedingly broad range of additional procedures and services. These may include planning and supervising diverse gang programming, contriving circumstances that minimize the possibility of intergang fighting, encouraging the gang's segmentation into conventional and delinquent subgroups when such a polarization naturally emerges and cannot be reconciled, providing direct instruction in conventional behaviors (e.g., what to say, when, to whom), and much more.[1]

Given the diverse, demanding, and multifaceted array of components constituting the job of detached worker, it is no wonder that Fox (1985), in an article aptly titled "Mission Impossible?" describes the qualifications for such persons in this way: "Dedicated, abundant energy, a sense of fun, good and quick intelligence, courage, inventiveness, ability to relate to suspicious teenagers, a degree of comfort with authority, and a firm set of values rooted in his own experience, all seem essential" (p. 26).

Four of the detached work programs thus operationalized are particularly relevant for further consideration here. With one exception, each program was formally and systematically evaluated for its effectiveness. Although unevaluated, the New York City Youth Board Project served as a springboard shaping the nature of other such programs. The Roxbury Project (Miller, 1974) was evaluated by means of a variety of effectiveness criteria and a series of comparison groups. Results on several intermediate criteria were favorable—worker relationships with gangs were established; recreational, educational, and occupational interests were stimulated. However, on the project's ultimate criterion, inhibition of law-violating or morally disapproved behavior (Quicker, 1983), no significant between-condition differences emerged. The Chicago Youth Development Project (Mattick & Caplan, 1962) was yet another apparent outcome failure on delinquency reduction criteria. Results indicated that an intensive worker-youth relationship was not, as had been predicted, positively related to a prosocial outcome. In fact, the youths who claimed to be closest to their detached workers were most in trouble with the police. The Los Angeles Group Guidance Project (Klein, 1968) was also fully evaluated, and it too proved to be a seemingly inadequate approach to rechanneling the values and behavior of delinquent gang youths. Gang member delinquency actually increased over the course of the project's life, especially for youths who received the fullest worker attention.

It is not often the case in social science research that such a clear confluence of results (positive or negative) emerges, and thus it is not surprising that gang researchers more or less unanimously concluded that the detached work approach ought not be pursued further. Klein (1968), in particular, urged this step, claiming that the consistently negative results were largely due to the manner in which detached work programming attended primarily to the gang as a group, and less to its individual members, thus enhancing gang cohesiveness, perpetuating and not rechanneling the gang, and drawing new recruits to its membership. Klein's programmatic response to these conclusions, the more individually oriented cohesiveness-reducing, gang-busting Ladino Hills Project, did succeed in reducing the absolute level of delinquency, mostly because the gangs diminished in size. This seemed to Klein and others to be the evidential nail in the detached work program's coffin.

Negative evidence notwithstanding, there is more to the evaluation story to be told. It is our belief that all detached work programs suffer from one, and typically several, failures of implementation. In each instance, both implementation plans and evaluation procedures seem adequate, but not the manner in which worker activities were actually conducted. If this is the case, program effectiveness remains indeterminate and conclusions regarding outcome efficacy must be suspended. There are five reasons for taking this position: (a) failure of program integrity, (b) failure of program intensity, (c) absence of techniques relevant to delinquency reduction, (d) failure of program prescriptiveness, and (e) failure of program comprehensiveness. The sections that follow will elaborate upon these evaluative shortfalls because they, and the conclusion of indeterminacy of program effectiveness, apply not only to detached work gang programming but also to a number of other approaches to gang intervention.

Program Integrity

Program integrity refers to the degree to which the intervention as actually implemented corresponds to or follows the intervention program as planned. As noted in the report from the New York State Task Force on Juvenile Gangs (New York State Division for Youth, 1990):

> If youth at risk of gang involvement are to be served adequately, it is critical that programs developed be actually implemented according to planned program procedures. Too often, mostly as a result of too few personnel or inadequate funding, programs of apparent substantial potential are actually implemented inadequately. (p. 44)

Failure of program integrity, as thus defined, appears to have been a relatively common characteristic of the detached work programs examined earlier. The New York City Youth Board Project, according to Gannon (1965), repeatedly suffered from high staff turnover, monumental red tape, low staff morale, worker role confusion, and a number of other kindred threats to program integrity. In the Chicago

Youth Development Project, "the workers found their jobs so demanding [that] they tend to swallow up the whole life of the person holding them" (Quicker, 1983, p. 69). Even more directly bearing on the correspondence between intervention plan and implementation, Klein (1968) notes with regard to the Group Guidance Project that its worker counseling policy component was confused, its planned parent group component largely nonexistent, its psychiatric intervention component inflexible. In addition, its supervisory plan, meant to promote program integrity, was severely inadequate in its actual implementation: Program supervisors wound up spending less than 30 minutes per worker per week in field supervision and observation. Responding to this fact, Klein (1968) comments that

> action in the street scene means, almost inevitably, lower levels of line supervision. . . . For the researcher, this supervisorial gap poses serious problems of data validity, discrepant views of the action, feedback mechanics, and proper implementation of program . . . procedures. In other words, there is little control, and certainly less than is found in most action-research settings. (p. 235)

Program Intensity

The intensity with which an intervention is delivered is its amount, level, or dosage. The New York State Task Force on Juvenile Gangs made this observation on program intensity:

> In general, it will be the case that "the more the better," whether referring to amount of youth contact with the interveners; amount of counseling time, recreational time or job skills training time; or amount of family or community involvement in programming for youth. (New York State Division for Youth, 1990, p. 44)

On this criterion of project adequacy, the detached work programs considered here do not do well. Worker-youth ratios were an acceptable 1 to 29 in the Roxbury Project, an unacceptable 1 to 78 in the New York City Youth Board Program, and a quite impossible 1 to 92 in the Chicago Youth Development Project. Such disproportionate caseloads usually meant that workers rarely met youths individually and almost always met them in groups. As Mulvihill, Tumin, and Curtis (1969) observe:

> How would a rational worker go about meeting and maintaining rapport with as many as a hundred youngsters much of whose lives are street oriented? Being on the street himself is not sufficient; too many boys are missed that way. The worker has little choice but to encourage group gatherings. (p. 1455)

These gatherings, as Dumpson (1949) noted in connection with the New York City Youth Board Project, can mean dealing with as many as 50 youths at a time!

Klein's (1968) data on the intensity of the Group Guidance Project are most telling on this topic. The project's detached workers, it seems, were in reality only partly detached. They spent 25 to 50 percent of their time (on average 38 percent or about two-fifths) in the project office and a considerable amount of time (on average 25 percent) alone (traveling, hanging around gathering spots). Thus, almost two-thirds of their typical working day was not spent with project youths. Klein pointedly comments:

> Whether one looks at this as an hour and a half a day, a day a week, or ten weeks out of a year, this is a fascinating piece of information. Gang workers in this project spent one-fifth of their time with gang members. . . . With 50 to 100 gang members in the neighborhood, and eight hours a week spent in contact with them, how much impact can reasonably be expected? It may be like squeezing blood out of a turnip to think that an average of five minutes per week per boy could somehow result in a reduction of delinquent behavior. (p. 163)

So much for intervention intensity!

Absence of Delinquency-Relevant Techniques

Well-designed evaluations of intervention programs often include both proximal and distal measures of the intervention's effectiveness. The former are tied directly to the content of the intervention: If remedial reading was the intervention, has the youth's reading level advanced? If social skills training was provided, is the youth more socially skilled? If employment interviewing behaviors were taught, how does the youth actually behave in a mock or real interview? Improvement on distal or more derivative outcome criteria is usually possible only if prior improvement on the proximal or more immediate criteria has first taken place. Thus, grade point average might well be a distal criterion of effectiveness in a remedial reading intervention employing the proximal criterion of change in reading level. Similarly, level of self-esteem might be the derivative criterion in a social skills intervention, and actual job attainment could be the distal measure in the instance of employment interviewee training. In the evaluation of detached work programs, a variety of appropriate proximal measures have been employed, but the criterion of distal effectiveness (and the programs' raison d'être) has consistently been change in delinquent behavior. Combined outcome evidence is fairly supportive of the proximal effectiveness of detached work but consistently unsupportive of its distal effectiveness, thus defined.

Though the potency of delinquency-altering techniques has improved since the era of detached work programming, it is still largely inappropriate to predict that any intervention targeted to behavior, attitude, or value A will be so potent that, in addition to changing A, it will also have significant impact on derivative criterion B. Available delinquency interventions are simply not that powerful. Klein (1968), in examining the outcome of his Group Guidance Project, comments in this regard:

Another weakness derives from the general lack of knowledge in the entire field of delinquency prevention, and the worker is the unfortunate bearer of this burden. I refer here to the lack of specific techniques for dealing with specific forms of delinquent behavior. An exception is the control of gang fighting in which worker visibility, the provision of face saving alternatives, and truce meetings are accepted procedures for avoiding territorial raids and retaliations. Unfortunately, few techniques exist that are comparably effective with theft, rape, malicious mischief, auto theft, truancy, and so on. This lack of specific behavior related techniques forces the worker to fall back upon general intervention procedures such as individual or family counseling, group activities, job development, and so on, procedures which at best have only an indirect relationship to delinquency producing situations. (p. 150)

In the Group Guidance Project, a diverse array of 241 (usually group) activities were conducted over the 2½ years of the program's life, an average of 2 activities per week. In spite of the activities' diversity, their contents were such that the evaluators concluded:

It was clear from our observations that the special activities were seldom used directly . . . for delinquency prevention. Any major positive impact on delinquency would have to be indirect, through self-discovered lessons about fair-play, the value of prosocial activity, and so on. (Klein, 1968, p. 169)

These absence-of-technique conclusions, in addition to eliciting admiration of Klein and his research team for their research acumen and remarkable candor should, we hope, serve as both insight and stimulus: insight regarding the need for more direct and potent delinquency interventions, stimulus for the effort to produce same.

Program Prescriptiveness

As delinquency reduction techniques are developed, become available, and are implemented with both integrity to plan and intensity of dosage, they must also be applied prescriptively. The detached work programs considered here, as is true of the vast majority of delinquency intervention programming of all kinds, were not employed in a differential, tailored, individualized, or prescriptive manner. The success of interventions such as detached work is likely to be substantially enhanced to the degree that the worker's techniques (and worker characteristics) are propitiously matched with qualities of the participating youths. Valuable leads in this regard already exist. They include notions urging different approaches to core versus marginal gang members (Yablonsky, 1967); to leaders versus followers

(Needle & Stapleton, 1982); to older versus younger youths (Spergel, Ross, Curry, & Chance, 1989); to youths from theft, conflict, or racket subcultures (Spergel et al., 1989); to youths with varying degrees of aggressiveness and gang involvement (Klein, 1968); and to youths classified as clique leaders, cohesiveness builders, or recruits (Klein, 1968). Moreover, different approaches may be chosen in response to diverse worker qualities. The last, an especially ignored but, we believe, especially outcome-relevant prescriptive ingredient, is described well by Spergel et al. (1989):

> A key objective should be to match the skills of the worker opti-
> mally with the needs of the group. For example, the worker who is
> particularly effective in setting limits should be assigned to a group
> which has great difficulty in controlling its aggressive impulses; a
> worker who is skilled at individual and group treatment should
> work with a group requiring therapeutic help; a worker who is
> talented at opening up and developing community resources for
> socioeconomically deprived youths should be assigned to a group
> needing access to appropriate opportunities. (p. 29)

In general, we are urging that the proper, if complex, prescriptive question to be addressed is, Which types of youths in which types of gangs being serviced by which types of detached workers will yield which types of prosocial outcomes?

Program Comprehensiveness

It was the intent of all of the detached work programs considered here to provide not only the main intervention components associated with worker-youth relationships but also comprehensive, multilevel programming to both individual youths and the systems of which they were a part. The New York City Youth Board Project (1960) had broad aspirations:

> It has been asked whether it is most productive to work with the
> group, with the individual in the group, or with the community
> itself, and through changes in the community, bring about changes
> in the group. Traditionally the work of the Street Club Project has
> been focused on all three: the group, the neighborhood and the
> individual members themselves. This stems from our conviction
> that delinquency is caused by a multiplicity of factors—both indi-
> vidual and social—and that an effective approach to the problem
> should incorporate both of these areas. (p. 118)

Given the long, formative, and frequently antisocial life histories of many gang youths and the levels of contemporary reinforcement they receive for continuing to engage in antisocial behavior, this aspiration to multipronged intervention seems most appropriate. Yet detached workers in the programs implemented were overworked and undertrained, and they had few resources at their disposal. Most of what was available to them was youth oriented, not system oriented, in aims and substance. Thus, rather than intervention comprehensiveness, what actually emerged

> targeted specific gangs and gang youth. It was not integrated into other service or community development approaches occurring at the same time. It concentrated on the development of worker-gang member relationships and recreational and group activities in somewhat isolated terms. It was a fairly unidimensional approach. (Klein, 1968, p. 52)

These several intervention implementation shortfalls—regarding program integrity, program intensity, delinquency reduction techniques, prescriptiveness of implementation, and program comprehensiveness—characterize not only the four detached work projects examined in this chapter but also other, similar programs. Given this reality, an examination of the nature and efficacy of detached work programming must conclude, as we believe is largely true for most other types of interventions with gang youths, that "the relevant evidence, instead of being interpreted as proof of lack of effectiveness, should more parsimoniously be viewed as indeterminate, generally neither adding to nor detracting from a conclusion of effectiveness or ineffectiveness" (Goldstein, Glick, Irwin, Pask-McCartney, & Rubama, 1989, p. 4).

OPPORTUNITIES PROVISION PROGRAMS

Gang intervention programming, whatever its major thrust, has always given at least some attention to enhancing extra-gang opportunity structures available to such youths. But in some eras, it has been decidedly minor attention. As noted previously, during the decades of detached work programming, for example, primary emphasis was consistently placed on the worker-youth relationship and on attempts to alter behavior by gang reorientation and values transformation, with relatively little effort directed toward system change (e.g., the enhancement of work, school, or family opportunity). Awareness of the incompleteness or asymmetry of this perspective, coupled with the purported gang cohesiveness and delinquency-enhancing effects of detached work programming—all in a context of increased general promotion in the United States of diverse social legislation—preceded and stimulated the opportunities provision phase of gang work. Spergel et al. (1989) describe this strategy as

> a series of large scale social resource infusions and efforts to change institutional structures, including schools, job opportunities, political employment . . . in the solution not only of delinquency, but poverty itself. Youth work strategies were regarded as

insufficient. Structural strain, lack of resources, and relative deprivation were the key ideas which explained delinquency, including
youth gang behavior. The structures of social and economic means
rather than the behavior of gangs and individual youth had to be
modified. (p. 147)

The proposed relevance of this strategy to gang youths in particular is captured
well by Morales (1981): "The gang is a symptom of certain noxious conditions found
in society. These conditions often include low wages, unemployment, lack of
recreational opportunities, inadequate schools, poor health, deteriorated housing and other factors contributing to urban decay and slums" (p. 4).

Quicker (1983) echoes this perspective, pointing even more directly to the need
for opportunities provision:

The development of gangs stems primarily from environmental
causes. It appears that the legitimate opportunity system is closed
to most lower class boys who, having internalized middle class
norms of success, are frustrated by their inability to succeed in
socially prescribed ways. Joining with other boys, similarly frustrated, they form gangs which provide some of them access to that
illegitimate opportunity system (an illegal economy) where they
are able to at least partially realize their aspirations. (p. 11)

Klein (1968), in joint response to the apparent failure of his detached work
Group Guidance Project and the subsequent greater success of his opportunities-
oriented Ladino Hill Project, expresses a similar view:

One of the difficulties encountered by many past programs stems
from the enormous complexity of the gang problem. It has been
assumed that a problem deriving its existence from a multitude of
sources (family, community, economic deprivation, individual deficiencies, etc.) must be dealt with on all levels. Yet most gang programs
have been of the detached worker variety, a form of intervention for
which this multilevel approach is inefficient at best, and in reality
almost impossible. Detached workers can have relatively little impact on individual character disorders or psychological deficiencies,
family relationships, poverty, educational and employment disadvantages, community disorganization and apathy, and so on. (p. 238)

The need for provision of practical and esteem-enhancing opportunities, of
course, was apparent as far back as Thrasher's (1927/1963) work and earlier. What
was different in the late 1960s and 1970s was the country's willingness to respond
to this need with a broad programmatic effort. Dozens of varied programs followed
to address the need for opportunities. Following is a roughly chronological sampler
of programs oriented in particular to gang youths:

- Mobilization for Youths (Cloward & Ohlin, 1960; Miller, 1974), which provided vocational guidance and the opportunity to gain small business work experience

- Spergel's (1965) street gang project, which included substantial involvement with gang members' families, employers and employment services, public school personnel, and a variety of youth agencies

- Klein's (1968) Ladino Hills Project, whose resource workers (rather than detached workers) sought to provide participating gang youth employment, improve school opportunities, and enhance access to recreational, health, and welfare resources

- Baca's (1988) Citywide Mural Project

- The 1973 New York Police Probation Diversion Project (Gardner, 1983), which provided special education and substance abuse prevention programming

- Krisberg's (1974) Urban Leadership Training Program, which attempted to train gang leaders for careers in community service

- DeLeon's (1977) corporation- and police-initiated scouting troops

- Haire's (1979) Rampart gang study, which mobilized a unified school district to provide expanded educational opportunities

- The Hire-a-Gang-Leader program (Amandes, 1979), which taught an array of job-seeking and job-keeping skills and pro-vided actual employment opportunities

- The Ocean Township Youth Volunteer Corps (Torchia, 1980), which offered both community service and diverse recreational possibilities to adjudicated gang youths

- Willman and Snortum's (1982) Project New Pride and Gang Employment Programs, and Falaka's House of Umoja (Gardner, 1983), all of which emphasized job training and employment opportunity programming

- Project SAY (Save-A-Youth), developed by Willis-Kistler (1988), which offered a full array of family, school, and recreational opportunities

- Thompson and Jason's (1988) school and after-school Project BUILD (Broader Urban Involvement and Leadership Development)

- The employment-oriented Community Access Team (California Youth Gang Task Force, 1981), Youth Enterprises of Long Beach (Quicker, 1983), and SEY Yes (Quicker, 1983) programs

- The school-oriented GREAT (Gang Resistance and Training; Los Angeles Unified School District, 1989); PREP (Preparation Through Responsive Education; Filipczak, Friedman, & Reese, 1979); and Gangs Network (college option generating; Needle & Stapleton, 1982) programs

- The family-oriented Family and School Consultation Project (Stuart, Jayaratne, & Tripoldi, 1976) and the Aggression Replacement Training project (Goldstein et al., 1989)

Prescriptive Evaluation

With very few exceptions (e.g., Klein, 1968; Thompson & Jason, 1988), opportunities provision gang programming has not been systematically evaluated. There is no concrete evidence whether, or to what extent, gang youths in general or particular subgroups thereof seek or accept the diverse opportunities provided. Thus, it is unknown whether they benefit in either proximal, opportunity-specific ways or more distally in terms of termination of gang membership, delinquency reduction, or future life path. There is no shortage of affirming impressionistic and anecdotal support—including a major 45-city survey seeking the views of both law enforcement and other agencies on the effectiveness of opportunities provision and other gang intervention approaches (Spergel et al., 1989)—but its heuristic value is limited, especially for determination of future programming.

Klein's (1968) Ladino Hills Project is an important exception; its careful evaluation sets a standard to which others should aspire. Especially noteworthy is its prescriptive feature, a systematic effort to develop a typology of gang youths to identify categories responsive to different patterns of programming, including opportunities provision. Klein's (1971) initial success in this attempt well deserves replication and elaboration by others. His gang member categories (clique leaders, cohesiveness builders, recruits, and best bets) make both intuitive and empirical sense.

Whether implemented prescriptively or not, the opportunities provision strategy should be responsive to the urging of Spergel et al. (1989) that opportunities be accompanied by sufficient support and organization. They comment:

> A general design for improved living in particularly deprived
> lower-class areas should be based on three concepts: opportunity,
> service, and organization. . . . Since the provision of basic social
> and economic opportunities is not enough, however, a variety of
> significant social supports, through services, must be developed to
> insure that the expanded opportunities which become available to

the child at school or to the parent through a better job are utilized. Social work, as well as psychological, psychiatric, health, and other community services, must be amply provided to many parents and children so that the basic opportunities are appropriately appreciated and used. . . . Even the provision of expanded opportunities and services may still not be enough to prevent social ills and to rehabilitate problem families and their children. Expanded opportunities and services must be efficiently organized. Too often, problem youngsters and their families are shunted from agency to agency. . . . [M]any programs in deprived neighborhoods lack quality, imagination, and flexibility. Untrained and poorly supervised personnel are presented with intolerably heavy and difficult assignments which they cannot handle effectively. Stereotyped and inferior practices at schools and agencies are little better than no teaching at all. (pp. 173–174)

The effectiveness of opportunities provision is thus seen as a joint function of the opportunities provided, the manner in which they are delivered, and the way they are coordinated, organized, or interrelated. Such thinking regarding the context, content, and relationship of opportunities provided also characterizes this chapter's primary conclusion—that a multifaceted, comprehensive orientation to gang intervention is required.

DETERRENCE/INCARCERATION PROGRAMS

As the 1970s drew to a close, the United States got tough. A combination of the heavy influx of drugs, growing levels of violence, purported failure of rehabilitative programming, and the rise of political and judicial conservatism all combined to usher in the era of deterrence/incarceration and usher out the provision of social, economic, and educational opportunities. Opportunities provision is not gone, but it is much less frequently the centerpiece of gang intervention programming. Social control—surveillance, deterrence, arrest, prosecution, incarceration—has largely replaced social improvement as the preeminent approach to gang youths:

A philosophy of increased social opportunity was replaced by growing conservatism. The gang was viewed as evil, a collecting place for sociopaths who were beyond the capacity of most social institutions to redirect or rehabilitate them. Protection of the community became the key goal. (Spergel et al., 1989, p. 148)

The deterrence/incarceration strategy came to guide the gang-related actions not only of law enforcement personnel but of others also. In Philadelphia's Crisis Intervention Network program, in Los Angeles's Community Youth Gang Services, and in the other similar crisis intervention programs that sprang up across the country, the resource worker—who had replaced the detached worker—was in turn replaced by the surveillance/deterrence worker. Working out of radio-dispatched automobiles and assigned to geographical areas rather than to specific gangs, surveillance/deterrence workers responded to crises, focusing on rumor control, dispute resolution, and, most centrally, violence reduction. Maxson and Klein (1983) capture well the essence of this strategy, contrasting it with the earlier values transformation approach:

> The transformation model fostered social group work in the streets with empathic and sympathetic orientations toward gang members as well as acceptance of gang misbehavior as far less of a problem than the alienating response of community residents and officials. By contrast, the deterrence model eschews an interest in minor gang predations and concentrates on the major ones, especially homicide. The worker is, in essence, part of a dramatically energized community control mechanism, a "firefighter" with a more balanced eye on the consequences as well as the cause of gang violence. Success is measured first in violence reduction, not in group or individual change. (p. 151)

Of course, the police and other agents of the criminal justice system are the primary implementers of the deterrence/incarceration approach to gang intervention. It is a largely suppressive approach, employing such tactics as surveillance, stake out, aggressive patrol, intelligence gathering, infiltration, investigation, prosecution, and incarceration. Its spirit is captured well by Hagedorn (1988): "The basic strategy for coping with gangs remains the iron fist, a strategy that moves the problem from visibility in the community to the invisibility of the prison" (p. 150).

COMPREHENSIVE PROGRAMS

It is a primary responsibility of society's officialdom to protect its citizens. Gang violence in its diverse and often intense forms must be monitored, deterred, and punished. But much more must be done. Gang youths are *our* youths. They are among us now, and, even if periodically incarcerated, most will be among us in the future. We deserve protection from their predations, but they deserve the opportunity to lead satisfying and contributory lives without resorting to individual or group violence. Punishment may be necessary, but punishment fails to teach new, alternative means to desired goals. Implementation of the deterrence/incarceration model may indeed be necessary in today's violence-prone United States, but it is far from sufficient. What is needed and appears to be emerging is a less unidimensional and more integrative gang intervention model, one with at least the potential to supplant exclusive employment of deterrence/incarceration. We term it The Comprehensive Model; it is similar in spirit and in most particulars to Spergel et al.'s

(1989) Model B, which incorporates and seeks prescriptively to apply major features of programming centered on detached workers, opportunities provision, and social control.[2] It is a multimodal, multilevel strategy requiring that substantial resources of diverse types be employed in a coordinated manner. We have described elsewhere the manner in which aggressive and antisocial behavior derives from complex causality and, hence, will yield most readily when approached with interventions of equivalent complexity (Goldstein, 1983). The same is true for gang aggression and antisocial behavior.

Comprehensive gang intervention programming, while occasionally approximated in the past, still remains much more an aspiration than a reality. Two state-level gang task forces, in New York and California, have each recently sought to detail the possible scope of this intervention strategy and the array of means available for its implementation. The New York report succinctly orients us to this strategy:

> Programming for youth at risk of gang involvement must be both youth- and system-oriented. Too often have such youths alone been targeted for intervention efforts, with program failure the result. Family-oriented youth programming must seek to impact on the entire family system of which the youth is a part. School-oriented programs must seek to alter both the youth's approach to school, and the school's approach to such youth. Job-oriented programs must seek to enhance the youth's job-related skills and motivations, but also increase training for and the availability of appropriate employment. (New York State Division for Youth, 1990, p. 42)

By highlighting the multiplicity of causes underlying youth gang involvement —including difficulties associated with family, school, employment, health, recreation, media influences, racism, and more—this report underscores both the specific targets appropriate for comprehensive gang intervention and the likely obstacles in successful implementation.

The California report (California Council on Criminal Justice, 1989) carries matters further by offering extensive recommendations in what is the most complete effort to date to operationalize a comprehensive gang intervention program strategy. A summary of recommendations is provided in the following pages. The reader is urged to consult the full report for elaboration.*

Law Enforcement Recommendations

1. Establish or consolidate gang and narcotics enforcement activities within a single, specialized gang and narcotics enforcement unit.

---

* Recommendations on the following pages are from the executive summary of *State Task Force on Gangs and Drugs: Final Report* by the California Council on Criminal Justice, 1989, Sacramento, CA: Author. Reprinted by permission.

2. Provide ongoing training to the appropriate officers on methods of gang and drug enforcement, patrol, and investigation, as well as on the need to integrate specialized operations with patrol and investigations.

3. Coordinate gang and drug enforcement and prevention within an inter-agency task force, including schools, prosecution, probation, corrections, and community organizations.

4. Coordinate efforts with fire marshals and health inspectors to abate crack houses (or other facilities used as gang gathering places) by enforcing local health, fire, building, and safety codes.

5. Recruit officers, both men and women, from a representative cross section of ethnic groups, possessing bilingual skills and sensitivity to special language or cultural needs.

6. Coordinate law enforcement efforts with business and community organizations as well as with outreach and awareness programs to encourage community participation and victim/witness cooperation.

7. Notify parents or guardians of their children's gang affiliations.

8. Increase the number of peace officers in law enforcement agencies to enhance patrol and field operation staffing, placing more officers on the street to protect the community and to suppress gang- and drug-related crime.

9. Establish a Serious Habitual Offender (SHO) Program within each law enforcement agency to coordinate with prosecution and probation operations in targeting the most serious offenders for apprehension, prosecution, and incarceration.

10. Establish a community advisory group within all law enforcement departments to coordinate and select community-based organization programs that will most effectively provide community service, prevention, intervention, and community mobilization programs that are necessary to address the gang and drug problem.

Prosecution Recommendations

1. Establish vertical prosecution units focused on gang and drug offender cases.

2. Target first-time gang and drug offenders for stricter prosecution to discourage their criminal behavior.

3. Provide training to specialized prosecution units on the unique aspects and methods of gang and drug case prosecution.

4. Participate in or encourage the development of local multiagency task forces directed toward the apprehension, prosecution, and incarceration of gang and drug offenders.

5. Request the courts to place no-bail holds on serious gang and drug offenders who may pose a danger to the community, victims, or witnesses.

Corrections Recommendations

1. Continue intelligence coordination between corrections and enforcement agencies.

2. Establish, under the direction of the California Department of Corrections and the Department of the Youth Authority, minimum-security state correctional facilities to house appropriate offenders in vacant or unused military facilities (as provided by the U. S. Department of Defense) to alleviate overcrowding and to permit the incarceration of violent, drug-dealing gang offenders. Inmates confined in these facilities should be assigned to work on job skills training that supports the renovation and maintenance of the grounds and buildings.

3. Continue to present programs within correctional facilities to classify and segregate gang members, and to provide for tattoo removal and assistance in returning the gang members to the community.

4. Implement gang drug treatment and prevention programs within correctional institutions and as an element of preparation for release on parole/probation.

5. Continue to provide correctional officers with training in gang and drug offender supervision, classification, and investigative techniques.

6. Modify construction standards for local jails to allow for quicker and less expensive facility construction without sacrificing safety and security.

7. Establish, under the direction of local jail corrections authorities, minimum-security county correctional facilities to house appropriate offenders in vacant or unused military facilities (as provided by the U. S. Department of Defense) to alleviate overcrowding and to permit the incarceration of violent, drug-dealing gang offenders. Inmates confined to these facilities should be assigned to work on job skills training that supports the renovation and maintenance of the grounds and buildings.

8. Recruit officers and agents, both men and women, from a representative cross section of ethnic groups possessing bilingual skills and sensitivity to special language or cultural needs.

Probation/Parole Recommendations

1. Continue or establish specialized vertical probation and parole supervision units with reduced caseloads, focusing on the gang drug-trafficking offender.

2. Develop standardized gang control probation and parole conditions in conjunction with the courts and paroling authorities to be used statewide that will preclude continuing gang and drug involvement and will provide enhanced ability for parolee/probationer tracking. Require that the conditions be listed on an identification card that must be carried by the probationer/parolee at all times and be presented to any peace officer on request. The card must also include the name of the probation or parole officer and a 24-hour contact phone number for that agency.

3. Establish a centralized statewide registry to maintain information on all probationers and parolees, listing the specific probation and parole terms and conditions that apply to each individual.

4. Implement gang and drug probation and parole programs to more effectively manage gang parolees and probationers.

5. Provide training to specialized probation and parole supervision personnel on the aspects of and methods for gang and drug offender supervision.

6. Recruit officers/agents, both men and women, from a representative cross section of ethnic groups possessing bilingual skills and sensitivity to special language or cultural needs.

Judicial Recommendations

1. Establish, through the California Center for Judicial Education and Research (CJER) and the State Judicial Council, a training program for judges to inform them of the unique aspects of gang and drug cases.

2. Establish regional courts to hear cases pertaining to a designated geographic/community area so that judges may become more aware of, and sensitive to, the crime problems occurring within a specific community.

3. Establish specialized courts, within larger communities, hearing only cases involving gangs and drugs so that judges may become more aware of the complex nature of the specific legal interpretations, criminal behavior, and sentencing requirements relating to these cases.

4. Ensure that gang and drug offenders violating their probation are returned to the judge who sentenced them.

5. Establish special night court sessions within either regional or specialized gang and drug case courts in order to offer a convenient time for juvenile offenders to attend court with their parents or guardians.

6. Develop, through the State Judicial Council and the Chief Probation Officers Association, uniform, statewide standards for setting probation conditions for serious gang and drug offenders.

Executive Recommendations

1. Consider the creation, through an executive order, of a Statewide Narcotics Enforcement Coordination Task Force.

2. Direct the California National Guard to concentrate surveillance and reconnaissance efforts along the California-Mexico border.

3. Direct the Governor's Office of Criminal Justice Planning to survey community-based organizations in order to establish a clearinghouse of information on successful models for prevention, intervention, and community mobilization programs and on methods for obtaining funding for such programs.

4. Direct the Commission on Peace Officer Standards and Training to provide instruction for law enforcement officers regarding the history, function, and safe handling of assault-type weapons. Also direct the Governor's Office of Criminal Justice Planning to provide prosecutors with similar training.

5. Establish a computer-based information system for compiling and organizing municipal, county, and statewide gang data, including gang-related narcotics trafficking intelligence.

Legislative Recommendations

1. Enact legislation that would provide stricter treatment of juveniles who commit serious crimes. The Task Force recommends the following changes to the Welfare and Institutions Code:

   a. Amend the Welfare and Institutions Code, including Section 707, as well as Section 190 *et seq.*, of the Penal Code, to mandate that any 16- or 17-year-old juvenile who is charged with a serious "Proposition 8" felony, as defined in Section 1192.7 of the Penal Code, or who is charged with the sale or possession for sale of any controlled substance, or who is charged with any offense involving the use of any type of firearm or possession of a firearm at the time of commission or arrest, shall be automatically tried as an adult and subject to the imposition of an adult sentence;

b. Amend Welfare and Institutions Code Section 707, as well as Section 190 *et seq.*, of the Penal Code, defining the crime of murder and its punishment to mandate that 16- or 17-year-old juveniles charged with the commission of special circumstances murder be subject to the term of life imprisonment without the possibility of parole;

c. Amend Section 707 of the Welfare and Institutions Code to provide, in cases involving other felony offenses, that juveniles 16 years of age or older involved in gang activity as defined by Penal Code Section 186.2 are rebuttably presumed to be unfit for treatment by the juvenile court, and are suitable to be tried as adults; and

d. Further amend the Welfare and Institutions Code to provide that 14- and 15-year-old minors who are charged with the commission of special circumstances murder are to be tried as adults and, upon conviction, shall serve a minimum term of 20 years, including automatic transfer from the Department of the Youth Authority to the Department of Corrections upon attaining the age of 21 years.

2. Enact a comprehensive Racketeer Influenced and Corrupt Organization Act (RICO) statute similar to the existing federal provisions.

3. Amend the state narcotics asset forfeiture laws to:

a. Eliminate the 1994 sunset clause from the statute language and make it identical to existing federal forfeiture provisions.

b. Provide for the forfeiture of any vehicle used in a drive-by shooting.

c. Commit an amount from the Asset Forfeiture Fund to the Gang Violence Suppression Program budget within the Governor's Office of Criminal Justice Planning.

4. Enact legislation to establish policy to provide stricter treatment of offenders who use weapons:

a. Amend Subdivision (a) of Section 245 of the Penal Code by adding a provision that would make assault with a machine gun punishable by a mandatory term of life imprisonment with the possibility of parole;

b. Amend Subdivision (a) of Section 245 to provide for a mandatory term of 4, 8, or 12 years of imprisonment for assault with a high-capacity, semiautomatic firearm;

c. Amend the Penal Code by adding a mandatory sentence enhancement section covering murder, shooting into a dwelling or vehicle, kidnapping, robbery, escape, or witness intimidation that would enhance the sentence for the underlying felony as follows:

 • Use of a machine gun by a principal—an additional term of 5, 10, or 15 years.

- Use of a high-capacity semiautomatic firearm by a principal—an additional term of 3, 4, or 5 years; and

- Any principal armed with a machine gun—an additional term of 3, 4, or 5 years.

Sections 1203.06 and 12022.5 of the Penal Code, which together compose California's "Use of Gun—Go to Prison" law, require that personal use of a firearm receives a mandatory state prison sentence and the most severe sentence enhancements;

d. Amend Section 1385 of the Penal Code to prohibit a judge from striking any sentence enhancement for misuse of a machine gun or high-capacity semiautomatic firearm;

e. Amend the Penal Code to provide that the punishment for an ex-felon who possesses a machine gun will be a mandatory term of 4, 8, or 12 years, and a term of 3, 6, or 9 years for possession of a high-capacity semiautomatic firearm by an ex-felon;

f. Amend the Penal Code to provide that carrying a semiautomatic firearm and an easily accessible, loaded high-capacity magazine for that specific semiautomatic firearm in an automobile be a felony punishable by a term of 1, 2, or 3 years;

g. Amend Section 12220 of the Penal Code to provide a term of imprisonment of 3, 4, or 5 years for illegal possession of a machine gun; and

h. Amend the Penal Code to provide that the intentional conversion of a firearm into a machine gun shall be punished by a term of imprisonment of 3, 4, or 5 years.

5. Amend Section 666 of the Penal Code by adding Section 11550 of the Health and Safety Code to the list of those violations that may be charged as an alternative felony/misdemeanor if the defendant has suffered a prior conviction for violation of Section 11550 or any of the offenses enumerated in Section 666.

6. Amend Section 11353.5 of the Health and Safety Code so that it conforms with Title 21 of the United States Code, Section 845a relating to the distribution or manufacturing of drugs in or near schools and colleges.

7. Enact legislation that would eliminate, by constitutional amendment, postindictment preliminary hearings in cases in which the defendants have already been indicted by a grand jury.

8. Enact legislation to enable and to fund the Governor's Office of Criminal Justice Planning in administering a training program for prosecutors, law

enforcement officers, and the judiciary regarding the investigative functions of a criminal grand jury.

9. Enact legislation that would allow hearsay testimony in the preliminary hearing.

10. Revise the provisions of the Penal Code and the Rules of the Court relating to sentencing in order to limit a trial court's discretion to grant probation to narcotics traffickers.

11. Enact legislation, through constitutional amendment, that would require judicial officers to consider the protection of the public in setting bail or allowing a defendant to be released on his or her own recognizance in all criminal prosecutions.

12. Enact legislation that would amend Section 1078 of the Penal Code to provide for judicial *voir dire* of prospective jurors in criminal trials.

13. Enact legislation that would amend the California Constitution to allow *voir dire* of prospective jurors in open court, in capital cases.

14. Enact legislation that will expand the designation of Enterprise Zones and Economic and Employment Incentive Areas in order to provide increased economic development and job opportunities within gang-affected communities.

15. Enact legislation to eliminate heroin and cocaine addiction and drug sales from any consideration for diversion to Penal Code Section 1000 drug programs and allow the program to concentrate on the drug users who can benefit from the educational and counseling concepts that are intended by these programs.

16. Enact legislation to place on the ballot a constitutional amendment that will require parents to be responsible for the costs of detaining their children within juvenile facilities.

17. Enact legislation to mandate that the Department of Corrections develop and implement a comprehensive narcotics treatment, education, and diversion program for inmates in all of its penal institutions.

18. Enact legislation to amend the current provisions of the state's electronic surveillance law to parallel the federal statute.

19. Enact legislation that will provide for the forfeiture of any leasehold, and attendant deposits, where there has been illegal narcotics-related activity in the leased or rented property.

20. Enact legislation to provide adequate funding for the expansion of the prison system and/or any California detention facility, including secure facilities for juvenile offenders.

21. Amend Penal Code Section 594 (Vandalism) to make gang-related graffiti, regardless of the dollar amount of damage, an alternate misdemeanor or felony with increased penalties.

22. Enact legislation to implement a statewide curfew law and to recommend that communities with current curfew ordinances make a renewed, concentrated enforcement effort in the area of juvenile curfew violations.

23. Enact legislation to require that the State Department of Education, the Governor's Office of Criminal Justice Planning, and the Department of the Youth Authority develop and implement a statewide mandated gang and drug prevention program within all public schools in the state to:

   a. Teach social values and self-esteem to youths, commencing with kindergarten;

   b. Teach social responsibility and, most importantly, family values and parenting skills;

   c. Teach students in all grades how to avoid involvement with gangs and drugs;

   d. Train teachers and administrators on how to implement this curriculum, and how to detect and intervene with gang- and drug-related or "at risk" behavior; and

   e. Mandate the California State Commission on Credentialing to require all teachers and administrators to complete the gang and drug prevention program as a requirement for certificate renewal.

24. Enact legislation to establish Juvenile Justice Centers within individual communities throughout the state.

25. Enact legislation to fund and establish Juvenile Assessment Centers through the Governor's Office of Criminal Justice Planning, the California Department of the Youth Authority Youth Services Bureau, the probation authority, and the juvenile court to screen juvenile status offenders. The process must take appropriate action within the current 6-hour time limit in which the juvenile can be legally detained.

26. Enact legislation to mandate that the State Department of Education establish a program to require testing of all juveniles in primary grades to determine physiological or psychological learning disabilities.

Federal Agency Recommendations

1. Increase the availability of federal resources to state and local gang- and drug-related case investigations.

2. Increase public awareness of the Internal Revenue Service's (IRS's) cash transaction reporting requirements for businesses, and enforce compliance with these regulations.

3. Increase the use of federal "cross designation" of local police officers and prosecutors to allow local authorities to use the federal system.

4. Coordinate Immigration and Naturalization Service (INS) investigations with state and local authorities to identify known offenders who may be suitable for deportation proceedings and also to increase the seizure of narcotics illegally imported across our borders.

5. Coordinate federal agency investigations with state and local authorities to identify opportunities for interdiction. Use military forces and their resources to interdict more effectively the flow of illegal narcotics into our country.

6. Conduct a nationwide investigation of gang relationships with international narcotics traffickers. Establish, through the Federal Bureau of Investigation (FBI), a nationwide data base for gang drug-trafficking case information.

7. Continue funding to support victim/witness protection and relocation.

8. Continue and expand funding to Head Start–type programs.

9. Adopt federal legislation that provides mandatory sentences for gang members, their associates, or others who cross interstate lines for the purpose of conducting gang-related drug activities.

10. Provide vacant or unused military facilities that would be suitable for the confinement of adult or juvenile inmates to the California Department of Corrections, the California Department of the Youth Authority, or local governments.

Local Government Recommendations

1. Expand gang intervention programs to prevent continuing gang and drug involvement.

2. Set local government budget priorities to allocate funds to gang and drug prevention and enforcement programs.

3. Direct the Community Redevelopment Agency to develop job-generating, inner-city projects to develop residential communities and business/industry zones within affected communities.

School Program Recommendations

1. Establish a required gang and drug prevention program, coordinated with local law enforcement, community, and business organizations.

2. Provide and require, for continuing certification, training for administrators and teachers to raise awareness of the gang and drug problem, and outline prevention education curricula.

3. Provide components in the school prevention education program to enhance parental awareness of gang and drug problems, and refer parents or guardians to community support groups.

4. Coordinate with community-based organizations and law enforcement agencies to develop and implement a parental skills training program.

5. Establish and enforce codes within the schools to prohibit the display of gang "colors" and the use of pagers or car phones on school grounds.

6. In cooperation with local government and state agencies, expand after-school, weekend, and summer youth programs to appeal to broader based groups, especially in the age range of 10 to 18 years.

7. Establish a program within all school systems to require the testing of juveniles in primary grades to determine physiological and psychological learning disabilities.

Community-Based Organizations Recommendations

1. Identify and recruit successful community members and business persons to serve as role models and mentors to youths.

2. Seek support from local businesses and industries for employment training and placement programs.

3. Provide for community mobilization and involvement through Neighborhood Watch programs to encourage citizen participation and victim/witness cooperation.

4. Encourage parental responsibility, establish parental support programs to increase awareness of gang and drug problems, and provide 24-hour hot lines and counseling. Enhancing parental skills is critical to mitigating the gang problem.

5. Establish, in coordination with local law enforcement agencies and the schools, a parental notification program to inform parents or guardians when their children are involved in gang and drug activity.

6. Establish, in coordination with religious organizations, a prevention and intervention program utilizing role models and mentors for counseling youths.

7. Establish prevention and intervention programs in communities with special language or cultural needs.

8. Implement programs to encourage teenagers to serve as role models and to participate in community development programs.

Business and Industry Recommendations

1. Expand opportunities for business development through the state's Enterprise Zones.

2. Engage in "adopt a school," youth sports team sponsorship, inner-city job placement, and executive volunteer job training and counseling programs.

3. Develop training programs and work experience opportunities for youths, targeting both gang members and potential gang members.

Media Recommendations

1. Cover all aspects of the gang and drug problem, including the success of intervention and prevention programs.

2. Provide public service announcements and programming for public education on gang and drug prevention and parenting responsibilities.

3. Ensure that gang-related reporting does not glorify the gang culture or attribute acts to any one gang by name.

SUMMARY

We have in this chapter traced the history and development of gang intervention efforts in the United States during the 20th century. Benign neglect of low level gang problems gave way in midcentury to the detached work approach. Evaluated as ineffective, though in fact never adequately implemented, it yielded to the opportunities provision strategy during the decades of the 1960s and early 1970s. The United States grew more conservative in its attitudes toward many social problems in the 1970s and 1980s, including the problem of juvenile gangs. The deterrence/incarceration era, still largely with us in the 1990s, predominated. However, there are the beginnings of a new constellation of these approaches, perhaps a more prescriptive and potent combination of "carrot and stick." We strongly support this comprehensive approach to gang intervention, as it appears more accurately than single-targeted approaches to respond to the multicausal complexity of gang formation and behavior.

NOTES

[1] Additional detailed descriptions of detached gang work are provided by Bernstein (1964); Crawford, Malamud, and Dumpson (1950); and Fox (1985).

[2] Spergel et al. (1989) comment that this model "assumes that the gang problem may be only partially amenable to police suppression. Gang interventions must be defined in broader terms. The youth gang suppression strategy must be incorporated as part of an interagency community collaborative approach which also gives due attention to prevention and social intervention" (p. 173).

REFERENCES

Amandes, R. B. (1979). Hire a gang leader: A delinquency prevention program that works. *Juvenile and Family Court Journal, 30,* 37–40.

Baca, C. (1988, June). *Juvenile gangs in Albuquerque.* Paper presented at the meeting of the Coordinating Council of the Albuquerque Police Department, Albuquerque, NM.

Bernstein, S. (1964). *Youth on the streets.* New York: Association Press.

Bremmer, R. H. (1976). Other people's children. *Journal of Social History, 16,* 83–103.

California Council on Criminal Justice. (1989). *State Task Force on Gangs and Drugs: Final Report.* Sacramento, CA: Author.

California Youth Gang Task Force. (1981). *Community access team.* Sacramento: Author.

Cloward, R. A., & Ohlin, L. E. (1960). *Delinquency and opportunity: A theory of delinquent gangs.* New York: Free Press.

Crawford, P. L., Malamud, D. I., & Dumpson, J. R. (1950). *Working with teen-age gangs. A report on the Central Harlem Street Clubs Project.* New York: Welfare Council of New York City.

DeLeon, R. V. (1977). Averting violence in the gang community. *The Police Chief, 44,* 52–53.

Dumpson, J. R. (1949). An approach to antisocial street gangs. *Federal Probation, 13,* 22–29.

Filipczak, J., Friedman, R. M., & Reese, S. C. (1979). PREP: Educational programming to prevent juvenile problems. In J. S. Stumphauzer (Ed.), *Progress in behavior therapy with delinquents.* Springfield, IL: Charles C Thomas.

Fox, J. R. (1985). Mission impossible? Social work practice with Black urban youth gangs. *Social Work, 30,* 25–31.

Furfey, P. H. (1926). *The gang age.* New York: Macmillan.

Gannon, T. M. (1965). *The changing role of the street worker in the Council of Social and Athletic Clubs.* New York City Youth Board Research Department.

Gardner, S. (1983). *Street gangs.* New York: Franklin Watts.

Goldstein, A. P. (1983). United States. In A. P. Goldstein & M. H. Segall (Eds.), *Aggression in global perspective.* Elmsford, NY: Pergamon.

Goldstein, A. P., Glick, B., Irwin, M. J., Pask-McCartney, C., & Rubama, I. (1989). *Reducing delinquency: Intervention in the community.* Elmsford, NY: Pergamon.

Hagedorn, J. (1988). *People and folks: Gangs, crime and the underclass in a rustbelt city.* Chicago: Lake View.

Haire, T. D. (1979). Street gangs: Some suggested remedies for violence and vandalism. *The Police Chief, 46,* 54–55.

Klein, M. W. (1968). *The Ladino Hills Project* (Final Report). Washington, DC: Office of Juvenile Delinquency and Youth Development.

Klein, M. W. (1971). *Street gangs and street workers.* Englewood Cliffs, NJ: Prentice-Hall.

Kobrin, S. (1959). The Chicago Area Project: A twenty-five-year assessment. *Annals of the American Academy of Political and Social Science, 322,* 136–151.

Krisberg, B. (1974). Gang youth and hustling: The psychology of survival. *Issues in Criminology, 9,* 243–255.

Los Angeles Unified School District. (1989). *GREAT: Gang Resistance Education and Training.* Los Angeles: Office of Instruction.

Mattick, H. W., & Caplan, N. S. (1962). *Chicago Youth Development Project: The Chicago Boys Club.* Ann Arbor, MI: Institute for Social Research.

Maxson, C. L., & Klein, M. W. (1983). Gangs—Why we couldn't stay away. In J. R. Kleugel (Ed.), *Evaluating juvenile justice.* Newbury Park, CA: Sage.

Miller, W. B. (1974). American youth gangs: Past and present. In A. Blumberg (Ed.), *Current perspectives on criminal behavior.* New York: Knopf.

Morales, A. (1981). *Treatment of Hispanic gang members.* Los Angeles: University of California, Neuropsychiatric Institute.

Mulvihill, D. J., Tumin, M. M., & Curtis, L. A. (1969). *Crimes of violence.* Washington, DC: National Commission on the Causes and Prevention of Violence.

Needle, J. A., & Stapleton, W. V. (1982). *Police handling of youth gangs.* Washington, DC: National Juvenile Justice Assessment Center.

New York City Youth Board. (1960). *Reaching the fighting gang.* New York: Author.

New York State Division for Youth. (1990). *Reaffirming prevention: Report of the Task Force on Juvenile Gangs.* Albany, NY: Author.

Puffer, J. A. (1912). *The boy and his gang.* Boston: Houghton Mifflin.

Quicker, J. C. (1983). *Seven decades of gangs.* Sacramento: State of California Commission on Crime Control and Violence Prevention.

Sheldon, W. H. (1949). *Varieties of delinquent youth.* New York: Harper.

Spergel, I. A. (1965). *Street gang work: Theory and practice.* Reading, MA: Addison-Wesley.

Spergel, I. A., Ross, R. E., Curry, G. D., & Chance, R. (1989). *Youth gangs: Problems and response.* Washington, DC: Office of Juvenile Justice and Delinquency Prevention.

Stuart, R. B., Jayaratne, S., & Tripoldi, T. (1976). Changing adolescent deviant behavior through reprogramming the behavior of parents and teachers. *Canadian Journal of Behavioral Science, 8,* 132–144.

Thompson, D. W., & Jason, L. A. (1988). Street gangs and preventive interventions. *Criminal Justice and Behavior, 15,* 323–333.

Thrasher, F. M. (1963). *The gang.* University of Chicago Press. (Original work published 1927)

Torchia, J. R. (1980, December). Ocean Township Youth Volunteer Corps. *Law and Order,* pp. 12–15.

Willis-Kistler, P. (1988, November). Fighting gangs with recreation. *P & R,* pp. 45–49.

Willman, M. T., & Snortum, J. R. (1982). A police program for employment of youth gang members. *International Journal of Offender Therapy and Comparative Criminology, 26,* 207–214.

Yablonsky, L. (1967). *The violent gang.* New York: Penguin.

PART II

Psychological Interventions

CHAPTER 3

Cognitive-Behavioral Interventions

Clive R. Hollin

Even a cursory glance at the literature reveals a wealth of research into gangs from many different disciplines and theoretical perspectives (Huff, 1990). For example, it is clear that gangs serve many different functions for gang members: To use a widely cited example, Yablonsky (1959) distinguished *violent, social,* and *delinquent* gangs. Indeed, the defining of different types of gangs has continued to inform research efforts, as illustrated by Goldstein's (1991) analysis of gangs as delinquents, gangs as hyperadolescents, gangs as groups, and gangs as communities. Some research has examined gang membership for broad sociodemographic characteristics, including gender (e.g., Campbell, 1984), city of origin (e.g., Moore, Vigil, & Garcia, 1983), and ethnicity (e.g., Chin, 1990). Other studies have considered specific forms of gang activity such as drug use (e.g., Fagan, 1989) and street violence (e.g., Klein & Maxson, 1989). A range of intervention alternatives, using psychological, law enforcement, and social policy strategies, has been undertaken to bring about change at individual, group, community, and state levels (Goldstein, 1991).

The aim of this chapter is to suggest how cognitive-behavioral theory and associated methods of intervention might be applied in gang intervention programs. Given the breadth of the gang research literature, I have selected the literature on delinquent behavior to illustrate the application of cognitive-behavioral theory. The first part of the chapter offers a review of this theory and of its application, at both theoretical and practical levels, to delinquency. The second part extrapolates from the literature on delinquency to recommend strategies for the implementation of effective gang intervention programs.

REVIEW

A review of basic principles associated with cognitive-behavioral theory will form the basis for an application of this theory to account for delinquent behavior. From this basis it will be possible to examine intervention strategies grounded in cognitive-behavioral theory and to consider the outcomes of such interventions with young offenders.

Cognitive-Behavioral Theory

Since ancient times, there have been explanations of human actions that locate the cause of behavior *inside* the person. Many philosophical and psychological theories emphasize an inner world—be it biological, mental, or spiritual—in seeking to explain human behavior. The genesis of a different way of explaining behavior can be traced to the turn of this century, with the discovery of *classical conditioning* by the Russian physiologist and Nobel Prize winner, Ivan Pavlov. The force of Pavlov's discovery lay in the conceptual shift toward an explanation of behavior in terms of an interaction between the individual and the outside world. Supplanting the view of behavior as necessarily the product of some biological or psychological force inside the person, a new understanding of the world took shape, with the emphasis on events *external* to the person. This idea was to revolutionize the discipline of psychology, in terms both of theory and of method, as researchers began examining *behavior* as a phenomenon worthy of study in its own right rather than treating it simply as a by-product of mysterious inner forces.

This new behavioral approach was adopted by John B. Watson, whose 1913 paper, "Psychology As the Behaviorist Views It," caught the mood of the times in an American university system seeking an alternative to unscientific mentalistic theories and methods of research. In essence, Watson argued that humans, like other animals, are born with innate stimulus-response reflexes and that through the process of classical conditioning we learn more and more complex chains of behavior. Although the study of classical conditioning continues to provide a rich source of ideas (Rescorla, 1988), with the benefit of hindsight we know that most human behavior is almost certainly too complex to be reduced to chains of associations built from innate reflexes. However, it is the line of thought evoked by Watson that is crucial: Watson, like Freud, set into motion a new way of thinking about the world, and as Freud's theories were modified by the post-Freudians, so Watson's ideas were in turn developed by the neobehaviorists.

The individual destined to be the most influential of the neobehaviorists was a young researcher at Harvard University who between 1930 and 1935 developed the basic principles for a revolutionary approach to understanding behavior. This new approach was called *behavior analysis,* and its champion was B. F. Skinner.

Behavior Analysis

As Kazdin (1979) notes, one of the great errors made in many textbooks is the dismissal of the principles of behavior analysis as simplistic and mechanistic. Although those principles are readily understandable, the associated philosophical and theoretical issues are complex. It is beyond the scope of this chapter to cover these issues; however, a number of excellent texts address them (Catania & Harnad, 1988; Hayes, 1989; Lee, 1988; Modgil & Modgil, 1987; Rachlin, 1991; Zuriff, 1985).

The basis for Skinner's contribution can be traced to a line of research concerning the relationship between the consequences of a behavior and the probability of that same behavior recurring in the future. Skinner's experimental studies led to the formulation of a number of key concepts. Behavior that operates on the environment to produce consequences was termed *operant behavior* by Skinner; the relationship between behavior and its consequences he called a *contingency.* Skinner described two types of contingency, which he named *reinforcement* and *punishment.*

A *reinforcement contingency* is one in which the consequences of a behavior increase the likelihood of that behavior occurring in the future. There are two types of reinforcement contingency: *Positive reinforcement* occurs when a behavior is maintained or increased because it leads to consequences that the individual finds rewarding; *negative reinforcement,* on the other hand, occurs when the consequence of the behavior is avoidance of or escape from an aversive situation. It is important to note that reinforcement and punishment are individually defined. It is easy to assume that some rewards, such as money or praise, have universal reinforcement properties, but this is not the case: For example, some individuals, perhaps adolescents in particular, find praise far from rewarding (Brophy, 1981). On the other hand, consequences that most people might find unrewarding or aversive, such as verbal or physical abuse, can be rewarding for some individuals in certain situations and hence can reinforce their behavior.

In operant terms, a *punishment contingency* is defined as one in which the consequences of a behavior lead to a decrease in the frequency of that behavior. (From the point of view of clarity, it is unfortunate that the term *punishment* has different meanings in the context of behavior analysis and in everyday usage.) As with reinforcement, there are two types of punishment: With *positive punishment,* an unpleasant outcome (which need not be physical pain) is contingent on the behavior; with *negative punishment,* the behavior leads to the loss of something the individual finds rewarding. As with rewarding outcomes, the experience of an aversive outcome must be understood in individual terms.

In addition to operant behavior and contingencies, this brief introduction to behavior analysis must include one final topic: *three-term contingency.* Behavior, in the main, does not happen at random; rather, environmental events signal that if a certain behavior is carried out, then it is likely to be reinforced or punished. For example, an unruly child who tends to shout in the classroom is unlikely to do so when the classroom is empty; it is more likely that a number of cues—the presence of certain other children, a particular teacher, a type of lesson—will set the scene for the shouting. The child has learned that shouting when these cues are present either produces rewarding consequences such as peer approval (positive reinforcement) or leads to the avoidance of events such as a disliked lesson (negative reinforcement). The relationship between the setting or antecedent events, the behavior, and the consequences is called a three-term contingency. This notion gives rise to the much-used A-B-C format—that is, antecedent-behavior-consequence.

Behavioral analysis is the attempt to arrive at an understanding of a behavior through the formulation of an A-B-C sequence. In essence, the goal of a behavioral analysis is to understand the function, in terms of reinforcement and punishment contingencies, of a behavior for the individual concerned. Hence an A-B-C formulation is properly termed a *functional analysis.*

The type of behavior analysis carried out in laboratory studies, sometimes with animals, is usually called *experimental* analysis of behavior. However, the task of *applied* behavior analysis is to move away from the laboratory and use the principles of functional analysis to understand human behavior in real-life settings. The departure from the highly controlled laboratory environment makes applied behavior analysis an immensely difficult task. The difficulties are twofold. First, the complexity of most people's lives makes it impossible to discover every event in their learning history and to appreciate every influence on their behavior. Hoffman's (1991) account of the way in which even the most subtle variations in parental behavior can produce marked differences in the behavior of children illustrates this point perfectly. Second, because people differ from animals in a variety of important ways—principally in our cognitive abilities, in our highly evolved use of verbal language, and in the nature of our social environment—there must be significant adjustments in some of the findings from laboratory studies (e.g., Lowe, 1983).

The struggle between theory and real life is perhaps nowhere more evident than in the attempts of behavior analysts to solve the "problem" of private events. As we will see, this search for a solution has divided the ranks of behavior analysts, giving rise to a modified behavioral approach called cognitive-behavioral theory. First, however, what is the problem?

The "Problem" of Private Events

The history of the problem can be traced back to Watson's view that because the private, internal world is impossible to study scientifically, it should not be of concern to psychology. An unfortunate legacy of this view is the criticism that behaviorism denies the existence of, or at best ignores, "private" events such as thoughts and feelings. Such criticism is misplaced if directed at contemporary behaviorism: As Skinner (1974) states, "A science of behavior must consider the place of private stimuli. . . . The question, then, is this: What is inside the skin and how do we know about it? The answer is, I believe, the heart of radical behaviorism" (pp. 211–212). In a partial answer to his own question, Skinner (1986a) has proposed a place for private events in a behavioral sequence: "In a given episode the environment acts upon the organism, something happens inside, the organism then acts upon the environment, and certain consequences follow" (p. 716).

The key issue that arises, and that is the essence of the "problem," is whether what happens inside the skin can be considered behavior and hence be part of behavior analysis or whether internal, private events should be accorded a separate, perhaps mentalistic, status and so fall outside the realm of behavior analysis. The position of behavior analysts is that private events are behaviors: That is, private events are seen as being established by a particular environment and maintained and modified by environmental consequences. Do private events cause behavior? Again Skinner is clear: "Private events . . . may be called causes, but not initiating causes" (see Catania & Harnad, 1988, p. 486). The initiation of operant behavior, including private behavior, is located in the environment, most often in our social world. However, once initiated, one behavior can lead to another and so on; thus private behavior can be the precursor to overt, observable behavior.

As is clear, accepting this approach to understanding human behavior means accepting a certain view of the world, our place within it, and the relative status of our own thoughts and feelings. However, behavior analysis is only one approach; of course, there are many others. In some cases there are few if any points of convergence between theories; in other cases some overlap exists. Albert Bandura recognized the overlap between traditional behavioral approaches and emerging cognitive psychology, blending the two to form the hybrid of social learning theory.

Social Learning Theory

Social learning theory is in part an extension of operant principles but with increased attention to cognition and with changes in the role and status of cognition (Bandura, 1986). The departure from mainstream behavioral thinking began with the studies that elucidated the phenomenon of learning by observation (e.g., Bandura, 1977). Whereas behavioral theory maintained that behavior was acquired through external reinforcement, the studies of Bandura and his colleagues suggested that learning could also take place at a purely cognitive level—that is, without the presence of reinforcement contingencies. Further, according to the principles of operant learning, maintenance of behavior depends on the environment. Bandura modified this view by introducing the concept of motivation rather than reinforcement as the force that maintains behavior. Motivation, in Bandura's view, takes three forms: *external reinforcement,* as in operant learning; *vicarious reinforcement,* which comes from observing other people; and *self-reinforcement,* as in a sense of personal pride or achievement. The introduction of motivation as a cause of behavior, as well as the concept of internal as well as external reinforcement, marked a clear divergence from traditional behaviorism.

Although social learning theory overlaps to some degree with behavior analysis, it is clear that the cognitive revolution in psychology has progressed at considerable speed (Baars, 1986). As psychologists increasingly have turned their attention to the study of cognition, so cognitive theories such as information processing theory have been developed. Social learning theory has, in a sense, been overthrown by the cognitive revolution, and the term *cognitive-behavioral theory* has now entered popular usage. The theoretical research and debate continue apace, and, as the theories advance, cognitive-behavioral theory continually mutates into new forms, seemingly with an ever more cognitive appearance.

Theory-Practice Links

The importance of theory becomes clear when attempts are made to translate theory into practice. As we will see, shifts in theory have in a few short years led to dramatic changes in treatment styles and methods. In little more than two decades, behavior therapy has been overtaken by cognitive-behavior therapy (Fishman, Rotgers, & Franks, 1988). Accompanying this development has been the rise of cognitive therapy, quite different in form and emphasis from its predecessors (Brewin, 1988).

The discerning reader will by now have realized that it is difficult if not impossible to offer a watertight definition of cognitive-behavioral theory. It follows that it will likewise be difficult to arrive at a universally agreed upon definition of cognitive-behavioral intervention. Kendall and Bacon (1988) have described the situation as follows:

> There have been many attempts to define cognitive behavior therapy and to define how it is similar to and different from traditional behavior therapy and other approaches (e.g., Beck, 1970; Kendall, 1985; Kendall & Hollon, 1979; Mahoney, 1977; Mahoney & Arkoff, 1978; Meichenbaum, 1977). All of these reviews come to a similar conclusion: it may be undesirable to specify with much precision what cognitive behavior therapy is and where its boundaries lie. Cognitive behavior therapy is a general perspective that lacks a single unifying theory. (p. 156)

Therefore, although one might have a favored perspective within the broad church of cognitive-behavioral theory, an applied cognitive-behavioral analysis must take heed of environmental factors, cognition, affect, and overt behavior. Such an analysis can be used to develop an understanding of all social behaviors, from the "micro" level of an individual to the "macro" level of a culture (Lamal, 1991; Skinner, 1986b), including delinquent behaviors.

Learning, Cognition, and Delinquent Behavior

Association and Reinforcement

If we trace the development of theories within mainstream criminology, the impact of behavioral theory is evident. Sutherland (1924) was perhaps the first to emphasize the role of learning in the acquisition of delinquent behavior; it is surely more than coincidence, given the time when he was writing, that his theory was called "differential *association* theory." While unequivocally holding the view that crime is socially defined by powerful individuals within society, Sutherland asked the awkward question of why some people become criminals whereas others do not. He suggested that the answer lies in learning, particularly learning that takes place in association with others who are favorably disposed toward lawbreaking (which need not mean actual criminals, although they would be included). Sutherland argued that the content of learning includes both the skills to commit specific offenses and the attitudes and motivations conducive to applying those skills. Sutherland's anticipation of many later theoretical developments is remarkable: His account encompasses social process and social structure, skills and cognitions, and a view that criminal behavior is an acquired behavior like any other and not a sign of some mysterious psychopathology.

Following Sutherland, Jeffery (1965) suggested that advances in operant learning could be used to refine differential association theory to produce a fresh approach called "differential reinforcement theory." Briefly, Jeffery proposed that delinquent behavior is an operant behavior acquired and maintained through the reinforcing consequences it produces for the individual concerned. In most delinquent acts the payoff is material and financial gain, although there can be social rewards such as peer approval and peer group status. Delinquent acts can, of course, also produce aversive consequences such as apprehension and loss of liberty, and these consequences can have a punishing (in an operant sense) effect on the delinquent behavior. In the final analysis, therefore, it is the balance of reinforcement and punishment in the individual's learning history that is important.

The application of concepts from learning theory to delinquent behavior continues to elicit interest and generate debate (Hollin, 1989; Morris & Braukmann, 1987). However, with the advent of social learning theory, theories of delinquent behavior based on association and reinforcement began to undergo significant changes.

Social Learning and Cognition

The ideas and concepts from social learning theory have been applied to the study of delinquent behavior both by psychologists (e.g., Nietzel, 1979) and by sociologists and criminologists (e.g., Akers, 1977; Krohn, Massey, & Skinner, 1987). From the standpoint of social learning theory, the acquisition of criminal behavior—including the attitudes conducive to the commission of offenses as well as the necessary skills—can be traced either to reinforcement through consequences or to modeling and imitation. Models for delinquent behavior can be found throughout the social environment: in the actions of parents, siblings, and peers; on television and in films; and in magazines and books. Maintenance of delinquent behavior can be attributed to the motivating factors of tangible gain, social reward, or personal reward such as a sense of pride and increased self-esteem following successful burglary of a house or avoidance of detection after a mugging.

In an increased acknowledgment of the role of cognition, Akers (1990) suggests that individuals develop definitions of their behavior that justify their actions. For example, a car thief may argue that it is justifiable to steal cars because no one gets hurt, the owners of the cars can stand the loss, and, in any case, they are insured, so no one loses. This neutralization, which obviously involves some cognitive processing, establishes the meaning of the delinquent behavior for the perpetrator. In this respect, cognitive processes constitute a highly personalized aspect of an individual's delinquency. Social learning theory offers perhaps the most psychologically sophisticated theory in mainstream criminology, as Akers notes:

> The full behavioral formula in social learning theory includes both positive and negative punishment and positive and negative reinforcement. It also includes schedules of reinforcement, imitation, associations, normative definitions (attitudes and rationalizations), discriminative stimuli, and other variables in both criminal and conforming behavior. (p. 660)

Following contemporary developments in psychological theory, studies of delinquent behavior have concentrated increasingly on the study of cognition.

Although one could rightly maintain that the study of cognitive ability as assessed via intelligence tests is a traditional concern in the study of delinquency, it is *social cognition* that attracts most contemporary interest. Social cognition can be defined as that aspect of cognition concerned with attitudes and beliefs about other people and their actions and with one's own social functioning in relation to others. This cognitive emphasis is not a theoretical departure from social learning or cognitive-behavioral theory; rather, it is the process of completing the necessary research *within* that paradigm.

The research itself can be loosely classified into two sorts, concerning styles of social cognition and social information processing.

Styles of Social Cognition

A variety of styles and characteristics of social cognition, outlined in the following sections, have been associated with delinquency (see Hollin, 1990a; Ross & Fabiano, 1985).

Empathy and role taking

The ability to see things from the other person's point of view and to display empathy is an important aspect of social cognition. A number of studies have suggested that delinquents score low on measures of empathy and role taking (e.g., Chandler, 1973; Kaplan & Arbuthnot, 1985), although other studies have found no consistent difference in empathy between delinquents and nondelinquents (e.g., Ellis, 1982; Lee & Prentice, 1988). This variation in findings across studies may be attributable to factors such as the type of measure used in the study; the subjects' age, sex, and length of criminal career; and the type of offense involved (DeWolfe, Jackson, & Winterberger, 1988).

Locus of control

Locus of control refers to the degree to which individuals believe their behavior to be under their own *internal* control or under the control of *external* factors such as luck, fate, or people in authority. A number of studies have suggested that delinquents tend toward external control—that is, they see their behavior as being controlled by factors outside their individual control (Beck & Ollendick, 1976; Kumchy & Sayer, 1980). However, not all studies have found a difference between delinquents and nondelinquents (Groh & Goldenberg, 1976). This result may be due to sample variations: For example, violent young offenders tend toward greater external control than do young offenders who are nonviolent (Hollin & Wheeler, 1982).

Moral reasoning

Kohlberg (1978) argues that moral development progresses through three levels, with two stages at each level. At the lower stages, moral reasoning is characterized by concreteness and egocentricity; at the higher stages, moral reasoning is guided by abstract notions such as "justice" and "rights" and is much more social in orientation. In this model, delinquent behavior is associated with a delay in the development of moral reasoning: Given the opportunity for crime, the individual lacks the ability to resist temptation. A number of researchers have examined this proposition, with the traditional result that the experimental outcomes are equivocal (Blasi, 1980; Jennings, Kilkenny, & Kohlberg, 1983; Jurkovic, 1980). However, in a recent meta-analysis, Nelson, Smith, and Dodd (1990) did report the overall conclusion from the data that delinquents are disadvantaged in moral reasoning ability. Nevertheless, Nelson et al. suggest that the strength of the relationship between moral reasoning and delinquent behavior depends on other factors. For example, moral reasoning is correlated with other cognitive developmental processes that should be controlled if research is to reveal true between-group differences in moral development. In addition, the heterogeneity of the offender population may suggest within-group differences that should be taken into account in the search for differences between offenders and nonoffenders.

The relationship of moral reasoning to other cognitive processes is made clear in a study of sociocognition in delinquents conducted by Lee and Prentice (1988). This study assessed a range of indices of cognitive functioning—including empathy, role-taking ability, logical cognition, and moral reasoning—in both delinquent and nondelinquent samples. Comparing across groups, the researchers found that the delinquents scored significantly lower on role taking, logical cognition, and moral reasoning, though not on empathy. However, when they examined the interrelations of these measures of sociocognition, they found significant correlations between role taking, logical cognition, and moral development. Lee and Prentice reached the conclusion that role taking actually plays a mediating role between logical cognition and moral reasoning. It appears, therefore, that the position is more complex than simply one of differences between delinquents and nondelinquents in respective levels of moral reasoning.

The importance of within-group differences in delinquent populations is illustrated by a study conducted by Thornton and Reid (1982). They found that convicted offenders who had committed crimes with no financial benefit (assault, murder, sex offenses) showed more mature moral judgment than those who transgressed for money (robbery, burglary, theft, fraud). Overall, it is safe to conclude that—although there are indications that young offenders use less mature moral reasoning than do nonoffenders—the association between moral development and delinquent behavior is unlikely to be either simple or linear.

Self-control

Low self-control, often linked with impulsive behavior, is described by Ross and Fabiano (1985) as the omission of thought between impulse and action. Poor self-control is characterized by a failure to stop and think, a failure to learn effective ways of thinking about social situations, and a failure to generate alternative courses of action. The empirical evidence is equivocal with respect to impulsivity in delinquent samples. Some studies have found higher levels of impulsivity in delinquents (e.g., Rotenberg & Nachshon, 1979); others, no difference between delinquent and nondelinquent samples (e.g., Saunders, Reppucci, & Sarata, 1973). The variation in findings is, again, probably due to the use of different measures of impulsivity in different studies and to the heterogeneity of the delinquent population (Arbuthnot, Gordon, & Jurkovic, 1987).

Social Information Processing

Dodge (1986) outlined four essential steps in the effective cognitive processing of social information: (a) encoding social cues, (b) cognitively representing and interpreting social cues, (c) searching for the appropriate response, and (d) deciding on the best option for making a response. This cognitive sequence culminates, of course, in the actual performance of the behavior itself. Deficits and biases at any of these stages can result in antisocial behavior, perhaps aggressive behavior in particular (Akhtar & Bradley, 1991).

Encoding and representation

The ability accurately to perceive, interpret, and comprehend social cues, perceived mainly in the form of nonverbal signals, is a fundamental component of social cognition. It demands attention to a wide array of cues in order to define the social situation before deciding on a suitable response. There is evidence that some individuals, particularly aggressive young people, search for and perceive fewer social cues than the norm (Dodge & Newman, 1981; Slaby & Guerra, 1988), have difficulty interpreting some basic nonverbal cues such as facial expression (McCown, Johnson, & Austin, 1986), and have a cognitive set that predisposes them consistently and erroneously to interpret the behavior of others as aggressive and hostile (Dodge & Frame, 1982).

Searching and deciding

Cognitively searching for suitable responses in a social situation and then deciding on the best course of action is sometimes called *social problem solving*. This cognitive process demands the ability in a given social situation to generate feasible courses of action, consider the various outcomes that might follow, and plan how to achieve the preferred outcome. In a typical study with young offenders, Freedman, Rosenthal, Donahoe, Schlundt, and McFall (1978) compared the social problem-solving ability of delinquents and nondelinquents, using the Adolescent Problem Inventory (API). The API consists of a series of social problem situations, such as an invitation from peers to join in a delinquent act; respondents say what their actions would be in the various situations. According to Freedman et al., the responses of a delinquent sample to the API items were rated as less socially competent than the responses of a matched nondelinquent group. The delinquents used a more limited range of alternatives to solve interpersonal problems, and they relied more on verbal and physical aggression. In another study using the API, Veneziano and Veneziano (1988) also found that delinquents scored lower than nondelinquents on the inventory, although they observed considerable within-group differences in performance for the delinquent sample. Similar findings have been reported by Higgins and Thies (1981) and, specifically concerning female delinquents, by Gaffney and McFall (1981) and Ward and McFall (1986).

With respect to the selection of responses in social situations, several studies have shown that delinquent and aggressive adolescents consider fewer consequences of their actions than do controls (Hains & Ryan, 1983; Slaby & Guerra, 1988). The final stage in Dodge's sequence refers, of course, to action rather than cognition, and it is appropriate to note that there is some evidence that delinquents do tend to have difficulty with social performance skills (Spence, 1981).

In summary, the implication of much of the research is that *some* delinquents experience a degree of difficulty in social functioning, including both social cognition and social performance (Hollin, 1990b). However, there are two cautionary points to emphasize. First, the number and range of empirical studies is not vast, and the artificiality of many experimental studies may make it prudent to treat the data as tentative rather than absolute. The second point refers to the heterogeneity of the delinquent population, as Veneziano and Veneziano (1988) suggest: "Delinquents are a diverse group with respect to their social skills, with a wide range of knowledge and presumably behavior" (p. 167). Indeed, Renwick and Emler (1991) did not find evidence of poor social skills in their sample of delinquents. It would be wrong, therefore, to make the assumption that all delinquents have social difficulties.

Cognitive-Behavioral Intervention

There is a long history of interventions with delinquents based on behavioral theory and using procedures such as token economies, contingency contracting, functional family therapy, and skills training. A number of summaries and reviews of this body of work are available (e.g., Blakely & Davidson, 1984; Feldman, 1977; Gendreau & Ross, 1987; Hollin, 1989; Milan, 1987a, 1987b; Nietzel, 1979; Stumphauzer, 1986). However, given the more recent developments in social learning theory and the new emphasis on cognition, there are fewer studies that might accurately be described as focusing on *cognitive*-behavioral interventions. Although summaries are available (Hollin, 1990a; Ross & Fabiano, 1985), a brief overview may be useful.

The evidence discussed earlier suggests that there are grounds (though by no means certain grounds) for believing that delinquents show less well developed social cognition than do nondelinquents. A number of intervention programs used with delinquents have therefore attempted to modify social cognition using cognitive-behavioral techniques. Focal areas have included role taking, moral reasoning, self-control, and social problem solving.

Role Taking

Chandler (1973) has reported the evaluation of an intervention program designed to encourage young male offenders to see themselves from other peoples' perspectives and so to develop their own role-taking abilities. The design compared three groups: a role-taking skills training group, a placebo treatment control group, and a no-treatment control group. The role-taking skills group took part in exercises such as drama and filmmaking to develop and enhance their ability both to see themselves from another perspective and to appreciate the views of others. The outcome data showed that the group's role-taking abilities were enhanced, and, at an 18-month follow-up, the skills group had committed fewer offenses than the controls. A similarly successful intervention program in social perspective-taking skills, conducted with female delinquents, has been described by Chalmers and Townsend (1990).

Moral Reasoning Development

As noted earlier, there is support for the proposition that delinquents are characterized by delayed or impaired moral reasoning. A number of intervention programs have therefore sought to modify moral reasoning with groups of offenders. In a typical study, Gibbs, Arnold, Cheesman, and Ahlborn (1984) evaluated a sociomoral reasoning development program for male and female institutionalized delinquents. The intervention took the form of small group discussions on various sociomoral dilemmas: The delinquents were encouraged to give their views and opinions on their moral choices, but they were also required to justify their thoughts and to engage in reaching a consensus on the best solution. Compared to a no-treatment control group, the intervention group showed a significant upward movement in moral reasoning as assessed by Kohlberg's stages of moral judgment. A similar study, although carried out with adolescents "at risk" for delinquency, also reported beneficial effects from a moral reasoning development program (Arbuthnot & Gordon, 1986). This latter program elicited not only improved moral reasoning but also improvement on a number of behavioral measures including academic performance and police/court contact.

Self-Control and Self-Instruction

The development of self-control in childhood follows three stages: (a) The child's behavior is controlled by the verbal community, (b) the child's own overt speech regulates his or her behavior, and (c) the child's covert or "inner" speech governs his or her actions (Luria, 1961). A failure to progress through this developmental sequence results in maladaptive regulatory self-statements, with an associated lack of self-control and tendency toward impulsive behavior. Techniques have been developed to train or modify self-control by changing the individual's self-statements; such self-instructional training has become popular, especially with child and adolescent populations (Dush, Hirt, & Schroeder, 1989).

Self-instructional training follows the developmental stages just described: First, a model performs a task and makes appropriate overt self-statements, then the trainee practices the same behavior. The trainee then progresses to whispered self-instruction and finally to covert, silent self-instruction. The trainee is encouraged to use self-statements to self-observe, self-evaluate, and self-reinforce appropriate overt behaviors (Kanfer, 1975).

A number of studies have used such cognitive behavior modification procedures with young offenders. In a typical study, Snyder and White (1979) used self-instructional training with a group of aggressive adolescents having histories of criminal behavior and living in a residential facility. (A control group received no such training.) The first step in the program was to assess the participants' self-statements immediately before aggressive episodes; the young people then were encouraged to consider the consequences of both their self-statements and their actions. According to self-instructional procedures, appropriate, less aggressive verbalizations were then modeled, rehearsed, and practiced, first overtly and then covertly: The new verbalizations included self-reinforcing statements for successful behavior. In the final stage of the program, homework assignments were used to develop further self-monitoring and self-reinforcement skills. On three outcome measures—absence from class, fulfillment of social and self-care duties, and frequency of impulsive behavior—the self-instruction group performed better than controls at both a posttraining evaluation and an 8-week follow-up. Snyder and White's findings show that the cognitive-behavioral intervention was a valuable addition to the institutional token economy in which all the young offenders, treatment and control groups alike, were participating.

Anger control

An extension of self-control procedures is the development of techniques specifically addressing the control of anger. Owing much to the work of Novaco (e.g., Novaco, 1975, 1985; Novaco & Welsh, 1989), anger management has become a popular clinical technique generating a large body of experimental-clinical literature. The goal of anger management is not the elimination of anger but the self-regulation of cognition, emotion, and behavior through self-control. A typical anger management program has three components: (a) *cognitive preparation,* which teaches individuals about their own anger and its causes and effects; (b) *skill acquisition,* in which coping strategies—including self-statement modification, relaxation, and assertion skills—are taught; and (c) *application training,* in which the newly acquired skills are practiced in a range of supervised in vivo and role-play settings. Considerable resources are available regarding anger management programs for adolescents (Feindler & Ecton, 1986; Goldstein & Keller, 1987).

Anger control techniques have been widely used with offenders, particularly violent offenders, of all ages (Howells, 1989). In a typical study with delinquents, Feindler, Marriott, and Iwata (1984) evaluated an anger management program for young people suspended from school because of their offenses. In comparison with a no-treatment control group, those in the anger management group showed a number of positive changes, including decreases in aggressive behavior, improvement in problem-solving skills, and increases in observer-rated self-control. Like Snyder and White (1979) in their study of self-instructional training, Feindler et al. found that the anger management program was a valuable addition to the token economy in which all the delinquents were participating.

Social Problem Solving

The problem-solving skills needed for successful social adjustment include sensitivity to interpersonal problems along with the ability to see the consequences of one's actions, generate solutions to social problems, and think in terms of means and ends in planning the steps toward successful outcomes (Spivack, Platt, & Shure, 1976). In problem-solving skills training, cognitive techniques, particularly self-instructional training, are blended with modeling, role-playing, and discussion to train skills such as recognizing and defining problems, generating solutions, and planning for outcomes (Camp & Bash, 1981). Problem-solving training has been used successfully with a variety of client groups, including heroin addict offenders (Platt, Perry, & Metzger, 1980). A study by Hains and Hains (1987) illustrates the use of this type of cognitive intervention. A group of five institutionalized delinquents were trained in social problem-solving skills. All five showed immediate improvement in problem-solving ability, but two immediately returned to baseline levels after the initial training. The remaining three continued at follow-up to show improvement over baseline performance. In addition, there were indications of improvement in other aspects of institutional performance following the problem-solving skills training.

Multimodal Programs

In several of the studies discussed earlier, cognitive-behavioral techniques were particularly effective when used in conjunction with other behavioral methods such as the token economy. A number of studies have investigated the potency of multimodal programs that include both cognitive-behavioral and behavioral interventions.

In one such study, Gross, Brigham, Hopper, and Bologna (1980) used a combination of social skills training, behavior therapy, and self-management training with female delinquents. The program succeeded in increasing self-control, decreasing the number of social problems, and reducing school absenteeism and suspensions. The outcome literature includes a number of similar studies, mostly demonstrating the efficacy of these more complex programs (e.g., Bowman & Auerbach, 1982; DeLange, Lanham, & Barton, 1981; Guerra & Slaby, 1990; Hollin, Huff, Clarkson, & Edmondson, 1986; McDougall, Barnett, Ashurst, & Willis, 1987).

Complementing these individual studies has been another recent trend, toward the design and evaluation of large-scale comprehensive multimodal treatment packages. The Reasoning and Rehabilitation Program described in detail by Ross and Fabiano (1985) provides an excellent model for conducting a cognitively based intervention with offenders. An empirical evaluation of the program, although conducted with adult, not juvenile, offenders, demonstrated that it can significantly reduce recidivism (Ross, Fabiano, & Ewles, 1988).

Aggression Replacement Training (ART) is one of the most recent and comprehensive multimodal programs (Goldstein & Glick, 1987; Goldstein, Glick, Irwin, Pask-McCartney, & Rubama, 1989). ART uses a number of cognitive-behavioral and behavioral techniques, which are grouped into three categories: structured learning (also known as Skillstreaming), including both social skills training and social problem-solving training; anger control training; and moral education. Glick and Goldstein (1987) evaluated the application of ART with young male offenders. The program was successful with those who had committed less serious offenses (theft, drug use): In comparison with controls, they improved in terms of skill acquisition and institutional behavior, and after discharge they merited improved ratings from probation and parole officers. However, youths who had committed more serious offenses (murder, sex offense, violent crime) showed less change in institutional performance, though they did display an improvement in moral reasoning that was not evident with the less serious offenders.

Evaluation of Outcomes

Before considering the outcome studies it is worth noting Roberts' (1987) observation that, despite the large-scale professional and financial commitments to the rehabilitation of juvenile offenders, remarkably few research and follow-up studies have been reported. Thus the published studies represent only a sample, probably a small sample, of the total array of programs. Further, even when evaluative research is undertaken, a measure of offending behavior is likely to be omitted from the evaluation (Blakely & Davidson, 1984). One hypothetical explanation for this weakness in evaluation design lies in the distinction, or lack of it, between *clinical* and *criminological* measures.

Clinical Measures

Many of the outcome studies discussed earlier used a wide range of cognitive and behavioral measures in the evaluation of cognitive-behavioral programs. In terms of clinical outcome—that is, as measures of personal change in program participants—such measures make obvious sense as dependent variables in an experimental investigation. As might be expected, most studies report substantial improvements on clinical outcome measures, a result that testifies to the general efficacy of cognitive-behavioral techniques. This trend in outcomes can justly be claimed as success in purely clinical terms and as evidence of effective intervention methods that can foster personal change in delinquents. However, in one sense clinical efficacy is not the issue: These studies were carried out with *delinquents*. The question then becomes, What do clinical outcome measures have to do with modification of offending behavior as a criterion for successful outcome?

Emery and Marholin (1977) argue strongly that the literature is dominated by a strategy of "targeting behaviours that are believed to be incompatible with delinquency" (p. 867). Implicit in such a strategy are two related assumptions: first, that the clinical target is functionally related to the offending behavior; second, that modifying the clinical target will in turn modify the offending behavior. Establishing a functional relationship between the clinical measure and the delinquent behavior is an empirical concern (a point that applies to any intervention strategy). While supporting the importance of individual differences within the delinquent population, the evidence on social problem solving, moral development, and so on discussed earlier does suggest that delinquents as a group may be characterized by certain types and levels of social cognition. It is, however, an inferential leap to suppose that sociocognitive functioning *causes* offending behavior and a further leap to assume that modifying cognitive functioning will affect that behavior.

Exactly the same point has been made concerning behavioral interventions with delinquents (Blakely & Davidson, 1984; Emery & Marholin, 1977). Indeed, as Blakely and Davidson suggest, programs that target behaviors *associated* those inferential leaps with delinquency: "Temporal, setting, and behavioral generalization were hypothesized in suggesting that behavioral procedures would affect delinquency rates" (p. 261). It is clear that the strategy of using offending behavior as a measure of generalization from cognitive-behavioral (or, indeed, any other) programs is not without problems.

In discussing this issue, Hollin and Henderson (1984) suggest that the important distinction is between *stimulus generalization* and *response generalization*. Stimulus generalization is the transfer of a newly learned response to situations other than those in which the learning took place; response generalization, on the other hand, occurs when changing one response changes other responses in an individual's behavioral repertoire. Thus, for example, if an institutionalized young offender is trained in anger management skills and after release applies these skills with his or her probation officer, then stimulus generalization has occurred. However, monitoring the delinquent behavior of the young offender after release implies that the researcher expects response generalization—in other words, that improvement in anger control will, in turn, modify the delinquent behavior. It is not difficult to construct a hypothesis that causally links anger management with offending behavior. However—and this is critical—such a hypothesis awaits large-scale empirical verification. It follows that, by conducting individual change programs without empirical support, practitioners are simply playing the percentages in gambling that the assumed link exists and hence that a given intervention with delinquents will be successful.

Social problem solving provides an example of the uncertainty of the relationship between social cognition and delinquent behavior. As noted earlier, Freedman et al. (1978) reported that delinquents' responses on the Adolescent Problem Inventory (API) were rated as less socially competent than those of a control group. A later study by Hunter and Kelley (1986) investigated the relationship between performance on the API and level of offending. For a sample of 60 young offenders, API score was correlated with various aspects of delinquent behavior such as type of offense and number of arrests. The API score failed to correlate significantly with any of the measures of delinquency. Similarly, Veneziano and Veneziano (1988) found no relationship between number and types of offenses and API performance. However, Ward and McFall (1986) found that the scores of female delinquents on a similar inventory, the Problem Inventory for Adolescent Girls (Gaffney & McFall, 1981), did correlate significantly with self-reported delinquency. It is clear from these few studies that much remains to be learned about the role of social cognition in the etiology and maintenance of delinquency.

Criminological Measures

In addition to problems with generalization, the use of criminological measures poses particular problems for evaluation. Criminological data can be gathered in many forms, including self-report, police cautions, reconviction rates, time to reconviction, and offense type. There are difficulties with both self-reported and official measures of crime, as illustrated by two studies with delinquents. Spence and Marzillier (1981) used both types of measure—police arrest data and self-report of offenses—following social skills training with delinquents. They reported that "the most noticeable finding was the large discrepancy between the number of police convictions . . . and the number of offenses reported by the boys" (p. 362). The young offenders who had taken part in the social skills training had the fewest officially reported offenses but the most self-reported offenses. Similarly, Davidson, Redner, Blakely, Mitchell, and Emshoff (1987), evaluating the outcome of a diversionary program for young offenders, found reduced recidivism following the intervention as measured by official indices such as police records and court petitions. Self-reports of offending behavior, on the other hand, failed to suggest any effect from the intervention.

Further, as the reviews note regularly, the behavioral outcome literature is sorely lacking in follow-up data concerning delinquent populations (Blakely & Davidson, 1984; Braukmann & Fixsen, 1975; Hollin, 1990a).

Follow-Up Studies

Why have comparatively few follow-up studies been conducted? Emery and Marholin (1977) have strong views on this failure:

> Because most researchers produce frequent permanent products (articles, chapters, books) in order to receive reinforcement in the form of raises, tenure, social acknowledgement by peers, editor-ships, and job offers, they are likely to avoid any delay in terminating a particular research effort, especially if the delay is as long as the 1 or 2 years often required to collect adequate follow-up data. (p. 869)

However, there are other reasons for the dearth of follow-up studies. It is relatively easy to collect data while running an intervention program, and this is done in most studies. Collection of follow-up data, in contrast, requires the time, funds, and other resources needed to track down offenders when they are no longer easily accessible. It is fair to say that most practitioners and researchers lack the resources that would make it feasible to carry out expensive and thorough follow-up studies.

As we turn to the findings of the outcome literature, it is important to consider them in the context of the limitations discussed.

Toward Rehabilitation: Analysis and Meta-Analysis

Over the years there has been a struggle, both philosophical and empirical, between proponents of punishment for offenders and proponents of rehabilitation. On one side in the conflict are those who stand for what might be called a "human science" explanation of criminal behavior—that is, an approach that values empirically informed, constructive strategies, including rehabilitation, in the formulation of policies for managing offenders. On the other side are those who base their argument either on neoclassical theory or on ideology and nonempirical analysis and who advocate policies that encompass punishment, retribution, and deterrence.

The decades between the 1940s and 1960s witnessed a profusion of programs for the intended rehabilitation of offenders. These programs incorporated individual psychotherapy, group therapy, education, behavior modification, and counseling. A landmark review of treatment outcome studies concerning offenders, published by Lipton, Martinson, and Wilks in 1975, cast grave doubts on the effectiveness of many rehabilitation programs. However, a paper anticipating this review and titled "What Works? Questions and Answers About Prison Reform" (Martinson, 1974) was to have the greatest influence. The message taken from Martinson's paper (a message not strictly accurate) was that "nothing works" in the rehabilitation of offenders. This nothing-works doctrine has, in the intervening years, been transformed from an interpretation of the existing data to a socially constructed "fact" seemingly accepted by academics and policymakers alike. Analyses of the contingencies that led to such a ready acceptance of the nothing-works position, though beyond the scope of this chapter, are available (Andrews, 1989, 1990; Andrews & Wormith, 1989; Cullen & Gendreau, 1989).

While the nothing-works ideology held sway, a voice of opposition—exemplified by Paul Gendreau and Robert Ross (e.g., Gendreau & Ross, 1979, 1987; Ross & Gendreau, 1980)—argued that the true message of the outcome studies was that effective rehabilitation was an attainable goal and cited examples of success. Thornton (1987) reinforced this view in a reexamination of the studies cited by Martinson in 1974, although Martinson (1979) had already begun to retreat from the notion that nothing works. Nonetheless, proponents of rehabilitation faced the difficulty of making a coherent case from a vast jumble of empirical findings. There are literally hundreds of outcome studies, and reviewers must confront the task of interpreting data produced by many different types of intervention, conducted in different settings, with different criteria for success.

Given such a wealth of data, it is very difficult if not impossible to draw meaningful conclusions about what works, for whom, and under what conditions simply by pooling the results of several hundred studies and "vote counting." However, the development of the statistical technique of meta-analysis has provided one way to produce a standardized overview of a large number of empirical studies. Briefly, as Izzo and Ross (1990) explain, meta-analysis is

> a technique that enables a reviewer to objectively and statistically
> analyze the findings of each study as data points. . . . The pro-
> cedure of meta-analysis involves collecting summary statistics,
> using the summary statistics from each study as units of analysis,
> and then analyzing the aggregated data in a quantitative manner
> using statistical tests. (p. 135)

A number of meta-analytic studies of the offender rehabilitation literature have been reported over the past 6 years. A summary of their findings follows.

The meta-analytic studies: A summary

The first meta-analysis, by Garrett (1985), included 111 studies reported between 1960 and 1983, involving a total of 13,055 young offenders who had participated in a range of residential treatment programs. Garrett's analysis showed that residential programs have a small but consistent effect in reducing delinquency, with cognitive-behavioral programs faring particularly well in comparison with other approaches such as psychodynamic therapies and life skills training. Further meta-analytic studies (Andrews et al., 1990a; Gottschalk, Davidson, Gensheimer, & Mayer, 1987; Izzo & Ross, 1990; Lipsey, 1992; Roberts & Camasso, 1991; Whitehead & Lab, 1989) followed Garrett's. Gendreau and Andrews (1990) offer an overview of those subsequent studies. As in most research, the later studies could build on their predecessors; therefore, the findings outlined here are taken from the most recent meta-analytic studies: Andrews et al. (1990a), Lipsey (1992), and Roberts and Camasso (1991). Though all three studies are important, the Lipsey study is a major undertaking, involving an analysis of 443 outcome studies in the field of juvenile delinquency.

Referring to a point made previously, meta-analysis offers insights into the effectiveness of programs according to both *clinical* and *criminological* outcome measures. In general, programs with specific clinical aims tend to produce beneficial outcomes in terms of clinical, personal change. However, a major contribution of the meta-analytic studies is that they begin to allow some firm statements to be made about what works in lowering recidivism. These are the findings that are of interest here.

The first point to emerge from Lipsey's study is that there is a substantial variability in treatment outcome. Some studies show significant effects of intervention on recidivism, in keeping perhaps with the position of writers such as Paul Gendreau and Robert Ross; on the other hand, numerous studies show either no treatment effects or even negative effects, in keeping with the nothing-works position. Given this broad distribution of treatment effects, it is understandable that different reviewers have reached different conclusions, reflecting their samplings of the distribution and their own definitions of success. To paraphrase Lipsey's metaphor, if the diversity of treatment effects in delinquency is as large as an elephant, it is little wonder that the reviewer grasping the trunk and the one clutching an ear describe different animals.

Nevertheless, meta-analytic studies make it possible to outline the characteristics of intervention programs that show significant effects *in terms of reduction of criminal behavior.*

1. Indiscriminate targeting of intervention programs is counterproductive in attempting to reduce recidivism. Important predictors of success are the selection of medium- to high-risk offenders and the focusing of programs on criminogenic areas.

2. The type of intervention program is important. The more structured and focused approaches, including behavioral, skill-oriented, and multimodal treatments, appear to be more effective than less structured and focused approaches, such as counseling.

3. The most successful interventions, though essentially behavioral, include a cognitive component that addresses the "attitudes, values, and beliefs that support anti-social behavior" (Gendreau & Andrews, 1990).

4. Andrews et al. (1990a) suggest that some approaches to intervention are not appropriate for general use with offenders. Specifically, they hold that "traditional psychodynamic and nondirective client-centered therapies are to be avoided within general samples of offenders" (p. 376).

5. Intervention programs conducted in the community have a greater effect on offending behavior than do residential programs. Although residential programs can be effective, they should be linked structurally with community-based interventions.

6. The most effective rehabilitation programs have high "treatment integrity" in that they are carried out by trained staff under effective management.

7. Roberts and Camasso (1991) report that interventions targeted at the family appear successful: "Rigorous studies of family treatment, involving large groups of 200 or more juveniles, demonstrated that this method of intervention was effective in reducing recidivism for at least one year post-treatment" (p. 438).

The meta-analytic studies suggest that intervention programs with all the characteristics outlined can bring about decreases in recidivism 20 to 40 percent greater than those obtained through the mainstream criminal sanctioning of offenders. On this basis it is fair to refute the notion that nothing works in attempts to rehabilitate offenders. Indeed, we can state confidently that rehabilitation programs based on the principles just enumerated can significantly reduce recidivism.

Still, the technique of meta-analysis is not foolproof. For instance, the analysis can be only as good as the data selected for analysis and the way in which the data are coded for analysis. Also, the interpretation of the findings is a point for debate rather than a given truth. Indeed, the meta-analysis reported by Andrews et al. (1990a) drew a critical response from Lab and Whitehead (1990), which in turn elicited a rejoinder from Andrews et al. (1990b). Nevertheless, meta-analysis allows a new look at the data and creates an opportunity to make positive recommendations for the design of effective offender rehabilitation programs.

RECOMMENDATIONS

To plan for success, it is necessary to identify the key areas where goals must be met and then, in as informed a manner as possible, devise strategies to achieve these goals. It seems to me that there are two key areas to consider: the client group selected for the rehabilitation program and the integrity of the treatment program.

In approaching this agenda, let us keep in mind that individually focused rehabilitation programs and broader social and cultural changes are not mutually exclusive. As West (1980) has said, "The crucial importance of economic, social and political factors in the definition and incidence of crime is undeniable, as is the need for socio-political change, but the part played by individual characteristics in determining who becomes a criminal should not be neglected" (p. 619). Indeed, a true cognitive-behavioral approach would imply that change in a person's behavior would result from modification of the environment as well as from changes within the individual.

Client Issues

The meta-analyses strongly suggest that rehabilitation is best delivered to high-risk groups—that is, to offenders whose patterns of offending indicate a high probability of recidivism. There are problems associated with programs targeted at low-risk groups, and some of these efforts appear counterproductive (e.g., McCord, 1978). Various theoretical explanations might account for this circumstance (cf. Palamara, Cullen, & Gersten, 1986), and the situation might well change when better early predictors of risk are defined. For the present it would seem prudent to take heed of this finding.

At a practical level, the selection of high-risk offenders may well yield groups of people who are unwilling to take part in rehabilitation programs. At one time such client resistance would have led to despair. However, with newer techniques such as motivational interviewing, practitioners now have means to engage and work with client resistance (Miller, 1985). The application of this motivational technique to offender populations is beginning to take shape. It is seen, for example, in the work of Perkins (1991) with sex offenders, a group characterized by denial and resistance to change. Perkins uses strategies based on the psychology of persuasion to encourage participation in rehabilitation programs. The extension of these methods to encourage gang members to participate in intervention programs is a project waiting to be launched. When the basic research is completed, the advantages to practitioners will be considerable.

Treatment Integrity

Treatment integrity is another important issue to emerge from the meta-analytic studies. To illustrate the point, Quay (1987) has commented on a study in which

> the majority of those responsible for carrying out the treatment were not convinced that it would affect recidivism (the major dependent variable of the study), and the group leaders (not professional counselors) were poorly trained. The treatment was not well implemented. (p. 246)

If treatment integrity is to be achieved, two areas must receive attention. The first is the actual delivery of the rehabilitation program; the second is program management. Each will be considered in turn.

Program Delivery

One requirement for effective program delivery is a highly trained staff. The meta-analyses have indicated that cognitive-behavioral techniques can be potent, especially in the broader context of multimodal programs in community and family settings, and this finding sets the agenda for training. A competent practitioner must be able to conduct a functional analysis, including a cognitive-behavioral assessment, of the offending behavior. This analysis should lead to the formulation of a specific—ideally individually tailored—program for the offender.

In terms of practical skills, staff members responsible for implementing a cognitive-behavioral program need not only the overall ability and awareness to work with young people but also a set of quite specific skills. To work in a multimodal program, the practitioner must have mastery of the basic behavioral techniques both to increase and to decrease behavior; the ability to conduct social skills training; and the ability to deliver instruction in anger management, moral reasoning, social problem solving, self-instruction, and other methods of cognitive change. Further, the practitioner working in a residential or institutional setting must understand the need to build generalization into the program (Burchard & Harrington, 1986; Gentry & Ostapiuk, 1989).

Adequate staff training is crucial for the development of these skills. The details of a full training program are beyond the scope of this chapter; however, I have given a thorough description of such training elsewhere (Hollin, 1990a).

Although practitioners' skills and their commitment to cognitive-behavioral programs are essential ingredients for success, they are not sufficient ones. As the meta-analyses indicate, it is also necessary to overcome organizational resistance—the obstacles that threaten to impede the progress that might be made with a properly implemented program, whether in a community or a residential setting. For example, Laws (1974) described the barriers he faced when attempting to implement a residential program with offenders. The barriers were plainly about control: control over the admission of offenders to the program, control over the time when offenders would leave the program, control over finances and other resources, and control over staff training. Laws, as have others, documented professional clashes with both administrators and fellow practitioners.

It would be foolish to suggest that such organizational issues can be smoothly and easily resolved, but in the principles defined by Reppucci (1973) some solutions begin to appear. Reppucci suggests that treatment integrity can be greatly enhanced if organizational policies can be formulated along the following lines: (a) a clear guiding philosophy that is understood by all involved in the program, (b) an organizational structure that facilitates communication and accountability, (c) an involvement of staff in decision making, (d) a community orientation, and (e) a limit on the time spent in developing and "tuning" programs, which would counteract the pressure to try to deal with too much in too short a time.

There are, I think, three points to be taken from Reppucci's list. As already noted, there is a pressing need for adequate training of staff in the theory and practice of effective intervention. There is need for organizational structures that facilitate rehabilitation work. Finally, there is need for management systems that can monitor the design, implementation, and progress of rehabilitation programs.

Program Management

My second major recommendation is for attention to management structures, perhaps along the lines just indicated. Attention to what Burchard (1987) terms "social and political contingencies" is becoming increasingly common among behavior analysts, who previously tended to devote their attention primarily to "therapeutic contingencies." Goldstein et al. (1989) have analyzed management issues according to different styles of administrative organization. Of the styles they define, a developmental/community structure is clearly preferable. Such a structure incorporates democratic decision making by all concerned, with shared responsibility for achieving program aims.

The Broader Context

To follow Burchard, we must look beyond organizational boundaries to legal and political issues. In the context of delinquent gangs, Goldstein (1991) offers a series of detailed recommendations for comprehensive state level intervention. Goldstein's list of recommendations targets law enforcement, prosecution, corrections, probation and parole systems, the judiciary, the executive and legislative branches, federal agencies, local government, school programs, community organizations, business and industry, and the media. This inclusion of a "macro" behavioral analysis of societies and cultures alongside the "micro" analysis of therapeutic contingencies is a major step forward. Spergel and Curry (1990) have argued that community and educational strategies are likely to be effective for intervention with delinquent youth gangs. Clearly, such approaches demand attention at the "macro" level of social policy and resource distribution. At the same time, the "micro" level approach should not be dismissed. For example, Agnew (1991) makes a point that is pertinent in instances when the gang serves a social function:

> It may not be necessary to remove adolescents from delinquent
> peer groups in order to reduce delinquency. One may also reduce
> delinquency by altering the relationship between the adolescent and
> delinquent peers. Strategies designed to reduce emotional closeness
> to delinquent peers and increase the ability to resist peer pressure,
> for example, may be effective in negating the influence of delin-
> quent peers. (p. 68)

The empirical studies and intervention methods discussed in this chapter provide the basis for a strategy to achieve Agnew's goal. Broadly speaking, when cognitive-behavioral interventions are nested within comprehensive legal and social initiatives for change, their true potential for precipitating individual change will be realized.

REFERENCES

Agnew, R. (1991). The interactive effects of peer variables on delinquency. *Criminology, 29,* 47–72.

Akers, R. L. (1977). *Deviant behavior: A social learning approach* (2nd ed.). Belmont, CA: Wadsworth.

Akers, R. L. (1990). Rational choice, deterrence, and social learning theory in criminology: The path not taken. *Journal of Criminal Law and Criminology, 81,* 653–676.

Akhtar, N., & Bradley, E. J. (1991). Social information processing deficits of aggressive children: Present findings and implications for social skills training. *Clinical Psychology Review, 11,* 621–644.

Andrews, D. A. (1989). Recidivism is predictable and can be influenced: Using risk assessment to reduce recidivism. *Forum on Corrections Research, 1,* 11–18.

Andrews, D. A. (1990). Some criminological sources of anti-rehabilitation bias in the Report of the Canadian Sentencing Commission. *Canadian Journal of Criminology, 32,* 511–524.

Andrews, D. A., & Wormith, J. S. (1989). Personality and crime: Knowledge destruction and construction in criminology. *Justice Quarterly, 6,* 289–309.

Andrews, D. A., Zinger, I., Hoge, R. D., Bonta, J., Gendreau, P., & Cullen, F. T. (1990a). Does correctional treatment work? A clinically relevant and psychologically informed meta-analysis. *Criminology, 28,* 369–404.

Andrews, D. A., Zinger, I., Hoge, R. D., Bonta, J., Gendreau, P., & Cullen, F. T. (1990b). A human science approach or more punishment and pessimism: A rejoinder to Lab and Whitehead. *Criminology, 28,* 419–429.

Arbuthnot, J., & Gordon, D. A. (1986). Behavioral and cognitive effects of a moral reasoning development intervention for high risk behavior-disordered adolescents. *Journal of Consulting and Clinical Psychology, 34,* 208–216.

Arbuthnot, J., Gordon, D. A., & Jurkovic, G. J. (1987). Personality. In H. C. Quay (Ed.), *Handbook of juvenile delinquency.* New York: Wiley.

Baars, B. J. (1986). *The cognitive revolution in psychology.* New York: Guilford.

Bandura, A. (1977). *Social learning theory.* New York: Prentice-Hall.

Bandura, A. (1986). *Social foundations of thought and action: A social cognitive theory.* Englewood Cliffs, NJ: Prentice-Hall.

Beck, A. T. (1970). Cognitive therapy: Nature and relation to behavior therapy. *Behavior Therapy, 1,* 184–200.

Beck, S. J., & Ollendick, T. H. (1976). Personal space, sex of experimenter, and locus of control in normal and delinquent adolescents. *Psychological Reports, 38,* 383–387.

Blakely, C. H., & Davidson, W. S. (1984). Behavioral approaches to delinquency: A review. In P. Karoly & J. J. Steffen (Eds.), *Adolescent behavior disorders: Foundations and contemporary concerns.* Lexington, MA: Lexington.

Blasi, A. (1980). Bridging moral cognition and moral action: A critical review of the literature. *Psychological Bulletin, 88,* 1–45.

Bowman, P. C., & Auerbach, S. M. (1982). Impulsive youthful offenders: A multimodal cognitive behavioral treatment program. *Criminal Justice and Behavior, 9,* 432–454.

Braukmann, C. J., & Fixsen, D. L. (1975). Behavior modification with delinquents. In M. Hersen, R. M. Eisler, & P. M. Miller (Eds.), *Progress in behavior modification* (Vol. 1). New York: Academic.

Brewin, C. R. (1988). *Cognitive foundations of clinical psychology.* London: Erlbaum.

Brophy, J. (1981). Teacher praise: A functional analysis. *Review of Educational Research, 51,* 5–32.

Burchard, J. D. (1987). Social policy and the role of the behavior analyst in the prevention of delinquent behavior. *The Behavior Analyst, 10,* 83–88.

Burchard, J. D., & Harrington, W. A. (1986). Deinstitutionalization: Programmed transition from the institution to the community. *Child & Family Behavior Therapy, 7,* 17–32.

Camp, B. W., & Bash, M. A. S. (1981). *Think aloud: Increasing social and cognitive skills— A problem-solving program for children.* Champaign, IL: Research Press.

Campbell, A. (1984). *The girls in the gang: A report from New York City.* Oxford: Blackwell.

Catania, A. C., & Harnad, S. (Eds.). (1988). *The selection of behavior: The operant behaviorism of B. F. Skinner: Comments and consequences.* Cambridge: Cambridge University Press.

Chalmers, J. B., & Townsend, M. A. R. (1990). The effects of training in social perspective taking on socially maladjusted girls. *Child Development, 61,* 178–190.

Chandler, M. J. (1973). Egocentrism and anti-social behavior: The assessment and training of social perspective-taking skills. *Developmental Psychology, 9,* 326–332.

Chin, K. (1990). Chinese gangs and extortion. In C. R. Huff (Ed.), *Gangs in America.* Newbury Park, CA: Sage.

Cullen, F. T., & Gendreau, P. (1989). The effectiveness of correctional rehabilitation: Reconsidering the "nothing works" debate. In L. Goodstein & D. L. MacKenzie (Eds.), *The American prison system: Issues in research and policy.* New York: Plenum.

Davidson, W. S., Redner, R., Blakely, C. H., Mitchell, C. M., & Emshoff, J. G. (1987). Diversion of juvenile offenders: An experimental comparison. *Journal of Consulting and Clinical Psychology, 55,* 68–75.

DeLange, J. M., Lanham, S. L., & Barton, J. A. (1981). Social skills training for juvenile offenders: Behavioral skill training and cognitive techniques. In D. Upper & S. Ross (Eds.), *Behavior group therapy: An annual review* (Vol. 3). Champaign, IL: Research Press.

DeWolfe, T. E., Jackson, L. A., & Winterberger, P. (1988). A comparison of moral reasoning and moral character in male and female incarcerated felons. *Sex Roles, 18,* 583–593.

Dodge, K. A. (1986). A social information processing model of social competence in children. In M. Perlmutter (Ed.), *Minnesota symposium on child psychology* (Vol. 18). Hillsdale, NJ: Erlbaum.

Dodge, K. A., & Frame, C. L. (1982). Social cognitive biases and deficits in aggressive boys. *Child Development, 53,* 620–635.

Dodge, K. A., & Newman, J. P. (1981). Biased decision-making processes in aggressive boys. *Journal of Abnormal Psychology, 90,* 375–379.

Dush, D. M., Hirt, M. L., & Schroeder, H. E. (1989). Self-statement modification in the treatment of child behavior disorders: A meta-analysis. *Psychological Bulletin, 106,* 97–106.

Ellis, P. L. (1982). Empathy: A factor in antisocial behavior. *Journal of Abnormal Child Psychology, 2,* 123–133.

Emery, R. E., & Marholin, D. (1977). An applied behavior analysis of delinquency: The irrelevancy of relevant behavior. *American Psychologist, 6,* 860–873.

Fagan, J. (1989). The social organization of drug use and drug dealing among urban gangs. *Criminology, 27,* 633–669.

Feindler, E. L., & Ecton, R. B. (1986). *Adolescent anger control: Cognitive-behavioral techniques.* Elmsford, NY: Pergamon.

Feindler, E. L., Marriott, S. A., & Iwata, M. (1984). Group anger control training for junior high school delinquents. *Cognitive Therapy and Research, 8,* 299–311.

Feldman, M. P. (1977). *Criminal behaviour: A psychological analysis.* Chichester, England: Wiley.

Fishman, D. B., Rotgers, F., & Franks, C. M. (Eds.). (1988). *Paradigms in behavior therapy: Present and promise.* New York: Springer.

Freedman, B. J., Rosenthal, L., Donahoe, C. P., Schlundt, D. G., & McFall, R. M. (1978). A social-behavioral analysis of skill deficits in delinquent and non-delinquent adolescent boys. *Journal of Consulting and Clinical Psychology, 46,* 1448–1462.

Gaffney, L. R., & McFall, R. M. (1981). A comparison of social skills in delinquent and nondelinquent girls using a role-playing inventory. *Journal of Consulting and Clinical Psychology, 49,* 959–967.

Garrett, C. J. (1985). Effects of residential treatment on adjudicated adolescents: A meta-analysis. *Journal of Research in Crime and Delinquency, 25,* 463–489.

Gendreau, P., & Andrews, D. A. (1990). What the meta-analyses of the offender treatment literature tell us about "what works." *Canadian Journal of Criminology, 32,* 173–184.

Gendreau, P., & Ross, R. R. (1979). Effective correctional treatment: Bibliotherapy for cynics. *Crime and Delinquency, 25,* 463–489.

Gendreau, P., & Ross, R. R. (1987). Revivification of rehabilitation: Evidence from the 1980s. *Justice Quarterly, 4,* 349–407.

Gentry, M., & Ostapiuk, E. B. (1989). Management of violence in a youth treatment centre. In K. Howells & C. R. Hollin (Eds.), *Clinical approaches to violence.* Chichester, England: Wiley.

Gibbs, J. C., Arnold, K. D., Cheesman, F. L., & Ahlborn, H. H. (1984). Facilitation of sociomoral reasoning in delinquents. *Journal of Consulting and Clinical Psychology, 52,* 37–45.

Glick, B., & Goldstein, A. P. (1987). Aggression Replacement Training. *Journal of Counseling and Development, 65,* 356–367.

Goldstein, A. P. (1991). *Delinquent gangs: A psychological perspective.* Champaign, IL: Research Press.

Goldstein, A. P., & Glick, B. (1987). *Aggression Replacement Training: A comprehension intervention for aggressive youth.* Champaign, IL: Research Press.

Goldstein, A. P., Glick, B., Irwin, M. J., Pask-McCartney, C., & Rubama, I. (1989). *Reducing delinquency: Intervention in the community.* Elmsford, NY: Pergamon.

Goldstein, A. P., & Keller, H. (1987). *Aggressive behavior: Assessment and intervention.* Elmsford, NY: Pergamon.

Gottschalk, R., Davidson, W. S., Gensheimer, L. K., & Mayer, J. (1987). Community-based interventions. In H. C. Quay (Ed.), *Handbook of juvenile delinquency.* New York: Wiley.

Groh, T. R., & Goldenberg, E. E. (1976). Locus of control with subgroups in a correctional population. *Criminal Justice and Behavior, 3,* 169–179.

Gross, A. M., Brigham, T. A., Hopper, C., & Bologna, N. C. (1980). Self-management and social skills training: A study with pre-delinquent and delinquent youth. *Criminal Justice and Behavior, 7,* 161–184.

Guerra, N. G., & Slaby, R. G. (1990). Cognitive mediators of aggression in adolescent offenders: Part II. Intervention. *Developmental Psychology, 26,* 269–277.

Hains, A. A., & Hains, A. H. (1987). The effects of a cognitive strategy intervention on the problem-solving abilities of delinquent youths. *Journal of Adolescence, 10,* 399–413.

Hains, A. A., & Ryan, E. B. (1983). The development of social cognitive processes among juvenile delinquents and nondelinquent peers. *Child Development, 54,* 1536–1544.

Hayes, S. C. (Ed.). (1989). *Rule-governed behavior: Cognition, contingencies, and instructional control.* New York: Plenum.

Higgins, J. P., & Thies, A. P. (1981). Social effectiveness and problem-solving thinking of reformatory inmates. *Journal of Offender Counseling, Services and Rehabilitation, 5,* 93–98.

Hoffman, L. W. (1991). The influence of the family environment on personality: Accounting for sibling differences. *Psychological Bulletin, 110,* 187–203.

Hollin, C. R. (1989). *Psychology and crime: An introduction to criminological psychology.* London: Routledge.

Hollin, C. R. (1990a). *Cognitive-behavioral interventions with young offenders.* Elmsford, NY: Pergamon.

Hollin, C. R. (1990b). Social skills training with delinquents: A look at the evidence and some recommendations for practice. *British Journal of Social Work, 20,* 483–493.

Hollin, C. R., & Henderson, M. (1984). Social skills training with young offenders: False expectations and the "failure of treatment." *Behavioural Psychotherapy, 12,* 331–341.

Hollin, C. R., Huff, G. J., Clarkson, F., & Edmondson, A. C. (1986). Social skills training with young offenders in a Borstal: An evaluative study. *Journal of Community Psychology, 14,* 289–299.

Hollin, C. R., & Wheeler, H. M. (1982). The violent young offender: A small group study of a Borstal population. *Journal of Adolescence, 5,* 247–257.

Howells, K. (1989). Anger-management methods in relation to the prevention of violent behaviour. In J. Archer & K. Browne (Eds.), *Human aggression: Naturalistic approaches.* London: Routledge.

Huff, C. R. (Ed.). (1990). *Gangs in America.* Newbury Park, CA: Sage.

Hunter, N., & Kelley, C. K. (1986). Examination of the validity of the Adolescent Problem Inventory among incarcerated juvenile delinquents. *Journal of Consulting and Clinical Psychology, 54,* 301–302.

Izzo, R. L., & Ross, R. R. (1990). Meta-analysis of rehabilitation programs for juvenile delinquents: A brief report. *Criminal Justice and Behavior, 17,* 134–142.

Jeffery, C. R. (1965). Criminal behavior and learning theory. *Journal of Criminal Law, Criminology and Police Science, 56,* 294–300.

Jennings, W. S., Kilkenny, R., & Kohlberg, L. (1983). Moral development theory and practice for youthful and adult offenders. In W. S. Laufer & J. M. Day (Eds.), *Personality theory, moral development, and criminal behavior.* Toronto: Lexington.

Jurkovic, G. J. (1980). The juvenile delinquent as moral philosopher: A structural-developmental approach. *Psychological Bulletin, 88,* 709–727.

Kanfer, F. H. (1975). Self-management methods. In F. H. Kanfer & A. P. Goldstein (Eds.), *Helping people change: A textbook of methods.* Elmsford, NY: Pergamon.

Kaplan, P. J., & Arbuthnot, J. (1985). Affective empathy and cognitive role-taking in delinquent and nondelinquent youth. *Adolescence, 20,* 323–333.

Kazdin, A. E. (1979). Fictions, factions and functions of behavior therapy. *Behavior Therapy, 10,* 629–654.

Kendall, P. C. (1985). Toward a cognitive-behavioral model of psychopathology and a critique of related interventions. *Journal of Abnormal Child Psychology, 13,* 357–372.

Kendall, P. C., & Bacon, S. F. (1988). Cognitive behavior therapy. In D. B. Fishman, F. Rotgers, & C. M. Franks (Eds.), *Paradigms in behavior therapy: Present and promise.* New York: Springer.

Kendall, P. C., & Hollon, S. D. (Eds.). (1979). *Assessment strategies for cognitive-behavioral intervention.* New York: Academic.

Klein, M. W., & Maxson, C. L. (1989). Street gang violence. In N. A. Weiner & M. E. Wolfgang (Eds.), *Violent crime, violent criminals.* Newbury Park, CA: Sage.

Kohlberg, L. (1978). Revisions in the theory and practice of mental development. In W. Damson (Ed.), *New directions in child development: Moral development.* San Francisco, CA: Jossey-Bass.

Krohn, M. D., Massey, J. L., & Skinner, W. F. (1987). A sociological theory of crime and delinquency: Social learning theory. In E. K. Morris & C. J. Braukmann (Eds.), *Behavioral approaches to crime and delinquency: A handbook of application, research, and concepts.* New York: Plenum.

Kumchy, C., & Sayer, L. A. (1980). Locus of control and delinquent adolescent populations. *Psychological Reports, 46,* 1307–1310.

Lab, S. P., & Whitehead, J. T. (1990). From "nothing works" to "the appropriate works": The latest stop on the search for the secular grail. *Criminology, 28,* 405–417.

Lamal, P. A. (Ed.). (1991). *Behavioral analysis of societies and cultural practices.* New York: Hemisphere.

Laws, D. R. (1974). The failure of a token economy. *Federal Probation, 38,* 33–38.

Lee, M., & Prentice, N. M. (1988). Interrelations of empathy, cognition, and moral reasoning with dimensions of juvenile delinquency. *Journal of Abnormal Child Psychology, 16,* 127–139.

Lee, V. L. (1988). *Beyond behaviorism.* Hillsdale, NJ: Erlbaum.

Lipsey, M. W. (1992). Juvenile delinquency treatment: A meta-analytic inquiry into the variability of effects. In T. D. Cook, H. Cooper, D. S. Cordray, H. Hartmann, L. V. Hedges, R. J. Light, T. A. Lovis, & S. M. Mosteller (Eds.), *Meta-analysis for explanation: A casebook.* New York: Russell Sage Foundation.

Lipton, D., Martinson, R., & Wilks, D. (1975). *The effectiveness of correctional treatment.* New York: Praeger.

Lowe, C. F. (1983). Radical behaviourism and human psychology. In G. C. L. Davey (Ed.), *Animal models of human behaviour.* Chichester, England: Wiley.

Luria, A. R. (1961). *The role of speech in the regulation of normal and abnormal behavior.* New York: Liveright.

Mahoney, M. J. (1977). Reflections on the cognitive-learning trend in psychotherapy. *American Psychologist, 32,* 5–13.

Mahoney, M. J., & Arkoff, D. B. (1978). Cognitive and self-control therapies. In S. L. Garfield & A. E. Bergin (Eds.), *Handbook of psychotherapy and behavior change: An empirical analysis.* New York: Wiley.

Martinson, R. (1974). What works? Questions and answers about prison reform. *The Public Interest, 35,* 22–54.

Martinson, R. (1979). New findings, new views: A note of caution regarding sentencing reform. *Hofstra Law Review, 7,* 243–258.

McCord, J. (1978). A thirty year follow up of treatment effects. *American Psychologist, 33,* 284–289.

McCown, W., Johnson, J., & Austin, S. (1986). Inability of delinquents to recognize facial affects. *Journal of Social Behavior and Personality, 1,* 489–496.

McDougall, C., Barnett, R. M., Ashurst, B., & Willis, B. (1987). Cognitive control of anger. In B. J. McGurk, D. M. Thornton, & M. Williams (Eds.), *Applying psychology to imprisonment: Theory & practice.* London: Her Majesty's Stationery Office.

Meichenbaum, D. (1977). *Cognitive behavior modification.* New York: Plenum.

Milan, M. A. (1987a). Basic behavioral procedures in closed institutions. In E. K. Morris & C. J. Braukmann (Eds.), *Behavioral approaches to crime and delinquency: A handbook of application, research, and concepts.* New York: Plenum.

Milan, M. A. (1987b). Token economy programs in closed institutions. In E. K. Morris & C. J. Braukmann (Eds.), *Behavioral approaches to crime and delinquency: A handbook of application, research, and concepts.* New York: Plenum.

Miller, W. R. (1985). Motivation for treatment: A review with special emphasis on alcoholism. *Psychological Bulletin, 98,* 84–107.

Modgil, S., & Modgil, C. (1987). *B. F. Skinner: Consensus and controversy.* New York: Falmer.

Moore, J., Vigil, D., & Garcia, R. (1983). Residence and territoriality in Chicago gangs. *Social Problems, 31,* 182–194.

Morris, E. K., & Braukmann, C. J. (Eds.). (1987). *Behavioral approaches to crime and delinquency: A handbook of application, research, and concepts.* New York: Plenum.

Nelson, J. R., Smith, D. J., & Dodd, J. (1990). The moral reasoning of juvenile delinquents: A meta-analysis. *Journal of Abnormal Child Psychology, 18,* 231–239.

Nietzel, M. T. (1979). *Crime and its modification: A social learning perspective.* Elmsford, NY: Pergamon.

Novaco, R. W. (1975). *Anger control: The development and evaluation of an experimental treatment.* Lexington, MA: Heath.

Novaco, R. W. (1985). Anger and its therapeutic regulation. In M. A. Chesney & R. H. Rosenman (Eds.), *Anger and hostility in cardiovascular and behavioral disorders.* New York: Hemisphere.

Novaco, R. W., & Welsh, W. N. (1989). Anger disturbances: Cognitive mediation and clinical prescriptions. In K. Howells & C. R. Hollin (Eds.), *Clinical approaches to violence.* Chichester, England: Wiley.

Palamara, F., Cullen, F. T., & Gersten, J. C. (1986). The effect of police and mental health intervention on juvenile deviance: Specifying contingencies in the impact of formal reaction. *Journal of Health and Social Behavior, 27,* 90–105.

Perkins, D. E. (1991). Clinical work with sex offenders in secure settings. In C. R. Hollin & K. Howells (Eds.), *Clinical approaches to sex offenders and their victims.* Chichester, England: Wiley.

Platt, J. J., Perry, G., & Metzger, D. (1980). The evaluation of a heroin addiction treatment program within a correctional setting. In R. R. Ross & P. Gendreau (Eds.), *Effective correctional treatment.* Toronto: Butterworths.

Quay, H. C. (1987). Institutional treatment. In H. C. Quay (Ed.), *Handbook of juvenile delinquency.* New York: Wiley.

Rachlin, H. (1991). *Introduction to modern behaviorism* (3rd ed.). New York: Freedman.

Renwick, S., & Emler, N. (1991). The relationship between social skills deficits and juvenile delinquency. *British Journal of Clinical Psychology, 30,* 61–71.

Reppucci, N. D. (1973). Social psychology of institutional change: General principles for intervention. *American Journal of Community Psychology, 1,* 330–341.

Rescorla, R. A. (1988). Classical conditioning: It's not what you think it is. *American Psychologist, 43,* 151–160.

Roberts, A. R. (1987). National survey and assessment of 66 treatment programs for juvenile offenders: Model programs and pseudomodels. *Juvenile and Family Court Journal, 38,* 39–45.

Roberts, A. R., & Camasso, M. J. (1991). The effect of juvenile offender treatment programs on recidivism: A meta-analysis of 46 studies. *Notre Dame Journal of Law, Ethics and Public Policy, 5,* 421–441.

Ross, R. R., & Fabiano, E. A. (1985). *Time to think: A cognitive model of delinquency prevention and offender rehabilitation.* Johnson City, TN: Institute of Social Sciences and Arts.

Ross, R. R., Fabiano, E. A., & Ewles, C. D. (1988). Reasoning and rehabilitation. *International Journal of Offender Therapy and Comparative Criminology, 20,* 29–35.

Ross, R. R., & Gendreau, P. (Eds.). (1980). *Effective correctional treatment.* Toronto: Butterworths.

Rotenberg, M., & Nachshon, I. (1979). Impulsiveness and aggression among Israeli delinquents. *British Journal of Social and Clinical Psychology, 18,* 59–63.

Saunders, J. T., Reppucci, N. D., & Sarata, B. P. (1973). An examination of impulsivity as a trait characterizing delinquent youth. *American Journal of Orthopsychiatry, 43,* 789–795.

Skinner, B. F. (1974). *About behaviorism.* London: Cape.

Skinner, B. F. (1986a). Is it behaviorism? *Behavioral and Brain Sciences, 9,* 716.

Skinner, B. F. (1986b). What is wrong with daily life in the Western world? *American Psychologist, 41,* 568–574.

Slaby, R. G., & Guerra, N. G. (1988). Cognitive mediators of aggression in adolescent offenders: Part 1. Assessment. *Developmental Psychology, 24,* 580–588.

Snyder, J. J., & White, M. J. (1979). The use of cognitive self-instruction in the treatment of behaviorally disturbed adolescents. *Behavior Therapy, 10,* 227–235.

Spence, S. H. (1981). Differences in social skills performance between institutionalized juvenile male offenders and a comparable group of boys without offence records. *British Journal of Clinical Psychology, 20,* 163–171.

Spence, S. H., & Marzillier, J. S. (1981). Social skills training with adolescent male offenders: Part 2. Short-term, long-term and generalized effects. *Behaviour Research and Therapy, 19,* 349–368.

Spergel, I. A., & Curry, G. D. (1990). Strategies and perceived agency effectiveness in dealing with the youth gang problem. In C. R. Huff (Ed.), *Gangs in America.* Newbury Park, CA: Sage.

Spivack, G., Platt, J. J., & Shure, M. B. (1976). *The problem-solving approach to adjustment: A guide to research and intervention.* San Francisco, CA: Jossey-Bass.

Stumphauzer, J. S. (1986). *Helping delinquents change: A treatment manual of social learning approaches.* New York: Haworth.

Sutherland, E. H. (1924). *Principles of criminology.* Philadelphia: Lippincott.

Thornton, D. M. (1987). Treatment effects on recidivism: A reappraisal of the "nothing works" doctrine. In B. J. McGurk, D. M. Thornton, & M. Williams (Eds.), *Applying psychology to imprisonment: Theory & practice.* London: Her Majesty's Stationery Office.

Thornton, D. M., & Reid, R. L. (1982). Moral reasoning and type of criminal offence. *British Journal of Social Psychology, 21,* 231–238.

Veneziano, C., & Veneziano, L. (1988). Knowledge of social skills among institutionalized juvenile offenders: An assessment. *Criminal Justice and Behavior, 15,* 152–171.

Ward, C. I., & McFall, R. M. (1986). Further validation of the Problem Inventory for Adolescent Girls: Comparing Caucasian and Black delinquents and nondelinquents. *Journal of Consulting and Clinical Psychology, 54,* 732–733.

Watson, J. B. (1913). Psychology as the behaviorist views it. *Psychological Review, 20,* 158–177.

West, D. J. (1980). The clinical approach to criminology. *Psychological Medicine, 10,* 619–631.

Whitehead, J. T., & Lab, S. P. (1989). A meta-analysis of juvenile correctional treatment. *Journal of Research in Crime and Delinquency, 26,* 276–295.

Yablonsky, L. (1959). The delinquent gang as a near-group. *Social Problems, 7,* 108–117.

Zuriff, G. E. (1985). *Behaviorism: A conceptual reconstruction.* New York: Columbia University Press.

CHAPTER 4

Interpersonal Skills Training Interventions

Arnold P. Goldstein

Our consideration of the actual and potential value of interpersonal skills training for gang intervention purposes appropriately begins with focus on a different, if related, class of intervention approaches—psychotherapy.

Until the early 1970s, there were primarily three major clusters of psychological and psychotherapeutic approaches designed to alter the behavior of aggressive, withdrawn, ineffective, or disturbed individuals: psychodynamic/psychoanalytic, humanistic/client-centered, and behavior modification. Each of these diverse orientations found concrete expression in individual and group interventions targeted to aggressive adolescents: The psychodynamic approach involved psychoanalytically oriented individual psychotherapy (Guttman, 1970), activity group therapy (Slavson, 1964), and the varied array of treatment procedures developed by Redl and Wineman (1957). The humanistic/client-centered approach found expression in applications with juvenile delinquents (e.g., Truax, Wargo, & Silber, 1966) of the client-centered psychotherapy of Carl Rogers (1957), the therapeutic community applications of Jones (1953), Guided Group Interaction (McCorkle, Elias, & Bixby, 1958), Positive Peer Culture (Vorrath & Brendtro, 1974), and the school discipline approach of Dreikurs, Grunwald, and Pepper (1971). Behavior modification involved a wide variety of interventions reflecting the systematic use of contingency management, contracting, and the training of teachers and parents as behavior change managers (O'Leary, O'Leary, & Becker, 1967; Patterson, Cobb, & Ray, 1973; Walker, 1979). Though each of these intervention philosophies differed from the others in several major respects, a significant commonality was the shared assumption that the client had somewhere within himself, as yet unexpressed, the effective, satisfying, nonaggressive, or prosocial behaviors whose expression was among the goals of the intervention. Such latent potentials, in all three approaches, would be realized by the client if the change agent were sufficiently skilled in reducing or removing obstacles to such realization. The psychodynamic therapist sought to do so by calling forth and interpreting unconscious material blocking progress-relevant awareness. The humanistic/client-centered change agent, who in particular believed that the potential for change resides within the client, sought to free this potential by providing a warm, empathic, maximally accepting helping environment. And the behavior modifier, by means of one or more contingency management procedures, attempted to ensure that when the latent desirable behaviors or approximations thereto did occur, the client would receive appropriate contingent reinforcement, thus increasing the probability that these behaviors would recur. Therefore, whether sought by means of interpretation, therapeutic climate, or contingent reward, all three approaches assumed that somewhere within the individual's repertoire resided the desired, effective goal behaviors.

INTERPERSONAL SKILLS TRAINING

In the early 1970s, an important new intervention approach began to emerge, an approach resting upon rather different assumptions—interpersonal skills training. Viewing the "helpee" more in educational, pedagogic terms than as a client in need of counseling or psychotherapy, the interpersonal skills trainer assumed that the individual was lacking, deficient, or at best weak in the skills necessary for effective and satisfying personal and interpersonal functioning. The task of the skills trainer became, therefore, not interpretation, reflection, or reinforcement, but the active and deliberate teaching of desirable behaviors. Rather than an intervention called *psychotherapy,* between a patient and psychotherapist, or counseling, between a client and counselor, what emerged was an intervention called *training,* between a trainee and an interpersonal skills trainer.

The roots of the interpersonal skills training movement lay in both education and psychology. The notion of seeking to teach desirable behaviors has often, if sporadically, been a significant goal of the educational establishment in the United States. The Character Education Movement of the 1920s and more contemporary moral education and values clarification programs are but a few possible examples. In addition to interest in skills training exhibited in the schools, numerous interpersonal and planning skills courses are taught in the more than 2,000 community colleges across the United States, and hundreds of self-help books focusing on similar skill-enhancement goals are available. Clearly, the formal and informal educational establishment has provided the fertile soil and stimulation necessary for the interpersonal skills training movement to grow.

Much the same can be said for psychology: Its prevailing philosophy and concrete interests also laid the groundwork for the development of this new movement. The learning process has, above all else, been the central theoretical and investigative concern of American psychology since the late 19th century. This focal interest also assumed major therapeutic form in the 1950s, as psychotherapy practitioners and researchers alike came to view psychotherapeutic treatment more and more in learning terms. The very healthy and still-expanding field of behavior modification grew from this joint learning-clinical focus and may be appropriately viewed as the immediately preceding context from which interpersonal skills training emerged. Concurrent with the growth of behavior modification, psychological thinking increasingly shifted from a strict emphasis on remediation to one equally concerned with prevention, and the bases for this shift included movement away from a medical model toward what may most aptly be called a psychoeducational theoretical stance. Both of these thrusts—heightened concern with prevention and a psychoeducational perspective—added impetus to the viability of the interpersonal skills training movement.

Perhaps psychology's most direct contribution to interpersonal skills training came from social learning theory—in particular, from work conducted or inspired by Albert Bandura. Regarding the same broad array of modeling, behavioral rehearsal, and social reinforcement investigations that helped stimulate and direct the development of our own approach to skills training, Bandura (1973) comments:

> The method that has yielded the most impressive results with diverse problems contains three major components. First, alternative modes of response are repeatedly modeled, preferably by several people who demonstrate how the new style of behavior can be used in dealing with a variety of . . . situations. Second, learners are provided with necessary guidance and ample opportunities to practice the modeled behavior under favorable conditions until they perform it skillfully and spontaneously. The latter procedures are ideally suited for developing new social skills, but they are unlikely to be adopted unless they produce rewarding consequences. Arrangement of success experiences particularly for initial efforts at behaving differently, constitute the third component in this powerful composite method. . . .
> Given adequate demonstration, guided practice, and success experiences, this method is almost certain to produce favorable results. (p. 253)

Other events of the 1970s provided still further stimulation for the growth of the interpersonal skills training movement. The inadequacy of prompting, shaping, and related operant procedures for adding *new* behaviors to individuals' behavioral repertoires was increasingly apparent. The widespread reliance upon deinstitutionalization that lay at the heart of the community mental health movement resulted in the discharge from public mental hospitals of approximately 400,000 persons, the majority of whom were substantially deficient in important daily functioning skills. In addition, it had become clear that what the mental health movement had available to offer clients from lower socioeconomic levels was grossly inadequate in meeting their psychotherapeutic needs. These factors (i.e., relevant supportive research, the incompleteness of operant approaches, large populations of grossly skill-deficient individuals, and the paucity of useful interventions for large segments of society), along with historically supportive roots in both education and psychology, suggested to several researchers and practitioners the need for a new intervention, something prescriptively responsive to these needs. Interpersonal skills training was the answer, and a movement was launched.

Our involvement in this movement, an interpersonal skills training approach we term Skillstreaming, began in the early 1970s. At that time, and for several years thereafter, our studies were conducted in public mental health hospitals with long-term, highly skill-deficient, chronic patients, especially those preparing for de-institutionalization into the community. As our research program progressed and demonstrated with regularity successful skill-enhancement effects (Goldstein, 1981), we shifted our focus from teaching a broad array of interpersonal and daily living skills to adult psychiatric inpatients to skills training for aggressive individuals. Our trainee groups included spouses engaged in family disputes violent enough to warrant police intervention (Goldstein, Monti, Sardino, & Green, 1979; Goldstein & Rosenbaum, 1982); child-abusing parents (Goldstein, Keller, & Erne, 1985; Solomon, 1977; Sturm, 1980); and, most especially, overtly aggressive adolescents (Goldstein & Pentz, 1984; Goldstein, Sherman, Gershaw, Sprafkin, & Glick, 1978; Goldstein, Sprafkin, Gershaw, & Klein, 1980).

Skill Deficiency and Juvenile Delinquency

A substantial body of literature has directly demonstrated that delinquent and other aggressive children and teenagers display widespread interpersonal, planning, aggression management, and other psychological skill deficiencies. Freedman, Rosenthal, Donahoe, Schlundt, and McFall (1978) examined the comparative skill competence levels of a group of juvenile delinquents and a matched group (age, IQ, socioeconomic background) of nonoffenders in response to a series of standardized role-play situations. The offender sample responded in a consistently less skillful manner. Spence (1981) constituted comparable offender and nonoffender samples and videotaped interviews of each adolescent with a previously unknown adult. The offender group evidenced significantly fewer instances of eye contact, appropriate head movements, and speech, as well as significantly more fiddling and gross body movement. Conger, Miller, and Walsmith (1975) added further to this picture of skill deficiency. They concluded from their evidence that juvenile delinquents, as compared to nondelinquent cohorts,

> had more difficulty in getting along with peers, both in individual one-to-one contacts and in group situations, and were less willing or able to treat others courteously and tactfully, and less able to be fair in dealing with them. In return, they were less well liked and accepted by their peers. (p. 442)

Not only is it possible to discriminate delinquents from their nondelinquent peers on a continuum of skill competence, much the same is true for youngsters who are chronically aggressive. Patterson, Reid, Jones, and Conger (1975) observe:

> The socialization process appears to be severely impeded for many aggressive youngsters. Their behavioral adjustments are often immature and they do not seem to have learned the key social skills necessary for initiating and maintaining positive social relationships

with others. Peer groups often reject, avoid, and/or punish aggressive children, thereby excluding them from positive learning experiences with others. (p. 4)

Mussen, Conger, Kagan, and Gerwitz (1979) confirm this observation. Boys in the Mussen et al. longitudinal study who became delinquent were appraised by their teachers as less well-adjusted socially than their classmates as early as third grade. They appeared less friendly, responsible, or fair in dealing with others and more impulsive and antagonistic to authority. Poor peer relations (showing less friendliness toward classmates, being less well liked by peers) were further developmental predictors of later delinquency. Thus, it may be safely concluded that psychological skill deficiencies of diverse—especially interpersonal—types characterize both predelinquent and delinquent youths to a degree that significantly differentiates them from their nondelinquent or nonaggressive peers. Furthermore, as Spence (1981) notes, the relationship between delinquent behavior and skill deficits is a complex one:

On the one hand it seems likely that adolescents who are delinquent in social skills may well resort to offending as a means of achieving the peer status and respect they would be unable to obtain by more socially acceptable means. Similarly, it seems probable that children who experience difficulty in interactions with teachers and/or peers at school are more likely to be truant, and thereby become more likely to commit offenses. To complicate matters further, evidence also suggests that when apprehended by the police, adolescents who are deficient in social skills will be more likely to be prosecuted or convicted for the offense than their socially skilled peers. (p. 108)

It is clear that the juvenile offender characteristically displays substantial deficits in a broad array of prosocial interpersonal skills. The remediation of such deficits looms as an especially valuable goal.

Overview of Interpersonal Skills Training Components

Interpersonal skills training may be operationalized via a variety of didactic procedures, but most such approaches revolve primarily around the four techniques that constitute Skillstreaming: modeling, role-playing, performance feedback, and transfer and maintenance of training. We will examine these procedures in greater detail later in this chapter; the following brief description of how these components apply with regard to our own Skillstreaming approach will provide the reader with an orienting overview of the methodology.

Modeling

Skillstreaming requires first that trainees be exposed to expert examples of the behaviors (i.e., skills) we wish them to learn. The five or six trainees constituting the Skillstreaming group are selected based upon their shared skill deficiencies.

Each skill is broken down into four to six different behavioral steps. The steps constitute the operational definition of the given skill. Either live acting by the group's trainers or audiovisual modeling displays portray the steps of that skill being used expertly in a variety of settings relevant to the trainees' daily life. Trainees are told to watch and listen closely to the way the actors in each vignette sequentially portray the skill's behavioral steps.

Role-Playing

A brief spontaneous discussion almost invariably follows the presentation of a modeling display. Trainees frequently comment on the steps, the actors, and how the situation or problem portrayed occurs in their own lives. Because our primary goal in role-playing is to encourage realistic behavioral rehearsal, a trainee's statements about her individual difficulties using the skill being taught can often develop into material for the first role-play. To enhance the realism of the portrayal, the main actor is asked to choose a second trainee (a coactor) to play the role of the person relevant to the skill problem.

The main actor is asked to describe briefly the real problem situation and the person(s) with whom she could try the behavioral steps in real life. The coactor is called by the name of the main actor's significant other during the role-play. The trainer then instructs the role-players to begin. It is the trainer's main responsibility, at this point, to be sure that the main actor keeps role-playing and that she attempts to follow the behavioral steps while doing so. Role-playing continues until all trainees in the group participate.

Performance Feedback

Upon completion of each role-play, a brief feedback period ensues. The goals of this activity are to let the main actor know how well she followed the skill's steps or in what ways she departed from them, to explore the psychological impact of the enactment on the coactor, and to provide the main actor with encouragement to try out her role-play behaviors in real life. Comments must point to the presence or absence of specific, concrete behaviors and not take the form of broad evaluative comments or generalities.

Transfer and Maintenance of Training

Several aspects of Skillstreaming have as a primary purpose augmentation of the likelihood that learning in the training setting will transfer to the trainee's real-life environment and will endure over time. These procedures include provision of general principles, response availability, identical elements, stimulus variability, and programmed reinforcement (Goldstein, 1981; Goldstein & Kanfer, 1979).

Other Interpersonal Skills Training Approaches

Concurrent with or following our development of the Skillstreaming approach, a number of similar programmatic attempts to enhance social competence emerged.

Those that have focused at least to some extent on aggressive youngsters and their prosocial training include Life Skills Education (Adkins, 1970), Social Skill Training (Argyle, Trower, & Bryant, 1974), AWARE: Activities for Social Development (Elardo & Cooper, 1977), Relationship Enhancement (Guerney, 1977), Teaching Conflict Resolution (Hare, 1976), Developing Human Potential (Hawley & Hawley, 1975), Interpersonal Communication (Heiman, 1973), and Directive Teaching (Stephens, 1976). The instructional techniques that constitute each of these skills-training efforts derive from social learning theory and typically consist of instructions, modeling, role-playing, and performance feedback, with ancillary use in some instances of contingent reinforcement, prompting, shaping, or related behavioral techniques.

Developing in part out of the empirical tradition of behavior modification, these interpersonal skills training efforts have come under early and continuing research scrutiny. The existing body of skills training investigations involving aggressive adolescent and preadolescent subjects is summarized in Table 4.1. Two-thirds of these studies are of multiple group design; the remainder are single-subject studies. Interpersonal skills training is operationally defined in an almost identical manner across all of these investigations as a combination of instructions, modeling, role-playing, and performance feedback. Subjects are either adjudicated juvenile delinquents, status offenders, or chronically aggressive youngsters studied in secondary school settings.

Although target skills have varied across investigations, for the most part they have concerned interpersonal behaviors, prosocial alternatives to aggression, and aggression management or aggression inhibition behaviors. As Spence (1981) has correctly noted, single case studies have tended toward microskill training targets (e.g., eye contact, head nods), and multiple group studies have sought to teach more macroskill competencies (e.g., coping with criticism, negotiation, problem solving). Results for skill acquisition have been consistently positive. Aggressive adolescents are able to learn a broad array of previously unavailable interpersonal, aggression management, affect-relevant, and related psychological competencies via the training methods examined here.

Evaluation for maintenance and transfer of acquired skills yields a rather different outcome. Many studies have tested for neither. Those studies that have looked at maintenance and transfer report a mixed result. Our own investigative efforts in this regard (Goldstein, 1981) point to the not surprising conclusion that generalization of skill competence across settings (transfer) and time (maintenance) are a direct function of the degree to which the investigator/trainer implements training procedures explicitly designed to enhance transfer and/or maintenance. We will examine an array of such procedures in a later section.

To summarize our view of empirical efforts to date, interpersonal skills training with aggressive adolescents rests on a firm investigative foundation. A variety of investigators, designs, subjects, settings, and target skills have resulted in a healthy examination of the effectiveness of such training. Skill acquisition is a reliable outcome, but the social validity of this consistent result is tempered substantially by the frequent failure—or at least indeterminacy—of transfer and maintenance.

Table 4.1 Psychological Skills Training Research With Adolescent and Preadolescent Trainees

Investigator	Design	Treatment	Trainees	N	Setting	Target skill	Outcome
Bornstein et al. (1980)	Single case: multiple baseline	Instructions Modeling Role-play Feedback	Aggressive adolescent inpatients	4	Psychiatric hospital	Assertiveness	Increase in skill performance contingent on training, decrease in aggression, maintained at 6 months
Braukmann et al. (1973)	Single case: multiple baseline	Instructions Modeling Role-play Feedback	Juvenile delinquents	2	Family group home	Heterosexual interaction skills (head nods, attending, etc.)	Increase in skill performance contingent on training, increase in female contact at parties
Braukmann et al. (1974)	Single case: multiple baseline	Instructions Modeling Role-play Feedback	Juvenile delinquents	6	Family group home	Interview skills (posture, eye contact, etc.)	Increase in skill performance contingent on training
DeLange et al. (1981)	Multiple group: training, no training	Instructions Modeling Role-play Feedback	Juvenile delinquents	50	Residential institution	Assertiveness	No significant between-condition differences

Study	Design	Population	Training components	N	Setting	Skills	Results
Elder et al. (1979)	Single case: multiple baseline	Aggressive adolescents	Instructions Modeling Role-play Feedback	4	Psychiatric hospital	Assertiveness, anger control	Increase in skill performance contingent on training, decrease in aggression, maintained at 6 months
Goldstein and Glick (1987)	Multiple group: training, motivation control, no-training control	Juvenile delinquents	Modeling Role-play Feedback Anger control Moral education	51	Residential institution	Dealing with accusations, responding to anger, dealing with group pressure, responding to failure, etc.	Training > control on 4 of 10 trained skills, anger control, moral reasoning level
Goldstein and Glick (1987)	Multiple group: training, motivation control, no-training control	Juvenile delinquents	Modeling Role-play Feedback Anger control Moral education	54	Residential institution	Dealing with accusations, responding to anger, dealing with group pressure, responding to failure, etc.	Training > controls on 5 of 10 trained skills, anger control, community adjustment
Goldstein et al. (1989)	Multiple group: youth and family training versus youth only training, no training	Juvenile delinquents	Modeling Role-play Feedback Anger control Moral education	84	Community	Empathy, preparing for stressful conversations, keeping out of fights, dealing with group pressure, etc.	Both training conditions > control on skill acquisition, anger control, and recidivism

Table 4.1 (cont.)

Investigator	Design	Treatment	Trainees	N	Setting	Target skill	Outcome
Greenleaf (1977)	Multiple group: training (present versus absent), transfer programming (present versus absent), attention control versus brief instructions control	Modeling Role-play Feedback	Aggressive adolescents	43	Secondary school	Helping others	Both training conditions > controls on study skill acquisition and maintenance
Gross et al. (1980)	Single group: multiple baseline	Instructions Modeling Role-play Shaping	Juvenile delinquents	10	Group home	Prosocial responsiveness (responding to criticism, responding to teasing)	Increase in skill performance contingent on training, reduced truancy at post, 2 months, and 1 year
Hazel et al. (1981)	Multiple group: training, no training	Instructions Discussion Modeling Role-play Feedback	Juvenile delinquents	24	Probation office	Giving feedback, negotiating, resisting peer pressure, etc.	Training > controls on study skills, maintained at 2 months
Hollin and Courtney (1983)	Multiple group: training–8 weeks, training–4 days, no-training control, nonreferred control	Instructions Modeling Role-play Feedback	Juvenile delinquents	15	Residential institution	Conversation skills (eye contact, listening, initiating), conflict avoidance skills	No significant between-condition differences

Study	Design	Components	Population	N	Setting	Skills	Results
Hollin and Henderson (1981)	Multiple group: no training	Instructions Modeling Role-play Feedback	Juvenile delinquents	14	Residential institution	Conversation skills, nonverbal communication skills	No significant between-condition differences
Hummel (1980)	Multiple group: training (single or combined skills), varied or constant stimulus conditions	Modeling Role-play Feedback	Aggressive adolescents	47	Secondary school	Negotiation, self-control	All training under varied stimulus conditions > all training under constant stimulus conditions
Kifer et al. (1974)	Single case: multiple baseline	Instructions Role-play Feedback	Juvenile delinquents and their parents	3	Family group home	Negotiation skills (expressing opinion, reaching agreement)	Increase in skill performance contingent on training
Lee et al. (1979)	Multiple group: training, attention control, no-training control	Instructions Modeling Role-play Feedback	Aggressive adolescents	30	Secondary school	Aggression control skills, assertiveness	Training > controls on assertiveness, no significant between-condition differences on aggression control skills
Litwack (1976)	Multiple group: training and anticipation of serving as a trainer, training, brief instructions control	Modeling Role-play Feedback	Aggressive adolescents	40	Secondary school	Following instructions, expressing a compliment	Both training conditions > controls on both study skills

Table 4.1 (cont.)

Investigator	Design	Treatment	Trainees	N	Setting	Target skill	Outcome
Maloney et al. (1976)	Single case: multiple baseline	Role-play Contingent reinforcement	Juvenile delinquents	4	Family group home	Conversation skills (posture, volunteering answers)	Increase in skill performance contingent on training by peers or by teaching parents
Matson et al. (1980)	Single case: multiple baseline	Instructions Modeling Role-play Feedback Contingent reinforcement	Aggressive adolescent inpatients	4	Residential institution	Conversation skills (eye contact, choosing content, etc.)	Increase in skill performance contingent on training, maintained at 3 months
Minkin et al. (1976)	Single case: multiple baseline	Instructions Modeling Role-play Feedback	Juvenile delinquents	4	Family group home	Conversation skills (asking questions, giving feedback)	Increase in skill performance contingent on training
Ollendick and Hersen (1979)	Multiple group: training, discussion control, no-training control	Instructions Modeling Role-play Feedback	Juvenile delinquents	27	Residential institution	Interpersonal accommodation skills, verbal and nonverbal	Training > controls on study skills, reduction in state anxiety, increase in internal locus of control

98

Study	Design	Training components	Population	N	Setting	Target skill	Results
Pentz (1980)	Multiple group: brief instruction control, no-training control; training by teacher, parent, or peer; aggressive versus passive trainees	Modeling Role-play Feedback	Aggressive unassertive adolescents	90	Secondary school	Assertiveness	All training conditions > controls on study skill acquisition and transfer, teacher trainers > parent or peer trainers on skill acquisition
Robin (1981)	Multiple group: training, family therapy, wait list control	Instructions Modeling Role-play Feedback	Adolescents from conflicted families	33	Clinic	Problem-solving communication skills	Training > controls on all study skills, training > therapy on behavioral skills, maintained at 10 weeks
Robin et al. (1977)	Multiple group: training, wait list control	Instructions Discussion Modeling Role-play Feedback	Adolescents from conflicted families and their parent	24	Clinic	Problem-solving communication skills	Training > controls on study skills, no transfer to home
Sarason and Ganzer (1973)	Multiple group: training, discussion control, no-training control	Modeling Role-play Feedback	Juvenile delinquents	192	Residential institution	Prosocial problem solving	Training > controls on study skills

Table 4.1 (cont.)

Investigator	Design	Treatment	Trainees	N	Setting	Target skill	Outcome
Sarason and Sarason (1981)	Multiple group: training–live modeling, training–video modeling, no-training control	Instructions Modeling Role-play Feedback	Adolescents in school with high dropout and delinquency levels	127	Secondary school	Job interviewing, resisting peer pressure, asking for help, dealing with frustration	Training–live modeling > controls on job interview skills, training (both types) > controls on problem-solving skills, no significant differences on other study skills
Shoemaker (1979)	Multiple group: training, discussion control, no-training control	Instructions Discussion Modeling Role-play Feedback Contingent reinforcement	Juvenile delinquents	30	Residential institution	Assertiveness	Training > controls on study skill, no generalization to interview situation
Spence and Marzillier (1981)	Multiple group: training, attention placebo control, no-training control	Instructions Modeling Role-play Feedback	Juvenile delinquents	76	Residential institution	Coping with criticism and teasing, inviting friendships	Training > controls on study skills

Study	Design	Training components	Population	N	Setting	Target skills	Outcome
Spence and Marzillier (1979)	Single case: multiple baseline	Instructions Modeling Role-play Feedback	Juvenile delinquents	5	Residential institution	Conversation skills (eye contact, head movement, listening)	Increase in nonverbal skills performance contingent on training, maintained at 2 weeks
Spence and Spence (1980)	Multiple group: training, attention control, no-training control	Modeling Role-play Feedback	Juvenile delinquents	44	Residential institution	Nonverbal skills (e.g., eye contact), interaction skills (e.g., dealing with teasing)	Training $>$ controls on study skills, not maintained at 6 months
Thelen et al. (1976)	Multiple group: training, didactic control, baseline control	Modeling Role-play Feedback	Juvenile delinquents	6	Group home	Conflict resolution skills (coping with accusations, expressing positive feelings)	Increase in skill performance contingent on training, not maintained at 2 weeks
Trief (1976)	Multiple group: training (cognitive, affective, or combined aspects of skill), attention control, brief instructions control	Modeling Role-play Feedback	Juvenile delinquents	58	Residential institution	Perspective taking	All training conditions $>$ controls on study skill acquisition and transfer
Werner et al. (1975)	Multiple group: training, no-training control	Instructions Modeling Role-play Feedback	Juvenile delinquents	6	Family group home	Prosocial communication with police (eye contact, cooperation, expression of reform)	Pre-post training increase on study skills for training and control groups

RESEARCH AND APPLICATION ISSUES

Experimental Design

Review of the preceding research highlights several issues that bear directly on the efficacy of interpersonal skills training with aggressive adolescents. These issues concern experimental design, prescriptive utilization of training, trainee motivation to learn new skills, and enhancement of skill transfer. As noted previously, existing interpersonal skills training research has relied upon either single subject or multiple group designs. The respective advantages and limitations of these two strategies have been amply considered elsewhere (Hersen & Barlow, 1976; Kazdin, 1978, 1980). Based on these considerations, it is suggested that future research focus on both strategies in combination rather than on one or the other for assessing the efficacy of skills training.

An additional experimental design question involves training package components. Most skills training efforts to date are defined operationally by the procedures of instruction, modeling, role-playing, and performance feedback. The modest success of skills training with regard to transfer and maintenance effects is sufficient basis for dissatisfaction with this customary operational definition. What needs to be added to or deleted from the "basic foursome" is best determined by the use of what Kazdin (1980) has described as constructive and dismantling treatment designs. Skillful utilization of combinations of these experimental designs reflects what we feel to be the optimal experimental design strategy at this stage in the development of interpersonal skills training research.

In implementing such designs, we believe there exist two planes along which potentially viable treatment components may be added and deleted experimentally. Horizontal additions and deletions refer to new treatment components utilized with the trainee. In our Skillstreaming research implementation of this approach, we sought via a constructive design strategy to discern whether the potency of our basic interpersonal skills training package (i.e., modeling, role-playing, performance feedback, transfer and maintenance training) could be significantly enhanced. In addition to our attention to the direct teaching of prosocial behavior (by the four components), we sought to teach prosocial values and aggression inhibitors. That is, we implemented and evaluated not only what to do instead of aggression (prosocial values and behaviors) but also how to manage or reduce aggression itself.

We labeled this intervention combination (Skillstreaming, moral education, and anger control training) Aggression Replacement Training and evaluated its efficacy in three separate investigations. The first two involved delinquent, low-income youths incarcerated at medium or maximum security facilities for adjudicated delinquents (Goldstein & Glick, 1987). The third study, community-based, sought similar efficacy information for this intervention employed with chronically aggressive youths residing in either their own or group homes (Goldstein, Glick, Irwin, Pask-McCartney, & Rubama, 1989). All three investigations yielded encouraging, positive outcomes. Skills were learned, aggression was reduced, and, in its most comprehensive implementation (the community-based evaluation), recidivism was reduced.

One may also intervene vertically and seek to achieve direct impact on any and all of those figures in the trainee's real world whose own behavior may significantly influence trainee skill competence. With reference to aggressive adolescents, our work *School Violence* (Goldstein, Apter, & Harootunian, 1984) is an example of such a systems or vertical intervention research strategy. School violence is hypothesized to yield most fully when, in addition to the several suggested interventions targeted directly toward the aggressive youngster, equally energetic attention is directed toward the teachers involved, the school's administration, the parents, the school board, and other relevant persons in the school community—even state and federal agencies. A second example of this strategy is the community-based evaluation of Aggression Replacement Training referred to previously (Goldstein et al., 1989). This intervention yielded its most potent outcomes when, simultaneous with the delinquent youth's participation in it, similar sessions were independently held for the youth's parents and younger siblings.

Prescriptive Utilization

Prescriptive utilization of training is a second issue relevant to enhancing the potency of interpersonal skills training. Prescriptive utilization refers to the identification and implementation of optimal characteristics of the training enterprise *for particular trainees.* This research and practice strategy parallels viewpoints advanced in other areas, such as education (Cronbach & Snow, 1969; Harootunian, 1978; Hunt, 1972; Stern, 1970) and psychotherapy (Goldstein, 1978; Goldstein & Stein, 1976; Magaro, 1969).

Two domains of trainee characteristics are especially noteworthy in this regard. One is the domain of individual trainee skill deficiencies. It is not enough, as Bellack (1979), Michelson and Wood (1980), and others have argued, to employ multimodal deficit assessment techniques (behavioral observation, role-play tests, skill inventories, structured interviews) in order to identify the skills in which a youngster is deficient. It is also necessary in remedial efforts to be prescriptively responsive to the fact that there are three different ways in which an individual may be deficient in any given skill. Ladd and Mize (1983) comment:

> First, children may lack knowledge or concepts of appropriate
> social behavior . . . or they may possess concepts atypical of their
> peer group. . . . At least three forms of social knowledge may be
> represented in a skill concept, each of which is viewed as neces-
> sary for effective social functioning: (a) knowledge of appropriate
> goals for social interaction, (b) knowledge of appropriate strategies
> for reaching a social goal, and (c) knowledge of the context(s) in
> which specific strategies may be appropriately applied. . . . Second,
> children may lack, perhaps as a result of insufficient practice of the
> skills, actual behavioral abilities. . . . Finally, some children may

be deficient in giving themselves feedback about their interpersonal encounters. Specifically, these children may lack the
ability (a) to monitor and evaluate their own behavior and its
effects on others . . . and (b) to make inferences or attributions
about their interpersonal successes and failures that are conducive
to continued effort, adaptation, and self-confidence in social interactions. (pp. 129–130)

Selection of target skills, it thus follows, might optimally reflect not only such
typical parameters as the skill(s) in which the trainee is deficient, the degree of
deficiency, and the interpersonal and environmental contexts in which the deficiency manifests itself but also the particular nature (knowledge, behavior, feedback) of the deficit.

The second prescriptive domain concerns the particular receptivity channels
and optimal learning styles of trainees. To respond to such trainee qualities, our
modeling displays have been audiotaped, videotaped, or live; role-playing has
varied in length, simplicity, and repetitiveness; performance feedback has been
directive, gentle, or of variable length; and transfer and maintenance training have
been operationalized as a function of the trainee's available community resources,
homework opportunities, and capacity for abstraction. With aggressive adolescents, we have in our practice prescriptively evolved toward (a) groups no larger
than five or six; (b) briefer initial structuring of group procedures; (c) live modeling
by trainers; (d) use of two or three different vignettes when modeling; (e) heightened
levels of trainer activity, directiveness, and control; (f) increased use of token or
material reinforcers; (g) employment of visual depictions of target skill steps;
(h) added reliance on preannounced rules for group management; (i) adolescent-
relevant target skills; and (j) skills trainers experienced with adolescents.

Trainee Motivation

In addition to experimental design and prescriptive utilization, a third issue is
trainee motivation. We believe that interpersonal skills training research and practice have not given sufficient attention to trainee motivation for skill competence and
development. In addition to appropriate contingent reinforcement, the functioning
of which in a skills-training context is well established, trainee motivation may
be enhanced in conjunction with three different events that unfold sequentially
during the skills-training process: (a) the establishment of the trainer-trainee relationship, (b) selection of appropriate target skills, and (c) establishment of certain
group parameters relevant to motivation.

A host of clinicians have speculated that therapeutic progress of diverse sorts
with aggressive adolescents would be advanced by a trainer-trainee relationship
involving low empathy, high impersonality, and careful avoidance of emotional
exploration (i.e., the opposite of the relationship expected to be helpful in traditional
psychotherapeutic interventions—Dean, 1958; Goldstein, Heller, & Sechrest,
1966; Schwitzgebel, 1967; Slack, 1960). Edelman and Goldstein (1984) examined

this proposition empirically and found substantial support for the prescriptive utility in such pairings of helper behavior involving low empathy (plus high genuineness). Precisely what other relationship qualities are optimal in this context remains very much at question—with, as just noted, considerable speculation and some preliminary evidence combining to point to a type of relationship quite different from that characteristically aspired to in most other change endeavors.

Which skills shall be taught, and who will select them?

This question is as much motivational as tactical. To the degree that the youngster is able to anticipate learning skill competencies that are in her own perception presently deficient and of likely utility in real-world relationships, her motivation is correspondingly enhanced. We have operationalized this perspective in Skill-streaming training by means of a process we call "negotiating the curriculum." Skills trainer and trainee compare, contrast, examine, and select skills to reflect both trainer beliefs about what the trainee needs and trainee beliefs about deficiencies and desired competencies.

Where are the group sessions held?

In addition to these intrinsic motivators, certain group parameters may be varied to act as extrinsic motivators for learning new skills. In most schools and institutions, we try to seek a special place, a place associated in the trainee's thinking with particular privileges or opportunities (e.g., teachers' lounge, student center, recreational area) and yet not so removed in its characteristics from the typical application settings in which trainees function as to reduce the likelihood of skill transfer.

When will the group meet?

If it is not judged to be too great an academic sacrifice, we attempt to schedule school-based skills-training sessions when what the youngster will have to miss is an activity he does not especially enjoy (including certain academic subjects), rather than free play, lunch, gym, or the like.

Who will lead the group?

Particularly for beginning sessions, we seek to utilize as trainers those teachers, cottage parents, members of the institutional staff, or others we deem to be most stimulating, most attuned to the needs and behaviors of aggressive adolescents (but, for reasons described earlier, not those who are most overtly empathic), and in general most able to capture and hold the attention of participating youngsters. This strategy often has beneficial motivational consequences for both the initial groups of trainees and, through the school or institutional grapevine, subsequent groups of trainees.

Which skill shall be taught first?

The first skill taught is optimally one likely to yield immediate, real-world rewards for the trainee. It must "work"; it must pay off. Some trainers prefer to begin with simpler conversational skills as a sort of warm-up. Our own preference is to try to achieve simplicity as well as reward potential.

Transfer and Maintenance

Trainee change in prosocial directions means rather little if such change is limited to the training setting. Failure to transfer gains from training to application settings constitutes one of the most significant—if not the most significant—unsolved problems in the field of skills training. Research points clearly to the conclusion that a substantial proportion of such change is limited to the training setting, with minimal real-life value accruing to the participant (Ford & Urban, 1963; Goldstein, 1973; Goldstein et al., 1966; Gruber, 1971; Kazdin, 1975). Although efforts at programming generalization by teaching systematic problem-solving skills and coping strategies (Mahoney, 1974; Walker & Buckley, 1972) or circumventing the need for transfer by providing in vivo training (Drum & Figler, 1973; Goldstein et al., 1966; Hsu, 1965; Weiner, Becker, & Friedman, 1967) have somewhat modified this pessimistic conclusion with reference to certain behavior modification approaches, it still largely applies. Thus, failure of transfer and maintenance remains a most serious and pervasive intervention problem.

Application of Skillstreaming, Aggression Replacement Training, and the Prepare Curriculum With Gang Youths

Extensive practitioner experience and substantial empirical research pointing to positive outcome efficacy combine to support the use of three interpersonal skills training approaches for youths either already involved in antisocial gang activities or at clear risk for doing so. These are the approaches developed and evaluated expressly for such youths by our own research group. Their sequential development is depicted in Table 4.2. As can be seen, our continuing attempt to enhance the potency and comprehensiveness of our skills-training program led to Skillstreaming's evolution into Aggression Replacement Training, which in turn grew into the Prepare Curriculum. Respective procedures for these approaches are described in the remainder of this chapter. First, however, it is important to note that whereas Skillstreaming has been widely employed with adjudicated juvenile delinquents in both residential and community settings, it has not to our knowledge been used with gangs as gangs. That is, although many of the youngsters with whom it has been employed are gang members—and certainly many others who have so participated aspire to gang membership—with one exception we know of no instances in which a Skillstreaming group consisted entirely of the membership of a gang. The exception is our own work in progress, which employs Skillstreaming as part of Aggression Replacement Training with four juvenile gangs in Brooklyn, New York (Goldstein, Glick, Blancero, & Carthan, in preparation). The participating gangs represent differing ethnicity, age levels, and core versus fringe gang status.

What special organizational, locational, trainer, or other arrangements will prove optimal for this latter trainee group remain to be determined. In our view, there exist no a priori reasons that the participation of gang members in Skillstreaming—or in Aggression Replacement Training or the Prepare Curriculum—need be precluded. Changes may be necessary, but they may, in fact, be changes more

Table 4.2   Evolution of Three Skills-Based Interventions

1973–1983

Skillstreaming

1984–1988

Aggression Replacement Training

- Skillstreaming
- Anger Control Training
- Moral Reasoning Training

1988–present

The Prepare Curriculum

- Skillstreaming
- Anger Control Training
- Moral Reasoning Training
- Problem-Solving Training
- Empathy Training
- Situational Perception Training
- Stress Management
- Cooperation Training
- Recruiting Supportive Models
- Understanding and Using Group Processes

---

in emphasis than in kind. The trainer-trainee relationship may be more crucial for success than in non–gang member groups. Trainer knowledge of gang structure and functioning may be more critical. Trainee input in skill selection may be more important. We hope such obstacles of emphasis will not deter others from implementing these approaches with gang and gang-aspiring youths. The generalization-enhancing principle of identical elements urges arrangements in which youths are trained in conjunction with the other persons with whom they regularly interact and toward whom their skill repertoire is regularly directed. For gang youths, the training group—their gang—may form such a unit.

SKILLSTREAMING

The purpose of this section is to provide the information needed to prepare and conduct effective Skillstreaming groups. The selection, preparation, and instruction of gang member or at-risk preadolescent and adolescent trainees will be our major focus. We will also attend to such organizational matters as the optimal number, length, timing, spacing, and location of the Skillstreaming sessions, as well as to such instructional concerns as implementing Skillstreaming procedures (modeling, role-playing, performance feedback, transfer and maintenance training) in opening and later sessions. Finally, group management problems and their resolution will be discussed.

Preparing for Skillstreaming

Selecting Trainers

A wide variety of individuals have served successfully as Skillstreaming trainers. Their educational backgrounds have been especially varied, ranging from high school diploma only through various graduate degrees. Although formal training in a helping profession is both useful and relevant to becoming a competent Skillstreaming trainer, we have found characteristics such as sensitivity, flexibility, and instructional talent to be considerably more important than formal education. We have made frequent and successful use of trainers best described as paraprofessionals, particularly with trainees from lower socioeconomic levels. In general, we select trainers based upon the nature and demands of the Skillstreaming group. Two types of trainer skills appear crucial for successfully conducting a Skillstreaming group. The first might be described as general trainer skills—that is, those skills requisite for success in almost any training or teaching effort. These include the following:

1. Oral communication and teaching ability

2. Flexibility and resourcefulness

3. Enthusiasm

4. Ability to work under pressure

5. Interpersonal sensitivity

6. Listening skills

7. Knowledge of the subject (adolescent development; aggression management; peer pressures on adolescents; gang organization, customary behavior, and goals; etc.)

The second type of skills necessary includes specific trainer skills—that is, those skills relevant to Skillstreaming in particular. These include the following:

1. Knowledge of Skillstreaming—its background, procedures, and goals

2. Ability to orient both trainees and supporting staff to Skillstreaming

3. Ability to plan and present live modeling displays

4. Ability to initiate and sustain role-playing

5. Ability to present material in concrete, behavioral form

6. Ability to deal with group management problems effectively

7. Accuracy and sensitivity in providing corrective feedback

How can we tell if potential trainers are skilled enough to become effective group leaders? We use behavioral observation, actually seeing how competently potential trainers lead mock and then actual Skillstreaming groups during our trainer preparation phase.

Preparing Trainers

We strongly believe in learning by doing. Our chief means of preparing trainers for Skillstreaming group leadership is, first, to have them participate in an intensive, 2-day workshop designed to provide the knowledge and experience needed for beginning competence. In the workshop, we use Skillstreaming to teach Skillstreaming. First, we assign relevant reading materials for background information. Next trainees observe skilled and experienced group leaders model the central modeling display presentation, role-playing, performance feedback, and transfer training and maintenance procedures that constitute the core elements of the Skillstreaming session. Then workshop participants role-play in pairs these group leadership behaviors and receive detailed feedback from the workshop leaders and others in the training group regarding the degree to which their group leadership behaviors match or depart from those modeled by the workshop leaders. To assist workshop learning in transferring smoothly and fully to the actual training setting, regular and continuing supervisory sessions are held after the workshop with the newly created Skillstreaming group leaders. These booster/monitoring/ supervision meetings, when added to the several opportunities available for trainer performance evaluation during the workshop itself, provide a larger sample of behaviors upon which to base a fair and appropriate trainer selection decision.

Selecting Trainees

Who belongs in the Skillstreaming group? We have long held that no therapy or training approach is optimal for all clients and that our effectiveness as helpers or trainers will grow to the degree that we become prescriptive in our helping efforts (Goldstein, 1978; Goldstein & Stein, 1976). As noted earlier, Skillstreaming grew originally from a behavior-deficit view of the asocial and antisocial behavior composing juvenile delinquency. If such behavior is due in substantial part to a lack of ability in a variety of alternative prosocial skills of an interpersonal, personal, aggression management, or related nature, our selection goal is defined for us. The Skillstreaming group should consist of youngsters weak or deficient in one or more clusters of skills that constitute the Skillstreaming curriculum. Optimally, this selection process will involve the use of interview, direct observation, and behavioral testing procedures and appropriate skill checklists (Goldstein et al., 1980).

Because the ultimate goal of Skillstreaming is change in overt behavior, the removal of skill deficits, and the learning of prosocial alternatives, the selection of trainees is based exclusively on the nature and level of skill deficiency. Largely or entirely irrelevant to the selection decision are most of the usual bases for training selection decisions. If the clients are skill deficient and possess a few very basic group participation skills, we are largely unconcerned with their age, sex, race, social class, or, within very broad limits, even their mental health. At times, we have had to exclude persons who were severely emotionally disturbed, too hyperactive for a 30-minute session, or so developmentally disabled that they lacked the rudimentary memory and imaginative abilities necessary for adequate group participation. But such persons have been relatively few and quite far between. Thus, although Skillstreaming is not a prescription designed for all youths in gangs or leaning toward gang involvement, all juvenile delinquents, or all aggressive adolescents, its range of appropriate use is nevertheless quite broad.

Skillstreaming Skills

The 50 skills that constitute the Skillstreaming curriculum for adolescents are as follows:

Group I: Beginning Social Skills

1. Listening
2. Starting a Conversation
3. Having a Conversation
4. Asking a Question
5. Saying Thank You
6. Introducing Yourself
7. Introducing Other People
8. Giving a Compliment

Group II: Advanced Social Skills

9. Asking for Help
10. Joining In
11. Giving Instructions
12. Following Instructions
13. Apologizing
14. Convincing Others

Group III: Skills for Dealing With Feelings

15. Knowing Your Feelings
16. Expressing Your Feelings
17. Understanding the Feelings of Others
18. Dealing With Someone Else's Anger
19. Expressing Affection
20. Dealing With Fear
21. Rewarding Yourself

Group IV: Skill Alternatives to Aggression

22. Asking Permission
23. Sharing Something
24. Helping Others
25. Negotiating
26. Using Self-Control
27. Standing Up for Your Rights
28. Responding to Teasing
29. Avoiding Trouble With Others
30. Keeping Out of Fights

Group V: Skills for Dealing With Stress

31. Making a Complaint
32. Answering a Complaint
33. Sportsmanship After the Game
34. Dealing With Embarrassment
35. Dealing With Being Left Out
36. Standing Up for a Friend
37. Responding to Persuasion
38. Responding to Failure
39. Dealing With Contradictory Messages
40. Dealing With an Accusation
41. Getting Ready for a Difficult Conversation
42. Dealing With Group Pressure

Group VI: Planning Skills

43. Deciding on Something to Do
44. Deciding What Caused a Problem
45. Setting a Goal
46. Deciding on Your Abilities
47. Gathering Information
48. Arranging Problems by Importance
49. Making a Decision
50. Concentrating on a Task

Each of these 50 skills is broken down into its constituent behavioral steps. The steps *are* the skill and as such form the specific basis and guide for the entire modeling, role-playing, feedback, and homework sequence. Component steps and guidelines for teaching the 50 skills are presented in Goldstein et al. (1980).

Group Organization

The preparation phase of the Skillstreaming group is completed by attention to those organizational details necessary for a smoothly initiated, appropriately paced, and highly instructional group to begin. Factors to be considered in organizing the group are number of trainees, number of trainers, number of sessions, spacing of sessions, and length and location of sessions.

Number of trainees

Because trainee behavior in a Skillstreaming group may vary greatly from person to person and group to group, it is not appropriate to recommend a single, specific number of trainees. Ideally, the number of trainees will permit all to role-play, will lead to optimal levels of group interactions, and will provide a diverse source of performance feedback opportunities. In our experience with delinquent adolescents, these goals have usually been met when the group's size was from five to seven trainees.

Number of trainers

The role-playing and feedback that make up most of each Skillstreaming session are a series of "action-reaction" sequences in which effective skill behaviors are first rehearsed (role-play) and then critiqued (feedback) in the context of not infrequent behavior management problems. Thus, the trainer must lead, observe, and manage. We have found that one trainer is hard pressed to do these tasks well all at the same time, and we strongly recommend that each session be led by a team of two trainers. One trainer can usually pay special attention to the main actor, helping the actor "set the stage" and enact the skill's behavioral steps. While this is occurring, the other trainer can attend to the remainder of the group and help them as they observe and evaluate the unfolding role-play. The two trainers can then exchange these responsibilities on the next role-play.

Number of sessions

Skillstreaming groups typically seek to cover one skill in one or two sessions. The central task is to make certain that every trainee in the group role-plays the given skill correctly at least once—preferably more than once. Most Skillstreaming groups have met this curriculum requirement by holding sessions once or twice per week. Groups have varied greatly in the total number of meetings held.

Spacing of sessions

The goal of Skillstreaming is not merely skill learning or acquisition; much more important is skill transfer. Performance of the skill in the training setting is desired, but performance of it in the facility or community is crucial. Several aspects of Skillstreaming, discussed later in this section, are designed to enhance the likelihood of such skill transfer. Session spacing is one such factor. As will be described, after the trainee role-plays successfully in the group and receives thorough performance feedback, she is assigned homework—that is, the task of carrying out in the real world the skill just performed correctly in the group. In order to ensure ample time and opportunity to carry out this very important task, Skillstreaming sessions must be scheduled at least a few days apart.

Length and location of sessions

One-hour sessions are the typical Skillstreaming format, though both somewhat briefer and somewhat longer sessions have been successful. In general, the session goal that must be met is successful role-playing and clarifying feedback for all participants, be it in 45 minutes, 1 hour, or 1½ hours.

In most agencies, a reasonably quiet and comfortable office, classroom, or similar setting can be found or created for the use of Skillstreaming groups. We suggest no special requirements for the meeting place beyond those that make sense for any kind of group instruction—that it be free of distraction and at least minimally equipped with chairs, chalkboard, and adequate lighting. How shall the room be arranged? Again, no single, fixed pattern is required, but one functional and comfortable layout is the horseshoe or U-shaped arrangement, with the role-players and the trainer guiding them at the front of the room. In this group arrangement, all observing trainees and the main actor can watch the trainer point to the given skill's behavioral steps, written on a chalkboard, while the role-play is taking place. In this manner, any necessary prompting is provided immediately. At the same time, the role-play is serving as an additional modeling display for observing trainees.

Meeting With Trainees Before the First Session

A final step that must be taken before holding the first session of a new Skillstreaming group is preparing the trainees who have been selected for what they ought to expect and what will be expected of them. What this premeeting might include follows.

1. *Describing what the purposes of the group will be as they relate to the trainee's specific skill deficits.* For example, the trainer might say, "Remember when you lost privileges because you thought Henry had insulted you and you got in a shoving match with him? Well, in Skillstreaming you'll be able to learn what to do in a situation like that so you can handle it without fighting and still settle calmly whatever is going on."

2. *Describing briefly the procedure that will be used.* Although we believe that trainees typically will not have a full understanding of what Skillstreaming is and what it can accomplish until after the group has begun and they have experienced it, verbal, pregroup structuring of procedures is a useful beginning. It conveys at least a part of the information necessary to help trainees know what to expect. The trainer might say, "In order to learn to handle these problem situations better, we're going to see and hear some examples of how different people handle them well. Then you will actually take turns trying some of these ways right here. We'll let you know how you did, and you'll have a chance to practice on your own."

3. *Describing some of the hoped-for benefits of active trainee participation in the group.* If the trainer has relevant information about a trainee, the

possible benefits described might appropriately be improved proficiency in the particular skills in which the trainee rates himself as especially deficient.

4. *Describing group rules.* These rules include whatever the trainer believes the group members must adhere to in order to function smoothly and effectively with regard to attendance, punctuality, confidentiality, completion of homework assignments, and so forth. At this premeeting stage, rule structuring should be brief and tentative. A fuller discussion of this matter should be reserved for the group's first session, in which all members can be encouraged to participate and in which rule changes can be made by consensus.

Conducting the Skillstreaming Group

We now wish to turn to a detailed, step-by-step description of the procedures that constitute the Skillstreaming session. The opening session will be considered first. The elements of this session that get the Skillstreaming group off to a good start will be emphasized. Next the procedures that constitute the bulk of most Skillstreaming sessions—modeling, role-playing, performance feedback, and transfer and maintenance training—will be described. Finally, an outline that can be followed for sessions after the first will be presented.

The opening session is designed to create a safe, nonthreatening environment for trainees, stimulate their interest in the group, and give more detailed information about Skillstreaming than was provided in the individual orientations. The trainers open the session with a brief warm-up period to help participants become comfortable when interacting with the group leaders and with one another. Content for this initial phase should be interesting and nonthreatening to the trainees. Next trainers introduce the Skillstreaming program by providing trainees with a brief description of what skills training is about. Typically, this introduction covers such topics as the importance of interpersonal skills for effective and satisfying living, examples of skills that will be taught, and ways these skills can be useful to trainees in their everyday lives. It is often helpful to expand this discussion of everyday skill use to emphasize the importance of the undertaking and the personal relevance of learning the skills. The specific training procedures (modeling, role-playing, performance feedback, and transfer training) are then described at a level that the group can easily understand. We recommend that trainers describe procedures briefly, with the expectation that trainees will understand them more fully once they have actually participated in their use.

A detailed outline of the procedures that ideally make up this opening session follows.

Outline of Opening Session Procedures

A. Introductions

1. Trainers introduce themselves.

2. Trainers invite trainees to introduce themselves if they are not all previously acquainted. As a way of relaxing trainees and beginning to familiarize them with one another, the trainer can elicit from each some nonprivate information, such as neighborhood of residence, school background, special interests or hobbies, and so forth.

B. Overview of Skillstreaming

Although some or all of this material may have been discussed in earlier individual meetings with trainees, a portion of the opening session should be devoted to a presentation and group discussion of the purposes, procedures, and potential benefits of Skillstreaming. The discussion of the group's purposes should stress the probable remediation of those skill deficits that trainees in the group are aware of, concerned about, and eager to change. The procedures that make up the typical Skillstreaming session should be explained again and discussed with give and take from the group. The language used to explain the procedures should be geared to the trainees' level of understanding—that is, the terms *show, try, discuss,* and *practice* should be respectively used for the words *modeling, role-playing, performance feedback,* and *transfer training.* Heaviest stress at this point should perhaps be placed on presenting and examining the potential benefits to trainees of their participation in Skillstreaming. Concrete examples of the diverse ways that skill proficiencies could, and probably will, have a positive effect on the lives of trainees should be the focus of this effort.

C. Discussion of group rules

The rules that will govern participation in the Skillstreaming group should be presented by the trainers during the opening session. If appropriate, this presentation should permit and encourage group discussion designed to give members a sense of participation in the group's decision making. That is, members should be encouraged to accept and live by those rules they agree with and seek to alter those they wish to change. Group rules may be necessary and appropriate concerning attendance, punctuality, size of the group, and time and place of the meetings. This is also a good time to provide reassurance to group members about concerns they may have, such as confidentiality, embarrassment, and fear of performing.

D. Introduction of the first interpersonal skill

Following introductions, the overview of Skillstreaming, and the presentation of group rules, the trainers should proceed to introducing and modeling the group's first skill, conducting role-plays on that skill, giving performance feedback, and encouraging transfer training. These activities make up all subsequent Skillstreaming sessions.

The following training procedures, illustrated in the opening session as they relate to the group's first skill performance, are also vital in the core procedures of later sessions.

Modeling

The modeling display presented to trainees should depict, in a clear and un-ambiguous manner, the behavioral steps that constitute the skill being taught. All of the steps making up the skill should be modeled in the correct sequence. Generally, the modeling will consist of live vignettes enacted by the two trainers. When two trainers are not available, a reasonably skillful trainee may serve as a model along with the trainer. In all instances, it is especially important that the trainers rehearse the vignettes carefully prior to the group meeting, making sure that all of the skill's steps are enacted correctly and in the proper sequence.

Trainers should plan their modeling display carefully. Content relevant to the immediate life situations of the trainees in the group should be selected. At least two examples should be modeled for each skill so that trainees are exposed to skill use in different situations. Thus, two or more different content areas are depicted. We have found that trainers usually do not have to write out scripts for the modeling display but can instead plan their roles and likely responses in outline form and rehearse them in their preclass preparations. These modeling display outlines should incorporate the following guidelines.

1. Each skill demonstration should involve at least two different situations. If a given skill is taught in more than one group meeting, two more new modeling displays should be developed.

2. Situations relevant to the trainees' real-life circumstances should be selected.

3. The main actor—that is, the person enacting the behavioral steps of the skill—should be portrayed as a person reasonably similar to group members in age, socioeconomic background, verbal ability, and other salient characteristics.

4. Modeling displays should depict only one skill at a time. All extraneous content should be eliminated.

5. Modeling displays should depict all the behavioral steps of the skill being modeled, in the correct sequence.

6. All modeling displays should depict positive outcomes. Displays should always end with reinforcement to the model.

In order to help trainees attend to the skill enactments, skill cards, or cards previously prepared including the name of the skill being taught and listing its behavioral steps, are distributed prior to the modeling display. Trainees are told to watch and listen closely as the models portray the skill. Particular care should be given to helping trainees identify the behavioral steps as they are presented in the context of the modeling vignettes. Trainers should also remind the trainees that, in order to depict some of the behavioral steps in certain skills, the actors will occasionally be "thinking out loud" statements that would ordinarily be thought silently and that this process is done to facilitate learning.

Role-Playing

Following the modeling display, discussion should focus on relating the modeled skill to the lives of trainees. Trainers should invite comments on the behavioral steps and how these steps might be useful in real-life situations that trainees encounter. It is most helpful to focus on current and future skill use rather than only on past events or general issues involving the skill. Role-playing in Skillstreaming is intended to serve as behavioral rehearsal or practice for future use of the skill. Role-playing of past events that have little relevance for future situations is of limited value to trainees. However, discussion of past events involving skill use can be relevant in stimulating trainees to think of times when a similar situation might occur in the future. The hypothetical future situation, rather than a reenactment of the past event, would be selected for role-playing.

Once a trainee has described a situation in her own life in which the skill might be helpful, that trainee is designated the main actor. She chooses a second trainee (the coactor) to play the role of the other person (mother, peer, staff member, etc.) in her life who is relevant to the situation. The trainee should be urged to pick as a coactor someone who resembles the real-life person in as many ways as possible—physically, expressively, and so forth. The trainers then elicit from the main actor any additional information needed to set the stage for role-playing. To make role-playing as realistic as possible, the trainers should obtain a description of the physical setting, the events immediately preceding the role-play, the manner the coactor should display, and any other information that would increase realism.

It is crucial that the main actor use the behavioral steps that have been modeled. This is the main purpose of role-playing. Before beginning the actual role-play, the trainer should go over each step as it applies to the particular role-play situation, thus preparing the main actor to make a successful effort. The main actor is told to refer to the skill card on which the behavioral steps are printed. (As noted previously, the behavioral steps are written on a chalkboard visible to the main actor as well as the rest of the group during the role-playing.) Before role-playing begins, trainers should remind all of the participants of their roles and responsibilities: The main actor is told to follow the behavioral steps; the coactor, to stay in the role of the other person; and the observers, to watch carefully for the enactment of the behavioral steps. At times, feedback from other trainees is facilitated by assigning each one a single behavioral step to focus and provide feedback on after the role-play. For the first several role-plays, the observers also can be coached on cues to observe (posture, tone of voice, content of speech, etc.).

During the role-play, it is the responsibility of one of the trainers to provide the main actor with whatever help, coaching, and encouragement she needs to keep the role-playing going according to the behavioral steps. Trainees who "break role" and begin to explain their behavior or make observer-like comments should be urged to get back into the role and explain later. If the role-play is clearly going astray from the behavioral steps, the scene can be stopped, needed instruction can be provided, and then the role-play can be restarted. One trainer should be positioned near the chalkboard in order to point to each of the behavioral steps in turn as the role-play unfolds, thus helping the main actor (as well as the other trainees) to follow each of the steps in order. The second trainer should sit with the observing trainees to be available as needed to keep them on task.

The role-playing should be continued until all trainees have had an opportunity to participate in the role of main actor. Sometimes this will require two or three sessions for a given skill. As suggested before, each session should begin with two new modeling vignettes for the chosen skill, even if the skill is not new to the group. It is important to note once again that, although the framework (behavioral steps) of each role-play in the series remains the same, the actual content can and should change from role-play to role-play. It is the problem as it actually occurs, or could occur, in each trainee's real-life environment that should be the content of the given role-play.

There are a few more ways to increase the effectiveness of role-playing. Role reversal is often a useful role-play procedure. A trainee role-playing a skill may on occasion have a difficult time perceiving the coactor's viewpoint and vice versa. Having the actors exchange roles and resume the role-play can be most helpful in this regard. At times, the trainer can also assume the coactor role in an effort to give the trainee the opportunity to handle types of reactions not otherwise role-played during the session. For example, it may be crucial to have a difficult coactor realistically portrayed. The trainer as coactor may also be particularly helpful when dealing with less verbal or more hesitant trainees.

Performance Feedback

A brief feedback period follows each role-play. This helps the main actor evaluate how he followed or departed from the behavioral steps. It also examines the psychological impact of the enactment on the coactor and provides the main actor with encouragement to try out the role-played behaviors in real life. The trainer should ask the main actor to wait until he has heard everyone's comments before responding to any of them.

The coactor is asked about his reactions first. Next the observers comment on how well the behavioral steps were followed and on other relevant aspects of the role-play. Then the trainers comment in particular on how well the behavioral steps were followed and provide social reinforcement (praise, approval, encouragement) for close following. To be most effective in their use of reinforcement, trainers should follow these guidelines.

1. Provide reinforcement only after role-plays that follow the behavioral steps.

2. Provide reinforcement at the earliest appropriate opportunity after role-plays that follow the behavioral steps.

3. Vary the specific content of the reinforcements offered—for example, praise particular aspects of the performance, such as tone of voice, posture, phrasing, and the like.

4. Provide enough role-playing activity for each group member to have sufficient opportunity to be reinforced.

5. Provide reinforcement in an amount consistent with the quality of the given role-play.

6. Provide no reinforcement when the role-play departs significantly from the behavioral steps (except for "trying" in the first session or two).

7. Provide reinforcement for an individual trainee's improvement over previous performances.

8. Always provide reinforcement to the coactor for being helpful, cooperative, and so forth.

In all aspects of feedback, it is crucial that the trainer maintain the behavioral focus of Skillstreaming. Both trainer and trainee comments should point to the presence or absence of specific, concrete behaviors and should not take the form of broad evaluations or generalities. Feedback may of course be positive or negative in content. A negative comment should always be followed by a constructive comment as to how a particular fault might be improved. At minimum, a "poor" performance can be praised as "a good try" at the same time that it is criticized for its faults. If at all possible, trainees failing to follow the relevant behavioral steps in their role-plays should be given the opportunity to role-play these same behavioral steps again after receiving corrective feedback. At times, as a further feedback procedure, we have audiotaped or videotaped entire role-plays. Giving trainees opportunities following role-play to observe themselves on tape can be an effective aid, enabling them to reflect on their own verbal and nonverbal behavior and its impact upon others.

Because a primary goal of Skillstreaming is skill flexibility, role-play enactments that depart somewhat from the behavioral steps may not be "wrong." That is, a different approach to the skill may in fact work in some situations. Trainers should stress that they are trying to teach effective alternatives and that the trainees would do well to have the behavioral steps being taught, or as collaboratively modified, in their repertoires of skill behaviors, available to use when appropriate.

Transfer and Maintenance Training

Several aspects of the training sessions have been designed to make it likely that learning in the training setting will transfer to the trainees' real-life environments and will be maintained there. Techniques for enhancing transfer and maintenance, as used in the sessions, follow.

Provision of general principles

It has been demonstrated that transfer and maintenance of training are facilitated by providing trainees with general mediating principles governing successful or competent performance in both the training and real-world settings. This idea has been operationalized in laboratory contexts by providing subjects with the organizing concepts, principles, strategies, or rationales that explain the stimulus-response relationships operating in both the training and application settings. General principles of skill selection and utilization are provided to trainees verbally, visually, and in written form.

Overlearning

Overlearning involves training in a skill beyond what is necessary to produce initial changes in behavior. The overlearning, or repetition of successful skill enactment, in the typical Skillstreaming session is quite substantial. Each skill taught and its behavioral steps are:

1. Modeled several times

2. Role-played one or more times by the trainee

3. Observed live by the trainee as every other group member role-plays

4. Read by the trainee from a chalkboard and a skill card

5. Practiced in real-life settings one or more times by the trainee as part of a formal homework assignment

Identical elements

In perhaps the earliest research on transfer enhancement, Thorndike and Woodworth (1901) concluded that when one habit facilitated another, it was to the extent that they shared identical elements. More recently, Ellis (1965) and Osgood (1953) have emphasized the importance for transfer of similarity between stimulus aspect of the training and application tasks. The greater the similarity of physical and interpersonal stimuli in the Skillstreaming setting and the home, community, or other setting in which the skill is to be applied, the greater the likelihood of transfer. Skillstreaming is made similar to real life in several ways. These include:

1. Designing the live modeling displays to be highly similar to what trainees face in their daily lives through the representative, relevant, and realistic portrayal of the models, protagonists, and situations.

2. Designing the role-plays to be similar to real-life situations through the use of props, the physical arrangement of the setting, and the choice of realistic coactors

3. Conducting the role-plays to be as responsive as possible to the real-life interpersonal stimuli to which the trainees must actually respond later with the given skill

4. Rehearsing of each skill in role-plays as the trainees actually plan to use it

5. Assigning of homework

Stimulus variability

Positive transfer is greater when a variety of relevant training stimuli are employed (Callantine & Warren, 1955; Duncan, 1958; Shore & Sechrest, 1961). Stimulus variability may be implemented in Skillstreaming sessions by use of the following:

1. Rotation of group leaders across groups

2. Rotation of trainees across groups

3. Role-playing of a given skill by trainees with several different coactors

4. Role-playing of a given skill by trainees across several relevant settings

5. Completion of multiple homework assignments for each given skill

Real-life reinforcement

Given successful implementation of both appropriate Skillstreaming procedures and transfer and maintenance enhancement procedures, positive transfer and maintenance may still fail to occur. As Agras (1967), Gruber (1971), Patterson and Anderson (1964), Tharp and Wetzel (1969), and dozens of other investigators have shown, stable and enduring performance of newly learned skills in application settings is very much at the mercy of real-life reinforcement contingencies. We have found it useful to implement several supplemental programs outside the Skillstreaming setting that can help to provide the rewards trainees need to maintain new behaviors. These programs include provision for both external social rewards (provided by people in the trainees' real-life environments) and self-rewards (provided by the trainees themselves). A particularly useful tool for transfer and maintenance enhancement—a tool combining the possibilities of identical elements, stimulus variability, and real-life reinforcement—is the skill homework assignment.

When possible, we urge use of a homework technique we have found to be successful with most groups. In this procedure, trainees are instructed to try in their own real-life settings the behaviors they have practiced during the session. The name of the person(s) with whom they will try the skill, the day, the place, and so forth are all discussed. The trainee is urged to take notes on her attempt to use the skill on the Homework Report Form (Figure 4.1). This form requests detailed information about what happened when the trainee attempted the homework assignment, how well she followed the relevant behavioral steps, the trainee's evaluation of her performance, and thoughts about what the next assignment might appropriately be.

It has often proven useful to start with relatively simple homework behaviors and, as mastery is achieved, work up to more complex and demanding assignments.

Figure 4.1   Homework Report Form

Name _____   Date _____

Group leaders _____

Fill in during this class

1. Homework assignment: _____

_____

    a. Skill: _____

    b. Use with whom: _____

    c. Use when: _____

    d. Use where: _____

2. Steps to be followed: _____

_____

Fill in before next class

3. Describe what happened when you did the homework assignment:

_____

_____

4. Steps you actually followed: _____

_____

5. Rate yourself on how well you used the skill (check one):

    Excellent ☐   Good ☐   Fair ☐   Poor ☐

6. Describe what you feel should be your next homework assignment:

_____

_____

This provides both the trainer and the people who are targets of the homework with an opportunity to reinforce each approximation of the more complex target behavior. Successful experiences at initial homework attempts are crucial in encouraging the trainee to make further attempts at real-life use of the skill.

The first part of each Skillstreaming session is devoted to presenting and discussing these homework reports. When trainees have made an effort to complete their homework assignments, trainers should provide social reinforcement. Failure to do homework should be met with some expressed disappointment, followed by support and encouragement to complete the assignment. It cannot be stressed too strongly that without these or similar attempts to maximize transfer, the value of the entire training effort is in severe jeopardy.

Much of the foregoing procedural material is conveniently summarized, for purposes of review, by the following outline.

Outline of Later Session Procedures

A. Trainer and trainees review homework.

B. Trainer presents overview of the skill.

    1. Introduces skill briefly prior to modeling display.

    2. Asks questions that will help trainees define the skill in their own language.

        Examples: "Who knows what _____ is?"

                  "What does _____ mean to you?"

                  "Who can define _____?"

    3. Postpones lengthier discussion until after trainees view the modeling display. If trainees want to engage in further discussion, the trainer might say, "Let's wait until after we've seen some examples of people using the skill before we talk about it in more detail."

    4. Makes a statement about what will follow the modeling display.

        Example: "After we see the examples, we will talk about times when you've had to use _____ and times when you may have to use that skill in the future."

    5. Distributes skill cards, asking a trainee to read the behavioral steps aloud.

    6. Asks trainees to follow each step in the modeling display as the step is depicted.

C. Trainer presents modeling display of two relevant examples of the skill in use, following its behavioral steps.

D. Trainer invites discussion of skill that has been modeled.

1. Invites comments on how the situation modeled may remind trainees of situations involving skill use in their own lives.

    Example: "Did any of the situations you just saw remind you of times when you have had to _____?"

2. Asks questions that encourage trainees to talk about skill use and problems involving skill use.

    Examples: "What do you do in situations where you have to _____?"

        "Have you ever had to _____?"

        "Have you ever had difficulty _____?"

E. Trainer organizes role-play.

1. Asks a trainee who has volunteered a situation to elaborate on his remarks, obtaining details on where, when, and with whom the skill might be useful in the future.

2. Designates this trainee as a main actor and asks the trainee to choose a coactor (someone who reminds the main actor of the person with whom the skill will be used in the real-life situation).

    Examples: "What does _____ look like?"

        "Who in the group reminds you of _____ in some way?"

3. Gets additional information from the main actor, if necessary, and sets the stage for role-playing (including props, furniture arrangement, etc.).

    Examples: "Where might you be talking to _____?"

        "How is the room furnished?"

        "Would you be standing or sitting?"

        "What time of day will it be?"

4. Rehearses with the main actor what he will say and do during the role-play.

    Examples: "What will you say for the first step of the skill?"

        "What will you do if the coactor does _____?"

5. Gives group members some final instructions as to their parts just prior to role-playing.

> *Examples:*   To the main actor: "Try to follow all of the steps as best you can."
>
> To the coactor: "Try to play the part of _____ as best you can. Say and do what you think _____ would do when _____ follows the skill's steps."
>
> To the other trainees in the group: "Watch how well _____ follows the steps so that we can talk about it after the role-play."

F. Trainer instructs the role-players to begin.

1. One trainer stands at the chalkboard and points to each step as it is enacted and provides whatever coaching or prompting is needed by the main actor or coactor.

2. The other trainer sits with the observing trainees to help keep them attending to the unfolding role-play.

3. In the event that the role-play strays markedly from the behavioral steps, the trainers stop the scene, provide needed instruction, and begin again.

G. Trainer invites feedback following role-play.

1. Asks the main actor to wait until he has heard everyone's comments before talking.

2. Asks the coactor, "In the role of _____, how did _____ make you feel? What were your reactions to him?"

3. Asks observing trainees: "How well were the behavioral steps followed?" "What specific things did you like or dislike?" "In what ways did the coactor do a good job?"

4. Comments on how the behavioral steps were followed, provides social reward, points out what was done well, and comments on what else might be done to make the enactment even better.

5. Asks the main actor: "Now that you have heard everyone's comments, how do you feel about the job you did?" "How do you think that following the steps worked out?"

H. Trainer helps role-player to plan homework.

1. Asks the main actor how, when, and with whom he might attempt the behavioral steps prior to the next class meeting.

2. As appropriate, assigns homework and gets a written commitment from the main actor to try out his new skill and report back to the group at the next meeting (see Figure 4.1).

3. Assigns homework to trainees who have not had a chance to role-play during a particular class, in the form of looking for situations relevant to the skill that they might role-play during the next class meeting.

Managing Problem Behaviors in the Skillstreaming Group

As is true for any type of treatment, training, or teaching group, management problems sometimes occur during Skillstreaming. Group management problems, at a general level, are any behaviors shown by one or more group members that interfere with, inhibit, deflect, or slow down the training procedures or goals of Skillstreaming. In this section, we will describe problems as they may occur in the Skillstreaming group. Some occur very rarely; others occur with greater frequency. All of the problems that we are presently aware of are included here in order to fully prepare trainers for behaviors they may have to deal with in actual groups. Our coverage should be considered comprehensive but not exhaustive—every time we conclude that we have seen everything in the Skillstreaming group, something new and challenging comes along. Our proposals for dealing with group management problems will usually suffice, but skilled trainers will be called upon from time to time to deal creatively with new challenges as they arise in even the most productive Skillstreaming groups. Most methods will need to be employed only as a temporary bridge between trainees' initial resistance and their subsequent acknowledgment that participation is useful, valuable, and personally relevant. These techniques, derived from research on skills-training group management as well as from our own and others' experiences with such groups, should help trainers deal with almost any difficulties that may arise.

Types of Group Management Problems

The following discussion reports the full range of group management problems that have occurred in Skillstreaming groups for delinquent or chronically aggressive adolescents.

Inactivity

Minimal participation involves trainees who seldom volunteer, provide only brief answers, and in general give the trainers a feeling that they are "pulling teeth" to keep the group at its various skills-training tasks.

A more extreme form of minimal participation is *apathy,* in which nearly everything the trainers do to direct, enliven, or activate the group is met with a lack of interest and spontaneity, and little if any progress toward group goals.

Although it is quite rare, *falling asleep* does occur from time to time. The sleepers need to be awakened, and the trainers might wisely inquire into the cause of the tiredness because boredom with the group, lack of sleep, and physical illness are all possible reasons, each one requiring a different trainer response.

Active resistance

Trainees involved in *participation but not as instructed* are off target. They may be trying to role-play, serve as coactor, give accurate feedback, or engage in other tasks required in Skillstreaming, but their own personal agendas or misperceptions interfere, and they wander off course to irrelevant or semirelevant topics.

Passive-aggressive isolation is not merely apathy, in which the trainees are simply uninterested in participating. Nor is it participation but not as instructed, in which trainees actively go off task and raise personal agendas. Passive-aggressive isolation is the purposeful, intentional withholding of appropriate participation, an active shutting down of involvement. It can be thought of as a largely nonverbal "crossing of one's arms" in order to display deliberate nonparticipation.

When displaying *negativism,* trainees signal more overtly, by word and deed, the wish to avoid participation in the Skillstreaming group. They may openly refuse to role-play, provide feedback, or complete homework assignments. Or they may not come to sessions, come late to sessions, or walk out in the middle of a session.

Disruptiveness encompasses active resistance behaviors more extreme than negativism, such as openly and perhaps energetically ridiculing the trainers, other trainees, or aspects of the Skillstreaming process. Or disruptiveness may be shown by gestures, movements, noises, or other distracting nonverbal behaviors characteristically symbolizing overt criticism and hostility.

Hyperactivity

Digression is related to participation but not as instructed, but in our experience is a more repetitive, more determined, and more strongly motivated moving away from the purposes and procedures of Skillstreaming. Here the trainees feel some emotion strongly, such as anger or anxiety or despair, and are determined to express it. Or the skill portrayed by the trainers or other trainees may set off associations with important recent experiences, which the trainees feel the need to present and discuss. Digression is also often characterized by "jumping out of role" in the role-play. Rather than merely wandering off track, in digression the trainees drive the train off its intended course.

Monopolizing involves subtle and not-so-subtle efforts by trainees to get more than a fair share of time during a Skillstreaming session. Long monologues, requests by the trainees to role-play again, elaborate feedback, and attention-seeking efforts to "remain on stage" are examples of monopolizing behavior.

Similar to monopolizing but more intrusive and insistent, *interruption* is literally breaking into the ongoing flow of a modeling display, role-play, or feedback period with comments, questions, suggestions, observations, or other statements. Interruptions may be overly assertive or angry, on the one hand, or they may take a more pseudo-benevolent guise of being offered as help to the trainer. In either event, such interruptions more often than not retard the group's progress toward its goals.

Excessive restlessness is a more extreme, more physical form of hyperactivity. The trainees may fidget while sitting; rock their chairs; get up and pace; smoke a great deal; drink soft drink after soft drink; or display other nonverbal, verbal, gestural, or postural signs of restlessness. Such behavior will typically be accompanied by digression, monopolizing, or interrupting behavior.

Cognitive inadequacies and emotional disturbance

Closely related at times to excessive restlessness, the *inability to pay attention* is often an apparent result of internal or external distractions, daydreaming, or other pressing agendas that command the trainees' attention. Inability to pay attention except for brief time spans may also be due to one or more forms of cognitive impairment.

Cognitive deficits due to developmental disability, intellectual inadequacy, impoverishment of experience, disease processes, or other sources may result in trainees' *inability to understand* aspects of the Skillstreaming process. Failure to understand can, of course, also result from errors in the clarity and complexity of statements presented by the trainers.

Material presented in the Skillstreaming group may be both attended to and understood by the trainees, but not remembered. *Inability to remember* may result not only in problems of skill transfer and maintenance but also in group management problems when what is forgotten includes rules and procedures for trainee participation, homework assignments, and so forth.

Bizarre behavior is not common, but when instances of it do occur they can be especially disruptive to group functioning. This type of group management problem may not only pull other trainees off task, it may also frighten them or make them highly anxious. The range of bizarre behavior possible is quite broad, including talking to oneself or inanimate objects, offering incoherent statements to the group, becoming angry for no apparent reason, hearing and responding to imaginary voices, and exhibiting peculiar mannerisms.

Reducing Group Management Problems

Most Skillstreaming sessions proceed rather smoothly, but the competent trainer is a prepared trainer. Preparation includes knowing both what problems might occur and what corrective steps to take when they do occur. The following discussion focuses on an array of methods for reducing group management problems.

Simplification methods

Reward minimal trainee accomplishments. Problematic trainee behavior can sometimes be altered by a process similar to shaping. For example, rather than responding positively to trainees only when they enact a complete and accurate role-play, reward in the form of praise and approval may be offered for lesser but still successful accomplishments. Perhaps only one or two behavioral steps were role-played correctly. Or, in the extreme example of rewarding minimal trainee accomplishment, praise may be offered for "trying" after a totally unsuccessful role-play or even for merely paying attention to someone else's role-play.

Shorten the role-play. A more direct means of simplifying the trainees' task is to ask less of them. One way of doing so is to shorten the role-play, usually by asking trainees to role-play only some (or one) of the behavioral steps that constitute the skill being taught.

Have the trainer "feed" sentences to the trainee. With trainees having a particularly difficult time participating appropriately in the Skillstreaming group, especially for reasons of cognitive inadequacy, the trainer may elect to take on the role of coach or prompter. There are a variety of ways this may be accomplished, perhaps the most direct of which involves a trainer's standing immediately behind the trainee and whispering the particular statements that constitute proper enactment of each behavioral step for the trainee to then say out loud.

Have the trainee read a prepared script. We personally have never used this approach to group management problems, but others report some success with it. In essence, it removes the burden of figuring out what to say from the trainees and makes the task of getting up in front of the group and acting out the skill's behavioral steps easier. Clearly, as with all simplification methods, using a prepared script should be seen as a temporary device, used to move trainees in the direction of role-playing with no such special assistance from the trainers.

Have the trainee play the coactor role first. An additional means of easing trainees into the responsibility of being the main actor in a role-play is to have them play the role of the coactor at first. This accustoms them more gradually to getting up before the group and speaking because the "spotlight" is mostly on someone else. As with the use of a prepared script, this method should be used only temporarily. Before moving on to the next skill, all trainees must always take on the role of the main actor with the particular skill.

Elicitation of response methods

Call for volunteers. Particularly in the early stages of the life of a Skillstreaming group, trainee participation may have to be actively elicited by the group's trainers. As trainees actually experience the group's procedures, find them personally relevant and valuable, and find support and acceptance from the trainers and from other group members, the need for such elicitation typically diminishes. The least directive form of such trainer activity is the straightforward calling for volunteers.

Introduce topics for discussion. Calling for volunteers, essentially an invitation to the group as a whole, may yield no response in the highly apathetic group. Under this circumstance, introducing topics that appear relevant to the needs, concerns, aspirations, and particular skill deficiencies of the participating members will often be an effective course of action.

Call on a specific trainee. If unsuccessful, the largely nondirective elicitation methods already presented may be followed by a more active and directive trainer intervention—that is, calling upon a particular trainee and requesting that trainee's participation. In doing so, it is often useful to select a trainee who by means of attentiveness, facial expression, eye contact, or other nonverbal signals communicates potential involvement and interest.

Reinstruct trainees by means of prompting and coaching. The trainer may have to become still more active and directive than mentioned already and, in a manner similar to our earlier discussion of feeding role-play lines to a trainee, prompt and coach the trainee to adequate participation. Such assistance may involve any aspect of the Skillstreaming process—attending to the modeling display, following a skill's behavioral steps during role-playing, providing useful performance feedback after someone else's role-play, completing homework assignments in the proper manner, and so forth.

Threat reduction methods

Employ additional live modeling by the trainers. When the Skillstreaming trainers engage in live modeling of a skill, they are doing more than just the main task of skill enactment. Such trainer behavior also makes it easier for trainees to get up and risk less than perfect performances in an effort to learn the skill. For trainees who are particularly anxious, inhibited, or reluctant to role-play, an additional portrayal or two of the same skill by the trainers may put them at ease. Such additional live modeling will also prove useful to those trainees having difficulty role-playing because of cognitive inadequacies.

Postpone the trainee's role-playing until last. This recommendation is a straightforward extension of the one just presented. The threat of role-playing may be reduced for a trainee if he is not required to role-play until the trainers' live modeling and role-playing by all other trainees are completed. It is crucial, though, that no trainee deficient in the skill be excused completely from role-playing that skill. To do so would run counter to the central skill-training purpose of Skillstreaming.

Provide reassurance to the trainee. This method of dealing with group management problems involves the trainers' providing one or more trainees with brief, straightforward, simple, but very often highly effective messages of encouragement and reassurance. "You can do it," "We'll help you as you go along," and "Take it a step at a time" are but a few examples of such frequently valuable reassurance.

Provide empathic encouragement to the trainee. This is a method we have used often, with good results. In the case of trainee reluctance to role-play, for example, the trainer may provide empathic encouragement by proceeding through the following steps:

Step 1: Offer the resistant trainee the opportunity to explain in greater detail her reluctance to role-play and listen nondefensively.

Step 2: Clearly express your understanding of the resistant trainee's feelings.

Step 3: If appropriate, respond that the trainee's view is a viable alternative.

Step 4: Present your own view in greater detail, with both supporting reasons and probable outcomes.

Step 5: Express the appropriateness of delaying a resolution of the trainer-trainee difference.

Step 6: Urge the trainee to try to role-play the given behavioral steps.

The identical procedure may be used effectively with a wide range of other trainee resistances.

Clarify threatening aspects of the trainee's task. Clarifying threatening aspects of tasks requires deeper explanations, repetition of earlier clarifications, and provision of further illustrations. In all instances, the task involved remains unchanged, but what is required of trainees to complete the task is further presented and made clear.

Restructure threatening aspects of the trainee's task. Unlike the method just discussed, in which the task remains unchanged and the trainers seek to clarify the trainee's understanding of it, in the present method the trainers may alter the trainee's task if it is seen as threatening. Behavioral steps may be changed, simplified, reorganized, deleted, or added. Role-plays may be shortened, lengthened, changed in content, merged with other skills, or otherwise altered. Aspects of performance feedback may be changed, too—the sequence of who delivers it, its generality versus specificity, its timing, its length, its focus. No aspect of Skill-streaming should be considered unchangeable. All treatment, training, and teaching methods should perpetually be open to revision as needed in the judgment of skilled and sensitive users. Most certainly, this also includes Skillstreaming.

Termination of response methods

Urge the trainee to remain on task. Trainees who wander away from the group's task may at times be gently but firmly brought back on track. The trainers can do this by reminders, cajoling, admonishing, or simply clearly pointing out to the trainee what he is doing incorrectly and what he ought to be doing instead.

Ignore trainee behavior. Certain inappropriate trainee behaviors can be terminated most effectively by simply ignoring them. This withdrawal of reinforcement, or extinction process, is best applied to those problem behaviors that the group can tolerate while still remaining on task as the extinction process is taking place. Behaviors such as pacing, whispering to oneself, and occasional interruptions are examples of behaviors perhaps best terminated by simply ignoring them. Behaviors that are more disruptive to the group's functioning, or even dangerous, will have to be dealt with more frontally.

Interrupt ongoing trainee behavior. This problem management method requires directive and assertive trainer behavior. We recommend interrupting ongoing trainee behavior primarily when other methods fail. Interrupting trainees' inappropriate, erroneous, or disruptive behavior should be carried out firmly, unequivocally, and with the clear message that the group has its tasks and that they must be gotten on with. In its extreme form, interrupting may even require removing trainees from groups for brief or extended periods of time.

This consideration of problem behaviors and their reduction completes our presentation of the procedures that constitute Skillstreaming. We turn now to the further interpersonal skills training intervention groupings into which Skillstreaming has evolved: Aggression Replacement Training and the Prepare Curriculum.

AGGRESSION REPLACEMENT TRAINING

As noted earlier, the frequent failure of transfer or maintenance of training gains is a common outcome not only across skills-training approaches, but in interventions of all types (Goldstein & Kanfer, 1979; Karoly & Steffen, 1980; Keeley, Shemberg, & Carbonell, 1976). This not uncommon failure of such gains to generalize across settings or time formed the primary motivation for our effort to expand our training intervention beyond Skillstreaming to an expanded program: Aggression Replacement Training. Many efforts designed to enhance transfer and maintenance have appropriately turned outward—to parents, employers, teachers, siblings, or other benign and gain-reinforcing persons available in trainees' real-world environments. One is rarely so fortunate with the type of trainee upon whom most of our work has focused—chronically aggressive youths. Far too often, parents are indifferent or unavailable; peers are the original tutors of antisocial, not prosocial, behavior; employers are nonexistent or too busy; and teachers have written off the youngsters years ago. To be sure, when and if one may mobilize the assistance of such persons, one should energetically do so. Much more often, however, one is left with a single transfer and maintenance enhancement option—working with the target youngster.

If, as seems the case with any interpersonal skills training method used alone, Skillstreaming alone fails to provide reliable transfer and maintenance outcomes, we reasoned, then our training intervention must be broadened, its coverage and potency increased in a fuller effort to arm the youngster with whatever is needed to want and be able to behave enduringly in constructive, nonaggressive, and still satisfying ways in the community. With this as our guiding philosophy, we constructed and evaluated Aggression Replacement Training, a training intervention involving three components: Skillstreaming, anger control training, and moral education. Table 4.3 illustrates the interaction among these three components. A full discussion of this intervention appears in Goldstein and Glick (1987).

Skillstreaming

As discussed earlier, Skillstreaming is a systematic psychoeducational intervention demonstrated across a great many investigations to teach a 50-skill curriculum

Table 4.3 Aggression Replacement Training Curriculum

Skillstreaming	Moral reasoning	Anger control
Skill: Expressing a Complaint	1. The Used Car	Introduction
1. Define what the problem is and who's responsible for it.	2. Dope Pusher	1. Rationale: Presentation and discussion
2. Decide how the problem might be solved.	3. Riots in Public Places	2. Rules: Presentation and discussion
3. Tell that person what the problem is and how it might be solved.		3. Training procedures: Presentation and discussion
4. Ask for a response.		4. Contracting for ACT participation
5. Show that you understand his or her feelings.		5. Initial history taking regarding antecedent provocations–behavioral response–consequences (A-B-C)
6. Come to agreement on the steps to be taken by each of you.		
Skill: Responding to the Feelings of Others (Empathy)	1. The Passenger Ship	Assessment
1. Observe the other person's words and actions.	2. The Case of Charles Manson	1. Hassle Log: Purposes and mechanics
2. Decide what the other person might be feeling and how strong the feelings are.	3. LSD	2. Anger self-assessment: Physiological cues
3. Decide whether it would be helpful to let the other person know you understand his or her feelings.		3. Anger Reducers
4. Tell the other person, in a warm and sincere manner, how you think he or she is feeling.		a. Reducer 1. Deep breathing training
		b. Reducer 2. Refocusing—backward counting
		c. Reducer 3. Peaceful imagery

133

Table 4.3 (cont.)

Skillstreaming	Moral reasoning	Anger control
Skill: Preparing for a Stressful Conversation	1. Shoplifting	Triggers
1. Imagine yourself in the stressful situation.	2. Booby Trap	1. Identification of provoking stimuli
2. Think about how you will feel and why you will feel that way.	3. Plagiarism	a. Direct triggers (from others)
3. Imagine the other person in the stressful situation. Think about how that person will feel and why.		b. Indirect triggers (from self)
4. Imagine yourself telling the other person what you want to say.		2. Role-play: Triggers + cues + anger reducers
5. Imagine what he or she will say.		3. Review of Hassle Logs
6. Repeat the above steps using as many approaches as you can think of.		
7. Choose the best approach.		
Skill: Responding to Anger	1. Toy Revolver	Reminders (Anger Reducer 4)
1. Listen openly to what the other person has to say.	2. Robin Hood Case	1. Introduction to self-instruction training
2. Show that you understand what the other person is feeling.	3. Drugs	2. Modeling use of reminders under pressure
3. Ask the other person to explain anything you don't understand.		3. Role-play: Triggers + cues + reminders + anger reducers
4. Show that you understand why the other person feels angry.		4. Homework assignments and review of Hassle Log
5. If it is appropriate, express your thoughts and feelings about the situation.		

134

Self-Evaluation

1. Review of reminder homework assignments
2. Self-evaluation of post-conflict reminders
   a. Self-reinforcement techniques
   b. Self-coaching techniques
3. Review of Hassle Log post-conflict reminders
4. Role-play: Triggers + cues + reminders + anger reducers + self-evaluation

Thinking Ahead (Anger Reducer 5)

1. Estimating future negative consequences for current acting out
2. Short-term versus long-term consequences
3. Worst to least consequences
4. Role-play: "If . . . then" thinking ahead
5. Role-play: Triggers + cues + reminders + anger reducers + self-evaluation + Skillstreaming skill

1. Private Country Road
2. New York Versus Gerald Young
3. Saving a Life

1. The Kidney Transplant
2. Bomb Shelter
3. Misrepresentation

Skill: Keeping Out of Fights

1. Stop and think about why you want to fight.
2. Decide what you want to happen in the long run.
3. Think about other ways to handle the situation besides fighting.
4. Decide on the best way to handle the situation and do it.

Skill: Helping Others

1. Decide if the other person might need and want your help.
2. Think of ways you could be helpful.
3. Ask the other person if he/she needs and wants your help.
4. Help the other person.

Table 4.3 (cont.)

Skillstreaming	Moral reasoning	Anger control
Skill: Dealing With an Accusation	1. Lieutenant Berg	The Angry Behavior Cycle
1. Think about what the other person has accused you of.	2. Perjury	1. Review of Hassle Logs
2. Think about why the person might have accused you.	3. Doctor's Responsibility	2. Identification of own anger-provoking behavior
3. Think about ways to answer the person's accusations.		3. Modification of own anger-provoking behavior
4. Choose the best way and do it.		4. Role-play: Triggers + cues + reminders + anger reducers + self-evaluation + Skillstreaming skill
Skill: Dealing With Group Pressure	1. Noisy Child	Full Sequence Rehearsal
1. Think about what the other people want you to do and why.	2. The Stolen Car	1. Review of Hassle Logs
2. Decide what you want to do.	3. Discrimination	2. Role-play: Triggers + cues + reminders + anger reducers + self-evaluation + Skillstreaming skill
3. Decide how to tell the other people what you want to do.		
4. Tell the group what you have decided.		

Skill: Expressing Affection
1. Decide if you have good feelings about the other person.
2. Decide whether the other person would like to know about your feelings.
3. Decide how you might best express your feelings.
4. Choose the right time and place to express your feelings.
5. Express affection in a warm and caring manner.

1. Defense of Other Persons
2. Lying in Order to Help Someone
3. Rockefeller's Suggestion

Full Sequence Rehearsal
1. Review of Hassle Logs
2. Role-play: Triggers + cues + reminders + anger reducers + self-evaluation + Skillstreaming skill

Skill: Responding to Failure
1. Decide if you have failed.
2. Think about both the personal reasons and the circumstances that have caused you to fail.
3. Decide how you might do things differently if you tried again.
4. Decide if you want to try again.
5. If it is appropriate, try again, using your revised approach.

1. The Desert
2. The Treat
3. Drunken Driving

Full Sequence Rehearsal
1. Review of Hassle Logs
2. Role-play: Triggers + cues + reminders + anger reducers + self-evaluation + Skillstreaming skill

of prosocial behaviors. Stated simply, in addition to other target behaviors, it teaches youngsters behaviors they may use instead of aggression in response to provocations they may experience.

Anger Control Training

Anger control training was developed by Feindler and her research group (Feindler, Marriott, & Iwata, 1984), based in part on the seminal anger control and stress inoculation research of Novaco (1975) and Meichenbaum (1977). In contrast to Skillstreaming, anger control training teaches the inhibition of anger, aggression, and, more generally, antisocial behavior. By means of its constituent components (e.g., identification of the physiological cues of anger and its external and internal triggers or instigators, self-statement disputation training, refocusing of anticipation or consequences), it teaches chronically angry and aggressive youths to respond to provocation (others' and their own) less impulsively, more reflectively, and with less likelihood of acting-out behavior. In short, anger control training teaches youngsters what not to do in anger-instigating situations.

Moral Education

Armed with both the ability to respond prosocially to the real world and with the skills necessary to stifle or at least diminish impulsive anger and aggression, will the chronically acting-out youngster in fact choose to do so? To enhance the likelihood that such will in fact be the youngster's choice, we believe one must enter into the realm of moral values (see chapter 5). In a long and pioneering series of investigations, Kohlberg (1969, 1973) demonstrated that exposing youngsters reasoning at differing levels of moral thinking to a group discussion of moral dilemmas arouses an experience of cognitive conflict whose resolution will frequently advance a youngster's moral reasoning to that of the higher level peers in the group. Although stage advancement is a reliable finding, as with other single interventions, efforts to utilize this technique by itself as a means of enhancing overt moral behavior have yielded only mixed success (Arbuthnot & Gordon, 1983; Zimmerman, 1983). We speculated that this was the case because such youngsters did not have in their behavioral repertoires the skill behaviors to act prosocially or to successfully inhibit the antisocial. We thus reasoned that, when coupled with Skillstreaming and anger control training, Kohlbergian moral education had marked potential for providing constructive motivation toward prosocial behavior and away from antisocial behavior.

As noted previously, each of our three evaluations of the efficacy of Aggression Replacement Training employed with chronically aggressive, delinquent youths yielded positive findings. To build further upon such outcomes, most recently we have moved beyond Aggression Replacement Training to a new, much more comprehensive expression of this intervention philosophy. We call it the Prepare Curriculum.

THE PREPARE CURRICULUM

Three of the courses included in the Prepare Curriculum (Goldstein, 1988), a 10-course intervention, are the same as for Aggression Replacement Training: Skillstreaming, anger control training, and moral education. A description of the additional seven courses follows.

Problem-Solving Training

Aggressive adolescents and younger children are frequently deficient in knowledge of and ability to use such prosocial competencies as the array of interpersonal skills and anger control techniques taught in Skillstreaming and anger control training, but they may also be deficient in other ways crucial to the use of prosocial behavior. They may, as Ladd and Mize (1983) point out, be deficient in such problem-solving competencies as "(a) knowledge of appropriate *goals* for social interaction, (b) knowledge of appropriate *strategies* for reaching a social goal, and (c) knowledge of the *contexts* in which specific strategies may be appropriately applied" (p. 130).

An analogous conclusion flows from the research program on interpersonal problem solving conducted by Spivack, Platt, and Shure (1976). At early and middle childhood, as well as in adolescence, chronically aggressive youngsters were less able than more typical youngsters to function effectively in most problem-solving subskills (e.g., identification of alternatives, consideration of consequences, determining causality, means-ends thinking, and perspective taking).

Several programs have been developed already in an effort to remediate such problem-solving deficiencies with the types of youngsters of concern here (DeLange, Lanham, & Barton, 1981; Giebink, Stover, & Fahl, 1968; Sarason & Sarason, 1981). Such programs represent a fine beginning, but problem-solving deficiency in such youths is substantial (Chandler, 1973; Selman, 1980; Spivack et al., 1976), and substantial deficiencies require longer term and more comprehensive interventions. The Prepare Curriculum's problem-solving training course, outlined in Table 4.4, seeks to provide just such an intervention. It is a longer term sequence of such graduated problem-solving skills as reflection, problem identification, information gathering, identification of alternatives, consideration of consequences, and decision-making. An initial evaluation of this sequence with an aggressive adolescent population has yielded significant gains in problem-solving skills thus defined, substantially encouraging further development of this course (Grant, 1986). These results give beginning substance to our earlier assertion that

> individuals can be provided systematic training in problem solving skills both for purposes of building general competence in meeting life's challenges, and as a specific means of supplying one more reliable, prosocial alternative to aggression. (Goldstein, 1981)

Table 4.4   Problem-Solving Training

Session 1	Introduction
Session 2	Stop and think
Session 3	Problem identification
Session 4	Gathering information (own perspective)
Session 5	Gathering information (others' perspectives)
Session 6	Identifying alternatives
Session 7	Evaluating consequences
Session 8	Review and practice

Empathy Training

For two reasons, we were especially interested in the inclusion in the Prepare Curriculum of a course designed to enhance participating youths' level of empathy. Expression of empathic understanding, it appears, can serve simultaneously as an inhibitor of negative interactions and as a facilitator of positive ones. Evidence clearly demonstrates that

> responding to another individual in an empathic manner and assuming temporarily their perspective decreases or inhibits one's potential for acting aggressively toward the other. . . . Stated otherwise, empathy and aggression are incompatible interpersonal responses, hence to be more skilled in the former serves as an aid to diminishing the latter. (Goldstein & Glick, 1987, pp. 241–242)

The notion of empathy as a facilitator of positive interpersonal relations stands on an even broader base of research evidence. Our recent review of the literally hundreds of investigations inquiring into the interpersonal consequences of empathic responding reveals such responding to be a consistently potent promotor of interpersonal attraction, dyadic openness, conflict resolution, and individual growth (Goldstein & Michaels, 1985). It is a most potent facilitator indeed.

This same review led us to define empathy as a multistage process of perception of emotional cues, affective reverberation of the emotions perceived, their cognitive labeling, and communication. Correspondingly, we developed the Prepare Curriculum multistage training program by which these four constituent components could be taught. This program is presented in outline form in Table 4.5, and in detail in *The Prepare Curriculum* (Goldstein, 1988).

Situational Perception Training

Once armed with the interpersonal skills necessary to respond prosocially to others, the problem-solving strategies underlying skill selection and use, and a fuller empathic sense of the other person's perspective, the chronically aggressive young-ster may still fail to behave prosocially because she "misreads" the context in which the behavior is to occur. A major thrust in psychology during the past 15 years has concerned the *situation* or *setting,* as perceived by the individual, and its im-portance in determining overt behavior. Morrison and Bellack (1981) comment, for example:

> Adequate social performance not only requires a repertoire of response
> skills, but knowledge about when and how these responses should
> be applied. Application of this knowledge, in turn, depends upon
> the ability to accurately "read" the social environment: determine
> the particular norms and conventions operating at the moment, and
> to understand the messages being sent . . . and intentions guiding
> the behavior of the interpersonal partner. (p. 70)

Dil (1972), Emery (1975), and Rothenberg (1970) have shown that emotionally disturbed youngsters, as well as those "socially maladjusted" in other ways, are characteristically deficient in such social perceptiveness. Furnham and Argyle (1981) observe:

> It has been found that people who are socially inadequate are
> unable to read everyday situations and respond appropriately. They
> are unable to perform or interpret nonverbal signals, unaware of
> the rules of social behavior, mystified by ritualized routines and
> conventions of self-presentation and self-disclosure, and are hence
> like foreigners in their own land. (p. 37)

Argyle, Furnham, and Graham (1981) and Backman (1979) have stressed this same social-perceptual deficit in their work with aggressive individuals. Dodge, Bates, and Pettit (1990) have done similarly, especially with reference to aggressive adolescents. In their study of the cycle of violence, they found

> that harmed children are likely to develop biased and deficient pat-
> terns of processing social information, including a failure to attend
> to relevant cues, a bias to attribute hostile intention to others, and a
> lack of competent behavioral strategies to solve interpersonal prob-
> lems. These patterns, in turn, were found to predict the develop-
> ment of aggressive behavior. (p. 1682)

We believe that the ability to accurately "read" social situations can be taught. To accomplish this goal, this course's contents are responsive to the valuable leads provided in this context by Brown and Fraser (1979), who propose three salient dimensions of accurate social perceptiveness, (a) the *setting* of the interaction and its associated rules and norms; (b) the *purpose* of the interaction and its goals, tasks, and topics; and (c) the *relationship* of the participants—their roles, responsibilities, expectations, and group memberships.

Table 4.5 Empathy Training: A Components Approach

A. Readiness Training

   1. Acquisition of empathy preparatory skills (Frank, 1977)

      a. Imagination skills to increase accurate identification
of implied meanings

      b. Behavioral observation skills to increase accurate prediction
of others' overt behavior

      c. Flexibility skills to increase differentiation ability in shifting
from *a* to *b*

   2. Elimination of empathy skill acquisition inhibitors

      a. Programmed self-instruction to understand one's perceptual biases
(Bullmer, 1972)

      b. Interpersonal Process Recall to reduce affect-associated anxiety
(Pereira, 1978)

B. Perceptual Training

   1. Programmed self-instruction (Bullmer, 1972) to increase interpersonal
perceptual accuracy and objectivity

   2. Observational sensitivity training (Smith, 1973) to increase competence
in recording sensory impressions and in discriminating them from
inferential, interpretive impressions

C. Affective Reverberation Training

   1. Meditation (Goleman, 1977; Lesh, 1970)

   2. Structural integration or Rolfing (Keen, 1970; Rolf, 1977)

   3. Reichian therapy (Lowen, 1967; Reich, 1933/1949)

   4. Bioenergetics (Lowen & Lowen, 1977)

   5. Alexander Technique (Alexander, 1969)

   6. Feldenkrais's Awareness Through Movement (Feldenkrais, 1970, 1972)

   7. Dance therapy (Bernstein, 1975; Pesso, 1969)

   8. Sensory awareness training (Brooks, 1974; Guenther, 1974)

   9. Focusing (Gendlin, 1981, 1984)

   10. Laban-Bartenieff method (Bartenieff & Lewis, 1980)

D. Cognitive Analysis Training

    1. Discrimination training (Carkhuff, 1969a, 1969b) in utilizing perceptual (B) and reverberatory (C) information

    2. Exposure (e.g., to facial expressions) plus guided practice and feedback on affective labeling accuracy (Allport, 1924; Davitz, 1964)

E. Communication Training

    1. Didactic-Experiential Training (Carkhuff, 1969a, 1969b)

    2. Interpersonal Living Laboratory (Egan, 1976)

    3. Relationship Enhancement (Guerney, 1977)

    4. Microtraining: Enriching Intimacy Program (Ivey & Authier, 1971)

    5. Structured Learning Training (Goldstein, 1981)

F. Transfer and Maintenance Training

    1. Provision of general principles (Duncan, 1958; Judd, 1902)

    2. Maximizing identical elements (Osgood, 1953; Thorndike & Woodworth, 1901)

    3. Maximizing response availability (Mandler, 1954; Underwood & Schultz, 1960)

    4. Maximizing stimulus variability (Callantine & Warren, 1955; Shore & Sechrest, 1961)

    5. Programmed, real-world reinforcement (Goldstein & Kanfer, 1979)

Stress Management

We have oriented each of the preceding courses toward either directly enhancing prosocial competency (e.g., Skillstreaming, moral education, situational perception training) or reducing qualities that inhibit previously learned or newly acquired prosocial competency (e.g., anger control training). The course we now describe is of this latter type. It has been demonstrated by Arkowitz, Lichtenstein, McGovern, and Hines (1975) and Curran (1977) that individuals may possess an array of prosocial skills in their repertoires but not employ them in particularly challenging or difficult situations because of anxiety. A youth may have learned well the Skillstreaming skill "Responding to Failure," but his embarrassment at a failing grade in front of his teacher or his missing a foul shot in front of his friends may engender a level of anxiety that inhibits proper use of this skill. A young woman may possess the problem-solving competency to plan well for a job interview but perform poorly in the interview when her anxiety takes over. Anxiety as a source of prosocially incompetent and unsatisfying behavior may be especially prevalent in the highly peer-conscious adolescent years.

A series of self-managed procedures exist to substantially reduce stress-induced anxiety. These procedures form the basis of the Prepare Curriculum stress management course. As outlined in Table 4.6, participating youngsters are taught systematic deep muscular relaxation (Benson, 1975; Jacobson, 1964); meditation techniques (Assagioli, 1973; Naranjo & Ornstein, 1971); thematic imagery (Anderson, 1978); exercise (Walker, 1975); and related means for the management, control, and reduction of stress.

Cooperation Training

Chronically aggressive youths have been shown to display a personality trait pattern high in egocentricity and competitiveness and low in concern for others and cooperativeness (Pepitone, 1985; Slavin et al., 1985). The Prepare Curriculum offers a course in cooperation training not only because enhanced cooperation among individuals is a valuable social goal but also because of the valuable concomitants and consequences of enhanced cooperation. An extended review of research on one major set of approaches to cooperation training—namely, cooperative learning—reveals outcomes of enhanced self-esteem, group cohesiveness, altruism, and cooperation, as well as reduced egocentricity. As long ago as 1929, Maller commented:

> The frequent staging of contests, the constant emphasis upon the making and breaking of records, and the glorification of the heroic individual achievement . . . in our present educational system lead toward the acquisition of competitiveness. The child is trained to look at members of his group as constant competitors and urged to put forth a maximum effort to excel them. The lack of practice in group activities and community projects in which the child works with his fellows for a common goal precludes the formation of habits of cooperativeness. (p. 163)

Table 4.6   Stress Management Training

1. Progressive relaxation training
2. Yogaform stretching
3. Breathing exercises
4. Physical exercises
5. Somatic focusing
6. Thematic imagery
7. Meditation

It was many years before the educational establishment responded concretely to this Deweyian challenge, but when it did it created a wide series of innovative, cooperation-enhancing methodologies, each of which deserves application and scrutiny both in general educational contexts and in work with particularly non-cooperative youths. Using shared materials, interdependent tasks, group rewards, and similar features, these methods (applied to any content area) have consistently yielded interpersonal, cooperation-enhancing group and individual benefits.

In developing our course, we attempted to sort through the existing methods, adding aspects of our own, and prescriptively tailored a cooperative learning sequence of special value for chronically aggressive youths. In doing so, we not only made use of the valuable features of the cooperative learning approaches but also responded to the orientation toward physical action typical of such youths by relying heavily on cooperative sports and games. This type of athletic activity, although not popular in the United States, does exist elsewhere (Orlick, 1978a, 1978b, 1982; Fluegelman, 1981). Collective score basketball, noncontact football, cross-team rotational hockey, collective fastest-time and best-score track meets, and other sports restructured to be what cooperative gaming creators term "all touch," "all play," "all positions," and "all shoot" may seem strange to the typical youth in this country, weaned on highly competitive, individualistic sports. However, such cooperative approaches appear to be a valuable way in which aggressive youths may be directed toward the goal of cooperation. To provide a sense of the specific contents of such cooperative gaming, sports, and simulations, we have listed in Table 4.7 a few of the activities that are part of this Prepare Curriculum course.

Recruiting Supportive Models

Typically, aggressive youths are regularly exposed to highly aggressive models in their interpersonal worlds. Parents, siblings, and peers are themselves frequently chronically aggressive (Knight & West, 1975; Loeber & Dishion, 1983; Osborn & West, 1979; Robins, West, & Herjanic, 1975). Simultaneously, there tend to be relatively few countervailing prosocial models available to be observed

Table 4.7   Cooperation Training

A. Cooperative Learning Methods

  1. Student Teams–Achievement Divisions (Slavin, 1980)
  2. Teams–Games–Tournaments (Slavin, 1980)
  3. Team Assisted Individualization (Slavin, Leavey, & Madden, 1982)
  4. Jigsaw I (Aronson, Blaney, Stephan, Sikes, & Snapp, 1978)
  5. Jigsaw II (Slavin, 1980)
  6. Learning Together (Johnson & Johnson, 1975)
  7. Group Investigation (Hertz-Lazarowitz, Sharan, & Steinberg, 1980)
  8. Co-op Co-op (Kagan, 1985)

B. Cooperative Games

  1. Ages 3–7

    a. Jack-in-the-Box Name Game (Harrison, 1975)
    b. Cooperative Hide-and-Seek (Orlick, 1978a)
    c. Partner Gymnastics (Orlick, 1978a)
    d. Frozen Bean Bag (Orlick, 1978a)

  2. Ages 8–12

    a. New Basketball (Deacove, 1978)
    b. Three-Sided Soccer (Deacove, 1978)
    c. Tug of Peace (Orlick, 1978a)
    d. All on One Side (Orlick, 1978a)

  3. Adolescent

    a. Strike-Outless Baseball (Deacove, 1978)
    b. Mutual Storytelling (Weinstein & Goodman, 1980)
    c. Octopus Massage (Weinstein & Goodman, 1980)
    d. Brussels Sprouts (Weinstein & Goodman, 1980)

and imitated. When they are, however, such prosocial models can make a tremendous difference in the daily lives and development of such youths. In support of this assertion, we turn not only to such community-based prosocial models as Big Brothers, the Police Athletic League, Boy Scouts, and the like, or to the laboratory research consistently showing that rewarded prosocial behaviors (e.g., sharing, altruism, cooperation) are quite often imitated (Bryan & Test, 1967; Canale, 1977; Evers & Schwarz, 1973). More direct evidence also exists. For example, Werner and Smith (1982), in their impressive longitudinal study of aggressive and non-aggressive youths, *Vulnerable but Invincible,* investigated youngsters growing up in a community characterized by high levels of crime, unemployment, and school drop out, as well as by a great number of aggressive models. Youths in this environment were able to develop into effective, satisfied, prosocially oriented individuals if they had sustained exposure to at least one significant prosocial model—be it parent, relative, or peer. Similar results have been reported by Ellis and Lane (1978); Hawkins and Fraser (1983); Kauffman, Gruenbaum, Cohler, and Gamer (1979); and Pines (1979).

Because such models are often scarce in the real-world environments of the youths the Prepare Curriculum is intended to serve, efforts must be put forth to help these youths identify, encourage, attract, elicit, and at times perhaps even create sources and attachments to others who function prosocially themselves and who can also serve as sustained sources of direct support for the youths' own prosocially oriented efforts.

Our course content for teaching youths to identify, encourage, attract, elicit, and create these types of supportive relationships relies in large part on the procedures and skills of the Skillstreaming curricula for adolescents (Goldstein et al., 1980) and younger children (McGinnis & Goldstein, 1984).

Understanding and Using Group Processes

That adolescents and preadolescents are acutely responsive to peer influences is a truism frequently drawn in both lay and professional literature on child development. It is a conclusion resting on a very solid research foundation (Baumrind, 1975; Field, 1981; Guralnick, 1981; Manaster, 1977; Moriarty & Toussieng, 1976; Rosenberg, 1975). As a curriculum designed to enhance prosocial competencies, it is especially important that the Prepare Curriculum include a segment giving special emphasis to group—especially peer—processes. The title of this course includes both *understanding* and *using* because both are clear goals. Participating youths are helped to understand such group forces and phenomena as peer pressure, clique formation and dissolution, leaders and leadership, cohesiveness, imitation, reciprocity, in-group versus out-group relations, developmental phases, competition, and within-group communication.

For such understanding to have real-world value for participating youths (the *using* component of the course title), this course's instructional format consists almost exclusively of experiential group activities in which participants learn means for effectively resisting group pressure, seeking and enacting a group leadership role, helping build and enjoy the fruits of group cohesiveness, and so forth. Examples drawn from the several dozen specific Prepare Curriculum activities that constitute this course are listed in Table 4.8.

SUMMARY

We have in this chapter evaluated and described in detail three progressively more comprehensive interpersonal skills training interventions: Skillstreaming, Aggression Replacement Training, and the Prepare Curriculum. Their successful employment with chronically aggressive, at-risk, and individual gang youths is well established. Their use with intact gangs has just begun and, based upon the foregoing efficacy evaluations, is to be strongly encouraged.

Table 4.8   Group Dynamics Training

A. Forming

    1. Who Am I? A Getting Acquainted Activity
    2. Group Conversation: Discussion Starters
    3. Group Development: A Graphic Analysis
    4. Verbal Activities Within Groups

B. Storming

    1. Conflict Resolution: A Collection of Tasks
    2. Discrimination: Simulation Activities
    3. Rumor Clinic
    4. Nonverbal Communication

C. Norming

    1. Group Self-Evaluations
    2. Group-on-Group: A Feedback Experience
    3. Styles of Leadership
    4. Dyadic Encounter

D. Performing

    1. Top Problems: A Consensus-Seeking Task
    2. Line Up and Power Inversion
    3. Stretching: Identifying and Taking Risks
    4. Cash Register: Group Decision Making

E. Adjourning

Note. The activities listed are drawn from *Handbook of Structured Experiences for Human Relations Training* (Vols. 1–5) by J. W. Pfeiffer and J. E. Jones, 1974, La Jolla, CA: University Associates.

REFERENCES

Adkins, W. R. (1970). Life skills: Structured counseling for the disadvantaged. *Personnel and Guidance Journal, 49,* 108–116.

Agras, W. S. (1967). Transfer during systematic desensitization therapy. *Behavior Research and Therapy, 5,* 193–199.

Alexander, F. M. (1969). *The resurrection of the body.* New York: Dell.

Allport, F. H. (1924). *Social psychology.* New York: Houghton Mifflin.

Anderson, R. A. (1978). *Stress power.* New York: Human Sciences.

Arbuthnot, J., & Gordon, D. A. (1983). Moral reasoning development in correctional intervention. *Journal of Correctional Education, 34,* 133–138.

Argyle, M., Furnham, A., & Graham, J. (1981). *Social situations.* Cambridge, England: Cambridge University Press.

Argyle, M., Trower, P., & Bryant, B. (1974). Explorations in the treatment of personality disorders and neuroses by social skill training. *British Journal of Medical Psychology, 47,* 63–72.

Arkowitz, H., Lichtenstein, E., McGovern, K., & Hines, P. (1975). The behavioral assessment of social competence in males. *Behavior Therapy, 6,* 3–13.

Aronson, E., Blaney, N., Stephan, C., Sikes, J., & Snapp, M. (1978). *The jigsaw classroom.* Newbury Park, CA: Sage.

Assagioli, R. (1973). *The act of will.* New York: Viking.

Backman, C. (1979). Epilogue: A new paradigm. In G. Ginsburg (Ed.), *Emerging strategies in social psychological research.* New York: Wiley.

Bandura, A. (1973). *Aggression: A social learning analysis.* Englewood Cliffs, NJ: Prentice-Hall.

Bartenieff, I., & Lewis, D. (1980). *Body movement: Coping with the environment.* New York: Gordon & Breach.

Baumrind, D. (1975). Early socialization and adolescent competence. In S. E. Dragastin & G. H. Elder (Eds.), *Adolescence in the life cycle.* Washington, DC: Hemisphere.

Bellack, A. S. (1979). Behavioral assessment of social skills. In A. S. Bellack & M. Hersen (Eds.), *Research and practice in social skills training.* New York: Plenum.

Benson, H. (1975). *The relaxation response.* New York: Avon.

Bernstein, P. (1975). *Theory and methods in dance-movement therapy.* Dubuque, IA: Kendall/Hunt.

Bornstein, M., Bellack, A. S., & Hersen, M. (1980). Social skills training for highly aggressive children: Treatment in an inpatient psychiatric setting. *Behavior Modification, 4,* 173–186.

Braukmann, C. J., Fixsen, D. L., Phillips, E. L., Wolf, M. M., & Maloney, D. M. (1974). An analysis of a selection interview training package for predelinquents at Achievement Place. *Criminal Justice and Behavior, 1,* 30–42.

Braukmann, C. J., Maloney, D. M., Phillips, E. L., & Wolf, M. M. (1973). *The measurement and modification of heterosexual interaction skills of predelinquents at Achievement Place.* Unpublished manuscript, University of Kansas, Lawrence.

Brooks, C. V. W. (1974). *Sensory awareness: The rediscovery of experiencing.* New York: Viking.

Brown, P., & Fraser, C. (1979). Speech as a marker of situations. In K. Scherer & H. Giles (Eds.), *Social markers in speech.* Cambridge, England: Cambridge University Press.

Bryan, J. H., & Test, M. A. (1967). Models and helping: Naturalistic studies in aiding behavior. *Journal of Personality and Social Psychology, 6,* 400–407.

Bullmer, K. (1972). Improving accuracy of interpersonal perception through a direct teaching method. *Journal of Counseling Psychology, 19,* 37–41.

Callantine, M. F., & Warren, J. M. (1955). Learning sets in human concept formation. *Psychological Reports, 1,* 363–367.

Canale, J. R. (1977). The effect of modeling and length of ownership on sharing behavior of children. *Social Behavior and Personality, 5,* 187–191.

Carkhuff, R. R. (1969a). *Helping and human relations: A primer for lay and professional helpers: Vol. 1. Selection and training.* Amherst, MA: Human Resource Development.

Carkhuff, R. R. (1969b). *Helping and human relations: A primer for lay and professional helpers: Vol. 2. Practice and research.* Amherst, MA: Human Resource Development.

Chandler, M. (1973). Egocentrism and antisocial behavior: The assessment and training of social perspective-taking skills. *Developmental Psychology, 9,* 326–332.

Conger, J. J., Miller, W. C., & Walsmith, C. R. (1975). Antecedents of delinquent personality, social class, and intelligence. In P. H. Mussen, J. J. Conger, & J. Kagan (Eds.), *Readings in child development and personality.* New York: Harper & Row.

Cronbach, L. J., & Snow, R. E. (1969). *Individual differences in learning ability as a function of instructional variables* (Office of Education Final Report). Stanford, CA: Stanford University Press.

Curran, J. P. (1977). Skills training as an approach to the treatment of heterosexual-social anxiety: A review. *Psychological Bulletin, 84,* 140–157.

Davitz, D. (1964). *The communication of emotional meaning.* New York: McGraw-Hill.

Deacove, J. (1978). *Sports manual of cooperative recreation.* Perth, Ontario: Family Pastimes.

Dean, S. I. (1958). Treatment of the reluctant client. *American Psychologist, 13,* 627–630.

DeLange, J. M., Lanham, S. L., & Barton, J. A. (1981). Social skills training for juvenile delinquents: Behavioral skill training and cognitive techniques. In D. Upper & S. Ross (Eds.), *Behavior group therapy, 1981: An annual review* (Vol. 3). Champaign, IL: Research Press.

Dil, N. (1972). *Sensitivity of emotionally disturbed and emotionally non-disturbed elementary school children to emotional meaning of facial expressions.* Unpublished doctoral dissertation, Indiana University, Bloomington.

Dodge, K. A., Bates, J. E., & Pettit, G. S. (1990). Mechanisms in the cycle of violence. *Science, 250,* 1678–1683.

Dreikurs, R., Grunwald, B. B., & Pepper, F. C. (1971). *Maintaining sanity in the classroom.* New York: Harper & Row.

Drum, D. J., & Figler, H. E. (1973). *Outreach in counseling.* New York: Intext Educational Publication.

Duncan, C. P. (1958). Transfer after training with single versus multiple tasks. *Journal of Experimental Psychology, 55,* 63–73.

Edelman, E. M., & Goldstein, A. P. (1984). Prescriptive relationship levels for juvenile delinquents in a psychotherapy analog. *Aggressive Behavior, 10,* 269–278.

Egan, G. (1976). *Interpersonal living: A skills/contract approach to human-relations training in groups.* Pacific Grove, CA: Brooks/Cole.

Elardo, P., & Cooper, M. (1977). *AWARE: Activities for Social Development.* Reading, MA: Addison-Wesley.

Elder, J. P., Edelstein, B. A., & Narick, M. M. (1979). Adolescent psychiatric patients: Modifying aggressive behavior with social skills training. *Behavior Modification, 3,* 161–178.

Ellis, H. (1965). *The transfer of learning.* New York: Macmillan.

Ellis, R. A., & Lane, W. C. (1978). Structural support for upward mobility. *American Sociological Review, 53,* 743–756.

Emery, J. E. (1975). *Social perception processes in normal and learning disabled children.* Unpublished doctoral dissertation, New York University.

Evers, W. L., & Schwarz, J. C. (1973). Modifying social withdrawal in preschoolers: The effects of filmed modeling and teacher praise. *Journal of Abnormal Child Psychology, 1,* 248–256.

Feindler, E. L., Marriott, S. Z., & Iwata, M. (1984). Group anger control training for junior high school delinquents. *Cognitive Therapy and Research, 8,* 299–311.

Feldenkrais, M. (1970). *Body and mature behavior.* New York: International Universities Press.

Feldenkrais, M. (1972). *Awareness Through Movement.* New York: Harper & Row.

Field, T. (1981). Early peer relations. In P. S. Strain (Ed.), *The utilization of classroom peers as behavior change agents.* New York: Plenum.

Fluegelman, A. (1981). *More new games.* Garden City, NY: Dolphin.

Ford, D. H., & Urban, H. B. (1963). *Systems of psychotherapy.* New York: Wiley.

Frank, S. J. (1977). *The facilitation of empathy through training in imagination.* Unpublished doctoral dissertation, Yale University, New Haven, CT.

Freedman, B. J., Rosenthal, L., Donahoe, C. P., Schlundt, D. G., & McFall, R. M. (1978). A social behavioral analysis of skill deficits in delinquent and nondelinquent adolescent boys. *Journal of Consulting and Clinical Psychology, 46,* 1448-1462.

Furnham, A., & Argyle, M. (1981). *The psychology of social situations.* Elmsford, NY: Pergamon.

Gendlin, E. (1981). *Focusing.* New York: Bantam.

Gendlin, E. (1984). The politics of giving therapy away: Listening and focusing. In D. Larson (Ed.), *Teaching psychological skills.* Pacific Grove, CA: Brooks/Cole.

Giebink, J. W., Stover, D. S., & Fahl, M. A. (1968). Teaching adaptive responses to frustration to emotionally disturbed boys. *Journal of Consulting and Clinical Psychology, 32,* 336-368.

Goldstein, A. P. (1973). *Structured learning therapy: Toward a psychotherapy for the poor.* New York: Academic.

Goldstein, A. P. (Ed.). (1978). *Prescriptions for child mental health and education.* Elmsford, NY: Pergamon.

Goldstein, A. P. (1981). *Psychological skill training: The structured learning technique.* Elmsford, NY: Pergamon.

Goldstein, A. P. (1988). *The Prepare Curriculum: Teaching prosocial competencies.* Champaign, IL: Research Press.

Goldstein, A. P., Apter, S. J., & Harootunian, B. (1984). *School violence.* Englewood Cliffs, NJ: Prentice-Hall.

Goldstein, A. P., & Glick, B. (1987). *Aggression Replacement Training: A comprehensive intervention for aggressive youth.* Champaign, IL: Research Press.

Goldstein, A. P., Glick, B., Blancero, D., & Carthan, W. (in preparation). *The prosocial gang.* Syracuse, NY: Syracuse University.

Goldstein, A. P., Glick, B., Irwin, M. J., Pask-McCartney, C., & Rubama, I. (1989). *Reducing delinquency: Intervention in the community.* Elmsford, NY: Pergamon.

Goldstein, A. P., Heller, K., & Sechrest, L. B. (1966). *Psychotherapy and the psychology of behavior change.* New York: Wiley.

Goldstein, A. P., & Kanfer, F. H. (1979). *Maximizing treatment gains.* New York: Academic.

Goldstein, A. P., Keller, H., & Erne, D. (1985). *Changing the abusive parent.* Champaign, IL: Research Press.

Goldstein, A. P., & Michaels, G. Y. (1985). *Empathy: Development, training and consequences.* Hillsdale, NJ: Erlbaum.

Goldstein, A. P., Monti, P. J., Sardino, T. J., & Green, D. (1979). *Police crisis intervention.* Elmsford, NY: Pergamon.

Goldstein, A. P., & Pentz, M. A. (1984). Psychological skill training and the aggressive adolescent. *School Psychology Review, 13,* 311-323.

Goldstein, A. P., & Rosenbaum, A. (1982). *Aggress-Less.* Englewood Cliffs, NJ: Prentice-Hall.

Goldstein, A. P., Sherman, M., Gershaw, N. J., Sprafkin, R. P., & Glick, B. (1978). Training aggressive adolescents in prosocial behavior. *Journal of Youth and Adolescence, 7,* 73-92.

Goldstein, A. P., Sprafkin, R. P., Gershaw, N. J., & Klein, P. (1980). *Skillstreaming the adolescent: A structured learning approach to teaching prosocial skills.* Champaign, IL: Research Press.

Goldstein, A. P., & Stein, N. (1976). *Prescriptive psychotherapies.* Elmsford, NY: Pergamon.

Goleman, D. (1977). *The varieties of the meditative experience.* New York: Dutton.

Grant, J. (1986). *An instructional training program for problem solving skill enhancement with delinquent youth.* Unpublished doctoral dissertation, Syracuse University, Syracuse, NY.

Greenleaf, D. (1977). *Peer reinforcement as transfer enhancement in structured learning therapy.* Unpublished master's thesis, Syracuse University, Syracuse, NY.

Gross, A. M., Brigham, T. A., Hopper, C., & Bologna, N. C. (1980). Self-management and social skills: A study with pre-delinquent and delinquent youth. *Criminal Justice and Behavior, 7,* 161–184.

Gruber, R. P. (1971). Behavior therapy: Problems in generalization. *Behavior Therapy, 2,* 361–368.

Guenther, H. V. (1974). *Philosophy and psychology in the Abhidharma.* Berkeley: Shambala.

Guerney, B. G., Jr. (1977). *Relationship enhancement.* San Francisco: Jossey-Bass.

Guralnick, M. J. (1981). Peer influences on the development of communicative competence. In P. S. Strain (Ed.), *The utilization of classroom peers as behavior change agents.* New York: Plenum.

Guttman, E. S. (1970). Effects of short-term psychiatric treatment for boys in two California Youth Authority institutions. In D. C. Gibbons (Ed.), *Delinquent behavior.* Englewood Cliffs, NJ: Prentice-Hall.

Hare, M. A. (1976, March). *Teaching conflict resolution situations.* Paper presented at the meeting of the Eastern Community Association, Philadelphia.

Harootunian, B. (1978). Teacher training. In A. P. Goldstein (Ed.), *Prescriptions for child mental health and education.* Elmsford, NY: Pergamon.

Harrison, M. (1975). *For the fun of it! Selected cooperative games for children and adults.* Philadelphia: Friend's Peace Committee.

Hawkins, J. D., & Fraser, M. W. (1983). Social support networks in delinquency prevention and treatment. In J. K. Wittaker & J. Garbarino (Eds.), *Social support networks.* New York: Aldine.

Hawley, R. C., & Hawley, I. L. (1975). *Developing Human Potential: A handbook of activities for personal and social growth.* Amherst, MA: Education Research Associates.

Hazel, J. S., Schumaker, J. B., Sherman, J. A., & Sheldon-Wildgen, J. (1981). *ASSET: A social skills program for adolescents.* Champaign, IL: Research Press.

Heiman, H. (1973). Teaching interpersonal communications. *North Dakota Speech and Theatre Association Bulletin, 2,* 7–29.

Hersen, M., & Barlow, D. H. (1976). *Single case experimental designs: Strategies for studying behavior change.* Elmsford, NY: Pergamon.

Hertz-Lazarowitz, R., Sharan, S., & Steinberg, R. (1980). Classroom learning styles and cooperative behavior of elementary school children. *Journal of Educational Psychology, 72,* 99–106.

Hollin, C. R., & Courtney, S. A. (1983). A skill training approach to the reduction of institutional offending. *Personality and Individual Differences, 4,* 257–264.

Hollin, C. R., & Henderson, M. (1981). The effects of social skills training on incarcerated delinquent adolescents. *International Journal of Behavioral Social Work, 1,* 145–155.

Hsu, J. J. (1965). Electro-conditioning treatment for alcoholics. *Quarterly Journal for the Study of Alcoholism, 26,* 449–459.

Hummel, J. (1980). *Session variability and skill content as transfer enhancers in structured learning training.* Unpublished doctoral dissertation, Syracuse University, Syracuse, NY.

Hunt, D. E. (1972). Matching models for teacher training. In B. R. Joyce & M. Weil (Eds.), *Perspectives for reform in teacher education.* Englewood Cliffs, NJ: Prentice-Hall.

Ivey, A. E., & Authier, J. (1971). *Microcounseling.* Springfield, IL: Charles C Thomas.

Jacobson, E. (1964). *Anxiety and tension control.* Philadelphia: Lippincott.

Johnson, D. W., & Johnson, R. T. (1975). *Learning together and alone.* Englewood Cliffs, NJ: Prentice-Hall.

Jones, M. (1953). *The therapeutic community.* New York: Basic.

Judd, C. H. (1902). Practice and its effects on the perception of illusions. *Psychological Review, 9,* 27–39.

Kagan, S. (1985). Co-op co-op: A flexible cooperative learning technique. In R. Slavin, S. Sharan, S. Kagan, R. Hertz-Lazarowitz, C. Wegg, & R. Schmuck (Eds.), *Learning to cooperate, cooperating to learn.* New York: Plenum.

Karoly, P., & Steffen, J. J. (Eds.). (1980). *Improving the long-term effects of psychotherapy.* New York: Gardner.

Kauffman, C., Grunebaum, H., Cohler, B. J., & Gamer, E. (1979). Superkids: Competent children of psychotic mothers. *American Journal of Psychiatry, 136,* 1398–1402.

Kazdin, A. (1975). *Behavior modification in applied settings.* Homewood, IL: Dorsey.

Kazdin, A. (1978). Methodological and interpretive problems of single-case experimental designs. *Journal of Consulting and Clinical Psychology, 46,* 629–642.

Kazdin, A. (1980). *Research designs in clinical psychology.* New York: Harper & Row.

Keeley, S. M., Shemberg, K. M., & Carbonell, J. (1976). Operant clinical intervention: Behavior management or beyond? Where are the data? *Behavior Therapy, 7,* 292–305.

Keen, S. (1970, October). Sing the body electric. *Psychology Today,* pp. 56–61.

Kifer, R. E., Lewis, M. A., Green, D., & Phillips, E. L. (1974). Training predelinquent youths and their parents to negotiate conflict situations. *Journal of Applied Behavior Analysis, 7,* 357–364.

Knight, B. J., & West, D. J. (1975). Temporary and continuing delinquency. *British Journal of Criminology, 15,* 43–50.

Kohlberg, L. (1969). Stage and sequence: The cognitive-developmental approach to socialization. In D. A. Goslin (Ed.), *Handbook of socialization theory and research.* Chicago: Rand McNally.

Kohlberg, L. (Ed.). (1973). *Collected papers on moral development and moral education.* Cambridge, MA: Harvard University, Center for Moral Education.

Ladd, G. W., & Mize, J. (1983). A cognitive-social learning model of social-skill training. *Psychological Review, 90,* 127–157.

Lee, D. Y., Hallberg, E. T., & Hassard, H. (1979). Effects of assertion training on aggressive behavior in adolescents. *Journal of Counseling Psychology, 26,* 459–461.

Lesh, T. V. (1970). Zen meditation and the development of empathy in counselors. *Journal of Humanistic Psychology, 10,* 39–74.

Litwack, S. E. (1976). *The use of the helper therapy principle to increase therapeutic effectiveness and reduce therapeutic resistance: Structured learning therapy with resistant adolescents.* Unpublished doctoral dissertation, Syracuse University, Syracuse, NY.

Loeber, R., & Dishion, T. (1983). Early predictors of male delinquency: A review. *Psychological Bulletin, 94,* 68–99.

Lowen, A. (1967). *The betrayal of the body.* New York: Macmillan.

Lowen, A., & Lowen, L. (1977). *The way to vibrant health: A manual of bioenergetic exercises.* New York: Harper & Row.

Magaro, P. A. (1969). A prescriptive treatment model based upon social class and premorbid adjustment. *Psychotherapy: Theory, Research and Practice, 6,* 57–70.

Mahoney, M. J. (1974). *Cognition and behavior modification.* Cambridge, MA: Ballinger.

Maller, J. B. (1929). *Cooperation and competition: An experimental study in motivation.* New York: Columbia University Teachers College.

Maloney, D. M., Harper, T. M., Braukmann, C. J., Fixsen, D. L., Phillips, E. L., & Wolf, M. M. (1976). Teaching conversation-related skills to predelinquent girls. *Journal of Applied Behavior Analysis, 9,* 371.

Manaster, G. J. (1977). *Adolescent development and the life tasks.* Boston: Allyn & Bacon.

Mandler, G. (1954). Transfer of training as a function of degree of response overlearning. *Journal of Experimental Psychology, 47,* 411–417.

Matson, J. L., Esveldt-Dawson, K., Andrasik, F., Ollendick, T. H., Petti, T., & Hersen, M. (1980). Direct, observational, and generalization effects of social skills training with emotionally disturbed children. *Behavior Therapy, 11,* 522–531.

McCorkle, L., Elias, A., & Bixby, F. (1958). *The Highfields story: A unique experiment in the treatment of juvenile delinquency.* New York: Holt.

McGinnis, E., & Goldstein, A. P. (1984). *Skillstreaming the elementary school child: A guide for teaching prosocial skills.* Champaign, IL: Research Press.

Meichenbaum, D. H. (1977). *Cognitive-behavior modification: An integration approach.* New York: Plenum.

Michelson, L., & Wood, R. (1980). Behavioral assessment and training of children's social skills. *Progress in Behavior Modification, 9,* 241–291.

Minkin, N., Braukmann, C. J., Minkin, B. L., Timbers, G. D., Timbers, B. J., Fixsen, D. L., Phillips, E. L., & Wolf, M. M. (1976). The social validation and training of conversation skills. *Journal of Applied Behavior Analysis, 9,* 127–139.

Moriarty, A. E., & Toussieng, P. W. (1976). *Adolescent coping.* New York: Grune & Stratton.

Morrison, R. L., & Bellack, A. S. (1981). The role of social perception in social skills. *Behavior Therapy, 12,* 69–79.

Mussen, P. H., Conger, J. J., Kagan, J., & Gerwitz, J. (1979). *Psychological development: A life span approach.* New York: Harper & Row.

Naranjo, C., & Ornstein, R. E. (1971). *On the psychology of meditation.* New York: Viking.

Novaco, R. W. (1975). *Anger control: The development and evaluation of an experimental treatment.* Lexington, MA: Heath.

O'Leary, K. D., O'Leary, S., & Becker, W. C. (1967). Modification of a deviant interaction pattern in the home. *Behavior Research and Therapy, 5,* 113–120.

Ollendick, T. H., & Hersen, M. (1979). Social skills training for juvenile delinquents. *Behavior Research and Therapy, 17,* 547–555.

Orlick, T. (1978a). *The cooperative sports and games book.* New York: Pantheon.

Orlick, T. (1978b). *Winning through cooperation.* Washington, DC: Acropolis.

Orlick, T. (1982). *The second cooperative sports and games book.* New York: Pantheon.

Osborn, S. G., & West, D. J. (1979). Conviction records of fathers and sons compared. *British Journal of Criminology, 19,* 120–133.

Osgood, C. E. (1953). *Method and theory in experimental psychology.* New York: Oxford University Press.

Patterson, G. R., & Anderson, D. (1964). Peers as social reinforcers. *Child Development, 35,* 951–960.

Patterson, G. R., Cobb, J. A., & Ray, R. S. (1973). A social engineering technology for retraining the families of aggressive boys. In H. E. Adams & I. P. Unikel (Eds.), *Issues and trends in behavior therapy.* Springfield, IL: Charles C Thomas.

Patterson, G. R., Reid, J., Jones, R. R., & Conger, R. E. (1975). *A social learning approach to family intervention.* Eugene, OR: Castalia.

Pentz, M. A. (1980). Assertion training and trainer effects on unassertive and aggressive adolescents. *Journal of Counseling Psychology, 27,* 76–83.

Pepitone, E. A. (1985). Children in cooperation and competition: Antecedents and consequences of self-orientation. In R. Slavin, S. Sharan, S. Kagan, R. Hertz-Lazarowitz, C. Wegg, & R. Schmuck (Eds.), *Learning to cooperate, cooperating to learn.* New York: Plenum.

Pereira, G. J. (1978). *Teaching empathy through skill building versus interpersonal anxiety reduction methods.* Unpublished doctoral dissertation, Catholic University of America, Washington, DC.

Pesso, A. (1969). *Movement in psychotherapy.* New York: New York University Press.

Pfeiffer, J. W., & Jones, J E. (1974). *A handbook of structured experiences for human relations training* (Vols. 1–5). La Jolla, CA: University Associates.

Pines, M. (1979, January). Superkids. *Psychology Today,* pp. 53–63.

Redl, F., & Wineman, D. (1957). *The aggressive child.* Glencoe, IL: Free Press.

Reich, W. (1949). *Character analysis.* New York: Farrar, Straus & Giroux. (Original work published 1933)

Robin, A. L. (1981). A controlled evaluation of problem-solving communication training with parent-adolescent conflict. *Behavior Therapy, 12,* 593–609.

Robin, A. L., Kent, R., O'Leary, K. D., Foster, S., & Prinz, R. (1977). An approach to teaching parents and adolescents problem-solving communication skills: A preliminary report. *Behavior Therapy, 8,* 639–643.

Robins, L. N., West, P. A., & Herjanic, B. L. (1975). Arrests and delinquency in two generations: A study of black urban families and their children. *Journal of Child Psychology and Psychiatry, 16,* 125–140.

Rogers, C. R. (1957). The necessary and sufficient conditions of therapeutic personality change. *Journal of Consulting Psychology, 21,* 95–103.

Rolf, I. (1977). *Rolfing: The integration of human structures.* Boulder, CO: The Rolf Institute.

Rosenberg, M. (1975). The dissonant context and the adolescent self-concept. In S. E. Dragastin & G. H. Elder (Eds.), *Adolescence in the life cycle.* Washington, DC: Hemisphere.

Rothenberg, B. B. (1970). Children's social sensitivity and the relationship to interpersonal competence, interpersonal comfort, and intellectual level. *Developmental Psychology, 2,* 335–350.

Sarason, I. G., & Ganzer, V. J. (1973). Modeling and group discussion in the rehabilitation of juvenile delinquents. *Journal of Counseling Psychology, 20,* 442–449.

Sarason, I. G., & Sarason, B. R. (1981). Teaching cognitive and social skills to high school students. *Journal of Consulting and Clinical Psychology, 49,* 908–918.

Schwitzgebel, R. L. (1967). Short term operant conditioning of adolescent offenders on socially relevant variables. *Journal of Abnormal Psychology, 72,* 134–142.

Selman, R. L. (1980). *The growth of interpersonal understanding: Developmental and clinical analyses.* New York: Academic.

Shoemaker, M. E. (1979). Group assertion training for institutionalized male delinquents. In J. S. Stumphauzer (Ed.), *Progress in behavior therapy with delinquents.* Springfield, IL: Charles C Thomas.

Shore, E., & Sechrest, L. (1961). Concept attainment as a function of number of positive instances presented. *Journal of Educational Psychology, 52,* 303–307.

Slack, C. W. (1960). Experimenter-subject psychotherapy: A new method of introducing intensive office treatment for unreachable cases. *Mental Hygiene, 44,* 238–256.

Slavin, R. E. (1980). Cooperative learning. *Review of Educational Research, 50,* 315–342.

Slavin, R. E., Leavey, M., & Madden, N. A. (1982, April). *Effects of student teams and individualized instruction on student mathematics achievement, attitudes, and behaviors.* Paper presented at the meeting of the American Educational Research Association, New York.

Slavin, R. E., Sharan, S., Kagan, S., Hertz-Lazarowitz, R., Webb, C., & Schmuck, R. (1985). *Learning to cooperate, cooperating to learn.* New York: Plenum.

Slavson, S. R. (1964). *A textbook in analytic group psychotherapy.* New York: International Universities Press.

Smith, H. C. (1973). *Sensitivity training.* New York: McGraw-Hill.

Solomon, E. (1977). *Structured learning therapy with abusive parents: Training in self-control.* Unpublished doctoral dissertation, Syracuse University, Syracuse, NY.

Spence, A. J., & Spence, S. H. (1980). Cognitive changes associated with social skills training. *Behaviour Research and Therapy, 18,* 265–272.

Spence, S. H. (1981). Differences in social skills performance between institutionalized juvenile male offenders and a comparable group of boys without offence records. *British Journal of Clinical Psychology, 20,* 163–171.

Spence, S. H., & Marzillier, J. S. (1979). Social skills training with adolescent male offenders: I. Short-term effects. *Behaviour Research and Therapy, 17,* 7–16.

Spence, S. H., & Marzillier, J. S. (1981). Social skills training with adolescent male offenders: II. Short-term, long-term and generalized effects. *Behaviour Research and Therapy, 19,* 349–368.

Spivack, G., Platt, J. J., & Shure, M. B. (1976). *The problem-solving approach to adjustment: A guide to research and intervention.* San Francisco: Jossey-Bass.

Stephens, T. M. (1976). *Directive teaching of children with learning and behavioral handicaps.* Columbus, OH: Merrill.

Stern, G. G. (1970). *People in context.* New York: Wiley.

Sturm, D. (1980). *Therapist aggression tolerance and dependence tolerance under standardized conditions of hostility and dependency.* Unpublished master's thesis, Syracuse University, Syracuse, NY.

Tharp, R. G., & Wetzel, R. J. (1969). *Behavior modification in the natural environment.* New York: Academic.

Thelen, M. H., Fry, R. A., Dollinger, S. J., & Paul, S. C. (1976). Use of videotaped models to improve the interpersonal adjustment of delinquents. *Journal of Consulting and Clinical Psychology, 44,* 492.

Thorndike, E. L., & Woodworth, R. S. (1901). The influence of improvement in one mental function upon the efficiency of other functions. *Psychological Review, 8,* 247–261.

Trief, P. (1976). *The reduction of egocentrism in acting-out adolescents by structured learning therapy.* Unpublished doctoral dissertation, Syracuse University, Syracuse, NY.

Truax, C. B., Wargo, D. G., & Silber, L. D. (1966). Effects of group psychotherapy with high accurate empathy and nonpossessive warmth upon female institutionalized delinquents. *Journal of Abnormal Psychology, 71,* 267–274.

Underwood, B. J., & Schultz, R. W. (1960). *Meaningfulness and verbal behavior.* New York: Lippincott.

Vorrath, H., & Brendtro, L. K. (1974). *Positive Peer Culture.* Chicago: Aldine.

Walker, C. E. (1975). *Learn to relax.* Englewood Cliffs, NJ: Prentice-Hall.

Walker, H. M. (1979). *The acting-out child: Coping with classroom disruption.* Boston: Allyn & Bacon.

Walker, H. M., & Buckley, N. K. (1972). Programming generalization and maintenance of treatment effects across time and across settings. *Journal of Applied Behavior Analysis, 5,* 209–224.

Weiner, L., Becker, A., & Friedman, T. T. (1967). *Home treatment.* University of Pittsburgh Press.

Weinstein, M., & Goodman, J. (1980). *Playfair: Everybody's guide to noncompetitive play.* San Luis Obispo, CA: Impact.

Werner, E. E., & Smith, R. S. (1982). *Vulnerable but invincible: A study of resilient children.* New York: McGraw-Hill.

Werner, J. S., Minkin, N., Minkin, B. L., Fixsen, D. L., Phillips, E. L., & Wolf, M. M. (1975). Intervention package: An analysis to prepare juvenile delinquents for encounters with police officers. *Criminal Justice and Behavior, 2,* 55–84.

Zimmerman, D. (1983). Moral education. In Center for Research on Aggression (Ed.), *Prevention and control of aggression.* Elmsford, NY: Pergamon.

CHAPTER 5

Moral-Cognitive Interventions

John C. Gibbs

On April 19, 1989, a young woman jogging in New York City's Central Park was attacked by a gang[1] of as many as 12 East Harlem youths aged 13 to 16. She was hit with rocks, beaten senseless with a metal pipe, stabbed in the head five times, and repeatedly raped and sodomized. By the time she was found several hours later, she had lost three-quarters of her blood and lapsed into a coma (she eventually awoke and to a miraculous extent recovered). The youths were subsequently arrested but showed little remorse for the attack.

How can one account for such a lack of remorse in the wake of such brutality? How might one intervene with gang-prone youths to prevent violent and other antisocial behavior? This chapter addresses such questions through a review of theories that posit a primary role for cognition in the motivation of moral or antisocial behavior. *Cognition* refers to basic patterns or "structures" of mature or immature thought in cognitive-developmental theory and to veridical or distorted attitudes or beliefs in social information processing theory. Cognitive-developmental interventions attempt to remediate developmental delays in social cognition or moral judgment, whereas information-processing interventions attempt to correct erroneous conduct-relevant attitudes or beliefs. Cognition that motivates moral behavior, then, is both mature and veridical. Adequate moral-cognitive intervention will require the assimilation of both cognitive-structural and information-processing theories into a multicomponent approach.

COGNITIVE-STRUCTURAL THEORY

According to cognitive-structural (or cognitive-developmental) theory (e.g., Kohlberg, 1984), remorseless antisocial behavior is attributable at least in part to sociomoral developmental delay—that is, the persistence beyond early childhood of (a) immature or superficial moral judgment and (b) pronounced "me-centeredness"

I thank Valerie Gibbs, Ginny Jelinek, Bud Potter, Mike Vasey, and Charles Wenar for their helpful comments on a preliminary version of this chapter.

(Lickona, 1983, p. 152) or egocentric bias. Cognitive-structural interventions attempt to provide social perspective-taking opportunities that can remedy both the superficial and egocentric aspects of sociomoral developmental delay.

Moral Judgment Development and Delay

In cognitive-structural theory, moral development involves a "construction" of progressively mature moral meaning. Kohlberg contended that, because of this constructive process, a cross-culturally standard sequence of stages in moral judgment development can be identified (see Kohlberg, 1971, 1984; Colby & Kohlberg, 1987; for a review of pertinent research, see Walker, 1988). Kohlberg's Stages 1 through 4 are adapted and used in Gibbs, Basinger, and Fuller's (1992) neo-Kohlbergian typology, which classifies the adapted stages into mature and immature developmental levels. Stages 1 and 2 represent immature or superficial moral judgment; an adolescent or adult evidencing only these stages should be considered developmentally delayed in moral reasoning. Stages 3 and 4, representing mature or profound moral judgment, should define the cognitive-structural norm for any culture. The adolescent or adult who has attained a relatively mature stage of moral meaning may hold, for example, that one should keep a promise to a friend to preserve the trust on which the friendship is based or to observe the mutual respect that is the basis for any relationship. Mature or profound moral understanding pertains not only to keeping promises, but to a broad spectrum of culturally pervasive moral norms and values such as telling the truth, refraining from stealing, helping others, and saving lives.

The superficiality of immature moral judgment is most readily illustrated by Stage 1, which reflects "the natural tendency of young children to embody . . . moral notions in concrete places or events" (Damon, 1988, p. 15). Stage 1 morality entails a physicalistic understanding of moral authority (e.g., "The father is the boss because he's bigger"; Kohlberg, 1984, p. 624) or of the moral worth of a human life (one of the subjects in Kohlberg's longitudinal study suggested that saving the life of more than one person is especially important because "one man has just one house, maybe a lot of furniture, but a whole bunch of people have an awful lot of furniture," p. 192). Similarly, the need to keep a promise might be justified by appeal to physical consequences (otherwise the person "will beat you up"). Perceptually impressive features of a situation (e.g., size, objects, or actions), then, tend to capture the young child's attention or imagination; it is these features that dominate the child's reasons for obeying authority, saving a life, keeping a promise, or adhering to other moral prescriptions.

Stage 2 reasoning goes beyond physical perceptions to interrelate psychological perspectives, but this stage as well can be characterized as superficial. Kohlberg (1984) describes the perspective at Stage 2 as

> pragmatic—to maximize satisfaction of one's needs and desires
> while minimizing negative consequences to the self. The assump-
> tion that the other is also operating from this premise leads to an

emphasis on instrumental exchange. . . . For example, it is seen
as important to keep promises to insure that others will keep their
promises to you and do nice things for you, or . . . in order to
keep them from getting mad at you. (pp. 626–628)

With the advent of Stage 3, moral judgment advances beyond superficiality
to a mature understanding of moral norms and values. Stage 3 is marked by an
interrelating of egoistic and instrumental perspectives sufficient to bring about
an understanding of the mutuality or trust that underlies mature interpersonal relationships. Kohlberg suggests that "Stage 3 reciprocity [allows] one to understand
reciprocity as going beyond concrete notions of equal exchange to maintaining relationships, mutuality of expectations, and sentiments of gratitude and obligation"
(Kohlberg, 1984, pp. 628–629). This progression in moral judgment from instrumental exchange ("You scratch my back, I'll scratch yours") to a "mutuality of
expectations" was also observed by Piaget (1932/1965), whose study of moral judgment was seminal for Kohlberg's work. Piaget characterized the progression as
a transition from "reciprocity as a fact" to "reciprocity as an ideal" or "do as you
would be done by" (p. 323).

Stage 3 moral judgment does not fully represent moral-cognitive adequacy or
maturity for individuals living in a society more complex than a small community.
As adolescents or adults move beyond local communities to universities or complex
work settings, they increasingly deal with anonymous individuals and relate to
individuals who have diverse or heterogeneous values. As a result of this experience and the reflection it stimulates, their appreciation of the need for mutual trust
(Stage 3) expands into an appreciation of the need for commonly accepted, consistent standards and requirements (Stage 4; cf. Edwards, 1975, 1982; Mason &
Gibbs, 1993). As a subject in Kohlberg's longitudinal study said, "You've got to
have certain understandings in things that everyone is going to abide by or else
you could never get anywhere in society, never do anything" (Colby et al., 1987,
p. 375). In the absence of commonly accepted "understandings" such as the responsibility to respect one another's rights and to contribute to society, not only will
society "never get anywhere," but (in the words of another of Kohlberg's longitudinal subjects) "chaos will ensue, since each person will be following his or her
own set of laws" (p. 375).

In sum, then, the child progresses in moral judgment from a relatively superficial (physicalistic, egoistic-instrumental) level to a more profound and mature
level entailing insight into the psychological meaning and functional bases of interpersonal relationships (mutuality of expectations) and human society (commonly
accepted standards and interdependencies). This age-related progression in moral
judgment has been found in longitudinal studies (Colby, Kohlberg, Gibbs, &
Lieberman, 1983; Page, 1981; Walker, 1989) and in cross-cultural research. In a
review of Kohlbergian moral judgment studies in 27 countries, Snarey (1985)
concluded that Kohlberg's Stages 1 through 4 are "represented in a wide range
of cultural groups" (p. 218).

Kohlberg (1984) emphasized the particular role of stimulating social interaction in the development of moral judgment:

> If moral development is fundamentally a process of the restructuring of modes of role-taking, then the fundamental social inputs stimulating moral development may be termed "role-taking opportunities." . . . Participation in various groups . . . [stimulates] development. . . . The child lives in a total social world in which perceptions of the law, of the peer group, and of parental teaching all influence one another. . . . Various people and groups . . . [stimulate] *general moral development*. . . . The more the social stimulation, the faster the rate of moral development. (pp. 74–78)

As children enter adolescence, those who have lacked the role-taking opportunities with which to construct an age-normative (i.e., at least Stage 3) understanding of human social life are left with an egoistic-instrumental worldview (Stage 2); such developmentally delayed young people are prone to behavior that is antisocial—and potentially dangerous, given the size, strength, independence, sex impulses, and ego capabilities of adolescents. As might be expected, controlled comparisons of delinquent or conduct-disordered children or adolescents with normal peers (Bear & Richards, 1981; Blasi, 1980; Campagna & Harter, 1975; Chandler & Moran, 1990; Gavaghan, Arnold, & Gibbs, 1983; Jennings, Kilkenny, & Kohlberg, 1983; Nelson, Smith, & Dodd, 1990; Trevethan & Walker, 1989) indicate that, at least on production measures, disproportionately higher percentages of delinquent or conduct-disordered young people are at Stage 2. In a study that analyzed moral judgment delay by area of moral value, Jelinek (1991) found evidence of pronounced delay in the reasons offered by both male and female delinquents for obeying the law.

Delinquents' delay in the development of moral judgment provides one interpretation of the absence or paucity of remorse noted among at least certain psychological types of juvenile offenders (e.g., the "undersocialized-aggressive" type; Quay, 1987). According to Kohlberg,

> guilt in its most precise sense is moral self-judgment, and it presupposes the formation of internal or mature [moral judgment]. . . . If a boy is a member of a delinquent gang, he will deny the anxiety in the pit of his stomach because it is "chicken" to fear the cops. If he has developed more mature modes of moral judgment, he will . . . say, "I could never do that, I'd hate myself if I did." (1984, p. 66)

It is interesting to speculate on the applicability of moral judgment theory to the East Harlem youths. Did they lack adequate social perspective-taking opportunities and hence fail to develop age-appropriate moral judgment? Is their lack of remorse accordingly attributable to a general moral-cognitive immaturity? One important manifestation of a lack of adequate social role-taking opportunities in a child's socialization history is a dysfunctional family rife with harsh, arbitrary power assertion (Gibbs, 1987, 1991a, 1991b). Journalistic investigations did find that most of the youths had a history of behavior problems. The extent to which the youths' families were dysfunctional is not clear, however. Although family instability was evident (five of seven case studies involved absent, criminal, or neglecting fathers), none of the families was on welfare or was especially poverty stricken (Kunen, 1989; Stone, 1989). The East Harlem youths may well have been delayed in areas of moral judgment development. Nonetheless, reports that their home lives may not have been especially dysfunctional prompts one to consider other factors as well in speculating about the Central Park crime.

Egocentric Bias and Social Decentration

Another aspect of the sociomoral developmental delay of antisocial youths is the persistence into adolescence of a high degree of "me-centeredness" (Lickona, 1983, p. 152) or egocentric bias. Egocentric bias is a natural feature of thought and behavior in early childhood. Damon (1977) found that young children's reasoning on distributive justice tasks confuses fairness with "the child's own desires": For instance, the child may assert, "I should get it because I want to have it" (p. 75). Lickona characterized the general orientation of the young child as "Whatever I want is what's fair!" (p. 91).

Piaget (1932/1965) and Flavell (1985) suggest that egocentric bias is especially prominent in early childhood because interchanges with peers and others have not yet prompted the child to "decenter" in attention from his or her own very salient needs, desires, and impulses. (It should be noted, however, that in the presence of a highly salient adult authority figure, the child may momentarily "recenter" on the adult; Stage 1 moral judgment pertains precisely to such circumstances. Young children also respond empathically on occasion, especially in response to physically salient distress cues; Hoffman, 1978.) Case (1985) has argued that centration in early childhood may be inevitable to some extent, given working memory limitations that restrict the young child's ability to consider multiple perspectives.

With accumulation of social perspective-taking experiences and maturation of working memory, children's egocentric bias and other centration tendencies generally decline. In a study of the evolution of children's reasons for obedience, Damon (1977) found later reasons to be "less egocentric . . . the self's welfare is still important, but at these later levels self-interest is increasingly seen in the context of the welfare of everyone in the relation" (p. 221). Although egocentric bias tends to decline with maturity, it may never disappear entirely. Flavell (1985) has pointed out that even as mature adults "we experience our own points of view more or less directly, whereas we must always attain the other person's in more or less indirect manners. . . . Furthermore, we are usually unable to turn our own viewpoints off completely, when trying to infer another's" (p. 125).

Egocentric bias is perhaps particularly evident in spontaneous Stage 2 moral judgment, as Lickona (1983) points out:

> Especially when Stage 2 is first breaking through, kids' energy
> tends to go into asserting *their* needs and desires and making the

world accommodate them. They have a supersensitive Unfairness Detector when it comes to finding all the ways that people are unfair to them. But they have a big blind spot when it comes to seeing all the ways *they* aren't fair to others and all the ways parents and others do things for them. (p. 149)

Even after Stage 2 has "broken through," the very nature of its instrumental egoism virtually invites egocentric bias: After all, self-interested exchanges are readily subvertible to self-interested *advantages* if the opportunity arises. The Stage 2 thinker may evaluate, say, obeying the law and not stealing as important, but the value is basically contingent on the individual's calculations and interests. Stage 2 thinking may support not stealing from someone if that person has done one favors or is likely to find out and retaliate; by the same token that thinking may support stealing if the would-be victim has not done any favors lately or if the chance of detection is low. Incarcerated juvenile felons in our intervention groups (Gibbs & Potter, 1991), when reflecting on their acts of shoplifting and other offenses, have recollected that their thoughts at the time concerned whether they could get what they wanted and get away successfully. Spontaneous references to victims of the offenses were totally absent.

Egocentric bias may be present even where "ego" expands to encompass certain close friends and relatives. Moral judgment may be age-appropriate in the immediate social context but delayed in areas where the referent for moral reasoning concerns acquaintances or strangers. Such a contextual difference may characterize delinquents' moral judgments about the value of life. One question on the recently developed Sociomoral Reflection Measure–Short Form (Gibbs, Basinger, & Fuller, 1992) is especially pertinent to this issue. Question 7 asks, "How important is it for a person [without losing his or her own life] to save the life of a stranger?" Jelinek (1991) found that male delinquents were less likely to evaluate this as important and showed particular delay in moral reasoning on this question (in addition to the previously noted delay in reasoning concerning the importance of obeying the law). The following were typical Stage 2 responses to the question about saving the life of a stranger: "If you hardly know them, then who cares?"; "That would be stupid, to help someone you don't know"; and "It doesn't matter, you won't see them again." In contrast, on Question 6, about saving the life of a friend, male delinquents did not evidence delayed moral judgment in comparison with the control group. (Male and female delinquents combined, however, were delayed on all questions.) The implication is that delinquents are capable of age-appropriate moral judgment in some areas, but they exhibit delay largely because they apply mature reasoning competence only to a restricted social sphere. Contributing to the developmental delay, then, is the narrowness of the valued social world: Juvenile offenders tend to be either "me-centered" or "me-and-my-few-friends-centered."

The restricted sociomoral frame of reference of delinquent young people can be applied in our speculative analysis of the East Harlem youths. Consider that the youths were male, African American or Hispanic, and adolescent; their victim was female, Caucasian, and adult. In addition to differences in gender, ethnicity, and age, the attackers may have perceived a difference in socioeconomic status vis-à-vis the victim. If susceptibility to delay in the development of moral judgment is linked to restriction of the moral sphere in juvenile offenders, then the victim certainly fell outside that sphere. In the minds of the delinquents, she was dehumanized as an out-group member to whom mature moral concern need not apply. But why was she so brutally victimized?

SOCIAL INFORMATION PROCESSING THEORY

Even if both immaturity of judgment and self-centeredness are present, sociomoral developmental delay may not lead to severely or criminally antisocial behavior unless certain defensive processes come into play. Another cognitive theory with relevance to moral or social behavior—social information processing theory— takes account of these processes.

Consider claims that virtually all individuals—even those evidencing sociomoral developmental delay and engaging in antisocial behavior—possess (a) some degree of empathic predisposition (Henggeler, 1989; Hoffman, 1978, 1981) and (b) a motivation to maintain self-consistency or avoid cognitive dissonance between behavior and self-concept (e.g., Blasi & Oresick, 1986; Kelman & Baron, 1968; cf. Steele, 1988). Indeed, particularly where harm to others is obvious and difficult to ignore, the youth engaging in antisocial behavior may encounter the psychological stresses of (a) incipient guilt from empathy aroused by salient victim distress cues and (b) cognitive dissonance between behavior that is unjustifiably harmful to others and a concept of the self as one who does not unjustifiably harm others (such a self-concept is clinically observed; in quantitative assessments, delinquents' self-esteem tends to be lower than nondelinquents'; Henggeler, 1989). The aversiveness of anticipated empathy-based guilt and threats to self-concept normally inhibit at least plainly antisocial behavior; why, then, the Central Park crime? By the same token, why do we have the violent gang member—or any severely recidivist offender? As Samenow (1984) put the question, "How is it possible for a criminal to believe that he is a good guy"—and, I would add, for a criminal not to be plagued by empathy-based guilt—"when he has left behind him a trail of destruction?" (p. 160). I believe that the answer takes us in the direction of social information processing theory (especially as articulated by Dodge, 1986).

Cognitive Distortions

Frequently underlying antisocial behavior are cognitive distortions, nonveridical attitudes or beliefs pertaining primarily to the self and one's social behavior. Although cognitive distortions may be self-destructive (see Dobson, 1988; Dryden & Golden, 1987), the antisocial youth typically develops certain self-serving cognitive distortions; these distortions may support sociomoral developmental delay and defend against empathic or cognitive-dissonance stresses and potential inhibitors. Egocentric bias itself in effect constitutes a distortive attitudinal posture in social motivation: For example, "Because I want it, that makes it mine" (cf. Damon, 1977; Lickona, 1983; Yochelson & Samenow, 1976, 1977). Because self-centered cognitive distortions stem directly from egocentric bias and may be antecedent to other distortions, they can be called *primary distortions.*

Subsequent or secondary cognitive distortions have been termed *rationalizations* (Sykes & Matza, 1957, p. 666). Again, our thesis is that (a) egocentrically biased behavior can lead to overt and unambiguous harm to others and (b) such harm or its anticipation normally generates certain psychological stresses (empathic guilt, dissonance with self-concept). Secondary distortions or rationalizations serve to preempt or neutralize the stresses, thereby extinguishing or at least attenuating their inhibitory power. In Bandura's (1991) cognitive social learning theory, distortions or rationalizations permit one to "disengage" from moral self-evaluation of one's detrimental or reprehensible conduct (p. 72). Primary and secondary distortions may form a reciprocally supportive network, strengthening any particular distortion—much as primitive and derived beliefs gain stability from being "functionally connected" according to Rokeach's cognitive personality theory (Rokeach, 1968, pp. 5–8).

In our work with antisocial youths (see Gibbs & Potter, 1987, 1991; Gibbs, Potter, & Goldstein, in press; Gibbs, Potter, & Leeman, 1989), my associates and I have been struck by the prevalence of two main categories of rationalization: externalized attribution of blame and mislabeling. I first encountered the problem of externalizing distortion several years ago during a moral discussion with male juvenile felons of a problem situation concerning shoplifting. During the discussion I was prompted to ask—rhetorically, I thought—"Who's to blame in this situation?" I thought it was obvious that the primary person to blame was the shoplifter. To my surprise, several of the boys in the group quite seriously answered that the store owner was at fault. Their reasoning was that if the store owner wasn't alert enough to spot and catch a shoplifter, he deserved to be robbed. "It's on him," as one group member put it.

Once I realized that my supposedly rhetorical question was not necessarily so rhetorical for this population, I started asking it in other problem situation discussions as well. In a discussion of a car theft situation, I learned that such a theft was the car owner's fault because, after all (it was stated in the problem situation), the owner had left the keys in the car. That made the owner a "fool"; anyone that careless or "stupid" deserved to get "ripped off." Similarly, I learned that a teacher who says she trusts a class taking a test and leaves the room for a few minutes is to blame for whatever cheating takes place. The teacher, for being such a trusting fool, has it coming if the students cheat.

In a similar vein, Vorrath and Brendtro (1985) note the "elaborate systems" of antisocial youths

> for displacing responsibility for their problems onto some other
> person or circumstance. When we ask a youth why he got into
> trouble he will say his parents were messed up, or he had the
> wrong friends, or the police were out to get him, or the teachers

hated him, or his luck turned bad. Projecting, denying, rationalizing, and avoiding, he becomes expert at escaping responsibility. (p. 37)

Externalized attribution of blame has been studied by Dodge and associates. Dodge (1986) conceptualizes the phenomenon of externalizing distortion in terms of social information processing theory, which accounts for variables hypothesized to mediate between incoming stimuli and overt behavioral responses: attending, encoding, representing, generating of possible responses and consequences, and selecting and monitoring of responses. As articulated by Dodge, social information processing theory can be related both to other information-processing approaches (Gardner, 1985) and to cognitive social learning theory (Bandura, 1991; Mischel & Mischel, 1976).

In experimental research, Dodge and associates (Dodge, 1980; Dodge, Price, Bachorowski, & Newman, 1990) studied the propensity of aggressive boys for unprovoked aggressive acts. Dodge (1980) found that, before committing aggressive acts toward other boys, the subjects apparently engaged in "distorted" (p. 167) thinking: Although the other boys' intentions were in fact ambiguous, the aggressive boys (unlike the otherwise comparable control subjects) interpreted their actions as hostile and gratuitously attributed aggressive intentions to the others. In the minds of the aggressive boys, their aggression against the others was thereby justified: "That guy has it in for me so whatever I do to him, he deserves it."

The relationship of externalizing distortion to aggressive behavior has also been found in other studies. Dodge, Price, et al. (1990) found higher levels of hostile attribution among severely aggressive juvenile offenders, and Kahn and Chambers (1991) found higher sexual recidivism rates among juvenile sex offenders who blamed their victims. In a recent longitudinal study, Dodge, Bates, and Pettit (1990) found young children's hostile attributional bias and other distortions to be (a) linked to prior physical abuse and (b) predictive of aggressive behavior in kindergarten. Dodge (1986) notes the long-term social difficulties engendered by such inaccurate processing of information in social transactions:

If a child responds in an inappropriately aggressive way to a social situation, the peer may be likely to process this information in a way which leads him or her to label the child as deviant and respond by rejecting the child. As a result, the child may acquire even more social difficulties. In this way, the cognitive operations of each child interact with each other's behavior in a transaction, as if in a chess match. (p. 87)

Sykes and Matza (1957) point out that externalizing rationalizations offer an obvious advantage to the offender: "By attacking others, the wrongfulness of his own behavior is more easily repressed or lost to view" (p. 668). Indeed, the delinquent tends to perceive himself not as a victimizer but as a victim (Samenow, 1984). The roles in the victimization process are reversed as the delinquent "moves himself into the position of an avenger and the victim is transformed into a wrongdoer"

(Sykes & Matza, 1957, p. 668). The offender's concept of self as a "good guy" (to recall Samenow's question) is thereby preserved. Furthermore, the offender need contend with little or no feeling of empathy because the true victim is not perceived as such. The neutralizing of guilt made possible by the blaming of the victim is almost explicit in the self-report of a 17-year-old concerning his recent break-ins: "If I started feeling bad, I'd say to myself, 'Tough rocks for him. He should have had his house locked better and the alarm on'" (Samenow, 1984, p. 115).

The second category of cognitive distortion is mislabeling—that is, constructing biased representations or interpretations of one's behavior and its effects. Like the externalizing of blame, mislabeling permits the antisocial youth psychologically to escape responsibility or at least to reduce cognitive dissonance, and to preempt or neutralize empathy-based guilt. Yochelson and Samenow (1976) describe the use of euphemistic or "minimizing" (p. 499) labels that permit the antisocial individual to claim that he or she "didn't really hurt anybody" (Sykes & Matza, 1957, p. 669). For example, serious vandalism can be passed off as "mischief" or a "prank" (pp. 667–668). Lickona (1983) notes that self-aggrandizing behavior that hurts others is often glorified as "cool" or "smart" by antisocial peer groups and even in the popular media (p. 152). As Bandura (1991) observes, "Euphemistic language . . . provides a convenient device for masking reprehensible activities or even conferring a respectable status upon them" (p. 79).

Like externalizing, mislabeling has been quite evident in our group work. For example, in discussing a problem concerning whether to make a drug delivery, several group members argued that making the delivery would be "helping out a friend"—despite a clear indication in the problem situation that the drug was illegal and quite harmful to those who would receive it. Also, group members often minimize the severity of their actions—for instance, by attempting to characterize an assault as "just screwing around." A group member who had grabbed a woman's purse dangling from a supermarket shopping cart recalled thinking that the theft taught the woman a good lesson, to be more careful in the future.

One can discern in the Central Park crime both categories of cognitive distortion. Several of the gang members suggested that they were just "wilding" or "having fun" (mislabeling and minimizing). The dehumanization of unfamiliar, dissimilar others described earlier also represents a kind of mislabeling, of seeing certain human beings as somehow outside the boundaries of what is "human." (Indeed, as the youths marauded through the park that evening, they yelled racial epithets at whites; Stone, 1989.) Externalization of blame is suggested by comments of the arrested youths' neighborhood peers: They suggested that blame for the attack rested with the woman; by being foolish enough to frequent Central Park at night, she "committed suicide." Such cognitive distortions are of course directly pertinent to the problem posed earlier of how to account for the lack of remorse in the wake of the brutal attack. One can speculatively paraphrase the words of the 17-year-old burglar quoted earlier: "*If I started to feel bad,* I'd say to myself, 'Tough rocks for her; she should have had more sense than to be alone in Central Park at night.'"

In general, then, the sociomoral developmental delay typical of antisocial youths is often associated with cognitive distortions. The delay itself generally consists of the persistence of egocentric bias as well as immature moral judgment. Persistent egocentric bias tends to consolidate into a self-serving attitude ("If I want something, I should have it"), termed a primary cognitive distortion. Where primary cognitive distortions generate aggressive actions with clearly harmful consequences, the need arises to defend against certain potentially inhibiting stresses (empathy for the victim, dissonance with self-concept). Defending against such stresses, and thereby permitting the maintenance of primary distortions, are secondary cognitive distortions (externalizing blame, mislabeling).

Finally, it should be noted that sociomoral developmental delay and cognitive distortion typically characterize the gang itself as well as the individual gang member. Classic characterizations (Cohen, 1955; Miller, 1958) of the gang subculture in terms of negativism, short-term hedonism, toughness, and "smartness" (the ability to get what one wants with minimum physical exertion) can be interpreted in developmental terms as representing a Stage 2 morality, in which self-centered behavior is euphemistically labeled and accorded status.

MORAL-COGNITIVE INTERVENTIONS

The problems of sociomoral developmental delay and cognitive distortion have implications for treatment or secondary prevention programs for youths who are high risk for gang involvement. Treatment work addressing these problems is reviewed next. Goldstein (1991), Kazdin (1987), and others have called for comprehensive treatment approaches that weave together promising, compatible component approaches into a multifaceted program. In the past 5 years, our own treatment work (Gibbs, 1987, 1991b; Gibbs & Potter, 1987; Gibbs et al., in press; Gibbs et al., 1989) has entailed the conceptual and practical interweaving of moral-cognitive theories.

Programs Remediating Sociomoral Developmental Delay

Treatment programs addressing the sociomoral developmental delay of high-risk youths have used mainly Kohlbergian stage of moral judgment as the referent for developmental delay. As noted earlier, a disproportionate percentage of antisocial youths demonstrate sociomoral reasoning at immature levels, especially at Stage 2. Accordingly, the treatment rationale is straightforward. To the extent that antisocial behavior results from a delay in moral judgment development, treatment of antisocial youth should entail remediation of the developmental delay.

In theoretical terms, moral judgment–delayed youths need an enriched, concentrated dosage of social perspective-taking opportunity to stimulate them to catch up to an age-appropriate level of moral judgment. Subjects are given opportunities to consider the perspectives of others vis-à-vis their own perspectives, in the context of either a macrointervention or a microintervention strategy. In the macrointervention or "Just Community" strategy, attempts are made to restructure the institution (school or correctional facility) in accordance with principles of democracy and justice so that subjects (students or inmates) participate as much as is feasible in the rule-making and enforcement processes that affect institutional life (e.g., Duguid, 1981; Hickey & Scharf, 1980; Higgins, 1991; Kohlberg & Higgins, 1987; Power, Higgins, & Kohlberg, 1989). The narrower microintervention strategy focuses on group discussion of relevant sociomoral dilemmas or problem situations as a stimulus for perspective-taking experiences. Subjects must justify the reasons for their problem-solving decisions in the face of challenges from more developmentally advanced peers and from group leaders (e.g., Gibbs, Arnold, Ahlborn, & Cheesman, 1984).

A Sample Problem Situation

"George's Problem Situation" is an example of the problem situations used in the Gibbs et al. (1984) microintervention:

> One day Jake tells his younger brother, George, a secret: Jake is selling drugs. George and Jake both know that the kind of drug Jake is selling causes lung and even brain damage and can even kill people. George asks his older brother Jake to stop dealing. But the family is poor, and Jake says he is only doing it to help out the family. Jake asks George not to tell on him.

The following excerpted discussion of George's problem situation is drawn from one of the Gibbs et al. groups, in this case a group of 10 male juvenile offenders. Pretesting showed that the group had an approximately equal mixture of Stage 2 and Stage 3 participants. The opening question, whether George should tell on his brother, juxtaposed the moral values of contract (George would be keeping a promise), affiliation (Jake was helping out the family), and property (the drugs were Jake's) against those of life (the drugs could kill people) and law (Jake's dealing was against the law). Although hypothetical, the problem situation sparked a very ego-involved discussion, with several participants spontaneously describing their own drug histories. Subjects challenged one another in sociomorally relevant ways in more than a dozen instances, and all but one of the challenges were initiated by the subjects themselves rather than by a session leader. Virtually all group members became substantively involved in the discussion. The group goal was to reach consensus on the "best decision" for each of seven questions about the problem situation, as well as the "best reason" for that decision. Whether or not the group reached consensus varied by question, but the referent for "best reason" consensus was generally the most advanced of the reasons offered in the discussion. Stage 2 participants seemed nonplussed at finding themselves overruled by the group majority, but they acquiesced on many questions to make consensus possible (despite being invited to block consensus if they still had "strong objections"). In terms of cognitive-structural theory, such accommodations may have stimulated reflection and advancement to a higher stage of moral reasoning. A detailed account of this illustrative session follows.

The group failed to achieve consensus on the opening question of whether or not George should tell, but there was agreement on the best respective reasons for each of the two positions. For not telling, a Transitional 2/3 justification (intermediate between Stage 2 and Stage 3: Jake was only trying to help out the family) was approved, even by those who had initially proposed a Stage 2 reason (George should mind his own business). Those in favor of telling agreed that the life consideration (Jake was in effect killing other people) was the best reason.

Discussion of the second question, "What if George finds out that Jake is selling the drug to the young kids at school?" yielded a consensus that George should tell in that case because the young kids "don't know what they're doing" (not scorable but higher than Stage 2), overriding an initial opinion that young kids could do whatever they wanted (Stage 2).

The third question, asking whether it is "ever right to tell a secret on someone," generated a discussion that became especially spirited as dissension frustrated the group's effort to reach a consensus. The group did select, as the best reason against telling, a Transition 2/3 consideration ("Nobody is going to trust you any more") over Stage 2 alternatives ("People dog you for the rest of your life if you tell a secret"; "You should mind your own business"). Those on the other side of the issue pointed out that it is sometimes right to tell a secret when a life may be at stake (e.g., if someone "told you he was going to pay back" another person by cracking his skull with a pool cue). One subject who favored warning the prospective victim explained, "I wouldn't want to see a dude laying on the ground with his head split open" (Stage 3). This prompted a challenge from a pretest Stage 2 participant: "If it's not you, what do you care?" The subject retorted, "I just wouldn't want to see it" and was supported by other pretest Stage 3 subjects: "What if no one cared in this world, what would it be like?" and "Look at it this way—if I knew he was going to split your head open when you weren't looking, wouldn't you appreciate [being told]?" Another pretest Stage 2 participant entered the discussion: "Then that guy'd be mad and split *your* head open." Even the Stage 2 participants agreed, however, that for the "telling" side of the issue, the best reason was that "you wouldn't want to see him get hurt" (Stage 3).

The final question, "What if George finds out that Jake isn't using any of the money at all to help out the family but instead is spending the money on booze and other things for himself? Then is George right not to tell?" also yielded a "can't decide." The reasons in favor of not telling were Stage 2: "If the guy's snitchin' it's his own business" and "I wouldn't want to take a risk, you know, and sell something and then have to give all my money away, you know."

Many of the final interchanges of the session were especially noteworthy:

Participant A: I think you should help the family with the money.

Participant B: In a way he did. He's out drinking and boozing it up, that way the family ain't got to feed him [Stage 2].

Participant C: How do you think that makes the parent feel [Stage 3], man?
. . . That hurts, man. . . . I wouldn't want to see my brother
like that [Stage 3], man. What's he going to become?

Participant B: If he's selling drugs, he's got all kinds of money.
What do you got? Nothin'.

Participant C: Nothing? Go out and get a job.

Participant D: He really don't care for himself and his family.
He really don't care.

Participant C: He's hurting himself and still he's hurting other people
[Transition 2/3] and plus he lied to his brother. [This
statement was selected by the group as the "best reason."]

Participant E: Narking on me, you know, and getting me in jail and
caring for me, you know, I don't want nobody caring
for me [that way].

Participant C: Somebody's caring for you right now, man.

Evaluation of Cognitive-Structural Interventions

Probably the most impressive study of moral-cognitive developmental progress
has been Arbuthnot and Gordon's (1986) microintervention, entailing a 4-month-
long weekly small group discussion program. This program involved antisocial
juveniles, identified as such by teachers. Participants showed gains not only in
moral judgment but also in behavior (in terms of disciplinary referrals, tardiness,
and grades), both on short-term assessments conducted 2 or 3 weeks after the intervention and on 1-year follow-up posttests, relative to a randomly assigned
passage-of-time control group. Several differences between the experimental group
and the control group increased on the follow-up assessment. Similarly, changes
in classroom conduct (in terms of absenteeism rates and teachers' ratings) did not
indicate significant improvement for the experimental group relative to the controls until the 1-year follow-up, suggesting a possible sleeper effect.

Other behavioral findings have been less impressive, however. Niles (1986),
in a similar study, found moral judgment gain but no conduct gain. Also, our follow-
up of our own (Gibbs et al., 1984) study found no conduct gains associated with
the moral judgment gains. Finally, reports of conduct gain in connection with Just
Community macrointervention programs (e.g., Power et al., 1989) are anecdotal
and are not based on comparisons with control groups.

Although moral-cognitive interventions generally seem to stimulate the development of more mature moral judgment, then, the reduction of antisocial behavior
does not necessarily follow. In theoretical terms, this finding suggests the insuffi-
ciency of cognitive-structural theory as a comprehensive theory and the need for
supplementation with other theories, such as social information processing theory.
Specifically, cognitive-structural interventions have attended to moral judgment

delays but not explicitly to egocentric bias or to primary and secondary distortions. I suspect that, although such interventions have facilitated gains in moral judgment, the self-centered orientation (in terms of both egocentric bias and distorted attitude) and associated secondary cognitive distortions have remained more or less in place. It may be possible for individuals to evidence Stage 3 moral judgment—and at the same time engage in seriously antisocial behavior—if egocentric bias and associated distortions preempt consideration of the legitimate expectations and feelings of others in actual social situations. As noted earlier, many delinquents show competence for Stage 3 moral judgment in certain areas but evidence Stage 2 moral judgment when unvalued others (mere acquaintances, strangers) are involved. Schnell's (1986) finding of pronounced antisocial attitudes among delinquents as compared to nondelinquents implies that distortions prominently characterize Stage 3 juvenile offenders. (Interestingly, however, Schnell also found higher levels of anxiety and guilt among *Stage 3* delinquents; this finding suggests that defensive attitudes and other distortions do not entirely neutralize the consciences of these subjects.)

It is noteworthy that Kohlberg himself encountered evidence of cognitive distortion in his macrointervention work. Kohlberg and Higgins (1987) found that students in a Just Community program in a Bronx, New York, high school

> were morally immobilized by what we call *counter-norms,* peer
> norms or expectations that violate not only conventional moral
> norms but the capacity to empathize with each other or take each
> other's viewpoint. . . . [One counter-norm was] "Look at me the
> wrong way and you're in for a fight." One of us accidentally brushed
> against a student in the hall and he angrily yelled and continued
> threatening even after an explanation and an apology. As far as the
> norm of trust [is concerned] . . . there was the counter-norm . . .
> "It's your fault if something is stolen—you were careless and
> tempting me." (p. 110)

Partly because of the discovery of these "counter-norms" or externalizing distortions, Kohlberg and Higgins (1987) suggest a multifaceted approach—that is, adding a "critical role" for "teacher structuring and teacher advocacy" to "Piaget's emphasis on non-interference with the spontaneous process of peer interaction as the center of developmental moral education" (p. 125).

One can find evidence for a movement toward multifaceted treatment not only in Kohlberg and Higgins's suggestion but also in Arbuthnot and Gordon's (1986) relatively successful microintervention, described earlier. Their treatment study incorporated 2 preintervention weeks devoted to exercises designed to promote group cohesiveness, openness, and rapport. In addition, Arbuthnot and Gordon spent "two sessions . . . on active listening and communication ('I' messages) skills, an unplanned diversion from dilemma discussions necessitated by the participants' general lack in these skills, a lack which appeared to impede effective discussions" (p. 210). Arbuthnot and Gordon concluded that a comprehensive program should encompass not only moral discussion but also therapeutic techniques to promote group cohesion and mutual caring and to develop "social skills (for translation of new reasoning into action)" (p. 215). Insofar as Arbuthnot and Gordon's intervention incorporated such techniques, their singular results in terms of conduct improvement may be partly attributable to social skills training. On the other hand, social skills training alone has not been found to produce durable behavioral effects (Hollin, 1990; Long & Sherer, 1985; but cf. Kazdin, Bass, Siegel, & Thomas, 1989; see also chapter 4 in this volume). A rationale for social skills training in the context of moral-cognitive interventions is suggested later.

Treatment for Cognitive Distortion: Positive Peer Culture

As stated earlier, antisocial youths generally evidence not only sociomoral developmental delay but also cognitive distortion. Accordingly, in theoretical terms, both cognitive-structural theory and social information processing theory should form the basis for moral-cognitive intervention. Cognitive-structural micro- and macrointerventions, then, should include a component dealing with cognitive distortions. Because cognitive-structural interventions are group interventions, the social information processing component would have to be group oriented. Fortunately, although some of the pertinent therapy literature (e.g., Beck et al., 1990; Glasser, 1965) emphasizes the treatment of individuals, most of the literature is group oriented (e.g., Guerra & Slaby, 1990; Kahn & Lafond, 1988; Vorrath & Brendtro, 1985; Yochelson & Samenow, 1976, 1977). The focus in the following review is on Positive Peer Culture (PPC; Vorrath & Brendtro, 1985), a group intervention for youths, although some other programs are mentioned as well.

PPC is an adult-guided but youth-run small group treatment approach for maladjusted or antisocial adolescents. PPC or Guided Group Interaction began as a grass roots movement among child care practitioners (see McCorkle, Elias, & Bixby, 1958; cf. Jones, 1953); however, its programmatic features can be interpreted and evaluated in theoretical terms. As Harstad (1976) notes, PPC's emphasis on the group as the primary vehicle for helping troubled youths is consistent with the symbolic interactionist (e.g., Mead, 1934) view of the self as an inherently social construction and of the development of the self as a product of interaction with significant others in groups. PPC's emphasis on the group is also consistent with the emphasis on social perspective-taking opportunities in cognitive-structural theory.

PPC programs generally feature groups of 8 to 10 juveniles who meet for 1 to 1½ hours, 5 days per week. In a typical meeting, each group member reports recent and recurring behavior problems; the group then "awards" the meeting to a particular member for discussion of his or her problem. To help members recognize problems in their own and others' behavior, the group learns to use a 12-category behavior problem list in the reporting of problems. Following are the problem categories: having a low self-image, being inconsiderate of others, being inconsiderate of self, having an authority problem, misleading others, being easily misled, aggravating others, being easily angered, stealing, having an alcohol or drug problem, lying, and fronting. In some instances, the heightened awareness of the harmfulness of one's behavior brought about by self-recognition is sufficient to motivate some change. For many antisocial youths, however, as Vorrath and Brendtro (1985) emphasize, denial and other defensive distortions must be explicitly confronted if self-recognition of problems is to produce genuine motivation to change. Hence, the group is taught to discern and challenge minimizing and externalizing distortions that can undermine honest problem reporting—for example, minimizing an assault as a disagreement or attributing one's "easily angered" problem to "the stupid things [another person] does" (pp. 88–89).

The problems of mislabeling and externalizing are further addressed by two techniques recommended by Vorrath and Brendtro (1985). *Reversing* involves "placing responsibility for action back on those who must do the changing rather than allowing them to project it outside themselves" (p. 39). A youth who asserts, "I got in trouble because both of my parents are alcoholics and don't care about me" should be countered or reversed with "Do you mean that all people with parents who have problems get in trouble?" (p. 39).

Relabeling counteracts the tendency of antisocial youths to engage in self-serving representations or interpretations—for instance, by placing a positive label on negative behavior. Thus, in the PPC program, "if stealing is seen as slick, then it should be relabeled" by the group leader—but increasingly by the group itself— "as 'sneaky and dumb' " (p. 23).

A third technique advocated by Vorrath and Brendtro (1985), *confronting,* entails addressing not only secondary but also primary (that is, self-centered) cognitive distortions by "making the student aware of the effect of his actions on others" (p. 109). Confronting, so defined, is essentially what Hoffman (1983) has characterized in the parental discipline context as induction. Like induction, confronting directs the recipient's attention to the harm to others resulting from his or her actions and thereby elicits and strengthens empathic responses. Such strengthening is therapeutically crucial if empathic responses (and related emotions such as empathy-based guilt) are to counteract egocentric bias and to penetrate primary and secondary cognitive distortions. In a similar vein, confronting relates to Yochelson and Samenow's (1977) recommendation that change agents challenge antisocial individuals to put themselves in another's position and to understand the "chain of injuries" (p. 223) resulting from every crime.

Through use of confronting and other techniques in a basically supportive group context, the PPC program aims to cultivate a group "climate for change" (Vorrath & Brendtro, 1985, p. 63) in which individuals turn from antisocial and self-destructive behavior to behavior that helps others and themselves. In residential settings, PPC groups form living units and even evaluate whether group members are deserving of privileges and ready for release. Recent research has found that PPC enhances juvenile inmates' amenability to treatment and therapeutic change (see Atwood & Osgood, 1987; Martin & Osgood, 1987; Osgood, Gruber, Archer, & Newcomb, 1985; Wasmund, 1988). On the other hand, PPC has not been shown by most studies to reduce recidivism (Gottfredson, 1987). Like the other moral-cognitive interventions reviewed, then, PPC used alone has strengths but also limited behavioral effectiveness.

The Role of Social Skills Training

Providing practice for antisocial youths in considering the legitimate expectations and feelings of others is a major feature of social skills training programs (see Little & Kendall, 1979). For example, in Goldstein and Glick's (1987) Aggression Replacement Training (see also Goldstein, 1988, and chapter 4 in this volume), social behavior skills are broken down into practical steps that are modeled, tried out, discussed, and practiced. One skill, "Expressing a Complaint," is broken down into six steps, the fifth of which is "Show that you understand his/her feelings." The third of six steps constituting "Preparing for a Stressful Conversation" is "Imagine the other person in the stressful situation. Think about what that person will feel and why." "Responding to Anger" includes "Listen openly to what the other person has to say," and "Dealing With an Accusation" includes "Think about why the person might have accused you." Other social skills are entirely devoted to perspective taking ("Responding to the Feelings of Others," "Helping Others," "Expressing Affection").

A social skill that is especially important in gang involvement prevention programs is "Dealing With Group Pressure," the first step of which is "Think about what the other people want you to do and why." Like other social skills, this skill provides the opportunity to develop an other-oriented or "decentered" cognitive mediation of one's behavior. This cognitive mediation view of social skills training renders it theoretically compatible with both cognitive-structural and information processing theories. Without cognitive mediation, a youth—such as those involved in the Central Park crime—is vulnerable not only to group pressure but in particular to the deindividuation and disinhibition processes entailed in collective violence (Prentice, 1990).

Fine-grained practice in taking others' perspectives in actual social situations may well be critical if moral-cognitive interventions are to be effective in ameliorating antisocial *behavior*. It is perhaps no accident that the one moral-cognitive intervention that yielded unequivocal behavioral outcome benefits (Arbuthnot & Gordon, 1986) incorporated social skills training—although, as noted, social skills training programs by themselves generally have only limited effectiveness.

Multicomponent Moral-Cognitive Intervention

A moral-cognitive intervention for antisocial youths should treat *in a single group program* both sociomoral developmental delay (egocentric bias, superficial moral judgment) and cognitive distortion. Positive Peer Culture is perhaps the optimal group format for moral-cognitive intervention. One of the strengths of PPC is its explicit attention to the power of adolescent peer climates to influence individual adolescents for good or ill. Gangs or other countercultures such as those that tend to develop in correctional institutions are "characterized by opposition to institutional rules and goals, norms against informing authorities about rule violations, and the use of physical coercion as a basis of influence among inmates" (Osgood et al., 1985, p. 71). PPC techniques for counteracting the externalizing, mislabeling distortions of the antisocial peer group represent a crucial contribution: Unless the antisocial peer culture can itself be transformed, any progress achieved on the individual level will almost inevitably be undermined by the countercultural influence. Conversely, once the adolescent group is successfully transformed from a Stage 2 counterculture of egocentric, antisocial, rationalizing individuals into a Stage 3 culture, a powerful climate for positive change exists.

The benefits do not flow unidirectionally from PPC to moral-cognitive interventions, however; moral-cognitive therapies, for their part, can equip the group with crucial skills and other cognitive resources for helping its members. Although Vorrath and Brendtro (1985) claim that group "members demonstrate great skill in helping the student who gets [i.e., is awarded] the meeting" (p. 92), others experienced in PPC programming have been skeptical. Carducci (1980) argues that, although PPC provides the motivation, it does not supply the maturity and skills youth groups would need to accomplish behaviorally effective preventive intervention for their members. In Carducci's view, the effectiveness of PPC has been hampered by the fact that antisocial juveniles are "frequently at a stage of arrested moral/ethical/social/emotional development" (p. 157; see research cited earlier). Furthermore, Carducci points out that such youths "usually do not know what steps to take to solve problems" (p. 158)—that is, they show social skill deficits. Similarly, Goldstein and Glick (1987) conclude on the basis of a research review that "delinquent and other aggressive children and teenagers display widespread interpersonal, planning, aggression management, and other psychological skills deficiencies" (p. 22).

Because of such delays and deficits (and, I would add, distortions), antisocial youths are often poorly equipped to help their peers accomplish change. That many antisocial adolescents are deficient in helping skills is suggested by survey research (Brendtro & Ness, 1982) on 10 PPC treatment programs in various United States cities. Staff members at 9 of these 10 PPC centers cited as a program problem "abuse of confrontation" (p. 311) in the youth group meetings, prompting the researchers—one of whom is the second author of *Positive Peer Culture*—to comment, "Harassment, name-calling, screaming in someone's face, hostile profanity, and physical intimidation have no place in a quality program" (p. 322). Yet such behavior is precisely what one should anticipate if (a) constructively helping antisocial adolescents requires a certain maturity in sociomoral reasoning, along with social skills and veridical social cognition and (b) those attempting to provide the help are other adolescents with similar backgrounds—that is, with delays, deficits, and distortions in precisely those crucial areas.

To the benefit of both moral-cognitive and PPC programs, then, we have integrated moral-cognitive interventions into a PPC group format (Gibbs, Potter, & Goldstein, in press). Our program is called Equipping Peers to Help One Another, or EQUIP. The EQUIP program shares with Goldstein and Glick's (1987)

Aggression Replacement Training a curriculum addressing moral judgment development, anger management, and social skills development. However, this material is not introduced until the group is genuinely receptive—that is, until group members "frown on negative behavior" (Vorrath & Brendtro, 1985, p. 49). In EQUIP, discussions of moral problem situations and other activities promote the emerging positive peer culture and develop the skills and other psychological resources the group will need if it is to be effective in helping individual members. We designate the moral discussion, anger management, or social skills sessions as "equipment meetings," meetings through which the group gains "equipment" for helping its members. Equipment meetings, held once or twice each week, provide not only psychological resources but some variety in the daily group sessions.

The EQUIP program not only adds equipment meetings to the usual PPC regimen but also enhances the problem reporting phase of the standard PPC meetings with an important innovation: Group members are asked to describe and label both a behavior problem and the underlying cognitive distortion. Requiring more analytical problem reporting limits the opportunity for youths to use problem reporting to externalize blame (a difficulty acknowledged by Vorrath and Brendtro themselves) or to engage in "mechanical verbalizations," the second most frequently cited problem with PPC (Brendtro & Ness, 1982, p. 313).

As a precondition for labeling and correcting their distortions, EQUIP groups learn not only the PPC problem list but also a list of four categories of "thinking errors" (the term for cognitive distortion used by Yochelson & Samenow, 1976, 1977). Youths entering an EQUIP group complete the How I Think Questionnaire (Gibbs, Potter, & Barriga, 1993), which can serve as a vehicle for teaching the four kinds of thinking errors. (The categories, with illustrative items from the questionnaire, are listed in Table 5.1.) Following each item, respondents indicate along a scale the extent to which the item describes how they think.

A group that has learned the four thinking errors has acquired important equipment for providing effective help to its members. For example, the requirement that members report (with the group's help if needed) the thinking error underlying each behavior problem often enhances group insight into the basis for individuals' behavior problems. One youth reported resisting and yelling profanities at a staff member who, in accordance with institutional policy, attempted to inspect his carrying bag. The designation of the incident as "authority problem" was easy enough. Identification of the underlying cognitive distortion required some discussion, but it provided a problem analysis that the group used later when the youth was awarded the meeting. The youth explained that the bag had contained something very special and irreplaceable—photographs of his grandmother—and he was not going to let anyone take them. In seeking to identify underlying thinking errors, the group learned important further information: Throughout the incident, the juvenile thought only of his photos; he did not for a moment consider the staff member's perspective (she was only carrying out institutional policy concerning inspection for contraband). Nor did he reflect that the staff member was in no way abusive and hence that he had no reason to fear that his photos would be confiscated. This explanation revealed that behind the "authority" behavior problem lay "being

**Table 5.1 How I Think Questionnaire Items:
Four Categories of Cognitive Distortion**

1. Self-centered

   If I see something I like, I take it.
   If I lie to people, that's nobody's business but my own.
   People should let me do whatever I want.
   If people don't cooperate with me, it's their fault if they get hurt.

2. Minimizing or mislabeling

   If you can get away with it, only a fool wouldn't steal.
   Everybody lies. It's no big deal.
   Laws are meant to be broken.
   Beating somebody up teaches them a good lesson.

3. Assuming the worst

   You might as well steal; people are going to steal from you anyway.
   I might as well lie—if I tell the truth, people aren't going to believe me anyway.
   You should hurt people first, before they hurt you.
   People are always trying to start fights with me.

4. Blaming others

   If someone is careless enough to lose a wallet, the person deserves
      to have it stolen.
   It's OK to tell a lie if someone is dumb enough to fall for it.
   If I hit someone, it's their fault for making me mad.
   If I make a mistake, it's not my fault if I got mixed up with the wrong crowd.

Note. From *The How I Think Questionnaire* by J. C. Gibbs, G. Potter, and A. G. Barriga (1993). Unpublished manuscript, The Ohio State University, Columbus. Copyright 1993 by the authors. Reprinted by permission.

self-centered" and "assuming the worst" cognitive problems. Furthermore, the youth's anger at staff for his subsequent disciplinary write-up was identified as an "easily angered" problem and attributed to a "blaming others" thinking error.

As the youth achieved these insights (and learned other self-monitoring skills) with his peers' help, his anger dissipated considerably. Perhaps most important, he began to regret his verbal assault on the staff member. I believe that his remorse was therapeutically crucial: He could now see the unfairness of his behavior toward her, empathize with her, and attribute blame to himself. Through this and other sessions, the youth's "authority" and "easily angered" problems were repeated less and less frequently. I surmise that the conduct improvement was attributable, at least in part, to the attenuation of cognitive distortion and the consequent activation of inhibitory factors such as empathy-based guilt and dissonance with self-concept. (The youth also benefited from developing certain social skills, especially that of expressing a complaint constructively.) This youth's conduct improvement partially illustrates the statistically significant results of a controlled study of

EQUIP, which found that EQUIP was effective both in dramatically improving institutional conduct and in reducing recidivism rates by better than half 1 year after release (Leeman, Gibbs, & Fuller, in press).

Cognitive theories imply that the "positive" in Positive Peer Culture should mean morally mature and veridical. Almost certainly, the sociomoral cognition of the East Harlem youths was neither mature nor veridical. In other words, they did not tell themselves or others the truth: namely, that they had committed a vicious, unprovoked, and cowardly attack on an innocent human being. Most likely, each youth's implicit attitudes or beliefs were: I can and should do whatever I feel like doing now[2]; we are merely being wild and having some fun; and any harm that comes to foolish strangers is their fault. The refreshing thesis of moral-cognitive interventions is that relativistic representations of the youths' cognitions as simply "different" or "their subjective reality" are misleading. Rather, those cognitions are *wrong* (nonveridical, distorted, faulty, erroneous, etc.). Extending Henggeler's (1989) conclusion that cognitive distortions play an important role in antisocial behavior, I conclude that the correction of cognitive distortions should be central in moral-cognitive interventions with antisocial, gang-prone youths.

NOTES

[1] Strictly speaking, this group did not constitute a gang because the group did not fulfill the usual gang criteria: a self-designated group name, recurring meetings, and self-designated territory or "turf" (see Goldstein, 1991). Nonetheless, the theories and research discussed in the chapter should apply to youths at high risk for involvement not only with spontaneous groups but also with gangs in the strict sense.

[2] A corollary distortion may be: Anyone who does not comply with my getting what I want is being unfair to me. Several of the East Harlem youths recollected group indignation and outrage that the woman attempted to resist their beatings (Stone, 1989). Similarly, an incarcerated offender who had murdered a sales clerk justified his lack of remorse in a recent television interview: He explained that the woman had refused to "cooperate" and "follow the rules" (i.e., resisted giving him the merchandise and money he demanded). Of course, the distorted use of "cooperation" in this context is another example of mislabeling (a word that means "working together toward a common end" is euphemistically misapplied to "giving me what I unfairly want").

REFERENCES

Arbuthnot, J., & Gordon, D. A. (1986). Behavioral and cognitive effects of a moral reasoning development intervention for high-risk behavior-disordered adolescents. *Journal of Consulting and Clinical Psychology, 85,* 1275–1301.

Atwood, R. O., & Osgood, D. W. (1987). Cooperation in group treatment programs for incarcerated adolescents. *Journal of Applied Social Psychology, 17,* 969–989.

Bandura, A. (1991). Social cognitive theory of moral thought and action. In W. M. Kurtines & J. L. Gewirtz (Eds.), *Handbook of moral behavior and development: Vol. 1. Theory.* Hillsdale, NJ: Erlbaum.

Bear, G. G., & Richards, H. C. (1981). Moral reasoning and conduct problems in the classroom. *Journal of Educational Psychology, 73,* 644–670.

Beck, A. T., Freeman, A. et al. (1990). *Cognitive therapy of personality disorders.* New York: Guilford.

Blasi, A. (1980). Bridging moral cognition and moral action: A critical review of the literature. *Psychological Bulletin, 88,* 1–45.

Blasi, A., & Oresick, R. J. (1986). Affect, cognition, and self in developmental psychology. In D. J. Bearison & H. Zimiles (Eds.), *Thought and emotion: Developmental perspectives.* Hillsdale, NJ: Erlbaum.

Brendtro, L. K., & Ness, A. E. (1982). Perspectives on peer group treatment: The use and abuse of Guided Group Interaction/Positive Peer Culture. *Children and Youth Services Review, 4,* 307–324.

Campagna, A. F., & Harter, S. (1975). Moral judgment in sociopathic and normal children. *Journal of Personality and Social Psychology, 31,* 199–205.

Carducci, D. J. (1980). Positive Peer Culture and assertiveness training: Complementary modalities for dealing with disturbed and disturbing adolescents in the classroom. *Behavioral Disorders, 5,* 156–162.

Case, R. (1985). *Intellectual development: Birth to adulthood.* New York: Academic.

Chandler, M., & Moran, T. (1990). Psychopathy and moral development: A comparative study of delinquent and nondelinquent youth. *Development and Psychopathology, 2,* 227–246.

Cohen, A. K. (1955). *Delinquent boys: The culture of the gang.* Glencoe, IL: Free Press.

Colby, A., & Kohlberg, L. (1987). *The measurement of moral judgment: Theoretical foundations and research validation* (Vol. 1). Cambridge, England: Cambridge University Press.

Colby, A., Kohlberg, L., Gibbs, J. C., & Lieberman, M. (1983). A longitudinal study of moral judgment. *Monographs of the Society for Research in Child Development, 48*(1–2, Serial No. 200).

Colby, A., Kohlberg, L., Speicher, B., Hewer, A., Candee, D., Gibbs, J., & Power, C. (1987). *The measurement of moral judgment: Vol 2. Standard issue scoring manual.* Cambridge, England: Cambridge University Press.

Damon, W. (1977). *The social world of the child.* San Francisco: Jossey-Bass.

Damon, W. (1988). *The moral child: Nurturing children's natural moral growth.* New York: Free Press.

Dobson, K. S. (Ed.). (1988). *Handbook of cognitive-behavioral therapies.* New York: Guilford.

Dodge, K. A. (1980). Social cognition and children's aggressive behavior. *Child Development, 51,* 162–170.

Dodge, K. A. (1986). A social informational processing model of social competence in children. In M. Perlmutter (Ed.), *Minnesota symposia on child psychology: Vol. 18. Cognitive perspectives on children's social and behavioral development.* Hillsdale, NJ: Erlbaum.

Dodge, K. A., Bates, J. E., & Pettit, G. S. (1990, December). Mechanisms in the cycle of violence. *Science,* pp. 1678–1685.

Dodge, K. A., Price, J. M., Bachorowski, J. A., & Newman, J. P. (1990). Hostile attributional biases in severely aggressive adolescents. *Journal of Abnormal Psychology, 99,* 385–392.

Dryden, W., & Golden, W. L. (Eds.). (1987). *Cognitive-behavioural approaches to psychotherapy.* Cambridge, England: Hemisphere/Harper & Row.

Duguid, S. (1981). Moral development, justice, and democracy in the prison. *Canadian Journal of Criminology, 23,* 147–163.

Edwards, C. P. (1975). Social complexity and moral development: A Kenyan study. *Ethos, 3,* 505–527.

Edwards, C. P. (1982). Moral development in comparative cultural perspective. In D. A. Wagner & H. Stevenson (Eds.), *Cultural perspectives on child development.* San Francisco: Freeman.

Flavell, J. H. (1985). *Cognitive development* (2nd ed.). Englewood Cliffs, NJ: Prentice-Hall.

Gardner, H. (1985). *The mind's new science: A history of the cognitive revolution.* New York: Basic.

Gavaghan, M. P., Arnold, K. D., & Gibbs, J. C. (1983). Moral judgment in delinquents and nondelinquents: Recognition versus production measures. *Journal of Psychology, 114,* 267–274.

Gibbs, J. C. (1987). Social processes in delinquency: The need to facilitate empathy as well as sociomoral reasoning. In W. M. Kurtines & J. L. Gewirtz (Eds.), *Moral development through social interaction.* New York: Wiley-Interscience.

Gibbs, J. C. (1991a). Sociomoral developmental delay and cognitive distortion: Implications for the treatment of antisocial youth. In W. M. Kurtines & J. L. Gewirtz (Eds.), *Handbook of moral behavior and development: Vol 3. Application.* Hillsdale, NJ: Erlbaum.

Gibbs, J. C. (1991b). Toward an integration of Kohlberg's and Hoffman's theories of morality. In W. M. Kurtines & J. L. Gewirtz (Eds.), *Handbook of moral behavior and development: Vol 1. Theory.* Hillsdale, NJ: Erlbaum.

Gibbs, J. C., Arnold, K. D., Ahlborn, H. H., & Cheesman, F. L. (1984). Facilitation of sociomoral reasoning in delinquents. *Journal of Consulting and Clinical Psychology, 52,* 37–45.

Gibbs, J. C., Basinger, K. S., & Fuller, D. (1992). *Moral maturity: Measuring the development of sociomoral reflection.* Hillsdale, NJ: Erlbaum.

Gibbs, J. C., & Potter, G. (1987, April). *Identify it/own it/replace it: Helping youth help one another.* Paper presented at the meeting of the Commission on Interprofessional Education and Practice, Columbus, OH.

Gibbs, J. C., & Potter, G. (1991, April). *Aggression Replacement Training in the context of Positive Peer Culture.* Paper presented at the meeting of the Ohio Council for Children With Behavioral Disorders, Columbus, OH.

Gibbs, J. C., Potter, G., & Barriga, A. (1993). *The How I Think Questionnaire.* Unpublished manuscript, The Ohio State University, Columbus.

Gibbs, J. C., Potter, G., & Goldstein, A. P. (in press). *EQUIP: Equipping youth to help one another.* Champaign, IL: Research Press.

Gibbs, J. C., Potter, G., & Leeman, L. W. (1989, October). *IOR: Equipping youth to help one another.* Workshop presented at the meeting of the National Association of Guided Peer Agencies, Columbus, OH.

Glasser, W. (1965). *Reality therapy: A new approach to psychiatry.* New York: Harper & Row.

Goldstein, A. P. (1988). *The Prepare Curriculum: Teaching prosocial competencies.* Champaign, IL: Research Press.

Goldstein, A. P. (1991). *Delinquent gangs: A psychological perspective.* Champaign, IL: Research Press.

Goldstein, A. P., & Glick, B. (1987). *Aggression Replacement Training: A comprehensive intervention for aggressive youth.* Champaign, IL: Research Press.

Gottfredson, G. D. (1987). Peer group interventions to reduce the risk of delinquent behavior: A selective review and a new evaluation. *Criminology, 25,* 671–714.

Guerra, N., & Slaby, R. G. (1990). Cognitive mediators of aggression in adolescent offenders: Part 2. Intervention. *Developmental Psychology, 26,* 269–277.

Harstad, C. D. (1976). Guided group interaction: Positive Peer Culture. *Child Care Quarterly, 5,* 109–120.

Henggeler, S. W. (1989). *Delinquency in adolescence.* Newbury Park, CA: Sage.

Hickey, J. E., & Scharf, P. L. (1980). *Toward a just correctional system.* San Francisco: Jossey-Bass.

Higgins, A. (1991). The Just Community approach to moral education: Evolution of the idea and recent findings. In W. M. Kurtines & J. L. Gewirtz (Eds.), *Handbook of moral behavior and development: Vol 3. Application.* Hillsdale, NJ: Erlbaum.

Hoffman, M. L. (1978). Empathy, its development and prosocial implications. In C. B. Keasey (Ed.), *Nebraska symposium on motivation* (Vol. 25). Lincoln: University of Nebraska Press.

Hoffman, M. L. (1981). Is altruism part of human nature? *Journal of Personality and Social Psychology, 40,* 121–137.

Hoffman, M. L. (1983). Affective and cognitive processes in moral internalization. In E. T. Higgins, D. N. Ruble, & W. W. Hartup (Eds.), *Social cognition and social development: A sociocultural perspective.* Cambridge, England: Cambridge University Press.

Hollin, C. R. (1990). Social skills training with delinquents: A look at the evidence and some recommendations for practice. *British Journal of Social Work, 20,* 483–493.

Jelinek, V. G. (1991). *Moral judgment developmental delay in female delinquents.* Unpublished master's thesis, The Ohio State University, Columbus.

Jennings, W. S., Kilkenny, R., & Kohlberg, L. (1983). Moral development theory and practice for youthful and adult offenders. In W. S. Laufer & J. M. Day (Eds.), *Personality theory, moral development and criminal behavior.* Lexington, MA: Lexington.

Jones, M. (1953). *The therapeutic community.* New York: Basic.

Kahn, T. J., & Chambers, H. J. (1991). Assessing reoffense risk with juvenile sexual offenders. *Child Welfare, 70,* 333–345.

Kahn, T. J., & Lafond, M. A. (1988). Treatment of the adolescent sexual offender. *Child and Adolescent Social Work, 5,* 135–148.

Kazdin, A. E. (1987). *Conduct disorders in childhood and adolescence.* Newbury Park, CA: Sage.

Kazdin, A. E., Bass, C., Siegel, T., & Thomas, C. (1989). Cognitive-behavioral therapy and relationship therapy in the treatment of children referred for antisocial behavior. *Journal of Consulting and Clinical Psychology, 57,* 522–535.

Kelman, H. C., & Baron, R. M. (1968). Determinants of modes of resolving inconsistency dilemmas: A functional analysis. In R. P. Abelson, E. Aronson, W. J. McGuire, T. M. Newcomb, M. J. Rosenberg, & P. H. Tannenbaum (Eds.), *Theories of cognitive consistency: A sourcebook.* Chicago: Rand McNally.

Kohlberg, L. (1971). From *is* to *ought:* How to commit the naturalistic fallacy and get away with it in the study of moral development. In T. Mischel (Ed.), *Cognitive development and epistemology.* New York: Academic.

Kohlberg, L. (1984). *The psychology of moral development: Essays on moral development* (Vol. 2). San Francisco: Harper & Row.

Kohlberg, L., & Higgins, A. (1987). School democracy and social interaction. In W. M. Kurtines & J. L. Gewirtz (Eds.), *Moral development through social interaction.* New York: Wiley-Interscience.

Kunen, J. S. (1989, May). Madness in the heart of the city. *People,* pp. 107–111.

Leeman, L. W., Gibbs, J. C., & Fuller, D. (in press). Evaluation of a multi-component treatment program for juvenile delinquents. *Aggressive Behavior.*

Lickona, T. (1983). *Raising good children.* Toronto: Bantam.

Little, V. L., & Kendall, P. C. (1979). Cognitive-behavioral interventions with delinquents: Problem-solving, role-taking, and self-control. In P. C. Kendall & S. D. Hollon (Eds.), *Cognitive-behavioral interventions: Theory, research, and procedures.* New York: Academic.

Long, S. J., & Sherer, M. (1985). Social skills training with juvenile offenders. *Child and Family Behavior Therapy, 6,* 1–11.

Martin, F. P., & Osgood, D. W. (1987). Autonomy as a source of prosocial influence among incarcerated adolescents. *Journal of Applied Social Psychology, 17,* 97–108.

Mason, M. W., & Gibbs, J. C. (1993). Social perspective-taking and moral judgment among college students. *Journal of Adolescent Research, 8,* 109–123.

McCorkle, L., Elias, A., & Bixby, F. L. (1958). *The Highfields story.* New York: Holt.

Mead, G. H. (1934). *Mind, self, and society.* University of Chicago Press.

Miller, W. (1958). Lower class culture as a generating milieu of gang delinquency. *Journal of Social Issues, 14,* 5–19.

Mischel, W., & Mischel, H. N. (1976). A cognitive social-learning approach to morality and self-regulation. In T. Lickona (Ed.), *Moral development and behavior: Theory, research, and social issues.* New York: Holt, Rinehart & Winston.

Nelson, J. R., Smith, D. J., & Dodd, J. (1990). The moral reasoning of juvenile delinquents: A meta-analysis. *Journal of Abnormal Child Psychology, 18,* 231–239.

Niles, W. J. (1986). Effects of a moral development discussion group on delinquent and predelinquent boys. *Journal of Counseling Psychology, 33,* 45–51.

Osgood, D. W., Gruber, E., Archer, M. A., & Newcomb, T. M. (1985). Autonomy for inmates: Counterculture or cooptation? *Criminal Justice and Behavior, 12,* 71–89.

Page, R. A. (1981). Longitudinal evidence for the sequentiality of Kohlberg's stages of moral judgment in adolescent males. *Journal of Genetic Psychology, 139,* 3–9.

Piaget, J. (1965). *Moral judgment of the child* (M. Gabain, Trans.). New York: Free Press. (Original work published 1932)

Power, C., Higgins, A., & Kohlberg, L. (1989). *Lawrence Kohlberg's approach to moral education.* New York: Columbia University Press.

Prentice, D. S. (1990). Perspectives on research classics: Two routes to collective violence. *Contemporary Social Psychology, 14,* 217–218.

Quay, H. C. (Ed.). (1987). *Handbook of juvenile delinquency.* New York: Wiley.

Rokeach, M. (1968). *Beliefs, attitudes, and values: A theory of organization and change.* San Francisco: Jossey-Bass.

Samenow, S. E. (1984). *Inside the criminal mind.* New York: Random House.

Schnell, S. V. (1986). *Delinquents with mature moral reasoning: A comparison with delayed delinquents and mature nondelinquents.* Unpublished doctoral dissertation, The Ohio State University, Columbus.

Snarey, J. (1985). The cross-cultural universality of social-moral development: A critical review of Kohlbergian research. *Psychological Bulletin, 97,* 202–232.

Steele, C. M. (1988). The psychology of self-affirmation: Sustaining the integrity of the self. In L. Berkowitz (Ed.), *Advances in experimental social psychology.* New York: Academic.

Stone, M. (1989, August 14). What really happened in Central Park. *New York,* 30–43.

Sykes, G. M., & Matza, D. (1957). Techniques of neutralization: A theory of delinquency. *American Sociological Review, 22,* 664–670.

Trevethan, S. D., & Walker, L. J. (1989). Hypothetical versus real-life moral reasoning among psychopathic and delinquent youth. *Development and Psychopathology, 1,* 91–103.

Vorrath, H. H., & Brendtro, L. K. (1985). *Positive Peer Culture* (2nd ed.). New York: Aldine.

Walker, L. J. (1988). Moral reasoning. In R. Vasta (Ed.), *Annals of child development* (Vol. 5). Greenwich, CT: JAI.

Walker, L. J. (1989). A longitudinal study of moral reasoning. *Child Development, 60,* 157–166.

Wasmund, W. C. (1988). The social climates of peer group and other residential programs. *Child and Youth Care Quarterly, 17,* 146–155.

Yochelson, S., & Samenow, S. E. (1976). *The criminal personality: A profile for change* (Vol. 1). New York: Aronson.

Yochelson, S., & Samenow, S. E. (1977). *The criminal personality: The change process* (Vol. 2). New York: Aronson.

PART III

Contextual Interventions

CHAPTER 6

Family-Based Interventions

Arthur M. Horne

Chronic and serious conduct problems during childhood and early adolescence present a major and costly problem for society. The Federal Bureau of Investigation reported that in 1987 more than 1.4 million juveniles were arrested for nonindex crimes (vandalism, drug abuse, running away) and almost 900,000 were arrested for index crimes (larceny, theft, robbery, assault, rape). The cost to society includes not only the funds required for the repair and/or replacement of material goods and the provision of necessary health services to victims but also the $1 billion needed each year to maintain the juvenile justice system. And, of course, the number of antisocial acts committed by children and adolescents resulting in monetary loss and/or physical suffering far exceeds the number of reported crimes. It is estimated that about 4% of boys under 18 have diagnosable conduct disorders and that approximately two-thirds of them will continue to display antisocial behavior into adulthood (American Psychiatric Association, 1987).

Behaviors associated with conduct disorders involve frequent violation of family, school, and societal rules through such acts as lying, stealing, and physical aggression. Youths engaging in these behaviors frequently have concomitant problems, such as social incompetence, rejection by peers, academic failure, and other mental health disorders including substance abuse and suicidal behavior. They are also at increased risk for physical injury and even death. Thus, the extent of their problems challenges personal, family, school, and community resources. Furthermore, once such problem behaviors become chronic, they are quite resistant to intervention, as evidenced by the high rates of recidivism among juvenile delinquents despite incarceration or rehabilitation efforts (Goldstein, 1991; Patterson, 1982; Ulrici, 1983) and by the failure of adolescent treatment programs to maintain improvement in seriously antisocial behavior (Henggeler, 1989; Jones, Weinrott, & Howard, 1981; Kazdin, 1987a, 1987b; Patterson, DeBaryske, & Ramsey, 1989; Wilson & Herrnstein, 1985).

Attempts to intervene with conduct-disordered adolescents have had minimal success. Although certain treatment programs targeting early to late adolescents have shown some initial success, the follow-up results have been less encouraging (Jones et al., 1981; Kazdin, 1987a; Patterson et al., 1989; Wilson & Herrnstein, 1985). More effective interventions have been those targeting younger children and involving others significant in the child's life: parents, teachers, and some-times peers (Fleischman, Horne, & Arthur, 1983; Griest, Forehand, Wells, & McMahon, 1980; Horne & Sayger, 1990; Patterson, Reid, Jones, & Conger, 1975).

Although the picture looks rather discouraging for changing well-established patterns of antisocial behavior in older adolescents, research in the last decade has provided some grounds for optimism about our ability to *prevent* the develop-ment of full-blown chronic delinquency in youth. First, well-designed empirical studies have yielded information about the developmental progressions likely to result in chronic conduct disorder, as well as correlates of the developing disorder. The studies have also identified clear markers of high-risk status in children. Second, a number of researchers have demonstrated the efficacy of several inter-ventions with a family emphasis for making at least short-term changes in specific types of antisocial behavior.

THE DEVELOPMENT OF DELINQUENT BEHAVIOR

Various models explain the developmental progression of antisocial behavior in children and adolescents and demonstrate a clear family connection. Patterson and his colleagues (Patterson, 1986; Patterson et al., 1989), for example, have indi-cated that a child's temperament can interact with poor parental discipline practices to produce a coercive parent-child relationship. Children in such relationships develop conduct problems early, are rejected by their peers, experience academic failure because they spend significant time off task, and fail to learn normal pro-social behavior during the elementary school years. Excluded by normal peers, they turn to deviant peer groups in late childhood or early adolescence, typically beginning in about the fourth grade. Patterson et al. (1989) have noted a number of contextual variables that contribute to disrupted family management practices in the families of such children: intergenerational antisocial behavior; demographic variables such as ethnicity, socioeconomic status, and parental education; and family stressors such as marital conflict, divorce, and unemployment.

A second model predicting delinquency has been developed by Loeber (1982). He reports that children with high rates of antisocial behavior are more likely to persist in delinquent acts than children with initially lower rates. Once a high level of antisocial behavior has been established, an individual tends to maintain that level rather than moderating the behavior, at least until late adolescence or early adulthood. Social and family variables that serve as predictors of delinquency include poor parental supervision, lack of parent involvement, poor disciplinary methods, parental rejection, parental criminality and aggressiveness, marital prob-lems, parental absence, poor parental health, composite family handicaps, and low socioeconomic status. Additionally, Loeber suggests that chronic delinquents tend, as children, to have been antisocial in more than one setting, shown a consider-able variety of antisocial behaviors, and acquired such behaviors at an early age.

Elliott, Huizinga, and Ageton (1985) have added to this developmental sequence the theory that children who have experienced strain and inadequate socialization through ineffective parent-child interactions fail to assimilate conventional behavioral norms and societal expectations. During early adolescence, when the peer group becomes a focal point of development, these youngsters reject societal norms and begin to associate with a deviant peer group. This deviant group provides a subculture in which antisocial behavior is socially accepted and reinforced and conventional social behavior is punished (Buehler, Patterson, & Furniss, 1966).

A Conceptual Framework

A conceptual framework for the development of delinquent behavior within a family context has been developed by Horne, Forehand, Frame, and Norsworthy (1990). This framework, described by Horne (1991), is shown in Figure 6.1.

The time line in the center of the illustration represents the developmental progression from birth through early and middle childhood and finally to adolescence. Above the time line is a flowchart of developmental steps that may lead to delinquency.

The Developmental Progression

The first component contributing to the development of delinquency is the child's inborn genetic and cognitive temperament. Innate predispositions, cognitive abilities, and temperament may lead directly to conduct problems, as children who are fussy or irritable are more difficult for parents to manage. This is particularly true for families that are headed by single parents, have inadequate income, or have few available resources (child care, health services, family support, etc.) for attending to the child. The child's temperament can also contribute to the development of a coercive parent-child interaction pattern. Children who are difficult at birth are perceived less positively by their parents; when this happens, parents and children are likely to develop a contentious rather than cooperative relationship.

When positive relationships fail to develop at the child's birth and in early childhood, there is a weakness in conventional bonding as well. In the absence of a bonding process through which the child comes to feel loved and cared for and develops self-esteem, the development of behavioral problems is accelerated. The child behaves in a way consistent with his or her perceived sense of self.

A pattern of coercive parent-child interaction established early and accompanied by weak conventional bonding within the family frequently results in a number of conduct problems. The child is likely to be oppositional, aggressive, hyperactive, and in general very difficult for adults to manage. Escalating coercive family interactions, as described by Patterson (1982), lead to frequent aggression, anger, and, at times, abusive behavior.

The child who has experienced coercive relations with parents and weak conventional bonding within the family, and who demonstrates conduct problems, generally fails to develop adequate social competence and is rejected by peers. In other words, the child who has low self-esteem, engages in escalating coercive

Figure 6.1 Conceptual Framework for Development and Prevention of Serious Conduct Disorders in Children

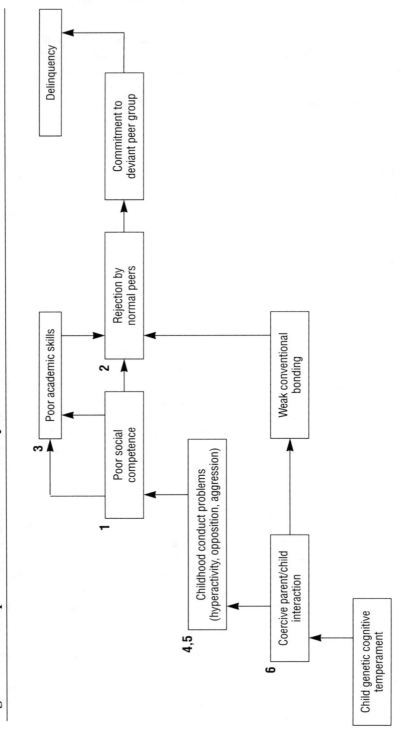

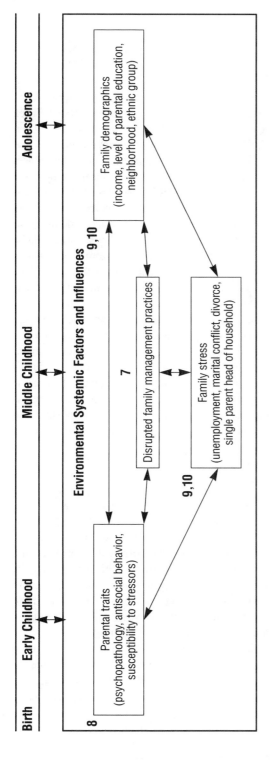

Birth — **Early Childhood** — **Middle Childhood** — **Adolescence**

Environmental Systemic Factors and Influences

8

Parental traits
(psychopathology, antisocial behavior,
susceptibility to stressors)

7

Disrupted family management practices

9,10

Family stress
(unemployment, marital conflict, divorce,
single parent head of household)

9,10

Family demographics
(income, level of parental education,
neighborhood, ethnic group)

Potential Interventions

1. Social competence enhancement (four levels)
2. Peer counseling
3. Academic remediation
4. Behavioral self-control strategies
5. Training teachers/educators in behavior management strategies
6. Parent training in child management skills
7. Social learning family therapy
8. Parent individual therapy
9. Couple/single parent counseling
10. Parent education/career–vocational/financial

Note. From "Social Learning Family Therapy" by A. M. Horne. In *Family Counseling and Therapy* (2nd ed., p. 481) edited by A. H. Horne and J. L. Passmore, 1991, Itasca, IL: Peacock. Copyright 1991 by Peacock Publishing Company. Adapted by permission.

patterns of behavior, lacks the ability to share and to understand others' perspectives, and cannot interact with others in socially acceptable ways will be ignored, ostracized, and directly rejected by normal peers.

A further exacerbating factor often accompanying the behavioral repertoire described is deficiency in academic skills. It is commonly believed that children develop behavior problems because they lack academic skills, but Cornwall and Bowden (1990) have reported the opposite: that antisocial behavior predates academic underachievement and that children who demonstrate conduct disorders and oppositional or defiant behaviors generally did so before entering school and before developing academic problems. Further, Griffin (1987) found that poor academic performance was a major factor related to violent and aggressive behaviors in adolescence. Although some researchers report that addressing academic problems will result in amelioration of problem behavior (MacMillan & Kavale, 1986), others have found that antisocial behavior does not necessarily diminish with academic remediation (Wilson & Herrnstein, 1985) and that attention to other skills— such as self-control for the young person, classroom management for the teacher, and child management for the parent—may be necessary.

The combination of temperament, parent-child interaction, poor bonding, problem behavior, inadequate social competence, academic failure, and peer rejection frequently leads a child with antisocial behaviors to develop a commitment to a deviant peer group, the gang. This participation in gang activities contributes to delinquency, the highest level of antisocial behavior represented in Figure 6.1.

This account, like the flowchart in Figure 6.1, has outlined a linear progression of the development of delinquent behavior from the child's point of view. The following are environmental systemic factors (shown below the time line in Figure 6.1) that contribute to this development.

Systemic Factors

Family characteristics have been well documented in studies of factors contributing to delinquency in young people (see Goldstein, 1991, and Horne & Sayger, 1990, for a review of relevant research). These factors include parental psychopathology and antisocial behavior. For instance, it has been well documented that children who suffer abuse most often are reared by parents who themselves were abused as children. Also, many parents become psychologically and emotionally unavailable to their children through drug and alcohol abuse. The combination of parental substance abuse and personality characteristics may result in poor parenting practices, abusive interactions, and escalating aggression.

Families with aggressive children are characterized by a high level of family stress. This may be the product of unemployment, marital conflict, divorce, or single parenthood, among other things. Parents experiencing chronic stress frequently turn to alcohol or drugs in an attempt at stress management. The likely result is inept parenting.

A further influence on a child's development and behavior patterns is family demographics. The parents' income and educational level are strongly linked to antisocial behavior in the child. The family's neighborhood and ethnic group likewise can help determine whether aggression develops and what form it will take if it does.

Parental traits, family stress, and demographic factors can interfere with effective family management practices. When the family system is disrupted—whether temporarily or chronically—the effect on the child can be dramatic. The environmental systemic factors just enumerated interact with the child's own developmental stages. Figure 6.2 presents a three-dimensional model that suggests the potency of this interaction.

OVERVIEW OF FAMILY-BASED INTERVENTIONS

A myriad of models have been developed for the treatment of delinquent behavior, though few models have emphasized family treatment. Indeed, many models from mainstream therapy that have been proposed for use with delinquency are decidedly not family oriented. An analytic model, for example, primarily emphasizes helping the individual develop responsible behavior by addressing early trauma; a component of treatment is transference, which is not compatible with a family emphasis. Other models, such as Adlerian therapy, have acknowledged the importance of the family in the development and treatment of problem behavior, but interventions most often have focused on helping the individual learn to understand the family of origin, the family life-style, and the roles of family members, as well as the private logic the individual uses to maintain his or her role and function within the family. Other models of therapy, such as Gestalt, rational-emotive, and person-centered, have generally been individual oriented as well. A number of other approaches, such as group therapy, detention, and incarceration, place the family in a tangential or minor role with respect to treatment.

Two major models of family intervention have been developed, applied, and evaluated for effectiveness in the treatment of delinquent behavior. Both models have been applied extensively with aggressive children in the family context. The first model, structural family therapy, was influenced by Salvadore Minuchin and his colleagues. The second, social learning family therapy, was influenced by Gerald Patterson and members of the Oregon Social Learning Center.

Structural Family Therapy

Salvadore Minuchin is a psychiatrist who worked at the Wiltwyck School for Boys, a correctional institution for young delinquents in the state of New York in the 1960s; later, he served as director of supervision and training in family therapy at the Philadelphia Child Guidance Center. At Wiltwyck the typical client was described as "the ghetto-living, urban, minority group member who is experiencing poverty, discrimination, fear, crowdedness, and streetliving" (Minuchin, Montalvo, Guerney, Rosman, & Schumer, 1967, p. 22). Minuchin et al. indicated that the clients' life-styles could be explained largely by social class variables:

Figure 6.2 Development of Conduct Disorders in Children

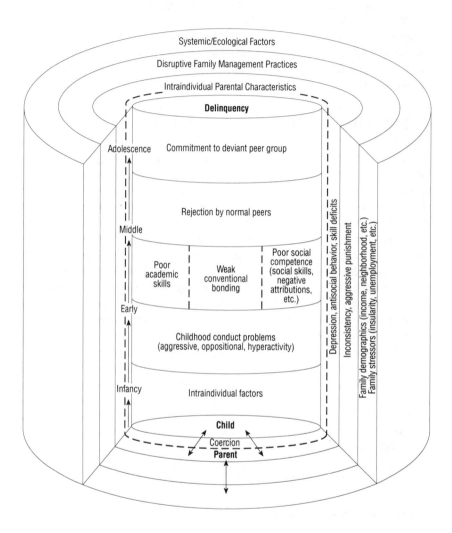

Note. From "Social Learning Family Therapy" by A. M. Horne. In *Family Counseling and Therapy* (2nd ed., p. 483) edited by A. H. Horne and J. L. Passmore, 1991, Itasca, IL: Peacock. Copyright 1991 by Peacock Publishing Company. Adapted by permission.

Action-excitement orientation, special styles of communication, limited number of usable roles, etc., seem to characterize low-income groups in a wide variety of social settings, and there is every reason to believe that ethnic and racial factors do not account for these characteristics, but that social class variables do. (p. 24)

The Wiltwyck treatment team, working from an initial position of lack of knowledge or training concerning this particular population, developed their own interventions and explanations for what worked. Their intervention process, structural family therapy, was described in *Families of the Slums.*

In the structural family therapy model, the emphasis is not on education or direct teaching but on restructuring the family. Several patterns characterize dysfunctional families: the disengaged, the enmeshed, the family with the peripheral male, the family with noninvolved parents, and the family with juvenile parents (Colapinto, 1991). Often more than one pattern may be present in a given family; the two most common patterns are the disengaged and the enmeshed.

Within families, patterns are defined by boundaries set for the family system (all members involved in the family) and for the family subsystems (the married subsystem, the parent subsystem, the sibling subsystem, etc.). The permeability of boundaries refers to the access to the family system or subsystems within the family. In some families, boundaries are quite permeable and allow for ready access to the family by societal influences (work, friends, school) or across subsystems by family members. Family boundaries may be very rigid and impermeable, providing for little external influence on the family or across family subsystems.

Minuchin (1981) has indicated that families may function anywhere along an axis, with one end having very closed, impermeable boundaries in which family members have very little contact with one another and operate as a collection of autonomous individuals rather than as an integrative and interactive family. Emotional distance among family members is great, and family members are generally emotionally and physically disengaged. At the other end of the continuum of the axis are families with highly diffused, permeable boundaries. Families with highly permeable boundaries among subsystems are referred to as enmeshed; there is excessive closeness among family members. With the enmeshed family, members are overinvolved with one another and subsystems are not clearly defined. This results in family members' not developing autonomy and personal responsibility. In disengaged and enmeshed families, the individual's symptoms serve to maintain the family structure for other family members, who need the symptom bearer to behave as he or she does to maintain equilibrium.

Delinquent behavior may evolve from either end of the continuum. With disengaged families, family members frequently have very little contact and leave one another to their own resources. Adolescents needing more involvement and leadership and more help with problems, are likely to reach out of the family to fulfill growth needs for support and involvement. The peer group frequently fills these needs, and those youths who turn to delinquent peers are highly influenced by them. Within the enmeshed family, characterized by high involvement with other family members and a lack of autonomy and privacy, adolescents frequently reach out to the peer group to find respite from family involvement.

A number of techniques have been developed specifically for working with families from a structural perspective. One of these, *joining,* involves a number of steps for joining with the family as they enter therapy. Through joining, the therapist aims to become accepted, temporarily, as a member of the family. This gives the therapist the right to confront and eventually challenge each family member.

The *family map* is a device for indicating

> the position of family members vis-à-vis one another. It reveals coalitions, affiliations, explicit and implicit conflicts, and the ways family members group themselves in conflict resolution. Maps identify family members who operate as detourers of conflict and family members who function as switchboards. The map charts the nurturers, healers, and scapegoaters. Its delineation of the boundaries between subsystems indicates what movement there is and suggests possible areas of strength or dysfunction. (Minuchin & Fishman, 1981, p. 69)

Another technique, *enactments,* entails having family members engage in scenarios, activities in which they try to address family problems. As they do, the therapist studies strengths and weaknesses to see how effective each member is at dealing with family stress. Minuchin uses enactment to *search for strength,* a technique for identifying competent behaviors as a way of defining the family. To illustrate the search for strength, Minuchin describes a critical mother who voices negative and judgmental evaluations of her children. Rather than being critical of the mother for her critical statements of the children, which indicated that the children refused to behave and stubbornly "did their own thing," the therapist presented the mother's statements as an indication of her ability to discern differences and respect developmental stages: "The mother's description is highly differentiated; she is clearly a sensitive person who is observant of the children's individual developmental processes" (Minuchin & Fishman, 1981, p. 106). Seeking strength even in characteristics frequently perceived as negative is a way of restructuring definitions of the family.

The technique of *reframing* involves defining the problem from a different perspective. The goal is to shift the focus from the symptom-bearing child to the transactional difficulties of the family. Rather than asking how the child behaves in a particular situation, the therapist would ask how the family managed their disagreements, clearly indicating that the problem resides not within the child but within the family interaction pattern.

Connectedness is a technique to pull disengaged families closer together. Exercises require family members to explore their interconnections. The opposite technique, *differentiation,* is designed for enmeshed families. The therapist uses activities to help family members become more individuated and separate.

Effectiveness of Structural Family Therapy

Structural family therapy began by addressing family issues surrounding delinquent youths. It has a long history of application in treatment of inner-city, low-income families characterized by aggressive behavior. The model does not lend itself well to empirical research, however, for the subject of evaluation has been family structural change rather than specific individual behaviors such as delinquency. Aponte and VanDeusen (1981) have summarized the research on the application of structural family therapy with families of delinquents. They report that the therapy was effective in more than half the cases and that, when the conventional therapy of the Wiltwyck Center was used as a control, roughly 50 to 55% of the families undergoing structural therapy had gains surpassing those of families experiencing conventional therapy. The families experiencing success were those characterized as enmeshed; however, families defined as disengaged failed to improve through therapy.

Structural family therapy and related family interventions, such as strategic family therapy, hold considerable promise for families with aggressive children. To date, however, the research support has not been sufficient to permit unqualified endorsement. Structural family therapy necessitates in-depth training and supervision. Its broader application will require more expertise than is currently available in most community agencies. Given the shortage of adequately trained therapists and the current lack of empirical support, structural family therapy is promising but not fully endorsed as a model for intervention.

Parent Education/Training

Of the intervention models that adopt a family focus in addressing delinquent and aggressive behavior, the one most extensively developed and studied is probably that of Gerald Patterson and his associates. On the basis of social learning theory, they have studied aggressive children in the family context for approximately three decades.

The 1950s and 1960s saw a growing interest in the application of social learning theory concepts—which had demonstrable relevance for individuals—to family situations (Bandura, 1969). During the 1950s almost two-thirds of all referrals of children to community mental health services were related to behavior problems (Roach, 1958), but only a small fraction of those referred actually received service (Bahm, Chandler, & Eisenburg, 1961). Those who were served generally received individual, traditional therapy, which provided little or no benefit to socially aggressive children (Levitt, 1971).

In the early 1960s, Gerald Patterson at the Oregon Social Learning Center began applying social learning concepts to aggressive children within a family context. Patterson's work comprised three stages for the therapist: (a) learning the concepts of behavioral theory, (b) learning to define deviant behavior and monitoring and recording its occurrence, and (c) learning to modify one or two of the child's problematic behaviors (Patterson et al., 1975). Movement from one stage to the next was contingent on successful completion of the preceding stage. Patterson's early work included use of basic point systems and instruction in modeling, contingent attention, and effective disciplinary techniques (Patterson et al., 1975).

Patterson developed a large-scale project in which 27 families with aggressive sons were treated. The treatment achieved at least a 30% reduction in aggressive behavior among two-thirds of the boys, and parents reported a 50% reduction in the occurrence of conduct problems of concern to them. The gains had been maintained at a 1-year follow-up of the families. At that time, positive results had also generalized to other children in the family; this finding indicated that parents were able to generalize their learnings (Arnold, Levine, & Patterson, 1975).

Following up on Patterson's 27-family study, members of the Oregon Social Learning Center conducted a series of studies leading to refinements in the treatment program. Their work incorporated research control measures needed for comparative clinical research. The results further demonstrated the effectiveness of behavioral parent training approaches (Walter & Gilmore, 1973; Wiltz & Patterson, 1974), and replication studies (Fleischman, 1981; Fleischman & Horne, 1979; Patterson & Reid, 1973) provided support for the model.

In related work at the University of Georgia, under the direction of Rex Forehand, a decade-long social learning parent training program involved more than 100 families with children who had noncompliance and other behavior problems. Forehand's work demonstrated (a) that parent training programs effectively modify selected parental behaviors and address noncompliance in clinic settings (Forehand & King, 1977); (b) that these changes generalize over time and to other settings, behaviors, and children (Wells, Forehand, & Griest, 1980); and (c) that teaching parents self-control techniques and social learning principles helps them generalize effective behaviors (McMahon, Forehand, & Griest, 1981). The long-term effectiveness of the treatment was documented by Baum and Forehand (1981), who found that posttreatment gains had been maintained 4½ years following treatment.

Although the parent training work was demonstrably effective for reducing *noncompliant* behavior in children, there were some shortcomings in terms of failure to generalize and to maintain treatment gains to other behavior problem areas. Further, there was difficulty in engaging family members in treatment and follow-up, and findings of the research center were not always generalizable to the natural settings: Aggressive behaviors occurring in the home and school settings were not always reduced as a result of intervention, and reductions in such behavior were not always maintained over time (Forehand & Long, 1991). This was particularly true when other factors, such as marital discord, economic crises, and related issues, interfered.

Griest and Wells (1983) stated, "It is only recently that the treatment vehicle in parent training has been identified as potentially requiring intervention in areas other than child-management skills" (p. 38). They recommended that therapy incorporate attention to additional components, including the parents' cognitive functioning, their physiological status, their marital circumstances and conflict, and social variables.

In the last decade, a series of studies have examined what happens when social learning family therapy addresses the additional variables highlighted by Griest and Wells. Griest et al. (1980), for example, found that the mother's personal adjustment was predictive of whether the child would be referred for treatment and that modifying the mother's perceptions should be a treatment goal. The importance of treating parental perceptions was also underscored by Morris et al. (1988), who found that fathers of aggressive boys (in comparison with fathers of nonaggressive boys) had significantly more negative thoughts toward their sons and reported more negative and fewer positive thoughts about their children and families.

Problem solving is another area that has been incorporated into social learning family therapy. Morris et al. (1988) found that fathers of well-behaved boys were more efficient problem solvers and more frequently modeled behavior designed to reach agreeable problem solutions than did fathers of aggressive boys.

Parental psychological variables and level of marital conflict have also proven important in social learning family therapy. Mothers of conduct-disordered children show higher levels of depression and anxiety than do mothers of normal children (Griest et al., 1980). Further, there is clearly a relationship between parents' marital problems and children's behavior problems (Johnson & Lobitz, 1974). This relationship can take different forms: Clinicians and researchers often assume that, when a relationship exists between marital discord and child behavior problems, the marital strife causes the conduct problems. In fact, the opposite may be true: The presence in the family of a conduct-disordered child may precipitate marital adjustment problems.

Social Learning Family Therapy

As social learning treatment interventions have become more responsive to additional factors (marital discord, parent cognitions and perceptions, social status variables), there has been a shift from parent training to family therapy. The goal has been to move from a simplistic educational model to a more sophisticated psychosocial educational model incorporating methods that address the family environment and the interactional patterns that create and maintain coercive relationships. Horne and Sayger (1990), having reviewed social learning treatment programs, list the following requirements for an effective social learning family therapy intervention:

1. Assessment must provide clear definitions of problem areas and identify treatment goals that correspond to the problems presented by the family.

2. There should be involvement with multiple systems, including parents, siblings, school personnel, and others.

3. Positive expectations for change should be established, and therapists should be skilled in interventions that will impact the environment.

4. Family members should learn effective problem-solving and self-control skills, which will provide parents and children with an alternative repertoire of stress- and conflict-management tools.

5. Disciplinary methods that are appropriate for all family members should be established.

6. Prosocial behaviors for children and parents should be a focal point of the intervention.

7. Provisions should be in place for intervening in other systems, including counseling for the extended family, training and other assistance for teachers and other school personnel, and consultation to community agencies.

8. All family members should learn skills for maintaining positive changes.

Evident in this list are the basic procedures of social learning family therapy. These include identifying and addressing the behavior(s) of persons involved, their cognitions or perceptual viewpoints, and the environmental circumstances that precede, maintain, and will contribute to changing behavior and consequences. Social learning theory assumes an interaction among people's behaviors, cognitions, and environment, an interaction that leads to the development and maintenance of family patterns. If therapy is to be effective, each of the components must be assessed and addressed.

A number of therapeutic programs fulfill the requirements outlined. They include programs developed by Patterson et al. (1975); Patterson and Forgatch (1987); Forgatch and Patterson (1989); Fleischman, Horne, and Arthur (1983); Forehand and McMahon (1981); Horne and Sayger (1990); and Blechman (1985). Following is a brief description of a social learning family therapy model specifically developed for families that have children with a high rate of aggressive behavior (Fleischman et al., 1983; Horne & Sayger, 1990).

Assessing Family Interaction

The first phase of social learning family therapy involves assessing current family interaction patterns. A variety of assessment procedures may be used; they frequently include in-home observations or structured interactions in the clinic setting that give the therapist insight into the antecedents and consequences of conflicts within the family. It is assumed that family stress situations or problems are not linear in their development, but rather that reciprocal relationships exist: For instance, one family member engages in behaviors that another perceives as aversive; this leads to a retaliatory behavior, which then contributes to an ongoing conflict that escalates and finds an outlet in extreme emotional or physical abuse.

In addition to observation of problem situations, assessment tools may include paper-and-pencil measures. Other assessment procedures may focus on the child, the parents, other family members such as siblings or grandparents who live in the home, teachers, and other important individuals. A number of authors (see Horne & Sayger, 1990) have described specific assessment procedures; the important point is that the assessment methods should be relevant to the presenting problem(s).

Initiating Treatment

Following assessment, the therapist initiates treatment with the family by establishing a therapeutic climate. This is frequently a difficult point because many families are not present voluntarily: The therapy may be court ordered or mandated by child protective services or another similar agency. Dealing with client resistance is crucial in social learning family therapy. It involves developing an alliance with the clients while using the social system to apply pressure for participation. Techniques for developing a therapeutic climate include normalizing problems rather than focusing on pathology, defining all family members as victims, and arriving at a therapy agenda that is relevant to all family members.

During the initiation stage, therapist and clients explore how individual family members perceive the family problems, what they do, how they think, and what they feel about the situation. The therapist characterizes the problems as family interaction patterns rather than as pathology. At this time the therapist also begins establishing contact with other agencies that are involved with the family. These may include the school, the juvenile justice system, welfare or child protective agencies, and other related organizations. The goal is to coordinate services and to keep other agencies informed about the type of intervention so that there is consistency in approaches.

Preparing for Success

The second stage of intervention is called "preparing for success." The family is helped to establish goals for change. The goals should be clear, and progress should be observable and able to be tracked or documented. A goal-setting form is used to make this step easier; ideal, acceptable, and unacceptable levels of behavior are specified on the form.

During this phase of treatment, family members are taught a number of specific skills, including the following:

1. *Rearranging the environment.* Are there things the family can do to prevent problems? These can range from moving a stereo to a higher shelf so young children can't reach the controls to helping an adolescent prepare a place to do homework.

2. *Developing consistent routines.* One quality that aggression-prone, dysfunctional families lack is consistency in family routines. Developing routines is a skill that most functional families understand but that needs to be taught to dysfunctional families.

3. *Making clear, polite statements.* Teaching parents to issue statements in a clear and polite manner is often difficult, particularly in families where anger and aggression are common and coercion is the norm. Teaching parents to treat their children and each other with respect and dignity is a very important but frequently very difficult task.

4. *Teaching new skills.* Often, children in dysfunctional families have never been taught the skills that are expected of them. Helping parents learn to present expectations in a concrete, clear manner and then to be consistent and persistent about performance is very important.

5. *Improving coordination between parents.* Children are expert at working parents against each other, particularly in situations of divorce or separation. Helping parents work toward coordinating their parenting styles, or at least not undercutting each other, is both possible and necessary for good progress.

6. *Strengthening marital ties if there is a marital relationship.* Helping the couple identify marital strengths and improve their relationship will help them coordinate parenting efforts and lead to a more enjoyable family environment. At this point in therapy redirection often occurs, and marital therapy becomes the focus for a time.

7. *Encouraging parental growth and well-being.* Wahler (1980) has determined that parents who are not doing well emotionally, physically, and socially are less likely to make and maintain positive change. Accordingly, facilitating change within the family requires attending to the growth and well-being of the parent. This attention may address a variety of needs, such as identifying vocational opportunities, overcoming substance abuse problems, managing family relationships better, and dealing more effectively with community agencies.

8. *Addressing fairness.* Children who are aggressive report as a prime concern that family members are not fair and that they, the children, are not treated the way they are expected to treat their parents. Although this perception generally is not accurate—there is reciprocity in family fairness—it is true that decisions frequently are based not on the notion of fairness but on the use of power and coercion.

Teaching Self-Control

A generalization that may be made about families with delinquent and aggressive children is that there is a general lack of emotional and behavioral self-control. As family members begin to change their pattern of interaction by using new skills, they are taught effective self-control techniques.

Instruction in self-control skills for the younger people is modeled on the Turtle Technique developed by Schneider and Robin (1976). Children are told a story about a turtle who formerly always got in trouble but then learned effective problem-solving and relaxation skills from a wise old tortoise. The instruction can take from one session to several weeks, depending upon the child's age and skill level.

For parents, self-control skills instruction takes a different direction. If their intellectual skills and level of understanding permit, they may learn a basic question drill for assessing the problem and doing something different: What is your goal? What are you doing now? Is what you are doing helping you to achieve your goal? If not, what could you be doing differently? This drill is followed by the therapist's providing relaxation training and giving parents permission to leave the conflict scene. For family members who can discuss cognitive beliefs and perceptions, a modified form of rational-emotive therapy is offered. They are taught ways of examining irrational beliefs (e.g., "This child is driving me crazy with fighting . . . he's just doing it because he's got the devil in him and he's an evil person") and developing alternative statements that will defuse the conflict ("I don't like what he's doing, but I can stand it because I'm getting help in learning how to manage his behavior more effectively. . . . He's learned to be the way he is, and we can teach him new ways of behaving"). During self-control instruction, parents also learn to use positive imagery, relaxation techniques, and positive problem-solving steps.

Introducing Appropriate Discipline

Once family members learn self-control skills, they are ready to move on to the next step, effective discipline. The disciplinary methods introduced are selected to fit the problems presented by the family. All family members are involved in each step of the learning process. Following are the most common forms of discipline taught:

Ignoring

This technique helps parents address minor problems such as whining and other attention-getting or annoying behaviors. It is not a good approach in dangerous situations or for parents who are unlikely to be able to carry it through.

Grandma's Law

This highly effective method simply requires that one complete a less pleasant activity before proceeding to a more pleasant one: "You may watch TV when you have finished your homework" or "Eat your peas—then you may have your dessert." The goal, as grandmothers have always known, is to make the anticipated behavior (watching television, eating dessert) contingent upon completion of the less favored one (doing homework, eating peas). Most families with aggressive children know Grandma's Law but reverse the process, allowing the positive experience before the negative: "OK, watch TV for a while, but then you've got to do your homework" or "OK, you can have your dessert now, but next time you have to eat your peas."

Natural and logical consequences

Allowing children to experience natural and logical consequences can be a very powerful teaching technique. Natural consequences are results that happen naturally, without human intervention. When a parent warns a child not to touch a hot stove and the child touches it, the child naturally gets burned. If the parent tells the child to wear a coat on a cold day and the child refuses, she naturally gets cold. A logical consequence, on the other hand, does not occur naturally but is rather a result of a rule or a guideline. For example, a student who fails to study may do poorly on an examination; a child who does not cooperate may be refused permission to do something he wants to do. For this method of discipline, the "punishment" should always fit the "crime."

Time-out

Time-out is a special type of logical consequence applied when a child fails to comply. Time-out removes the child from a reinforcing or pleasurable activity; it is not meant as a punishment. The break in activity is generally very brief: "You did not do what I asked, and so you are to take 5 minutes time-out, now. When you are through, come back and I'll expect you to do what was asked." Time-out means placing the child in a safe, nonreinforcing room or location. The child's bedroom, with toys and games, would not be appropriate. A longer time-out period would likewise not be effective; the child might spend the time being angry and considering ways of seeking revenge.

The time-out technique is based partly on the fact that people generally enjoy spending time in the company of others. If that were not the case in a particular family, the technique would be less effective. This problem would be recognized during the selection of discipline methods.

Extra chores

The imposition of extra chores is another, more intensive form of logical consequence to be used when other methods such as time-out do not work. When the behavior problems are manifested at school, for example, and time-out would not be appropriate, extra chores tailored to the problem behavior can be an effective consequence.

Loss of privileges

This form of logical consequence calls for removing a privilege that the child enjoys—for example, watching television, participating in activities, or going out on weekends. This method is particularly useful as a backup for other approaches that may not work. When time-out is ignored, for example, and the parent needs a more powerful intervention, removing privileges is very helpful.

Developing positive family interactions

When the family has mastered new disciplinary methods, the next step commonly is to teach them how to establish and maintain effective family interactions. The family learns ways of reinforcing appropriate behavior or "catching the child being good." Like other aspects of the intervention, this process is adapted to developmental levels and types of dysfunction within the family. Various formal reward procedures are effective for reinforcing behavior:

- *Point systems.* Point systems are used for charting and graphing behaviors, sometimes with the aid of colorful, amusing stickers. Accumulation of points is linked to a tangible reinforcer such as a sum of money, a favorite food, or a preferred activity.

- *Allowances.* An allowance system appropriate for somewhat older children is a more advanced form of point system: Each week the child earns the allowance for doing what was agreed upon by the family. Money is a very powerful reinforcer.

- *Contracts.* In contracting, parents and children draw up a contract together. Family members agree to cooperate on tasks and to show confidence in and respect for one another in the process.

Beyond formal procedures, some powerful informal methods, called social interactions or social reinforcers, can help create a more positive environment in the home. Following are some examples:

- *Verbal attending.* Verbal attending is spending time with and listening to others. Very often family members, parents in particular, ignore or attend in a very condescending manner to the others, especially children. Verbal attending means showing appreciation for and interest in what other family members say.

- *Nonverbal attending.* James (1987), investigating patterns of physical touching among family members, observed about the same numbers of "touches" within functional and dysfunctional families. There were significant differences between the two groups, however, in the ways in which family members touched. Functional families touched in affectionate and supportive ways, whereas dysfunctional families used touch as a means of control and discipline. Teaching family members positive nonverbal attending skills—constructive ways of touching—can help change interaction patterns.

Teaching Active Listening

A number of programs are available for developing active listening skills. Members of dysfunctional families often lack these skills and generally cannot attend to the content and affect being communicated by the others. In reviewing a decade's studies from the Family Therapy Research Project at Indiana State University, Horne and Sayger (1990) noted that active listening skills were either absent or not demonstrated in the majority of dysfunctional families studied. Functional families used active listening: Members were able to identify the content and affect of one another's spoken communications, and they could repeat the information to the speaker. They also conveyed praise, encouragement, humor, and support in their statements to other family members. In dysfunctional families, on the other hand, members were unable to identify the content and affect of what the others said, frequently spoke over the discourse of others, and conveyed criticism, sarcasm, and complaints in their responses.

Social learning family therapy generally begins by addressing family problems that occur within the home, such as fighting among siblings, noncompliance, lying, and property destruction. Parents have difficulty applying behavior management procedures effectively outside the home if they have not first attended to problems at home. Once parents have successfully addressed family problems in the home setting, though, the treatment focus should move to problems outside the home, such as conflicts at school or in the neighborhood. When positive family functioning has been attained at home, parents can be more effective with their children in most other situations. It is important to build in training for generalizing and maintaining change.

All stages in the social learning family therapy process should include a number of essential steps. First, the therapist should outline the procedures clearly and explain why they will be important. Then the procedures should be modeled, preferably with the involvement of all family members. Modeling should be followed by in-session behavioral rehearsals so that all family members will know the procedures and be adept at using them. The therapist should ask the family to anticipate potential problems: "We have covered the use of natural and logical consequences. You've agreed to use the process this week. Now tell me, what do you think could come up that would prevent you from following through? Are there situations that may occur that will stop you from doing this?" If likely problems are identified, the therapist and the family should discuss ways of dealing with them. Another important step is to address the children's concerns, for they frequently believe they are being singled out to do all of the work. Finally, the therapist should alert family members to problems or concerns that may affect their participation in treatment: "You know, this week we can expect Bill's behavior to get worse rather than better—that generally happens when we introduce a new discipline method like natural and logical consequences."

The components of this version of social learning family therapy may be offered in a variety of ways. The specific problems to be addressed—which vary considerably from family to family—must be determined at intake. The order of what is taught likewise depends on the family's needs. For some families, marital therapy will be the first consideration. Other families will need immediate attention to disciplinary steps. Still others may need to detour entirely to address concerns not covered here, such as alcohol or drug dependency, which must be met before other aspects of treatment are begun.

Functional Family Therapy

Functional family therapy (FFT; Alexander & Parsons, 1982; Barton & Alexander, 1981) is an integrative family intervention model with a background and developmental history in behavioral and social learning approaches, but with a systemic perspective on the function of behavior within the family structure. It incorporates the best of social learning family therapy and systemic approaches to family treatment. In recent years the model has expanded to include a cognitive component that allows therapists to address the individual and the family from behavioral, cognitive, and systemic perspectives. Behaviors are seen as having roles and functions for the individual, but problems are also viewed in terms of the functions they serve in the family system. Childhood behavior problems, then, are seen as fulfilling interpersonal functions, such as intimacy and distancing, within the family. A goal of functional family therapy, therefore, is to teach more effective communication patterns so that families can function in more adaptive ways.

The functional family therapist attempts to determine the function of a behavior; whether it causes family members to move closer together (merging), to move farther apart (separating), or to be at a midpoint where both merging and separating are possible. The therapist attends to behaviors, cognitions, and the functional role of each person in the family system.

As the therapist works with the family, several goals emerge. First, the therapist tries to clarify the meaning of each family member's behavior within the context of the observed interactions. Second, he or she tries to relabel behaviors to help family members understand how their behaviors function within the system. Third, to clarify interactions and relationships, the therapist helps family members see the interdependence of their behaviors and emotions.

To help families address their issues, functional family therapists provide specific activities and exercises that family members can use to help fulfill the functions of problem behaviors (e.g., to separate or to merge) but in a more effective and less conflictual way. The therapist and the family work to understand where each person is on the merge-and-separate continuum, and family members learn to negotiate ways of fulfilling the needs. In one family, for example, a daughter wanted to be less intimate and to differentiate from the family; at the same time the father sought to continue engaging in father-daughter activities. The therapist helped them adapt an activity they had shared for years, fishing together from a boat on a lake. Father and daughter changed their fishing practice to become trout fishers, starting several miles apart on the river and working toward each other. The overall companionship of the activity satisfied the father, while the separateness of place allowed for individuation on the part of the daughter.

Alexander (1988) has thoroughly examined the skills therapists need in order to use the FFT model effectively. The therapist must possess the qualities and relationship skills essential to therapy in general (empathy, warmth, genuineness, concreteness, congruence, humor, self-disclosure) but also must have good structuring skills (clarity, directiveness). According to Alexander, the steps in therapeutic intervention include introducing the therapy to the family, assessing family

interactions and the purposes of behaviors, motivating family members to participate in change, developing specific behavior change interventions, and terminating
therapy. The focus is on increasing positive interactions among family members:
The therapist helps them specify behaviors they desire from one another, negotiate
changes sought, and develop solutions to interpersonal problems. Family members
learn to reinforce one another for changes that occur within the family. Most of
the work is done in the clinic setting, where the therapist can intervene directly
to change communication patterns.

Alexander's (1988) research has focused on two matters, understanding functional and dysfunctional families and applying functional family therapy methods
to help dysfunctional families become healthier. Regarding the first matter, Alexander has shown that there are considerable differences in the ways families interact. For instance, in families with delinquent or aggressive teenagers, there is a
less egalitarian distribution of conversational time, whereas adaptive families with
adolescents share conversation more democratically. Adaptive families are supportive, whereas families with delinquents are less supportive and more blaming
and defensive. Adaptive families work together to develop cohesion and cooperation, whereas dysfunctional families work to dismantle the family structure. The
goal of functional family therapy is to help dysfunctional families address the
specific areas in which they are deficient.

The FFT model seems to work very effectively. There is considerable empirical support for its application with families that have delinquent children. Alexander
and Parsons (1973) compared families receiving FFT with families receiving client-
centered therapy, psychodynamically oriented family therapy, and no treatment.
Use of the FFT model yielded significantly greater changes within the families
and significantly lower recidivism rates for the adolescents. The changes were
maintained at 18 months posttreatment, and at a 2½-year follow-up the siblings
of the delinquent adolescents had significantly lower rates of referral to juvenile
courts. Continued research and evaluation of the model with delinquents have been
part of the evolving theory and practice of functional family therapy.

RECOMMENDED INTERVENTIONS
FOR SPECIFIC FAMILY PROBLEMS

Figure 6.1 presents a conceptual framework for the development and prevention
of serious conduct disorders in children. Following are potential interventions for
the various factors that may contribute to the development of delinquency.

Coercive Parent/Child Interaction

Parent training in child management skills is the recommended intervention for
coercive parent/child interactions. This level of intervention is mostly educational
and gives parents specific skills for dealing with parenting problems. Resources

such as Patterson's *Families* (1979), Fleischman et al.'s *Troubled Families* (1983), and Blechman's *Solving Child Behavior Problems at Home and at School* (1985) are appropriate for this type of intervention.

Childhood Conduct Problems

Behavioral self-control strategies are needed to help children address and manage problem behaviors associated with hyperactivity, opposition, and aggression. The Turtle Technique, described earlier, is very useful at this stage, as are other strategies developed for children with oppositional or impulsive tendencies. Kirby and Grimley (1986) and Kendall and Braswell (1985), for example, describe treatment programs that target attention deficit disorder and behavior problems associated with hyperactivity.

Another intervention process that is relevant to this stage is the training of teachers in behavior management strategies. Most teacher training programs today do not provide adequate training in classroom management skills. With resources shrinking and class sizes expanding, teachers frequently are not equipped to handle a class with several behavior-disordered children. It is highly recommended that teachers receive assistance in developing some of these intervention skills.

Poor Social Competence of Child

Clearly, children who lack social competence will fail to develop appropriate relations with peers. A number of programs have been developed to facilitate the teaching of social skills to children. Matson and Ollendick (1988) describe the assessment and training of children with social deficits. They recommend a particular curriculum that may be offered either in a regular classroom or in a special clinical setting, such as a community mental health center or juvenile justice center. They also provide guidelines for use of the curriculum with special populations.

A model of social skills training developed specifically for children with behavior problems is Structured Learning, also known as Skillstreaming. Materials include *Skillstreaming the Elementary School Child* (McGinnis & Goldstein, 1984) and *Skillstreaming the Adolescent* (Goldstein, Sprafkin, Gershaw, & Klein, 1980). In these materials, Goldstein and colleagues present a model for identifying skill deficits and developing a structured learning program to address these deficits. Skillstreaming learning is seen more as an educational training program than a therapeutic intervention. A third contribution, the Prepare Curriculum (Goldstein, 1988), presents modules to be mastered by young people. Specific modules include training in problem solving, interpersonal skills, anger control, moral reasoning, stress management, situational perception, empathy, cooperation, and recruiting support. All of these interventions may be conducted with individuals, with families, or in a school or clinic setting. (For more about these approaches, see chapter 4.)

Rejection of Child by Normal Peers

The programs developed by Matson and Ollendick and by Goldstein and colleagues can be used to help young people overcome problems concerning interpersonal relationships with peers. Though all children have some difficulty developing good peer skills, most children are able to learn effective ways of getting along with age-mates. Children with histories of aggression, however, tend to attribute aggression to others, even when it is not demonstrated in others' behavior (Dodge, 1991). Intervention requires special attention to the mastery of personal relationships. A recently developed model, the Earlscourt Social Skills Group Program, is based on Goldstein's Skillstreaming model with the addition of components on reinforcement and charting and includes content and features from an information-processing approach to aggressive behavior (Pepler, King, & Byrd, 1991). An advantage of the Earlscourt program is that it is developed for use with groups of children. To encourage generalization, it also incorporates parental involvement and training as well as teacher participation.

Parental Issues

A number of adult issues impact the development of children and can contribute to aggressive tendencies. Such parental traits as psychopathology, antisocial behavior, and susceptibility to stressors need careful assessment; generally they are best addressed through individual therapy with the parent. Substance abuse problems require specialized and direct intervention.

Family Stress

Unemployment, marital conflict, divorce, and single parenthood are all contributors to family stress. Remedies may include parent education and assistance with educational, career, and financial issues, though these will frequently require services from another source or agency. Vocational and career support, for example, is very important for low-income families but generally is outside the purview of family therapists.

In cases of family stress, couples counseling is often needed to address marital or relationship issues not dealt with in other interventions. Therapists have a number of marital therapy models to draw on, but the work of Jacobson and Margolin (1979) and Stuart (1980) is particularly relevant. They address couples' concerns from a social learning perspective, making the treatment focus similar to that recommended for addressing children's issues. A single parent who heads a household may need assistance with family management skills and stress reduction. Not all single-parent households have aggressive children, nor do they all experience highly stressful parent-child interactions (Horne, 1981). For those that do, however, parenting programs tailored for single parents are helpful. The therapist can also help the parent establish a support network and find other means of managing stressful circumstances.

Family Demographics

Family income, level of parental education, neighborhood, and ethnic group are additional factors that may influence the development of aggressive behavior in children. Parental counseling and education can address some of these demographic factors. Vocational, career, and financial counseling are also appropriate. For families that may be immigrants or for other reasons are not yet acculturated to the United States, a multicultural approach, which includes support groups, education, and specific assistance in deficit areas, is recommended. In such a situation, it may be crucial to have a therapist who understands the family's cultural background and can help them bridge the gap between their original culture and their new culture of residence. An especially important issue is the child's alienation from the family as he or she moves toward identifying with the new majority culture. Children in immigrant families frequently feel embarrassed by or angry toward their unacculturated parents. Rejecting their parents, they may demonstrate these feelings through aggression or participation in minority gang activities.

Disrupted Family Management Practices

The degree of the disruption of family management, the age of the child, and the nature of the particular problems will determine the type of intervention needed. Interventions can range from parent education—as in the models offered by Patterson et al. (1975); Patterson and Forgatch (1987); Fleischman, Horne, and Arthur (1983); Forehand and McMahon (1981); Horne and Sayger (1990); and Blechman (1985)—to structural family therapy (Minuchin, 1981). However, for the intensive work needed by highly aggressive, dysfunctional families, the functional family therapy model developed by Alexander and associates is recommended. FFT is backed by considerable empirical research and is particularly effective for families with highly aggressive, destructive children who are involved in juvenile gang activity.

The interventions mentioned may be viewed along the continuum presented in Figure 6.3, from most structured to least structured. They vary in the amount of training required for their implementation and in the amount of empirical support available.

CONCLUSIONS

The intervention models described in this chapter are oriented toward helping families. Although these models have not been directly applied to the problem of gang involvement and the treatment of delinquent behavior in the gang setting, there is evidence that the development of aggressive behavior leading toward gang involvement is strongly influenced by family factors. These factors must be addressed if delinquent and gang behavior are to be prevented: Interventions that bypass family problems, though often effective initially, do not result in durable improvement.

Figure 6.3   Continuum of Family Treatment Approaches

Most Structured	Least Structured
Least Training Required	Most Training Required
Most Empirical Research Support	Least Empirical Research Support

◄───►

Parent education/training	Social learning family therapy	Functional family therapy	Structural family therapy

This chapter has focused more on prevention than on treatment, for it is far more effective and efficient to prevent delinquency than it is to remediate it after it has developed. Prevention, however, requires a certain commitment from the community in terms of resources to support family change. In a society in which significant numbers of adults feel disenfranchised and lack hope for a better life for themselves or their children, many turn to self-medication to ease their pain. The prevalence of substance abuse, combined with inadequate access to needed resources, results in situations where parents cannot provide the love, support, structure, and discipline their children need to become normal, contributing, and healthy members of society. Communities need to provide additional resources to all families in the following forms:

- Child and adolescent counseling regarding healthy family life-styles

- Premarital or presexual counseling about birth control and family planning

- Prenatal medical and social support

- Parent training and family development information and support

- Preschool child care and early education opportunities such as Head Start

- Ongoing support for families as their children progress through developmental stages in the family, the school, and the community

The research on the treatment of childhood aggression has demonstrated that efforts at behavioral change must be multifocused, addressing the child specifically but also including the family, the school, and community agencies. Interventions too often have focused on a single component, with the result being less than effective. Communities need to coordinate services so that all personnel and agencies addressing aggressive child behavior can work together systematically.

REFERENCES

Alexander, J. (1988). Phases of family therapy process: A framework for clinicians and researchers. In L. C. Wynne (Ed.), *The state of the art in family therapy research: Controversies and recommendations.* New York: Family Process.

Alexander, J., & Parsons, B. (1973). Short-term behavioral interventions with delinquent families: Impact on family process and recidivism. *Abnormal Psychology, 81,* 219–225.

Alexander, J., & Parsons, B. (1982). *Functional family therapy.* Pacific Grove, CA: Brooks/Cole.

American Psychiatric Association. (1987). *The diagnostic and statistical manual of mental disorders* (3rd ed. rev.). Washington, DC: Author.

Aponte, H., & VanDeusen, J. (1981). Structural family therapy. In A. Gurman & A. Kniskern (Eds.), *Handbook of family therapy.* New York: Brunner/Mazel.

Arnold, J., Levine, A., & Patterson, G. R. (1975). Changes in sibling behavior following family intervention. *Journal of Consulting and Clinical Psychology, 43,* 683–688.

Bahm, A., Chandler, C., & Eisenberg, L. (1961). *Diagnostic characteristics related to service of psychiatric clinics for children.* Paper presented at the 38th Annual Convention of Orthopsychiatry, Munich, Germany.

Bandura, A. (1969). *Principles of behavior modification.* New York: Holt, Rinehart & Winston.

Barton, C., & Alexander, J. (1981). Functional family therapy. In A. Gurman & D. Kniskern (Eds.), *Handbook of family therapy.* New York: Brunner/Mazel.

Baum, C., & Forehand, R. (1981). Long term follow-up assessment of parent training by use of multiple outcome measures. *Behavior Therapy, 12,* 643–652.

Blechman, E. (1985). *Solving child behavior problems at home and at school.* Champaign, IL: Research Press.

Buehler, R., Patterson, G., & Furniss, J. (1966). The reinforcement of behavior in institutional settings. *Behavior Research and Therapy, 4,* 157–167.

Colapinto, J. (1991). Structural family therapy. In A. Gurman & D. Kniskern (Eds.), *Handbook of family therapy* (Vol. 2). New York: Brunner/Mazel.

Cornwall, A., & Bowden, H. (1990). *Learning disabilities and aggression: A critical review.* Unpublished manuscript. Halifax, Nova Scotia: Isaac Walton Killam Hospital for Children.

Dodge, K. A. (1991). The structure and function of reactive and proactive aggression. In D. Pepler & K. Rubin (Eds.), *The development and treatment of childhood aggression.* Hillsdale, NJ: Erlbaum.

Elliott, D., Huizinga, D., & Ageton, S. (1985). *Explaining delinquency and drug use.* Newbury Park, CA: Sage.

Fleischman, J. J. (1981). A replication of Patterson's "Intervention for boys with conduct problems." *Journal of Consulting and Clinical Psychology, 49,* 342–351.

Fleischman, M. J., & Horne, A. M. (1979). Working with families: A social learning approach. *Contemporary Education, 1,* 66–71.

Fleischman, M. J., Horne, A. M., & Arthur, J. L. (1983). *Troubled families: A treatment program.* Champaign, IL: Research Press.

Forehand, R., & King, H. (1977). Noncompliant children: Effects of parent training on behavior and attitude change. *Behavior Modification, 1,* 93–108.

Forehand, R., & Long, N. (1991). Prevention of aggression and other behavior problems in early adolescent years. In D. Pepler & K. Rubin, *The development and treatment of childhood aggression.* Hillsdale, NJ: Erlbaum.

Forehand, R., & McMahon, R. (1981). *Helping the noncompliant child: A clinician's guide to effective parent training.* New York: Guilford.

Forgatch, M. S., & Patterson, G. R. (1989). *Parents and adolescents living together: Part 2. Family problem solving.* Eugene, OR: Castalia.

Goldstein, A. P. (1988). *The Prepare Curriculum: Teaching prosocial competencies.* Champaign, IL: Research Press.

Goldstein, A. P. (1991). *Gangs: A psychological perspective.* Champaign, IL: Research Press.

Goldstein, A. P., Sprafkin, R. P., Gershaw, N. J., & Klein, P. (1980). *Skillstreaming the adolescent: A structured learning approach to teaching prosocial skills.* Champaign, IL: Research Press.

Griest, D., Forehand, R., Wells, K., & McMahon, R. (1980). An examination of differences between nonclinic and behavior problem clinic-referred children and their mothers. *Journal of Abnormal Psychology, 89,* 497–500.

Griest, D., & Wells, K. (1983). Behavioral family therapy with conduct disorders in children. *Behavior Therapy, 14,* 37–53.

Griffin, G. (1987). Childhood predictive characteristics of aggressive adolescents. *Exceptional Children, 54,* 246–252.

Henggeler, S. (1989). *Delinquency in adolescence.* Newbury Park, CA: Sage.

Horne, A. M. (1981). Aggressive behavior in normal and deviant members of intact versus mother-only families. *Journal of Abnormal Child Psychology, 9,* 283–290.

Horne, A. M. (1991). Social learning family therapy. In A. M. Horne & J. L. Passmore (Eds.), *Family counseling and therapy* (2nd ed.). Itasca, IL: Peacock.

Horne, A. M., Forehand, R., Frame, C., & Norsworthy, K. (1990). *A conceptual framework for development and prevention of serious conduct disorders in children.* Unpublished manuscript, University of Georgia, Athens.

Horne, A. M., & Sayger, T. (1990). *Treating conduct and oppositional deficit disorders in children.* New York: Pergamon.

Jacobson, J., & Margolin, G. (1979). *Marital therapy.* New York: Brunner/Mazel.

James, L. C. (1987). *A study of the differences in touch patterns between functional and dysfunctional families.* Unpublished doctoral dissertation, Indiana State University, Terre Haute.

Johnson, S., & Lobitz, G. (1974). The personal and marital adjustment of parents as related to observed child deviance and parenting behaviors. *Journal of Abnormal Child Psychology, 2,* 192–207.

Jones, R., Weinrott, M., & Howard, K. (1981). *The national evaluation of the teaching family model.* Unpublished manuscript, Evaluation Research Group, Eugene, OR.

Kazdin, A. E. (1987a). *Conduct disorders in childhood and adolescence.* Newbury Park, CA: Sage.

Kazdin, A. E. (1987b). Treatment of antisocial behavior in children: Current status and future directions. *Psychological Bulletin, 102,* 187–203.

Kendall, P., & Braswell, L. (1985). *Cognitive-behavioral therapy for impulsive children.* New York: Guilford.

Kirby, E., & Grimley, L. (1986). *Understanding and treating attention deficit disorder.* New York: Pergamon.

Levitt, E. (1971). Research on psychotherapy with children. In A. Bergin & S. Garfield (Eds.), *Handbook of psychotherapy and behavior change.* New York: Wiley.

Loeber, R. (1982). The stability of antisocial and delinquent child behavior: A review. *Child Development, 53,* 1431–1446.

MacMillan, D. L., & Kavale, K. A. (1986). Educational intervention. In H. C. Quay & J. S. Werry (Eds.), *Psychopathological disorders of childhood* (3rd ed.). New York: Wiley.

Matson, J., & Ollendick, T. (1988). *Enhancing children's social skills.* New York: Pergamon.

McGinnis, E., & Goldstein, A. P. (1984). *Skillstreaming the elementary school child: A guide for teaching prosocial skills.* Champaign, IL: Research Press.

McMahon, R., Forehand, R., & Griest, D. (1981). Effects of knowledge of social learning principles on enhancing treatment outcome and generalization in a parent training program. *Journal of Consulting and Clinical Psychology, 49,* 526–532.

Minuchin, S. (1981). *Families and family therapy.* Cambridge, MA: Harvard University Press.

Minuchin, S., & Fishman, C. (1981). *Family therapy technique.* Cambridge, MA: Harvard University Press.

Minuchin, S., Montalvo, B., Guerney, B., Rosman, B., & Schumer, F. (1967). *Families of the slums.* New York: Basic.

Morris, P. W., Horne, A. M., Jessell, J. C., Passmore, J. L., Walker, J. M., & Sayger, T. V. (1988). Behavioral and cognitive characteristics of fathers of aggressive and well-behaved boys. *Journal of Cognitive Psychotherapy: An International Quarterly, 2,* 251–265.

Patterson, G. R. (1979). *Families: Applications of social learning to family life.* Champaign, IL: Research Press.

Patterson, G. R. (1982). *Coercive family process.* Eugene, OR: Castalia.

Patterson, G. R. (1986). Performance models for antisocial boys. *American Psychologist, 41,* 432–444.

Patterson, G. R., DeBaryske, B., & Ramsey, E. (1989). A developmental perspective of antisocial behavior. *American Psychologist, 44,* 329–335.

Patterson, G. R., & Forgatch, M. S. (1987). *Parents and adolescents living together: Part 1. The basics.* Eugene, OR: Castalia.

Patterson, G. R., & Reid, J. B. (1973). Interventions for families of aggressive children: A replication study. *Behaviour Research and Therapy, 11,* 383–394.

Patterson, G. R., Reid, J. B., Jones, R. R., & Conger, R. E. (1975). *A social learning approach to family intervention* (Vol. 1). Eugene, OR: Castalia.

Pepler, D., King, G., & Byrd, W. (1991). A social-cognitively based social skills training program for aggressive children. In D. Pepler & K. Rubin (Eds.), *The development and treatment of childhood aggression.* Hillsdale, NJ: Erlbaum.

Roach, J. (1958). Some social psychological characteristics of child clinic caseloads. *Journal of Consulting Psychology, 22,* 183–186.

Schneider, M., & Robin, A. (1976). The Turtle Technique: A method for the self-control of impulsive behavior. In J. Krumboltz & C. Thompson (Eds.), *Counseling methods.* New York: Holt, Rinehart & Winston.

Stuart, R. (1980). *Helping couples change.* New York: Guilford.

Ulrici, D. K. (1983). The effects of behavioral and family interventions on juvenile recidivism. *Family Therapy, 10,* 25–36.

Wahler, R. G. (1980). The insular mother: Her problems in parent-child treatment. *Journal of Applied Behavior Analysis, 13,* 207–219.

Walter, H., & Gilmore, S. K. (1973). Placebo versus social learning effects of parent training procedures designed to alter the behavior of socially aggressive boys. *Behaviour Research and Therapy, 11,* 361–377.

Wells, K. C., Forehand, R., & Griest, D. (1980). Generality of treatment effects from treated to untreated behaviors resulting from a parent training program. *Journal of Clinical Child Psychology, 8,* 217–219.

Wilson, J. Q., & Herrnstein, R. J. (1985). *Crime and human nature.* New York: Simon & Schuster.

Wiltz, N. A., & Patterson, G. R. (1974). An evaluation of parent training procedures to alter inappropriate aggressive behavior of boys. *Behavior Therapy, 5,* 215–221.

CHAPTER 7

School-Based Interventions: Safety and Security

Ronald D. Stephens

INTRODUCTION

Although youth gangs have been a part of American life since the early 18th century, today's gangs pose a greater threat to public safety and order than at any time in recent history. Youth gangs, whose organization and existence at one time had primarily a social basis, now are motivated by violence, extortion, intimidation, and illegal trafficking in drugs and weapons. Today's gangs are better organized, remain active for longer periods, and are much more mobile; they also have access to sophisticated weaponry.

Gangs Going Corporate

Gangs are going corporate, franchising various regions of the country and developing their own specialists in money laundering, marketing, tax evasion, and strategic planning. Law enforcement officials recently caught a group of Los Angeles Crips conducting a drug sales seminar in St. Louis, Missouri. Some gangs are even sending their homeboys to college to equip them with the latest in high-tech skills. Many gangs have learned new ways to avoid prosecution legally and increasingly sophisticated ways to traffic drugs.

The National School Safety Center, a program of the United States Departments of Justice and Education and Pepperdine University, works with law enforcement and education agencies nationwide in developing effective gang prevention and gang intervention strategies. In addition to publishing written resources, the center provides customized training and technical assistance programs. For further information, write to the National School Safety Center, c/o Pepperdine University, Malibu, CA 90263, or call (805) 373-9977.

Coming to a Community Near You

Gangs are on the move to every possible location throughout the United States. They are motivated to seek out new communities where they can get more money for their drugs, where law enforcement is less prepared to deal with them, and where potential rivals are fewer and easier to intimidate. Quite frankly, many gang members are tired of the crime and violence of the inner city. They too want safer environments.

Law enforcement officials in various cities indicate that New York has about 50 gangs with 5,000 members; Chicago has 125 gangs with 12,500 members; Dallas has 225 gangs; and Los Angeles has more than 900 gangs with about 100,000 members. Miami has reported a 1,000% increase in gangs and gang membership during the past 5 years. In Los Angeles alone, nearly 780 gang-related killings occurred in 1991, and preliminary figures for 1992 indicate a continuing increase.

More Than a Big-City Problem

Youth gangs are not simply a big-city or inner-city problem, nor are they a problem of a particular race or culture. Gang membership crosses all ethnic, racial, and geographic boundaries. Hispanic, African American, Caucasian, Asian, and the new hybrid gangs are spreading rapidly to a host of midsize and smaller cities. Suburban and rural communities provide attractive alternatives for recruiting members, marketing drugs, and finding safety from rival gangs.

Parents, students, educators, law enforcers, legislators, judges, prosecutors, community and religious leaders, and others are in a unique position to stem the threatening tide of gang violence that is spreading across the country.

SCHOOL INVOLVEMENT WITH YOUTH GANGS

Drugs, gangs, and weapons in schools are intricately related. Gangs market drugs and routinely use guns as the tools of their trade. Schools become involved with youth gangs for several reasons. Because many current and potential gang members are students, the school has become a prime recruiting ground.

Gang members engaged in selling drugs also can find a natural market outlet for their wares at the schools. One gang member even stated, "The reason I go to school is to sell drugs." Another student was asked, "Do you have a drug problem in your school?" She replied, "No, I can get all the drugs I want."

Gang members often stake out specific areas at a school as their turf, a practice that can lead to violence on the campus. In one Los Angeles high school a local gang claimed a specific public telephone booth as its turf. When a non–gang member used it, the ensuing argument was settled by a gun; a student's death resulted. After the student was killed, 35 students withdrew from the school because of fear.

Gang members also extort fees from other students for the opportunity to use certain school facilities, to walk to and from school, or to obtain protection. One Asian gang in San Francisco was charging a restaurant owner 1,000 dollars per month simply for protection. Several gangs are well organized in this regard and have established clear guidelines for their protection racket.

Although drug-free school zone programs are working in many areas of the country, the cooperative support of students, parents, school administrators, and law enforcement is essential. Drug-free school zone laws provide for enhanced mandatory minimum sanctions against any person who sells, traffics in, or uses drugs or who commits a drug-related crime within the drug-free zone. Drug-free zones generally include the school's perimeter plus territory within a 1,000-foot radius. Alabama currently has the most aggressive law—territory within 3 miles of a school is declared drug free.

A Gang Assessment Tool

Because school or law enforcement officials may not want to acknowledge the presence of gangs and gang members, I developed a questionnaire, the Gang Assessment Tool, to assist local school and community officials in the evaluation process ("Gangs vs. Schools," 1992). Each of the following questions has a point value.

1. Do you have graffiti on or near your campus? (5 points)

   Graffiti is one of the first warning signs of gang activity. If you have graffiti in your community or on your campus, you probably have gang activity.

2. Do you have crossed-out graffiti on or near your campus? (10 points)

   At an elementary school in Los Angeles, five different graffiti monikers were present on the schoolhouse door. Each of the previous ones had been crossed out. The principal apologized for the graffiti, stating that the painters had not been to the campus since the previous Friday; this was only Monday. Crossed-out graffiti indicates that more than one gang is in the community and the likelihood of gang warfare is higher.

3. Do your students wear colors, jewelry, or clothing; flash hand signals; or display other behavior that may be gang related? (10 points)

   Dress styles, hand signs, jewelry, and other identifying marks reinforce members' affiliation with a particular gang. More and more school districts are establishing dress codes that prohibit the wearing of gang symbols, gang colors, or disruptive dress styles. Parents should be particularly aware of gang styles and colors and make certain their children do not wear them. It is all too easy to be mistaken for a gang member and end up as another fatal statistic.

4. Are drugs available at or near your school? (5 points)

   Drugs and gangs are inseparably related. Some gangs are developing tremendous expertise in drug trafficking and sales. They have their own experts in money laundering, marketing, distribution, recruiting, and law. A gang will move into a community and provide the rent, utilities, telephone, and a starter kit of supplies to help members get the drug-trafficking operation going. Gangs are on the move and looking for new opportunities, perhaps in your community.

5. Has there been a significant increase in the number of physical confrontations/staredowns within the past 12 months in or near your school? (5 points)

   Fights symbolize the increasing conflict on many campuses. School violence and intimidation encourage gang formation and gang-related activity. Increasing violence may signal a growing tendency toward gang violence. It is important to clearly communicate, consistently enforce, and fairly apply reasonable behavior standards.

6. Are weapons increasingly present in your community? (10 points)

   Weapons are the tools of the trade for gangs. Wherever gangs are found, weapons will follow. Unfortunately, when a weapon is used, an irreversible consequence and a chain reaction often result. A fistfight is one thing, but a gunfight can have a tragic outcome— and the violence usually only escalates.

7. Do your students use beepers, pagers, or cellular phones? (10 points)

   The trend is for schools increasingly to outlaw the use of such devices by students. Most students are not doctors or lawyers and do not need beepers. Except in rare cases, beepers and pagers are inappropriate and unnecessary for students.

8. Has there been a drive-by shooting at or near your school? (15 points)

   Drive-by shootings reflect more advanced gang-related problems. It is possible to have a gang presence in your community without drive-by shootings. Most of those shootings are the result of competition between rival gangs for drug turf or territorial control of a specific area. Once gang rivalry begins, it often escalates to increasing levels of violence. If you have had a drive-by shooting on or near your school campus, conditions are grave and gang activity in your community has escalated to its most serious state.

9. Have you had a "show-by" display of weapons at or near your school? (10 points)

   Before you have a drive-by shooting, a "show-by"—a flashing of weapons—usually will occur. About the best course of action when such an incident happens is to duck and look for cover.

   The head football coach in a suburban Portland, Oregon, community told of a recent incident in which a group of Crips, dressed in blue, came speeding through his school's fieldhouse parking lot. It was near the end of the day. His team was with him when he shouted, "Slow it down, fellas." They did, only to pull out a semiautomatic weapon and point it at the coach and his team. The coach had the good judgment to hit the deck and order his team to drop for cover. The coach said, "I thought I had bought the farm. Fortunately, they didn't pull the trigger. In my 20 years of teaching, I have never been afraid until this year."

A North Carolina teacher, a veteran of 18 years, related that her mother had offered to buy out her teaching contract if only she would leave the profession. School violence has motivated some of the nation's best teachers to pull out.

10. Is your truancy rate increasing? (5 points)

There is a high correlation between truancy and daytime burglary. Excellent examples of truancy prevention and intervention programs are in effect in Houston, Texas; Rohnert Park, California; and Honolulu, Hawaii. Youngsters who are not in school often are terrorizing the community. Cooperation between schools and law enforcement to keep kids in school is important.

11. Is an increasing number of racial incidents occurring in your community or school? (5 points)

A high correlation exists between gang membership and racial conflict. We have often treated new immigrants and people from diverse cultural and ethnic backgrounds poorly and thus have encouraged the formation of gangs. Many gangs are formed along racial and ethnic lines for pur-poses of protection and affiliation. Sometimes friendship and affiliation take a backseat to criminal acts of violence and intimidation. People want to be respected and appreciated. It is important to cultivate multicultural understanding and respect that embraces diversity.

12. Does your community have a history of gangs? (10 points)

Gangs are not a new phenomenon. They have been around for decades—in some cases, for several generations. Youth gangs are even mentioned in the Bible (2 Kings 2:23). If your community has a history of gangs, your children are much more likely to be influenced by them.

13. Is there an increasing presence of informal social groups with unusual names like "the Woodland Heights Posse," "Rip Off a Rule," "Kappa Phi Nasty," "18th Street Crew," or "Females Simply Chillin"? (15 points)

The development of hard-core gang members often begins in groups with innocent and yet revealing names. Youngsters in these groups often become primary recruiting targets for hard-core gang members.

A score of 15 points or less indicates that the school or community does not have a significant gang problem and there is no need for alarm. A score of 20 to 40 points indicates an emerging gang problem. Gang factors and related incidents should be closely monitored, and a gang plan should be developed. A score of 45 to 60 points indicates the need to immediately establish a comprehensive, systematic gang prevention and intervention plan. A score of 65 points or more indicates an acute gang problem that merits a total gang prevention, intervention, and suppression program.

COMMON GANG MYTHS

For school and community gang suppression strategies to work effectively, common myths about gangs need to be dispelled. The myths were originally compiled by Lorne Kramer, chief of police in Colorado Springs, Colorado, then reported and discussed as follows ("Gang Membership," 1991).

Myth 1: The majority of street gang members are juveniles. Juveniles—those 18 years old or younger—actually constitute a minority of gang membership. In Los Angeles County, juveniles represent only about 20% of gang members. Across the nation, the age range of gang members is broadening; members are as young as 9 to 10 and as old as 40 or more. Money, drugs, and lax juvenile laws are key factors behind this move to attract children to gangs at younger ages.

Myth 2: The majority of gang-related crimes involve gangs versus gangs. In more than half of gang-related homicides, innocent victims who have no gang affiliation are killed or assaulted.

Myth 3: All street gangs are turf oriented. Some gangs may not claim any specific turf, whereas other gangs operate in multiple locations or even in very unsuspecting small cities. One Asian gang that operated crime rings from Florida to California had its headquarters in a small Pennsylvania town of less than 4,500 residents.

Myth 4: Females are not allowed to join gangs. Females are joining gangs in record numbers and often are extremely violent. In times past, females were thought of simply as mules—transporters of weapons or drugs—or as innocent bystanders. Females now make up about 5% of gang members. Both the number of female gang members and the violence of their acts are increasing.

Myth 5: Gang weapons usually consist of chains, knives, and tire irons. Perhaps brass knuckles, knives, and chains were the key weapons of the gangs of yesteryear, but today Uzis, AK–47s, and semiautomatics are the weapons of choice.

Myth 6: All gangs have a single leader and a tight structure. Most gangs are loosely knit groups and likely have several leaders. If one leader is killed, several other potential leaders seem to be waiting in the wings.

Myth 7: Graffiti is merely an art form. Graffiti is much more than an art form. It is a message that proclaims the gangs' presence and challenges rivals. Graffiti also serves as an instrument of intimidation and control—a form of advertising.

Myth 8: One way to cure gang membership is to lock the gang member away.
Incarceration and rehabilitation of hard-core gang members have not proven effective. Changing criminal behavior patterns is difficult. Prisons often serve as command centers and institutions of higher crime learning and preparation for ongoing gang-related activities. Often prisoners are forced to take sides with one group or another simply for protection.

Myth 9: Gangs are a law enforcement problem. Gangs are a problem for everyone. Communities need to develop effective, comprehensive, systemwide programs for gang prevention, intervention, and suppression.

SCHOOL-BASED STRATEGIES

Gang Prevention Curriculum

Gangs in school took on special significance for the Los Angeles Unified School District in the spring of 1988 when a 13-year-old boy was confronted by a group of Crips members for wearing a blue baseball cap to school. Because blue is the Crips' color, they told the boy he couldn't wear the hat to school; he wore it anyway. In retaliation, gang members unloaded 26 rounds from an AK–47 into the boy's home, killing his father and 6-year-old sister.

This event spurred school officials to develop an antigang curriculum for use in elementary schools. The program, developed under the leadership of Dr. Lila "Lulu" López, was implemented in September 1991. Called Mission SOAR (Set Objectives, Achieve Results), it focuses on building self-esteem, achieving goals, practicing group problem-solving, and learning how to resist gang involvement and pursue positive alternatives. Exhibit A presents introductory materials from the SOAR program.

Beginning prevention programs in the early grades is a key to long-term success. School curricula that focus on nonviolence, conflict resolution, and peer mediation are particularly valuable.

Gang Awareness

The school has a responsibility to heighten students' awareness of the consequences of gang membership and involvement. There are several things gang members do not tell their recruits. First, a new member inherits all the enemies of the established gang, perhaps dozens or even hundreds of enemies. A new gang member suddenly becomes a rival to other gangs. It is often blood in—blood out. Many acts of school crime and violence are gang-motivated rites of passage. It is not uncommon for a prospective gang member to shoot or stab someone in order to be "jumped" or initiated into the gang. Likely consequences of gang membership include going to prison, being seriously injured—perhaps permanently paralyzed—or even dying. Quitting is seldom an option: Although an individual may quit the gang, members of rival gangs may not know it. His own gang may require some blood— his own. Youngsters need to understand the vicious cycle of gang membership.

Clear Behavioral Expectations

Schools can take a number of measures to curb gang activity on campus. Most important, administrators should establish clear behavioral guidelines that specifically prohibit gang activity and encourage responsible citizenship.

A Model Dress Code

Several school districts forbid the wearing of any gang paraphernalia or apparel that identifies a student as a gang member. Sometimes just wearing the wrong colors can place a youngster in jeopardy. In Indianapolis, for instance, a 13-year-old student mistaken for a gang member was shot while riding the school bus. Model discipline and dress policies are crucial. More and more school districts are implementing model dress codes that clarify and define acceptable appearance standards. In creating such guidelines, administrators must take great care to maintain the delicate balance between an individual's First Amendment right of free expression and the school's responsibility to provide a safe and secure educational environment.

The Inglewood, California, Unified School District's dress code prohibits

> any apparel, jewelry, accessory, notebook or manner of grooming which, by virtue of its color, arrangement, trademark or any other attribute, denotes membership in such a group that advocates drug use or exhibits behaviors that interfere with the normal and orderly operation of a school. ("Inglewood School District," 1990)

Though the language of this policy is instructive, it should be seen as only one possible approach. Policies must be developed or adapted to meet local needs. The district's legal counsel should review all policies and procedures to ensure propriety, fairness, and consistency with other local laws.

Understanding Graffiti

More than simply a form of vandalism, graffiti is a message board that often will alert educators, law enforcers, and rival gangs to things "going down" in the community. School administrators need "gang savvy" to understand these messages. Maintaining a graffiti log book, as well as a glossary of unique gang terms and definitions, will help in crime tracking and record keeping.

Reading, Recording, and Removing Graffiti

The three Rs of graffiti eradication are read, record, and remove. It is essential to photograph and record any graffiti found on campus. Such evidence could be important in resolving other school offenses or tracking crime trends on campus. Graffiti removal is equally critical. The San Diego Unified School District has a graffiti removal team that works 24 hours a day to eradicate immediately any gang symbols or evidence of vandalism that may undermine a school's positive climate.

A Gang Crime Reporting Hot Line

The school should establish an anonymous gang crime reporting hot line in cooperation with law enforcement officials. Students have some of the best gang intelligence to offer. Make it easy, practical, and safe for them to report not only gang crimes but other school crimes as well.

Support and Protection for Victims

Providing adequate support and protection for victims of gang violence is crucial. If students or staff members do not feel safe in reporting gang crimes, the situation will only worsen. Counseling and other services can offer victims much-needed support.

Inservice Training

Teachers and staff members need inservice training to recognize gang activity. One teacher, after attending a training session on gang prevention in a major urban center, was embarrassed to realize that she had unknowingly been feeding the gang mentality. In response, she said that she intended to change the name of her classroom's pet goldfish, called "Homegirl," a gang term for girls. Another teacher in a wood shop class was unknowingly providing supervision, tools, instruction, and materials to assist a student in routing out his gang's name on a piece of lumber.

A Visitor Screening Policy

Every school campus should be monitored for signs of gang activity. Visitor screening procedures should be established. Administrators should maintain a visitors' log book, require valid visitor identification, and know the purpose of any visitor on the campus. Signs posted in English and other applicable languages can let visitors know that they must register with the office. Additional screening and evaluation criteria should be established.

Adequate Adult Supervision

All staff members should be trained to help in supervising the campus and preventing gang activity at school. Encourage parents and community leaders to get involved as well. Although many school districts employ uniformed or plainclothes resource officers or school peace officers to work on their campuses, school safety is everyone's business. It is all too easy for teachers and administrators to become complacent when a school police officer is hired.

Community Networking

Students, parents, law enforcement, the courts, and community leaders should be involved in developing a gang prevention and intervention plan that is unique to their locale. Timing is a critical consideration in planning: Imagine the public relations impact if school administrators waited until September—when parents had already purchased back-to-school clothing—to announce that certain colors or dress styles were prohibited.

Parent Notification

Parents need to know when their children are participating in gang-related activities. The San Diego Unified School District has designed a parent notification letter, translated into Spanish, Vietnamese, Hmong, and several other languages so that parents can be accurately informed in their native tongue about their child's activities. See Exhibit B for the text of this letter.

Parenting Classes

Schools can offer evening or weekend classes or programs that inform parents about gang activity and offer them skills and techniques to divert their children from gang membership. Hawaii's antitruancy program, sponsored jointly by the Hawaii Police Department and the State Department of Education, is an excellent model (see Exhibit C).

Parents should be suspicious if their children come home wearing new types of clothing or if they insist on wearing the same style or color each day. New, unexplained sums of money should also raise questions. Parents should create opportunities for ongoing communication by keeping in touch with their children and spending time with them. Knowing where children are and whom they are with is crucial in keeping them out of gang activity.

Cooperation With Law Enforcement

Any viable gang prevention and intervention plan depends on close coordination with law enforcement officials. They represent valuable resources in the areas of inservice training, crisis management, and truancy prevention. By working closely with the schools in truancy intervention programs, the Houston Police Department reduced community daytime burglaries by 70%. Similar programs in California and Louisiana have brought about comparable reductions in crime.

Attractive Extracurricular Programs

One of the main reasons young people join gangs is that they want something to do. In the absence of school-sponsored programs, young people are more likely to gravitate to gangs. Vital and interesting extracurricular programs will encourage youngsters to use their time in more positive ways.

Community Service Programs

Several school districts, including public schools in Washington, D. C., have implemented community service programs for their students. These programs encourage young people to get involved with senior citizens, child care centers, neighborhood cleanups, hospitals, and other community undertakings. Washington students are required to give 100 hours in community service to meet high school graduation requirements. Maryland has become the first state in the nation to mandate community service as a condition for receiving a high school diploma. Community service fosters feelings of ownership, pride, and self-worth—three important qualities that counterbalance gang involvement.

GANG MEMBERSHIP

A Working Definition for Educators

Although different regions of the country may have different definitions of gang membership, a good working description of a gang is a group of three or more individuals who share a unique name and identifiable marks or symbols, claim a territory or turf, associate on a regular basis, and engage in criminal or antisocial behavior.

Establishing a Local Definition

Often parents and school administrators do not admit that their children or their students are involved in gang activity because they think it makes them look bad or they simply do not want to acknowledge gang presence. Police agencies in Ventura County, California, use 15 criteria for identifying youths as gang members. Their criteria, which can also help parents and educators ascertain gang involvement, are as follows:

- Having gang tattoos

- Wearing gang garb, which could include color of clothing, types of clothing, head coverings, or methods of grooming

- Displaying gang markings or slogans on personal property or clothing

- Possessing gang literature that indicates membership

- Admitting gang membership

- Being arrested with known gang members

- Attending functions sponsored by the gang or known gang members

- Being cited by a reliable informant

- Being identified by relatives as a gang member

- Being named by law enforcement agencies as a gang member

- Exhibiting behavior fitting police profiles of gang-related drug dealing

- Being stopped by police with a known gang member

- Loitering, riding, or meeting with a known gang member

- Selling or distributing drugs for a known gang member

- Helping a known gang member commit a crime

It takes only one of these indications to be considered a gang wannabe or hanger-on; two can cause a youth to be labeled as an associate gang member, and five or more can cause police to label the individual as a hard-core gang member. At a time when gang attire is often more a matter of fashion than a statement of membership, it is important to apply a range of criteria.

Immediate Intervention Strategies

When a gang member enrolls in a school or when an enrolled student is identified as a gang member, special intervention strategies should be considered. These might include additional supervision, appropriate locker placement (perhaps near the principal's office), teacher selection and training, parent consultation, pertinent classroom assignments, special counseling, and records review. The gang member or wannabe generally needs extra time and attention, which will be claimed either from the educational system or from the criminal justice system. Teachers who work with gang members need special training in classroom management, conflict resolution, crisis management, and safe school planning.

STRATEGIES FOR PARENTS

Enhanced Supervision

In areas where gang activity is high, responsible adult supervision is critical. Chicago residents have established parent patrols that escort youngsters to and from school. Parents in Orange County, California, have established a similar program, called Operation Safe Corridors. Many Los Angeles high schools encourage parent volunteers to visit the school and provide extra supervision of playgrounds, hallways, restrooms, and other potential trouble areas.

Education About Early Warning Signs

Parents must learn about the early signs of gang involvement and must spend quality time with their children, listening to them and providing good role models. Parents need to become educated about the gang mentality. One mother, for instance, couldn't understand why her son—whose waist size was 32—wanted her to buy him size 44 pants. As it turned out, baggy pants were simply the dress style for his particular gang. Many gang members find it much easier to conceal contraband and weapons in baggy clothing.

Unusual nicknames or monikers—such as "Sniper," "Flaco," or "Ice Pick"—should not be overlooked. Unexplained possession of money, change of dress style, presence of tattoos, withdrawal, or any other unusual behavior should arouse suspicion. It is crucial for parents to stay in touch with their children, asking them about the school day, visiting the school, and participating in special programs. In addition to taking an interest in their children, parents should take time to know their children's friends. Parents need to know where their children are and let their children know where they themselves can be reached. Children need discipline, direction, and—most of all—time. The parental gift of time can make an indelible and lasting impression on children.

The school should help parents assess their children's tendency to be involved with gang activity. The Gang Banger Test for Parents, shown in Exhibit D, is an excellent evaluation tool for this purpose.

Gang Awareness Training

Parents need assistance in understanding the gang mentality and learning what they can do to prevent the growth of gangs in their community. A support group of parents who have lost their children as a result of gang crime constitutes one valuable resource.

Partnerships With Business

Job placement for young people is one of the strongest gang prevention strategies available. Young people are bound to work at something, whether it be criminal activity on the streets or employment activity where they can learn specific skills with responsible adult supervision and positive role models.

LAW ENFORCEMENT CONNECTION WITH SCHOOLS

Law enforcement strategies for dealing with gangs in schools include establishing a visible patrol, developing accurate gang intelligence, following up on rumors, cooperating with school personnel, and, most important, keeping abreast of the latest information on gangs from around the country.

Gangs like to infiltrate communities where law enforcement officers are not as well trained to work with gangs, where their own enterprise is easier and more profitable, and where there is less gang rivalry. For example, the gang detail commander in Minneapolis reported several Los Angeles gang members operating in that city. The gangs call it "Money-apolis" because they can get three to four times the usual price per kilo of crack (they net the standard 13,000 dollars in Los Angeles).

Because gangs have expanded across the country, a national gang information network is needed. Profiling and documenting of gang members is critical, as is police officer training that covers effective gang investigation techniques, interpretation of graffiti, tracking of pending gang conflicts, and classification of gang symbols and language.

The Los Angeles County Sheriff's Department has one of the finest models anywhere in the country for tracking information about gang members. Called GREAT (for Gang Reporting, Evaluation, and Tracking system), the information network maintains files on more than 100,000 gang members. The GREAT data base is capable of maintaining color mug shots, fingerprints, and up to 150 pieces of information about each individual. Authorized operators of the system include law enforcement officials or resource officers assigned to each school.

The Los Angeles Sheriff's Office has been very willing to work with law enforcement officers in other jurisdictions to help them set up their own systems. Colorado maintains a statewide gang information network. The development of a national tracking system would make it much more difficult for gang members to commit crimes in new communities and be treated as first-time offenders.

JUDICIAL STRATEGIES

Effective gang prosecution strategies include vertical prosecution, witness protection plans, and information networks. Many jurisdictions now are doing a better job of enforcing existing laws concerning safe school/park zones, national and state drug laws, and local curfew ordinances. A relatively new federal law, the Gun-Free School Zones Act 1990, enhanced punishments for individuals who use, possess, or sell guns on or near a school campus. It is an effective measure for dealing with weapon-wielding perpetrators.

Better sharing of juvenile records also can be a powerful tool for curbing gang activity. For this reason, on March 13, 1989, C. Robert Jameson, presiding juvenile court judge in the Superior Court in Orange County, California, issued a landmark order addressing the gang issue:

WHEREAS, youth gangs clearly imperil the safety of both students and campuses, and;

WHEREAS, the Court has been informed that concerns about "confidentiality" have often hampered or prevented communication among educators, law enforcement, the District Attorney, and probation personnel; this lack of communication among the various professionals dealing with the same child impedes the solving and prosecution of crimes, as well as the evaluation and placement of juveniles who have committed crimes, depriving educators of information needed to insure safer schools.

THEREFORE IT IS ORDERED, that all school districts in Orange County, all police departments in Orange County, and the Orange

County District Attorney may release information to each other regarding any minor when any person employed by such a department, office, or school district indicates that there is a reasonable belief that this minor is a gang member or at significant risk of becoming a gang member.

Probation and parole strategies include enhanced supervision and counseling as well as increased surveillance.

DEVELOPING GANG SAVVY

Gang savvy is essential for understanding the language, graffiti, and symbols used by gang members. A prosecutor in a major city told about his first gang case. He asked the gang member, "Tell me what happened" and received a short, derogatory response. The attorney then said, "Look, I can't help you unless you tell me what happened." The gang member replied, "Well, Cuz, what it was, was we was peepin' out a lick when some slobs rolled up in a bucket and started diss'n us with red laces. They pulled out their gats, so we pulled out our roscoes and busted on 'em. But Babylon was waitin' down the street, so we got ghost. A strawberry dropped a dime on us, and, hey, we wound up in jail." The attorney realized that he had not understood a word the gang member said. The initial "Cuz" is the common word for a fellow gang member identified as a Crip or a "bro" (brother). The rest of the account translates thus:

> We were watching a robbery go down when some members of a rival gang drove up in an old jalopy—a beat-up car. They were wearing the colors of a rival gang, that is, red shoe laces. [Crips wear blue, and they view red as offensive. The mere presence of red is considered disrespectful.] They pulled out their semiautomatic weapons, so we pulled out our guns and shot at them. The police were observed nearby, so we left. A prostitute (strawberry) "dropped a dime"—called the police—on us, and we wound up in jail.

Gang language is in constant flux, and understanding it requires continual updating. Attorneys in the city where this encounter took place now spend a certain amount of time in street training to better understand and serve their clients.

A SYSTEMATIC APPROACH TO GANGS

Gangs are a community problem and a national challenge. Responding to gangs requires a systematic, comprehensive, and collaborative approach that incorporates prevention, intervention, and suppression strategies. Although each strategy has a specific vision and a pressing mandate, the greatest hope is in prevention: Only by keeping children from joining gangs in the first place will we be able to halt the rising tide of terror and violence that gangs represent.

ESTABLISHING A GANG PREVENTION/ INTERVENTION TEAM

Gangs are not simply a law enforcement problem. Several key players from the community should be included on the gang prevention/intervention team. The following is a starting list of possible professional and lay representatives, but others undoubtedly will be identified as well:

- Educators

- Law enforcement officers

- Students

- Parents

- Local judges

- Prosecutors

- Social services personnel

- Parks and recreation employees

- Probation and corrections officers

- Members of local churches and synagogues

- Business leaders

- Elected officials

- Child protective services personnel

- Emergency personnel

- Counselors

- Local hospital representatives

As a community creates its own gang prevention and intervention plan, a number of programs around the country can serve as models and provide assistance. The remaining exhibits (E through I) in this chapter present materials from these programs.

EXHIBIT A   Mission SOAR (Set Objectives, Achieve Results)

CONTENTS

Preliminaries
>   Acknowledgments
>   Preface
>   Introduction
>   To the Student

Lessons
>   1. Student Leadership Survey, Part 1
>   2. We Are More Alike Than Different
>   3. Expressing Feelings
>   4. Values
>   5. Giver's Gain
>   6. WHAM (What's Hot About Me), Part 1
>   7. The Gift That Each Student Brings to School
>   8. A Sharing Circle About "Put-Ups"
>   9. WHAM (What's Hot About Me), Part 2
>   10. Relaxing
>   11. Class Dream
>   12. Making Resolutions—Any Time of the Year
>   13. Formula for SMART
>   14. Treasure Mapping
>   15. Four Thinkers
>   16. Go for It
>   17. Intention Versus Mechanism
>   18. Are You Listening?
>   19. Taking a Stand
>   20. Win-Win
>   21. Become a Superstar
>   22. Happy Endings
>   23. Fighting Fair, Part 1
>   24. Fighting Fair, Part 2: Game Plan
>   25. Fighting Fair, Part 3: Practice the Game Plan
>   26. Stress Stoppers
>   27. Buddy Teams
>   28. Teamwork
>   29. Responsible Leadership
>   30. Commitments and Agreements

PREFACE

Welcome to this opportunity to continue to make a significant and positive difference in the lives of your students. This nontraditional approach is designed to help them choose alternatives to negative behavior—such as street gang involvement, alcohol and drug abuse, and dropping out of school—and to find in themselves the motivation for positive goal achievement.

The philosophy that supports this curriculum holds students to be innately able and, with your guidance, capable of increasing their own sense of responsibility and self-worth and potential for leadership and goal achievement. The desired outcome is for students to feel that they have unconditional acceptance just for being who they are. They will be listened to without judgment and will learn techniques that will enable them to make positive choices and take appropriate risks in achieving their goals.

The techniques that students will acquire in this curriculum will build a base for success that can last them throughout their lives, if they so choose. You have this unique opportunity to draw out the creativity in all your students as you move them through these lessons.

Best wishes for an enjoyable experience as you help plant the seeds of greatness in your students and nurture them—the students—so they can blossom into productive, self-actualized participants in our society.

Lila "Lulu" López, PhD
Project Director
Youth Gang Prevention Program
Office of Instruction

INTRODUCTION

Welcome to Mission SOAR (Set Objectives, Achieve Results)

1. Why do we need Mission SOAR?

Street gangs are becoming a serious problem in all neighborhoods of our district. Today, more and more students are coming to school with many nonacademic problems that did not exist 10 to 20 years ago, or did not exist with such intensity. These problems strongly influence their school achievement. Teachers have rarely been trained to deal with such nonacademic problems, yet teachers have the final responsibility for the education of all of their students. Mission SOAR was developed to address some of these nonacademic problems and deal with obstacles standing in the way of academic achievement.

2. Why focus on Self-Esteem?

Webster's *Ninth New Collegiate Dictionary* defines self-esteem as "confidence and satisfaction in oneself." According to recent findings of the California Task Force to Promote Self-Esteem and Personal and Social Responsibility, the lack of self-esteem leads people to use alcohol and drugs to deaden the pain of feeling worthless. Child abuse, gang membership, teenage pregnancy, and welfare dependence are also by-products. Dr. Neil Smelser, a University of California sociology professor who summarized the research on self-esteem for the Task Force, states that people who lack self-esteem are incapable of being personally and socially responsible (*Toward a State of Esteem,* Sacramento, California: Office of State Printing, 1990).

Mission SOAR develops or rebuilds self-esteem by guiding students to become responsible for themselves and to avoid negative people, destructive activities, and harmful substances. With high self-esteem, people can function better, feel better, think more positively, and have more fulfilling relationships in life. As they develop, these people are more readily accepted by employers, associates, friends, and family, and they are more likely to become a positive influence on others.

3. How do you use Mission SOAR?

The suggested way to use this curriculum is to follow the lessons in the given order. Some of the activities and games can be omitted, but each lesson has a specific purpose and lays the foundation for another lesson or concept. The environment, music, and teacher's attitude are especially important in setting the right tone so that students take an active role in each lesson by solving problems, creating goals, organizing their thoughts, and interacting with others.

If a specific situation arises and there is a lesson that is pertinent, then use the lesson that very day. Similarly, some lessons may be inappropriate for your particular class. Use your best judgment. Your goal is to develop *your* class as effectively as you can. In the same vein, if some examples used here do not apply to your students, modify them.

Mission SOAR, while originally developed for third and fourth graders with reinforcement activities for grades 5 and 6, can also be modified for pre-K to adult use. Spanish translations of key teacher responses and student sections are provided in bold letters for your convenience.

4. What concepts are covered in Mission SOAR?

Self-esteem
- Leadership
- Positive self-image
- Self-motivation
- Positive attitude and positive thinking
- Overcoming negativity
- Developing self-confidence
- Responsibility for self
- Acceptance and trust of self and others
- Respecting self and others

Achieving goals
- Goal planning and achievement
- Imagination
- Creativity

Problem solving
- Handling conflict
- Stress reduction and relaxation
- Taking risks

Communication
- Creating win-win situations
- Keeping agreements and rules—and why they work
- Keeping promises
- Communicating with and relating to others

Gangs
- Awareness
- Peer pressure
- Alternatives

5. What methods and procedures does Mission SOAR use?

- Cooperative learning
- Multimodal approaches
    Auditory
    Visual
    Kinesthetic
- Experiential approaches
- Group processes: pairs and teams
- Oral and written communication
- Role-playing
- Games
- Demonstration and participation
- Individualization
- Lecture and discussion

TO THE STUDENT

Street gangs are becoming a real problem in many neighborhoods in our school district today. This year, we are going to work on a series of lessons that will help you be the best that you can be—lessons that will help you choose alternatives to street gangs by giving you better choices. In these lessons, you will visualize your dreams and learn techniques to help you obtain them. You will learn ways to cope with problems here at school and at home. You will become the best possible *you* as you experience Mission SOAR (Set Objectives, Achieve Results) and learn to become greater than you already are. Best wishes for a successful life.

Note. This can be read to the students, as appropriate.

EXHIBIT B   Parent Letter, San Diego Public Schools

Dear Parent:

Your child has been participating in gang-related activity on the _____
_____ school campus. Your son/daughter may be
involved in one or more of the following:

1. *Showing colors:* Blue, red, black, or beige—for example, wearing a blue cap, blue
   shirt, white T-shirt, black pants and/or a Raiders jacket. These clothes are worn in
   such a way as to align the student with a particular gang. This includes exposing
   initials of designers. Many gangs have assigned their own definitions to certain
   initials.
2. *Hand signs:* Making particular hand gestures to signal gang affiliation or action.
3. *Stare downs:* Challenges to provoke fights.
4. *Nicknames:* Individual gang names given, which are usually attached to some
   perceived attribute this member may have, for gang purposes. The nickname tends
   to fit physical or psychological characteristics.
5. *Tattoos:* Most gang-related tattoos are on hands, forearms, and occasionally the
   face. They vary depending on the age of the gang member.
6. *Graffiti:* Written and/or spray painted challenges.
7. *Physical confrontations:* These may be one or more members against rival
   members.

_____ school takes the stance that hitting, slap-
ping, punching, kicking, or any other method used to inflict physical injury is an assault.
An assault may result in suspension leading to expulsion, an arrest, and a civil lawsuit
for damages. When both students participate, it is then a fight, and both are responsible
for punishments associated with physical violence.

Gang-related activity in the community, or on the way to and from school,
usually finds its way to our campus the following day or soon thereafter. Please
monitor your child's activities.

Fortunately, only a small percentage of students are active in these types of
actions. However, those who are affect the safety and learning atmosphere for *all*
students and staff. _____ school is serious in its
responsibility to educate students in a safe environment. It is a parent's responsibility
to monitor and provide guidance for minors under the age of 18 and over the age of 18
while attending public school and living at home.

In light of these obligations, this letter serves as official notice that if this student
participates in gang-related activities on this campus, he/she may ultimately be
expelled from school.

Students make choices continually. They make a conscious, clear choice when
deciding to commit themselves to a gang, regardless of motivation. It is now time for
your child to reevaluate his or her choices.

We would like to end this activity before your son/daughter loses the opportunity
to enjoy his/her school experience. We can achieve this by working together.

If I or any member of my staff can be of assistance to you, please feel free to
contact me at _____.

Sincerely,

Principal

_____

Note. Reprinted by permission of the San Diego, California, Public Schools.

EXHIBIT C   School Attendance Program (SAP) Materials

DOE/HPD TRUANCY PROGRAM

TO _____
     Parent/Guardian

RE _____
     Name of student

Kalakaua Intermediate School has begun a new School Attendance/Truancy Program in cooperation with the Juvenile Crime Prevention Division of the Honolulu Police Department. This program holds students accountable for unexcused absence.

Your child has accumulated a minimum of 4 unexcused hours of school time. Therefore, you are hereby notified to accompany your child to:

    PLACE   *Dole Intermediate School Cafeteria*
    ADDRESS   *1803 Kam. IV Road, Honolulu, 96819*
    DATE   _____
    TIME   *Saturday, 8:00 A.M. to 12 noon*

Please be on time! Both you and your child will be required to stay for the entire 4 hours.

For any additional information, you may call the Juvenile Crime Prevention Division, School Attendance Detail at _____.

FAILURE TO ATTEND THIS PROGRAM MAY RESULT IN YOUR CHILD'S BEING ARRESTED FOR TRUANCY AND THIS CASE REFERRED TO THE FAMILY COURT.

_____   _____
School Principal   Date/Time

_____   _____
Officer/ID#   Date/Time

_____

Note. Reprinted by permission of the Honolulu, Hawaii, Police Department.

SANFORD B. DOLE INTERMEDIATE SCHOOL PARENT BULLETIN

January 11, 1991

Message from Mrs. Ichimura:

Dear Parents,

I hope that your holiday season was a happy one. We are sending this Parent Bulletin out to you to keep you informed of some new programs on our Dole Intermediate campus. On these pages you will find details about the HPD-DOE Truancy and Prime Time programs. We are looking forward to a great year in 1991.

Honolulu Police Department–Department of Education Truancy Program.

The Honolulu Police Department and Department of Education, with support from the Family Court, will be piloting this new program at S. B. Dole and Walpahu Intermediate schools beginning January 14, 1991. Students who accumulate a minimum of 4 hours of unexcused absence will be required to report with their parents for a 4-hour session on Saturday at our cafeteria. The Saturday 4-hour session will be under the supervision of the Honolulu Police Department/Juvenile Crime Division Unit officers. JCPD officers will notify parents and student as to the date they should report for their Saturday session. The time for each Saturday session is 8:00 A.M.–12:00 P.M. It is the intent of this program to reduce the number of juveniles referred to the juvenile justice system for the offense of truancy.

The administration and staff would like to ask for your assistance and support of this program primarily by advising your child to attend his/her classes every day. Also, should your child be absent due to illness/personal reasons please make certain a note from you or a doctor is submitted to his/her homeroom teacher on the first day back to school.

1991–1992 School Registration.   We have begun the process of registering our students for the next school year. Please ask your child to show you his or her registration form. Should you have any questions please contact your child's grade level counselor.

Prime Time Program.   This program is a partnership of the Department of Parks and Recreation, City and County of Honolulu, and the State Office of Children and Youth to provide constructive, supervised after-school activities for young adolescents.

Schedule: Monday through Friday from 2:30 P.M.–5:30 P.M.
            Wednesday 1:30 P.M.–5:30 P.M.
Cost: Free
Location: S. B. Dole Campus

For more information call Mr. Roger Watanabe at _____.

Holidays.   No school on: Friday, January 18, 1991 (End first semester)
                            Monday January 21, 1992 (Martin Luther King Day)

EXHIBIT D   Gang Banger Test for Parents

PARENTAL USE ONLY: NOT MY CHILD?

Circle the best answer:

Dress

a. My child constantly wears all black, blue, or red (sportswear: caps and jackets).
b. My child constantly wears a mixture of reds with black and blues with black.
c. My child wears his clothes too large (sagging).
d. My child doesn't fit any of these categories.

Body (Physical Appearance)

a. My child constantly wears his hair in braids or ponytails.
b. My child has tattoos of the street he lives on on his body (also teardrop tattoos).
c. My child has unexplainable scars and bruises on his body.
d. My child keeps his hair clean-cut, has no scars or tattoos.

Language (Oral or Written)

a. My child constantly talks in slang terms (cuzz, book, homie, O.G., etc.).
b. My child writes his letters backwards and crosses out or refuses to write certain letters (usually *B* or *C*).
c. My child constantly uses profanity and writes graffiti.
d. My child speaks and writes normally.

Associates

a. My child's friends are always older than he is.
b. My child never lets me meet his friends.
c. My child seems to care more about his friends than his family.
d. I know all my child's friends and their activities.

Behavior

a. My child is constantly in trouble with the law.
b. My child stays out late and refuses to tell me where he has been.
c. My child uses disrespectful language in front of me and my friends.
d. My child is respectful and rarely gets in trouble.

Explanation of lettering system:

a = 10 points	42 to 50 = Hard-Core Gang Banger
b = 8 points	31 to 41 = Gang Affiliations
c = 7 points	15 to 30 = Wannabe
d = 1 point	14 or Less = Safe Zone

a. Your child has a 99% chance of being a hard-core gang member.
   Open your eyes and get some help!

b. Your child is likely to have some gang affiliations, but you haven't lost him yet.
   You may need to take some drastic steps to get your child back. Move out of the
   neighborhood. Have your child live with a relative. Pray.

c. Your child is in the wannabe stage. This is a critical time for you and your child.
   Pay more attention to the child and immediately correct inappropriate behavior.

d. Your child is *probably* not a gang member, but don't take anything for granted.
   Stay aware of your child's behavior and activities.

Note. Reprinted from *Gang Violence and an Eternity of Silence* by permission
of Michael Dennis, Tri-Community Education Center, Carson, California.

EXHIBIT E   Gang Intervention: A Ten-Step Plan

1. *Be honest.* Admit to the potential for problems in your school.

2. *Get smart.* School administrators and staff need to become aware of the myriad of gang symbols and paraphernalia. In the SAISD [San Antonio Independent School District], our School District Police Department puts on gang awareness programs for school staff, PTA groups, and other community groups.

3. *Identify your school's gang leaders.* Once identified, get them on your side.

4. *Don't close your doors at 3:15.* To address the needs of marginal students who might be vulnerable to gangs, devise ways to keep students involved after regular school hours with activities that promote school spirit and give them something to take pride in.

5. *Work with the police.* The SAISD Police Department has initiated a Middle School Intervention Officer Program. The program places peace officers on the middle school campuses, where they can interact with the faculty, staff, and most important, the students themselves. The officers not only serve as role models but act as friends to the student who may be at a point where he or she could be susceptible to the lure of gang activities.

6. *Involve transfer students.* Students who have been transferred to your school because they were involved in gang-related activities at another school need special attention.

7. *Get the parents on your side.* Parent support is critical to eliminating gang influence in your schools. We should educate the parents so that they can recognize the early signs of gang involvement. Dress codes should eliminate gang attire from your campus. Ask the parents to support your decisions to enforce the school dress code.

8. *Find role models.* Youngsters need more positive role models. Help them find positive role models. Our students need someone to look up to other than drug dealers and gang members.

9. *Work together.* We must all work together as a team. Our fragmented efforts will not be enough to combat the gang problem. The police must work with the educators, who must work with the civic groups, who must work with the parents, who must work with the children, and so on and so on.

10. *Recognize and believe that we can make a difference.*

Note. Compiled by the San Antonio Independent School District Police Department, Special Operations Group. Reprinted by permission of the San Antonio, Texas, Independent School District.

EXHIBIT F   Gang Affiliation/Activity Procedures

The principals of all district schools shall ensure that

1. School policies are prepared and adopted in accordance with the provisions of Education Code Section 35291.5, said policies to encompass the provisions detailed in the first two paragraphs of Board Policy 5338;

2. Adopted school policies are included in printed rules and regulations provided students and parents;

3. All site staff, certificated and classified, are aware of the provisions of Board Policy 5338 and of the responsibilities they have for complying with the provisions, these to include

   a. Ensuring continuing staff, parent, and student awareness of the signs of gang affiliation/activity, with programs to inform students of the potential dangers gang involvement poses;

   b. A referral policy to the principal/designee for any student considered to be in violation of the letter and/or spirit of the policy;

   c. Procedures to provide intervention(s) with students found to be in violation of the provisions of Policy 5338;

   d. Provisions to recommend expulsion of any student who, after being involved with intervention strategies and admonished regarding the provisions of Policy 5338, engages in gang-related activity as defined in said policy.

4. Students identified as being possibly involved in gang-related activity are served by programs which enhance self-esteem, encourage interest and participation in wholesome activities, and promote membership in authorized student organizations.

   Training to provide increased awareness of the threat to the safety of students and staff which gang-related activity poses shall be provided each August or September by the Director, Pupil Personnel Services, to all newly hired staff. Additional presentations shall be made available to individual school site staff on request of the principal. All presentations shall provide training in current identification symbols used by students involved in gang-related activity, and shall include the identification of hand signals, apparel, jewelry, and any other significant gang-related material/information.

Note. Reprinted by permission of the New Haven, California, Unified School District (Administrative Regulation for Board Policy 5338).

Attachment 1: Gang Affiliation and Activity

The governing board intends to maintain campuses which are safe for students and staff in accordance with the mandate of the Constitution of the State of California. In meeting this commitment, the governing board finds that gangs which initiate or advocate activities which threaten the safety and well-being of persons or property on school campuses are harmful to the educational purposes for which the schools are operated. The Board further finds that the use of hand signals and the presence of any apparel, jewelry, accessory, book, or manner of grooming which, by virtue of its color, arrangement, trademark, symbol, or any other attribute, denotes membership in such a group creates a clear and present danger of the commission of unlawful acts on school premises or the violation of lawful school regulations, or the substantial disruption of the orderly operation of the school.

The Board further finds that incidents involving initiations, hazings, intimidations, and/or related activities of such group affiliations are likely to cause bodily danger, physical harm, or personal degradation or disgrace resulting in physical or mental harm to students and are prohibited.

The Superintendent or designee shall develop appropriate regulations to ensure that any student wearing, carrying, or displaying gang paraphernalia, or making gestures which symbolize gang membership, or causing an incident affecting the school attendance of another student shall be subject to appropriate disciplinary action.

The Superintendent or designee shall provide staff inservice training in gang recognition and communicate to all staff current symbols of gang membership.

The Superintendent or designee shall establish programs designed to enhance individual self-esteem, to foster interest in a variety of wholesome activities, and to promote membership in authorized student organizations in order to counter gang membership.

Legal Reference:

California Constitution, Article I, Section 28(c)
California Education Code
32050 Hazing Definition
32051 Hazing Definition
48907 Student Rights and School
48900 Grounds for Suspension and Expulsion (General)
48900.5 Suspension by Principal

First Reading: March 7, 1989
Second Reading: March 21, 1989

EXHIBIT G   Crime Control Act of 1990
(S.3266, Title XVII—General Provisions)

SEC. 1702: GUN-FREE SCHOOL ZONES ACT OF 1990

(a) SHORT TITLE—This section may be cited as the "GUN-FREE SCHOOL ZONES ACT of 1990."

(b) PROHIBITIONS AGAINST POSSESSION OR DISCHARGE OF A FIREARM IN A SCHOOL ZONE—

(I) IN GENERAL—Section 922 of title 18, United States Code, is amended by adding at the end the following new subsection: "(q) (1) (A) It shall be unlawful for any individual knowingly to possess a firearm at a place that the individual knows, or has reasonable cause to believe, is a school zone.

"(B) Subparagraph (A) shall not apply to the possession of a firearm—

"(i) on private property not part of the school grounds;

"(ii) if the individual possessing the firearm is licensed to do so by the State in which the school zone is located or a political subdivision requires that, before an individual obtain such a license, the law enforcement authorities of the State or political subdivision verify that the individual is qualified under law to receive the license;

"(iii) which is—

"(I) not loaded; and

"(II) in a locked container, or a locked firearms rack which is on a motor vehicle;

"(iv) by an individual for use in a program approved by a school in the school zone;

"(v) by an individual in accordance with a contract entered into between a school in the school zone and the individual or an employer of the individual;

"(vi) by a law enforcement officer acting in his or her official capacity; or

"(vii) that is unloaded and is possessed by an individual while traversing school premises for the purpose of gaining access to public or private lands open to hunting, if the entry on school premises is authorized by school authorities.

"(2) (A) Except as provided in subparagraph (B), it shall be unlawful for any person, knowingly or with reckless disregard for the safety of another, to discharge or attempt to discharge a firearm at a place that the person knows is a school zone.

"(B) Subparagraph (A) shall not apply to the discharge of a firearm—

"(i) on private property not part of school grounds;

"(ii) as part of a program approved by a school in the school zone, by an individual who is participating in the program;

"(iii) by an individual in accordance with a contract entered into between a school in a school zone and the individual or an employer of the individual; or

"(iv) by a law enforcement officer acting in his or her official capacity.

"(3) Nothing in this subsection shall be construed as preempting or preventing a State or local government from enacting a statute establishing gun-free school zones as provided in this subsection."

Note. This Act amends several sections of title 18 of the United States Code, which is on Crimes and Criminal Procedure. The amended sections are from Part I on Crimes, Chapter 44 on Firearms.

(2) DEFINITIONS—Section 921(a) of such title is amended by adding at the end thereof the following new paragraphs:

"(25) The term 'school zone' means—

"(A) in, or on the grounds of, a public, parochial or private school; or

"(B) within a distance of 1,000 feet from the grounds of a public, parochial or private school.

"(26) The term 'school' means a school which provides elementary or secondary education, as determined under State law.

"(27) The term 'motor vehicle' has the meaning given such term in section 10102 of title 49, United States Code."

(3) PENALTY—Section 924(a) of such title is amended by adding at the end thereof the following new paragraph:

"(4) Whoever violates section 922(q) shall be fined not more than $5,000, imprisoned for not more than 5 years, or both. Notwithstanding any other provision of law, the term of imprisonment imposed under this paragraph shall not run concurrently with any other term of imprisonment imposed under any other provision of law. Except for the authorization of a term of imprisonment of not more than 5 years made in this paragraph, for the purpose of any other law a violation of section 922(q) shall be deemed to be a misdemeanor."

(4) EFFECTIVE DATE—The amendments made by this section shall apply to conduct engaged in after the end of the 60-day period beginning on the date of the enactment of this Act.

(5) GUN-FREE ZONE SIGNS—Federal, State, and local authorities are encouraged to cause signs to be posted around school zones giving warning of prohibition of the possession of firearms in a school zone.

EXHIBIT H   Street Smart Gang Information

Awareness is the first step in helping youths to stay out of drugs and gangs and in preventing drug/gang involvement and activity on the school campus. The purpose of this information booklet is to help you as parents, staff, and administrators to help stop the problems with drugs and gangs in our community and school campuses.

Characteristics of Gangs and Gang Members

1. A gang is two or more people who form an allegiance for a common purpose and engage, individually or collectively, in violence and other criminal activity.

2. Gangs have identifiable leadership and internal organization. They identify with or claim control over territory in a community. Gangs usually form along ethnic and socioeconomic boundaries. They are located in the inner cities and other urban, suburban, and rural areas.

3. The typical gang member may be uneducated but intelligent. Gang members are street smart, able to fend for themselves and accomplished in the art of manipulation.

4. They follow strict codes of conduct and ethics as defined by the gang. They are concerned about proving themselves, being recognized for their work, and establishing a reputation. They are loyal and protective of their turf.

5. They often come from uninvolved families, have other family members involved in gangs, and are disenfranchised from a system that values employment skills and economic security. Gangs are now found in all types of communities and socio-economic levels.

Four Types of Gang Members

1. Hard-core gang members make up approximately 10% of the group. They have been in the gang for the longest period of time. They are frequently in and out of jail, are often unemployed, and use or sell drugs. They are very influential in directing the gang.

2. Regular gang members are younger, usually 14–20 years old. They have been initiated into the gang, often back up the hard-core members in word and action, and are potential hard-core members.

Note. Excerpted from the *Street Smart Gang Information Packet* by permission of Greg Zavala, Anti-Drug Suppression Specialist, Stockton, Colorado, Unified School District. Preparation funded through the Office of Criminal Justice Planning.

3. Wannabes vary in age but average 10–13 years. These youths are not official members of the gang, but they act as or claim to be part of the gang. They often dress in gang attire, spend time with gang members, and write or draw the graffiti associated with the gang.

4. Potentials are potential gang members. They live in or close to areas where there are active gangs, or they have a family member who is already a gang member. They can freely choose other alternatives, thus avoiding gang affiliation completely.

Other Associated Gang Elements

1. Peripheral gang members are people who move in and out of the gang on the basis of their own personal interests or gains. This movement is dependent on the direction of the gang's activities at the moment.

2. Cliques are subgroups of the larger gangs, whose territory covers several city blocks. Many cliques are organized by age, school, or geographical areas.

3. Veteranos are former gang members who are no longer active in the day-to-day activities of the gang. However, they still may reside in the "neighborhood"; and if the "homeboys" become involved in territorial confrontation with a rival gang, the veteranos could become active and assist in the defense of the barrio.

Gangs activity can be prevented and overcome if school staff members can identify, understand, and remove risk factors that encourage gang involvement.

References: National School Safety Center.

Mixed Ethnic Gangs

Gangs usually form ethnic and racial boundaries, although there is a new trend of youths joining gangs for economic motives rather than ethnic differences. The traditional youth gangs that are structured along ethnic lines include those for Hispanic, Asian (e.g., Vietnamese, Filipino), Black, Samoan, and White (e.g., Stoners, Satanic, Punk, Heavy Metal) youths.

Identification of Gangs

Several warning factors exist that indicate a possibility of gang involvement on or off campus. If any of the warning signs are present on a school campus, administrators and staff members should be ready with appropriate prevention and intervention strategies.

Warning Factors

1. An "informal" dress code that is followed by a few students
   (e.g., hats, scarves, jewelry, shoelaces, colors, insignias)

2. Hand signs passed back and forth among students

3. Use of new nicknames

4. The appearance of graffiti on school property, book covers, notebooks

5. Newly acquired and unexplained "wealth" often displayed or shared with peers

6. Increased violent actions on campus, including an increase in the number of referrals for assaults, batteries, and unlawful fighting; weapons on campus; use, sale, or possession of drugs

7. Tattoos on students' hands or arms

8. Expressed racism or hatred of religious groups and certain sexual preferences

Reasons for Joining Gangs

Every youth has basic needs for feelings of self-worth, identity, acceptance, recognition, companionship, belonging, purpose, and security. When families, schools, churches, and communities do not meet these needs, gangs may. Gangs can often supply what traditional systems have failed to provide.

Consequences of Gang Membership

Youths who fall prey to gang seduction pay a high price for membership. Initiation rites often involve committing serious criminal—usually violent—acts to "prove" loyalty.

Gang membership almost guarantees one a criminal record, not to mention the physical risks and dangers of violent activities.

Moreover, gangs often depend upon the youngest members to carry out the most serious offenses because juveniles receive more lenient treatment and lesser penalties when found guilty of a crime.

EXHIBIT I   Graffiti Removal Ordinance

AN ORDINANCE to amend Chapter 18 of the Omaha Municipal Code by adding thereto a new Article VI entitled "Graffiti"; to provide for intent and purpose; to provide for legislative determination; to provide definitions; to provide for prohibition of graffiti; to provide for violations; to provide for penalty; to provide notice for graffiti removal; to provide for lien; to provide for appeal; to provide for removal; to provide for consent; and to provide the effective date hereof.

BE IT ORDAINED BY THE CITY COUNCIL OF THE CITY OF OMAHA:

Section 1. That Chapter 18 of the Omaha Municipal Code is hereby amended, by adding a new Article VI, to read as follows:

"Article VI. Graffiti.

Sections:

18-60 Intent and Purpose
18-61 Legislative Determination
18-62 Definitions
18-63 Prohibition of Graffiti
18-64 Violation—Penalty
18-65 Graffiti—Notice of Removal
18-66 City's Costs Declared Lien
18-67 Appeal
18-68 Removal
18-69 Private Property Consent

18-60. Intent and Purpose

Graffiti on public and private property is a blighting factor which not only depreciates the value of the property which has been the target of such malicious vandalism, but also depreciates the value of the adjacent and surrounding properties, and in so doing, negatively impacts upon the entire community. The City has in the past undertaken to remove graffiti from public property but has been unable to mount a successful program for encouraging the owners of private property to undertake to remove graffiti and other inscribed materials from walls, structures, etc. The legislation of the State of Nebraska has authorized the City to *define, regulate, suppress,* and *prevent* nuisance and to declare what shall constitute a nuisance and to abate and remove the same.

18-61. Legislative Determination

The City Council finds and determines that graffiti is a nuisance and unless it and other inscribed material is removed from public and private properties, it tends to remain; and other properties are then in the target of graffiti with the result that entire neighborhoods and indeed the community is depreciated in value and made a less desirable place to be. The City Council therefore determines that it is appropriate that the City of Omaha develop procedures to implement the provisions of the Revised Statutes of Nebraska, 1943, as amended, and provide for the removal of graffiti and other inscribed material from both public and private property under the circumstances set forth hereinafter.

Note. Passed January 9, 1990, Ordinance No. 31976 of the Omaha, Nebraska, Municipal Code.

The City Council hereby declares as a matter of legislative determination that:

(1) The increasing incidents of the defacement of public and private property through the application of graffiti upon walls, rocks, bridges, buildings, fences, gates, other structures, trees and other real and personal property within the corporate boundaries of the City constitutes a blight on this community, and, in the interests of the health, safety, and general welfare of the residents and taxpayers of the City, immediate steps must be taken to remove this blight.

(2) When appropriate, the courts should require those who commit acts of defacement of public or private property through the application of graffiti to restore the property so defaced, damaged or destroyed.

(3) Obtaining convictions for the application of graffiti is difficult due to the fact that the offense can be committed so very quickly and secretively that witnesses to the act are frequently nonexistent.

(4) The public should be encouraged to cooperate in the elimination of graffiti by reporting to the proper authorities the incidents of the application of graffiti which the members thereof observe.

18-62. Definitions

Whenever the following terms are used in this Chapter, they shall have the meaning established by this section:

a. "Graffiti" means the defacing, damaging, or destroying by spraying of paint or marking of ink, chalk, dye, or other similar substances on public and private buildings, structures, and places.

b. "Graffiti abatement procedure" means an abatement procedure which identifies graffiti, issues notice to the landowner to abate the graffiti, and cures in absence of response.

c. "Private contractor" means any person with whom the City shall have duly contracted to remove graffiti.

18-63. Graffiti–Prohibited

It shall be unlawful for any person to write, paint or draw upon any wall, rock, bridge, building, fence, gate, other structure, tree or other real or personal property, either publicly or privately owned, any drawing, inscription, figure or mark of the type which is commonly know and referred to as "graffiti" within the City of Omaha.

18-64. Graffiti–Violation Penalty

Any person who is convicted of violating Section 18-63 of the Chapter shall be punished by a fine of not exceeding Five Hundred Dollars ($500.00) or by imprisonment not to exceed six (6) months or both such fine and imprisonment. In addition to such punishment, the court may, in imposing sentence, order the defendant to restore the property so defaced, damaged or destroyed.

18–65. Graffiti–Notice of Removal

Whenever the Public Works Director or his/her designated representative determines that graffiti exists on any public and private buildings, structures and
places which are visible to any person utilizing any public right-of-way in this
City, be this road, parkway, alley, or otherwise and that seasonal temperatures
permit the painting of exterior surfaces, the Public Works Director or his/her
designated representative shall cause a notice to be issued to abate such nuisance.
The property owner shall have thirty (30) days after the date of the notice to
remove the graffiti, or the same will be subject to abatement by the City.

The notice to abate graffiti pursuant to this section shall cause a written notice to
be served upon the owner(s) of the affected premises, as such owner's name and
address appears on the last property tax assessment rolls of the County of
Douglas. If there is no known address for the owner, the notice shall be sent in
care of the property address. The notice required by this Section may be served in
any one of the following manners:

  a. By personal service on the owner, occupant or person in charge or
      control of the property.

  b. By registered or certified mail addressed to the owner at the last known
      address of said owner. If this address is unknown, the notice will be sent
      to the property address.

The notice shall be substantially in the following form:

NOTICE OF INTENT TO REMOVE GRAFFITI

Date:

NOTICE IS HEREBY GIVEN that you are required by law at your
expense to remove or paint over the graffiti located on the property
commonly known as _____, Omaha, Nebraska, which is
visible to public view, within thirty (30) days after the date of this notice;
or, if you fail to do so, City employees or private contractors employed by
the City will enter upon your property and abate the public nuisance by
removal or painting over the graffiti. The cost of the abatement by the
City employees or its private contractors will be assessed upon your
property and such costs will constitute a lien upon the land until paid.

All persons having any objection to, or interest in said matters are hereby
notified to submit any objections or comments to the Public Works Director of the City of Omaha or his/her designated representatives within ten
(10) days from the date of this notice. At the conclusion of this thirty (30)
day period the City may proceed with the abatement of the graffiti inscribed on your property at your expense without further notice.

18-66. City's Costs Declared Lien

Any and all costs incurred by the City in the abatement of the graffiti nuisance under the provisions of this Article may constitute a lien against the property upon which such nuisance existed.

18-67. Appeal

Within ten (10) days from the mailing or personal service of the notice, the owner or person occupying or controlling such premises or lot affected may appeal to the Administrative Appeals Board.

18-68. Removal by City

Upon failure of persons to comply with the notice by the designated date, or such continued date thereafter as the Public Works Director or his/her designated representative approves, then the Public Works Director is authorized and directed to cause the graffiti to be abated by City forces or private contract, and the City or its private contractor is expressly authorized to enter upon the premises for such purposes. All reasonable efforts to minimize damage from such entry shall be taken by the City, and any paint used to obliterate graffiti shall be as close as practicable to background color(s). If the Public Works Director provides for the removal of the graffiti or other inscribed material, he shall not authorize nor undertake to provide for the painting or repair of any more extensive area than that where the graffiti or other inscribed material is located.

18-69. Private Property Consent Forms

Property owners in the City of Omaha may consent in advance to City entry onto private property for graffiti removal purposes. The City will make forms for such consent available.

Section 2. This Ordinance shall be in full force and take effect fifteen (15) days from and after the date of its passage.

REFERENCES

Gang membership crosses cultural, geographic bounds. (1991, November). *School Safety Update* (National School Safety Center News Service), pp. 2–3.

Gangs vs. schools: Assessing the score in your community. (1992, March). *School Safety Update* (National School Safety Center News Service), p. 8.

Inglewood School District adopts measures to combat gang activity. (1990, January 14). *Los Angeles Times*, p. 15.

CHAPTER 8

School-Based Interventions: Best Practices and Critical Issues

Donald W. Kodluboy
Loren A. Evenrud

INTRODUCTION

The past decade has seen alarming trends in the composition and activities of youth gangs. Planners, providers, and consumers of school-based interventions need to know about these trends. This chapter will describe the problems that street gangs present for elementary and secondary schools, review typical gang intervention and prevention programs, and emphasize the importance of a "best practice" approach to developing, implementing, and monitoring gang intervention and prevention programs in a school setting. We will discuss critical issues relevant to school-based intervention programs, including academic and social/behavioral "school variables," gang-related behavior viewed as a handicapping condition, school-family interactions, use of contingency management in school settings, program intensity issues, and group processes. Guidelines for interacting with social service agencies and the juvenile justice system will conclude the chapter.

Every large urban school district is affected to some degree by street gang activity. The National Youth Gang Survey revealed that 21 large urban areas currently have gang problems and another 24 have emerging gang problems (Spergel & Curry, 1990). Gangs are present within the boundaries of virtually every major school district in the United States.

District officials rarely report their schools to be "out of control" or irretrievably damaged by the presence of street gangs on campus or in the adjacent neighborhood. City officials tend to underplay the presence of gangs within their jurisdictions for fear of negative perceptions (Hagedorn, 1988, 1990; Huff, 1990). School officials also commonly first deny and then downplay criminal activity on or near campus (Stover, 1987; Rubel & Ames, 1986). Independent evidence suggests, however, that even though gang violence within schools is not common, the influence of gangs within and near schools is significant (Gaustad, 1990; Lopez, 1989; Nebgen, 1990; Prophet, 1990; Spergel, 1990; Stephens, 1991; Thompson & Jason,

1988). Armed children continue to appear at the schoolhouse door as fear escalates in many communities. Gang activity has brought the threat of violence to student life to an alarming extent: It is estimated that over 135,000 children bring guns to school every day in the United States (Children's Defense Fund, 1991). Burke (1991) reports that in a recent locker search following trouble in a San Francisco Bay Area high school, 62 guns were found, 40 of them in the lockers of female students. Rowland, Fountain, and Martinez (1991) report the growing presence of marginal and some core gang members in suburban Chicago schools. The exact relationship between gang presence in the community and the phenomenon of armed students is unknown. It is certain, however, that gangs contribute to a culture of fear and heighten students' perceived need to go to school armed to defend themselves in case of attack. Spergel (1990) reports that fear is indeed one of the major effects of gang presence in a community.

Definitions

In this discussion of school-based interventions, the focus will be on school-age gang members. However, though most street gang members join at an early age, they tend to stay involved well into adulthood (Spergel & Chance, 1991).

A youth or street gang is defined as a closely or loosely organized association of individuals who express their identification through private language, symbolic behavior, and the wearing of "colors" and who commonly claim territory in a neighborhood. The gang and its individual members tend to engage in criminal behavior primarily, though not exclusively, as a function of the association; this distinguishes them from conventional age-mates or nongang delinquents (Fagan, 1989). The gang is generally, though not always, ethnically homogeneous. It is primarily a male institution; females rarely represent a significant percentage of members (Spergel & Chance, 1991).

Behavioral expectations for gang members are usually expressed through some form of directive gang leadership, whether hierarchical or consensual. Individual members may be rewarded or sanctioned for compliance or noncompliance with those expectations. When school-age youths join gangs, they most commonly do so in a natural search for adolescent social interaction more than through any formal recruitment process (Fagan, 1989). Recruitment, sometimes formal but usually in the form of simple proximity or "hanging out" with gang members (Fagan, 1989), commonly takes place in or near the schoolyard of the new member (Spergel, 1990).

Percentages

The number of school-age gang members in a geographic area may vary greatly according to the demographic characteristics of the area. In areas where geographic, social, and economic isolation of ethnic populations is extreme, numbers are likely to be high. Spergel (1990) notes that the typical percentage of age-eligible youths involved in gangs ranges from 3 to 10%. Baker (1988; cited in Spergel, 1990) found that in one assessment, 25% of a sample alleged gang affiliation. Where Asian youth gangs are concerned, the figure is commonly below 1%, though it may be rising to as high as 3% among some recent Southeast Asian immigrants (S. Hahn, personal communication, November 22, 1991). The significance of this finding, consistent across the nation, is that most school-age youths do not join street gangs, even though they experience many of the same structural and cultural stressors as those who do.

Motivation

The most commonly cited reasons for joining a gang also vary markedly by gang type. They include protection, status and identity, access to friends, a feeling of family, protection of the neighborhood, and access to girls (Fagan, 1989). Gang prevention programs often attempt to offer at-risk youth socially acceptable, motivational equivalents to gang membership. School officials planning such programs as school-based interventions are advised to analyze carefully the specific reasons youths in a given neighborhood express for joining a gang. Broad theory as to why youths join gangs must not determine which components will be included in any specific program. Rather, program decisions should be based on direct ecological analysis of specific situations and individuals encountered. Not all gang-affiliated youths join gangs for the same reasons, even within a given community. Moreover, experience suggests that gang-involved youngsters will often accommodate researchers' and service providers' suggestions regarding their behavior and will sometimes be other than truthful (Hagedorn, 1988; Jankowski, 1991). Consider, for example, planners of an intervention program that offers constructive recreation opportunities: They may assume that achieving a "family feeling" is local youths' primary motivation for joining a gang. Gang members are likely to echo that philosophy to maintain access to the recreation program, even if it does not reflect their true sentiments.

Recruitment

The primary age range for recruitment into street gangs is 11 to 15 years. This is also the age at which students are most likely to begin truanting from school, affiliating more closely with peers than with family, and spending more time away from direct adult supervision. When these latter factors are present for at-risk youths who live in gang-influenced communities, opportunities for gang involvement are plentiful. When enough at-risk youths are present in a given area to increase the probability of interaction with gang members through simple proximity, the result is a "critical mass" that fuels gang development and maintenance.

Geography

The geographic range of street gangs has broadened to include most large (and, increasingly, many smaller) urban centers across the nation (Gaustad, 1990;

National School Safety Center, 1988; Spergel, 1990). Los Angeles street gang contingents and "home-grown," largely independent variants of several Los Angeles gangs—notably the Crips and Bloods—are found as far north of Los Angeles as Seattle and as far east-northeast as Minnesota (Midwest Gang Investigators Association [MGIA], 1990). Chicago-based gangs are seen over much of the Midwest, occasionally as far south and southeast as the gulf and mid-Atlantic states; even small towns located along interstate highways that connect large cities are affected (MGIA, 1990). Highly mobile Asian youth gangs have affected primarily Asian communities from New York City to Long Beach, California, to as far north as Edmonton, Alberta (Burke & O'Rear, 1990; Shilliday, 1991).

In each town hosting more than a transient visit by gang members, school-age youths are affected both directly and indirectly. Direct effects range from victimization through criminal activity to coercion into gang membership (Spergel, 1990). Indirect effects include the obligation to adapt to an environment of fear, threats, and intimidation (Zinsmeister, 1990).

Many students have problems in academic performance, social behavior, and connectedness to the life of the school. When such students cluster in areas characterized by social, economic, and racial isolation and marginalization, the critical mass necessary for gang formation exists. When this marginalization occurs within both the dominant ethnic subpopulation and the greater community, there is increased probability that a pervasive gang culture will thrive. School-age youths in such a community are exposed daily to gang-related activities and gang subcultural values to a significant degree (Lemann, 1986a). In affected communities where gang subculture is often increasingly intergenerational, as in some Hispanic communities of Los Angeles (Jankowski, 1991; Vigil, 1990) and in many of the "ghetto poor" or "underclass" African American communities of the Midwest, the pervasive influence of gang life on young people is apparent. Although the manifestations and specific influence of intergenerational, ethnic, and subcultural variables differ considerably across gangs and geographic locations, the behavioral outcomes for school-age youths are remarkably consistent.

Problem Behaviors

The range of gang-related problem behaviors seen in schools is broad. The most common behavior is "representing" or "flying colors": wearing clothes of particular colors or styles. Associated with flying colors is "signing" or using hand signals specific to the gang, as well as using gang-specific language or argot (such as the Crips' "What's the buzz, Cuz") and displaying gang nicknames or tags (such as "Shorty Mac"). Such displays increase gang cohesion, strengthen group identity, and allow individuals to assume the social status of the group while in school.

Gang-related criminal behaviors typically include physical and verbal threats and intimidation of nongang peers or rival gang members, simple assault, extortion, drug sale, and theft. Less common are aggravated assault and the display and use of weapons, including firearms. Criminal behaviors may be considered gang related when they are done at the direction of the gang, benefit the gang, or constitute specific responses by a potential victim to threats from a rival gang.

NATURE OF THE PROBLEM FOR SCHOOL SYSTEMS

Although administrators nationwide express grave concern over gang activity in schools (Stephens, 1989), few studies or reports from school districts provide clear data on or distinctions between gang and nongang problem behavior affecting schools. Unfortunately, either that distinction is not made in incident reports or the reports making the distinction are unreliable because reporting procedures vary. For example, the Chicago Police Department reported in 1985 and 1986 that 10 to 11% of gang-related incidents occurred on or near school campuses, whereas the Chicago public schools reports for the same period show that "only 2% of discipline code violations were gang related" (Spergel, 1990). This discrepancy may reflect differences in focus of attention of school and police officials, gang members' taking action out of view of school officials, or both.

The broad range of antisocial or asocial behaviors among current youth gang members has been well documented (Fagan, 1989; Huff, 1990; Jankowski, 1991; Sibley, 1989; Spergel, 1990; Taylor, 1990). This body of research suggests that there are many types of gangs, developing and either persisting or breaking up, lasting a few years or several generations, their longevity depending on the cultural, geographic, economic, and social attributes of the environment where they first appear. As a school district recognizes and responds to gang presence in the community, the specific problems encountered will depend on the type of gang; the stage of its evolution; the response of school, community, and business; and the degree of social, economic, and racial isolation in the greater community. Therefore, the lessons learned and experiences documented must be reviewed within the context of each community or city.

Fagan's 1989 analysis of gang social organization is an excellent and thorough examination of the range of problem behaviors exhibited by gang-affiliated youths and of their reasons for joining gangs. Fagan ascertained that, among gang members, drug use is common, indeed the norm; that in most gangs, violent behaviors occur; and that a disproportionate number of gang members are involved in delinquent acts when compared with delinquent youths who are not gang affiliated. The increase in gang-related activity across communities is apparent (Spergel & Chance, 1991), as are the disturbing and highly public types of crime commonly associated with gang violence—that is, drive-by shootings and gang homicides (Curry & Spergel, 1988; Maxson, Gordon, & Klein, 1985; Meyer, 1991). Fortunately for the school-based professional, these phenomena typically occur in the vicinity rather than in the school itself, but the impact on students is nonetheless great, and several tragic gang-related assaults have occurred on school property (Burke, 1991; Prophet, 1990; Stephens, 1989; Witkin, 1991).

Basic Concepts Central to Intervention

To be effective, intervention must be responsive to the particular situation. The social learning approach to gang-related behavior provides both an appropriate means of analysis and a guide for intervention. School-based interventions for youth gangs must be neither too much nor too little, neither overreaction nor under-reaction, and more objective than emotional. The role and nature of school-related gang activity vary greatly from place to place, from generation to generation, and even from year to year. A one-size-fits-all approach to intervention is doomed to failure. Any approach that is disproportionate to the measurable, observable impact of gang activity on a school or community is likely to be counterproductive and prejudicial. An objective, culturally sensitive and prescriptive, data-based approach is called for.

This chapter is based on a social learning systems approach to gang problems. This model is well researched and well documented in both the basic and the clinical-applied research literature. It incorporates recognized standards of measurement and evaluation and has demonstrated reliability and validity as well as a strong empirical base. Although for certain individuals some concern about "within-child pathology" may be appropriate, few data exist to support broad application of such notions or analyses in interventions with gang-affiliated youth (Goldstein, 1991; Jankowski, 1991; Spergel, 1990). Psychopathological approaches are generally not recommended. Instead, we advocate a balanced psychological perspective, as characterized by Goldstein (1991), in which each individual is assessed and prescriptive educational and psychological intervention planned on the basis of assessment results. The importance of using a social learning model in analyzing and responding to the problems of behavior-disordered and delinquent youths is well documented in the literature (Bernal, Klinnert, & Schultz, 1980; Goldstein, 1991; Jenson, Clark, Walker, & Kehle, 1991; Kelley & Stokes, 1982; Kirigin, Braukmann, Atwater, & Wolf, 1982; Reid & Patterson, 1991; Welch & Holborn, 1988; Wolf, Braukmann, & Ramp, 1987). School officials, in reviewing programs for systematic replication within their districts, can be guided by this literature and the derived practices of direct assessment, intervention, and monitoring of observable behaviors for progress, as opposed to indirect measures of psychoeducational concepts. Earlier chapters in this book cite both the reliability and social validity of social learning concepts in gang-related interventions. This chapter will discuss the adaptation of those concepts to school systems in their roles as direct service providers and collaborative agencies.

The social learning approach recognizes that individuals learn gang-related behaviors in the same way as they learn all other behaviors. No underlying individual psychopathology is assumed as either a prerequisite or a necessary outcome of learning and displaying gang-related behaviors. Review of the literature suggests that few generalizations can be made about individual psychopathology as a cause of such behaviors (Jankowski, 1991; Spergel, 1990). Once learned, gang-related behaviors are expressed; they are rewarded and thereby enhanced, or discouraged and thereby eliminated, by individuals and institutions in the community where the behaviors occur.

Impact of Gangs

What is the specific impact of gangs on students, schools, and the school community, and what is the role of educators in responding to the gang problem in the United States? The National Education Association (NEA) refers to gang-related activity in its 1991–1992 resolutions. That organization holds that gang activity is a function of economic isolation and inadequate educational opportunity and supports collaboration among family, school, community, business, and law enforcement agencies in the effort to reduce gang-related crime (NEA Representative Assembly, 1991). Specifically, programs that promote positive self-image and academic success, such as dropout prevention programs, before- and after-school programs, and job training programs, are recommended. Law enforcement is viewed as supplemental to education, and the business community is encouraged to provide meaningful job opportunities.

Because of inadequacies and inconsistencies in the reporting of school "incidents" as gang related or not gang related, it is impossible to determine the exact numbers of such incidents or their significance nationwide or even within a given school district. There is no system for uniformly documenting gang-related incidents in public school settings. It is recommended that schools record and report problem behavior and behavior that violates local criminal codes, and that they follow best practice recommendations in this area (Spergel & Chance, 1991) in deciding whether to code incidents as gang related.

Behavior may be coded as gang related when (a) the behavior is directed by gang leadership or by consensus of gang members; (b) the behavior benefits the gang and not just the individual offender; (c) gang motivation is present as indicated (for example, by displaying of colors, shouting of gang phrases, or displaying of gang symbols during the act); or (d) the behavior is a direct response to gang activity (for instance, when a student brings a weapon to school in direct response to a gang threat or is truant out of fear based on a specific gang threat).

Assuming a "best practice" model of analysis and drawing on the literature concerning the generalization of social behavior learned in one setting to another setting, we can state the following: The probability that students will exhibit gang-related criminal behavior in school will depend on the degree to which the school environment resembles the environment where the students typically engage in gang-related behavior. Hence, the likelihood of those problem behaviors occurring in the school will be determined by their presence in the community and the presence or absence of school conditions that encourage, maintain, or discourage gang identification.

The impact of youth gangs on schools can be inferred from numerous reports of violence in and, especially, near the schoolyard. According to Witkin (1991), the National School Safety Center estimates that 135,000 students carried guns to school daily in 1987. Stephens (1989) reports that a 1988 survey of superintendents and representatives of 17 of the nation's major school districts identified the three major safety problems in these districts as drugs, gangs, and weapons. Stover (1988) observes that the severity of violence has increased particularly with the impact of drugs and gangs.

The 1987 National Adolescent Health Survey, cited in Zinsmeister (1990), revealed that 8% of all urban junior and senior high school students surveyed missed at least 1 school day per month out of fear and that 13% had been attacked one or more times in the previous year. Busch, Zagar, Hughes, Arbit, & Bussell (1990), in a study of adolescents who commit homicide, reports the four strongest predictors of adolescent homicide to be presence of a criminally violent family member, membership in a gang, abuse of drugs or alcohol, and presence of an educational handicap such as a learning disability. Urban educators will recognize this constellation of circumstances among many of their students. Pynoos and Eth (1985) and Batchelor and Wicks (1985; both cited in Bell & Jenkins, 1990), examining causes of homicide among African Americans, report that in Los Angeles and Detroit, 10 to 20% of all murders are witnessed by school-age youngsters. Jenkins and Thompson (1986) found that 25% of 536 elementary school children had seen someone shot. According to Shakoor and Chalmers (in press; cited in Bell & Jenkins, 1990), in "a survey of 1000 high school students, 23% had seen someone killed and 40% of those victims were family, friends, classmates, or neighbors" (p. 154).

Observing trends in Portland, Oregon, Prophet (1990) reports an increase in gang activities, activities linked primarily to the drug trade and Los Angeles street gang emigrés. Enrollment declined at three Portland high schools because of gang activity on or near the school campuses. In Chicago, according to Thompson and Jason (1988), although current gangs are of long standing, there has been a recent increase in activity, with the public schools providing youths of prime recruitment age. They cite reports of 40,000 schoolchildren attacked or threatened by gang members in 1981. Spergel (1990), in his major review of street gangs, notes that in the Chicago public schools, typically 5% of elementary students, 10% of high school students, 20% of special program students, and 35% of dropouts aged 16 to 19 are gang members. From these figures, Spergel concludes that 38,000 Chicago students were gang members during 1985.

Graffiti, a very common but often unrecognized representation of gang affiliation, appears near, on, or in school buildings. Graffiti generally advertises the presence of gang affiliates in a school or reflects conflict over gang territory. Spergel (1990) states that graffiti expresses ownership or control of schools, parks, and adjacent areas. Acknowledging that school gang recruitment data are of unknown reliability, he reports that in two high schools studied, 45% of males and 22% of females were asked to join gangs in or near their schools and that 25% of students who dropped out did so because of gang activity in the schools. In Chicago, 10% of students reported fearing street gang members while in school. Lemann (1986a, 1986b) and Spergel (1990) both note that fear is one of the most insidious effects of gangs on a community.

In 1987, the Detroit public schools closed for 2 days in the wake of the shooting of 102 youngsters, aged 16 and under, during a 4-month period (Zinsmeister, 1990). Gaustad (1990) describes an environment of pervasive fear, in which nongang students sometimes bring weapons to school for protection from gang members. Stephens (1989) reports that in one Los Angeles high school, a gang claimed a public phone booth as its turf and then shot and killed a nongang student who tried to use the phone. Bazar (1990) notes that in Long Beach, California, the 1989 gang drive-by shooting toll rose to 69, with 34 killed in such incidents in that single year. In Compton, California, one of the Los Angeles area communities most severely affected by gangs, the school system was besieged by gang activity during most of the 1980s (Putka, 1991). Also in Compton, in 1983 five students were shot at

Dominguez Hills High School, in 1987 a school security officer was killed, and in 1990 a janitor was killed at a grade school; all these were gang-related shootings. In the first 6 months of 1991, Chicago police confiscated 158 firearms in or near the city's public schools (Blau, 1991).

The National Crime Survey (U. S. Department of Justice, 1991) reveals that school-age youths aged 12 to 19 are far more likely than adults to be victims of violence and theft. At the same time, this population is the least likely to report crime to school or law enforcement officials (McDermott, 1979). Schools and contiguous streets and parks are frequently places of victimization for school-age youths (U. S. Department of Justice, 1991).

PROGRAMS, PAST AND PRESENT

The literature regarding gangs in schools and school-affiliated gang intervention programs describes numerous programs designed to prevent or reduce gang affiliation and related problem behavior (Goldstein, 1991; Huff, 1990; Spergel, 1990). However, both Goldstein and Spergel, reviewing organized responses to gangs, note a significant lack of reliable data on the effectiveness of such programs. Additionally, most programs reviewed do not focus specifically on outcomes of school-based interventions. Most studies and reports lack independent evaluation of the reliability and generality of reported positive effects and systematic replications of promising programs. In this section we will discuss a sample of activities currently being implemented in school districts nationwide and will review the literature related to such programs.

Goldstein's (1991) review of street gang programs cites numerous current programs, specifically in California and New York state, as promising, while recognizing that systematic evaluation is as yet lacking. Miller (1990) notes the chaotic and often parochial nature of poorly funded and uncoordinated responses to gangs in the United States. Although aspects of some past programs hint at useful strategies, complete and cohesive prescriptive models remain elusive.

Although no single program has demonstrated complete success, selected elements of many programs are noteworthy and deserve consideration for systematic replication elsewhere. The apparent dramatic effectiveness of the Perry Preschool Project (Huff, 1990) in reducing later adolescent delinquency is encouraging but is rarely emphasized in gang prevention literature. The beneficial aspects of the educational component of the Chicago Youth Authority Project, aimed at helping youths adjust to school (Spergel, 1990), may be both replicable in new programs and effective for preventing gang affiliation. Kohn and Shelly (1991) recently reported a reduction of gang affiliation achieved through the Young Horizons program in Long Beach, California, results that merit further analysis for replicability and applicability to other settings. The often-cited Paramount California Program reports remarkable success as measured by attitude surveys of young participants (Spergel, 1990), but independent direct measures of actual gang membership or figures on concurrent gang-related delinquent behavior in the community are not generally available.

In a recent survey, the Dade County, Florida, public schools counted an estimated 55 street gangs with 3,000 members within the school district boundaries (L. Harris, personal communication, September 22, 1991). Within that school district a uniform code of conduct addresses specific student behavior problems, designated staff members allocate a percentage of their time to gang-related issues, and staff receive inservice training including a gang resource document that communicates basic expectations and lists support resources. The district participates in the Dade County Juvenile Gang Intervention Project. The Dallas public school district has adopted a similar approach for dealing with a reported 200 gangs with 2,000 members (L. Harris, personal communication, September 22, 1991). The Dallas school district also provides staff training directed toward early identification and prevention and cooperates closely with local police departments in sharing information.

The Los Angeles County Office of Education designates an educational representative to the Los Angeles County Interagency Gang Task Force. The task force disseminates information to interested education agencies to foster the exchange of information on gang prevention and intervention. The county office of education is currently involved in implementing, monitoring, and evaluating 14 pilot programs as part of the major Gang Risk Intervention Pilot Program (GRIPP). Los Angeles, Dallas, Dade County, New York, Chicago, Portland, and most other large urban districts now have some formal, ongoing activities in place to prevent and respond to gang-related problems in schools and the nearby community. Most of these programs establish formal linkages with social service agencies and with law enforcement, juvenile justice, and juvenile parole and probation authorities. Some cities and school districts are forming linkages with the business community as well to enhance the social validity of prevention and intervention programs.

The Orange County public schools have recently embarked on an ambitious antidrug/gang violence collaborative model for grades 3, 5, and 7. The model integrates a variety of materials and strategies into the core English–language arts and history–social science frameworks already in place in all schools. Prevention, recognition of cultural diversity, and alternatives for students are emphasized (Orange County Department of Education, 1991).

In Portland, Oregon, the GRIT (Gang Resource and Intervention Team) program was conceived in 1989 to respond to gang-involved youths. In addition to improving communication between juvenile justice and law enforcement personnel, the program aims to direct gang-involved youths to alternative educational programs and enhance cooperation between juvenile authorities and the Portland public schools. Teacher training and development of a gang resistance curriculum are part of the GRIT program (Multnomah County of Oregon Juvenile Justice Division, 1989).

In the recent past, some researchers, such as Hagedorn (1988), have been interpreted as viewing law enforcement strategies for suppressing gang activity as essentially antithetical to effective prevention and intervention efforts. Huff (1990), in extending the analysis, notes the failure of "stand alone" law enforcement suppression approaches in the absence of concurrent collaboration with social service agencies. Perhaps owing to the severity of current gang-related criminal behavior, some school districts now have either voluntary or court-authorized exchange of information between school officials and parole, probation, law enforcement, and criminal justice personnel. Rapp, Stephens, and Clontz (1989) advocate facilitating access to juvenile justice, school, and criminal records on a need-to-know basis for concerned professionals involved with students at risk for, or engaging in, criminal behavior. Many large school districts see law enforcement and criminal justice agencies as having more than the "supplemental" role recently suggested by the National Education Association (NEA Representative Assembly, 1991). The Mountain View school district in Los Angeles County, recognizing that "law enforcement plays a pivotal role," has developed a program to foster a "proactive, positive relationship between police and youth at risk" as a way of addressing gang involvement (Ybarra, 1991, p. 2). In Burbank, California, the public schools, Police Department, and court services have sited collaborative personnel in the Burbank Unified Outreach Center to facilitate comprehensive planning for students at risk (M. Rosoff, personal communication, June 10, 1991). The St. Paul, Minnesota, Police Department has begun a community crime prevention program called ACOP (A Community Outreach Program) in four public housing communities. Its activities consist of community outreach and education, prompt diversion of first-time offenders, and school liaison in the Southeast Asian immigrant community recently affected by gangs (J. Mollner, personal communication, November 20, 1991).

A promising trend in these and other programs may be the recognition that educational and law enforcement personnel can find a common focus on prevention and alternative educational strategies. A forced choice between educational and suppression strategies is viewed as unnecessary and counterproductive in the context of a social learning, collaborative-prescriptive model. Best practice assumes collaboration among all agencies that interact with gang-affiliated youths and that serve gang-influenced communities.

A review of the outcome literature regarding gang prevention and intervention programs reveals several components that are part of most school systems. Conclusions and suggestions for further research and development of pilot programs follow from the outcome data. With the increasingly broad mandate of the nation's public school systems to interact with a widening range of external resources and agencies, school-based prevention and intervention programs clearly must be collaborative with these agencies. It is important to review programs commonly implemented by school personnel, both independently and in collaborative efforts.

BEST PRACTICE

We advise a literature-based best practice approach for school district officials analyzing and responding to perceived gang problems. This approach gives decision makers a conceptual and operational framework within which to evaluate, select, and modify programs. Simple, direct replication in one district of previously developed programs from another district is generally inadvisable unless critical implementation issues are first understood. A clear view of what constitutes best practice with regard to all aspects of program development and evaluation will allow districts to select appropriate programs and adapt them to their particular needs.

Best practice assumes that prevention and intervention strategies to be included under the broad umbrella of school-based interventions will meet common minimum professional standards. Best practice also means that the empirical literature on programs or program components will be examined and used as appropriate for the school district. Independent objective evaluation of program effects is central to a best practice model (McConnell, 1990). Careful attention to individual, community, and societal concerns about gangs is necessary to ensure the social validity of selected programs. Strong ethical regard for each individual client's best long-term interest is also an essential feature of best practice.

Any gang-focused program to be implemented within the public schools or in a collaboration between public schools and community agencies should:

1. Be related to and share the common mission and objectives of the school and school district

2. Be public and accountable

3. Be based on established standards of the profession or social service agency involved

4. Have specific, written projected outcomes

5. Have reasonable timelines for attaining the projected outcomes and meeting commitments

6. Monitor progress toward individual and agency objectives, using simple, direct measures

7. Be subject to external review

8. Demonstrate social validity through broad-based community involvement of all interested parties, such as businesses, neighborhood representatives, and others

9. Be free of cultural bias and consistent with prevailing prosocial community goals and norms

The absence of any of these qualities in a program may make outcome data less generalizable and make comparisons between programs unreliable. Perhaps the most critical variables, especially for a new program, are measurement variables. The time-tested measurement aphorism, "When you don't know where you are going, any road will take you there," is the main reason we know so little about what works and what does not work in gang prevention and intervention.

Antimeasurement bias can undercut the effectiveness of these critically important programs. Those implementing any gang prevention or intervention program within the public schools are urged to follow established principles and procedures of educational research.

For best practice in evaluation, McConnell (1990) recommends (a) working knowledge of research design, (b) description of critical aspects of expected student performance, (c) collection of data in a standardized and reliable manner, and (d) data analysis and interpretation that are meaningful to a wide audience. It is further recommended that ongoing formative evaluation, as well as summative evaluation, be used whenever possible. Both types of measurement are necessary, especially with programs that are politically sensitive and socially significant.

Conceptual Definitions of School Variables

Identifying several relevant and accessible school variables, such as delinquency in school and student values regarding school, allows educators to focus on only those variables that are most likely to affect student gang affiliation. This effort should lead to more efficient allocation of services and simplification of program evaluations.

Although there is an established data base on delinquent behavior per se, Spergel's (1990) review of youth gang research suggests that the problem of delinquent gangs in the specific context of schools has not been adequately studied. Data on school-based intervention and prevention programs are at best inconclusive. What is discernible from Spergel's review is that gang members tend to be relatively alienated from school. Spergel cites research showing that 80% of gang members in one large city in Florida are dropouts and estimates that in Chicago 35% of dropouts between 16 and 19 years of age are gang members. A higher dropout rate for gang members, along with a lack of connectedness with school, is a common finding in current research and in itself does not differentiate gang and nongang dropouts. Moreover, it is not certain what proportion of students drop out as opposed to being "pushed out" for gang-related behavior in school, nor is it clear at which age either reason predominates. Fagan (1989), interviewing members of four different types of gangs, found that 22 to 67% expressed some conventional values with regard to school. Such statements as "School is important to me" and "School is important to the gang" drew affirmative responses from youths representing all identified gang types. These findings suggest that gang members are likely to hold some conventional school-related values, which school personnel may be able to reinforce. Taylor (1990) suggests that vigilant school staffs and supportive school environments are necessary to counteract the impact of gangs and drugs in besieged communities.

Clements' (1988) analysis of delinquency prevention and treatment, though it does not deal specifically with predicting risk for gang membership, is illuminating in the context of street gangs. Among other findings, Clements suggests that (a) there is a strong correlation between school variables and delinquency; (b) parental supervision is inversely related to delinquency; and (c) the prime locus of prevention, control, and treatment is the local community. Walker and Sylvester (1991), in a review of research from the Oregon Social Learning Center, note that the "single best predictor of adolescent criminal behavior is a long established pattern of early school antisocial behavior" (p. 14). Further, speaking of antisocial adolescents affiliating with a peer group that supports delinquent acts, they observe that a "member of such a deviant group has an almost 70% chance of experiencing a first felony arrest within two years" (p. 14). Reid and Patterson (1991) state that measures of aggression are extremely stable over time, suggesting that early school intervention is critically important.

Among the three major foci of school, family, and community, the school exists as a constant link. Accordingly, the school is in prime position to coordinate and, in fact, shape collaborative services.

School Climate and Gang-Related Behavior

Before any gang intervention program can be successfully implemented, basic issues regarding school climate must be addressed. These issues involve physical facilities, personal interactions, and school policies concerning behavior and dress standards, discipline, and gang graffiti.

School climate may be described as the physical and social-interactive conditions in a school that (a) signal to students which behaviors are acceptable and which are not acceptable; (b) clearly demarcate school areas where (or times of day when) certain behaviors will be rewarded or sanctioned; (c) demarcate which school microenvironments are supervised and which unsupervised (and at which times); and (d) indicate to students which adults in which school settings will provide support, assistance, feedback, supervision, and—in some instances— protection. A positive school climate is a necessary first step for decreasing the probability that gang activity will occur on a school campus (National School Safety Center, 1988; Nebgen, 1990; Riley, 1991; Rubel & Ames, 1986; Stover, 1988; Taylor, 1990). Reliable and predictable adults, present in all environments where students are found, provide students with necessary supervision and feedback on their behavior.

The principal is often cited as the primary influence in establishing a positive, safe school climate (Rubel & Ames, 1986). Strong relationships between staff and students likewise support a positive climate. Students should participate actively with faculty in developing activities and strategies to ensure that all students have equal access to learning and social opportunities. Students may assist in developing dress and behavior codes. They should be assured that consequences for appropriate and inappropriate social behavior will be applied equitably. Other elements of climate that are important to all students' academic achievement are relevant curriculum, including active teaching and reinforcement of prosocial behavior; instruction at levels appropriate to student functioning; and strong parent involvement.

In addition to positive interactions between students and staff, certain basic physical attributes of schools facilitate prosocial behavior and discourage gang-related behavior. These physical features include (a) clear sight lines so that supervising adults can see all areas in which students congregate or travel; (b) ample natural or artificial lighting to facilitate supervision and monitoring; (c) an absence of physical, visual barriers that would allow disruptive student behavior to go unnoticed; (d) perimeter security to prevent unsupervised access to or unimpeded egress from campus for both students and nonstudents; (e) conspicuous presence of adult security personnel; (f) obvious visual reminders of student activities, work products, projects, and social activities on walls and bulletin boards; (g) a high rate of brief, positive social interaction between staff and students during passing times.

Gang-safe schools are kept free of all gang graffiti (National School Safety Center, 1988; Riley, 1991); graffiti, when found, must be removed immediately. This practice discourages further graffiti and signals to students that the school is a safe, gang behavior–free environment, in which gang-involved students are not allowed to claim visually any school space. In severely affected areas, the presence of gang graffiti is often intimidating to nongang students. For gang-involved students, such graffiti is often a challenge to confrontation. Students from one gang may refuse to attend school when graffiti from a rival gang is allowed to persist on school property.

To keep the school graffiti-free, the staff should be trained to recognize and report all known or suspected graffiti to school officials. Gang graffiti is commonly found in classrooms on surfaces visible to students but not to teachers. Class-room walls, doorjambs at eye level, desks, and maps are common graffiti targets. School lavatories, isolated building entrances, and locker rooms are also favored locations. The graffiti may be gang logos or personal "tags" of individual gang members' nicknames, printed in stylized fashion. Gang graffiti may decorate the name tags of kindergartners, the worksheets or books of middle school students, or the jewelry of secondary students. Staff vigilance and continuing education are crucial to effectively implementing a zero tolerance policy regarding gang graffiti.

In safe schools, staff are highly visible at all times in areas where students travel, congregate, or receive instruction. Students receive positive, personal attention from adults at a high rate. The range of positive, constructive, prosocial activities for students is wide and is developed with the cooperation of representative students and their families.

Whenever new school colors, banners, logos, or themes are selected, the context of the community should be considered. In established gang neighbor-hoods, school officials must be aware of gang traditions so they can avoid inadvertent use of gang colors or symbols. When a gang arrives in a neighborhood long after school colors or symbols are established, officials should try to block gang commandeering of the color or symbol by supporting its appropriate use by students and discussing its misuse frankly and privately with gang-involved students.

Similarly, staff should be aware of gang traditions in dress and language and avoid inadvertently "representing" gang colors, dress, or language themselves (Taylor, 1990). Gang-involved students note such unintended behavior on the part of adults and sometimes gauge a teacher's awareness by his or her dress and language. These students find considerable amusement in teachers who unknowingly wear gang colors, favored clothing items such as starter jackets, or certain kinds of earrings, or who use gang terms—such as "Cuz" in the west or "People" or "Folks" in the Midwest—in conversations with students.

Perhaps the most controversial school district response to gang activity on school campuses is the institution of strict dress and behavior codes. Although some feel that control of gang "representing" in the form of dress, language, or hand signs is unnecessary, the dominant opinion strongly supports the use of such codes in decreasing or preventing gang-related problem behavior in schools. It is clearly established that students who are gang members will use gang colors, clothing, and symbolism of speech and hand signs to claim territory, issue challenges, or insult rival gang members in school.

Although dress codes are often used effectively in districts where gang-related criminal behavior is common, a district with an emerging gang problem may be hesitant to issue a formal policy. The arguments against such dress codes generally revolve around students' right to self-expression through dress as a measure of free speech. The courts, however, have indicated that such rights are more limited than educators commonly assume. Two major court cases address this issue directly. In *Bethel School District No. 403 v. Fraser* (106 S. Ct. 3159, 1986), the court recognized the right of the school board to limit student rights to expression. Specifically, this case involved a student's right to use offensive language in a speech delivered to the student body in an assembly. The court found that the right of students to advocate controversial views "must be balanced against society's countervailing interest in teaching students boundaries of socially appropriate behavior" (at 3159). In writing the majority opinion, Justice Burger wrote:

> Nothing in constitution prohibits states from insisting that certain modes of expression are inappropriate and subject to sanctions, furthermore, inculcation of these values is truly work of schools and determination of what manner of speech in classroom or school assembly is inappropriate properly rests with school board. (at 3161)

Burger further wrote, "Given school's need to be able to impose disciplinary sanctions for wide range of unanticipated conduct disruptive of educational process, school disciplinary rules need not be as detailed as criminal code which imposes criminal sanctions" (at 3160). The key aspect of this decision for implementation of dress codes is the school district's responsibility to determine that a certain kind of behavior is disruptive of the educational environment.

Because gang-related behavior often is substantially disruptive and a material interference with the school environment, sanctions may prohibit further such behavior when the disruption can be demonstrated. Disruption might be observed, for example, when students refuse to walk a hallway dominated by others who congregate there wearing gang colors and issuing gang-related comments such as "This is Folks' territory"; when student altercations break out as a result of gang symbols being displayed in school; or when students refuse to enter a classroom or use a playground because gang-affiliated students display gang colors or use gang language.

School officials considering implementing dress codes to prevent gang conflict are referred to *Oleson v. Board of Education of School District No. 228* (676 F. Supp. 820; N. D. Ill., 1987), which involved a student's right to wear a gang-favored earring to school. The student commonly associated with a known gang, the Simon City Royals, and the earring he wore was a known gang symbol. In this case a pattern of gang-related behavior in the school and community disruptive to the educational process was established, and the district policy on "Prohibiting Gangs and Gang Activities" was cited. The court, in referencing *Bethel v. Fraser*, emphasized the right of the school board to direct the instruction of young people about their role in a democratic society. The court argued that "students are also expected to learn the rules which govern their behavior not only in school but in society. They are taught that they have individual rights and that those rights must be balanced with the rights of others" (at 822). Of central interest to school districts considering affirmative or prohibitive dress codes is the requirement that they show a "rational connection" between the dress code and the "accomplishment of a public purpose." A policy that does not have such a rational connection to a public purpose will not withstand court challenge (*Pence v. Rosenquist*, 573 F. 2d. 395, 7th Cir., 1978). When a relationship can be established such that (a) a form of student behavior or expression substantially disrupts and materially interferes with the educational process and (b) a conduct code addresses that behavior via a rational connection between elements of the code and accomplishment of the public purpose of providing a safe effective school environment, the courts are likely to support such a code. Specific review of a proposed conduct or dress code by the school board attorney is always advised prior to implementation.

Despite the support of the courts in this matter, it is always preferable to establish codes of conduct such as dress codes in a positive, affirmative manner to the extent possible. Gang-related displays of clothing, jewelry, or graffiti are best first addressed in private, personal discussion with the student; at the same time, the student's parent(s) should be informed about this high-risk behavior. Not all such displays mean that the student is gang involved or even gang informed. Gang fashion —"gangster chic"—is common in the music videos and music magazines popular with school-age youth. School officials should remember that many students who appear to be "representing" gang affiliation by dress or action are not, in reality, so involved. The unfortunate trend toward media glamorizing of gangster chic has resulted in the marketing of gang clothing styles and behavior among youth in general. Hence, school officials must be extremely cautious to avoid inadvertently labeling, stigmatizing, or accusing students of gang activity without careful, private consideration of each instance. A marginally affiliated student falsely labeled as a gang member may react by forming true linkages with the gang.

Academic Intervention

Academic intervention should be a primary objective of any gang prevention or intervention program. Relevant matters to consider are the literature on academic intervention and behavior disorders, the significance of academics for youthful offenders, and specific measurement issues.

Rutherford, Nelson, and Wolford (1985) note the importance of appropriate academic programs for youthful offenders. DiGangi, Perryman, and Rutherford (1990), in a descriptive analysis of youths in contact with juvenile corrections systems, discuss the importance of academic deficiencies and their remediation in a population of youthful offenders and at-risk youths. Spergel (1990), Goldstein (1991), and Pink (1984) further emphasize the need for more school-based academic interventions, among other strategies, in the treatment of at-risk and criminally active youths. Clements (1988) suggests that for older youth, school-based interventions should focus on improving academic performance, as poor performance is a strong predictor of later delinquency. For younger students, he recommends cognitive and behavioral control programs along with efforts aimed at enhancing academic success.

Academic intervention may well be the first accessible vector of behavior change for both prevention and intervention programs. Jenson et al. (1991), Dishion (1989; cited in Stoner, Shinn, & Walker, 1991), and Shapiro (1989) all note that academic enhancement and intervention are basic to effective social behavior programs. Kesler (1985; cited in Jenson et al.) notes research to support the assumption that direct instruction in reading results in substantial benefit for behavior disordered students. Doyle (1984; cited in Wittrock, 1985) comments that effective classroom managers focus on academic task expectations and academic assignment rules rather than directly on discipline issues. Gettinger (1990) reports that increasing academic learning time is fundamental to increasing achievement for low-achieving and at-risk students. Dishion (1989; cited in Jenson et al.) succinctly summarizes: "One of the strongest correlates of antisocial behavior in adolescents is basic academic skills deficit" (p. 775).

As the trend in education moves further in the direction of authentic or direct assessment and intervention, of both academic and behavior skills (Shapiro, 1989), the best practice nature and the utility of such strategies for gang prevention may become apparent. Research on effective instruction in either academic or social behavior (Stoner et al., 1991; Thomas & Grimes, 1990; Wittrock, 1985) consistently supports the development and implementation of instructional strategies based on clear expectations. Such strategies as guided practice, corrective feedback, signaled student responding, reinforced and increased opportunities to respond, increased time spent actively engaged in academics, peer tutoring, and group and individual contingencies are recommended for use in all academic settings in which the at-risk student is engaged. The use of age-appropriate, high-interest materials, especially in reading, is recommended, as are fluency-building activities, which are essential for comprehension.

For students who are gang involved or at risk for gang involvement, the experience of academic success is essential. Although such success is not in itself a guarantee, in the absence of academic success any other intervention is highly unlikely to be effective. Cost-effective and "student-palatable" strategies based on small-group instruction and tutorial assistance can be developed with the assistance of community volunteers and of cross-age and same-age peer tutors for all academic areas. Volunteers should be sought both in the immediate neighborhood and in the extended community, including the business community. Volunteer programs increase students' opportunities to respond academically; interact with high-status, conventional peers; and come in contact with adult role models and potential mentors from the business community.

School variables such as academic success are commonly cited as critical to delinquency and, by extension, to the prevention of gang-related delinquency. Recommendations on making school activities more relevant for delinquent and at-risk youths are also frequently cited (DiGangi et al., 1990; Rubel & Ames, 1986). However, little research suggests a strong causal relationship between school success alone and gang membership specifically. If the solution is as direct and uncomplicated as enhancing academic and other kinds of success in school, then it is necessary to explain why more and more youths are joining gangs at younger ages, staying involved longer, and engaging in more seriously antisocial behavior. The research on effective instruction is available to teachers and should be applied wherever possible. Analyses of academic enhancement clearly are inadequate in themselves to explain the rise in gang membership and activity and are equally inadequate for guiding comprehensive interventions. Academic success may best be viewed as a necessary but not sufficient condition for helping students avoid gang involvement.

School-Student-Family Interaction

The sociological and criminal justice literature on gangs has paid systematic attention to the roles of family variables related to delinquent behavior (Fagan & Wexler, 1987; Loeber & Le Blanc, 1990; Loeber & Stouthamer-Loeber, 1986; Schwartz, 1989; Shamsie, 1981). A subset of recent research examines the specific interactive relationship among student, school, and family variables that increases a young person's risk for school failure and lack of connectedness to school. Patterson (1982); Reid and Patterson (1991); Wahler (1980); Wahler and Dumas (1986); Walker, Stieber, Ramsey, and O'Neill (1991); and Kazdin (1985) analyzed interactions between parents' child-rearing practices and their children's subsequent adjustment to school and community. Their research demonstrated that parental child-rearing style is one powerful predictor of child antisocial behavior and later success, or lack of it, in school.

An especially malignant child-rearing style, the coercive-countercoercive pattern of parent-child interaction noted by Patterson (1982), has direct implications for educators. This pattern is one in which parent and child reciprocally teach each other to effect control and countercontrol by means of escalating negative interactions. Walker et al. (1991) have determined from a review of the literature that the "social ecologies" of such families may interact with school and student variables to maintain and sometimes even encourage antisocial behavior. Youngsters reared in homes with coercive practices, harsh discipline, and poor supervision are less likely than peers to be successful in school settings. According to Loeber and Dishion (1983; cited in Reid & Patterson, 1991), harsh discipline, poor supervision, and low parental involvement are the best predictors of later delinquency and criminality. Students exposed to those practices are likely to have family-derived negative social interactions with teachers and peers, with equally negative outcomes. Further, students who exhibit antisocial behavior tend to develop relationships with peer groups that support delinquent antisocial behavior (Walker & Sylvester, 1991), and participation in such groups is highly predictive of later criminal justice involvement. Reid and Patterson (1991) note that children from families characterized by coercive-countercoercive processes are likely to continue such behaviors in school by "induc[ing] microsocial interactional coercive pattern[s]" with teachers and students alike (p. 734). Paulson, Coombs, and Landsverk (1990) report that, although aggressive behavior toward parents is a rarity among Hispanic families, Hispanic gang members who do assault their parents are most likely to come from homes where there is "ineffective intrafamilial socialization, inadequate youth supervision, and minimal displays of affection" (p. 131). This youth-family interaction influences and is in turn influenced by school variables. School, family, and community are inextricably interconnected. Best practice in gang prevention therefore requires concurrent analysis of all these variables in instances where students in dysfunctional families are also being exposed to gang activities in the community.

Following within-school variables, school-student-family interactive variables may be the most accessible vector of change for school-based collaborative interventions. Collectively, the interactions may lead to low achievement and lack of appropriate social behavior as well as the development of antisocial behavior. Because at adolescence the influence of family declines and the peer group becomes at least equally important in shaping and maintaining behavior, it is apparent that school-based interventions often must be based on a collaborative model that addresses home and school ecology (Walker et al., 1991; Walker & Sylvester, 1991).

The common debate about the relative importance of individual psychodynamic variables and environmental socioeconomic structures as contributors to gang involvement (Jankowski, 1991; Miller, 1990) is of minimal importance in actual attempts to intervene with individual students. The psychological characteristics of a youth involved in a gang or considered at risk may be less important than the way those characteristics interact with school and home influences. This interaction will serve to discourage, encourage, or maintain appropriate social and academic behaviors in the school setting, with a resultant impact on the young person's connectedness to school.

As best practice, therefore, we recommend prescriptive, comprehensive, direct assessment of both academic and social behavioral needs within the context of family variables. This assessment should examine the social-instructional and behavior maintenance characteristics of both school and home environments to the maximum extent possible (Reid & Patterson, 1991; Walker et al., 1991; Walker & Sylvester, 1991). A direct assessment of antecedent instructional and behavior-maintaining stimuli (i.e., rewards and punishers), which prompt the student to engage in antisocial gang-related behaviors in school and at home, may be prerequisite to progress in either domain.

A comprehensive analysis may reveal that it is necessary to provide direct support to the parents of the gang-involved student. A parent training program should teach the parents how to

> (a) closely monitor a child's whereabouts, activities and friends; (b) actively participate in a child's life; (c) use such positive techniques as encouragement, praise, and approval to manage a child's home behavior; (d) ensure that discipline is fair, timely, and appropriate to the offense; and (e) use effective conflict-resolution and problem-solving strategies. (Walker & Sylvester, 1991, pp. 15–16)

Walker and Sylvester (1991) further recommend home reward systems to encourage academic success for at-risk students and a tracking/monitoring system for close home and school communication. The active involvement of parents in the social instruction, monitoring, and supervision of their gang-involved or at-risk youths is important to program success.

Gang Behavior as Part of a Handicapping Condition

An issue rarely discussed in public school systems is that of the gang member with a related social-emotional, educational disability. Commonly, gang-related behavior is viewed as a social maladjustment and therefore disqualifies a student from eligibility for special education services. Students who exhibit significantly inappropriate social behavior along with poor academic performance often escape assessment for learning disability because of the attention given to their overriding problem behavior. Recently, Nelson, Rutherford, Center, and Walker (1991) examined this issue, concluding that "research, scholarly opinion and professional practices consistently have indicated that this exclusionary clause is ill founded" (p. 406). Wolf, Braukmann, and Ramp (1987) also conclude from their research that seriously delinquent behavior may be part of a significantly handicapping condition. Often, school officials view gang-related delinquent behavior as willful and therefore subject only to disciplinary sanctions, without considering that these behaviors may indicate an emotional/behavioral disability.

Another factor prejudicial to a reasoned referral of some gang-involved students for special education assessment is that most gang members represent ethnic minorities and as such may be subject to cultural bias in assessment (Council for Children With Behavioral Disorders, 1989; Henderson, 1980; Lethermon, Williamson, Moody, & Wozniak, 1986). The poorly defined exclusionary concept of "socially maladjusted," the urgent social need to respond to school-age youths who have severe behavior disorders, and the problem of cultural bias in assessing an at-risk population comprising primarily students of color argue for reconsideration of current assessment practices, at least in some cases.

It is recommended as best practice to review instances and especially patterns of gang-related, severe, school-based problem behavior as possible indicators of an educationally relevant social-emotional disorder. Such behavior patterns may be reviewed for assessment under state and federal special education guidelines. Nelson et al. (1991) persuasively argue that antisocial students exhibiting behavior problems formerly thought to indicate social maladjustment rather than educational disability should be included under the special education guidelines. It is further recommended that school districts review the Council for Children With Behavioral Disorders white paper (1989) to determine best practice in assessment of culturally diverse populations. Application of common and traditional assessment instruments may lead to inaccurate conclusions about the etiology and current status of behavior problems and about interventions as well. Although not every school-based gang-related behavior problem will represent an educational disability, some most certainly will. For this reason, each student who exhibits severe problem behavior in school should be considered for possible assessment, irrespective of casual opinion of exclusion on the basis of gang affiliation.

Contingency Management in School-Based Settings

Although contingency management was discussed at length in chapter 3, the application of these powerful techniques in school-based collaborative interventions requires further comment. First, in light of the complex interaction between school-related and family variables, awareness of this interactive effect is a necessary consideration for anyone planning a behavioral intervention.

The efficacy of contingency management in preventing problem behaviors, whether in the classroom, on the playground, at recess, or on the school bus; in teaching social skills; and in enhancing academic responses is well established (Dougherty, Fowler, & Paine, 1985; Kirigin et al., 1982; McConnell, 1987; Welch & Holborn, 1988; White & Bailey, 1990; Wolf et al., 1987). Issues regarding both short- and long-term generalization of learned behaviors to other settings have also been researched (Foxx, McMorrow, Bittle, & Ness, 1986; Rhode, Morgan, & Young, 1983). Planners of school-based programs thus have the necessary technology and methodological caveats to develop both cost-effective and efficient programs. Recent expansions of behavioral procedures to include cognitive behavior modification (Kendall & Braswell, 1985) have added new techniques to the educator's repertoire.

Especially relevant to contingency management in school settings are concerns of social validity, cultural sensitivity, and habilitative acceptability to clients and other direct and indirect consumers. Such concerns also address the basic issue of fairness with regard to the highly emotional and often politically charged issue of youth gangs. Best practice implies developing observation and measurement systems that are as sensitive and objective as possible with respect to race, gender, and subculture. Target behaviors to be increased or decreased should be defined in terms of their importance to academic and social success for all students. The literature on racial and gender differences suggests the following important factors for staff to consider in developing programs for students whose race, culture, and environment may be different: (a) Race-related differences in interpretation of specific student behaviors are more likely to occur as measurement variables become more subjective than objective; (b) the more objective behavioral definitions are, the more likely it is that specific interventions can be defined; and (c) accurate interpretation of a particular behavior of a given student must refer to the student's cultural context (Henderson, 1980; Lethermon et al., 1986).

To individuals who view gangs as sociopolitical entities, gang prevention and suppression programs may appear antithetical to their goal of values transformation—that is, transformation of criminal gangs into positive social structures. To those who view gang behavior as an expression of individual sociopathy, intervention via social learning strategies may appear inadequate to deal with the assumed psychological problems of gang members. For educators who are, by training and practice, natural (if often unconfessed) social learning practitioners, a social learning approach—which emphasizes teaching new, appropriate behaviors and eliminating old, inappropriate ones—is a natural extension of daily school activity.

Reconciliation of these seemingly disparate positions is necessary if schools are to implement effective programs during the school day and to selectively support collaborative community-based programs. Because schools emphasize the teaching of academic and social skills, we recommended that schools develop and support programs that most closely approximate a teaching model. This means that school-based interventions should incorporate literature-based academic and social behavior contingency management systems, both traditional and cognitive-behavioral, within the context of socially validated beliefs of the greater community.

Social validity refers to the accuracy and significance of a term, concept, objective, or intervention within the full context of the culture or community affected by it. To achieve social validity, program developers must meet the concerns of both direct and indirect consumers of program services. Both groups should be considered as program goals and desired long-term outcomes are established. Direct consumers are the students involved in gangs or directly affected by gang presence. They are immediate participants in programs, as are their families. Other parties may be viewed as extended direct consumers; they include school administrators, teachers, employers of students, neighborhood residents, and others who observe, interact with, and respond to student behavior daily in a given context. It can be assumed that their expectations, in terms of both immediate social behavior and long-term behavioral outcomes, are relevant to social validity. Indirect consumers are all persons who react to student gang-related behavior mainly though secondary channels and less often through direct interaction—for example, through newspaper or broadcast media reports rather than through direct contact with students.

If the test of social validity is to be met, competing interests of disparate groups of direct and indirect consumers must be reconciled with reference to the school district's mission and goals and broad community values. No group necessarily has a greater stake in effective programming than another. The potential influence of any interested party on the planning or evaluation of a gang program for the school or district must be openly and thoughtfully assessed. The definition of "interested parties" is generally much broader than single-issue, vested interests are likely to acknowledge.

On the other hand, interventions and target behaviors must be consistent with the district's and the school's mission, goals, and objectives. Schools should not react reflexively when pressured by small but often vocal sources, who might represent an even smaller percentage of all the consumers affected by program planning decisions. For example, if a certain small group assumes that gangs are a legitimate, acceptable response of youths to social injustice in the United States and therefore should be allowed great latitude on a school campus, that opinion must be balanced against the views of all other consumer groups, both direct and indirect, and weighed against the need for maintaining order in a school and the safety concerns of other students, parents, employers, and so on.

In summary, it is recommended as best practice that school personnel, when planning group or individual interventions to prevent gang involvement or remediate gang-related behavior, consider the following criteria:

1. All primary systems must first focus on immediate improvement in academic performance for all at-risk or gang-involved students. In the absence of academic progress commensurate with grade expectations, other programs are unlikely to be maximally effective and will at best lack an essential component of social validity.

2. Individual behavior management systems must focus on active teaching of positive social behaviors, include plans for promoting generalization across school settings, and include maintenance components for long-term persistence of newly acquired social skills.

3. Behavior reduction strategies are necessary but only when used concurrently with written, positive, prosocial skills teaching programs. Behavior reduction systems do not supplant but rather supplement positive programs.

4. Depending on the age of the student(s) directly concerned, an appropriate degree of active student involvement in program planning and monitoring should be encouraged. An informed, involved student is more likely to be a compliant and satisfied participant. Involve the student whenever possible.

5. Behavior management programs must specify both short-term and long-term outcomes, referenced to the mission, goals, and objectives of the school and the community at large.

6. Behavior management programs are best implemented in the environment where the behavior is expected to occur naturally. Implementing programs directly in all school settings decreases the need for programming aimed specifically at generalization of behavior to the school setting.

7. Progress monitoring of target behaviors should use brief, direct, simple measures. The use of time-series data, taken weekly, for example, is

recommended. For a student who habitually missed or came late to all classes because he was associating with gang-related peers elsewhere in the building, formative evaluation might entail weekly charting of the number of classes attended on time. Staff might ask a formerly gang-affiliated student to self-report the number of social events attended in the company of gang-involved peers versus those where gang-involved peers were absent or in the minority. Building-wide measures might include such weekly items as the number of new graffiti reported, the number of students observed "representing" by wearing gang colors, the amount of student time devoted to extracurricular school activities or jobs, or the number of aggressive encounters where gang affiliation was a factor. Formative evaluation is preferred to summative evaluation alone.

8. Focusing on indirect measures not corroborated by direct observation of social behavior in naturalistic settings is discouraged. For example, verbal behavior of students involved in a values transformation group may not be accompanied by any observable, appropriate social behavior in school or in the community. Gang members are more influenced by what they do than by what they say (Spergel, 1990). Hagedorn's (1988) observation that gang members are highly facile in lying to social service agency representatives is advisory.

9. Parental collaboration and parent training programs are essential to both enhancing academic success and improving social competencies. A strong parent outreach component with specific activities to improve parents' skills in positive discipline and supervision, and to encourage involvement in their children's lives is recommended.

Program Intensity

School districts need to develop measured, prescriptive, positive responses to the gang involvement observed in the communities they serve. The premise of this chapter is that intervention based on directly assessed need, rather than a one-size-fits-all approach based on an individual's or agency's philosophy, is needed. Best practice is represented by the following hierarchy of program intensity, reflecting varying types and degrees of gang involvement.

For school-age youths in communities where gang influence is new and evolving, prevention and early intervention efforts should be focused almost totally on young "wannabes" and loosely committed, marginal adolescent members (Spergel, 1990). Less attention and fewer resources should be devoted to hardcore or more seriously offending gang members. The kinds of efforts likely to be fruitful in such communities include preschool social skills and academic readiness programs, gang avoidance skills training programs, parent awareness programs, alternative programs for evening and weekend recreation, in-school academic enhancement programs, social skills training programs, and job readiness and jobs programs for adolescents.

Values transformation or similar programs, which focus on the gang as a legitimate social structure and work within that structure, may be unnecessary where gang identity is not strongly established and where the community does not accommodate gangs as valid social entities. Indeed, officially recognizing a loose gang structure and increasing the time that unconventional, gang-involved youths spend together may inadvertently increase the gang's cohesion and reinforce its presence in the community (Spergel, 1990). In such communities, seriously gang-involved youths should be addressed on a highly individualized, prescriptive basis so as to recognize and support the individual and deemphasize that individual's identification with the gang.

In communities where gang influence is established and strong, and greater numbers of young people are involved, the requirements are different. There should be prevention and intervention efforts along the lines just discussed. In addition, there must be greater emphasis on, and more time and money dedicated to, direct gang intervention programs used on a highly prescriptive basis. Such programs might feature intensive supervision of youths by parents, school personnel, and community agency staff; individualized, intensive academic and social skills programming; referral of some students for special education evaluation; mentoring by community members; priority access to jobs programs; and direct community and school support to families to increase their skills in supervision and positive interaction (Spergel, 1990). For the more seriously gang-involved youthful offenders, both persuasive and coercive controls should be implemented.

For communities in which gang activity is highly significant and occurs on the school campus and in the immediate community outside of school hours, all those programs are recommended, along with increased emphasis on police-community liaison. Values transformation efforts addressing the behavior of small core groups of gang members may be necessary; these should be concurrent with other positive strategies emphasizing education and job training. School safety concerns, discussed in chapter 7, will be critical when gang influence, especially in violent or intimidating forms, is apparent on campus.

The basic principle of school-based intervention is "First do no harm." But harm can result from both over- and underidentifying and over- and underresponding to gang-related behavior. Direct assessment and prescriptive intervention through data-based programs satisfy this concern and increase the likelihood of success of both prevention and intervention efforts.

Group Process and Activities

Several types of group processes and activities are relevant in school-based gang intervention. Results of research on Positive Peer Culture (PPC), social skills training groups, friendship groups, and cognitive behavior training models form the basis for our best practice recommendations concerning preferred ways to establish group programs.

Traditional group processes are popular approaches both with youthful offenders and with gang and nongang delinquent youths (Goldstein, 1991; Gottfredson, 1987). To a large extent, however, group processes and activities addressing delinquency or gang activity remain unreferenced to a supportive independent data base (Shamsie, 1981; Spergel, 1990). The assumption behind group programming for nonconventional, delinquent youths is that because the peer group is influential, often disproportionately so, the group is the best agent for behavior change. Shamsie (1981), however, reported that group treatment for antisocial youths was rarely effective, with fewer than a third of the studies reviewed documenting positive change and none showing generalization to the community environment. In comparing traditional group and psychotherapeutic residential programs with behavioral treatment programs, Kirigin and colleagues (1982) found that the latter yielded better results. However, follow-up revealed that, in the absence of behavior maintenance programs in the community, generalization and long-term persistence of benefits remained low. McConnell (1987) notes that generalization of social behavior skills to the natural environment depends on the similarity of the teaching environment to the maintenance environment.

More recently, social skills training programs (Goldstein, 1991; Walker et al., 1983) have been developed and implemented in a variety of settings. Based on social learning rather than psychodynamic principles, such programs are recommended for group processes in school settings. Chapter 4 in this volume, on interpersonal skills training, addresses this form of intervention in greater detail. When such programs are to be implemented in a school setting, programming for generalization must be developed before training begins. All staff in the school building must be prepared to support behavioral gains made in such skills training groups so that newly acquired skills will be transferred to a broader environment.

Gottfredson's (1987) major review of favored peer group interventions has direct implications for school personnel. The programs reviewed—specifically, guided group interaction and PPC—remain popular with educators despite a near total absence of data to back their use. Supportive outcome data from the use of PPC in the Omaha, Nebraska, public schools appear, upon independent review, to be minimal concerning improvement of student attendance, absent concerning improvement of participants' academic grades, and unreliable because of the inclusion of nonequivalent comparison groups in the evaluation design. Describing the Rock Island, Illinois, experience with PPC, Gottfredson notes that the selection of participants was so erratic as to compromise severely the value of conclusions. Such outcome data as self-reports of delinquent behavior are also compromised by threats to validity like regression artifacts and maturation artifacts, and thus they are of limited use as well. Gottfredson found enough threats to validity to make firm conclusions, let alone suggestions for generalization or replication, impossible.

Gottfredson (1987) reviewed similar programs attempted in the Berrien County, Michigan, schools; the Chicago public schools; and St. John School in Chicago. Again, he found that the numerous serious threats to validity affecting both attempted "true" experiments and less structured clinical trials in these districts far outweighed the useful data collected. The analyses of the data from these programs were greatly hampered by the poor designs employed, and the few observable outcomes were both complex and confusing. One attempt at a true experimental implementation of PPC occurred during the 1982–1983 school year at St. John. Apparently, subjects were assigned to treatment and control groups in truly random fashion. The results were disconcerting at best. For high school students, the results implied an adverse effect of treatment. Greater "waywardness," more tardiness, less attachment to parents, and increases in self-reported delinquent behavior were observed for the treatment group. For elementary school students, no significant differences were found between treatment and control students. Generalizing from Gottfredson's work, we conclude that school-based gang prevention or intervention programs had best avoid a traditional peer culture approach. An important exception to this otherwise justified conclusion is the effective use of PPC in combination with complementary models designed to develop such competencies as anger control and diverse interpersonal skills. This multimodal approach is described by Gibbs in chapter 5.

Measurement of Group Effects

When in-school behavior change groups, such as "friendship groups" designed to help students develop conventional prosocial peer skills, are implemented, objective outcomes must be specified and progress measured. What a student with problem behavior or gang affiliation says in a group does not necessarily correspond to what the student actually does. It is the purpose, often unspoken, of most groups to improve the correlation between "saying" and "doing" (Karlan & Rusch, 1982). To determine the effectiveness of a group, therefore, planners and facilitators must write specific, observable behavioral goals for each group member early in the group process and modify them as the group progresses. Frequent, direct measurement of the target behavior should then be conducted. The behavior should be observed not only in the group but also in the student's natural environment—that is, the school setting and the community. Both self-reports and secondary reports from parents, community residents, and employers might supplement these objective measures of change.

The following paradigm illustrates the evaluation of a group process designed to remedy deficiencies in self-esteem, one commonly assumed cause of gang affiliation. Use of one or more of the recently published self-esteem scales is one acceptable approach, but it is not in itself sufficient to monitor progress or indicate success of the group. Improvement over time on such a scale is meaningless if the student continues to affiliate with a gang, engage in or tolerate gang criminal behavior, and do poorly in school. Concurrent validation must be sought through direct school and community measures of the student's self-esteem. Following are examples of such direct measures:

1. The number of positive self-statements, made by the student and overheard by others or recorded in a journal, regarding his or her prosocial behaviors in academic, social, artistic, or athletic realms

2. The number of days the student attended school

3. The number of days the student arrived at school punctually

4. Prosocial behaviors observed outside the group and the school and reported verbally or in writing by adults such as parents, teachers, employers, and others in the community

5. Direct measures of academic, social, artistic, or athletic behavior in school and community

6. A decrease in self-reports (or reports from police, corrections, or other social monitors) of criminal or delinquent gang-related behavior in the community

It is not uncommon for gang-affiliated students to express high self-esteem verbally but show little or no concurrent improvement in social behavior. Thus, it is essential to have independent measures from relevant environments.

Issues of group leadership are of special concern in group intervention with gang-involved students. Because leadership systems and expectations vary among gangs (Fagan, 1989; Jankowski, 1991), leadership in social skills or other groups for gang-affiliated youth must be closely guided. Larson (1991) describes a school-based violence prevention program in the Milwaukee public schools, a cognitive-behavioral program called "Think First." In "Think First," the adult remains responsible for guiding the group and providing a reference point for the discussions. Participants receive clear explanations of specific rules for travel to the group meeting place during school time, topics presented and discussed during group sessions, and group processes themselves. Social and cultural sensitivity issues are specifically addressed.

Mendelsohn (1991) describes a gang mediation program in which the adult leader takes a less directive but nonetheless specific role as clarifier of options for gang youths involved in aggressive disputes on and near the school campus. In one application, the mediation has resulted in a very promising 15 months of stable interaction between rival factions. Independent, concurrent community-referenced data are unavailable; they would be of great importance for educators wishing to systematically replicate the programs elsewhere. Spergel (1990) reports less encouraging results of gang mediation, noting that the result of mediation, generally a truce between factions, rarely is sustained over time. Haskel and Yablonski (1982; cited in Spergel, 1990) further suggest that recognizing and negotiating with a gang as a valid social entity legitimizes it and thereby stabilizes and further entrenches it in the community.

It is probable that mediation with gang members or gang leaders may sometimes be necessary to forestall immediate violence or prevent loss of life. It is also probable that such mediation increases the risk of validating the gang as a legitimate social entity, thus buying short-term peace at the price of long-term persistence of the gang. When such mediation is undertaken, responsible parties are obligated also to (a) immediately implement programs to prevent entry of more youths into the gangs involved in the mediation; (b) attempt to draw away members who are likely to leave the gang; and (c) collaborate with all interested agencies, especially schools and corrections, to enhance the school success of involved youths and concurrently to suppress criminal or delinquent gang-related behavior in the community. Merely to mediate gang disputes without undertaking major, concurrent prevention and intervention efforts focused on the gangs in question is to rob Peter to pay Paul. Because mediation may inadvertently increase the cohesion and permanence of the gangs, intensive efforts toward decreasing gang cohesion are ethically required and pragmatically necessary to protect the school and the community.

One researcher reports that efforts to co-opt a gang through recreational activity backfired. According to Yablonsky (1962; cited in Spergel, 1990), attempts to pull gang members in Morningside Heights, New York, away from the gang through baseball only served to pull more conventional young baseball players into the gang. Well-meaning but inadequately designed or supervised programs involving forced proximity of gang and nongang youths may lead conventional youths to aspire to gang membership. The importance of preventing this is obvious.

Despite the concerns and risks associated with peer group intervention, such programs—both new and promising ones and older programs of questionable social and scientific validity—will most surely be implemented within the public schools. Our best practice recommendation is that if peer group programs are to be used in a school system, officials should be aware of the limitations as well as the strengths of such programs.

The following considerations should guide the implementation of peer group programs: First, conventional peers (i.e., non-gang-affiliated students) rather than nonconventional peers (i.e., currently active gang members) are preferable as role models (Spergel, 1990), group leaders, conflict mediators, reinforcement mediators, and same- or cross-age tutors. Gang-affiliated youths should assume leadership roles only when conventional peer leaders are not forthcoming in the group, and they should serve in such roles only with close supervision. Should a group "elect" a gang-involved youth as its leader, the adult leader must be highly skilled and vigilant in directing and monitoring the group. Recognition and reinforcement of prosocial behaviors of gang members, whether observed in a group, in school, or in the community, is of course always appropriate and highly advised.

Adult leaders or mediators must reinforce and shape appropriate prosocial behavior of target youths, discouraging any emphasis on or reward of their gang status. Also, the adults must closely monitor the behavior of the gang-involved youths in the community to detect any concurrent gang-related criminal or delinquent behavior. Failure to do so may result in conventional peers noting and reporting that gang-involved students enjoy adult approval, status, and influence in the school setting despite their continued criminal or delinquent behavior in the community.

Finally, close supervision of adolescent group processes is necessary to maintain accountability in school systems and to guide the development of prosocial and leadership skills in the young people involved. Group outcomes are best measured directly in natural settings in school and in the community.

SCHOOL INTERACTION
WITH SOCIAL SERVICE AGENCIES

Social service agencies have a long history of responding to gang activity in communities. Throughout this history, however, a lack of coordination of services and an absence of accountability characterize many agency efforts to prevent or remediate gang affiliation and criminal gang behavior (Huff, 1990; Jankowski, 1991). Outcomes, when reported, tend to be anecdotal and lack concurrent independent validation. In this section we will examine critical issues for school districts attempting to forge effective collaborative relationships with community agencies.

The school is the key agency in the coordination of services for school-age at-risk or gang-affiliated youth. Except for cases of incarceration, no other agency than a school has as much daily responsibility for, or spends as much time with, such young people. Plas and Williams (1985) and Guthrie and Guthrie (1991) offer models of effective collaboration between schools and community agencies. Spergel (1990), in his policy recommendations, suggests that the schools in gang-impacted neighborhoods assume "responsibility for the development of programs directed to social control of youths, especially those between ten and fifteen years, in the middle grades who are beginning to take on gang roles and are already engaged in law-violating behaviors" (p. 262). Spergel further recommends that the school assume primacy in collaborating with law enforcement and school-community advisory groups to develop intervention and prevention programs.

Interagency collaboration assumes two general forms: first, school district support for detached programs not implemented within the school but involving students and, second, support for programs staffed partially or totally by outside agencies but implemented within the school building. Researchers agree that collaboration is critical and that both formal liaison with professional organizations and cooperation with and use of paraprofessionals from the community are necessary (Clements, 1988; Spergel, 1990; Huff, 1990; Rubel & Ames, 1986).

Because of the significant risks involved in programming for gang prevention and intervention, educators are advised to follow closely all best practice guidelines discussed earlier, with the following additions, relevant to community collaboration. Any agency that seeks support from, or that proposes to work within, the public school district must (a) specify how its mission, practices, and projected intervention outcomes relate to the mission of the school district; (b) specify oversight and accountability practices; (c) specify the empirical basis for the program to be implemented and address the philosophical basis for the intervention; (d) provide evidence of the reliability and validity of measurement practices to be employed; (e) maintain positive relationships with other agencies that may be cooperating with the school district; and (f) accept a relationship with school district employees concerning direct collaboration, monitoring, and supervision.

It is recommended that school district employees monitor or supervise non-district agency personnel, sometimes directly, while the latter are providing services to students on school grounds. Whether the collaborative program is a law enforcement program (e.g., DARE) or a traditional community-based, gang outreach, detached-worker program, the district should retain an oversight function and have the right of access and input to both developing and ongoing programs. An outside agency should never direct practice or policy within the school on the basis of perceived or actual expertise; rather, the agency should assume a true advisory and collaborative position within the school district's policy- and decision-making structure.

At all times, the rights of parents must be respected. Parents of directly involved students should have the opportunity to grant true informed consent for their children's participation in any gang intervention or prevention programs. Parents of students who are not directly involved in an intervention are nonetheless indirect consumers of the service by virtue of the presence of outside agency personnel within their children's school. These parents also have the right to know about the in-school activities.

A special caveat is necessary regarding the popular practice of inviting inspirational speakers who are former or current gang leaders to address school assemblies. The United States Department of Education (1988) has recommended that formerly drug-addicted or recovering persons not be employed as motivational speakers within drug abuse prevention programs. The recommendation was based on the recognition that such speakers do little to enhance drug abuse prevention efforts and may even have an opposite effect. Students sometimes see in such individuals a reason to assume that they too may abuse drugs while young and yet turn out to be successful and even in demand, perhaps as motivational speakers! Although no data yet exist to indicate that this recommendation should be generalized to gang intervention programs, the parallels are obvious. As current best practice, we discourage the use of former or current gang members as motivational speakers during school-wide assemblies devoted to gang prevention.

The role of former gang members in interventions with youths who are active members also is controversial. It is reasonable to suggest that, if the only job qualification of a former gang member now employed in a youth service agency is prior gang affiliation, the employing agency is not a preferred candidate for smooth interagency collaboration. More fruitful collaboration is likely if the agency hiring former gang members requires them to complete college or other relevant training before allowing them access to school-age youths. Some agencies employ qualified social service workers, members of the clergy, law enforcement officers, social workers, or other personnel whose past gang experience is incidental to their current professional status; such agencies are best situated to collaborate effectively with school systems.

Like former addicts or recovering persons, former gang members may play an important role in specific, prescriptive prevention and intervention efforts for specifically identified at-risk or gang-affiliated youth. There is no research available to suggest a role for current gang members in the public schools as motivational speakers, crisis counselors, or conflict mediators. It is reasonable to assume that the risks in exposing school-age youths to current gang leaders or associates as role models far exceed any foreseeable gain.

It is recommended as best practice that school districts seeking outreach workers or youth leaders for gang prevention and intervention programs first enlist individuals who have not been gang members but who are highly informed on gang issues. Occasionally it is necessary or, in specific instances, desirable to employ former gang members in youth leadership roles, especially in school districts where gang affiliation is common and gang activity pervasive. However, this is generally not the preferred practice, and even when necessary or desirable, such individuals should have advanced education or training as youth leaders as well as close supervision by school district personnel.

School districts that elect to employ former gang members in their programs are urged to follow these best practice guidelines:

1. Verify their status as former, rather than active, current gang members.

2. Determine that they have the educational, professional, or paraprofessional skills to interact with students in a manner acceptable to school personnel.

3. Require some direct supervision or monitoring by school district employees.

4. Consult parents of both directly and indirectly involved students who will be exposed to these individuals.

5. Monitor the direct and indirect short-term and long-term effects of these individuals' activities on student behavior and school climate.

6. Determine the impact on school relationships with other agencies such as law enforcement, parole, probation, and corrections.

7. Monitor the behavior of involved students in the community over time.

SCHOOL INTERACTION WITH JUVENILE JUSTICE AGENCIES

With the increases in the number and range of crimes committed in or near schools, the importance of collaboration between schools and juvenile justice agencies has increased as well. Interactions with law enforcement, parole, and probation agencies are commonplace for large urban school districts. With the broadening geographic distribution of youth gangs, street drug trade, and weapons use, it is more important than ever to inform educators about best practice in this area. They need to be up-to-date on crime reporting in schools; gang-, weapon-, and drug-free school practices; collaboration with parole, probation, and youth diversion services; and data reporting to juvenile justice officials.

Reporting of gang-related crime occurring in or near the school is crucial to a safe educational environment. The best school-based academic, social-behavioral, or parent-community-based programming delivered during the school day cannot in itself overcome the environment of fear in a surrounding community controlled by street gangs. Successful gang prevention and intervention efforts depend on improved crime reporting. Typically, victims and witnesses fail to report school-based crime for a variety of reasons, including the perception that nothing can be done within the legal system and the fear that reprisal may result (U. S. Department of Justice, 1983). The so-called "dark figure" of unreported crime (Skogan, 1977) has been recognized as one of the major obstacles to the effective operation of our criminal justice system. Spergel (1990) and Stover (1987) note the significant problem of inadequate data on school-based, gang-related crime due to school personnel's denial of problems, simple lack of awareness, or self-imposed isolation from gang-related problems.

Students must be encouraged to report crimes. Improved reporting can produce such positive results in the school and community as appropriate allocation of resources, swifter application of legal sanctions, a greater empowerment of individuals and communities, and more accurate and systematic collection of school-related crime data. To avoid a complete breakdown of the system and the development of a parallel, gang justice–driven retaliatory system in response to school-related crime, comprehensive victim and witness support is needed in both the school and criminal justice systems. Accountability for increasingly serious, violent criminal behavior is at an all-time low as violators are shielded from legal consequences through underreporting of crimes. Because the detailed reporting of a crime is a victim's only legitimate power, it is critical that all school professionals encourage and support the victims and witnesses who "make the call" in the face of gang-inspired intimidation and overt aggression.

Improved crime reporting can empower victims. Although the response of the criminal justice system may appear inadequate and impersonal to the victim, it is a fact that a criminal act will not be addressed unless it is officially reported to law enforcement authorities. The invisible victims of gang-inspired crime in the school and the surrounding community are entitled to the full support of our legal system, which is designed to protect life and preserve order.

The current debate over the appropriate definition of a gang or gang-related crime distracts from the recurrent cycle of victimization that is central to the gang subculture. Whether tightly bonded and directed by a charismatic, manipulative leader or loosely organized around the protection of local turf, the contemporary gang is an increasingly destructive element in the lives of young students. Exposure to gang violence through early involvement in predatory crime and participation in gang initiation rites often begins a cycle of fear that can debilitate an individual for a lifetime.

Research on school crime in the United States points to a serious lack of reporting. The landmark Safe School Study (National Institute of Education, 1978) conducted nationwide from 1976 to 1977, revealed that over two-thirds of all in-school crime was not reported and consequently not accurately reflected in local, state, and national crime statistics such as the Uniform Crime Reports. A comparable lack of reporting was also revealed by the independent National Crime Survey (NCS), which found that 9 of 10 crimes against students and 3 of 4 crimes against teachers were not officially reported to authorities (U. S. Department of Justice, 1991).

NCS results indicated that young people aged 12 to 19 are far more likely than adults to be victims of crimes of violence and theft. At the same time, this population is the least likely to report crime to school or law enforcement officials (U. S. Department of Justice, 1989). Schools and contiguous streets and parks are frequently places of victimization for school-age persons (U. S. Department of Justice, 1991). Menacker, Weldon, and Hurwitz (1989), in a follow-up of the 1978 HEW/NIE study, discerned the following alarming trends in school-based criminal activity:

> Eight percent of students reported being threatened by someone with a gun or knife, 4% were beaten so badly as to require medical treatment, 32% had carried a weapon to school at least once, 10% reported using a weapon at least once during the school year, 15% reported hitting a teacher. Of teachers, 3% reported being physically attacked, 42% reported that they had hesitated to confront problem students "out of fear for their own safety" and 39% reported theft of or damage to personal property. Regarding near-school crime, 19% of students reported taking the shortest route to school out of safety fears, 20% avoided school parking lots and other school areas out of fear, 98% of teachers reported school neighborhoods were threatening in terms of vandalism, attack and theft and "18% of teachers felt 'very unsafe' in the parking lot, and 22.9% felt 'very unsafe' elsewhere outside of school grounds." (p. 40)

It is recommended as best practice that school systems establish formal relationships with local law enforcement agencies. It may be necessary to develop a standard format for systematic reporting, data collection, and follow-up of school-related criminal gang behavior affecting staff and students. Individuals in each school should be designated and trained to provide complete and systematic crime reports to the local law enforcement agency. At the same time, within each police precinct, division, or team, one or more individuals should be designated to respond to each report of criminal gang behavior by telephone, personal visit, or written communication to the victim. Designation of individuals within the school system and the local law enforcement system will personalize the reporting process, introduce personal accountability, and ensure continuity and consistency.

It is imperative to institute a consistent approach to the reporting of gang crime on or near campus, while carefully observing the school district's data privacy provisions. Social learning principles apply to crime-reporting behavior as to any other: If students or staff are not reinforced or—worse—are punished for reporting crime, the rate of reporting will decrease. When this occurs, prevailing gang structures will quickly respond to gang crime via the traditional retaliation practices, and the violence and intimidation central to gang justice will escalate.

A second important aspect of collaboration between schools and juvenile justice agencies is the implementation of "gang-free" programs and practices. We have discussed several aspects of direct intervention, such as prohibition of gang colors or other symbols (Menacker et al., 1989), immediate eradication of gang graffiti (Rubel & Ames, 1986), and other immediate responses to blatant, disruptive gang representation on campus. In this section we will consider school participation in and support for the development of drug-free and weapon-free zones around schools and, often, adjacent parks. Lane (1991) reports that "gang or drug disputes were the leading cause of school gun violence" (p. 31).

The Federal Crime Control Act of 1990 includes Title XVII, the Gun-Free School Zones Act. This legislation "prohibits the possession or discharge of a firearm on or within 1,000 feet from private, parochial or public school grounds" (cited in Stevens & Evans, 1991, p. 32). This act is directly supported by the Drug-Free School Zones Act, section 860 of Title XXI, the Controlled Substances Act, which prescribes enhanced penalties for drug crimes committed within 1,000 feet of a school. Local or state ordinances that parallel these federal acts have been implemented in several jurisdictions, including Minnesota, and are highly recommended as supportive of school-based gang prevention and intervention efforts.

States such as California, Florida, Illinois, New Jersey, and Minnesota have enacted legislation that enables the courts to increase significantly the penalties for the possession, sale, and use of controlled substances and dangerous weapons in and around schools, parks, and other areas presumed to be safe environments. Because illegal weapons possession and use, along with drug sales, are common among current street gangs, such legislation has strong implications for school safety. As an example, recent legislation in Minnesota, 1991 Minn. Laws, 279, establishes drug- and weapon-free zones with boundaries one city block or 300 feet from any school, park, or public housing project. Along with other new legislation aimed at curtailing crimes committed for gang benefit as well as assaults on school officials, the Minnesota safe zone initiative has enhanced the efforts of school and law enforcement agencies to curb gang influence.

Local education authorities are urged to directly support the implementation of drug- and weapon-free zones around schools and parks, as this will enhance the effectiveness of school-based programs. The testimony of these authorities at local or state government hearings in support of relevant legislation is crucial. The existence of consistent and concurrent federal, state, and local sanctions for gang-related crime on or near school grounds increases the probability that such crime will be prosecuted and, it is hoped, will serve as at least a geographic deterrent to gang crime. Although schools are in no position to resolve all of the societal problems (racism, poverty, marginalization, and development of a gang subculture in the nation's urban areas) that engender gangs, school officials can come forward to support legislation that attempts to move the problems some distance from the schoolhouse door.

Systematic collaboration with parole, probation, and court diversion services is an important responsibility of school personnel. Young gang-involved students commonly are placed under court supervision. Court monitors, to effect meaningful change in the behavior of their charges, need current information about the students' school behavior. Court and school officials are currently hampered by a lack of knowledge regarding juveniles' prior adjudications in other counties and states. Statewide, cross-referenced central recording systems to track juvenile felony adjudications are extremely rare or nonexistent. Because young gang members are frequently highly mobile and are sometimes used by the gang to transport weapons and drugs, it is prudent and sound policy for school personnel, law enforcement officials, juvenile justice officials, and, particularly, juvenile liaison officers to cooperate and monitor movement of such youths.

A demonstration program sponsored by the United States Departments of Justice and Education (Rubel & Ames, 1986) offers a model of an information system designed to track the incidence of problem behavior and crime in schools. At the core of this program is an interagency team comprising representatives from local schools, courts, law enforcement agencies, and clinical service agencies. Emphasis is placed on improving the school climate and accurately recording school-related incidents that constitute violations of school discipline policy or of public law. Computerized summary reports enable the interagency team to make immediate decisions regarding action to address unacceptable behavior. This program, which includes an emphasis on legitimate community and student involvement, demonstrates a much-needed focus on system accountability and a genuine effort to address the need, felt by students and staff alike, for a safe school environment.

It is recommended that schools develop a common format for the reporting of data to court monitors. After seeking written permission and informed consent from parents or courts, as appropriate, for exchange of information, the school should designate an individual to provide weekly data on student progress to the court monitor. The data, provided in a format common to all schools in the system, should cover attendance, academic performance, social behavior, participation in extracurricular activities, and participation in student support groups such as chemical dependency or anger control training groups. For each court-monitored student, specific direct measures of performance should be developed and communicated to the student and family. Progress should be recorded and the records transmitted to all interested parties (provided that permission to exchange information has been secured). A time-series data base on observable behaviors will give court officials a basis for formative evaluation and decision making.

A systematic approach to coordination among schools, juvenile justice officials, and community social service agencies is central to decreasing—and, in some communities, largely eliminating—gang behavior as a major disruptive force. Spergel (1985), discussing gang activity in the Chicago public schools, urges that school boards "require that all levels of administration, especially principals in high schools, maximally involve parents, community organizations and neighborhood groups in the school's responsibility for social education, student discipline and gang activity reduction programs" (p. 202).

It is recommended as best practice that schools consider the proposals in Spergel's (1990) major work on street gangs, *Youth Gangs: Continuity and Change,* and actively participate in and support coordinated community efforts toward gang prevention and intervention. Leadership of a coordinated advisory group is best directed by "an official agency with a tradition of rehabilitation, community education and involvement, and offender supervision" such as a probation, parole, or law-enforcement agency (Spergel, 1990, p. 261). A further recommendation is that focus should be primarily on younger gang-involved students and secondarily on older involved youths. Early identification and intervention efforts are best directed by the local educational administrative unit, in close collaboration with all interested agencies and community groups. Perhaps least acknowledged by school personnel and educators in general is Spergel's final point on the need for both "persuasive," or educational, controls and "coercive" controls, or those effected by legal force, in responding to gang-related problems in the nation's schools. Although it may appear to contradict educational philosophy to coerce when one is schooled to persuade, the loss of students to street gangs and communities to despair compels school personnel to acknowledge the real outcomes of our stubborn adherence to ineffective philosophy. Skilled use of positive educational practices, combined with necessary coercive legal controls, applied prescriptively, yields a behavioral contrast that should increase the efficacy of both approaches.

As educators, we can advance beyond our current philosophy and practice to become a greater part of the solution, or we can stay bound to past practice and remain part of the problem. Best practice and systematic replication of the best programs that the education data base has to offer can only benefit schools, students, and the greater community. Nothing less than the future of a generation hangs in the balance.

REFERENCES

Bazar, J. (1990, June). Psychologists can help youth stay out of gangs. *APA Monitor,* p. 39.

Bell, C., & Jenkins, E. (1990). Preventing black homicide. In J. Dewart, *The state of black America.* New York: National Urban League, Inc.

Bernal, M., Klinnert, M., & Schultz, L. (1980). Outcome evaluation of behavioral parent training and client-centered parent counseling for children with conduct problems. *Journal of Applied Behavior Analysis, 13,* 677–691.

Blau, R. (1991, May 26). Guns taking deadly aim at youth. *Chicago Tribune,* pp. 1, 16.

Burke, J. (1991). Teenagers, clothes, and violence. *Educational Leadership: Journal of the Association for Supervision and Curriculum Development, 49*(1), 11–13.

Burke, T. W., & O'Rear, C. E. (1990). Home invaders: Asian gangs in America. *Police Studies: The International Review of Police Development, 13*(4), 154–156.

Busch, K., Zagar, R., Hughes, J., Arbit, J., & Bussell, R. (1990). Adolescents who kill. *Journal of Clinical Psychology, 46,* 472–485.

Children's Defense Fund. (1991). *The state of America's children 1991.* Washington, DC: Author.

Clements, C. (1988). Delinquency prevention and treatment: A community-centered perspective. *Criminal Justice and Behavior, 15,* 286–305.

Council for Children With Behavioral Disorders. (1989). White paper: Best assessment practices for students with behavioral disorders: Accommodation to cultural diversity and individual differences. *Behavioral Disorders, 14,* 263–278.

Curry, G. D., & Spergel, I. A. (1988). Gang homicide, delinquency and community. *Criminology, 26,* 381–405.

DiGangi, S., Perryman, P., & Rutherford, R. (1990, Summer). Juvenile offenders in the 90s: A descriptive analysis. *Perceptions,* pp. 5–8.

Dougherty, S., Fowler, S., & Paine, S. (1985). The use of peer monitors to reduce negative interaction during recess. *Journal of Applied Behavior Analysis, 18,* 141–153.

Fagan, J. (1989). The social organization of drug use and drug dealing among urban gangs. *Criminology, 27,* 633–667.

Fagan, J., & Wexler, S. (1987). Family origins of violent delinquents. *Criminology, 25,* 643–669.

Foxx, R., McMorrow, J., Bittle, R., & Ness, J. (1986). An analysis of social skills generalization in two natural settings. *Journal of Applied Behavior Analysis, 19,* 299–305.

Gaustad, J. (1990). *Gangs* (ERIC Digest No. EA 52). Eugene, OR: ERIC Clearinghouse on Educational Management.

Gettinger, M. (1990). Best practices in increasing academic learning time. In A. Thomas & J. Grimes (Eds.), *Best practices in school psychology.* Kent, OH: National Association of School Psychologists.

Goldstein, A. (1991). *Delinquent gangs: A psychological perspective.* Champaign, IL: Research Press.

Gottfredson, G. (1987). Peer group interventions to reduce the risk of delinquent behavior: A selective review and a new evaluation. *Criminology, 25,* 671–714.

Guthrie, G., & Guthrie, L. (1991). Streamlining interagency collaboration for youth at risk. *Educational Leadership: Journal of the Association for Supervision and Curriculum Development, 49*(1), 17–22.

Hagedorn, J. (1988). *People and folks: Gangs, crime and the underclass in a rustbelt city.* Chicago: Lake View.

Hagedorn, J. (1990). Back in the field again: Gang research in the nineties. In C. R. Huff (Ed.), *Gangs in America.* Newbury Park, CA: Sage.

Henderson, R. (1980). Social and emotional needs of culturally diverse children. *Exceptional Children, 46*(8), 598–605.

Huff, C. R. (1990). *Gangs in America.* Newbury Park, CA: Sage.

Jankowski, M. S. (1991). *Islands in the street: Gangs and American urban society.* Berkeley: University of California Press.

Jenkins, E., & Thompson, B. (1986). *Children talk about violence: Preliminary findings from a survey of Black elementary school children.* Paper presented at the annual convention of the Association of Black Psychologists, Oakland, CA.

Jenson, W., Clark, E., Walker, H., & Kehle, T. (1991). Behavior disorders: Training needs for school psychologists. In G. Stoner, M. Shinn, & H. Walker (Eds.), *Interventions for achievement and behavior problems.* Kent, OH: National Association of School Psychologists.

Karlan, G., & Rusch, F. (1982). Correspondence between saying and doing: Some thoughts on defining correspondence and future directions for application. *Journal of Applied Behavior Analysis, 15,* 151–162.

Kazdin, A. (1985). *Treatment of antisocial behavior in children and adolescents.* Homewood, IL: Dorsey.

Kelley, M., & Stokes, T. (1982). Contingency contracting with disadvantaged youths: Improving classroom performance. *Journal of Applied Behavior Analysis, 15,* 447–454.

Kendall, P., & Braswell, L. (1985). *Cognitive behavioral therapy for impulsive children.* New York: Guilford.

Kirigin, K., Braukmann, C., Atwater, J., & Wolf, M. (1982). An evaluation of teaching-family (Achievement Place) group homes for juvenile offenders. *Journal of Applied Behavior Analysis, 15,* 1–16.

Kohn, G., & Shelly, C. (1991, August). *Juveniles and gangs.* Paper presented at the annual convention of the American Psychological Association, San Francisco.

Lane, J. (1991, Spring). Schools caught in the crossfire. *School Safety,* 31–32.

Larson, J. (1991, September). School psychologists in Milwaukee use CBT groups to treat aggressive youth. *Communique* (Publication of the National Association of School Psychologists), pp. 4–6.

Lemann, N. (1986a, June). The origins of the underclass. *The Atlantic Monthly,* pp. 31–55.

Lemann, N. (1986b, July). The origins of the underclass. *The Atlantic Monthly,* pp. 54–68.

Lethermon, V., Williamson, D., Moody, S., & Wozniak, P. (1986). Racial bias in behavioral assessment of children's social skills. *Journal of Psychopathology and Behavioral Assessment, 8,* 329–337.

Loeber, R., & Le Blanc, M. (1990). Toward a developmental criminology. In M. Tonry & N. Morris (Eds.), *Crime and justice: A review of research* (Vol. 12). University of Chicago Press.

Loeber, R., & Stouthamer-Loeber, M. (1986). Family factors as correlates and predictors of juvenile conduct problems and delinquency. In M. Tonry & N. Morris (Eds.), *Crime and justice: An annual review of research* (Vol. 7). University of Chicago Press.

Lopez, L. (1989). *Gangs in Denver: A resource booklet.* Denver, CO: Author.

Maxson, C., Gordon, M., & Klein, M. (1985). Differences between gang and nongang homicides. *Criminology, 23,* 209–222.

McConnell, S. (1987). Entrapment effects and the generalization and maintenance of social skills training for elementary school students with behavioral disorders. *Behavioral Disorders, 12,* 252–263.

McConnell, S. (1990). Best practices in evaluating educational programs. In A. Thomas & J. Grimes (Eds.), *Best practices in school psychology II.* Kent, OH: National Association of School Psychologists.

McDermott, M. (1979). *Criminal victimization in urban schools.* Washington, DC: U. S. Government Printing Office.

Menacker, J., Weldon, W., & Hurwitz, E. (1989, September). School order and safety as community issues. *Phi Delta Kappan,* pp. 39–40, 55–56.

Mendelsohn, D. (1991). Mediation: A gang prevention strategy. *Conciliation Quarterly, 19*(1), 5–7.

Meyer, J. (1991, July 29). Gangs blamed for rising crime in Hollywood. *Los Angeles Times,* pp. 1, 16, 17.

Midwest Gang Investigators Association (MGIA). (1990). *Gang crimes seminar* [Handbook]. Bloomington, MN: Author.

Miller, W. B. (1990). Why the United States has failed to solve its youth gang problem. In C. R. Huff (Ed.), *Gangs in America.* Newbury Park, CA: Sage.

Multnomah County of Oregon Juvenile Justice Division. (1989). *Gang Resource Intervention Team: GRIT.* Portland, OR: Portland Police Department.

National Institute of Education. (1978). *Violent schools, safe schools: The Safe School Study report to Congress* (Vols. 1–3). Washington, DC: U. S. Government Printing Office.

National School Safety Center. (1988). *Gangs in schools: Breaking up is hard to do*. Malibu, CA: Pepperdine University.

National School Safety Center. (1989). *School crisis prevention and response* (NSSC Resource Paper). Malibu, CA: Pepperdine University.

NEA Representative Assembly. (1991). The 1991-1992 resolutions of the National Education Association. *NEA Today, 10,* 20.

Nebgen, M. (1990). Safe streets in Tacoma. *The American School Board Journal 177*(10), 26-27.

Nelson, C., Rutherford, R., Center, D., & Walker, H. (1991). Do public schools have an obligation to serve troubled children and youth? *Exceptional Children 57,* 407-415.

Orange County Department of Education. (1991). *Project Yes! The anti-drug/gang violence curriculum project*. Costa Mesa, CA: Author.

Patterson, G. R. (1982). *Coercive family process*. Eugene, OR: Castalia.

Paulson, M., Coombs, R., & Landsverk, J. (1990). Youth who physically assault their parents. *Journal of Family Violence, 5,* 121-133.

Pink, W. (1984). Schools, youth and justice. *Crime and Delinquency, 34,* 439-461.

Plas, J., & Williams, B. (1985). Best practices in working with community agencies. In A. Thomas & J. Grimes (Eds.), *Best practices in school psychology*. Kent, OH: National Association of School Psychologists.

Prophet, M. (1990). Safe schools in Portland. *American School Board Journal, 177*(10), 28-30.

Putka, G. (1991, April 23). Combatting gangs: As fears are driven from the classroom, students start to learn. *The Wall Street Journal,* pp. 1, 8.

Rapp, J., Stephens, R., & Clontz, D. (1989). *The need to know: Juvenile records sharing*. Malibu, CA: Pepperdine University, National School Safety Center.

Reid, J., & Patterson, G. R. (1991). Early prevention and intervention with conduct problems: A social interactional model for the integration of research and practice. In G. Stoner, M. Shinn, & H. Walker (Eds.), *Interventions for achievement and behavior problems*. Kent, OH: National Association of School Psychologists.

Rhode, G., Morgan, D., & Young, K. (1983). Generalization and maintenance of treatment gains of behaviorally handicapped students from resource rooms to regular classrooms using self-evaluation procedures. *Journal of Applied Behavior Analysis, 16,* 171-188.

Riley, K. (1991). *Street gangs and the schools: A blueprint for intervention*. Bloomington, IN: Phi Delta Kappa Educational Foundation.

Rowland, D., Fountain, J., & Martinez, M. (1991, September 22). Suburbs are waking up to threat of gangs. *Chicago Tribune,* pp. 1, 16.

Rubel, R., & Ames, N. (1986). *Reducing school crime and student misbehavior: A problem-solving strategy. Issues and practices*. Washington, DC: U. S. Department of Justice, National Institute of Justice, Office of Communication and Research Utilization.

Rutherford, R., Nelson, C., & Wolford, B. (1985). Special education in the most restrictive environment: Correctional/special education. *The Journal of Special Education, 19,* 59-71.

Schwartz, M. (1989). Family violence as a cause of crime: Rethinking our priorities. *Criminal Justice Policy Review, 3,* 115-132.

Shamsie, S. (1981). Antisocial adolescents: Our treatments do not work—where do we go from here? *Canadian Journal of Psychiatry, 26,* 357-364.

Shapiro, E. (1989). *Academic skills problems: Direct assessment and intervention*. New York: Guilford.

Shilliday, G. (1991, June 24). The new streets of Saigon. *Alberta Reporter,* pp. 42-46.

Sibley, J. (1989). Gang violence: Response of the criminal justice system to the growing threat. *Criminal Justice Journal, 11,* 403–422.

Skogan, W. (1977). Dimensions of the dark figure of unreported crime. *Crime and Delinquency, 23,* 41–50.

Spergel, I. A. (1985). *Youth gang activity and the Chicago public schools.* Unpublished manuscript, written for the Illinois State Board of Education in collaboration with the Chicago public schools.

Spergel, I. A. (1990). Youth gangs: Continuity and change. In M. Tonry & N. Morris (Eds.), *Crime and justice: A review of research.* (Vol. 12). University of Chicago Press.

Spergel, I. A., & Chance, R. L. (1991). National Youth Gang Suppression and Intervention Program. *National Institute of Justice Review, 224,* 21–24.

Spergel, I. A., & Curry, G. D. (1990). Strategies and perceived agency effectiveness in dealing with the youth gang problem. In C. R. Huff (Ed.), *Gangs in America.* Newbury Park, CA: Sage.

Stephens, R. D. (1989, Fall). Gangs, guns and drugs. *School Safety,* pp. 16–17.

Stephens, R. D. (1991, July 17). Testimony before the House Judiciary Committee on Crime and Criminal Justice, Rayburn House Office Building.

Stevens, J. B., & Evans, J. L. (1991, Spring). Warning: No guns allowed. *School Safety,* p. 32.

Stoner, G., Shinn, M., & Walker, H. (Eds.). (1991). *Interventions for achievement and behavior problems.* Kent, OH: National Association of School Psychologists.

Stover, D. (1987, February). Dealing with youth gangs in the schools. *The Education Digest,* pp. 30–33.

Stover, D. (1988, October). Armed and dangerous: School violence is rising and your staff is the target. *The Executive Educator,* pp. 15–21, 33.

Taylor, C. (1990). *Dangerous society.* East Lansing: Michigan State University Press.

Thomas, A., & Grimes, J. (Eds.). (1990). *Best practices in school psychology II.* Kent, OH: National Association of School Psychologists.

Thompson, D., & Jason, L. (1988). Street gangs and preventive interventions. *Criminal Justice and Behavior, 15,* 323–333.

U. S. Department of Education. (1988). *Drug prevention curricula: A guide to selection and implementation.* Washington, DC: Office of Educational Research and Improvement.

U. S. Department of Justice. (1983). *Police handling of youth gangs* (Reports of the National Juvenile Justice Assessment Centers). Washington, DC: U. S. Government Printing Office.

U. S. Department of Justice. (1989). *Criminal victimization in the U. S.* Washington, DC: U. S. Government Printing Office.

U. S. Department of Justice. (1991). *Teenage victims.* Washington, DC: U. S. Government Printing Office.

Vigil, J. (1990). Cholos and gangs: Culture change and street youth in Los Angeles. In C. R. Huff (Ed.), *Gangs in America.* Newbury Park, CA: Sage.

Wahler, R. (1980). The insular mother: Her problems in parent-child treatment. *Journal of Applied Behavior Analysis, 13,* 207–219.

Wahler, R., & Dumas, J. (1986). "A chip off the old block": Some interpersonal characteristics of coercive children across generations. In P. Strain, M. Guralnick, & H. Walker (Eds.), *Children's social behavior: Development, assessment and modification.* New York: Academic.

Walker, H., McConnell, S., Holmes, D., Todis, B., Walker, J., & Golden, N. (1983). *The Walker social skills curriculum: The ACCEPTS Program.* Austin, TX: PRO-ED.

Walker, H., Stieber, S., Ramsey, E., & O'Neill, R. E. (1991). Longitudinal prediction of the school achievement, adjustment and delinquency of antisocial versus at-risk boys. *Remedial and Special Education, 12*(4), 43–51.

Walker, H., & Sylvester, R. (1991). Where is school along the path to prison? *Educational Leadership: Journal of the Association for Supervision and Curriculum Development, 49*(1), 14–16.

Welch, S., & Holborn, S. (1988). Contingency contracting with delinquents: Effects of a brief training manual on staff contract negotiation and writing skills. *Journal of Applied Behavior Analysis, 21,* 357–368.

White, A., & Bailey, J. (1990). Reducing disruptive behaviors of elementary physical education students with sit and watch. *Journal of Applied Behavior Analysis, 23,* 353–359.

Witkin, G. (1991, April 8). Kids who kill. *U. S. News and World Report,* pp. 26–32.

Wittrock, M. (Ed.). (1985). *Handbook of research on teaching* (3rd ed.). New York: Macmillan.

Wolf, M., Braukmann, C., & Ramp, K. (1987). Serious delinquent behavior as part of a significantly handicapping condition: Cures and supportive environments. *Journal of Applied Behavior Analysis, 20,* 347–359.

Ybarra, W. (1991). *Response to gang violence: L. A. pilots new programs.* Los Angeles, CA: Los Angeles County Office of Education.

Zinsmeister, K. (1990, June). Growing up scared. *The Atlantic Monthly,* pp. 49–66.

CHAPTER 9

Employment Training Interventions

Joanne Y. Corsica

This chapter discusses innovative employment training programs and strategies that show promise for intervention with at-risk youth in mid- to late adolescence (aged 16 to 23). Any selection necessarily reflects bias, and this one is no exception. In my own view, the interventions most likely to succeed are comprehensive programs that are holistic in approach—that is, person centered, culturally sensitive, and flexibly structured to meet the participants' individual needs. They are also more likely to be smaller programs that are initiated through local community efforts, are funded either privately or with a mix of private and government monies, are limited in geographical scope, network actively with other youth service providers, and involve participants actively in decisions and processes that affect them, such as program design and operation.

There is already a recent and extensive body of literature examining the relative success of federally funded second-chance employment and training programs for hard-to-serve youth (Bassi & Ashenfelter, 1986; Cedillos, 1990; Danziger, Haveman, & Plotnick, 1986; Katz, 1989; Mangum, 1988; Smith, Walker, & Baker, 1988). Thus, such federal efforts will be discussed only briefly here. The federal programs often deemed successful, such as the Job Corps, the Neighborhood Youth Corps, or the Job Training Partnership Act (JTPA), typically provide comprehensive services including work readiness training, work experience, remedial education, counseling, and job placement. Success is assessed in terms of cost-benefit ratios calculated on a number of criteria such as job placement rates; reductions in criminal activity and welfare dependency; and employment-related measures including postprogram earnings and taxable income, unemployment insurance usage, and the like. Historically, poor trainee retention, postprogram employment in secondary labor markets, and job loss are factors not generally considered in program evaluations.

The author's research for and preparation of this chapter were supported by a national Institute of Alcohol Abuse and Alcoholism Training Grant (#T32–AA07240) to the Alcohol Research Group and Prevention Research Center, School of Public Health, University of California at Berkeley.

Federal employment training initiatives frequently have been less successful than other programs in developing innovative strategies because they often have been subject to the shifting political philosophies that govern policies, requirements, regulations, and funding levels. Premised alternately on a "culture of poverty" thesis or a "structural unemployment" thesis, federal programs tend to target specific groups and hence are less flexibly structured and more standardized in the range and type of services provided. Whereas person-centered programs are designed to focus on individual responses to structural, cultural, and personal issues within the context of the community, many federal programs are politically negotiated policy initiatives implemented in response to social issues, but only when those issues are perceived to have become national problems. Federal policy has been inconsistent, and funding has been inadequate relative to both the scope of needed services and the numbers of young people needing them.

Because ethnographic data can illuminate events from the informant's perspective, I have given such data extra weight in identifying program strategies likely to be effective with the at-risk population of concern here. Although some may criticize this emphasis on ethnographic and experiential data as being somewhat subjective, very little sound experimental research is available to inform policy and program design relevant to employment training. What does exist may be suggestive but is flawed nevertheless. The ethical and logistic problems of randomized group assignment, inherent in the topic of study, have forced quantitative researchers to use designs that lack adequate experimental controls.

ECONOMICS, ADOLESCENCE, AND GANG FORMATION

> The image of gangs inspires fear, not pity. No Hollywood entertainer has organized a "Gang-Aid" concert and none are likely to do so. Our sympathies are not often extended to those who actively rebel against their station in life, especially those who do so non-politically and destructively. . . . The lack of "good jobs" is clearly the major factor that has transformed the gang problem in the past few decades. (Hagedorn, 1988, p. 166)

Youths at all socioeconomic levels are finding the transition to adulthood difficult. The ambiguity and liminal status of adolescence, rooted in our economic and social history, reflect the lack of formal structures and rituals designed to integrate youths into society and to facilitate their transition from adolescence to adulthood. Also rooted in our economic and social history is the deterioration of informal social supports for the growing-up process traditionally found in family, kin, and community relations. Lacking systematic, formal cultural recognition of this developmental process and facing diminished informal social support, adolescents have become increasingly isolated and socially segmented in their experiences of the culture and its changing expectations of them. Strong peer associations (including more formalized associations such as gangs), which once were viewed as adaptive social responses to the tasks of adolescent development, now appear to be reactions to the increased social isolation that recent cultural and economic changes have effected.

A successful training program recognizes that the factors underlying gangs as organizations involved in illegal economic enterprises are related to but not inseparable from the factors underlying gangs as adolescent social reactions to increased structural isolation. Poverty and employment issues may drive the gang's drug business, but the difficult transition issues of adolescence—issues that are greatly exacerbated by the social dislocations associated with poverty—must be addressed as well. These shared issues were articulated very well by two young people I interviewed recently. One grew up in a suburban community; the other, in an inner-city ghetto. The drug business brought them together.

The following comments are from M. K., a 23-year-old white, middle-class, college-educated female who has had no gang affiliations. However, she has been a drug user. She is now in a rehabilitation program.

> The part that's so depressing is that there's so much to change that there's no way to make change happen . . . it would be so slow and take so long to happen that it just wouldn't work . . . so the only way is destruction. But at the same time nobody wants to take on the responsibility for the destruction, so you get apathetic and frustrated. . . . You don't want to be a part of it, except you are a part of it. . . . What good is a college education unless you're into computers or business? . . . There's no point in a college education in terms of jobs . . . the more you know, the more depressed you get. . . . Once you get into the work force you feel like you're not getting anywhere . . . like this isn't helping me, not furthering me, but you stick with it and stick with it and get frustrated with it. You think about working to save money so you can quit working, but you really live paycheck to paycheck. Where I work they offer promises of progress, but they keep me doing what I'm doing and you get fed up and you want to quit. You're in an entry level position and you do learn a lot, but you get responsibility so slowly. What you've learned isn't recognized, and because you're so readily available to do the shit work, you're always going to do the shit work. Call it entry level or call it shit level, it's the same thing— and that's pretty much where you're going to stay.
>
> You stick with it, your job, your plans, life in general, when you have hope in finding hope and faith in finding faith. When I get down it's because I have lost faith in finding faith and have no hope for finding hope. Belonging creates a kind of faith because you have a sense of connection. Belonging—that's your colors, your

identity. Everything is so fragmented now. It's a rush of images
coming at you in everyday life. Television, that's a lot of garbage
imagery coming at you. It's like—flash, flash, flash—so many
things at once, but that's how it is. It's sort of like a dream state,
but you live in it now as well as when you sleep. Things come so
fast and there's no connection. You're being overwhelmed with
imagery, people, and colors—flash, flash, flash—especially in the
city. You're constantly taking in all this stuff and you try to figure
out how to deal with it, how to get it organized. The best way to
get it organized is to try to organize yourself into a niche that you
can fit into and that becomes your community, whether it's gangs,
cults [like modern primitive culture], or whatever. And gradually
you take on the set of beliefs that the culture you're participating
in dictates to you.

R. G. is a 23-year-old poor Hispanic male with a high school education. He formerly was a member of a large midwestern gang; his older brother and that brother's
father were members of the same gang. Like M. K., R. G. is now in a rehabilitation program. Here are some of his observations.

Most people I know feel the same way, but they just come right to
the point and say, Yeah, man, the world is fucked. What M. K.
says, it's like that with gangs to a point. You grow up with a bunch
of guys; you all play in the neighborhood together, play ball and
stuff, and as you get older a couple of your friends will get into
[gangs] and then you join, too. At first maybe you don't get into the
whole thing—hitting someone with a baseball bat isn't something
you want to do—but slowly you get into it. People have the concept
that gangs exist because of the drug business. There's gangs in the
suburbs. The city limits aren't boundaries anymore. Richer sections have gangs. Look at the mall gangs . . . mall posses. If everybody had a job there would still be gangs. It's not all economics
even though that's a big part of it. Gangs have always been businesses. Look at the Mafia—look at the corporate world, it's a gang.
So of course there's economic reasons for gangs. But gangs give
you a sense of security, of belonging to the neighborhood. These
guys you're growing up with, they're there; they've got the girls,
they're cool . . . they have some bucks to spend on the girls.
They're respected, they're feared. You get a sense of being
somebody, of being respected for who you are, and you get
known and praised. They praise each other. It's almost tribal.
When people are in, it's like they're part of a family, and you
go from being a "peewee" or a "future" to being a full member,
and you're a member for life.

When I was young, my relatives—my brother, uncles, and cousins, all gangbangers—ran this little drug ring, and I used to hang out with them. My mom used to drink a lot, and sometimes she'd be gone for a week at a time, and my cousins and their friends —all these gangbangers—would hang out at the house and party and smoke weed and stuff and drink. I knew I didn't want to live like this for the rest of my life, and I knew the only way to get out was through school . . . I knew no one would carry me out; I'd have to get out myself. I was good at this school stuff, and I got a lot of rewards for doing well when I was young. I wound up in gifted classes, so the high school I went to didn't have a gang problem. Because there were so many different gang factions represented at the school, no one gang could really dominate. Besides, the kids at this school were more into books. I thought about a career, and then in 12th grade I got disillusioned and said fuck it, and I dropped out. School got really boring, and I got frustrated with the teachers. It seemed like they were picking on me because they knew I was dealing . . . and things were getting more messed up at home. So I quit school and hung out and partied. But I saw that wasn't going anywhere either. Gang behavior is a symptom of a larger disease, like teen suicides—the whole thing is wrong. Kids are learning most of what they know from peers—from older brothers and sisters and older friends. It's like parents are obsolete. It's no different for the middle-class kids I know, except they have money to spend and we don't; their parents don't give them time either. You're looking at this like it's all poverty level; there's gangs everywhere . . . it doesn't stop with poverty.

M. K. and R. G. have learned from each other that, despite very dissimilar backgrounds, they share similar difficulties in the transition to adulthood: isolation, confusion, disorganization, discontinuity and fragmentation, a need for connection, a search for a worldview that makes sense. Middle-class youths experiencing significant distress during adolescence are likely to internalize their feelings in self-destructive actions (suicide, drug use) and to form or join retreatist or separatist peer groups and associations. Inner-city minority youths, on the other hand, are more likely to externalize their feelings in destructive acts of violence against one another and to form or join criminal gangs. Successful approaches to intervention with economically disadvantaged minority youth at risk for criminal activity or gang involvement recognize these behavior patterns as inherently antisocial and destructive but do not view them as inherently deviant or psychopathological patterns rooted in a culture of poverty or structural unemployment. In a word, such programs understand that these young people, and young people in general, don't need to be "fixed." They do need jobs with growth opportunities and an empirically grounded sense that—with training, learning, and effort—meaningful employment and a reasonably sound financial future are possible. They do need adult support that not only facilitates learning but fosters a sense of personal connection to community as they begin to assume adult roles and responsibilities.

Whereas social, demographic, and economic changes have affected communities and families at all levels of culture in the United States, such changes have wrought a profound social transformation among inner-city minority neighborhoods and economically disadvantaged families—a transformation that is reflected in dramatic increases in social problems and social dislocation. The structural transformation of the American economy set the stage for the internally fueled social transformation of the inner-city ghetto. The rapid growth and expansion of inner-city minority gangs (including posses and crews) as economic enterprises and the increase in gang-related crime are frequent consequences of this transformation (Anderson, 1990; Hagedorn, 1988; Jankowski, 1991; Katz, 1989; Wilson, 1987).

GANG MEMBERS' ATTITUDES TOWARD EMPLOYMENT

Although theoretical orientations may differ, there is remarkable consistency among ethnographic accounts of gang members' attitudes toward work and job training programs and gang members' perceptions of the long-term opportunities such programs afford participants.

Hagedorn (1988) conducted an ethnographic investigation of gangs in Milwaukee in 1985. The gang founders approached in the study expressed feelings of bitterness and alienation toward community service agencies and perceived such agencies more as part of the problem than as part of the solution. Gang founders felt that agencies, though they used the gang issue to secure funding for employment training and other youth programs, were insincere and ambivalent in subsequently providing services to gang members. Hagedorn collected information on 260 gang members, most then in their early 20s. Follow-up interviews with 47 gang founders, conducted 5 to 8 years later, indicated that the majority of male gang founders in the original cohort were unemployed and still affiliated with the gang. Interview data suggest that Milwaukee's gangs "are becoming 'institutionalized' in poor black and Hispanic neighborhoods, not only as an adolescent adaptation, but as a means for young adults to cope with a jobless reality as well" (Hagedorn, 1988, p. 128).

Weisfeld and Feldman (1982) worked with a single informant in their ethnographic research. On the basis of their work with this former gang leader, these investigators asserted that the limited job opportunities available to urban youth are

> insufficiently appealing to compete effectively with the attractions
> of street crime and its associated value system. . . . Young people
> will respond to reasonable alternatives . . . they do not engage in
> crime out of some personality defect that would be refractory to

counseling efforts. . . . If the differential opportunity structure were altered appropriately, the appeal of legitimate employment would be stronger. (p. 581)

In his 10-year study of gangs in New York, Boston, and Los Angeles, Jankowski (1991) found a pattern of limited cooperation between gangs and job training program providers. He characterizes this pattern as "prudent-exchange relationships," sustained reciprocal relationships between social groups that become institutionalized or perpetuated because they are mutually beneficial. According to Jankowski, gang members cooperate with job program personnel for three reasons: The stipends paid to program participants help gang members pay their dues to the gang; some gang members hope to make connections to well-paying corporate jobs through participation in the program; and cooperation helps the gang establish or improve relationships with members of the wider community in which it operates. Jankowski also found that training program outcomes for gang members followed predictable patterns: termination of participation before completion of training, completion of training followed by a short period of employment voluntarily terminated by the gang member, or completion of training followed by refusal to accept a job. He explains these patterns thus:

From the beginning, many of the youths never intended to stay in the program or to take a job associated with the training. They had participated in the program . . . to obtain a little spending money during financially difficult times, or as part of the gang's efforts to help the community. . . . For those gang members who did intend to finish the program and possibly assume a job afterwards, the primary reason they did not take a job was because most of the jobs they were being trained for were the type most gang members were trying to avoid . . . most of the gang members were trying to secure the type of job that would catapult them from poor or working-class conditions into the upper-middle class. When a job was a skilled manual job or one that paid only a modest amount of money, they would quit and revert to efforts to accumulate large amounts of capital through one of their illegal business ventures. (p. 240)

THE NEED FOR REAL OPPORTUNITIES

Jankowski observed that

there needs to be diversification in employment programs . . . and success in job placement. . . . Some gang members use programs for the real thing—they are tired and have become fearful of the streets, so they will in fact enter job programs with great anticipation and relief, but they end up dropping out or finishing and either not getting placed or getting placed in a job with such appallingly low wages that they quit feeling disillusioned—like they've been taken. . . . A successful program is one that trains and places people in entry-level jobs where there is potential for mobility. . . . Success is an occupational trajectory . . . people may be placed at entry level, but what happens after that? . . . Placement is a big issue; too few funds go into placement . . . and training must address social skills as well as occupational skills. (M. S. Jankowski, personal communication, September 18, 1991)

The research of Elijah Anderson also speaks to the need not just for jobs, but for job opportunities:

Older youths should receive remedial education on demand, including job training that is long range and of high quality. Ideally, this would be on-the-job training with major employers, but it must be some form of gainful employment with an orientation toward growth and an incentive structure of benefits and rewards tied to an individual's development. . . . Legal employment for idle youths would improve the quality of life for all of us who inhabit the inner city by increasing the tax base, giving these youths a clear stake in the legitimate economy, and encouraging the formation of nuclear families. (Anderson, 1990, p. 254)

I recently conducted an ethnographic study of a comprehensive educational and work training program serving unemployed out-of-school youths (Corsica, 1991). The overwhelming majority of trainees included in the study were African American and Latino men aged 18 to 23 who lived in areas of persistent poverty in a large urban center. Many were school dropouts with histories of criminal justice system involvement. The program's success in retaining the trainees and in connecting them with work opportunities beyond the secondary labor market was quite limited; its success in fostering cognitive skills development and academic achievement was somewhat more marked. Perhaps what this project demonstrates best, however, is the great difficulty in retaining trainees in programs, in administering such programs as planned, and in having a positive impact on the work life of trainees in the face of myriad social, economic, and legal difficulties.

The program was highly structured and involved trainees in 32 paid hours of supervised on-the-job training and 8 nonpaid hours of required education each week. Trainees worked in small groups under staff supervision. The program's emphasis was basic education and work readiness or job skills training. Work readiness training emphasized discipline (e.g., getting to work regularly and punctually) and good work attitudes (e.g., working cooperatively in a group, following directions and orders); it did not include preparation in specific job skills.

Counseling staff—career counselors and social workers—were available to trainees by appointment during uncommitted time, before or after work and school.

The program serves approximately 150 youths annually; 24 American-born youths participated in this study. Among the first 10 trainees interviewed at program entry, only 1 trainee remained with the program for more than 4 months. Most were either fired or quit the program within 2 months. Of the 7 males in this initial group of 10, 6 had been arrested, 2 admitted to selling drugs, and 4 admitted to prior gang involvement. Among the 9 trainees who left the program before completing their training, only 1 left for another opportunity—another training program; the others left with no jobs. The next phase of the study included 14 trainees. Of this number, 8 out of 12 males had been arrested, all for drug-related offenses. Eight of this group of 14 left the program before completing it. Four of the 8 left for other opportunities: 2 went on to school, 1 took a job as a construction laborer, 1 took a job in car repair, and 1 took a temporary position with the postal service. Four simply left. Of the 6 trainees who essentially completed the program, only 2 went on to jobs that offered growth opportunities; 2 have no jobs, and 2 are still with the program but are looking for other opportunities through the agency's career counseling staff.

Of the 24 study participants, 9 entered the program as high school graduates. Of these 9, only 1 had achieved at least a 12th-grade level in reading, math, and language skills. Four of the 9 raised their academic skill levels to the 12th-grade level before leaving the program. Only 1 of the 9 is still with the program and working on improving his skills. Fifteen of the 24 study participants entered the program as high school dropouts. Of this number, 8 have taken and passed all or most of the tests required for the GED.

The difficulties encountered in the program just described are presaged in a report by the Social Action Research Center (1980). Reviewing evaluation findings for 17 Youth Participation and Community Services job development demonstration projects, the center found the following common problems: high staff turnover, low youth retention rates, concerns and uncertainties among youths about the value of employment and educational experiences relative to their job prospects, and false expectations about job opportunities. However, the research literature also indicates that, although such programs may achieve limited success in terms of job placement and job retention, programs that are holistic in approach and combine work experience, education, and counseling demonstrate some degree of effectiveness in dealing with high-risk youths (Blake, 1988; Lacey, 1988; Smith, Walker, & Baker, 1988; vanNagel, Foley, Dixon, & Kauffman, 1986).

RECOMMENDED PROGRAMS

Four employment training programs selected for fuller examination in this chapter take a holistic approach in providing comprehensive services to economically disadvantaged youths. Further, beyond providing holistic and comprehensive

services, these programs share at least most of the following additional characteristics: a highly individualized, person-centered approach, which allows program
participants to proceed at their own pace and according to their own interests; a
long-term commitment to participants; active involvement of participants in decisions that affect them; an orienting philosophy that views youths as valuable
resources and adults as mentors; a sensitivity to cultural and personal issues; a
structural flexibility that allows the program to accommodate participants' diverse
needs; and linkages to a network of community resources. The four programs,
which demonstrate the operationalization of these characteristics in very different
models, are YouthBuild/YAP, in East Harlem (YAP, or Youth Action Program,
is the prototype for the national YouthBuild program); GANG PEACE/FIRST,
Inc., in Roxbury, Massachusetts; the Bay Area Youth Employment Project, in
northern California; and Project Match, in Chicago.

YouthBuild/YAP

The original YouthBuild model was developed in 1978 through the efforts of the
Youth Action Program (YAP) of the East Harlem Block Schools, a community-
based organization, in partnership with neighborhood youths.

A group of youths approached East Harlem Block Schools staff with an idea:
The young people wanted to renovate an abandoned building, but they did not know
how to get either the funds or the training needed for such a construction project.
The encounter was the beginning of YAP. This grass-roots-initiated, community-
based program was staffed initially with volunteers from the school in cooperation
with East Harlem youths. Within 8 months, YAP received a $250,000 grant from
the Carter Administration's Community Crime Prevention Program. Eighteen
months later another $500,000 grant followed as YAP was designated a demonstra-
tion youth employment program. This program received one more federal grant
before the Reagan years began and federal funding ceased. Then, after 2 years of
fund-raising efforts, YAP succeeded in obtaining funding through state and city
governments and from private sources. These are still the program's principal
sources of revenue.

The National YouthBuild Coalition, established in 1988, is an organization
providing training and technical assistance to programs attempting to replicate the
YouthBuild model. The first successful replication of the YAP program occurred
in 1984 with the establishment of the Banana Kelly Community Improvement Association in the South Bronx. Since 1988, YouthBuild programs have been established
in Boston, Cleveland, St. Louis, San Francisco, and Tallahassee. A 3-year evaluation of YouthBuild/YAP programs was initiated in July of 1991. Currently, no
quantitative data documenting the program's impact on trainees are available.

Though all YouthBuild programs recruit at-risk youth, only the San Francisco
YouthBuild program has made a point of recruiting gang members. Program staff
have reached out to both California Youth Authority ranches and San Francisco
streets. In the first month of program operation (October 1991), 34 young people
were recruited. Of the 34 recruits, 8 had gang affiliations, 11 had been incarcerated

for felonies, and 9 were currently on parole. Program staff do not try to draw youths out of gangs; rather, they work with the youths "to reflect on what is positive about gang values . . . and develop with them a sense that the program is a real community by being with them . . . being there for them" (YouthBuild staff, personal communication, October 1991).

YouthBuild/YAP programs are for out-of-school low-income youths aged 16 to 23 who need employment training and education. Time in the program is evenly divided between work and education; one week participants work at a construction site, and the next week they are based at the agency for education and youth development activities. The education program emphasizes cognitive skills development and the application of those skills to the work site. Participants are paid only for their construction site work. They learn construction skills in on-the-job training under the direct supervision of a skilled site supervisor and in the classroom. The youths work in small crews on building renovation projects in their own community; the buildings are abandoned city-owned properties. Once a building is completed, it is designated for homeless and low-income tenants and is owned and managed by a local nonprofit organization. The program stresses leadership training; it involves youths in program governance through participation in the program's policy committee, the body responsible for staffing, program policy, budget, and community action.

Participants receive regular individual and group counseling, as well as career counseling, initial job placement, and 6 months of job placement follow-up services. Youths are encouraged to continue to use job placement services as needed and for as long as needed after they leave the program. Youths also participate in peer counseling and complete an intensive 2-week leadership development program. Staff also complete an intensive 2-week training program on supervision skills and human development.

Trainees not drawn to construction as a career are encouraged to complete the program but, at any point along the way, can get assistance in finding jobs related to their career goals. Those interested in continuing in the construction trades after program completion are helped to secure positions with labor unions and private contractors. The program is essentially a 12-month experience, but many youths are involved for as short a time as 6 months or as long as 18 months.

From the beginning, the emphasis of the YouthBuild program has been youth development through leadership training and participation in program governance; it is a partnership with youth. Adults act as mentors in facilitating development and guiding learning. The mentorship situation is grounded in the belief that trainees have valuable ideas about their community's needs and that adults can best help by sharing their know-how with young people. In this process, youths learn about accountability and responsibility—for self, others, the program, the community, and the wider world; they also learn work readiness skills, acquire marketable technical skills, and develop cognitive skills. Staff and young people together work to create a supportive, family-like community, a place of connection and belonging. Further, trainees have access to a range of community support services outside the program: Building on the East Harlem Block Schools' established resource network, YAP extended and strengthened that network.

To argue that the YouthBuild program is limited because it provides work experience only in the construction trades is to miss the point of the program: youth leadership development. The structure of this program and its underlying philosophy give youths a stake in the program, in the community, and in the legitimate economy.

GANG PEACE/FIRST, Inc.

GANG PEACE/FIRST, Inc. is a grass-roots, community-based program that grew largely out of the efforts of its founder, Rodney Dailey. The program, in operation since 1989 and serving youths in Roxbury, Massachusetts, is staffed by five paid employees and 30 volunteers, of whom many are neighborhood youths. The services GANG PEACE provides are health education, neighborhood outreach and youth advocacy, staff-facilitated peer counseling, tutoring, job finding, and "sober" recreational activities. Between staff and volunteers, the agency manages a caseload of approximately 150 youths. Staff, paid or volunteer, are in contact with program participants at least weekly. The agency is open all day and into the early evening. In the words of its founder, "Contact isn't hard because the youth don't have any other place to go" (R. Dailey, personal communication, October-November 1991). The program receives private foundation and United Way support. Like YouthBuild trainees, GANG PEACE youths play a significant role in the agency's operation.

Program responsibilities are distributed among seven departments: outreach, fund-raising, public relations, education workshops, clothing, donations, and volunteers. Departments are staffed by member-volunteers and paid workers. The services of the program are available to all area youths regardless of their membership status, but all are encouraged to become members of the agency. Youths receive services for as long as they need them.

Most of the young people served, most of the member-volunteer youths, and most of the paid staff are, or have been, gang members or otherwise affected by gangs. The agency's philosophy is not to break gangs, but to redirect their activities. Involvement in GANG PEACE operations is one avenue of redirection. Outreach workers recruit members by informing them about program services and telling them what they can learn. Outreach workers have recruited from the streets and through public relations efforts conducted in the schools and other public forums.

Counselor-advocates provide referrals and follow up on those referrals. GANG PEACE networks with agencies providing substance abuse counseling, housing, health care, job training, and education. GANG PEACE, for example, has placed five young people with YouthBuild Boston. The agency has also placed youths with employment programs under city sponsorship, such as the Boston Youth Campaign, and in JTPA job slots through the Private Industrial Council. It has helped a small number of young people find private-sector jobs (30 youths were placed; 20 of them were fired); a small group of GANG PEACE youths participate in a summer internship and training program with the Boston Film/Video Foundation.

Because the program maintains regular contact with participants, staff are able to continue working with those who are having difficulties at work or have been fired from employment. GANG PEACE works through its resource network to develop jobs with area employers, and it maintains a placement data base to assist neighborhood youths in the job search. A resource data base on starting small businesses has been developed to help young people learn about entrepreneurship. The program also conducts educational workshops on ways to get a job and keep it; politics and political participation; community subculture; drugs, violence, and AIDS; youth and drugs; and youth, the American dream, and entrepreneurship. GANG PEACE gives young people a place to be and an opportunity to learn about choices. The program makes a commitment to those it serves for as long as the youths feel the need of services. GANG PEACE makes no promises, but it supports opportunity through education and dialogue, individual attention to members, peer support and peer counseling, and strong advocacy through its resource network.

GANG PEACE is a grass-roots organization with a solid understanding of the community and a strong community presence. Currently, the program appears to be driven by the energies and vision of its founder, and in this sense it is personality dependent. It has not yet been systematically evaluated. The features of the model—a grass-roots, community base; involvement of youths in program development and operations; a long-term commitment to providing members with needed services; an individualized approach to members; cultural sensitivity; and service flexibility based on a well-developed resource network—are not personality dependent and can be replicated.

Bay Area Youth Employment Project Consortium/ Youth Opportunity Program

The Bay Area Youth Employment Project Consortium (BAYE) is a relatively recent (1988) replication of Stanford University's Youth Opportunity Program (YOP), implemented in 1968. The project provides opportunities for disabled, minority, and economically disadvantaged young people to have meaningful employment on a college or university campus, and it supports their continued education. Participating institutions include Stanford University, the University of California at Berkeley, Laney College in Oakland, and Santa Clara University. A number of foundations provided the financial support needed for the expansion. Each campus also provides program support through in-kind services and line-item budgets for BAYE.

The BAYE Project counselors have established a strong resource network with area youth service professionals and with local high school guidance personnel. This network is the referral source for the program. Any young person aged 14 to 21 and meeting the criteria (being economically disadvantaged, belonging to a minority, or having a handicap) is eligible for the program. There are no academic requirements; thus, both students and out-of-school youths are eligible. Out-of-school youths participating in this program are required to enroll in an educational program appropriate to their academic needs and skill levels. The program works to screen people in rather than out. To apply, the potential candidate must interview with the BAYE counselor, fill out an application form, and obtain a letter of recommendation from an adult friend, employer, or teacher. The counselor makes a selection decision by assessing whether or not the applicant is likely to benefit from the program.

Taking into account the young person's career interests, needs, and skill level, the counselor makes a referral to a specific campus job. Placement in the job is not a given; the individual must receive a job offer. BAYE staff work to develop campus jobs in all college or university departments, jobs that will provide opportunities to learn and to acquire skills. Once a participant is offered a job, he or she becomes a part-time employee of the college or university, working 10 hours a week during the school year and 20 to 30 hours a week in the summer in a job that typically pays about $5.00 per hour. Each individual in the program is matched with a mentor. The mentor, who may be the participant's supervisor, a faculty member, or an enrolled student, provides guidance, support, and assistance as needed. BAYE participants regularly visit other campuses involved in the project and have an opportunity to meet with other BAYE participants and with faculty and staff from other institutions. They also attend biweekly career and college workshops at their home campuses.

Each participant works with a counselor in developing an academic plan and a time frame for accomplishing specific goals and meets regularly with the counselor to discuss academic progress. All participants, including out-of-school youths, are counseled into academic programs. Participants stay in the program as long as they are benefiting from participation; tenure is open-ended.

> The failure of other programs is the stringency of eligibility requirements. We do not have hard-and-fast standards. We underscore personal responsibility issues, but you can't do that in isolation . . . students need counselor and teacher support. . . . The absenteeism and tardiness typical in other programs doesn't happen. . . . It's not seen as another job, it's seen as much more . . . there has to be more than structure in employment and training programs . . . it's the support—personal people contact. You get up in the morning because somebody cares (S. Griffin, personal communication, October 1991)

The retention rate in this program is very high. Approximately 60 individuals are in the full-year BAYE program, and 225 are in the summer program. Of the 16 program participants who were high school seniors in 1990, 14 graduated from high school and have been accepted to college. Of the 12 BAYE participants who were seniors in 1991, 12 were accepted to college. The program is popular and receives three applications for each available slot.

Some individuals in the BAYE program are at-risk youths who are on probation. Through court diversion, they are referred to alternative high schools that are BAYE feeder high schools; the young people are thus referred to the BAYE program.

Project Match

Project Match in Chicago is a second-chance employment assistance program that targets young people at risk for sustained unemployment and welfare dependency. The project consists of a direct service component, supported by the Illinois Department of Public Aid, and a research component supported by foundations and individual contributors. The project is run under the auspices of Northwestern University's Center for Urban Affairs and Policy Research. The service component is based in Chicago's Cabrini Green community and is affiliated with a health center in the same area. The project was established as an urban laboratory that would allow testing of various strategies designed to help program participants achieve stable employment and economic self-sufficiency.

Project Match uses a highly individualized case management approach to help participants "stay on track." Each participant is assigned to a single Project Match case manager, who assesses the person's service needs and job placement possibilities and then links the person to appropriate services and available jobs. The case manager brokers and coordinates services, which are organized in terms of the participant's specific goals and developed as a career plan, and helps the participant obtain the services. The intensity of the support services that case managers provide varies with individual participants' needs at different times. Services other than case management and job development are provided off site, but the case manager closely monitors the delivery of services provided through referral. The program makes a long-term commitment to participants, following them as they progress toward their goals and staying with them when they fail. The success of the case management approach resides in the personal relationship between case manager and participant.

Project Match uses a computerized participant tracking system as a support for daily service delivery, as a case management tool, and as a source of data on program outcomes for individual participants and for the program as a whole. The data thus collected allow research staff to assess the effectiveness, over time, of career route strategies developed with each participant and to identify patterns of incremental achievement for the total service population. At the individual level, these data are important to participant assessment; in the aggregate, they are important in the development of policy.

Analysis of data disclosed a high rate of rapid job loss and a significant problem in keeping participants on-track. Treating job retention as the dependent variable, Project Match research staff analyzed the relationships of a number of variables (age, gender, education, parenting status, prior training, prior work, starting wages, and hours worked) to this outcome. They found that, although low wages and youth were the best predictors of job loss, the variation could not be explained fully by these easily quantified independent variables. The researchers therefore conducted a qualitative study to explore job loss from the perspective of program participants and their employers. On the basis of their findings in both research efforts, they concluded that

> the problem of frequent job loss is one example of the truth being
> more complicated than policy makers have wanted to admit. The

> labor market, class and racial tensions, family pressures, and in-
> adequate skills are among the interrelated reasons people might
> have difficulty staying attached to the work force. (Olson, Berg, &
> Conrad, 1990, p. 42)

In response to such conclusions, service staff adopted an incremental approach
to self-sufficiency in developing career plans with clients. Crucial dimensions of
this approach include type of activity, time commitment, and sequence. An incremental approach allows clients to take multiple routes in working toward stable
employment. It includes a broader array of activities than are typically considered
in employment programs, and it treats time commitment and strategy sequences
with more flexibility.

> For disadvantaged groups, the struggle for economic self-sufficiency
> is a long-term process. Thus, solutions should be long-term in
> nature. . . . Successful programs will do more than provide pre-
> employment training or place people in jobs. They will provide
> comprehensive services and long-lasting involvement. They will
> "recycle" those who fail and celebrate small, yet critical victories.
> (Olson et al., 1990, p. 46)

CONCLUSIONS

The employment training programs that have been described are designed to build
bridges of experience that allow socially isolated youths to connect with supportive adults and communities fostering personal, social, and career growth. The
social integration of youths that occurs through these various kinds of relationships is a function of the strategies used in delivering holistic and comprehensive
services. The values and attitudes flowing from these strategies reflect a profound
respect for youths as individuals; a cultural sensitivity grounded in understanding
and appreciation of the impacts of cultural isolation and poverty; and an awareness
that the development of a mature, independent, and economically self-sufficient
adult can happen only in the context of a family-like community. It is not simply
the provision of holistic and comprehensive services that makes these programs
innovative and promising. It is also the way in which the services are defined, designed, organized, and delivered.

Although we still have much to learn about youth employment programs in
general and about second-chance employment training programs for at-risk, economically disadvantaged minority youths in particular, it is possible to design effective programs with the limited knowledge available. Clearly, what we need is not
negotiation of political ideologies but a coordinated and appropriately funded
national policy that reflects what is known.

REFERENCES

Anderson, E. (1990). *Streetwise: Race, class and change in an urban community.* University of Chicago Press.

Bassi, L. J., & Ashenfelter, O. (1986). The effect of direct job creation and training programs on low-skilled workers. In S. H. Danziger & D. H. Weinberg (Eds.), *Fighting poverty.* Cambridge, MA: Harvard University Press.

Blake, G. (1988). Education and the employability of youth. *Youth Policy, 10,* 26–28.

Cedillos, J. H. (1990). Job Corps—A socialization perspective. *Journal of Vocational Education Research, 15,* 25–40.

Corsica, J. Y. (1991). *Evaluation of a youth education and employment program.* Unpublished manuscript.

Danziger, S. H., Haveman, R. H., & Plotnick, R. D. (1986). Antipoverty policy: Effects on the poor and the non-poor. In S. H. Danziger & D. H. Weinberg (Eds.), *Fighting poverty.* Cambridge, MA: Harvard University Press.

Hagedorn, J. M. (1988). *People and folks: Gangs, crime and the underclass in a rustbelt city.* Chicago: Lake View.

Jankowski, M. S. (1991). *Islands in the street: Gangs and American urban society.* Berkeley: University of California Press.

Katz, M. B. (1989). *The undeserving poor.* New York: Pantheon.

Lacey, R. A. (1988). *Building the watertable of youth employability: Collaboration to support children and youth at risk between ages nine and fifteen* (No. RR–88–08). Washington, DC: National Commission for Employment Policy.

Mangum, G. L. (1988). *Youth transition from adolescence to the world of work.* Washington, DC: William T. Grant Foundation Commission on Work, Family and Citizenship.

Olson, L., Berg, L., & Conrad, A. (1990). *High job turnover among the urban poor: The Project Match experience.* Evanston, IL: Northwestern University, Center for Urban Affairs and Policy Research.

Smith, T. J., Walker, G. C., & Baker, R. A. (1988). *Youth and the hard-to-serve.* Philadelphia: Public/Private Ventures.

Social Action Research Center. (1980). *Provision of technical assistance and short-term training and the conduct of an evaluation of the youth participation and community services job development demonstration projects: Vol. 3. A final evaluation report.* Berkeley, CA: Author.

vanNagel, C. J., Foley, L. A., Dixon, M., & Kauffman, J. (1986). Review of treatment methods for the rehabilitation of juvenile delinquents. *Journal of Correctional Education, 37,* 140–145.

Weisfeld, G. E., & Feldman, R. (1982, October). A former street gang leader reinterviewed eight years later. *Crime and Delinquency,* pp. 567–581.

Wilson, W. J. (1987). *The truly disadvantaged.* University of Chicago Press.

CHAPTER 10

Recreational Interventions

Rick Lovell
Carl E. Pope

The constellation of problems related to gang and group delinquency in the United States is growing. In addition to direct costs borne by crime victims, the community as a whole absorbs significant costs for law enforcement measures, trials and other judicial proceedings, and correctional efforts (Thompson & Jason, 1988). Furthermore, large numbers of the nation's youth, especially in our inner cities, are slipping into a quagmire from which escape is extremely difficult.

The extent of the gang and group delinquency problem is difficult to grasp; even rough estimates fluctuate with differing perspectives and conceptions. For example, those concerned with gang delinquency must decide whether to focus on identified or identifiable organized gangs (characterized by a committed core, distinct leadership, gang paraphernalia, and concerted and relatively continuous activities) or to include more loosely organized delinquent groups (characterized by collections of youths "hanging together," involved primarily in spontaneous activities and lacking the commitment and paraphernalia associated with organized gangs). Whatever parameters are adopted, the overall picture is serious and growing more so.

Beyond those who are involved in delinquent gangs or groups, a significant number of American youths, especially in inner cities, are at risk. These youths are on the verge of becoming gang or group delinquents. As individuals they may or may not have committed offenses, may or may not have been sporadically involved in delinquent activities. But in a country where tens of millions partake of abundance, these youths live in conditions where access to developmental opportunities is quite different from that enjoyed by their better situated peers.

Our purpose in this chapter is to discuss recreational interventions as one set of strategies for addressing gang and group delinquency problems. We are concerned with youths at risk as well as with gang and group delinquents. We also think it necessary to concentrate our attention on urban areas where recreational and cultural resources are not a normal feature of young people's lives. In an aggregate sense, most United States cities and counties appear to have much to offer recreationally and culturally. However, if we disaggregate the image, we find large numbers of youths whose practical boundaries are their central city neighborhoods, where few or perhaps no such resources are available.

THE SOCIAL CONTEXT OF GANG ACTIVITY

Before examining recreational interventions with gang-affiliated youths, let us place the nature and location of gang activity in context. As gang activity and youth violence increase, we need to understand the underlying structural and economic factors. Failure to do so may compromise the effectiveness of any intervention activity, recreational or otherwise.

Over a decade ago, William Julius Wilson (1978) examined the relationship of African Americans to the economic structure of society from both historical and contemporary perspectives. He identified three stages of race relations: The first encompassed the period of antebellum slavery and the early postbellum era, the second extended from the last quarter of the 19th century to the time of the New Deal, and the third covered the post–World War II industrial era. Wilson argued that during the first two stages, African Americans were systematically excluded from meaningful participation in the economy because of their race. Through the end of the New Deal era, he held, labor markets were characterized by a system of institutional racism. However, the advent of World War II opened up expanded job opportunities for African Americans, ushering in a period of progressive transition from race inequality to class inequality. In sum, Wilson argued that class position had become as important as race, if not more so, in determining the life chances of African Americans. Unfortunately, economic opportunities for many African Americans, and for other minorities as well, have diminished greatly as their class position and race have excluded them from meaningful participation in the labor market.

What began in the 1960s and has continued into the 1990s is the formation of a permanently entrenched "ghetto underclass" (Wilson, 1978). The structural transformation of the economy (i.e., the decline in industrial and manufacturing jobs, the erosion of unskilled entry-level positions, and the growth of the service economy) has helped to create a separate class whose members have little chance of successfully competing in an advanced technological society. Many of these people, unable to subsist within the legal economy, take refuge in the illegal subeconomy and engage in such activities as prostitution, gambling, drugs, and the like (Fagan, Piper, & Moore, 1986; Miller, 1986). Frequently they vent their frustration in acts of expressive and instrumental violence, as witnessed in the resurgence of youth gang activity (Hagedorn, 1988). As a result, members of the underclass make up the bulk of juvenile and adult institutionalized populations and represent the most frequent clients of the juvenile justice system.

Expanding on Wilson's thesis, Lemann (1986a, 1986b) has examined the origin of the underclass, focusing on the city of Chicago and identifying a series of migration patterns that began in the early 1900s. The first migrations involved the movement of large numbers of African Americans from rural southern plantations to the industrialized north. They moved principally to improve their economic position by obtaining jobs in the industries of northern cities such as Chicago. In the second migration, occurring during the 1960s, large numbers of middle- and working-class African Americans left the inner city. Seeking a better quality of life, they often relocated to the suburbs, where they found improved housing, schools, and other services. As Silberman (1978) notes, an indirect effect of this second migration was the removal of African American leadership, role models, and economic power from the inner city. In one sense, then, certain inner-city areas were left to stagnate and perpetuate a vicious cycle of pathology, disorganization, poverty, and crime.

Wilson (1987) again drew attention to the problem with the publication of *The Truly Disadvantaged*, which identified numerous pathologies characterizing the lives of the ghetto underclass, outlined the social processes leading to such destruction, and detailed an agenda to ameliorate the ills. Wacquant and Wilson (1989), examining Chicago's high-poverty inner-city areas, assert that problems associated with both joblessness and economic exclusion have triggered a process that they term "hyperghettoization." In this process, the stabilizing forces of the inner city have deteriorated:

> Social ills that have long been associated with segregated poverty—violent crime, drugs, housing deterioration, family disruption, commercial blight and educational failure—have reached qualitatively different proportions and have become articulated into a new configuration that endows each with a more deadly impact than before. (p. 15)

The decline of business and industry, the reduction in the number of entry-level positions, the movement toward a service economy, and the like have created stagnating urban pockets that breed despair and hopelessness. Though such conditions affect all members of the underclass, they are more pronounced and have more serious implications for African American adolescents (Hawkins & Jones, 1989).

Unfortunately, for many minority and poor white youths who reside in the nation's inner cities, there are few alternatives to the streets. Thus, for many, drugs, gangs, and violence have become a way of life. Within many major metropolitan areas, school systems have become warehouses for troublesome youths. Rather than preparing students for their future as parents and labor force participants, schools instead serve as institutions of containment. Similarly, as communities deteriorate, young people develop little sense of belonging and attachment. Informal systems of social control that influenced and monitored youthful behavior in the past no longer prove effective. Many youths, as well as adults, have become estranged within their own communities. Anderson's (1990) recent ethnographic study of poor urban communities illustrates the point. Older generation African Americans (the "old heads") have become ineffective as role models and guides for the younger generation of African American males. Indeed, the streets and the peer group have replaced them as tutors. Thus, gangs and other groups of problem youths have taken control and provide one alternative to hopelessness, despair, and poverty.

DEFINING RECREATION

The Office of Juvenile Justice and Delinquency Prevention (OJJDP) has "identified prevention, intervention, and supervision as the three major components of the system that must be involved in developing and implementing a strategy [to address the problem of gangs]" (Bryant, 1989, p. 4). Accordingly, Bryant has noted for OJJDP that "law enforcement, prosecution, and the courts are included in the intervention component, while the supervision component includes correctional agencies, probation, and parole" (p. 4). As to the third component, "the institutions within prevention include schools, law enforcement, recreation, mental health, housing, community agencies, and churches" (p. 4).

The basis for the OJJDP three-component conceptualization is an awareness that certain communities need a comprehensive strategy that is coordinated and involves diverse organizations, agencies, and efforts across these components. The components may not be truly discrete but may overlap, as when a probation officer with a heavy caseload (or a normal caseload, for that matter) requires an adjudicated offender to participate in a structured recreation program as a matter of "correction" or "supervision." We do not wish to debate the conceptualization; rather, we wish to point out that the OJJDP conceptualization is one among others possible. What we do find important is the clear recognition that recreation is a part of an overall strategy to deal with gangs and/or potential gang participation.

The term *recreation* carries a broad set of connotations for most people. Most probably think of some activity or activities that are diverting, pleasing, and refreshing mentally and/or physically. Such activities could be of many sorts—for example, attending a sporting event, participating in a ball game, jogging, or any of a vast number of other possibilities. Mirroring the concern of a report from Milwaukee's Public Policy Forum, we center our interest on activities that are expressly intended to be developmentally significant and are therefore appropriate in the context of prevention or intervention efforts. Our concern is with efforts intended to "shape and enable" positive and developmental behaviors and to "offer opportunities for individuals to take control over their experiences and to participate in community life" (Public Policy Forum, 1991, p. 2).

Recreational activities may be categorized in various ways. As observed in the Public Policy Forum report:

Recreation activities can be grouped in three large categories:

- independent activities, some of which may involve facilities or centers (e.g., parks)

- minimal structure and supervision activities, which require planning, staff and facilities (e.g., aquatics programs)

- targeted leadership activities, which serve specific and well-defined purposes (e.g., learning a skill, increasing social abilities) (1991, p. 2)

Like the OJJDP conceptualization discussed earlier, this classification is one among many ways of categorizing. Also, in a particular application, hybridization may occur, producing subcategories or new categories. Again, our point here is not analysis of a particular scheme. Rather, we wish to direct attention to the multidimensional nature and potential variety of recreational activities and their intended purposes.

Within a developmental conception of recreation fit such activities as team and individual sports, classes in visual and performing arts and associated skills, camping programs, wilderness education and conditioning programs, various activities offered at drop-in centers, and many other sorts of social activities (see Public Policy Forum, 1991).

As we observed earlier, most larger cities and counties in the United States appear to offer many recreational and cultural opportunities. But availability and access may be uneven, and different conceptions may prevail. "Market orientations to recreation (where people seek out opportunities and, if appropriate, purchase services) or standard methods by which children acquire recreation or related social skills (e.g., clubs, classes, etc.) seem to work well in middle class [areas]" (Public Policy Forum, 1991, p. 3). Providers of recreational services may be public or private, and they may be nonprofit or profit-making organizations. In any case, most are established as just described—providing a variety of services for those who seek them, who can conveniently access the facilities, and who most often can pay fees for membership or use. Here, a middle-class conception of recreation prevails.

However, "in low income neighborhoods [particularly inner-city neighborhoods where at-risk youths are concentrated], the same conditions which challenge the traditional performance of schools likewise require different approaches to the organization of recreation services" (Public Policy Forum, 1991, p. 3). Because of those conditions, the conception of recreation suiting the needs of inner-city youths requires attention.

You've got to know the territory. You've got to know the folks who live here. . . . What "fits" adolescent inner city youth [may] differ in some important ways from approaches usually supported by existing policies and programs intended to benefit [these] groups. (Irby & McLaughlin, 1990, p. 37)

Organization and delivery of services may exclude those who need them most (Public Policy Forum, 1991).

RECREATIONAL INTERVENTION PROGRAMS: TRENDS AND MODELS

The literature on recreational intervention and/or prevention efforts is rather sparse. Much of it consists of anecdotal accounts of limited programs or efforts. Some of the literature involves largely theoretical discussions of policies, guidelines, or potential models aimed at recreation professionals rather than "practice based results" (Public Policy Forum, 1991, p. 28). Finally, as Thompson and Jason reported in 1988, the literature conspicuously lacks discussions of reasonably comprehensive and rigorous evaluations of programs in which recreation is central.

Nonetheless, there is sufficient information available to reveal certain trends regarding recreational interventions. For one thing, as pointed out by the Public Policy Forum (1991), a number of models for delivering recreational services have emerged nationally. With these, "recreation is less the issue . . . than the larger models which serve to integrate urban services and within which recreation functions as a significant element" (p. 28). Following are descriptions of three such comprehensive programs, each subsuming a significant recreational component as part of a larger effort.

New Jersey's School-Based Youth Services Program

New Jersey's youth services program began in the mid-1980s as a coordinated program run through community centers at the high schools in order to reduce various social service costs.* The plan derives to some extent from Milwaukee's own lighted schoolhouse approach as well as Los Angeles County's youth services program, which uses school buildings as activity centers in the afternoons and evenings. The New Jersey program involved an infusion of funds and technical assistance to increase the recreation and activity services in the after-school hours as well as providing linkages to health and other human services.

The program's overall purpose is to provide the adolescent population (ages 13 to 19), especially high-risk youths, with the opportunity to complete their education, to obtain skills that lead to employment or further education, and to lead physically and mentally healthy, drug-free lives.

Under the former system, there existed a fragmented assortment of programs that were narrow in scope, often located in inconvenient places or in settings that were socially unacceptable to the adolescent population; therefore, services were underutilized. Schools were found to be one of the most effective means of reaching the largest number of adolescents on a regular basis, with sites available during and after school hours, on weekends, and during summer vacation months.

---

* The descriptions of these three programs originally appeared in *The Serious Business of Play: A Focus on Recreation in the Milwaukee Agenda* (pp. 28–29) by the Public Policy Forum, 1991, Milwaukee: Author. Copyright 1991 by the Public Policy Forum. Reprinted by permission.

Each site offers a comprehensive "core package" of services, including

- Employment counseling, training, and placement
- Summer and part-time job development
- Drug and alcohol abuse counseling
- Academic counseling
- Primary and preventive health services
- Recreation
- Referrals to health and social services

In 1989, the School-Based Youth Services Program had already served over 19,000 teenagers. Over half of those served each month are considered at high risk for academic trouble, delinquency, family crises, and other social and health problems.

The Boston Safe Neighborhoods Program

About a year ago, in response to the alarming growth of homicides and the deterioration of inner-city neighborhoods, Boston began its Safe Neighborhoods program. The components were built around three basic goals:

- To expand economic opportunity in the inner city
- To foster community and parental responsibility
  for the actions of youths
- To coordinate law enforcement activities and streamline
  the criminal justice system

The city recognized the complex social conditions and networks that had led to the current situation and targeted activities to build support within the community. Recreation services have played a major role in the plans to the extent that they support the development of social and cultural networks at the community level. Through any number of classes, athletics, and cultural events, the opportunities for people to do things have increased significantly. These opportunities have increased alongside other action plans for employment opportunities and law enforcement ("community policing").

Planning and implementation have included high involvement from neighborhood organizations as well as cross-departmental staffing (e.g., a Parks Department manager as a staff member in the Mayor's Office program). This means that "everyone owns a piece of the solution."

Because of the expectation that the real impact of the project will grow from complex involvements (i.e., from various social, economic, and bureaucratic sources), the initial evaluation has focused primarily on accountability for simple measures—that is, were particular activities implemented as planned. The more basic outcomes will be looked at in terms of long-range factors such as crime incidents and school performance. These have been promising, but staff are cautious, waiting for longer term measures.

El Puente

El Puente (the Bridge) is a community-based youth center in Brooklyn, New York. It considers its program of services to be holistic, emphasizing the integration of recreation, education, and social service projects to enrich the minds, bodies, and spirits of its participants. The program is supported by city and state grants and by private foundations.

The recreational programming includes dance, drama, art, culture club, ethnic dance, athletics (e.g., basketball, boxing), and an Outward Bound Program, in which youths participate in wilderness skill training and in a community service project.

The educational programming involves GED (Graduate Equivalency Degree) and English-as-a-second-language courses, homework assistance, counseling, the New York–based "I Have a Dream" program, and combined learning and service projects (e.g., murals on such topics as AIDS, Young Latinos for Peace).

The holistic programming provides and supports the personal growth of young people. There are peer counselors, short- and long-term goals for each participant, and a medical unit to see to health needs.

Primarily through local initiatives, public and private, a variety of limited-scope recreation-focused programs have emerged across the United States. Such programs involve varying target groups (e.g., gangs, group delinquents, at-risk youths), emphases (i.e., prevention or intervention), structures, and levels of funding. Overall, these efforts are too few, often have quite limited resources, and may or may not have found the keys to success with particular populations.

THE ROLE OF RECREATIONAL STRATEGIES

The problems of gangs, group delinquents, and at-risk youths, as well as proposals for addressing these problems, are multidimensional. Expectations for a single set of strategies to have widespread impact are unrealistic. However, within existing limitations, there must be a concerted attempt to find effective strategies and approaches. Those who have focused on recreational strategies have generally aimed at intervention (targeting current gang members) and/or prevention (targeting at-risk youths and/or wannabes—prime candidates for gang membership or serious group delinquency problems).

In general, recreational strategies center on attempts to provide positive activities as alternatives to delinquent behaviors and activities; most include at least some attention to the idea of personal development. A constellation of positive aims guides general thinking about recreational strategies. For example, a common aim involves inducing young people to join positive activities in planned locations at times (e.g., after school, evenings, late at night, on weekends) when they may be most vulnerable to involvement in delinquent activities. The idea is straightforward: If a youth is engaged in a positive activity at a given time, he or she is, at least for that time, diverted from participation in undesirable activities. The aim may be as explicit as that underlying a South Central Los Angeles late-night basketball league: "By putting a few members of the Six Little Deuce Brims or Little Hoovers on the basketball court a few hours each week, the hope is there will be that many fewer people on the street, that many fewer drive-by shootings" (Armstrong, 1990, p. 1).

As stated, additional aims usually accompany the concerns of place, time, and positive activity. These aims may not be explicitly programmed for; rather, they may be hoped-for benefits thought to accrue from participation in positive recreational activities. For example, there may be a generalized expectation of benefits from positive association and teamwork, perhaps also from exposure, even if limited, to positive role models. In addition, recreation programming has been suggested as a means of providing a positive outlet for youthful energies, building self-esteem and self-confidence, enhancing social skills, developing responsibility and self-discipline, engendering respect for self and others, equipping youths to deal with peer pressure, and building leadership qualities.

THE QUESTION OF FIT

Any strategy for recreational intervention must be tailored to fit the context in which it will be implemented. To better appreciate the need for appropriate fit, consider variations from one city to another. For example, Atlanta's West End area, where there are several inner-city public housing developments, is characterized by group delinquency and activities involving "instrumental gangs" (groups loosely organized and induced to participate in and facilitate particular illegal activities, primarily drug sales) rather than extensive organized turf gang activity. The population of these developments is almost entirely African American.

Philadelphia presents a rather different, and mixed, scene. In North Philadelphia, organized gang activity is more prevalent. In South Philadelphia, the primarily Italian core neighborhood is adjoined by badly deteriorated housing developments populated primarily by African Americans; there is a large Asian population as well. The "problem" in South Philadelphia could best be described as a group delinquency problem. Youths "hang out" together, especially during evening hours, in loosely organized peer groups, often engaging in spontaneous delinquent acts or in haphazardly planned activities. There is instrumental organization of youths by others in connection with drug sales. Graffiti and the paraphernalia associated with organized youth gangs are largely absent. Drugs, alcohol, and gambling are key problems. Poverty is abundant in the housing developments, and deteriorating family structure is apparent. A host of factors contribute to extremely poor life conditions for many youths, and racial tension among members of the Italian neighborhood, the African American population, and the Asian population is very evident.

East Los Angeles has the more familiar organized youth gang problem, along with instrumental gang activity and adult involvement. Elsewhere, many cities' suburbs are beginning to evidence more significant group delinquency, instrumental group and gang activity, and gang formation. Although some important basic similarities (including poverty, deterioration of family structure, ethnic and racial strife, and the essential realization that virtually all youths living in such conditions are at risk) underlie all these situations, the situations do differ. The differences require thorough understanding of the difficulties in a given area and enlightened planning of recreational or other efforts to address them.

Irby and McLaughlin (1990) make a further observation about fit: "What 'fits' adolescent [and preadolescent] inner city youth differs in some important ways from approaches supported by existing policies and programs intended to benefit this group" (p. 37). Intervention strategies based on conventional wisdom about access to services and market-oriented approaches, particularly regarding recreation efforts, can certainly fail to fit an inner-city situation.

> Imported structures, or goals and routines "foreign" to the habits
> or interests of youth, almost certainly will fall short of expectations.
> Meaningful association in terms of the particular youth served,
> respect for their ethnicity, and responsiveness to local realities
> seem to be criterion [*sic*] for acceptance. (Irby & McLaughlin,
> 1990, p. 37)

Irby and McLaughlin (1990) take this prescriptive viewpoint in reviewing the operation of the Jesse White Tumbling Team, an inner-city organization serving at-risk youths since 1959 on the outskirts of Chicago's Cabrini Green housing development. They report that this organization is "designed from the point of view of the adolescent," stressing "positive aspects and interests of youth" that counter the appeal and function of gangs (p. 37). Athletics is a central dimension of the organization, but the approach is much broader; it is also developmental in the sense of intentionally promoting peer approval, community status for the young people, group cohesiveness, and interpersonal support, as well as creating the expectation of a positive pipeline out of the housing area.

Irby and McLaughlin (1990) conclude that "this positive and developmental perspective operates in clear distinction from programs and policies that try to 'manage' the negative or problematic aspects of adolescents—substance abuse, crime, school failure, teenage pregnancy and so on" (p. 38). The Jesse White Tumbling Team goes beyond the stereotypical image of a recreation effort. It is not a "program" in the usual sense of a particularized venture of definite duration. Instead, it is an organization in operation for more than 30 years, located where it needs to be, its founder and staff pursuing a developmental approach based on athletics and personal interaction, engendering changes in youths' attitudes and values over time.

Thinking both about the role of recreation and about fit leads us to several points. Gangs and at-risk youths are heavily concentrated in inner cities. It is clear that limited strategies such as recreational efforts intended primarily as a temporary antidote to violence may have some positive effect, but the effect is very likely to be minimal. For example, basketball participation alone, although a positive recreational experience, is highly unlikely to have major, long-term beneficial effects. Where prevention is the aim, recreation may be one aspect or the central aspect of an overall effort. However, the effort required is actually one of *youth development,* in which a full service organization addresses a youth's many developmental needs in a way that retains the person's participation and interest over time.

"Yet funders and policymakers generally continue to find more attractive those programs that aim to 'prevent' or 'stop' or 'remediate' some aspect of adolescent behavior than they do the more comprehensive, youth-focused, developmental approaches" (Irby & McLaughlin, 1990, p. 38). Long-term developmental approaches, whatever their central dimensions, are difficult to implement. The major problem is that there are few organizations in our inner cities that both are attractive to youths and can carry out developmental efforts. Many organizations that could possibly meet these requirements have retreated from the inner cities, relocating to less problem-ridden areas and adopting middle-class market orientations. This situation poses a major national dilemma.

An attempt to address the dilemma is under way. The Office of Juvenile Justice and Delinquency Prevention has funded a targeted outreach effort being conducted by the Boys and Girls Clubs of America (BGCA) in 33 cities. This effort is aimed at developing and assessing means for reaching the most vulnerable inner-city youths and deterring them from involvement in gangs and gang activities. The scope and nature of this outreach, as well as its possibilities, deserve further attention.

BOYS AND GIRLS CLUBS: TARGETED OUTREACH

In the targeted outreach project, local BGCA organizations are charged with implementing efforts tailored to "the community, the needs of their members, and the severity of the youth gang problem locally" (OJJDP, 1991, p. 3). Thirty clubs, designated as prevention sites, have received funding to implement efforts to "deter youth from becoming involved in gangs, with a primary focus aimed at 7 to 11 year olds" (p. 3). Three clubs received enhanced funding to focus on developing a community consortium with the aim of building a strong network with other public and private organizations. Three other clubs, designated as intervention sites, received additional funding to "develop and document model gang intervention programs focusing on activities for youth 12 to 16 years old" (p. 3).

These combined efforts constitute an attempt at finding ways to undertake prevention and intervention on a national basis. There are more than 1,100 Boys and Girls Clubs nationwide. "Typically, Club members live in large or medium-sized cities; have three or more siblings; are from minority populations; and have families whose annual income is less than $12,000" (OJJDP, 1991, p. 1). Local clubs are typically located in or adjacent to housing developments in urban areas where the most at-risk youths reside. Many local clubs have been in existence for decades, and they generally operate under a philosophy of youth development. In other words, although recreation is central to operation, a number of additional initiatives are typically undertaken to involve members in educational and personal skills development activities, to draw parents and other community volunteers into positive interactions with youths, and to educate the community about the needs of its youths.

Guided by program principles and recommendations, and with support from the national Boys and Girls Clubs of America, the designated clubs have launched their particular efforts. It is instructive to examine a few of those efforts. Following are descriptions of one prevention effort, one prevention/consortium effort, and one intervention effort.

The general strategy for each designated club involves recruiting 35 at-risk youths from the immediate area. For prevention efforts, *risk* is defined as any one of the following: having had two or more behavioral contacts with school authorities; being truant frequently; being abused or neglected; having a record of nonfelony offenses; and failing two or more school subjects. For intervention efforts, any one of the following constitutes risk: being a wannabe or fringe gang member; having family members in a gang; having been taken into custody by the juvenile system; being abused or neglected; and being identified as a substance abuser.

One representative prevention effort is being implemented in a medium-sized midwestern city; it is operated primarily from a location in an inner-city housing development. The area has organized gang activity and some instrumental gang activity; generally, poor conditions prevail. The main prevention activity is after-school programming. Young people participate in a tutoring/homework assistance session, which is followed by organized sports, field trips, group discussions (on relevant topics such as substance abuse), and other activities. A primary goal is to keep these youths involved beyond the project time period and to retain them as club members. Programming continues through the summer months, with various planned activities offered as alternatives to the streets.

A representative consortium effort is being implemented in a large city in the northeast. The designated club is located amidst several housing developments that have organized gang activity, instrumental gang activity, and generally very poor conditions. Beyond providing after-school activities of the sort just described, the club works intensively to involve other community organizations in a network associated with its effort, as well as to involve parents on a regular basis (e.g., in regular discussion sessions built around an evening meal). The network includes direct links with a local middle school (to increase monitoring and expand beyond homework assistance to creative educational activities that dovetail with school curriculum), with housing authority police and other local law enforcement personnel (to help identify potential difficulties in the area), and with other organizations. One of the club's links is with a local advertising firm. The firm made production facilities and technical assistance available to young people, who created video and graphic advertisements in an award-winning campaign against gangs. In addition, this effort has focused on providing recreational and educational activities that expose participants to experiences beyond the inner city. Field trips, overnight campouts, and other excursions are intended literally to take participants beyond the limits of the neighborhoods or housing areas where they spend most of their time. As in all the designated efforts, club staff work to make the facility a safe and neutral place, sheltered from the danger of the surrounding area.

One of the intervention efforts is situated in a large western city, in an area with extensive gang activity. Targeting older youths, this effort involves after-school activities, including tutorials and various recreational opportunities. Much attention is devoted to organizing and conducting sports-related outings and educational trips, such as museum visits and the like. Part of the club effort entails transporting gang-involved youths to a camp setting, where local deputy sheriffs participate in the camp situation. The purpose of this experience is to provide positive individual contact and attention and, ultimately, to promote changes in attitude. Club staff also visit probation detention facilities, where they help incarcerated youths maintain contact with family and friends and facilitate visits. Staff assist the young people in planning for their return to the community, searching for employment, and dealing with other issues. The aim is twofold: to advocate for youths and to convey a message of community concern.

The Boys and Girls Clubs efforts hold promise. Like the Jesse White Tumbling Team, these are organizations located in areas where most young people may be considered at risk. As Irby and McLaughlin (1990) point out, positive developmental approaches focused on the interests of youths are essential in countering both the appeal of gangs and the conditions of our inner cities.

CONCLUSIONS

As we suggested at the beginning of this chapter, life conditions are poor for many of this country's youths. Hundreds of thousands are at risk and vulnerable to the inducements offered by gangs. Tens of thousands have already taken the step of joining gangs or participating in gang activities. Reality demands coordinated national efforts focused on prevention as well as intervention. Although recreation-centered efforts hold promise, the promise is very limited unless such efforts are seen as but part of a multifaceted approach to youth development.

As noted earlier, devising concepts and strategies is only a first step. Any effort must take into account local realities and must be implemented with attention to youths' real life circumstances. Some basic elements must be addressed in each situation. First, especially in inner-city areas, any development effort must provide a safe haven, a physical location where youths can feel and be safe from potentially dangerous circumstances and experience a positive environment. Second, knowledgeable, empathic, and dedicated staff are critical in any effort. The personal factor cannot be overemphasized. Staff must be able to relate to youths, to communicate with youths, to serve as role models who motivate youths to pursue positive interests and to learn positive values. Third, development efforts must be seen as long-term, multistage processes in which youths are mainstreamed into a broad range of developmental activities and experiences. Fourth, youth programming must be a community consortium effort. Collaboration among public and private organizations to provide youths a community network and to furnish the resources and opportunities to support developmental aims offers the only hope of achieving more than transient successes.

As important as such comprehensive efforts are in interrupting the gang cycle, they alone will not resolve our national dilemma. Conditions in the United States are such that the gates to undesirable consequences are wide open. Nothing less than a revision of national priorities to address inner-city conditions, unemployment, and the effects of social and political tension will suffice. Moreover, little will change unless, and until, we end individual and political denial of the conditions prevalent in our inner cities, until we clearly realize that too many citizens— especially children—are living desperate and hopeless lives in conditions not of their own choosing. It is time to face the facts.

REFERENCES

Anderson, E. (1990). *Streetwise: Race, class and change in an urban community.* University of Chicago Press.

Armstrong, S. (1990, May 17). L.A. fights gangs with basketballs. *The Christian Science Monitor,* p. 10.

Bryant, D. (1989, September). Communitywide responses crucial for dealing with youth gangs. *Juvenile Justice Bulletin,* pp. 1–6.

Fagan, J., Piper, E., & Moore, M. (1986). Violent delinquents and urban youth. *Criminology, 24,* 439–471.

Hagedorn, J. (1988). *People and folks: Gangs, crime and the underclass in a rustbelt city.* Chicago: Lake View.

Hawkins, D., & Jones, N.E. (1989). Black adolescents and the criminal justice system. In R.L. Jones (Ed.), *Black adolescents.* New York: Cobb & Henry.

Irby, M., & McLaughlin, M. (1990). When is a gang not a gang? When it's a tumbling team. *Future Choices, 2*(2), 31–39.

Lemann, N. (1986a, June). The origins of the underclass. *The Atlantic Monthly,* pp. 31–55.

Lemann, N. (1986b, July). The origins of the underclass. *The Atlantic Monthly,* pp. 55–68.

Miller, E. (1986). *Street women.* Philadelphia: Temple University Press.

Office of Juvenile Justice and Delinquency Prevention (OJJDP). (1991, July). OJJDP and Boys and Girls Clubs of America: Public housing and high-risk youth. *Juvenile Justice Bulletin,* pp. 1-4.

Public Policy Forum. (1991). The serious business of play: A focus on recreation in the Milwaukee agenda. Milwaukee: Author.

Silberman, C.E. (1978). *Criminal violence, criminal justice.* New York: Vantage.

Thompson, D., & Jason, L. (1988). Street gangs and preventive interventions. *Criminal Justice and Behavior, 15,* 323-333.

Wacquant, L., & Wilson, W.J. (1989). The cost of racial and class exclusion in the inner city. *The Annals, 501,* 8–25.

Wilson, W.J. (1978). *The declining significance of race.* University of Chicago Press.

Wilson, W.J. (1987). *The truly disadvantaged: The inner city, the underclass and public policy.* University of Chicago Press.

CHAPTER 11

Community Change Interventions

Kurt M. Ribisl
William S. Davidson II

It is often necessary to make a decision on the basis of knowledge
sufficient for action but insufficient to satisfy the intellect.
—*Immanuel Kant*

Though attention to the topic of youth gangs stalled in the late 1960s and the 1970s
(Bookin-Weiner & Horowitz, 1983; Jackson, 1989), the problems associated with
those gangs have continued to have adverse consequences for youths themselves
and for their communities (Klein & Maxson, 1989). The problems today also
present greater challenges to researchers and interventionists alike because it appears that the nature of gangs may have changed. Gangs now involve their members
for longer periods, are more involved in drug use and trafficking, are more violent,
and use more sophisticated weapons (Bensinger, 1984; Klein & Maxson, 1989;
Miller, 1990; Short, 1990). Given the conclusions of Klein and Maxson that the
outcomes of past gang intervention programs have been "realistically quite discouraging" (p. 226) and that gangs have changed fundamentally to become even
more destructive (Goldstein, 1991; Hagedorn, 1990), the challenges now confronting both researchers and practitioners addressing the problem of youth gangs are
even more serious than previously thought.

   This chapter has four goals: first, to outline the problem and give a brief historical overview of gang intervention and research in the context of community perspectives on juvenile delinquency; second, to discuss the promise and possible
shortcomings of community programs that have been tried; third, to delineate issues
that practitioners would likely face in developing a program for community intervention with youth gangs; and finally, to describe how programs of this type could
be evaluated.

EXTENT OF THE PROBLEM

The number of total arrests of juveniles for violent crimes has escalated over the
past two decades, although the number of juvenile arrests for property crimes is

nearly the same as it was 20 years ago. Data from the FBI Uniform Crime Reports show that the total number of arrests for violent crimes for individuals aged 12 to 17 was 54,596 in 1970 and 86,220 in 1980. By 1990, juvenile arrests for violent crimes had climbed even higher, to 91,317; this represents a 67% increase over the 20-year period. By contrast, the total number of juvenile arrests for property crimes went from 531,818 in 1970 up to 703,428 in 1980 and back down to 564,060 in 1990 (Federal Bureau of Investigation, 1970, 1980, 1990). The difference in property crime arrests from 1970 to 1990 only amounts to a 6% overall increase, despite considerable volatility in the interim.

Although the rise in arrests of juveniles for violent crime seems alarming, the proportion of such arrests involving juveniles has actually been *decreasing* when compared to adults. In 1970, juveniles accounted for 22.6% of all arrests for violent crimes; by 1990 that figure had dropped to 16.2%. Not surprisingly, the same pattern holds true for property crimes. In 1970, juveniles were involved in 51.7% of all arrests for property crimes but only 31.9% by 1990.

In summary, the number of juvenile arrests for violent crimes has increased significantly over the last 20 years; however, the proportion of arrests for which juveniles are responsible has been declining. Although these data are for juveniles in general, they may be viewed as a possible estimate of trends in criminal activity attributable to gangs, which typically are composed of individuals in this same 12- to 17-year-old age group. Some caution is warranted in the face of evidence that people stay in gangs longer, which contributes to an increase in the average age of members (Spergel et al., 1989). Direct evidence of gang activity is very difficult to ascertain on a national level because of variations in local definitions of gang behavior (Klein, Gordon, & Maxson, 1986; Spergel, 1990).

These trends in arrest rates should themselves be viewed with caution. For example, demographic shifts associated with the baby boom may have had a substantial impact on particular crime rates. The population bulge attributable to the baby boom has moved out of the juvenile years and is now in the era when those composing it may contribute to adult crime statistics (Steffensmeier & Harer, 1991).

With these caveats in mind, we can note changes in the types of crime attributable to gangs. Early reports showed that gangs were involved in less serious offenses, such as fighting, burglary, and perhaps vandalism. However, in the last two decades, the problem of serious gang violence has escalated (Goldstein, 1991). The past decade has seen increases in gang homicides (Klein & Maxson, 1989). According to data from UCLA and the Centers for Disease Control, from 1970 to 1979 there were 240 homicides in Los Angeles that were related to gang violence (Loya, 1985). Other more recent data show a dramatic increase in gang-related homicides: There were over 1,500 gang-related homicides in Los Angeles during the 1985–1990 period alone (Gott, 1989). Although the actual numbers represented by these two sets of statistics may not be directly comparable (because the sources are different and the more recent data may be influenced by increased awareness and reporting of gang violence), the toll in human lives is still heavy. Further, it appears that the problem of gang violence is not confined to large urban areas in a handful of states. Gangs are emerging in smaller cities and have been found in every region and practically every state in the nation (Knox, 1991; Spergel, 1990).

The issue of gang activity has received a good deal of political attention. Communities are concerned with and frightened by gangs. The chair of the California State Task Force on Gangs and Drugs called today's gangs "urban terrorists [who] are turning our streets and neighborhoods into war zones, where it takes an act of courage simply to walk to the corner store" (California Council on Criminal Justice, 1989, p. viii). A survey of community members in Racine, Wisconsin, showed that 81% of adults perceived a gang problem in their city (Takata & Zevitz, 1990). Interestingly, only 30% of adults felt that there were gangs in their own neighborhoods, and only 24% reported direct contact with gangs. Those reporting gang activity in their neighborhoods were asked how they knew about those activities. The most common response (39%) was that they learned about gangs from the media. Communities may in some instances overreact to sensational media accounts and thus exaggerate the extent of gang presence and activity; gangs are nevertheless a menace to many communities.

Although the amount of violence perpetrated by gang members reportedly is only a small proportion of the overall violence (Morash, 1990; Spergel et al., 1989) and victims are typically other gang members (Klein & Maxson, 1989), many citizens feel strongly that gangs have taken over and that their streets are unsafe. Ironically, many individuals join gangs because they fear victimization by gangs or they hope to protect their neighborhoods (Fagan, 1989), even though gang membership ultimately increases their chances for victimization (Morash, 1990), exposes them to more dangerous environments, and involves them in more perilous routine activities (Fagan, 1990).

The California Task Force on Gangs and Drugs has argued that gang violence is not just a problem for the criminal justice system but that gangs are a major community problem and responsibility and that "the solution to the problem lies in the community itself" (California Council on Criminal Justice, 1989, p. ix). In a similar vein, Knox (1991) holds that the community is the last defense against gang crime if the family cannot be relied on as an effective agent of socialization; indeed, he notes, the community may also be our best defense.

Given the increase in gang-related violence and the strain that gangs place on communities, what can be done? The question of how to respond to gang activity is one of scientific as well as practical concern.

Since the end of the 1970s, government's approach to crime in general as well as to the gang problem has shifted from rehabilitation to deterrence and incapacitation (Goldstein, 1991). In fact, total prison admissions reached an all-time high in 1984 (U. S. Department of Justice, 1988). However, the punitive approach has had limited effectiveness in curbing the epidemic of violence (Morash, 1990). Although the debate on the efficacy of deterrence and incapacitation continues, there is little debate about the immense cost of such approaches. In the current fiscal crisis, their utility is being seriously questioned. In the face of frustration with traditional approaches to the problem of gangs, promising community intervention alternatives deserve serious consideration.

HISTORY OF COMMUNITY APPROACHES

To date, there have been few evaluations of systematic interventions with youth gangs (Klein & Maxson, 1989; Spergel, 1990) and correspondingly few reports of positive evaluations. The pool nearly evaporates when it is limited to interventions from a community perspective. In addition, the evidence from existing juvenile delinquency programs is not cause for optimism. Wright and Dixon's (1977) review of community interventions for juvenile delinquents showed that most past efforts had been largely ineffective. A meta-analysis of community-based interventions for juveniles by Gottschalk, Davidson, Gensheimer, and Mayer (1987) revealed that treatments in community settings generally did not have a significant effect on outcomes. Nevertheless, particular program characteristics were associated with desired outcomes. Hence, in our prescriptions for community interventions, we must be highly specific and consider the characteristics of successful interventions.

PROMISING COMMUNITY INTERVENTION APPROACHES

This section will describe three exemplary community approaches to gang delinquency. Just as definitional inconsistency has clouded the idea of what a "gang" is and created difficulty in accurately attributing crimes to gangs (Klein & Maxson, 1989; Knox, 1991), there has been little consensus as to what interventions are considered community interventions. We consider community interventions as being one or more of the following: multisystem, multilevel, preventive, and other than individually focused and based on verbal exchange. In surveying programs, we did not consider work with prison gangs or motorcycle gangs. Most of the articles we reviewed concern interventions with youth gangs, although we have included exemplary work with juvenile delinquents or those at risk to expand the knowledge base for prescribed intervention models. More comprehensive reviews of community initiatives for combating gang violence can be found in Goldstein (1991), Knox (1991), and Spergel (1990).

In our study, three models emerged as promising: Project BUILD, the Crisis Intervention Services Project, and the behavioral-ecological model of intervention. Each was selected on the basis of three criteria: First, the program must be a community intervention, as defined earlier; second, there must be some evidence of the program's effectiveness; and third, the program must be sufficiently well detailed that dissemination and replication are possible. We will describe each model, detailing the critical program ingredients and paying particular attention to the credibility of the evidence for the program's efficacy.

Project BUILD

Program Description

Thompson and Jason (1988) evaluated a preventive intervention whose goal was to prevent youths from joining gangs in Chicago. The program, part of Project Broader Urban Involvement and Leadership Development (BUILD), was based on social development theory and on the propositions of social opportunity theory as articulated by Weis and Hawkins (1981). Drawing on Weis and Hawkins' perspective, Thompson and Jason note that "prevention programs must teach requisite social and educational skills and then facilitate their use and subsequent reinforcement in an appropriate manner" (p. 325). The prevention program focused on diverting youngsters from gang membership by providing educational presentations, as well as access to and reinforcement for alternative prosocial activities.

The program was offered through public schools to youths considered at risk for gang membership based on teacher ratings and BUILD staff perceptions. Classes participated in 12 sessions on gang theory, the realities and consequences of gang membership, the dangers of substance abuse, and values clarification. The goals of the sessions were to alert youths to the tactics of gang recruitment and the processes of gang involvement and to deter them from future gang membership by pointing out its negative consequences. Speakers from minority racial backgrounds conducted a number of the class sessions.

The program also sought to provide alternative prosocial activities, thereby minimizing the opportunity for gang involvement. Every attempt was made to provide activities selected by participants themselves. Common after-school program activities included sports, travel, recreation, and job skills workshops.

Evidence of Effectiveness

A total of 121 students from six public grade schools participated in the study. Although schools were not randomly assigned to conditions, there were three experimental and three control schools. None of the sample was a current gang member, as ascertained by confidential rosters of gang members known to BUILD staff. Program participants included the targeted youths and all of their classmates.

At the end of the intervention, the names of the targeted youths were compared with those on the confidential gang rosters. Youths thus identified as gang members were categorized as failures. Those not on the roster of active gang members were considered successes. At follow-up, only 1 of 74 experimental participants and 4 of 43 controls were gang members. These results were reported as marginally significant.

Crisis Intervention Services Project

Program Description

The Crisis Intervention Services Project (CRISP) was initiated in response to the increase in problems associated with gang violence in Chicago (Spergel, 1986). The program was based on a similar program in Philadelphia that proponents claimed was highly successful. The CRISP program was multifaceted in approach and was based on four components: crisis intervention and mediation with gangs in the streets, intensive individual work with gang members, mobilization of local community groups to deal with the gang problem, and development of an advisory group to deal with local issues and needed resources. The program model was eclectic and drawn from the theoretical perspectives of sociocultural disorganization, opportunity theory, community development, social control, and differential association.

The multifaceted CRISP intervention attacked gang violence directly as well as indirectly. In order to have systematic information on gang violence as it occurred or escalated, gang workers were on the streets from 6:00 P. M. to midnight. Gang workers all carried communication pagers in the event of crises. Their surveillance was part of the crisis intervention component. Whenever they became aware of potentially violent situations or violence in progress, they tried to intervene to prevent or stop it.

Another responsibility of the gang workers brought them into direct contact with youths in need. This involved providing direct, informal counseling on the streets when necessary and making referrals to community human services when appropriate.

A third set of activities was aimed at involving targeted youths in community development activities. Several community development projects, such as a major graffiti-expunging effort, were undertaken. A specific neighborhood group was mobilized for each community development project. Further, a project advisory committee worked for more general solutions to community issues.

Evidence of Effectiveness

The CRISP program focused on several target areas within four police precincts selected for their high incidence of gang activity. A matched set of non-target areas was used for comparison. For evaluation purposes, the numbers and types of gang incidents in the target and nontarget areas were compared over time. Offenses were categorized as Type I offenses, serious violent crimes (e.g., homicide, robbery), or as Type II offenses, less serious violent crimes (e.g., simple assault, intimidation, gang recruitment).

Comparison of offenses in the preproject period and the project period showed a significant reduction in the rate of increase in Type I gang offenses in the target areas compared to the control areas. Regarding Type II offenses, there was little difference between the two areas. In addition, reports from the Chicago Gang Crime Unit indicated a significant reduction in the seriousness of gang activity in the target area. The proportion of the more serious Type I offenses dropped in the target area but rose in the nontarget area during the project period.

Comparisons of the target areas themselves suggested that the effects of the program were greater in the areas where more intense intervention had taken place. Finally, reports on violent offenses by individual youths receiving specialized counseling and referrals suggested that the intervention reduced offenses officially recognized as gang related but had no impact on total violent offenses or those not gang related.

Behavioral-Ecological Model of Intervention

Program Description

Hunsaker (1981) describes a unique community intervention with Chicano gang members, based on a behavioral-ecological model that has not often been applied to gang behavior. In this model, the entire community is viewed as an individual client, and the community's weaknesses and strengths are diagnosed. Interventions are designed to shape the behavior of the community so that it provides a more adaptive setting for its members. In this application, a reversal of power positions is implied: An attempt was made to have gang members directly and positively influence those in power.

The intervention took place in a densely populated city with six Chicano youth gangs. A private, nonprofit community-based agency served as the change agent. The intervention began with a number of assessments: First, an initial problem analysis identified problem situations, behaviors, and consequences. Second, problem clarification provided further specification of the surrounding events. Next, a motivational analysis revealed the outcomes that gang members sought when they engaged in illegal behavior. Relatedly, a developmental analysis showed the pattern of gang activity over time, with its consistency and its variations. Next, project staff assessed the degree to which self-control procedures might ameliorate the problems. Further, the social relationships intertwined with and supportive of group activities were analyzed. Finally, important environmental supports for gang activity were examined.

Gang members reported that they felt other community members were uninterested in their input and often harassed them. The community at large viewed gang members as doing poorly in school, committing crimes, writing offensive graffiti, and using psychoactive substances. In the community's eyes, the gang members' assets lay in their artistic talents and their skill in customizing cars.

Interventions were based on the strengths and weaknesses of both the community and the gang members. Most of the interventions employed behavioral techniques. Interventions included initiating a job program, starting satellite schools in neutral territory (so students could attend school without going into gang territory), and establishing a youth service bureau to provide educational experiences to school dropouts.

Evidence of Effectiveness

Hunsaker (1981) concluded that the goals of the program were partially met. Formal evaluation data were not yet available; evidence concerning the effectiveness of this intervention consisted mostly of descriptive information about the process of initiating and maintaining the program. Also, because the time frame of the program was restricted, interventions were begun before a thorough functional analysis was completed. The author noted the many problems arising from this limitation. The youth service bureau was dismantled toward the end of the intervention owing to a lack of funding. In sum, Hunsaker's report describes an interesting community approach to the gang problem. Most gang intervention programs operate from a deficit model, based on the notion that gang members are lacking something; this program, by contrast, shows that creative programming can integrate gang members' strengths into the intervention.

ISSUES FOR COMMUNITY CHANGE PROGRAMS

Given the broad scope of the gang problem and its seemingly unbreakable grip on many of our communities, comprehensive and multidisciplinary programs operating at multiple levels within the community are needed. When a community approach is to be adopted, a number of issues must be addressed. These include identifying a target population, selecting a level of intervention, choosing a theoretical model to guide the intervention, specifying appropriate characteristics of the change agents, and determining the organizational affiliation of the intervention effort.

Identifying the Target Population

The aim of a gang intervention program will have a major impact on the population that will be reached and on the overall characteristics of the program. A program aimed at preventing gang involvement will generally reach younger individuals, most likely in a school setting. On the other hand, a program aimed at rehabilitating current gang members is more likely to involve individuals in a wider age range. Further, reclamation efforts could take place in many institutions, such as the court system, youth center, or a private organization.

There are three basic types of prevention programs: primary, secondary, and tertiary (Bolman, 1969; Caplan, 1964). Primary prevention, which seeks to ensure that young people never become affiliated with gangs, focuses on all youths in a community or setting. Educational campaigns are generally in the category of primary prevention. An example is the Partners in Prevention Program (Boyle & Gonzales, 1989), initiated by the Sacramento Police Department. Its aim is to educate youths about the pitfalls of gang and drug involvement.

Secondary prevention seeks to terminate or lessen the involvement of individuals who are at high risk for association with gangs. Project BUILD (Thompson

& Jason, 1988) is one of the few secondary gang prevention efforts that have been evaluated. This program targeted youths considered at risk for gang involvement by teachers and project staff. This is the key distinction between primary and secondary prevention: The targets of change are individuals who are have certain predisposing risk factors, not the general population. Given the difficulties in trying to predict who will be delinquent or violent and the potential negative effects of labeling, caution is warranted in programming for youths at risk (Blakely & Davidson, 1981; Goldstein, 1991; Klein & Maxson, 1989). A commendable aspect of the Thompson and Jason intervention is that it involved entire classrooms instead of isolated youths. This approach minimized potential labeling and stigmatization of participants.

Noting a possibility for prevention, Klein and Maxson (1989) observe that it is probably more effective to reduce the attractiveness of the gang for the *newer* members and choose other strategies for older members. In addition, secondary prevention can be applied at the gang level. Taylor (1990), who studied Detroit gangs, suggests that gangs progress through stages. Intervention can be initiated with gangs identified to be in the first stage, the "scavenger stage." Gangs in this stage have few common goals and little cohesion. Programming could be aimed at preventing further development of the group into either a "territorial" or an "organized/corporate" gang.

Tertiary prevention seeks to terminate or lessen the involvement of core gang members. Klein and Maxson (1989) warn that this should be done carefully so that greater gang cohesion does not result. They recommend reinforcing alternative activities, such as jobs or education, for older members. Such an approach may be seen as an effort to draw on the strengths of the gang's cohesion but to turn it to prosocial ends. Wall, Hawkins, Lishner, and Fraser (1981) offer an overview of 36 different juvenile delinquency prevention programs that might be adapted to gang prevention.

Selecting the Level of Intervention

A critical step in planning is to determine the level of the intervention. Juvenile delinquency and youth gang programs have reflected remarkable variety in levels of intervention. At one end of the spectrum are programs that deal explicitly with individual youths, often employing either a behavior change or a values transformation approach. At the other end of the spectrum are interventions aimed at improving the opportunity structure of the community, on the assumption that the effects will trickle down and improve the situations of individual youths. Examples of programs at different levels will be described briefly.

Individual Level

The individual counseling aspect of the Spergel (1986) program illustrates focus at the individual level. The goal of this program was to identify individuals in need of community services and refer them to appropriate agencies. Another recent example of individual-level intervention focused on sociomoral cognitive development (Arbuthnot & Gordon, 1989). These programs attempted to alter delinquent youths' moral reasoning, with the ultimate aim of decreasing delinquent behavior. Although the authors present an interesting theoretical rationale for their approach, it has yet to be tested on more seriously delinquent youths such as gang members.

Group Level

Intervention can also be initiated at the group or neighborhood level. The group might be a social network of youths or even an intact gang. One approach to identifying groups, discussed earlier, was demonstrated by Thompson and Jason (1988), who asked teachers to identify youths whom they considered at high risk for later delinquent behavior. Intervention was administered to the entire class of which each targeted individual was a member. An advantage of group-level intervention is that it reaches more individuals and enhances the opportunity for broad impact. In addition, a youth's social group is a very important influence on delinquent behavior (Elliott, Huizinga, & Ageton, 1985), and reshaping group norms may lead to desirable outcomes for individuals.

Community Level

Interventions at the community level were more common in the 1960s, when the sociopolitical climate was more supportive of large-scale social programs. Many such programs were broad, aimed at increasing access to jobs and education and fostering community cohesion. Klein and Maxson (1989) recommend that gang intervention be programmed for geographic areas rather than for individual gangs. Several programs we reviewed were broadly based and also included an individual gang component. However, Spergel (1990) notes that the broad-scale programs of earlier years generally did not have much impact on gang membership and gang violence. Given the substantial capital outlay that such programs require, it is doubtful that they will be replicated in the current sociopolitical environment. Still, there are many community-level programs that would not need extensive funding.

Neighborhood and community watch programs have become increasingly popular as communities have grown more concerned about crime prevention. Local citizens have also involved themselves more actively in surveillance programs—to the extent that some citizens have acted almost as "vigilantes" in their neighborhoods (Spergel et al., 1989).

Choosing a Theoretical Model

From the outset, planners need to identify a theoretical model of delinquency that can act as a blueprint for the intervention. Lipsey (1988) remarks that "although a certain amount of trial-and-error testing of clinical hunches may well open up promising avenues, this approach has too many problems to justify its popularity"

(p. 74). Lipsey provides several reasons why atheoretical approaches are limited: They do not specify the optimal intervention points, they provide few criteria for sufficient treatment, they have limited explanatory power concerning the reasons why the treatment succeeded or failed, and they offer little guidance as to what variables are important and what outcomes might be expected.

Few gang control interventions have been developed from explicit theoretical formulations (Miller, 1990). Many reports on interventions are so vague that the theoretical model is blurred. Other reports seem to reflect a motley collection of radically different treatment approaches selected in cafeteria style. When two or three theoretical models are implicated in one intervention, it is practically impossible to disentangle the effects, if there are any.

In summary, community-based gang interventions need to be guided by a sound intervention theory. Knox (1991) describes how the absence of a clear theory of delinquency underlying the Boston Midcity Project (Miller, 1962) led to increased organization of gangs. Clements (1988) offers more guidance on some theoretical models for community delinquency prevention and treatment programs. A sound theory should have some empirical basis, be clear enough to guide program implementation, and provide specific predictions about long- and short-range outcomes.

Specifying Change Agent Characteristics

Affiliation of Change Agents

In past gang interventions, the characteristics of change agents have been quite diverse. Frequently, individuals with professional training have been used, as in many of the early detached worker programs (Cooper, 1967). Other programs have employed paraprofessionals (e.g., Davidson, Redner, Amdur, & Mitchell, 1990), and still others have recruited persons indigenous to the community, such as former gang leaders or members (Spergel, 1986; Torres, 1981). This simple classification into three groups is primarily heuristic and will not always be accurate, because many interventions employ individuals from different categories. We will briefly discuss the advantages and disadvantages of using change agents from these three categories.

Because many gang intervention projects require considerable resources to operate, they are often government funded and organized either by government agencies or by university-based researchers. Such programs are often staffed by professionals: psychologists, law enforcement representatives, social workers, and others. One advantage of employing professionals is that their ties with formal social service agencies may facilitate access to community resources. In addition, they may have greater perceived credibility. On the other hand, many gang members are suspicious of authority, and this could undermine the effectiveness of professional change agents. Gang members may also be suspicious of individuals whom they see as associated with government. Further, many professionals are not familiar with the subculture of gangs or the nature of life on the streets. This can severely limit their ability to deal effectively with situations as they arise.

Paraprofessionals may also serve as change agents in interventions. Parapro-fessionals have been involved in such diverse efforts as crisis hot lines, advocacy for troubled youths, job counseling, and weight loss programs. Durlak (1979) sur-veyed the effectiveness of paraprofessionals in many different types of programs and interventions and concluded that, in the studies he reviewed, professionals proved no more effective overall than paraprofessionals. He also detailed many studies showing nonprofessionals to be more effective.

There are many advantages in employing paraprofessionals in intervention projects. First, because resources are almost always scarce, paraprofessionals usually provide an economical alternative. Second, they are often members of the community where the intervention takes place and hence might be perceived more as "insiders" than professionals would be. Third, using paraprofessionals can mini-mize the social distance between the agents and the targets of change. Finally, para-professionals generally are no less effective than professionals in fulfilling their tasks.

The third source of change agents is the community's indigenous population. For example, some programs employ former (or current) gang members or leaders. A meta-analysis of treatments for juvenile offenders indicated that interventions involving change agents who were part of the setting were more likely to produce positive results (Davidson et al., 1990); this finding can also be applied to interven-tions with youth gangs.

Over 30 years ago, Kobrin (1959) cited many advantages of using indigenous workers in the Chicago Area Project: They knew the local society, they could communicate better with residents, their involvement demonstrated the project's confidence in the competence of local residents, and they probably had greater access to delinquent boys in the neighborhood. Current or former gang members provided good role models for those trying to disengage themselves from gangs. Further, it appeared that gang youths serving as change agents themselves benefited through what Reissman (1965) called the "helper principle," whereby the individual helping others receives direct benefits by doing so.

On the other hand, the use of indigenous individuals does have some draw-backs. Ironically, it appears that they may sometimes have less credibility than professionals in the eyes of gang members. Also, the past history of gang mem-bers employed in interventions may pose some problems. Spergel (1986) notes that former gang members working for CRISP in Chicago were often harassed by law enforcement officials who knew the indigenous workers from their past ac-tivities. Somewhat surprisingly, rival gang members even shot at the former gang members or their vehicles; luckily, no injuries were reported. A report on the Community Youth Gang Services Project (Maxson & Klein, 1983) also mentions some internal conflict between project staff members who were formerly in rival gangs.

The Chicago YMCA Detached Worker Project (Cooper, 1967) was notable in using individuals from several diverse groups. The project staff comprised 16 full-time professionals and 63 part-time indigenous youths and adults. The detached workers used counseling to prevent and alleviate destructive activities such as fighting or drug use; they were instructed to take action when the opportunity arose but not to put themselves in compromising positions. The indigenous workers, as part of the Youth Consultant Project, were expected to help plan and carry out legitimate group activities and to keep their groups under control. Consultants helped the detached workers organize athletic teams and tournaments and assisted with tours, camping trips, and dances. They also published a newspaper for the youths. The consultants were paid a small sum and invited on an annual project-sponsored trip to New York City. Consultants were expected to be good role models and warned that they would be fired if involved in any further illegal activity.

Ethnicity and Gender of Change Agents

Many researchers have observed that gangs are ethnically homogeneous (Klein & Maxson, 1989; Knox, 1991; Miller, 1974). Thrasher (1927/1963) identified many ethnic varieties of gangs (e.g., Polish, Italian, Jewish, African American) in his early work in Chicago. The broad ethnic diversity of Chicago gangs has not changed significantly since Thrasher's time. It appears that street gangs have been identified with practically every ethnic group in that city. The Chicago Police Department and the Cook County State's Attorney's Office estimated that Chicago was home to 50 Hispanic gangs, 40 African American gangs, and 14 white gangs (Bensinger, 1984). There has been a change, however, in that fewer gangs reflect European ethnic origins; almost all gangs today represent minority groups (Miller, 1990).

The cultural traditions of the ethnic group play a role in the development of a particular gang. Vigil and Long (1990) describe Chicano traditions that have woven their way into contemporary Chicano gangs. Also, there is some evidence of differences in gangs and gang behavior among different ethnic groups (Jackson, 1989). For instance, Spergel et al. (1989) observe that African American gangs are more involved in drug trafficking, Hispanic gangs in turf-related violence, Asian gangs in assorted property crimes, and white gangs in both organized property crime and vandalism. In addition, different ethnic groups may traffic in different types of drugs (Spergel, 1990). Chin (1990) highlights some commonalities and differences between Chinese gangs and gangs of other ethnic origins. Short (1989) contrasts white gangs and African American gangs. It is reasonable to conclude that ethnicity is a meaningful part of gang identity and is related to patterns of gang activity.

Gang programming should be diverse to mirror the diversity of the types of ethnic gangs themselves. The interaction of different types of treatment with different categories of young people needs more attention (Glenwick, 1988): With certain types of juvenile delinquents, only certain types of treatment programs may be effective (Sechrest & Rosenblatt, 1987). An intervention should be prescribed to alter the undesirable outcomes experienced by the particular ethnic group or individual gang. In addition, the choice of intervention tactics should be based on the cultural traditions and beliefs of the target group. Miller (1990) has suggested dividing minority gangs into "newcomer" (e.g., Latin American, Asian) and "established" (e.g., African, Mexican, Puerto Rican) groups on the basis of their recency of immigration to this country. Reasons for the formation and continuation of youth gangs differ for these groups, and one should consider different remedial strategies accordingly.

Given the importance of ethnicity to gang involvement, it is likely that the ethnic background of the change agent in an intervention program would make a difference to the gang members. Spergel has contributed to our understanding of this issue by examining the relationship between the change agent's ethnicity and the program's effectiveness. He found that the ethnicity of the staff appeared to have an important impact on participants in the Chicago CRISP intervention (Spergel, 1986). In areas intensively served by Hispanic workers well known in the Hispanic community, there were reductions in arrests of Hispanic youths for less serious gang crimes. A corresponding trend was not observed for African American participants; in fact, offenses generally increased in this group. Spergel noted two factors that may have contributed to these trends: The Hispanic workers paid little attention to non-Hispanic gangs and gang members, and there was an influx of African American families and youths into the target area.

Gender is another important characteristic of the change agent. Although male gang members outnumber females 20 to 1 (Goldstein, 1991), females do participate, generally as members of female gangs that are auxiliary to male groups (Campbell, 1990). The importance of gender for program implementation and effectiveness is difficult to discern; it clearly is an area that needs considerably more systematic study. Females may have vastly different motivations than males for gang involvement. Intervention strategies could be customized to meet the needs of female gang members. It seems likely that important work in this area will emerge.

The impact of the characteristics of the change agent has received little attention in the literature on the treatment of juvenile delinquency (Davidson et al., 1990). This issue clearly should be explored in more detail, particularly in the area of gangs, where opinion on the matter far outpaces known fact.

Determining the Organizational Affiliation of the Program

Another key consideration is the organizational affiliation of the gang intervention program. Programs that are affiliated within the established system have the advantages of greater credibility and greater likelihood of survival. Such programs may also be much easier to launch. Programs that are managed from outside the system have greater freedom to innovate but are less likely to survive. For example, uncertainty of funding threatened the survival of the youth service bureau component of the behavioral-ecological intervention described by Hunsaker (1981).

The problems of initiating, implementing, and maintaining a community gang control program outside the established criminal justice system have been described by Maxson and Klein (1983). Their program encountered conflicts with the traditional justice system. Criminal justice officials expected indigenous gang workers also to fulfill an expanded role as street informants. Program officials, on the other hand, felt that this would reduce their workers' credibility or place them in danger and would compromise the integrity of the program. In other words, they were reluctant to undermine the rapport with the gangs just to "keep the system happy," and they felt that such a dual role requirement would violate the intent of the program. Further tensions resulted from the need to establish boundaries so that the program did not infringe on police work. Surprisingly, another issue arose when gang homicides decreased. Although the decrease appeared to be real, both the program officials and the police claimed credit for the decline.

Characteristics of Promising Program Models

Given the current state of data on gang control interventions, it is not yet possible to delineate proven and efficacious techniques for reducing gang violence. However, promising interventions are characterized by certain approaches that should be more widely applied.

Interventions should target the proximal causes of the undesirable outcomes associated with gangs. The large-scale programs of previous decades required massive resources yet yielded relatively minimal returns. Miller (1990) observes that trying to change such an immense entity as the circumstances of lower class life to prevent gangs is like "trying to kill a gnat with a pile driver" (p. 281). In contrast to past practices, contemporary programs will probably focus more on the specific issues of gang violence than on broad-scale community development. Because the local conditions of gangs vary from city to city, interventions should be tailored to the unique strengths, weaknesses, and circumstances of the community. The input of current and former gang members, youths, and adult citizens must be sought in an effort to understand their varying perceptions of the local conditions.

Morash (1983) surveyed youths from two diverse communities in Boston who had participated in different community programs. The youths felt that the programs were not delivered in a way that would strengthen the social bonds among them—the purpose of many of the programs. In fact, the young people perceived the programs quite negatively. They felt that relationships with staff were practically nonexistent and found staff to be hostile, impersonal, and formal. Youths frequently reported being expelled from programs. If these survey results typify young people's thinking about our treatment programs, we will have difficulty drawing them away from the interesting exploits that gang involvement offers. Knox (1991) stresses that if we expect gang members to defect, we need to provide genuine alternatives to the perceived benefits of the gang.

Interventions should also be structured to provide treatment of adequate intensity and duration. Goldstein (1991) holds that some of our failures in developing effective gang intervention programs may be due to administration of "weak" treatments. What constitutes adequate intensity and duration remains to be determined. Meanwhile, program planners should be alert to the problem and avoid treatments that give participants only minimal exposure.

Because a substantial number of current gang members are from ethnic minority groups (Hagedorn, 1988; Miller, 1975, 1981), the use of culturally specific gang interventions shows promise. Though not specifically geared to gang youths, two major categories of interventions with African American youths are already in place (Watts, 1991). Manhood development programs for African American youths employ an array of rituals and customs drawn from African traditions. Mentoring programs, which do not necessarily have an Afrocentric perspective, match youths with adult role models. Such programs could be adopted for prevention and intervention efforts with African American youths, and similar approaches could be used with other minority youths. Manhood development approaches may be especially relevant to gang programming: Some intergang fighting occurs because insecure males wish to "demonstrate manliness to self and others" (Vigil & Long, 1990, p. 64). As yet, there are few other reports of culturally specific interventions for gang youths. One exception is the House of Umoja in Philadelphia (Woodson, 1981), where some African and African American traditions have influenced the nature and style of treatment.

If the ethnic backgrounds of the change agent and the gang member are matched, the intervention will more likely be sensitive to the youth's ethnic tradition. In addition, incorporation of elements of popular culture, such as rap music, into culturally specific interventions has been shown to capture the attention of ethnic urban youth (Abdul-Adil, in press). However, popular culture needs to be applied carefully: Huff (1989) notes that in Ohio, some new gangs emerged from competing break-dancing and rap groups.

CHALLENGES TO THE EVALUATOR OF YOUTH GANG INTERVENTIONS

Given the many difficulties in conducting evaluations with youth gangs, it is no wonder that there is a serious shortage of quality evaluations of gang interventions. There is a serious need for more extensive work to expand the current knowledge base on gangs. However, without a serious increase in the number of systematic interventions conducted with gangs, the accumulation of additional prescriptive knowledge will not be possible. In an excellent article on the gang work that needs to be done in the 1990s, Hagedorn (1990) makes an impassioned plea for gang researchers to get back into the field. He provides a strong rationale for the necessity for field studies, illustrates the limitations of "courthouse criminology" and "surrogate sociology," and suggests ways to overcome the perceived technical and professional objections to undertaking field studies of gangs. This section will touch on some of the difficulties in conducting evaluations with gangs and will offer suggestions for minimizing the difficulties.

Establishing the Setting

Hagedorn (1990) provides some excellent suggestions for gaining access to gangs and their members. Building rapport and establishing credibility is not easy. Further, gaining access to gang activities takes a good deal of time, often at unconventional hours: Gang members likely to assist in this effort "do not restrict their important activities to weekdays or 9 A.M. to 5 P.M." (Bookin-Weiner & Horowitz, 1983, p. 590). Anne Campbell (1991) reports that, for her book *Girls in the Gang,* she spent 6 months with each of three gangs while collecting data focusing on three female gang members. On a positive note, Hagedorn (1990) asserts that "any good field researcher, committed to learning about gangs and willing to spend long hours necessary to develop good informants, can solve the problem of access" (p. 251). Perseverance, flexibility, and availability appear to be the key ingredients in gaining access to gangs.

Ensuring Safety in Data Collection

The process of collecting data through either interviews or observational methods is not without risk. As Hagedorn (1990) points out, "There is clearly more danger of getting shot on urban streets than in a university library" (p. 255). However, if proper precautions are taken, data collection can occur without incident. Numerous large-scale studies with juvenile delinquents in major urban areas have been conducted without serious threat of harm to interviewers or participants (e.g., Davidson et al., 1990).

Certain procedures will help ensure the safety of interviewers. Many researchers have employed former and even current gang members to organize and conduct interviews (see Horowitz, 1990). For example, Hagedorn wrote his 1988 book *People and Folks: Gangs, Crime and the Underclass in a Rustbelt City* with the assistance of Perry Macon, a former gang member who helped in the interview process. Former gang members will be more familiar with the area and know where participants might be found; they may also provide a measure of protection. On the other hand, current or former gang members may draw trouble, especially while they are on rival turf. Potential rivalries should be anticipated.

Interviews should be scheduled on neutral turf and in public places if possible. Interviewers could carry communication devices and check in at prearranged times. If the interview will be conducted in a setting where there is a phone nearby (e.g., in a home), the interviewer might check in with project staff before and after the interview to have the security of knowing that somebody knows his or her location. The interviewer can make dummy phone calls to give the impression of surveillance even if nobody is at the other end of the line. Additional safety measures for the data collection process are discussed by Hagedorn (1990) and by Moore, Garcia, Garcia, Cerda, and Valencia (1978).

Evaluation Design

The design of the evaluation will have important implications for the possible conclusions about the efficacy of the intervention. In the ideal design, individual youths or individual gangs would be assigned either to a treatment or to a control (or treatment-as-usual) condition; this would allow for the least ambiguous interpretation of the outcome data (Campbell & Stanley, 1963). Depending on the nature of the intervention, a quasi-experimental approach may be necessary.

When the intervention targets individuals, it may be possible to employ a strict experimental approach, in which each youth is assigned randomly to an identifiable/specifiable intervention or a control group. Although experimental designs appear straightforward in theory, many complications and unintended side effects can result when these designs are brought to the field (see Schneider, 1986). These will need to be anticipated and addressed when they occur.

Not all interventions focus on individuals, and it is likely that in many instances, the gang itself will be the target. When the intervention is conducted on an intact group such as an entire gang or a particular neighborhood or community, that group must become the unit of analysis for evaluation purposes. For an experimental approach, this means randomly assigning groups or neighborhoods to an intervention. Randomization is feasible only to the extent that a reasonably large number of sampling units (gangs or neighborhoods) are available for involvement in the project; otherwise, a quasi-experimental approach will be needed. And with a true community-level intervention, it will be extremely difficult to employ an experimental approach. It is typically not possible for a program to include enough different communities to make evaluation comparisons meaningful.

Measures and Outcomes

An important advance in the area of measures and outcomes involves basing gang interventions on specific theoretical models. This would have at least two advantages. First, it would allow careful specification of the intervention in a publicly understandable way. Second, careful specification of the intervention model would help guide the selection of measures. The model should specify expected short-term as well as long-term outcomes, and the selection of process and outcome measures should be suited to the intended causal mechanisms and consequences of the intervention. Following is a brief discussion and critique of some measures commonly applied to delinquency and gang interventions.

Ideally, the evaluation will include process measures to test the basic theoretical model; these are useful to help confirm the integrity of the intervention. In other words, the first task in an evaluation is to determine if the intervention operated according to plan. Assuming it did, specific short- and long-term outcomes can more accurately be interpreted. If it is discovered that the intervention lacked fidelity, the results must be interpreted accordingly. One must also be aware of possible unintended processes in the intervention. Keeping evaluation procedures open to unintended as well as intended processes is very important in an area such as gang intervention.

A wide variety of outcome criteria can be employed; the choice will depend on the goals of the intervention. A basic criterion is delinquency or, more specifically, delinquent behavior or officially recognized delinquency. Because reducing the frequency and intensity of delinquent behaviors is likely to be a goal of most intervention programs, it is difficult to imagine circumstances in which evaluation would not address delinquency. There are four basic sources for this evaluative information: self-report ratings of delinquency (Fagan, Piper, & Moore,

1986; Hindelang, Hirschi, & Weis, 1981), official records of delinquency, collateral ratings of behavior, and observed delinquent behavior. Each has advantages and limitations.

Self-reports of delinquency are useful because the participants best know their own behaviors. In fact, a good deal of illegal behavior is private and unobserved by others. The principal drawbacks of self-reported delinquency ratings are their subjective nature and the fact that the participant's perceptions may be distorted, unintentionally or on purpose. Gang members have been known to give misinformation to police and social workers (Hagedorn, 1988) and may do the same for evaluators. There is some evidence that self-reports may be less valid among certain ethnic groups; therefore, comparisons within an ethnic group may be more accurate than comparisons across groups (Hindelang et al., 1981) when program effectiveness is examined. Also, self-reports may over- or underestimate delinquent behavior, depending on the conditions of measurement (Lipsey, 1988).

Official records of delinquency are obtained from either the police or the court system. Although these records are generally deemed objective, they often provide a gross underestimate of the "true" extent of delinquent acts: Most delinquent behaviors escape detection by the criminal justice system (Lipsey, 1988). Moreover, official definitions of gang-related crime vary greatly by city and are commonly influenced by the wishes of authorities who could benefit by the presence or absence of a gang problem (Klein et al., 1986). There is reason to ponder whether "official" delinquency is a measure of delinquent behavior or of the behavior of the criminal justice system. On a more positive note, there is good evidence that for some types of crime, official indicators of "gang relatedness" are fairly accurate. For example, the fact that a homicide is labeled gang related does not appear to have much impact on police investigation methods because characteristics of the settings and the participants are better predictors of the course of the investigation (Klein et al., 1986).

Other gang members, family, and friends are examples of collateral informants who may be able to shed light on the extent of delinquency for a given participant. Project BUILD (Thompson & Jason, 1988) used input from informants from several different gangs in generating confidential gang rosters that were used in evaluating the prevention program. Though collaterals might not make the most accurate assessment of the participant's behavior, their input nevertheless can be a useful adjunct to information on delinquency collected by other means (Davidson et al., 1990).

Observation is certainly the most resource-consuming method of obtaining data. However, observational techniques may provide a rich source of information regarding delinquency and other behaviors. Anthropologists and sociologists have used observational methods to study a variety of phenomena such as gang interactions. These methods were more common in the large-scale early studies in the Chicago school tradition.

In summary, each method of collecting information on delinquency has advantages and shortcomings, and collecting information from two or more sources can minimize the disadvantages associated with relying on a single method. However, the results of data from different sources do not always converge. Evaluators are advised to carefully articulate the anticipated outcomes of the intervention and specify whether behavioral, arrest, or group activity changes are desired (Davidson, Redner, Blakely, Mitchell, & Emshoff, 1987).

For some interventions, outcomes other than delinquency are the focus. For instance, one program may aim to lessen a member's involvement with the gang; another may seek to increase job or educational opportunities for gang members. Each evaluation should correspond to the program's particular aims and objectives —the possibilities are endless.

CONCLUSIONS

As the introductory quotation from Kant suggests, sometimes the urgent need for action means that we must proceed in the absence of complete information. This is the case with gang intervention efforts today. Many interventions were undertaken three decades ago with little tangible success. Indications are that the contemporary gang problem has worsened while our knowledge base has at worst eroded or at best remained static. Nevertheless, there are some promising directions for community intervention with youth gangs.

We have discussed several interventions and approaches that show promise. Good work in the area of prevention is needed, given the powerful grip of many gangs upon their members. Interventions should take account of the strengths of gangs and the weaknesses of the community, and not only the reverse. Programs need clearer theoretical rationales. Ethnicity is a meaningful part of the identity of gangs and their members; however, few interventions have used culturally specific approaches. Such approaches, though largely untested with this population, may help reduce the appeal of youth gangs and curb their destructive influence on our communities and young people.

REFERENCES

Abdul-Adil, J. K. (in press). Rap music: Towards a culture-specific model of empowerment. *The Community Psychologist.*

Arbuthnot, J., & Gordon, D. A. (1989). Crime and cognition: Community applications of sociomoral reasoning development. *Criminal Justice and Behavior, 15,* 379–393.

Bensinger, G. J. (1984). Chicago youth gangs: A new old problem. *Crime and Justice, 7,* 1–16.

Blakely, C., & Davidson, W. S. (1981). Prevention of aggression. In A. P. Goldstein, E. G. Carr, W. S. Davidson, & P. Wehr (Eds.), *In response to aggression.* New York: Pergamon.

Bolman, W. M. (1969). Toward realizing the prevention of mental illness. In L. Bellak & H. Barten (Eds.), *Progress in community mental health* (Vol. 1). New York: Grune & Stratton.

Bookin-Weiner, H., & Horowitz, R. (1983). The end of the youth gang: Fad or fact? *Criminology, 21,* 584–602.

Boyle, J., & Gonzales, A. (1989). Using proactive programs to impact gangs and drugs. *Law and Order, 37*(8), 62–64.

California Council on Criminal Justice. (1989). *State Task Force on Gangs and Drugs: Final report.* Sacramento, CA: Author.

Campbell, A. (1990). Female participation in gangs. In C. R. Huff (Ed.), *Gangs in America.* Newbury Park, CA: Sage.

Campbell, A. (1991). *The girls in the gang.* Oxford: Blackwell.

Campbell, D. T., & Stanley, J. C. (1963). *Experimental and quasi-experimental designs for research.* Boston: Houghton Mifflin.

Caplan, G. (1964). *Principles of preventive psychiatry.* New York: Basic.

Chin, K. (1990). Chinese gangs and extortion. In C. R. Huff (Ed.), *Gangs in America.* Newbury Park, CA: Sage.

Clements, C. B. (1988). Delinquency prevention and treatment: A community-centered perspective. *Criminal Justice and Behavior, 15,* 286–305.

Cooper, C. N. (1967). The Chicago YMCA detached workers: Current status of an action program. In M. W. Klein (Ed.), *Juvenile gangs in context: Theory, research, and action.* Englewood Cliffs, NJ: Prentice-Hall.

Davidson, W. S., Redner, R., Amdur, R. L., & Mitchell, C. M. (1990). *Alternative treatments for troubled youth: The case of diversion from the justice system.* New York: Plenum.

Davidson, W. S., Redner, R., Blakely, C. H., Mitchell, C. M., & Emshoff, J. G. (1987). Diversion of juvenile offenders: An experimental comparison. *Journal of Consulting and Clinical Psychology, 55,* 68–75.

Durlak, J. A. (1979). Comparative effectiveness of paraprofessional and professional helpers. *Psychological Bulletin, 86,* 80–92.

Elliott, D. S., Huizinga, D., & Ageton, S. S. (1985). *Explaining delinquency and drug use.* Newbury Park, CA: Sage.

Fagan, J. (1989). The social organization of drug use and drug dealing among urban gangs. *Criminology, 27,* 633–669.

Fagan, J. (1990). Social processes of delinquency and drug use among urban gangs. In C. R. Huff (Ed.), *Gangs in America.* Newbury Park, CA: Sage.

Fagan, J., Piper, E., & Moore, M. (1986). Violent delinquents and urban youths. *Criminology, 24,* 439–471.

Federal Bureau of Investigation. (1970). *Uniform Crime Report, 1970.* Washington, DC: U. S. Government Printing Office.

Federal Bureau of Investigation. (1980). *Uniform Crime Report, 1980.* Washington, DC: U. S. Government Printing Office.

Federal Bureau of Investigation. (1990). *Uniform Crime Report, 1990.* Washington, DC: U. S. Government Printing Office.

Glenwick, D. S. (1988). Community psychology perspectives on delinquency: An introduction to the special issue. *Criminal Justice and Behavior, 15,* 276–285.

Goldstein, A. P. (1991). *Delinquent gangs: A psychological perspective.* Champaign, IL: Research Press.

Gott, R. (1989, May). *Juvenile gangs.* Paper presented at the Conference on Juvenile Crime, Eastern Kentucky University, Richmond.

Gottschalk, R., Davidson, W. S., Gensheimer, L. K., & Mayer, J. P. (1987). Community-based interventions. In H. C. Quay (Ed.), *Handbook of juvenile delinquency.* New York: Wiley.

Hagedorn, J. M. (1988). *People and folks: Gangs, crime and the underclass in a rustbelt city.* Chicago: Lake View.

Hagedorn, J. M. (1990). Back in the field again: Gang research in the nineties. In C. R. Huff (Ed.), *Gangs in America.* Newbury Park, CA: Sage.

Hindelang, M. J., Hirschi, T., & Weis, J. G. (1981). *Measuring delinquency.* Newbury Park, CA: Sage.

Horowitz, R. (1990). Sociological perspectives on gangs: Conflicting definitions and concepts. In C. R. Huff (Ed.), *Gangs in America.* Newbury Park, CA: Sage.

Huff, C. R. (1989). Youth gangs and public policy. *Crime and Delinquency, 35,* 524–537.

Hunsaker, A. (1981). The behavioral-ecological model of intervention with Chicano gang delinquents. *Hispanic Journal of Behavioral Sciences, 3,* 225–239.

Jackson, P. G. (1989). Theories and findings about youth gangs. *Criminal Justice Abstracts, 21,* 313–329.

Klein, M. W., Gordon, M. A., & Maxson, C. L. (1986). The impact of police investigations on police-reported rates of gang and nongang homicides. *Criminology, 24,* 489–511.

Klein, M. W., & Maxson, C. L. (1989). Street gang violence. In N. A. Weiner & M. E. Wolfgang (Eds.), *Violent crime, violent criminals.* Newbury Park, CA: Sage.

Knox, G. W. (1991). *An introduction to gangs.* Berrien Springs, MI: Vande Vere.

Kobrin, S. (1959). The Chicago Area Project: A 25-year assessment. *The Annals of the American Academy of Political and Social Science, 322,* 19–29.

Lipsey, M. W. (1988). Juvenile delinquency intervention. *New Directions for Program Evaluation, 37,* 63–84.

Loya, F. (1985). *The epidemiology of homicide in the city of Los Angeles 1970–1979: A collaborative study.* Atlanta, GA: Centers for Disease Control, Violence Epidemiology Branch.

Maxson, C. L., & Klein, M. W. (1983). Gangs: Why we couldn't stay away. In J. R. Kluegel (Ed.), *Evaluating juvenile justice.* Newbury Park, CA: Sage.

Miller, W. B. (1962). The impact of a "total community" delinquency control project. *Social Problems, 10,* 168–191.

Miller, W. B. (1974). American youth gangs: Past and present. In A. Blumberg (Ed.), *Current perspectives on criminal behavior.* New York: Knopf.

Miller, W. B. (1975). *Violence by youth gangs and youth groups as a crime problem in major American cities.* Washington, DC: National Institute for Juvenile Justice and Delinquency Prevention.

Miller, W. B. (1981). American youth gangs: Past and present. In A. S. Blumberg (Ed.), *Current perspectives on criminal behavior: Essays on criminology.* New York: Knopf.

Miller, W. B. (1990). Why the United States has failed to solve its youth gang problem. In C. R. Huff (Ed.), *Gangs in America.* Newbury Park, CA: Sage.

Moore, J. W., Garcia, R., Garcia, C., Cerda, L., & Valencia, F. (1978). *Homeboys, gangs, drugs, and prison in the barrios of Los Angeles.* Philadelphia: Temple University Press.

Morash, M. (1983). Two models of community corrections: One for the ideal world, one for the real world. In J. R. Kluegel (Ed.), *Evaluating juvenile justice.* Newbury Park, CA: Sage.

Morash, M. (1990). *Gangs and violence.* Unpublished manuscript. East Lansing: Michigan State University.

Reissman, F. (1965). The "helper-therapy" principle. *Social Work, 10,* 27–32.

Schneider, A. L. (1986). Restitution and recidivism rates of juvenile offenders: Results from four experimental studies. *Criminology, 24,* 533–552.

Sechrest, L., & Rosenblatt, A. (1987). Research methods. In H. C. Quay (Ed.), *Handbook of juvenile delinquency.* New York: Wiley.

Short, J. F. (1989). Exploring integration of theoretical levels of explanation: Notes on gang delinquency. In S. F. Messner, M. D. Krohn, & A. E. Liska (Eds.), *Theoretical integration in the study of deviance and crime: Problems and prospects.* Albany: State University of New York Press.

Short, J. F. (1990). New wine in old bottles? Change and continuity in American gangs. In C. R. Huff (Ed.), *Gangs in America.* Newbury Park, CA: Sage.

Spergel, I. A. (1986). The violent gang problem in Chicago: A local community approach. *Social Service Review, 60,* 94–131.

Spergel, I. A. (1990). Youth gangs: Continuity and change. In M. Tonry & N. Morris (Eds.), *Crime and justice: A review of research* (Vol. 12). University of Chicago Press.

Spergel, I. A., Curry, G. D., Chance, R., Alexander, A., Seed, D., Kane, C., Ross, R. E., Rodriguez, P., & Simmons, E. (1989). *Youth gangs: Problem and response: A review of the literature, executive summary.* Washington, DC: U. S. Department of Justice, Office of Juvenile Justice and Delinquency Prevention.

Steffensmeier, D., & Harer, M. D. (1991). Did crime rise or fall during the Reagan presidency? The effects of an "aging" U. S. population on the nation's crime rate. *Journal of Research in Crime and Delinquency, 28,* 330–359.

Takata, S. R., & Zevitz, R. G. (1990). Divergent perceptions of group delinquency in a midwestern community: Racine's gang problem. *Youth and Society, 21,* 282–305.

Taylor, C. S. (1990). Gang imperialism. In C. R. Huff (Ed.), *Gangs in America.* Newbury Park, CA: Sage.

Thompson, D. W., & Jason, L. A. (1988). Street gangs and preventive interventions. *Criminal Justice and Behavior, 15,* 323–333.

Thrasher, F. M. (1963). *The gang.* University of Chicago Press. (Original work published 1927)

Torres, D. M. (1981). *Gang Violence Reduction Project: Fourth evaluation report* (July 1979–June 1980). Sacramento: California Department of the Youth Authority.

U. S. Department of Justice. (1988). *Report to the nation on crime and justice* (GPO Stock No. 027-000-01295-7). Washington, DC: U. S. Department of Justice, Bureau of Justice Statistics.

Vigil, J. D., & Long, J. M. (1990). Emic and etic perspectives on gang culture: The Chicano case. In C. R. Huff (Ed.), *Gangs in America.* Newbury Park, CA: Sage.

Wall, J. S., Hawkins, J. D., Lishner, D., & Fraser, M. (1981). *Juvenile delinquency prevention: A compendium of 36 program models.* Washington, DC: Office of Juvenile Justice and Delinquency Prevention.

Watts, R. J. (1991, June). *Manhood development for African-American boys: Program and organization development.* Paper presented at the meeting of the Society for Community Research and Action, Tempe, AZ.

Weis, J. G., & Hawkins, J. D. (1981). *Preventing delinquency.* Washington, DC: Government Printing Office.

Woodson, R. L. (1981). *A summons to life: Mediating structures and the prevention of youth crime.* Cambridge, MA: Ballinger.

Wright, W. E., & Dixon, M. C. (1977). Community prevention and treatment of juvenile delinquency. *Journal of Research in Crime and Delinquency, 14,* 35–67.

PART IV

Criminal Justice
Interventions

CHAPTER 12

The National Youth Gang Survey: A Research and Development Process

Irving A. Spergel
G. David Curry

There is evidence of an increase of gangs, violent gang activity, and gang-member-related drug trafficking in a growing number of large and small cities, suburban areas, and even some small towns and rural areas. There are claims that the number and proportion of females in gangs and the severity of their crimes may be increasing. The literature on gangs has recently proliferated, mainly through the publication of many participant observation studies (Spergel, 1991). Quantitative analyses and surveys of the gang problem are also increasing, although at a slower pace to date. Federal and state agencies are funding an assortment of gang prevention, intervention, and suppression programs. However, there appears to be limited coordination or integration of various research studies, policies, and intervention programs bearing on the complex problem of youth gangs. One preliminary integrative research and development effort has been the National Youth Gang Suppression and Intervention Program, of which an important component was the National Youth Gang Survey.

BACKGROUND

In 1987, the University of Chicago's School of Social Service Administration entered into a cooperative agreement with the United States Department of Justice's Office of Juvenile Justice and Delinquency Prevention (OJJDP) to establish the National Youth Gang Suppression and Intervention Program. The research and development program's primary goals, addressed in corresponding stages, were

Prepared under Grant No. 90–JD–CX–K001 from the Office of Juvenile Justice and Delinquency Prevention, Office of Justice Programs, United States Department of Justice. Points of view or opinions in this document are those of the authors and do not necessarily represent the official position or policies of the U. S. Department of Justice.

(a) to identify and assess promising approaches and strategies for dealing with the youth gang problem, (b) to develop prototypes or models from the information thereby gained, and (c) to produce technical assistance manuals for those who would implement the models.

During the first 2 years of the 4-year project, a survey gathered information on organized programs in the continental United States. Data were collected from 254 criminal justice and community-based agencies and grass-roots organizations in 45 cities and at six special program sites. The survey was intended to encompass every agency in the country that was currently or recently engaged in organized responses specifically intended to deal with gang crime problems. Categories of data collected concerned the nature and scope of the problem; its onset and development; the basis on which the problem was defined; the kind of goals, strategies, program structures, and activities developed; and the results of such interventions.

This chapter will deal primarily with the methodology and selected findings of the survey, which was an integral part of our program's assessment stage. It will conclude with a discussion of other aspects of the program, including an annotated bibliography of publications that resulted from program activities at various stages. Specifically, these stages included the following: assessment (Stage 1); prototype development (Stage 2); and development of technical assistance manuals of the National Youth Gang Suppression and Intervention Program, with collaboration in the research and development process by policymakers, administrators, and practitioners, as well as current or former gang members (Stage 3).

In the present volume on intervention, our chapter has a dual role. On one hand, the National Youth Gang Survey is an intensive, nationwide study of the range of existing interventions. On the other, the survey and, even more, related and subsequent components of the larger research and development program exemplify research itself as intervention.

STUDY SITES AND AGENCIES SURVEYED

Survey sites were selected in a process that began with the screening of 101 cities. Selection criteria included (a) presence and recognition of a youth gang problem and (b) presence of a youth gang program as an organized response to the problem. In itself, the division of the cities according to 1987 data on gang problems and organized responses serves as a baseline for future national surveys of the distribution of such problems and responses. Table 12.1 lists all cities screened, showing those that were included and those excluded.

In each city, a key agency, usually the police, was contacted initially by phone, and direct contact with an informed representative of the agency was established. The representative was asked two kinds of questions: The first was designed to ascertain the existence of a youth gang crime problem, and the second was intended to establish the existence of an organized agency or community response. A youth gang crime problem was simply one perceived or identified as such and eliciting a special agency and community reaction. An organized response was regarded

Table 12.1 Sites Screened for the National Youth Gang Survey

INCLUDED IN THE SURVEY

Chronic gang problem cities ($n = 21$)

Albuquerque, NM	Long Beach, CA	Phoenix, AZ
Chicago, IL	Los Angeles, CA	San Diego, CA
Chino, CA	Los Angeles County, CA	San Francisco, CA
Detroit, MI	New York, NY	San Jose, CA
East Los Angeles, CA	Oakland, CA	Santa Ana, CA
El Monte, CA	Pomona, CA	Stockton, CA
Inglewood, CA	Philadelphia, PA	Tucson, AZ

Emerging gang problem cities ($n = 24$)

Atlanta, GA	Hialeah, FL	Reno, NV
Benton Harbor, MI	Indianapolis, IN	Rockford, IL
Cicero, IL	Jackson, MS	Sacramento, CA
Columbus, OH	Louisville, KY	Salt Lake City, UT
Evanston, IL	Madison, WI	Seattle, WA
Flint, MI	Miami, FL	Shreveport, LA
Fort Wayne, IN	Milwaukee, WI	Sterling, IL
Fort Worth, TX	Minneapolis, MN	Tallahassee, FL

EXCLUDED FROM THE SURVEY

No declared organized youth gangs or gang activity ($n = 24$)

Albany, NY	Des Moines, IA	New Orleans, LA
Baltimore, MD	Fresno, CA	Pasadena, CA
Buffalo, NY	Greenville, MS	Pittsburgh, PA
Cambridge, MA	Houston, TX	Portsmouth, ME
Charleston, SC	Jersey City, NJ	Racine, WI
Charlotte, NC	Kansas City, KS	San Antonio, TX
Chattanooga, TN	Lincoln, NE	Tulsa, OK
Denver, CO	Memphis, TN	Washington, DC

No organized response ($n = 29$)

Anaheim, CA	Gary, IN	Omaha, NE
Berkeley, CA	Glendale, CA	Orlando, FL
Boston, MA	Hartford, CT	St. Petersburg, FL
Cincinnati, OH	Huntington Beach, CA	St. Louis, MO
Cleveland, OH	Jacksonville, FL	Spartanburg, SC
Compton, CA	Joliet, IL	San Bernardino, CA
East St. Louis, IL	Kansas City, MO	San Pedro, CA
El Paso, TX	Kenosha, WI	Springfield, MA
Fort Lauderdale, FL	Lakewood, CA	Wilmington, DE
Garden City, CA	Las Vegas, NV	

Excluded because outside U. S. mainland ($n = 4$)

Honolulu, HI	Tonga
San Juan, PR	Samoa

as a program in existence for at least a year, having a current or recent set of articulated program goals, demonstrating a response to the problem that was more than simplistic and unitary (e.g., either police arrests alone or a youth gang recreation program alone), and possessing some means to describe the program's impact. Several cities were excluded from the analysis because information gathered indicated that, in 1987, the agency or city administration did not recognize the existence of a gang problem. Many of the excluded agencies and cities have since recognized the problem, or ceased to deny it. In fact, some of these cities have developed large-scale, sophisticated approaches to the problem. At this point in the survey, we had a population of 98 cities or localities. Of these, 74, or slightly more than three-quarters, reported the presence of organized youth gangs or gang activities. Of those cities or jurisdictions reporting a gang problem, 29, or 39.2%, had no organized response to the problem as just defined. This left 45 cities meeting the two selection criteria.

To explore all promising programs that we could possibly identify, we also considered a number of programs that were not part of a community-level response. Six of these single-program sites, listed in Table 12.2, were eventually included in the survey. The California Department of the Youth Authority is a state correctional agency that maintains contact with officials in several California cities or counties and offers a number of unique programs for gang-identified youths. The Sunrise House is a social service agency with a tradition of meeting the needs of gang youths. The Paramount public school system has a gang program that has received national recognition. The other three sites mentioned in Table 12.2 are correctional agencies with special programs designed for incarcerated gang youths.

Our survey analyses are based on the 45 cities (one a county area) and the six sites identified through the initial screening. Clearly, this is not a systematic sample from a known population of eligible cities or agencies. Rather, it is a fairly large group of cities and agencies generally recognized to have youth gang problems and organized programs to address them. Relatively complete individual agency and cross-agency and community group level data were carefully collected.

Our survey concerned the gang problem, and organized responses to it, in two types of cities: chronic gang problem cities, which often had a long history of serious gang problems, and emerging gang problem cities, often smaller cities that had recognized and begun to deal with a usually less serious but often acute gang problem since 1980. In chronic problem cities or contexts, gangs tended to be better organized and involved in more serious crime and drug trafficking activity. Of the 45 localities, 21 were classified as chronic and 24 as emerging youth gang problem cities (see Table 12.1). A somewhat greater proportion of the chronic problem cities had large or very large populations, but the category included a sizable number of small cities as well. Most of the cities in the emerging problem category were smaller, although some had populations of over 500,000. We also classified the correctional schools and special agency programs or sites under these two rubrics (see Table 12.2).

This distinction between chronic and emerging sites was a valuable component of the analyses reported here and has since been refined and elaborated.

Table 12.2   Sites Included in the National Youth Gang Survey

Chronic gang problem sites ($n = 2$)	Emerging gang problem sites ($n = 4$)
California Department of the Youth Authority Sunrise House (CA)	Ethan Allen School (WI) Glen Mills School (PA) McClaren School (OR) Paramount School (CA)

Although our classification is mainly a temporal one, referring to the onset of the problem, we have observed that in some cities the gang crime problem was serious or violent at emergence and that in some chronic problem cities the problem subsided and reemerged later. Furthermore, the nature of the agency's or city's response to the gang crime problem helps determine whether it is in the emerging or chronic category.

STUDY PROCEDURES AND RESULTS

Once a city or jurisdiction was selected for inclusion in the survey, a snowball sampling technique was employed. The initial informed respondent was asked for a list of other key agencies involved in the community's organized gang response. An informed respondent at each of these agencies was then contacted and also asked for such a list; the interviewer for that city continued to contact respondents until all respondents' lists were exhausted. The response rate was 70.5%. Lack of response most commonly was associated with a respondent's determining, upon reflection, that his or her agency did not fall within the aims of our study.

We classified the 254 respondents into three major categories, with six criminal justice subcategories (see Table 12.3): law enforcement, mainly police (20.5%); prosecutors (10.2%); judges (5.5%); probation (12.6%); corrections (3.1%); parole (4.3%); school (13.3%), subdivided into academic and security personnel; community/service agencies (24.4%), subdivided into youth service, youth and family service/treatment, grass-roots groups, and comprehensive crisis intervention; community, county, or state planners (4.7%); and others (0.8%).

From these results, we know that the gang problem is addressed with some degree of complexity by a great variety of organizations located in small as well as large cities and jurisdictions in a number of states in the Union. We also know from federal agency reports (e.g., Drug Enforcement Administration, 1988; current research sponsored by the National Institute of Justice, 1991; and work of other federal and local agencies, including the Department of Health and Human Services) that the problem is widespread throughout almost all the states. Although the gang crime problem is national in scope, the development of organized community response programs probably lags behind the spreading problem.

Table 12.3   Respondent Categories

	CATEGORY		SUBCATEGORY	
	n	%[a]	*n*	%[a]
Law enforcement	52	20.5		
Prosecutors	26	10.2		
Judges	14	5.5		
Probation	32	12.6		
Corrections	8	3.1		
Parole	11	4.3		
School	35	13.8		
Academic			26	74.3
Security			9	25.7
Community/service	62	24.4		
Youth service agency			46	74.2
Youth and Family Service			8	12.9
Grass-roots			5	8.1
Comprehensive			3	4.8
Community planning	12	4.7		
Other	2	0.8		
	254	100.0		

[a] % = percent of all respondents.

Issues of Definition

To a large degree the definitions of *gang, gang member,* and *gang incident,* particularly by the police, shape the perceptions and strategies of those who confront the gang problem (Spergel, 1990; Spergel & Chance, 1991). Definitions are important for classification, intervention planning, and program evaluation. A policy or program that is effective for one kind of gang or delinquent group may not work for another kind.

We asked each respondent to define a gang, a gang member, and a gang-related incident and then subjected the open-ended responses to content analysis. We anticipated that some respondents would be unable to provide their own definitions and would use those of other agencies. The following represents a systematic effort to identify and decompose the various definitions of the three concepts—gang, gang member, and gang incident—in their various usages.

The Gang

In response to the item, "What is your organization's definition of a gang?" 236 respondents indicated the existence of an agency definition and stated it. The responses were first content analyzed according to 48 descriptors or indicators mentioned. The definitions included group structural characteristics, criminal and noncriminal behaviors, and symbolic behaviors. Faced with many possible ways of combining these dichotomous variables for analysis, we chose 12 conceptual groupings (see Table 12.4) relevant to various definitions and theoretical issues (Spergel, 1990) already articulated in the literature.

The first grouping represented general group characteristics. We tried to select a set of structural and behavioral characteristics that might fit the delinquent group as well as the gang (Cartwright, Tomson, & Schwartz, 1975; Klein, 1971; Taylor, 1990). Of the 236 respondents who defined a gang, 186 (78.8%) included general group characteristics in their definitions. The next grouping of structural-behavioral characteristics included those that may distinguish the gang from the delinquent group; we labeled them organizational characteristics. This distinction assumes that the gang may have a higher degree of organization than the delinquent group (Jacobs, 1977; Miller, 1975, 1982; Spergel, 1984). A majority (120, or 50.8%) of the respondents offering definitions included both general organizational characteristics and other structural characteristics such as an established identity and established relationships with other gangs. The third grouping of characteristics comprised noncriminal group activities. Very few respondents (14, or 5.9%) thought of the gangs they dealt with in terms of noncriminal behavior.

The second set of definitional criteria included criminal behavior. A general reference to crime or antisocial activity elicited responses relating to three types of crime: crimes of violence, drug crimes, and property crimes. The drug crimes of use and sale were joined for our analysis. Whereas a majority of respondents (149, or 63.1%) offered definitions with a general reference to crime or antisocial behavior, references to the three specific kinds of crime were less common. Allusions to violence were most frequent (22.0%), followed by references to drug crime (16.1%) and property crime (8.9%). A substantial majority of all respondents (180, or 76.3%) made either a general or a specific reference to criminal behavior.

An effort to deal with the many references to symbols led us at this point in the analysis to establish a general category and to separate symbols into three subcategories: references to the general gang culture (88, or 37.3%), references to symbols that are specific to particular types of gangs (173, or 73.3%), and references to symbols that are more personal (53, or 22.5%). (Personal symbols include such items as nicknames.) More than three-quarters of our respondents (181, or 76.7%) offered definitions of the gang that mentioned some kind of symbols.

Two further definitions emerged from variables that were combined with other subsets. They were theoretically and policy-relevant variables: age-role integration (Cloward & Ohlin, 1960; Spergel, 1964) and ecology or migration patterns (Moore, 1978; Skolnick, 1990). Eleven respondents (4.7%) specifically mentioned adult members in defining the gang, and 35 respondents (14.8%) stressed that gang members resided in the same community or locale.

Analysis of covariance is often used to make sense of diversity among a number of responses across a set of variables. Principal components analysis also can be used to produce a set of linear combinations that are unrelated to each other to

Table 12.4 Dichotomous Variables Derived From Content Analysis of Definition of a Gang (by Percent of Total Person Responses)

General group characteristics (n = 186, 78.8%)

Group	Certain number of members
Leadership	Loosely knit structure
Regular association	Common behavior

Gang organization characteristics (n = 120, 50.8%)

Affiliations with other gangs	Organized structure
Goals/purpose	Maintenance of unity
Established identity	Recruitment
Exclusion of nonmembers	Conflict with other gangs
Membership rules	

Noncriminal activities (n = 14, 5.9%)

Protection of selves/community	Sports activities
Recreation	Some nonviolent activities

General criminal or antisocial behavior (n = 149, 63.1%)

Crimes of violence (n = 52, 22.0%)

Violence	Shooting
Rape	Robbery
Intimidation	Armed members
Drive-by shooting	

Drug crime (n = 38, 16.1%)

Drug use	Drug sales

Property crimes (n = 21, 8.9%)

Vandalism	Theft
Burglary	Auto theft

General reference to symbols (n = 88, 37.3%)

Collective symbols (n = 173, 73.3%)

Gang name	Graffiti
Controlling of turf	Gang logo
Colors	Initiation
Rituals	

Personal symbols (n = 53, 22.5%)

Hand signs	Clothing
Tattoos	Member nicknames

Adult members (n = 11, 4.7%)

Residence in same locale (n = 35, 14.8%)

reduce the number of concepts with which we must cope. Principal components analysis assures us that we have broken our concepts down into a viable, non-redundant set of interpretive components (Johnson & Wichern, 1982). When certain items in a set of measures are really measures of some underlying construct, the eigenstructure of the correlation matrix produces a number of eigenvalues that approach zero. Our analysis of the matrix of tetrachoric correlation coefficients for our 12 definitional categories produces 12 eigenvalues, none of which approaches zero. (The smallest of the 12 eigenvalues is 0.47.) This suggests that each of our 12 components measures a unique dimension in the process by which agencies define youth gangs. The result also illustrates the diversity of our respondents' definitions of the gang.

Variations in definitions of gangs cannot be attributed to geographic location or respondent category, nor can variation in definitional criteria be attributed to the ethnicity of the gang members with which the agency deals or the race or ethnicity of the respondent. Spergel and Curry (1990) present several descriptive multivariate approaches to analyzing the 236 definitions of gang, but they conclude that a more restricted definition, one on which a greater number of agencies and sites could reach consensus, would be a valuable contribution to the formulation of a national gang policy.

The Gang Member

The concept of gang member, like that of gang, carries a negative attribution, particularly if the individual is suspected of criminal behavior. The label of "gang member" itself can, if substantiated, result in an enhanced sentence for a youth convicted of criminal activity, on the basis of recent law in several states. The source of information and the method of identifying youths as gang members can have implications for the breadth of the perceived problem in a particular community. In other words, the reliability of the data and the number and kind of different elements used in identifying a youth as a gang member are keys to meaningful theory-based research and effective policy.

In our study, 11 respondents either did not distinguish between gang members and nongang members or chose not to respond to our item "What are your organization's principal ways of identifying a gang member or gang case?" Content analysis of the 243 open-ended responses made revealed nine different methods of identifying gang members, as shown in Table 12.5. The methods fell into two overarching categories. The first involved an assessment of an individual or a case founded on direct observation or information recorded by the respondent's agency. This included identifications based—usually in overlapping fashion—on symbols or symbolic behavior (51% of the respondents), self-admission on the part of gang members (46.5%), observed association with known gang members (38.7%), involvement in specific types of criminal behavior (33.7%), and location or residence in a particular place (14%). The second general approach to identifying gang members was based on reports of membership from other agencies. The most common methods were identification by police (42%) and reports by other informants

Table 12.5   Methods of Identifying a Gang Member

Method	Respondents citing	% of respondents citing
Symbols/symbolic behavior	124	51.0
Self-admission	113	46.5
Association with gang members	94	38.7
Type of criminal behavior	82	33.7
Location or residence	34	14.0
Police identification	102	42.0
Informant identification	97	39.9
Other legal identification	46	18.9
Other institutional identification	39	16.0

(39.9%). Smaller proportions of respondents relied on identification by a specific criminal justice agency other than the police (for example, the court, probation, or prosecutor's office; 18.9%) or other institutional identifications such as those from schools or social service agencies (16.0%).

Attempts to identify underlying components of the matrix of tetrachoric correlation coefficients led us to the same conclusion that we reached in categorizing components of gang definitions. There are no nonzero eigenvalues, and there are no underlying structures that can contribute to our understanding of how different kinds of agencies in diverse locations identify gang members. Our nine categories are, however, nonredundant. Exploratory analyses of associations between these nine methods of identifying gang members and agency type, location, and type and dimensions of the gang problem reveal no identifiable patterns that explain the great variation in agencies' methods of identifying gang members. Spergel and Curry (1990) present several descriptive multivariate approaches to analyzing the 243 methods of identification but conclude that more precise identification methods are needed.

Attention also should be directed to the issue of gang member typologies, which become a further basis not only for identifying youths as gang members but for delivering types of law enforcement or human service suppression or intervention. Criteria for hard-core, peripheral, wannabe, and, especially, associate gang members have not been systematically developed. The term *associate* may in fact mean that a youth who happens to be in a particular location when a gang incident occurs but may have no relation to it is labeled and entered into a computer file as an associate or even a gang member. For the human service agency, a youth may become eligible for preventive services only if he is first labeled a fringe member or wannabe, when in fact he may have little contact with a gang or no interest in gang membership.

The Gang Incident

The gang incident, especially as defined by police, is the most important criterion for determining the scope of the gang problem in a particular locality. The city or agency (including the police) and the community say that a gang problem exists when a sufficient number of serious gang crime incidents occur and are officially or explicitly recognized. Of our 254 respondents, 233 provided the definition of *gang incident* used by their agencies. Content analysis of these responses suggested nine definitional components or subsets of characteristics of a gang incident (see Table 12.6). The presence or involvement of a gang member was the most frequently reported criterion for identifying an incident as gang related and was cited by 64.4% of respondents. Furthering gang function (i.e., the incident is related to gang member motivation or gang interest) was the next most common criterion (39.1%). Gang modus operandi was mentioned by 37.8% of the respondents. Certain crimes such as drive-by shootings are almost universally regarded as gang incidents, though the modus operandi varies considerably. Some respondents reported treating all auto thefts as gang related. One reported considering all drug crimes as gang related. The classic reference to conflict gangs is based on the notion of intergang rivalry. This was mentioned sufficiently often to warrant a separate category. Certain gangs and gang members clearly flaunt the intergang rivalry aspect of particular incidents. Again, principal components analysis revealed no nonzero eigenvalues. Our nine categories are nonredundant and cannot reasonably be collapsed into underlying subsets.

The distinction between a definition based mainly on gang membership criteria (e.g., as used by the Los Angeles County Sheriff's Department) and one based on gang motivation or interest criteria (e.g., as used by the Chicago Police Department) is significant in the determination of the scale of the gang problem. Maxson and Klein (1990) indicate that applying the broader definition of gang membership to the Chicago gang problem doubles the number of gang incidents, at least gang homicides, recorded (see also Spergel, 1990). When we look at these two approaches as reported among our 233 responses, we find that the two are not significantly related in a statistical sense *either positively or negatively.*

Although we found no differences in methods of identifying gang incidents that could be linked to agency type or geographical location, we did find a difference between chronic and emerging gang problem cities in the breadth of definitions of gang incident. To measure the breadth of identification methods, we used Rasch modeling (Wright & Masters, 1982) to assess the scalability of our nine methods of identifying a gang incident. Rasch modeling produced the calibrations for the nine items listed in Table 12.6 and showed our nine items to have an item-separable reliability coefficient of 0.97. This finding lets us treat the nine measures as conformable to addition and then compare means across subpopulations of respondents. The average approach to identifying a gang incident for respondents from chronic gang cities includes 1.9 of the methods listed in Table 12.6; for respondents from emerging gang cities, the average approach includes 2.3 methods. The t statistic for this difference is 3.21 and is statistically significant at the 0.005

Table 12.6   Methods of Identifying a Gang-Related Incident

Criterion	Respondents citing	%[a]	Rasch calibration
Gang member involved	150	64.4	−2.45
Furthers gang function	91	39.1	−1.18
Gang modus operandi	88	37.8	−1.24
Incident involves multiple offenders	37	15.9	0.15
Rival gangs involved	37	15.9	0.15
Youth involved	10	4.3	1.70
Gang claims incident	11	4.7	1.60
Other institution/group identifies	26	11.2	0.61
Location of incident identifies	25	10.7	0.65

[a] % = percent of respondents citing.

level. This finding could indicate that cities that have longer experience of gang problems have moved toward a narrower definition of a gang incident, whereas those with relatively recent problems tend to work with broader definitions. In other words, when the gang problem is first recognized there is a greater tendency to interpret a variety of deviant or criminal behaviors as gang behaviors than at a later time or when the problem is chronic. We do not find this difference in breadth of definition for the definition of either a gang or a gang member.

Programmatic Strategies

Each agency or community organization responds to a problem such as gang crime in terms of its mission, goals, and objectives. Often abstract or highly generalized terms justify and sustain the programs and activities that these entities—public, private, nonprofit, and sectarian—carry out. Most respondents in our study represented organizations established to deal with issues and problems broader than gangs and gang crime and to conduct a corresponding range of activities. We, however, attempted to develop measures of the goals and objectives, key programs, or activities underlying the organizations' efforts to deal specifically with the gang problem. We have termed these measures strategies of intervention. Conceptually, they are situated between broad mission or goal statements and specific or discrete program activities.

Social problems wax and wane, but most organizations seek to sustain their missions and strategies as long as possible. Sooner or later, an organization must clarify the relationship between gang problem and strategy of intervention, for the sake of logic or common sense as well as public relations—and very often to justify requests for additional funding for gang problem initiatives. There is some evidence that a human service or social intervention strategy in respect to the youth gang problem, predominant in the 1950s and 1960s, gave way to a law enforcement or suppression strategy in the 1970s and 1980s. This occurred for a variety of reasons not yet fully researched (see Spergel, 1992).

To understand the current dynamics and structure of organizations' responses to gangs, we tried to describe and analyze their strategies and to discover how strategies were interrelated across types of organizations in a particular locality and how they might vary across localities. Our survey respondents answered five open-ended questionnaire items intended to elicit information on program activities, priority of strategies employed, and estimates of effectiveness of agency efforts. These items were as follows:

Item IV-1. What are your unit's or organization's goals and objectives in regard to the gang problem?

Item VI-2. What has your department (or unit) done that you feel has been particularly successful in dealing with gangs? Please provide statistics, if relevant and available.

Item VI-3. What has your department (or unit) done that you feel has been least effective in dealing with gangs?

Item VI-6. What do you think are the five best ways employed by your department or organization for dealing with the gang problem? (Rank in order of priority.)

Item IV-14. What activities do gang or special personnel perform in dealing with the problem? [Probe by telephone interviewers later to determine how these are tied to the problem as described and goals/objectives.]

We used the answers to these items to construct an empirically based and theoretically sensitive set of five underlying strategies. Our analysis relied most heavily on the responses to Item VI-6. The strategies to emerge were community organization or community mobilization, social intervention, opportunities provision, suppression, and organizational change and development (see Table 12.7). The strategies are defined and their indicators—that is, the statements or phrases of the respondents—are classified as follows.

Community Organization

Spergel's (1991) literature review, described later in this chapter, names community organization, or neighborhood mobilization, as one of four major strategies employed historically in efforts to deal with the gang problem: "Community organization is the term used to describe efforts to bring about adjustment, development, or change among groups and organizations in regard to community problems or social needs" (p. 3). Earlier, Spergel (1969) used the term *interorganizing,* a key dimension of community organization or community organizing, to refer to "efforts at enhancing, modification, or change in intergroup or interorganizational relationships to cope with a community problem" (p. 20). Issues of coordination as well as mobilization across neighborhood, organization, and governmental levels are addressed in this formulation.

Table 12.7   Distribution of Strategy Rankings: Number of Responses (% of Total Responses) for Each Priority Category

| | STRATEGY RANK | | | | | |
	1	2	3	4	5	Total
Community organization	22 (8.9%)	58 (23.4%)	35 (14.1%)	5 (2.0%)	1 (0.4%)	121 (21.2%)
Social intervention	78 (31.5%)	46 (18.5%)	19 (7.7%)	3 (1.2%)	0	146 (25.5%)
Opportunities provision	12 (4.8%)	38 (15.3%)	15 (6.0%)	4 (1.6%)	0	69 (12.0%)
Suppression	109 (44.0%)	35 (14.1%)	16 (6.5%)	4 (1.6%)	1 (0.4%)	165 (28.8%)
Organizational change and development	27 (10.9%)	21 (8.5%)	18 (7.3%)	5 (2.0%)	0	71 (12.4%)

Respondents used key words and phrases that at times clearly could be included in this community organization category and at other times could not. Decisions for inclusion of items in a category had to be based on some appropriate rationale. For example, the contemporary term *networking* was classified within the community organization strategy unless it referred to networking among law enforcement agencies, in which case it was classified under suppression. References to *prevention*, when they implied program or policy efforts across agencies, were coded as community organization. All references to meeting with community leaders and attending meetings of community organizations were regarded as reflecting a community organization strategy. After much consideration, we included advocacy for victims under the strategy of suppression rather than community organization because it can be viewed as part of a more basic strategy of crime control. Following are additional key words indicating goals or activities encompassed by the community organization strategy:

Cleaning up the community
Involving the schools
Mobilizing community
Building community trust
Involving parents (families)
Educating the community
Changing the community

Social Intervention

Spergel's literature review (1991) identifies youth agency outreach and street work as a second major gang program strategy. According to Spergel (1966), street work is

> the practice variously labeled detached work, street club, gang work, area work, extension youth work, corner work . . . the systematic effort of an agency worker, through social work or treatment techniques within the neighborhood context, to help a group of young people who are described as delinquent or partially delinquent to achieve a conventional adaptation. (p. 27)

This strategy involves the redirection or conversion of youth gangs to legitimate social gangs or conventional organizations. This requires the agent to work with or manipulate the people or other agency representatives who interact critically with members of the delinquent group.

The notion of traditional street work may be somewhat outdated and has now become part of a larger strategy of social intervention that focuses on individual behavioral rather than group value change or transformation (Klein, 1971). Therefore, we place street work under the more general category of social intervention, which also encompasses recreational and sports activities. Social intervention also includes counseling or direct attempts—informational or guidance oriented—to change youths' values in such a way as to make gang involvement less likely. Actions to improve general, specialized, remedial, or basic alternative educational programs are included under opportunities provision. Advocacy for individual gang members is classified as a social intervention goal. The following indicators fall in the social intervention category:

Crisis intervention
Service activities
Diversion
Outreach
Provision of role models
Leadership development
Intergang mediation
Group counseling
Temporary shelter
Tattoo removal
Referrals for services
Religious conversion
Counseling of gang members
Drug prevention/treatment
All psychological approaches
All social work approaches

Postsentence social services
Working with gang structure
Helping members leave gang

Opportunities Provision

Spergel (1991) names provision of opportunities in terms of employment, job training, and education as a third major gang strategy. Under this approach are included "large scale resource infusions and efforts to change institutional structures including schools, job opportunities, political participation, and the development of a new relationship between the federal government and local neighborhoods in the solution not only of delinquency but of poverty itself" (p. 7). This strategy encompasses efforts to stimulate the development of new and improved schools, special training and job programs, and business and industry involvement in the social and economic advancement of people, efforts directed toward gang youths in disadvantaged inner-city and rural areas. Following are key words or phrases included under opportunities provision:

Job preparation
Job training
Job placement
Job development
Assistance with school
Tutoring
Education of gang youths

Suppression

As the fourth major gang program strategy, Spergel (1991) identifies suppression—formal and informal social control, which includes arrest, incarceration, and other forms of criminal justice, along with youth agency or community group supervision. Under this approach gang members may be arrested, prosecuted, and removed from the community for short or long prison sentences. Tactical patrols by police gang units, vertical prosecution, intensive supervision and vertical case management by probation departments, legislation targeted at gang members, and interagency task forces involving criminal justice actors are placed in this category. Also included are information systems (i.e., gathering/collecting and maintaining information), as well as information sharing, or the distribution or publishing of information on gangs that facilitates law enforcement. Suppression, however, should be distinguished from law enforcement: Suppression is a broader concept, which therefore includes social agency monitoring or targeting of youths for special forms of supervision with the aim of controlling gang behaviors. The following other key words or phrases are included under suppression:

Enforcement
Neutralization

Investigation
Adjudication
Apprehension
Monitoring
Restraint
Arrest
Discipline
Intelligence
Identification
Legal consequences
Removal from community
Correctional placement
Law enforcement liaison
Supervision
Setting limits

Organizational Change and Development

A fifth category, which has a modified or limited agency structural or program developmental quality, has been added. It includes organizational adaptations and changes that facilitate the application of the other strategies. Especially characteristic is specialization that enables an organization to deal with the gang problem—for example, formation of a special gang unit within a police department. This strategy includes needs assessment and evaluation, along with the following other approaches:

Internal agency coordination
Improvement of organizational efficiency
Program development
Advocacy for legislation
Specialized training
Additional resources
Case management
Use of media

Classification of Strategies

Using written guidelines regarding the five strategies, the two senior members of the research team, working separately, classified the responses of the 254 respondents and interpreted the rankings of the strategies. We agreed independently on approximately 70% of the classifications of the hundreds of separate items. After hours of case-by-case discussion, we reached agreement on all item rankings. Not all respondents provided items for five separate strategies, and some items essentially repeated a particular strategy. If an item repeated a strategy already ranked, it was eliminated. Each item was ranked into one strategy only.

Distribution of Strategies

Table 12.7 shows the distribution of strategies by rank for all of the respondents. The most common first or primary strategy of agencies in our survey was suppression (44% of agencies), followed by social intervention (31.5%). Organizational change and development (10.9%) and community organization (8.9%) were comparably less common as first or primary strategies. Opportunities provision as a primary strategy was infrequent (4.8%). Over the total listing of strategies in the five categories—primary, secondary, and so on—suppression was still the most often chosen, and opportunities and organizational change and development were the least often chosen. Because the majority of respondents were from criminal justice agencies, this distribution is not surprising. In the aggregate analysis of all the categories of strategies, opportunities provision rose in the number of times mentioned, but it obviously was not a priority strategy.

Type of Strategy Across Communities

In this part of the analysis, we were interested in the community rather than the agency level. We concentrated on each agency's primary strategy. Our locality or site level measure reflects the proportion of agencies in each community using each of our five strategies as the primary strategy. As Table 12.8 shows, there were significant differences between chronic and emerging gang cities in the use of three of the five gang program strategies—community organization, social intervention, and opportunities provision—as primary.

A multivariate analysis of variance for the differences across community by gang problem type was significant at the 0.05 level. Discriminant analysis to generate a function that separated communities by gang problem type on the basis of these three primary strategies produced a function that could be used successfully to reclassify two-thirds (66.7%) of the communities by problem type. There is, therefore, at least tentative empirical support for the notion that primary strategy choices vary by community or city type.

Perceived Causes of the Gang Problem

Our first attempt to determine whether these strategies were effective in reducing or controlling the youth gang problem took place at the logical-conceptual level. We assumed that strategic intervention in a social problem should be related in some common-sense way to the cause of the problem. Effectiveness in addressing a problem ordinarily signified success in addressing its cause. On the one hand, we assumed that organizational strategies for a problem such as gangs were dependent on organizational mission, political-economic interests, specific disciplinary approaches, and contemporary ideology and fashion. On the other hand, we considered it likely that perceptions of cause of a problem might not be closely related to strategic interventions selected to ameliorate it. Furthermore, determination of the cause of a social problem might not be closely dependent on the organization's mission and political interest. To the extent that the strategy was not related

Table 12.8   Mean Proportion of Respondents per Site Exhibiting Primary Strategy by City Type

	Chronic gang problem cities (n = 20)	Emerging gang problem cities (n = 22)
Community organization	.65	.160[a]
Social intervention	.283	.142[a]
Opportunities provision	.071	.017[a]
Suppression	.454	.573
Organizational change and development	.107	.085

[a] Student's t test significant at 0.05 level.

to cause of the problem, it seemed logical to anticipate that the problem would not be addressed adequately and therefore not alleviated.

Thus, from a research and policy development perspective, we thought it important to elicit from the survey respondents some expression of causes of the gang problem and a ranking of such perceived causes. We asked the following question: "What do you think are the five most important causes of the gang problem in your city? (Rank in order of priority.)"

From our 254 respondents, we received 244 open-ended responses to this question. As with strategy determinations, the two senior members of the research team first classified all answers separately. The minimal conflicts in classification arising from these two separate content analyses were resolved through case-by-case discussion. This process yielded 23 categories of perceived cause, which we further grouped into 4 major categories (see Table 12.9).

The first set of perceived causes of the gang problem involved broad problems at the level of the social system, such as poverty, unemployment, criminal opportunities, increased prevalence and profitability of drug sales, patterns of migration and changes in population composition, and other conditions of urban life. The second set of causes related to the failure of basic institutions, the family and the schools in particular. The third set of causes focused on the individual and peer group, and included substance abuse, psychological explanations (most frequently lack of self-esteem or personal pathology), peer influence, and fear coupled with the desire for self-protection through gang affiliation. Finally, many of our respondents recognized the existence of the gang problem within the context of numerous attempts to resolve it. In other words, there was a perception that community agency responses themselves might be inappropriate or inadequate. Respondents expressed this perception by citing failure of the police, the courts, or other representatives of the legal system; liberalism; failure of community

Table 12.9   Perceived Causes of the Gang Problem

	Respondents citing	% of respondents citing
Social system problems		
(Selecting)	222	91.0
(Ranking primary)	106	43.4
Poverty/unemployment	163	66.8
Criminal opportunity	33	13.5
Drug phenomena	101	41.4
Migration/demographics	20	8.2
Urban ecology	12	4.9
Institutional failure		
(Selecting)	183	75.0
(Ranking primary)	74	30.3
Family breakdown/failure	135	53.1
School failure/dropout	114	46.7
Lack of role models	13	5.3
Individual and peer group level problems		
(Selecting)	125	49.2
(Ranking primary)	31	12.7
Drug/alcohol use	17	6.7
Psychological explanations	84	33.1
Peer/gang influence	55	22.5
Self-protection/fear	29	11.9
Response effects		
(Selecting)	152	62.3
(Ranking primary)	33	13.5
Legal system failure	25	10.2
Liberalism	3	1.2
Community failure	48	19.7
Lack of services/programs	73	28.7
Media	13	5.3
Discrimination/race relations	27	11.1
Labeling	1	0.4
Lack of committed resources	12	4.9
Politics	4	1.6
Denial	11	4.5
Adult exploitation of juvenile justice system	3	1.2

No response = 10

participation; lack of social services and recreational programs for youth; media influence; discrimination and race relations; the labeling phenomenon; lack of resources committed to dealing with the gang problem; politicians' use of the gang problem to fulfill their personal ambitions; denial that a gang problem exists; and exploitation of the legal system by adults using youths to perform criminal acts.

Analysis of the ranking of perceived causes showed that system level causes were deemed most important by 43.4% of our respondents. Another 30.3% blamed major institutions for not meeting the needs of youths. The remainder, a little more than one-fourth of the respondents, attributed their gang problems to individual or peer-group level cause (12.7%) or response effects (13.5%). Poverty and unemployment, drug trafficking, family breakdown, and school system failure were viewed as the key causes of the gang problem.

Relationship Between Perceived Causes and Primary Strategies

Of particular interest for policy development is the degree of relationship between perceived causes and strategies selected to deal with the gang problem. Table 12.10 shows no observable relationship between perceived primary cause and primary response strategy. Chi-square tests of the distribution of each set of strategies by each perceived cause indicate that none of them is significantly different (at the 0.10 level) from the distribution of strategies for the entire population. Some researchers (Huff, 1989; Moore, 1988) have suggested that quick action, whether a police sweep or an expansion of a social intervention program, tends to follow upon a series of publicized crisis events. A systematic causal analysis did not often precede a course of agency action. There was little evidence of strategies based on logically related causes. Our analysis indicated, even on the basis of post hoc discussion with respondents, that coordination of cause and strategy was probably not occurring.

Measuring Program Effectiveness

In the absence of measures of direct program effectiveness, we examined three measures of perceived program effectiveness: perceived improvement in the gang problem since 1980, perceived agency effectiveness in 1987, and perceived community level effectiveness. Later, we will present and analyze independently gathered data that served as a validity check on perceptual data.

We used the following items to generate the perceptual measures:

Item III-18. Has the gang situation changed since 1980?

Item III-19. If yes, how?

Item V-1. How effective do you think your unit was in 1987 in dealing with the gang problem?

very effective ☐ moderately effective ☐ hardly effective ☐
not at all effective ☐

Table 12.10 Primary Strategy by Primary Perceived Cause: Number (Percent) of Responses per Perceived Cause

PRIMARY CAUSE	PRIMARY STRATEGY				
	Community organization	Social intervention	Opportunities provision	Suppression	Organizational change and development
Social system problems	10 (9.5%)	26 (24.8%)	7 (6.7%)	48 (45.7%)	14 (13.3%)
Institutional failure	6 (8.3%)	24 (33.3%)	3 (4.2%)	31 (43.1%)	8 (11.1%)
Individual level problems	3 (9.7%)	11 (35.5%)	0 (0.0%)	14 (45.2.%)	3 (9.7%)
Response effects	3 (9.1%)	16 (48.5%)	1 (3.0%)	11 (33.3%)	2 (6.1%)

Item IV-8. Are there any interagency task forces or community-wide organizations that attempted to coordinate efforts to deal with the gang problem in 1987?

Item IV-9. If yes, were these efforts:

very effective ☐ somewhat effective ☐ hardly effective ☐ not at all effective ☐ ?

We content analyzed the item concerning change since 1980 to produce a dichotomous variable of improvement versus nonimprovement. In transforming these three measures into a single evaluation measure, we chose not to give equal weight to each of these three variables, believing that the variables merited separate weights. We felt that these weights should be derived empirically from the structure of their covariation in this particular set of respondents. At the agency level, one of these variables was dichotomous, and the other two were sets of ordered categories. We chose to normalize these measures at the agency level using PC-PRELIS to generate normalized (PROBIT) scores for each of our categorical variables (see Table 12.11). A principal components analysis of the normalized (PROBIT) scores for the three measures resulted in the three eigenvalues, none of which approached zero. We used the first and largest of these eigenvalues (accounting for 45.5% of the variance) to generate the set of principal components coefficients to be used as weights for our three normalized measures (see Table 12.12).

The score generated for improvement since 1980, an agency rating of very effective, and a rating of very effective community level program is −2.18001. By adding 3.18001 to each score, one can easily transform this value so that it is equal to 1.0 and all subsequent values are positive. The result is a set of general effectiveness scores ranging from 1.0 to 5.87. It must be remembered in the analyses that follow that the lower the value of this measure of perceived general effectiveness, the greater the perceived effectiveness.

Program Strategies and Perceived Effectiveness

By regressing our measure of perceived general effectiveness on the proportion of agencies within each locality exhibiting each strategy as primary, we were able to compare relationships between perceived effectiveness and primary strategy. (In moving toward a city level of analysis we included the statewide site, the California Department of the Youth Authority, along with the cities.)

Table 12.13 presents analysis of covariance results for each strategy by type of city (i.e., with chronic vs. emerging gang problem). A negative slope as indicated by the sign of the regression coefficient indicates a positive relationship between the proportion of agencies in each city exhibiting an expressed strategy and the strategy's perceived general effectiveness. Conversely, a positive regression coefficient indicates a negative relationship between the proportion of agencies in each city exhibiting a particular strategy and perceived general effectiveness.

Table 12.11 Normalized (PROBIT) Scores for Three Gang Program Effectiveness Measures

IMPROVEMENT SINCE 1980

Yes = −1.63   No = 0.24

EVALUATION OF PROGRAM EFFECTIVENESS IN 1987

	Agency level	Community level
Very effective	−0.86	−1.02
Moderately effective	0.48	0.30
Hardly effective	1.52	1.22
Not at all effective	2.37	1.88

Table 12.12 Coefficients for First Principal Component

	Coefficient	% of variance explained
Improvement since 1980	0.411	31.5
Agency effectiveness	0.531	52.5
Community program effectiveness	0.531	52.4

Caution in interpreting these findings is justified by several conditions of the results. If the subsets of the cities were regarded as samples rather than populations, only two of the regression slopes—priority of community organization strategy in emerging problem settings and priority of opportunities provision strategy in chronic problem settings—would differ significantly from zero. Given the structural dependence that is built into the creation of the strategy measures and the assumptions of statistical techniques that decompose variance, the covariance scores inevitably will be negative, but this in fact indicates that a particular primary strategy is positively associated with the perception of general effectiveness.

In the context of these caveats, community organization as a primary strategy appears to be associated with greater perceived general effectiveness in emerging than in chronic problem settings. Social intervention as a primary strategy is differentially associated with lower perceived effectiveness in emerging and in chronic problem settings. Opportunities provision as a primary strategy is associated with greater perceived general effectiveness in chronic problem settings. (From Table 12.8, we know that opportunities provision is seldom exhibited as a primary strategy in emerging problem settings.)

The final step in our analysis at this point was construction of regression models of perceived general effectiveness. Though we considered a wide range of variables in our extended analyses of these data (Spergel & Curry, 1990), primary

Table 12.13   Analysis of Covariance Results:
General Effectiveness Score by City Type
With Primary Strategy as a Covariate

PRIMARY STRATEGY	REGRESSION COEFFICIENT		SIGNIFICANCE OF COVARIATE
	Chronic	Emerging	
Community organization	−2.14	−3.01[a]	0.001
Social intervention	0.34	2.03	0.05
Opportunities provision	−3.62[b]	−2.70	
Suppression	0.48	0.67	
Organizational change and development	0.89	1.84	

[a] Significant at the 0.05 level.
[b] Significant at the 0.01 level.

program strategy dominated any regression model of perceived general effectiveness regardless of type of problem setting. Table 12.14 shows the multiple regression models for predicting perceived general effectiveness from the proportion of agencies exhibiting a primary strategy. The findings suggest that different combinations of strategies were associated with a reduction in the youth gang problem in different kinds of cities.

In cities with chronic youth gang problems, agencies and community groups perceived a significant general effectiveness in reduction of the problem, mainly when the primary response strategy was the provision of social opportunities. Community organization or mobilization was also significantly related to perceived general effectiveness in reduction of the problem, but only when social opportunities were provided as well. When we look at the use of these two strategies together, we can explain almost 50% of the variance on the dependent variable. In the emerging youth gang problem cities, only community organization or community mobilization shows up as a significant independent variable, explaining 31% of the variance on the dependent variable, perceived general effectiveness.

Other Factors Contributing to Perceived Effectiveness

In an earlier paper (Curry & Spergel, 1988), we proposed that social disorganization, interacting with poverty variables, could account for much of the variance in the presence of gang problems in inner-city areas. It may be helpful to elaborate what we mean by social disorganization. The origin of what is called social disorganization theory is usually credited to Thomas and Znaniecki (1927) and their studies of the Chicago communities inhabited by Polish immigrants shortly after the turn of the century. The two social researchers whose work is most identified with ecological research, Shaw and McKay (1972), expanded the concept in

Table 12.14   Multiple Regression Models for Perceived General Effectiveness by Type of City or Jurisdiction

Problem setting type	Independent variable	b	Beta	R^2
Chronic gang problem cities	Proportion of agencies per community exhibiting opportunities provision as primary strategy	-4.18^a	-0.634	0.497
	Proportion of agencies per community exhibiting community organization as primary strategy	-2.91^b	-0.450	
Emerging gang problem cities	Proportion of agencies per community exhibiting community organization as primary strategy	-3.01^a	-0.558	0.311

[a] Significant at the 0.01 level.
[b] Significant at the 0.05 level.

explaining the distribution of delinquency and gang crime in the urban setting; eventually they came to substitute "differential social organization" for "social disorganization." Sutherland (1947) elaborates:

> The term "social disorganization" is not entirely satisfactory and it seems preferable to substitute for it the term "differential social organization." The postulate on which this theory is based, regardless of the name, is that crime is rooted in the social organization and is an expression of that social organization. A group may be organized for criminal behavior or organized against criminal behavior. Most communities are organized both for criminal and anticriminal behavior and in that sense the crime rate is an expression of the differential group organization. (p. 9)

As we use the concept, social disorganization remains linked to social, economic, and cultural transitions or disruptions such as population movements and changing labor market conditions. Social disorganization or "differential social organization" also signifies a lack of integration across key components of social life. Differences in goals, motivations, norms, values, and activities divide and sometimes create conflict between individual personalities, families, peer groupings, institutions, and segments of communities and the larger society. It should not be surprising that gang involvement is most likely to occur or begin in the interstitial period that is adolescence. Changes that weaken established ties to school, peers, and family can be critical. For example, there are seasonal rises in gang activity each fall as youths begin school, just before and after holiday periods, and during the late spring period of transition to summer vacation.

We feel that this approach does not make us vulnerable to criticisms of social disorganization such as those of Jankowski (1991), who argues that all social disorganization theories of gang formation assume "a lack of social control" (p. 22). We do not feel that our use of social disorganization requires us to reject Jankowski's hypothesis that

> low-income areas in American cities are, in fact, organized, but they are organized around an intense competition for, and conflict over, the scarce resources that exist in these areas. They comprise an alternative social order. In this Hobbesian world, the gang emerges as one organizational response—but not the only one— seeking to improve the competitive advantage of its members in obtaining an increase in material resources. (p. 22)

Social disorganization, as we define it, may or may not be related to racism, culture conflict (e.g., differences between an immigrant group's culture and that of the dominant community group), social isolation (e.g., environmental separation of a housing project from the neighborhood or the neighborhood from the city), or poverty. In fact, we believe that it is the interaction of at least two of these sets of variables, especially social disorganization and poverty, that creates high risks for different patterns of gang-related crime.

Our regression models, described earlier, showed that the one strategy associated with effectiveness in dealing with the youth gang problem, in both chronic and emerging problem areas, was community mobilization. We also expected other measures of community mobilization or of efforts toward community cohesion to be significantly associated with perceived general effectiveness, to the degree to which these responses reduced social disorganization. Although the possible combinations of variables are plentiful, several other variables in our national survey data that were designed to assess the level of community interorganizational relationship are worth examining for possible guidance in developing productive community responses to the gang problem.

One such variable is the presence of independent advisory boards or councils for individual organizations or agencies attempting to deal with the problem. Such boards usually comprise representatives of other agencies and community groups. We believe that the existence of such an external board indicates a connection of the agency's program with the community's system of concern and contributes to the integration of community efforts to address the problem. Table 12.15 shows the average general effectiveness scores for agencies in chronic and emerging gang problem cities. (Lower numeric scores indicate greater positive perception of general effectiveness in dealing with the gang problem.) There is a statistically significant difference between the effectiveness scores of agencies dealing with the gang problem in the two types of cities. Likewise, the significant differences across agencies choosing specific primary strategies that we saw in our regression analyses show up in the one-way analysis of variance results. The difference in average general effectiveness scores between agencies with and without external advisory boards is also statistically significant but does not seem so great.

Table 12.15   Mean General Effectiveness Scores by Categories of City and Primary Strategy Types and Presence of External Advisory Board

CATEGORY	n	MEAN[a]	STANDARD DEVIATION	SIGNIFICANCE OF DIFFERENCE[b]
Agencies by type of city				
Chronic	74	3.34	0.91	0.024
Emerging	56	2.94	1.07	
Primary strategy				
Community organization	11	2.54	1.33	0.001
Social intervention	45	3.54	0.90	
Opportunities provision	3	1.94	0.24	
Suppression	55	3.13	0.90	
Organizational change and development	17	2.87	0.77	
External advisory board				
Yes	79	3.02	0.95	0.034
No	53	3.40	1.01	

[a] The lower the mean score, the greater the perception of general effectiveness in dealing with the gang problem.
[b] t test or analysis of variance result.

It is only when we look at specific combinations of city type, primary strategy, and presence or absence of an external advisory board (see Table 12.16) that we see the most extreme differences in mean general effectiveness score. Presence of an external advisory board is associated with high levels of perceived effectiveness for respondents in chronic gang problem cities with opportunities provision as primary strategy and for respondents in emerging gang problem cities with community organization as primary strategy. In other words, the perceived effectiveness of select primary strategies can be enhanced significantly by the presence of external advisory boards that inevitably involve multiple interagency contacts and thereby extend community mobilization.

Validity Check

To minimize potential criticism that our analysis was based only on perceptual data and to tie it to more concrete evidence of actual reduction in the gang problem, we recontacted law enforcement agencies in a random sample of 21 cities in our survey, 11 drawn from the 15 with the highest general effectiveness scores and 10 from the 15 with lowest general effectiveness scores. We obtained information on changes between 1980 and 1987 in five empirical indicators: numbers

Table 12.16 **Mean General Effectiveness Scores by Presence of External Advisory Board Across City Type and Primary Strategy: Comparing Two Types of Cities and Three Types of Primary Strategies**

Presence of external advisory board	n	Mean[a]	Standard deviation	Significance of difference
Emerging gang problem city, social intervention as primary strategy, no external board	4	3.86	0.83	0.0006[b]
Chronic gang problem city, social intervention as primary strategy, no external board	12	3.84	0.87	
Emerging gang problem city, community organization as primary strategy, external board	6	1.88	1.01	
Chronic gang problem city, opportunities provision as primary strategy, external board	2	1.80	0	

[a] The lower the mean score, the greater the perception of general effectiveness in dealing with the gang problem.
[b] Analysis of variance result.

of gangs, gang members, gang-related homicides, gang-related assaults, and gang-related narcotic incidents. The data or numerical estimates were reasonably complete for most of the variables except number of gang-related narcotic incidents.

We found that the associations between perception of increased general effectiveness in reduction of the problem and actual or concrete data were perfectly correlated across the five empirical indicators—whether of improvement or deterioration in the gang situation—for 18 of the 21 cities or locations, a correspondence rate of 85.7%. A Fisher's Exact Test revealed that the hypothesis of no correspondence between perceptions and the set of empirical measures could be rejected at the 0.05 level of statistical significance. We thus have evidence that the perceptual data are grounded in the empirical world and that our causal models can now be accepted.

IMPLICATIONS FOR THEORY AND POLICY

The National Youth Gang Survey, conducted by the National Youth Gang Intervention and Suppression Program, may have a significant impact on future research on gangs. Of greater present concern is the influence it may have on gang policy and intervention programs. Many of the products of the research and development program reflect and grow from the findings of the survey. The prototypes/models and the technical assistance manuals are vehicles for directly linking the survey results to specific agency and community action approaches. Here we reiterate the major implications of those findings and documents for gang intervention planning and policy.

Resolution of Definitional Questions

In surveying 254 agencies engaged in coordinated community-based responses to the gang problem, we obtained almost as many distinct definitions of a gang, a gang member, and a gang incident. The literature review, field visits, and law enforcement conferences disclosed a need for common definitions within and across jurisdictions. The most immediate need of policy formulation and decision making is for consensus on what constitutes a gang incident. Salient examples are the definition based on gang function used by the Chicago Police Department and the definition based on gang member involvement used by the Los Angeles Police Department and Sheriff's Department. Comparable and useful estimates of the gang problem within communities and across the country depend on such consensus. In the absence of consensus, a clear understanding of the two most prominent definitions of *gang incident* would be a step in the right direction.

Definitions of the term *youth gang* or its equivalent vary widely and depend on particular agency, city or region of the country, race or ethnicity, and generational and cultural factors. Delinquent groups, gangs, and criminal organizations may also change their character over time. Distinctions among these deviant groups may be more of degree than of kind. Horowitz (1990) has argued for the advantages of not defining the gang itself. Even the adjective modifying the term *gang* has been a subject of concern within the criminal justice establishment. The inclusion of the designation *youth* by the National Youth Gang Intervention and Suppression Program has resulted in some criticism. Law enforcement officials prefer the term *street gang* because it includes both juveniles and adults and emphasizes the location of the gang and most of its criminal behavior. We who constitute the program's senior project staff suggest considering or using the following categories of gangs and related groups for policy and program design purposes.

Gang

The term *gang* generally refers to a group or collectivity of persons with a common identity who interact in cliques or sometimes as a whole group on a fairly regular basis and whose activities the community may view in varying degrees as legitimate, illegitimate, criminal, or some combination thereof. What distinguishes the gang from other groups is its communal or "fraternal," different, or special interstitial character.

Street gang

The term *street gang* refers to a group or collectivity of persons engaged in significant illegitimate or criminal activities, mainly threatening and violent. This term emphasizes the location of gang members and their gang-related activities.

Traditional youth gang

The traditional term *youth gang* refers mainly to a youth or adolescent gang and often to the youth sector of a street gang. Such a group is concerned primarily with issues of status, prestige, and turf protection. The youth gang may have a name and a location, be relatively well organized, and persist over time. Traditional youth gangs often have leadership structure (implicit or explicit), codes of conduct, colors, special dress, signs, symbols, and the like. Traditional gangs may vary across time in characteristics of age, gender, community, race/ethnicity, or generation, as well as in scope and nature of delinquent or criminal activities. Thus, the traditional gang subsumes many subtypes; it is still prevalent today and overlaps with other evolving youth gang and delinquent group phenomena.

Posse/crew

The term *posse* or *crew* is sometimes made equivalent to street or youth gang. The posse or crew, more often than the traditional youth gang, is characterized by a commitment to criminal activity for economic gain, particularly drug trafficking. This group may be loosely organized and/or connected to an adult criminal organization. It has fewer social-status-related or symbolic interests or characteristics.

Other youth gangs

Other types of deviant groups (e.g., stoners, punk rockers, neo-Nazi skinheads, satanic groups, motorcycle gangs, prison gangs) may resemble or be related to traditional youth or street gangs in various ways. They may also be distinguished by special behavioral, age, racial/ethnic, or location characteristics, as well as by cultural, political, or religious life-styles, perspectives, or biases. They may engage in group-oriented violent behavior to sustain or defend their beliefs. Such deviant groups also may be characterized by distinctive dress, leadership structure, and concern with status and turf.

Other considerations regarding youth gangs or groups

It is important to distinguish the foregoing gangs and gang-style groups from *youth* or *street groups* prevalent in an earlier era and still present today. These groups have been called street clubs, youth organizations, and social or athletic clubs. Such youth groups were and are less violent or delinquent, generally have fewer regular members, and are usually not viewed as delinquent youth gangs by the community. They serve to socialize lower income, working-class youths—and often first-generation "born-in-America" adolescents—in transition from childhood to adulthood. Activities of these groups may constitute acceptable behaviors and relatively normal rites of passage in their particular communities.

Copycat gangs may be increasingly present in some lower income and middle-class communities, often in smaller cities and suburban and rural areas. Youths in these groups may identify with and attempt to emulate the mannerisms and behaviors of youth gang members in urban centers. Copycat gang behaviors may have serious criminal consequences. Identification with gang culture—fostered in significant measure through media influence—may be a source of excitement, offer a novel experience, and constitute a challenge to authority in communities where rapid school or population change is occurring and family disorganization is increasing.

Most of these copycat gangs are ephemeral, engage in relatively minor delinquent acts, and have little if any actual or ongoing contact with criminal juvenile or adult groups. Policymakers should carefully assess the threat that the groups pose to the community and to the needs for social development of their members in order to avoid exaggerating and creating a problem where there is very little or no evidence of sustainable serious gang activity.

Delinquent Group

The term *delinquent group* refers to a group or collectivity, mainly of juveniles and/or adolescents, usually engaging in law-violating behaviors that are less serious, violent, or persistent than those of youth gangs, posses, or crews. The delinquent group usually is less organized and more ephemeral than a youth gang and has none of the special gang characteristics such as significant commitment to violence, turf, distinctive dress, colors, and signs or symbols. The delinquent group is the most prevalent of all deviant youth groups in most communities.

Criminal (Youth and/or Adult) Organization

The *criminal organization* is usually a relatively well organized, stable, and sophisticated clique, group, or organization of youths and/or adults committed primarily to systematic income-producing activity of a criminal nature. Its members are essentially employees of a criminal business organization. The criminal organization may at times use intimidation and violence to further or protect its economic interests. Such organizations often provide employment for current or former gang members and may offer services or goods to, and acquire rewards from, community members in mutually acceptable and reinforcing ways.

Gang Clique, Set, Klika

The *gang clique* or *set* may or may not be smaller than a youth gang. It can represent a separately named but closely related gang faction. On the other hand, the West Coast *klika* may represent an entire cohort or age sector of youths (e.g., 13- and 14-year-old males) who join or are "jumped into" a street gang. The clique in its smaller version may signify a "tight" grouping of two or three youths with similar characteristics or criminal interests. The terms *gang, clique,* and *set* are sometimes used interchangeably. Cliques are the key cohesive building blocks of the more diffuse gang structure.

Use of Assessment Procedures to Select Program Strategies

The literature review conducted by the National Youth Gang Intervention and Suppression Program (Spergel, 1991) suggested that the predominant strategy for dealing with the gang problem during the 1950s and 1960s was social intervention, whereas the predominant strategy during the 1970s and 1980s was suppression. The analysis of data from the National Youth Gang Survey produced little evidence documenting the efficacy of either approach as a primary strategy for either chronic or emerging gang problem cities. On the other hand, strategies showing some promise of efficacy are community organization in emerging gang problem cities and opportunities provision in chronic gang problem cities. The survey results, the literature review, the field visit studies, and the various regional conferences of policymakers and practitioners engaged in testing the program's models and manuals all point to the importance of a collective awareness of appropriate and complementary strategies, especially when their implementation involves a division of labor across agencies.

Our analysis implies that both community disorganization and poverty are necessary but not sufficient causes of the gang problem. In other words, both must be present in some variable combination for the gang problem to emerge and develop (Curry & Spergel, 1988). A more direct conclusion of the analysis is that adequate resources and improved interagency or community cohesion are needed, again in some variable and appropriate combination, if the problem is to be reduced. This is especially true in cities where the gang problem has been chronic and is probably most severe. It is likely that a concerted, coordinated community attack on the problem, with federal support and accompanied by provision of educational, training, and job opportunities for gang or high-risk youths, would help alleviate the problem.

Caution is needed, however. Our analysis, while highlighting the promise in certain strategies, did not indicate that suppression of gang violence and gang-member-related drug trafficking is unimportant or that various forms of social intervention are unimportant. We found, rather, that these actions per se are less important and do not contribute to increased effectiveness in dealing with the problem. The strength of our community mobilization variable clearly indicates the need for various community organizations, including law enforcement and youth agencies, to play important interactive and collective roles in both emerging and chronic problem cities. But collective action alone—even assuming that it is genuine—may itself be insufficient, particularly in chronic problem cities, without the infusion of additional resources targeted appropriately to the problem.

A basic consideration may be that the proliferation of the gang problem signifies a progressive weakening of basic institutions of socialization, especially the family but also the schools and other community organizations. Secondary institutions in the community, particularly police, schools, and youth agencies, must assume additional support and control functions that perhaps formerly were fulfilled by families. At the least, these institutions must support families and one another in better carrying out those functions critical to the youth socialization process, especially in low-income areas. The process of community mobilization and resource development must aim not only to strengthen these secondary institutions but, in doing so, to nurture a coherent community in which problematic or at-risk youths can play a constructive and meaningful role. Such involvement can provide an alternative to the criminal youth gang as a source of social status and self-esteem.

Analysis of our survey data revealed no evidence that most agencies or community programs attempted to link selected primary strategies to perceived causes of the gang problem. Yet, the literature review (Spergel, 1991) and the analysis of socialization patterns (Curry & Spergel, 1992) mandate a concern for such linkage. The field visit reports (Spergel & Chance, 1990) further confirm the utility of tailoring organizational solutions to the unique social context in which gang problems emerge. For this reason, the guidelines offered in the technical assistance manuals of the National Youth Gang Suppression and Intervention Program treat assessment as crucial in constructing a locally successful response.

Testing of Intervention Models

One way to perpetuate the development of poorly coordinated, ill-focused gang response programs at the local level is to continue to start from scratch as each emerging gang problem is recognized. One way to avoid hastily contrived, crisis-spawned patchwork responses is to have a nationally coordinated, systematic paradigm for dealing with the gang problem. Although any effective national gang program must take into account the locally unique social, political, and economic factors that define a gang problem, such a program must also limit itself to a set of well-defined models or prototypes with proven potential for success.

Each experimental program that is initiated must be accompanied by technical support that emphasizes effective model implementation and information system construction. Only if these conditions are met can stringent program evaluations be developed. Methodical application and testing of models and prototypes is necessary if we are to move toward a systematic national gang program guided by rational policy decisions based on valid information about the evolving problem.

THE NATIONAL YOUTH GANG SUPPRESSION AND INTERVENTION PROGRAM: STATUS AND PRODUCTS

Our National Youth Gang Suppression and Intervention Program, a cooperative venture of the OJJDP and the School of Social Service Administration at the University of Chicago, has been not only an exercise in the search for (and, we believe, the development of) promising approaches to the youth gang problem but a process in which expert policymakers, administrators, and practitioners from a wide variety of agencies and community groups have contributed ideas about the problem, indicating what works and what does not. These experts have also begun to test and refine our project ideas almost as they have been enunciated.

In the research and development process, we have attempted to integrate academic interests, research skills, and program experience of project staff, policymakers, and practitioners. Local and national level experts representing police, prosecution, the judiciary, probation, corrections, parole, schools, grass-roots organizations, employers, and government have been engaged. These integrative efforts have produced not only conferences, symposia, surveys, models, and implementation manuals but significant policy and program efforts to test related policies and procedures almost from the start.

In many respects, OJJDP's sanction, research and development planning, and funding for systematic testing of the models and manuals have been preempted as other national agencies and local communities have moved rapidly ahead. The Administration for Children and Families of the United States Department of Health and Human Services, along with a variety of city and state programs, some with Justice Department funding, have moved ahead using a community mobilization approach, albeit with limited additional funding targeted to gang youths. A variety of agencies, particularly in law enforcement, have eagerly sought out manuals produced by our program for help in dealing with emerging youth gang problems.

Systematic demonstration and testing of the models and manuals; the development of relevant structure, policies, and procedures; and especially the differential emphasis on community mobilization and opportunities provision strategies in emerging and chronic gang problem cities have not yet begun. Such testing may be initiated by the OJJDP and the Bureau of Justice Assistance Program. It is regrettable that, due to a change in its administrator, OJJDP did not follow through on its original plan for a Stage 4 field testing of the models. Nevertheless, we believe, the National Youth Gang Suppression and Intervention Program has already exceeded original expectations as a nationwide research and development effort—in large measure because of the extraordinary concern and involvement on the part of individuals and agencies who have confronted the problem in recent years.

Annotated Bibliography

The following publications are products of the National Youth Gang Suppression and Intervention Program. They are available from the United States Department of Justice, Office of Juvenile Justice and Delinquency Prevention. Many of these documents may also become available in the near future from the United States Government Printing Office, Washington, DC.

Stage 1: Assessment

A series of tasks were undertaken to assess the nature and extent of the gang problem in the United States and the variety of responses and approaches to it. Emphasis has been less on assessment of the problem itself than on the discovery and creation of promising approaches for dealing with it.

Youth Gangs: Problem and Response, 1991 (357 pp.), by I. A. Spergel

This comprehensive review of the literature on youth gangs encompasses theories, historical analyses, research, policy and program materials, evaluations, and recommendations. Topics covered include estimates of the number of youth gangs and their members; the geographic distribution of gangs; the demographic characteristics of gang membership; the role of violence in gang activity; gang involvement in drug trafficking; the social evolution and organization of gangs; and the association between the development of gangs and other community social factors such as families, schools, political organization, organized crime among adults, and socioeconomic characteristics. Criminal justice system community organization and grass-roots approaches and programs for dealing with the problem are also examined.

The literature review includes a number of findings that aid our understanding of gangs as a national problem. For example, gang homicides, regardless of the method of identification, have reached all-time officially recorded highs in major urban centers. Several kinds of evidence indicate that arrested gang offenders engage in more serious, chronic, and violent illegal activity than arrested non-gang offenders. On the other hand, the relationship between gangs, violence, and drug trafficking appears highly variable: The rise in drug trafficking or youth violence cannot simply be attributed to increased youth gang activity. For the most part, the gang problem develops in low-income, newcomer or transitional, and sometimes lower-middle-class communities. Different forms of gang organization and gang crime may be associated with these different community characteristics, which also may include race/ethnicity, age, generational factors, and criminal opportunity.

In an examination of the history of gang programs, the literature review identifies youth outreach and social or crisis intervention as the primary response to youth gangs in the 1950s and 1960s. In the 1970s and 1980s, however, a police suppression approach became the primary strategy for responding to the problem. A condensation of an early version of the literature review, with limited reference to policy and program responses, is found in Spergel (1990).

Report of the Law Enforcement Youth Gang Symposium, 1988
(152 pp.), edited by I. A. Spergel, C. Kane, R. L. Chance,
M. Hyatt, R. Ross, and P. Rodriguez

This report, a transcript of the first of two law enforcement conferences bringing together researchers and practitioners, facilitated the development of the literature review and the national survey. Almost every theme addressed in the survey and in the documents described in the next section grew out of this initial conference.

*Survey of Youth Gang Problems and Programs in 45 Cities
and 6 Sites,* 1990 (297 pp.), by I. A. Spergel and G. D. Curry (with
R. E. Ross and R. Chance)

This survey is the full study on which the present chapter is based. It involved 254 respondents representing 14 categories of criminal justice agencies, community-based agencies, grass-roots groups, and other types of organizations, who were extensively questioned through prescreening, questionnaires, and telephone interviews. The survey, conducted in 1988 and 1989, was the first national and comprehensive survey of organized agency and community group responses to gang problems in the United States.

The survey report contains data, analysis, and discussion concerning many aspects of the problem, including definition of terms (e.g., gang, gang member, and gang incident); gang characteristics, such as extent of the recognized problem, demographics, criminality, and organization, with special attention to gang-drug organized crime connections; agencies' gang-oriented policies, training procedures, and program mechanisms; advisory and interagency structures; perceived causes of the problem and strategies established to deal with it, including institutional and community network characteristics; and effectiveness of intervention—that is, perceived changes in the dimensions of the problem between 1980 and 1987, organizational and interorganizational effectiveness, differences between chronic and emerging problem cities and jurisdictions and their patterned responses to the problem, and the construction of causal regression models.

Community and Institutional Responses to the Youth Gang Problem, 1990 (184 pp.), by I. A. Spergel and R. L. Chance

Using the perceived effectiveness scores just mentioned, we selected five cities and one correctional site for field visits and more careful qualitative observation. For each locality or site, all of the respondents interviewed in the national survey as well as others were contacted and their programs observed. These critical on-site examinations of programs in action confirmed much of what had emerged from the national survey but also revealed accomplishments and shortcomings of local programs that were not easily illuminated by survey methodology. Some specific conclusions resulted from the field visits:

1. In cities with an emerging gang problem, clear and forthright recognition of the problem rather than denial is crucial in developing an effective response.

2. A promising response requires the proactive and sustained leadership of one or several key community activists and agency representatives.

3. Genuine collaboration among law enforcement, justice, corrections, and community-based and grass-roots agencies focused on effectively dealing with the youth gang problem is needed. Fundamental to such collaboration are mutual trust among agencies, interagency communication, shared perceptions of the nature of the problem, and a willingness to commit to complementary strategies in dealing with the gang problem. Success of this local mobilization approach was not always assured. Sometimes gang violence problems were transformed into drug trafficking problems. Sometimes street gang violence returned after a decade or more of peace. External factors such as intrusion of new populations, changing socioeconomic conditions, and shifts in national social policy affected the success of local responses.

Law Enforcement Definitional Conference Transcript, 1990
(138 pp.), edited by I. A. Spergel and L. Bobrowski

The findings of the National Youth Gang Survey, the field visits, and earlier discussions with law enforcement officials revealed marked differences in definition of key operational concepts, such as *gang* and *gang incident.* A special definitional conference was held for project researchers and law enforcement representatives at practitioner, administrative, and policy levels from Los Angeles, Los Angeles County, Chicago, and New York City. These localities were selected because they had the longest and most sophisticated—and sometimes most successful— experience with gangs. More important, they had been responsible for the construction of influential, but different, operational definitions of the terms *gang* and *gang incident,* definitions used throughout the country.

*The Youth Gang Problem: Perceptions of Former Youth Gang
Influentials, Transcripts of Two Symposia,* 1990 (139 pp.),
edited by I. A. Spergel

To address the preliminary findings and conclusions of the program from the perspective of gang members themselves, the principal investigator organized two symposia of former Chicago gang influentials. Nine African American and eight Hispanic (Puerto Rican and Mexican American) former gang leaders in their 20s, 30s, and 40s participated in separate all-day conferences to discuss the problem and consider what should be done about it. Both symposium transcripts present in detail a wealth of untapped, sometimes unstructured information from individuals whose lives have been shaped by youth gangs. Former key perpetrators and, sometimes, victims of gang violence illuminate the day-to-day realities of life in communities dominated by gang presence.

Reactions to and criticisms of various kinds of gang intervention and suppression programs were both personal and frank. The perceptions of the causes of the problem and of strategies for dealing with it were somewhat different and in large measure reflected racial or ethnic differences. Although for both groups personal needs and socialization factors appeared to have been important in prompting entry into gangs, economic need seemed to be an important additional motivation for the African American participants, and social pressures seemed relatively more urgent for the Hispanic participants. The African American former gang leaders viewed massive social and economic development programs as more important responses to the current youth gang problem, whereas the Hispanic participants saw additional services and restraints on the police as more important.

Client Evaluation of Youth Gang Services, 1990 (53 pp.),
by G. D. Curry

In coordination with the field visits mentioned earlier, a survey of current and former gang members utilizing intervention services at seven field agencies was conducted. Analysis of survey results yielded profiles by agency, ethnicity, and gender that distinguished these clients' perceptions of the effectiveness of different services. It was possible to compare active gang members with former gang members on a number of criteria. An analysis of former gang members' reasons for leaving the gang revealed several differences in motivation between Hispanic and African American respondents. The salient findings were as follows. The most commonly received services, according to clients' reports, were recreation and sports; these services, along with job placement, were also regarded as most helpful in curtailing gang activity. There were significant demographic differences in the proportions of youths receiving services from program agencies: Male gang members under age 21 reported receiving more services than non–gang members or older gang members; Hispanic youths reported receiving fewer services than either African Americans or whites, although Hispanics rated the services they received as more helpful. African Americans were more likely to report leaving the gang because of arrest or fear of violence; Hispanics more often reported that they had left the gang because of drug involvement (use and trafficking). In general, the two most frequently cited reasons for leaving the gang were getting older (42.4%) and getting arrested (37.3%).

Preventing Involvement in Youth Gang Crime, 1990 (173 pp.), by G. D. Curry and I. A. Spergel

The cooperative agreement between the United States Department of Justice and the University of Chicago required that we focus on suppression and intervention. However, it seemed extremely important also to address prevention in respect to the youth gang problem, at least on a limited basis. Policy and practice in the community usually cut across the levels of prevention, intervention, and suppression, and it was difficult for a variety of reasons to separate them. Our conceptions of suppression and intervention were broad, as indicated earlier. Our conception of early intervention somewhat overlapped the notion of prevention at the individual level, and our notion of opportunities provision encompassed much of what was needed to address the gang problem at the structural level.

The issue of socialization of youth to gangs has policy implications for prevention in many respects. We had available a data set resulting from prior research on a population of preteens and young adolescents in a high-gang-crime area, a project supported by the Office of Educational Research and Improvement of the United States Department of Education (Spergel & Curry, 1988). The present OJJDP-sponsored report is a comprehensive reanalysis of that data set, concerning socialization to gangs, in the context of a literature review on gang prevention programs. The data set contained survey and official record information on 439 male adolescents in grades 6 through 8 from four middle schools in four contiguous Chicago neighborhoods. The nature of the information facilitated the development of comparative models of gang involvement and delinquency for Hispanics and African Americans. From the reanalysis, we concluded that systematically different prevention programs may be required for communities with different ethnic and socioeconomic characteristics. More limited age parameters, along with greater importance of peer group and school-related self-esteem factors, helped explain gang and delinquent behavior among Hispanic youths. For African American youths, the pervasive presence of other gang members and groups involved in drug use and sales did more to explain gang and delinquent behavior.

Stage 2: Prototype Development

The second major stage of the program was the development of 12 prototypes for gang suppression and intervention.

Prototype/Models for Gang Intervention and Suppression, 1992 (517 pp.), by I. A. Spergel, R. L. Chance, K. Ehrensaft, T. Regulus, C. Kane, and A. Alexander

The separate prototypes or models, each centered around a key type of agency or focus, are as follows: Police, Prosecution, Judges, Probation, Corrections, Parole, Schools, Youth Employment, Community-Based Youth Agency, and Grass-Roots Organization. Two additional cross-cutting, systemwide models that encompass planning and interaction efforts, including interagency coordination, are General Community Design and Community Mobilization. These models are available as foundations for collaborative community-based programs in a variety of gang problem contexts, whether in cities or institutions. The models emphasize the development of complementary strategies, within and across organizations, which are meant both to support and to control high-risk gang-prone and gang member youths as they move toward a conventional adaptation.

The model identifies rationales, policies, procedures, and leadership roles appropriate for carrying out these strategies in each of the key types of criminal justice, community-based, and grass-roots organizations. Suppression, intervention, and prevention patterns should vary according to the type of organization as well as the type of community gang problem context. For example, although in the context of enforcement the primary strategy would be suppression, it should be carried out within a framework of community mobilization and have a strong secondary emphasis on strategies of social intervention, including referral of gang-prone youths or gang members for services and provision of opportunities through such efforts as job development or referral targeted directly or indirectly at gang youths. The application of this pattern of strategies would differ somewhat, depending on whether the community's gang problems were chronic and serious or emerging and modest.

Stage 3: Technical Assistance Manuals

The third major stage of the program was the development of technical assistance manuals to guide the implementation of specific models at the local level.

Technical Assistance Manuals, 1992 (approximately 1,200 pp.), by I. A. Spergel, R. L. Chance, K. Ehrensaft, T. Regulus, C. Kane, and R. Laseter

These 12 manuals, corresponding to the 12 prototypes, provide a common introduction, and each outlines precise steps for implementation of a particular model. Emphasis is on distinctive community context and organizational mission. Each manual furnishes guidelines for assessing the problem from a community-organizational mission perspective. Procedures for the development of local goals and objectives are described, and program mechanisms and procedures are catalogued. A concern with the categories of youths to be targeted is maintained throughout each manual.

The manuals emphasize mobilizing community interest, concern, and resources in a way that neither exaggerates nor denies the youth gang problem and that also encourages consensus among key actors on the nature and causes of the problem and on ways to deal with it. A variety of program activities, organizational arrangements, and other action steps are delineated for each type of organization. The manuals tell how to establish appropriate gang information data systems and raise issues related to information sharing across agencies and collaboration with the media. Matters of training, research and evaluation, and funding, as well as necessary cautions, are addressed.

REFERENCES

Cartwright, D. S., Tomson, B., & Schwartz, H. (1975). *Gang delinquency*. Pacific Grove, CA: Brooks/Cole.

Cloward, R. A., & Ohlin, L. E. (1960). *Delinquency and opportunity*. Glencoe, IL: Free Press.

Curry, G. D., & Spergel, I. A. (1988). Gang homicide, delinquency and community. *Criminology, 26,* 381-405.

Curry, G. D., & Spergel, I. A. (1992). Gang involvement and delinquency among Hispanic and African American males. *Journal of Research in Crime and Delinquency, 29,* 273-291.

Drug Enforcement Administration. (1988). *Crack cocaine availability and trafficking in the United States*. Washington, DC: U. S. Department of Justice, Drug Enforcement Administration, Cocaine Investigation Section.

Horowitz, R. (1990). Sociological perspectives on gangs: Conflicting definitions and concepts. In C. R. Huff (Ed.), *Gangs in America*. Newbury Park, CA: Sage.

Huff, C. R. (1989). Youth gangs and public policy. *Crime and Delinquency, 35,* 524-537.

Jacobs, J. B. (1977). *Stateville: The penitentiary in mass society*. University of Chicago Press.

Jankowski, M. S. (1991). *Islands in the street: Gangs and American urban society*. Berkeley: University of California Press.

Johnson, R. A., & Wichern, D. W. (1982). *Applied multivariate statistical analysis*. Englewood Cliffs, NJ: Prentice-Hall.

Klein, M. W. (1971). *Street gangs and street workers*. Englewood Cliffs, NJ: Prentice-Hall.

Maxson, C. L., & Klein, M. W. (1990). Defining and measuring gang violence. In C. R. Huff (Ed.), *Gangs in America*. Newbury Park, CA: Sage.

Miller, W. B. (1975). *Violence by youth gangs and youth groups as a crime problem in major American cities*. Washington, DC: U. S. Government Printing Office.

Miller, W. B. (1982, February). *Crime by youth gangs and groups in the United States* (Draft). Washington, DC: U. S. Department of Justice, National Institute of Juvenile Justice and Delinquency Prevention.

Moore, J. W. (1978). *Homeboys: Gangs, drugs and prison in the barrios of Los Angeles.* Philadelphia: Temple University Press.

Moore, J. W. (1988). Introduction: Gangs and the underclass: A comparative perspective. In J. M. Hagedorn, *People and folks: Gangs, crime and the underclass in a rustbelt city.* Chicago: Lake View.

National Institute of Justice. (1991, November 14). *NIJ FY 1991 gangs projects* (Research on Gangs). Washington, DC: U. S. Department of Justice.

Shaw, C. R., & McKay, H. D. (1972). *Juvenile delinquency in urban areas.* University of Chicago Press.

Skolnick, J. H. (1990). *Gang organization and migration.* Berkeley: University of California, Center for the Study of Law and Society.

Spergel, I. A. (1964). *Racketville, Slumtown, Haulburg.* University of Chicago Press.

Spergel, I. A. (1966). *Street gang work: Theory and practice.* Reading, MA: Addison-Wesley.

Spergel, I. A. (1969). *Problem solving: The delinquency example.* University of Chicago Press.

Spergel, I. A. (1984). Violent gangs in Chicago: In search of social policy. *Social Service Review, 58,* pp. 199–226.

Spergel, I. A. (1990). Youth gangs: Continuity and change. In M. Tonry & N. Morris (Eds.), *Crime and justice: A review of research* (Vol. 12). University of Chicago Press.

Spergel, I. A. (1991). *Youth gangs: Problem and response.* Washington, DC: U. S. Department of Justice, Office of Juvenile Justice and Delinquency Prevention.

Spergel, I. A. (1992). Youth gangs: An essay review. *Social Service Review, 66,* 121–140.

Spergel, I. A., & Chance, R. L. (1990). *Community and institutional responses to the youth gang problem.* University of Chicago, School of Social Service Administration.

Spergel, I. A., & Chance, R. L. (1991). National Youth Gang Suppression and Intervention Program. *National Institute of Justice Review, 224,* 21–24.

Spergel, I. A., & Curry, G. D. (1988). *Socialization to gangs: Baseline preliminary report.* University of Chicago, School of Social Service Administration.

Spergel, I. A., & Curry, G. D. (1990). *Survey of youth gang problems and programs in 45 cities and 6 sites* (National Youth Gang Suppression and Intervention Program). Washington, DC: U. S. Department of Justice, Office of Juvenile Justice and Delinquency Prevention.

Sutherland, E. H. (1947). *Principles of criminology.* New York: Lippincott.

Taylor, C. S. (1990). *Dangerous society.* East Lansing: Michigan State University Press.

Thomas, W. I., & Znaniecki, F. (1927). *The Polish peasant in Europe and America.* New York: Knopf.

Wright, B. D., & Masters, G. N. (1982). *Rating scale analysis: Rasch measurement.* Chicago: MESA.

CHAPTER 13

Gangs and the Police

C. Ronald Huff
Wesley D. Mcbride

PART I—GANGS AND POLICE ORGANIZATIONS: RETHINKING STRUCTURE AND FUNCTIONS

—C. Ronald Huff

Gangs pose a significant challenge to law enforcement agencies as well as to citizens, schools, and the quality of life in our communities. Comparatively little research has been published on the role of law enforcement with respect to gangs. However, it is worthwhile in this volume to assess briefly the challenges to law enforcement arising from the growth of gangs in the United States and to ask whether traditional organizational arrangements are equal to these challenges. In Part I of this chapter, I will discuss my own view of these evolving challenges to law enforcement and provide some recommendations based on the existing literature and on my own research and consulting experience with several major police departments over the past 6 years.[1] In Part II, Wesley McBride describes one major law enforcement agency's approach in dealing with gangs.

Little has changed since Needle and Stapleton concluded that "the body of gang literature is inadequate for researching the police role vis-à-vis youth gangs" (1983, p. 2). We do indeed have a more extensive literature on gangs themselves, but very little in that literature helps us understand much about the function of police with respect to gangs. Exceptions include recent research demonstrating that the police response must be part of a broader community-based strategy (Kramer, 1986; Spergel & Curry, 1990 and chapter 12 of this volume) and that specialized gang unit involvement can be an important asset in the investigative process—for example, in determining what is a gang-related homicide (Klein, Gordon, & Maxson, 1986). What *has* changed in the past decade, of course, is that the gang problem has spread throughout the nation. Whereas Needle and Stapleton found that 27 of 60 police departments acknowledged the presence of youth gangs in their communities, it is more likely now that almost all large, urban departments will acknowledge that such gangs exist (and when they don't acknowledge it, this may not mean an absence of gangs; it may just as often signal politically motivated denial because cities do not relish the image of having a gang problem). In fact, the willingness of political leaders to acknowledge the existence of a gang problem is one of two important variables determining the extent to which law enforcement can be effective in dealing with gang-related crime. The other factor is the organizational and resource allocation structure of the law enforcement agency.

New Challenges to Old Structures

Since at least 1829, when Sir Robert Peel organized the London Metropolitan Police, urban police departments typically have been characterized by rigid organizational structures that are highly resistant to change. In fact, the paramilitary nature of police organizations makes them even more restrictive than Weber's (1946) ideal bureaucracy. As is the case for "scientific management" (Taylor, 1911) and administrative organizational theory (Fayol, 1916/1930), the paramilitary model fails to consider many dimensions of organizational behavior, assumes that the organization's members always act rationally in pursuing organizational goals, assumes that the needs of the organization and those of its members are identical, assumes that goals and activities can be prescribed and outlined by superiors in advance of task execution, assumes that there is one best way to do things, and assumes that the organization's subsystems are undifferentiated and homogeneous.

As Bordua and Reiss (1966), Guyot (1979), and others have observed, the paramilitary organizational model has severe defects, in both descriptive and prescriptive terms: It neither describes accurately the day-to-day, real world of police work nor prescribes a model that is likely to work, because it presents the imagery of police as an "army" engaged in a "war on crime" in which citizens are cast as potential enemies. The reality, of course, is that most decision making by police officers occurs on the streets, without benefit of advance review by superiors. Furthermore, most citizens are not "the enemy" but are at least valuable potential allies of the police who may be alienated by being cast in that oppositional role.

The typical law enforcement organization is not well structured to deal with youth gangs. Traditional police departments rely on existing units (patrol, investigations, crime prevention, juvenile bureau, community relations) to respond to gang behavior. In recent years, several specialized forms of gang control have appeared more frequently (Needle & Stapleton, 1983). They include the following:

1. The *youth service program,* in which traditional police unit personnel (usually from the juvenile bureau) are assigned gang control responsibility, along with other duties

2. The *gang detail,* in which one or more officers of a traditional unit are given exclusive responsibility for gang control

3. The *gang unit,* in which one or more officers are in a unit established solely to cope with gang problems.

There are, of course, a number of permutations and combinations of these three models, including various arrangements for sharing and support among units. The more serious the gang problem in a given community, the more likely it is that a specialized gang control unit will emerge within the department (Needle & Stapleton, 1983). However, the emergence of such a special unit may be a two-edged sword, as will become clear later in this discussion.

There are four important types of activities that constitute the gang control aspect of police work: (a) intelligence and information processing, (b) prevention, (c) enforcement, and (d) follow-up investigation. One of the most unexpected findings of research on police handling of youth gangs has been the diffusion of gang control functions across multiple organizational units within the same department (Needle & Stapleton, 1983). Even in large departments that have specialized gang control units, these four activities generally have not been consolidated within one unit.

For departments that preserve the traditional organizational structure, the problems posed by youth gangs can be formidable. Compared with gang members of the 1950s, contemporary gang youths have a great deal more geographic mobility owing to the proliferation of automobiles and the efficiency of the freeway system in our major metropolitan areas. It is not at all uncommon for members of one gang to be observed by multiple law enforcement agencies during the same evening at locations that are 25 to 50 miles apart. The gangs in this scenario are far different from the turf-oriented gangs portrayed in *West Side Story*. *Turf* today does not necessarily mean neighborhoods, although this is often still the case for low-income housing projects. Turf now includes regional shopping malls; girls; skating rinks; and other persons, places, or things constituting possible objects of dominance. Recent research (Huff, 1989) suggests that one unintended consequence of massive citywide busing aimed at remedying segregation has been to exacerbate the gang problem in the schools. Rather than a neighborhood school with, perhaps, a neighborhood gang, we now have multiple rival gangs in the same school thanks to crosstown busing. Gang members may arrive at school as early as 7:00 A.M., commit a series of "B & Es" (breaking and entering), and still be in school when attendance is taken. They have a good alibi, while the police are left to solve a series of property crimes committed by gang members who do not even live in the area.

Recommendation 1: Consolidate all four major gang control functions—intelligence, prevention, enforcement, and follow-up— within one citywide gang unit.

In light of what we know about (a) efforts on the part of traditionally organized law enforcement agencies to control gangs and (b) the greatly increased geographic mobility and range of activity of contemporary gangs, it is clear that the four critical gang control elements should be placed in one citywide unit, which cooperates closely with countywide law enforcement agencies. In some major cities a citywide unit will need multiple substations in different geographic districts, but the officers should nonetheless be members of the same gang unit; this will foster closer cooperation, sharing of information, and development of collective and coordinated strategies and tactics. These strategies and tactics must, of course, be both appropriately timed and culturally sensitive (see Soriano, chapter 16 of this volume), taking into account such issues as the current social climate of the neighborhood and the city as well as the cultural or subcultural meanings of specific acts and the general perspective toward authority figures such as the police.

New Requirements for Information/Intelligence

Recommendation 2: Establish a comprehensive data base and information system especially designed for gangs and gang members.

Just as the increased geographic distribution and mobility of gangs and the changing nature of turf have combined to pose a challenge to traditional organizational structures in law enforcement, the increasing diversity and mobility of gangs pose a challenge to law enforcement information systems and intelligence operations. For example, when I began my own research on gangs in the mid-1980s, I quickly discovered that law enforcement agencies were typically not prepared to provide data on gang members or gang-related crimes. They simply did not have data bases or information systems that included these categories of information. Much of the data that I was able to collect during that time was the result of customized requests from computerized crime reporting systems within the agencies (e.g., requests for printouts of crime reports that mentioned "gangs" or "gang members").

This situation changed, of course, with the development of the Gang Reporting, Evaluation, and Tracking (GREAT) information system in Los Angeles County. Since the mid-1980s this system has become increasingly sophisticated and comprehensive. It now incorporates data from the Los Angeles County Sheriff's Department, the Los Angeles Police Department, and the Los Angeles County Probation Department. The data base includes many different data elements, or fields of information, for each gang member (or associate) identified. The system can be accessed by law enforcement and criminal justice user agencies throughout the nation and permits them to obtain information directly from system files. The system is nationally and regionally coordinated through advisory committees that are responsible for quality control and enforcement of operating agreements specifying terms of access, permitted uses of information, and other important parameters to prevent misuse of the information.[2] This system has been very useful to agencies across the nation in situations involving, for example, the migration of Los Angeles gang members to other cities.

A more recent computerized information system is in the final stages of testing in Broward County, Florida. Known as MAGIC, this multiagency system for tracking gangs is similar to the GREAT system in many features, is easy to use, and has data requirements that parallel, in important respects, Florida's STEP (Street

Terrorism Enforcement and Prevention) Act. Briefly, the system requires that a user have hard data in the form of appropriate answers to onscreen prompts before he or she can add an individual's name to the gang data base. Because the requirements for input of gang members' names are relatively stringent, this approach, which in effect establishes an audit trail, is useful in ensuring that the data base can survive potential court challenges.[3]

In states that have a STEP act (or comparable legislation defining a criminal street gang or similar organizational designation), this type of computerized information system can be valuable in helping law enforcement officers target individuals for arrest and in helping prosecutors establish adequate proof of continuing illegal activity. For example, the data base will reflect the date on which an individual is notified (in some states, actually served with notice) that he is recognized as a member of a criminal street gang and record any subsequent arrests after that date, showing continuing involvement following formal notification. Further, such an information system can be programmed, through the computer's internal clock, to move from active to inactive status the files of gang members or associates who have had no contact with law enforcement for a prescribed period (e.g., a year). In this way the data base stays current on active gang members and associates without losing the valuable information in the files of those who have become inactive. Similarly, inactive files can be removed from the data base after a designated period of inactivity, juveniles' records can be purged automatically when the data base shows that they have reached the age of majority, and so forth.

Whether the GREAT system, the MAGIC system, or another dedicated information system is adopted, it should be user-friendly, all users should receive training until they are quite comfortable with the system, interagency sharing should be promoted on at least a regional basis, and the system should be designed to track with the major components of criminal street gang acts in states that have such legislation.

Recommendation 3: Develop timely and accurate intelligence concerning gangs' organizational structures, leadership, rituals, and cultural belief systems.

Closely related to data on gang membership is the need for intelligence concerning gang organizational structures, distribution of power, initiation rituals, cultural beliefs, coalitions and rivalries, and other important features. Given the increasing diversity of and lethal conflict among gangs, such intelligence is a critical component of a successful law enforcement program. For example, the gang unit should strive to learn about each gang's leadership structure in instances where that structure is well developed. This information can be very useful when a gang's current leader is killed or arrested and may help answer some key questions: Who is likely to take over next? What is his background? Does he have a record of recent "specialization" in any particular type of crime? If so, the gang may be influenced by its leader's emphases and may focus on new, or at least different, types of crime. Will the succession of leadership be likely to result in more or less violence? Will it create an internal battle for control that may be destabilizing and thus offer law enforcement an opportunity to develop internal informants? If a gang member is killed, do the gang's cultural beliefs require immediate revenge? More subtle, delayed revenge? Such questions cannot always be answered, but the goal should be to acquire intelligence that will assist in answering them. The public's safety, as well as that of police and gang members themselves, may depend on it.

Recommendation 4: Use the data base to monitor such basic indicators as the age distribution of members and their ethnic/racial identities.

A further important function of the data base is to track each gang's age distribution, racial/ethnic composition, and other important demographic variables. Collecting and monitoring these indicators over time, and keeping current profiles of each gang, can be of strategic value in detecting significant shifts in membership and in allocating resources. For example, these data may indicate whether a gang is replenishing its membership by recruiting younger members or reveal possible coalitions among different groups.

The gang unit can also call on the data base in deciding which gangs should receive priority for intervention. For example, if all else is relatively equal (especially with respect to violent crimes committed) and given the resource limitations confronting most police agencies, it may be most effective to concentrate efforts on those gangs with a broad age distribution (e.g., 12 to 32) because the demographic data suggest that these gangs are perpetuating themselves by recruiting or attracting new, young members.

From Denial to Overreaction

In earlier research (Huff, 1989, 1990), I have noted that cities tend to move from an immobilizing stage I call denial (i.e., denial that the community has a gang problem) to an equally dangerous stage that I call overreaction. Whereas the denial stage includes what I call political paralysis, in which the police and other organizations have great difficulty working together to address emerging gangs, overreaction typically defines the gang problem as one for the police to solve. I liken this to blaming physicians for a disease: They can help prevent it and can treat it when it occurs, but they alone cannot be held responsible for its existence.

Recommendation 5: Avoid overlabeling and prematurely classifying individuals as gang members.

Although gangs are a product of societal and communitywide forces (and, as such, require broad, integrative intervention strategies), law enforcement organizations, once the community turns to them to solve the gang problem, typically undertake aggressive identification and classification of gangs and their members. During this stage, an officer who sees an individual interacting with a particular gang is likely to consider the individual at least an associate of that gang and may enter his name in the gang file. Research, however, consistently demonstrates that many such individuals are not confirmed gang members but are instead experimenting; they are typically wannabes who aspire to gang membership. In fact, some gang members have attributed their first real, confirmed identification with a gang to overlabeling by law enforcement (see, for example, Hagedorn, 1988; Huff, 1989, 1990): If, for example, a youth is seen with the Crips gang and is labeled a Crip, word may get out that he is a Crip. At this point he may feel compelled to join the Crips simply for protection from the Bloods. Overlabeling is particularly dangerous with respect to wannabes, who often experiment with various gangs—even rival gangs—and may or may not actually join one.

Overlabeling individuals and prematurely classifying them as gang members may backfire by driving them into particular gangs and may thus, by inflating estimates of gang membership, contribute to a dangerous spiral of escalating gang conflict and recruiting wars in which innocent citizens (and police) can get caught up, injured, or even killed. Law enforcement officers may be seduced into this practice because of the perceived need to document the magnitude of the problem so that additional resources (personnel, equipment, finances) can be acquired. They should resist this temptation, however: Overestimates of gang membership will be discovered eventually, coming to the attention of the public and of the politicians who control funding. This will call into question the agency's integrity and create the impression that it is willing to mislead the public and its leaders for self-serving reasons.

Overcoming Police Turf Battles

Recommendation 6: Rotate officers, at least briefly, among the gang, narcotics, patrol, homicide, and organized crime units. Also, ensure that officers receive cross-training across these units, help respond to backup calls, provide information for briefings, and participate on multiunit investigative task forces.

Internal and external turf wars constitute one of the most common problems facing police agencies. In some cases, law enforcement agencies pay more attention to turf than do gangs! It is not uncommon for agencies to resist sharing information or resources, working together, and so forth. Likewise, turf battles between different units of an agency can create major problems within the agency.

To deal successfully with contemporary gangs, it is increasingly necessary not only to establish a gang unit but also to ensure that the gang unit can work closely with the narcotics bureau, the juvenile bureau, patrol officers, and even homicide and organized crime units. These practices can help break down the turf barriers and foster greater cooperation and a collective sense of shared mission. Gang units, like other specialized units, may encounter some jealousy when they are initially formed, and they may develop some elitist and isolationist practices that, if left unchecked, can undermine departmental efficiency and effectiveness. By contrast, if the gang unit prepares a weekly newsletter for patrol officers, helps brief patrol officers on current gang activities and threats, and helps respond to backup calls when it is in the area, the esprit de corps is strengthened.[4]

Networking With Other Community Agencies and Using Nonarrest Situations to Build Relationships

Recommendation 7: Adopt a balanced, comprehensive approach to gang intervention, including suppression, prevention, and referral to community agencies.

As demonstrated by Spergel and Curry (1990 and Chapter 12 of this volume), the best strategies for long-term success in the prevention and control of gang-related crime appear to involve broad-based; community networking approaches. A broader approach to the problem, linking law enforcement with other community agencies and including community organization and expanded opportunities for youth, is more likely to achieve durable results than is a narrower focus on suppression.

Law enforcement agencies that rely solely on suppression are unlikely to be very effective in the longer term because (a) new gang members may simply replace those arrested owing to similar unmet needs and the continuing availability of criminal opportunities and (b) where incarceration follows conviction, the gang problem often is partially displaced into the correctional system as gang members become active inside the institutions, then return to the community and resume their activities with the gang. On the other hand, law enforcement agencies that recognize the importance of a balanced, comprehensive approach, including community organization and opportunities provision as well as suppression, are more likely to be successful in deterring and/or permanently diverting individuals from gang involvement. This broader approach is also quite consistent with the contemporary emphasis on both community-oriented and problem-oriented policing (see, for example, discussions by Brown, 1985, and Davis, 1985).

The recommended balanced approach includes both sticks (the deterrent threat of arrest) and carrots (prevention programs, expanded opportunities, counseling, and other positive programs). In recognition of this fact, the Los Angeles Police Department formulated the Drug Abuse Resistance Education (DARE) program, and the Los Angeles County Sheriff's Department developed its Substance Abuse and Narcotic Education (SANE) program—two initiatives that have been widely adopted around the country. In addition, many other police agencies have developed midnight basketball leagues, Police Athletic League (PAL) programs, truancy prevention programs,[5] and other positive programmatic initiatives.

Recommendation 8: Make a conscious effort to interact with current and potential gang members in nonarrest situations.

In addition to getting involved in community networking, police officers can make greater use of nonarrest situations to influence the lives of current and would-be gang members. A continuing display of professionalism, personal concern, and fairness—both on the streets and during incarceration—can help curb gang involvement and encourage cooperation with law enforcement's gang control efforts.

In my earlier research (Huff, 1989), I reported that gang members sometimes cited individual police officers as sources of positive influence. When questioned about this matter, they would frequently emphasize that it was the officer's professional behavior, fairness, and concern that stood out. They were positively affected, emotionally and psychologically, when officers demonstrated personal concern for them or their families, refrained from unnecessary roughness, and treated them fairly. Even though the same officer might have arrested a young gang member or wannabe when he deserved it, meaningful interaction in a nonarrest situation could have a powerful impact on his life. Gang-involved youths may not act as if they appreciate the interest shown by officers (just as typical adolescents seldom acknowledge with appreciation their parents' expression of concern), but they will admit this confidentially when asked by a researcher.

Finally, officers who demonstrate a genuine interest in young people, even those who are gang involved, can develop a certain level of trust that is much more likely to lead to cooperation and useful information. Furthermore, when a gang member is arrested and incarcerated, it is predictably the case that his homeboys will not visit him or deposit money in his account, despite their earlier assertions of "brotherhood" and "loyalty." If the officer maintains a personal interest in the young person, even visiting him during incarceration, this continuing expression of positive concern may make the youth more amenable to leaving the gang and/or providing information that could be helpful in deterring others from involvement.

Improving the Investigative Process

Recommendation 9: Improve the investigative process by (a) establishing a specialized gang unit and involving it in the investigation of potential gang-related crimes; (b) cultivating positive personal relationships with gang members; and (c) basing investigative procedures on a sound knowledge of the gang's features and practices, and of potential value tensions between gang leaders and noncore members.

As indicated earlier, Klein et al. (1986) demonstrated that the existence of a specialized gang unit can improve the investigative process in determining, for example, whether a homicide is gang-related. In addition to involving a specialized unit in crimes that are potentially gang related and maintaining relationships with gang members based on personal concern, law enforcement agencies conducting gang investigations have learned other important ways to increase their effectiveness.

The Baltimore Police Department has accumulated significant experience in the investigation of gang members and gang-related crimes. On the basis of a review of the existing literature, that department's approach appears to be one of the best examples of an attempt to differentiate between the youth gang and the more typical drug organizations. Baltimore's approach can be summarized as follows:

1. Identify each gang's membership, acts of violence, and victims.

2. Learn the gang's folklore.

3. Develop informants.

4. Target members outside the nucleus of the gang.

5. Place these targets in real or imagined jeopardy via controlled arrest situations, interviews of randomly arrested members, and/or the use of the grand jury.

6. Interview to determine if a particular gang member approves or opposes his gang's use of violence. Members often are opposed but get caught up in the gang's dynamics.

7. Use this tension to create the belief that the gang leader is threatening the gang's survival by the use of violence, thus putting the entire gang in jeopardy.

8. Grant immunity to establish self-interest on the part of the potential witness.

9. Allow no perception of neutral ground. The message should be that the gang member can either cooperate, have his case presented to the grand jury, or be targeted for investigation himself. (Burns & Deakin, 1989)

The strategic thrust of Baltimore's investigative procedure is based on the psychodynamics of the gang. What this strategy does, it appears, is to create cognitive dissonance for the targeted gang member, whose power position is outside the gang's nucleus. The process, as described by Burns and Deakin (1989), places the individual gang member in a position where he is confronted with two conflicting and mutually incompatible beliefs: (a) that the gang's survival is vital and (b) that the use of violence by the gang's leader has called forth police pressure and thus threatened the gang's survival. The first point is likely to be given heavier weight than the second point, assuming both that the individual is committed to the gang's safety and survival and that he is uncomfortable with the use of violence. In such a situation, the investigator often has the opportunity to exploit differences ("value tensions") between gang leaders and noncore members.

Part I of this chapter has placed the issue of police intervention with gangs in a broad context, emphasizing the importance of community networking, sound organizational design, and the formulation of strategies targeted to the special dynamics of youth gangs. Part II will provide a closer look at the efforts of one of our nation's largest and most prominent law enforcement agencies, the Los Angeles County Sheriff's Department. Given the magnitude of the gang problem in metropolitan Los Angeles, the discussion of this department's experience and its initiatives will illustrate and underscore the importance of adopting a broad, community-based approach to gang prevention and control.

PART II—POLICE DEPARTMENTS AND GANG INTER-
VENTION: THE OPERATION SAFE STREETS CONCEPT

—*Wesley D. McBride*

Gang violence has created an atmosphere of fear and foreboding throughout all levels of our society. A sort of gang phobia has spread across the country, with many segments of the population living in fear of street gangs. Certain groups adjust their daily life-styles because of this fear. Many citizens avoid beaches, neighborhood parks, or amusement centers for fear of being confronted by gangs. Much of this gang phobia is the result of paranoia; yet, in some communities, the fear is well founded.

Across this nation, street gang crime is increasing at an alarming rate, with little sign of abatement. The rate of gang-related murder climbs each year to set a new all-time record. During 1990 in Los Angeles County, 690 persons were slain because of gang violence; law enforcement sources estimate that over 5,000 were injured. The next year, 1991, showed no sign of improvement, with over 700 dead and approximately 7,000 injured.

Today's excessive gang violence is not simply due to the failure of law enforcement techniques, but is attributable to society's failure to respond adequately to growing societal problems. Underfunding of both law enforcement programs and community programs that innovatively address the issue of gangs has contributed to the growing influence of street gangs on the communities they inhabit.

The current trend is the continued exportation of Los Angeles–style street gang activity across the country, along with the excessive violence associated with such activity. Street gangs are becoming a major concern in middle-class suburbia. Gang activity is becoming markedly more violent, with a definite disregard on the part of the gangster for the innocent person's suffering. One gang's display of gratuitous violence seems to challenge another to commit even more heinous acts.

Gang members have become more bold in their defiance of the law and their affronts to public order. Field reports from officers in communities across the nation confirm this new rebellious attitude among street gangsters. The newly discovered bravado manifests the gang member's assumption that he can display total contempt for the public and violate the law with impunity. This attitude is part of a serious trend that may cause even more violent confrontations with law enforcement, further undermining legitimate efforts to combat the problem by making each issue a political event for aspiring politicos and activists.

Experts generally agree that, although obliteration of the street gang is a worthy goal, the goal is probably not attainable in today's free society. Theoretically, if one could dramatically decrease the rate of gang activity and recruitment levels, one could slowly starve the gang out of existence by drying up the recruitment pool of eager young neophyte gangsters.

How can law enforcement confront this problem and reinforce the common citizen's belief in a lawful society? First, we must recognize that street gangs are identifiable groups that inflict more heinous and tragic crimes on society than most other identifiable groups. Local governments must acknowledge that street gangs are malignant entities and that, like any other malignancy, they must not be ignored. Gang activity may be contained and managed, but only through aggressive interaction between the community and law enforcement agencies.

Police/Community Programs

Law enforcement agencies have traditionally sponsored youth programs within the communities that they policed. These programs have assumed various formats involving either direct participation of police officers in daily program operations or some form of departmental oversight. Most traditional police/community programs were based on the Police Athletic League concept and were established by individuals within law enforcement agencies to provide alternative activities to at-risk youths in inner-city communities.

In recent years, other programs have evolved that place law enforcement officers in the classroom. Known by various acronyms such as SANE (Substance Abuse and Narcotic Education) or DARE (Drug Abuse Resistance Education), these programs are designed to educate youths about the consequences of drug abuse. Given the heavy influence of street gangs in the world of narcotics, many of these programs have introduced antigang modules into their lesson plans.

Quantifiable evidence of such programs' success is as yet difficult to obtain. Whereas other types of "student and the law" programs have been used for many years, these drug- and gang-specific programs are relatively recent. The prevention messages they deliver are designed to influence the elementary school student population over successive generations.

Traditional law enforcement approaches that involve arrest and incarceration generally are not associated with delinquency prevention programs. Nonetheless, experienced gang investigators believe that in the world of street gangs, where power and intimidation are part of the basic makeup of the gangster mystique, those traditional measures play a major role in the prevention, or deterrence, of gang violence.

Operation Safe Streets

One innovative law enforcement effort that has produced dramatic results from its inception is the Operation Safe Streets (OSS) program instituted by the Los Angeles County Sheriff's Department in 1979. This program, funded by a grant from California's Office of Criminal Justice Planning, funded 14 gang investigators to concentrate on gang-related crime and provide criminal intelligence.

These deputy sheriffs were divided into four teams, assigned to four sheriff's station areas that were suffering a tremendous amount of gang violence. Applying a targeting concept, each investigative team selected the most active gang in its area and concentrated its law enforcement efforts solely on the targeted gang and its members. The intent of such targeting was to help the department utilize limited personnel resources to address a growing gang problem. By selecting specific gangs rather than addressing the activity of all of the nearly 200 identified gangs in the Sheriff's Department's jurisdiction, the OSS teams were able to apply intense scrutiny to individual gang members.

Closely tied to the investigative and prosecutorial efforts of the OSS teams was an equally important component involving prosecutors devoted totally to the prosecution of gang-related cases. These prosecutors designed and implemented a system of vertical prosecution (see chapter 14 of this volume) that allowed the same prosecutor or team to handle the case from its inception to conviction and sentencing. Continuity and singleness of purpose were thus infused into the philosophy of gang prosecution, whereas previously little time or effort had been devoted to prosecuting gang-related cases because of the difficulties routinely encountered in such cases.

Another important initial ingredient of OSS was the early involvement of the Los Angeles County Probation Department. Members of gangs targeted by OSS were assigned to specific probation officers who were part of a specialized gang unit within the probation department. The specialized gang probation officers had reduced caseloads, which allowed them time to supervise their probationers intensively.

The result of the combination of these three vital elements of law enforcement —targeting, vertical prosecution, and intensive probation supervision—produced dramatic decreases in gang violence when directed at the targeted street gangs. Many of the gangs targeted early in the program showed a 50% decrease in overall activity.

Investigators were able to establish rapport with the gang members by maintaining consistent contact with the gangs. Frequently, this personal contact was not in an adversarial context and permitted amiable exchanges of information, or rap sessions, between the officers and the gang members. Such exchanges personalized the contact and penetrated the cloak of anonymity that the street gangs had so carefully woven, thus removing from the gang one of its most effective methods of neighborhood control. The investigators found that, as they applied firm but fair law enforcement and used their personal knowledge of the gang members backed by a demonstrated humanitarian concern for the status of the individual, violence within the targeted gangs began to decline.

Once the street gang members became known to the authorities, several unexpected results were obtained. The investigators themselves developed some empathy for the gang members through their more personal knowledge of these youths and their family circumstances. Scrutiny revealed that, in many cases, the dysfunctional family and the absolutely desperate societal conditions to which the gang member was subjected limited his ability to function in normal society. This knowledge moved the gang investigators to provide more than just police and investigatory services to the community. They began actively seeking educational and job placement programs, along with family counseling, that might fill the needs of the gang members.

The interaction of the officers with the community as a whole began to pay off with the development of a network of concerned citizens. The information exchanged between law enforcement and concerned citizens, along with information gleaned from rap sessions with gang members, contributed to an intelligence data base on gangs that enabled law enforcement to better combat the growing violence in the community.

The Operation Safe Streets program proved to be a viable and innovative tool for combating gang violence. It allowed good use of limited resources while producing a demonstrable reduction in crime rates within the targeted gang areas. The program's philosophy, involving the targeting concept and greater interaction between the Sheriff's Department and the community as a whole, has been emulated in various jurisdictions with similar results.

The OSS concept is not without limitations, but the limitations are imposed by the program originators. The main problems lie in personnel allocation, personnel selection, identification of areas to target, and administration of the unit rather than in actual daily police routine. The problems encountered can be minimized through the development of an implementation plan.

Police prevention programs, no matter what concept underlies them, must have substantial departmental and community support to be successful. If one element is missing, long-term success is impossible.

NOTES

[1] Research and consulting activities involving gangs and police organizations have included projects in Columbus and Cleveland, Ohio; Denver and Aurora, Colorado; Broward County (Fort Lauderdale area), Florida; Little Rock, Arkansas; and Honolulu, Hawaii.

[2] For more information concerning the GREAT system, contact Bob Foy, Director, Law Enforcement Communication Network, PO Box 3098, Torrance, CA 90510. Telephone: (213) 543-3195.

[3] For more information concerning the MAGIC system, contact Gary Killam, Davie (Florida) Police Department, 6901 Orange Drive, Davie, FL 33314 Telephone: (305) 797-1205.

[4] These practices were employed by the youth gang unit of the Columbus, Ohio, Division of Police during my field research.

[5] One of the most innovative truancy prevention programs (tied to gang prevention, as well) is operated jointly by the Honolulu Police Department and the Hawaii Department of Education. Students in 16 participating schools who miss 4 hours of school without an acceptable excuse are required to attend, along with their parents or guardians, a special half-day class the next Saturday. These classes are taught primarily by Honolulu Police Department officers who have been certified as substitute teachers. The classes focus on the relationship between truancy and delinquency, juvenile status laws, responsibilities of parents and children, academic and social skills, gang activities in metropolitan Honolulu, drug abuse and trafficking, and other topics in the general area of youth and the law. The program also offers

mediation services for students and their parents. Evaluative data thus far are generally positive concerning both general and specific deterrence, although students with chronic histories of truancy were not significantly helped by the program (Chesney-Lind et al., 1992). For additional information about the Honolulu Police Department's experience in implementing this program, contact David Del Rosario or Rodney Goo, Honolulu Police Department, 1455 South Beretania Street, Honolulu, HI 96814. Telephone: (808) 943-3201.

REFERENCES

Bordua, D. J., & Reiss, A. J., Jr. (1966). Command control and charisma: Reflections on police bureaucracy. *American Journal of Sociology, 72,* 68–76.

Brown, L. P. (1985). Police-community power sharing. In W. A. Geller (Ed.), *Police leadership in America.* New York: Praeger.

Burns, E., & Deakin, T. J. (1989). A new investigative approach to youth gangs. *FBI Law Enforcement Bulletin, 58*(10), 20–25.

Chesney-Lind, M. et al. (1992). *An evaluation of Act 189: Hawaii's response to youth gangs.* Honolulu: University of Hawaii at Manoa, Center for Youth Research.

Davis, R. C. (1985). Organizing the community for improved policing. In W. A. Geller (Ed.), *Police leadership in America.* New York: Praeger.

Fayol, H. (1930). *Industrial and general administration.* London: Pittman. (Original work published 1916)

Guyot, D. (1979). Bending granite: Attempts to change the rank structure of American police departments. *Journal of Police Science and Administration, 7,* 253–284.

Hagedorn, J. M. (1988). *People and folks: Gangs, crime and the underclass in a rustbelt city.* Chicago: Lake View.

Huff, C. R. (1989). Youth gangs and public policy. *Crime and Delinquency, 34,* 524–537.

Huff, C. R. (1990). *Gangs in America.* Newbury Park, CA: Sage.

Klein, M. W., Gordon, M. A., & Maxson, C. L. (1986). The impact of police investigations on police-reported rates of gang and nongang homicides. *Criminology, 24,* 489–512.

Kramer, L. C. (1986). *How will changes in the Asian population impact street gang–related crime in California?* Sacramento: California Commission on Peace Officer Standards and Training.

Needle, J. A., & Stapleton, W. V. (1983). *Police handling of youth gangs.* Washington, DC: National Institute of Justice.

Spergel, I. A., & Curry, G. D. (1990). *Survey of youth gang problems and programs in 45 cities and 6 sites* (National Youth Gang Suppression and Intervention Program). Washington, DC: U. S. Department of Justice, Office of Juvenile Justice and Delinquency Prevention.

Taylor, F. W. (1911). *The principles of scientific management.* New York: Harper.

Weber, M. (1946). *Essays in sociology* (H. H. Gerth & C. W. Mills, Eds. and Trans.). New York: Oxford University Press.

CHAPTER 14

Gang Prosecutions:
The Hardest Game in Town

Michael Genelin

The word *gang* brings shudders to the community and community law enforcement officials alike. Mention gangs and the media go wild, disseminating images of vicious young thugs roaming neighborhoods and preying on unsuspecting citizens. Certainly, gangs are dangerous. And granted, gangs are cause for public concern—particularly, law enforcement concern. But gang offenses can be dealt with, contained, policed, and prosecuted. The questions are, How do we deal with the gang issue in terms of both public awareness and police and prosecution concerns? How do we successfully identify, prosecute, and incarcerate the criminal gang member? and, How can we "partner" with the public to help us in this endeavor?

Gangs are a unique problem in prosecution. We know that multiple criminals acting with a singularity of purpose create greater problems than criminals acting alone. Conspiracies, or multiple felons acting together, have a larger, longer reach. We certainly know that group action can terrorize. At the street gang level, the use of gang colors, gang clothing, gang signs, graffiti plastered all over buildings, and the gang's willingness to use force can intimidate neighborhoods. The fact is that the "key responsibility for bringing . . . gang offenders to justice, protecting the community, and thereby serving its best interest, has been placed on the county prosecutor or district attorney in conjunction with the police officer" (Ehrensoft, 1990). The question then becomes, How do we exercise that responsibility?

One underlying problem concerns reluctance on the part of government authorities to confess that a gang crime issue exists. Acknowledging a problem might bring citizen protest or criticism and a possible challenge at the polls. However, research has revealed that gang members are more likely to commit a multitude of crimes—and commit them more often—than are non–gang members. And the more dedicated members are to the gang, the more hard-core, the more likely those gang members are to commit many more crimes (Fagan, 1990). Essentially, hard-core gang members are charged with 70% more offenses than other gang members (Klein, 1968). Before such individuals can be successfully identified and prosecuted, all of the agencies concerned must agree that an issue confronts them.

Only then may the extent of the gang threat in any given jurisdiction be determined and a systematic approach to gang intervention be undertaken.

With this goal in mind, there are three areas that you, as a public prosecutor, must consider: (a) development of a program within your office that is geared toward assessing and dealing with the local gang problem; (b) initiation and maintenance of interactive processes with other agencies, both public and private, to obtain intelligence, generate an ongoing assessment of the gang process, and provide mutual programmatic support; and (c) development of a prosecutor's outreach program that takes a proactive stance within the community to enhance gang suppression. A discussion of each of these approaches is in order.

INTERNAL PROSECUTION PROGRAMMING

Assess Your Program

Development of your internal prosecution program depends first upon an assessment of the prosecution process. The local police department is the agency that has first contact with gangs. Make sure that when the police agency comes in for a filing they identify gang members for you. Even the development of a simple form or box check on an intake sheet or filing data-process form is enough. Your follow-up is then essential. Track the case through the prosecution system so that you can observe the results. If you have a large number of gang members in prosecution you may wish to computerize the tracking. Once prosecution results are obtained, assess them. This assessment will allow you to determine exactly what resources you need to prosecute gang members successfully (e.g., How many gang prosecutors should you assign to this function? Will a simple policy adjustment do the job?). It will also tell you how successful the individuals who carry out your prosecutions are.

Set a Policy

An assessment of your program will help you determine a policy toward gang prosecution in your department. Following assessment, you may decide you do not need gang prosecutors per se. Or you may decide to assign permanent vertical gang prosecutors to do gang prosecutions. Possibly, you may persuade the judicial system to set up a special judge or court to deal with the problem. Considering the danger for repeat offenses with gang members, you may wish to authorize only maximum pleas on gang cases and demand maximum sentences. In any case, you will be required to determine how you are going to deal with gang members.

An example of a policy toward gang prosecutions can be taken from the Los Angeles County District Attorney's Office. The stated objective was to use every opportunity to remove gang members from the streets. This objective was achieved by identifying street gang members at the time of filing. Their gang membership was then used as an aggravating factor at the time of sentencing to minimize case settlements and aggressively seek maximum sentences.

On the basis of perceived public need, certain assumptions were made in promulgating the policy. It was assumed that gang members are more dangerous than typical individual criminals. It logically followed, then, that they should be incarcerated for as long as possible. This policy was to be followed with identified gang members *irrespective of whether the current offense was gang related*—even at the misdemeanor level. Four program stages were established: (a) the identification of a defendant as a member of a criminal street gang, (b) special guidelines for filing and case settlement, (c) advocacy for maximum custody at sentencing, and (d) a probation violation program for gang offenders. Every effort was made to keep the defendant in custody during the pendency of the case through the use of high bail. Further, if the defendant was convicted and placed on probation, special conditions of probation were instituted (i.e., the defendant could not associate with other members of the gang, was prohibited from wearing colors, was subject to search conditions).

The Los Angeles policy was based on an assessment of what gang members are and how the agency wanted to deal with them, as well as on an acknowledgment that there are not enough gang prosecutors in Los Angeles to prosecute all the gang members committing crimes. Through this strict approach to case settlement and sentencing postures, a tone for gang prosecutions for the entire office was set. The policy also served as a declaration for the courts and the public about what was needed in the gang prosecution and sentencing processes.

Establish a Gang Prosecution Group

A policy declaration, no matter how well followed, is generally not enough. Expertise, and its utilization, is the next step. Why? Because gang cases are unique. They require special prosecutors who have been trained in gang prosecution techniques and who can vertically prosecute gang members.

Vertical Prosecution

Vertical prosecution units have existed for some time. The career criminal units set up in the 1960s to prosecute violent recidivists had a similar rationale: The prosecutor who files a case, interviews the witnesses, and commences conserving and enhancing the evidence throughout the prosecution knows that case from the ground up. The expertise of this prosecutor, then, will maximize case results. For example, we know that gang members intimidate witnesses. A prosecutor's early rapport with these witnesses is essential to counter the fear factor. In addition, gang members speak street jargon (e.g., Caló) that a trained prosecutor can understand and use. Witness protection in gang cases is another consideration that requires the trained gang prosecutor's experience.

There are two types of vertical prosecution. One method involves individual prosecutors' taking a case from the beginning through sentencing. But unit vertical prosecution, where members of a gang-trained division pick up cases at a date after filing, can also be employed. Both methods are dependent upon trained prosecutors.

Trained Prosecutors

The trained prosecutor is more than an attorney who knows how to file a criminal case. There are special considerations in gang cases that he or she must be aware of and know how to handle. Although this chapter is not about filing and trial techniques, an examination of some factual and procedural processes in relation to gang cases should illustrate why gang knowledge is needed and why vertical prosecution by a trained attorney is essential.

Filing considerations

Are your witnesses fearful? Is there an actual threat that must be dealt with? How do you protect witnesses from a gang? Is residence relocation of a witness necessary? Does a witness have to be put in custody? Should witness statements be recorded? If statements are recorded, should audiotaping or videotaping be used? What techniques should be used in the taping process? Do you need to employ conditional testimony to preserve against possible flight or unavailability?

Proof considerations

How can the case be proved to be gang related? What do gang signs or graffiti mean? Can the gang member's guilt be proven? Can a gang expert be employed to explain to the jury about gang processes, gang mentality, or even the psychology of the specific gang member involved in the case?

Legal considerations

Were accomplices involved? If so, can their testimony be used? Must you give leniency to one gang member for his or her testimony? How far can the rules of conspiracy be taken in a gang case? How high can bail be set for a gang member? Do multiple gang members bring joinder problems? Are there accomplice corroboration issues? Can the involvement of a gang allow for the use of broader search warrants? How do you deal with witnesses who recant their testimony? How do you use "Green" evidence and hearsay to prove the gang member's guilt? (As established in *California v. Green,* 399 U. S. 149 (1970) evidence of a statement made by a witness previously is not made inadmissible by the hearsay rule if that statement is inconsistent with his or her testimony at trial.)

Courtroom security considerations

Will the gang try to intimidate witnesses in the courthouse? How do you secure the corridors and the courtroom? Should you establish a videotape protection process at the courtroom door? How do you stop the "hard looks" in court? How do you deal with gang members who are going to be called as defense witnesses?

Clearly, gang prosecution presents myriad problems for the prosecutor. As a result, a prosecutor familiar with gang cases and vertical prosecution techniques is absolutely essential for successful gang prosecution. An internal prosecution program that integrates experienced prosecutors with a well-thought-out policy process has made significant progress toward dealing with gangs.

INTERACTIVE PROCESSES WITH OTHER AGENCIES: LOS ANGELES COUNTY INTERAGENCY GANG TASK FORCE

Once your own agency is set up to deal with gangs, you can begin to network with other agencies to maximize gang intervention efforts in your community. The initial goal should be the establishment of an interagency task force. If the police, probation department, or any of the other agencies that should be concerned with gang problems deny that gangs exist in the community, you may be able to go no further. However, if these agencies can openly articulate a gang problem, they should be willing to interact on an ongoing basis to share problems, information, and potential solutions. An example, again, can be taken from a group currently in existence in Los Angeles—the Los Angeles Interagency Gang Task Force.

In 1980 gang violence in Los Angeles rose to new heights. The agencies concerned with gang suppression formed gang-specific units to target the problem: the District Attorney's Office formed its Hardcore Prosecution Division, the Sheriff's Department formed Operation Safe Streets, the Los Angeles Police Department formed its Community Resources Against Street Hoodlums (CRASH) Division, and the Probation Department formed high-intensity suppression units to supervise gang members. Division representatives from these groups decided to meet on an ongoing basis as the Los Angeles Interagency Gang Task Force. A permanent liaison was established with the schools, the Mayor's Office, the Department of Paroles, the Board of Supervisors, the Los Angeles City Attorney's Office, and other agencies. This group continues to meet once a month. Subgroups within the task force meet independently between the monthly meetings.

Through the years, the task force has evolved from being an interagency communication group to being proactive in its approach to gang violence. It has expanded its focus, producing yearly reports on the state of gangs within the county for the government and the public and making recommendations for the reformation of the juvenile justice system.

The task force also recognized a need for special training across agencies to deal with criminal street gangs. In an effort to address this need, task force members began mutual training processes—the Los Angeles County Sheriff's Department and Los Angeles Police Department now assist in training gang prosecutors, and experienced prosecutors reciprocate by training police at their academies. This type of interactive gang training is now carried forward on a statewide basis by the California District Attorney's Association.

The Gang Reporting Evaluation and Tracking Program

A concrete result of agencies' involvement in the task force has been the development of the Gang Reporting, Evaluation, and Tracking (GREAT) information system. All identified gang members in Los Angeles are logged into the program's computer, along with their known associates (homeboys), aliases, and family—virtually all the information on the individual pertinent to his or her gang membership and criminality. As a result of the GREAT program, police can immediately tap into a gang member's background. Prosecutors know exactly what type of defendant or defense witness is being called and can more clearly articulate how gang membership relates to the crime in question.

But what has this continuing consortium of gang-interested groups meant to the community? The task force recognized the alienation between police and the communities that they serve, so it strongly urged that law enforcement agencies in the county adopt community-based policy strategies within their jurisdictions. It also recognized the need for community mobilization and suggested that law enforcement agencies initiate and facilitate community gang prevention efforts as a means of reducing that alienation. This policy has led to the development of focused, reasoned responses targeted toward specific problem-solving efforts. A closer look is in order.

The Reduction of Street Violence Program

The Reduction of Street Violence Program (RSVP) approach was created as a result of planning suggested by the task force. In this particular case, a high-risk gang area was the focus. The police in this area interacted on a daily basis with local, nongovernmental gang-interested groups to determine where danger zones existed in the community. As a result of the information obtained, the police shifted more personnel to these areas. Extra patrols were also established in parks to provide community residents with safe havens. In addition, school antigang programs were developed and instituted in conjunction with antidrug programs such as DARE (Drug Abuse Resistance Education) and SANE (Substance Abuse Narcotics Education). Gang violence counselors and the police attempted to cool off gang animosities. The results of these cooperative efforts were that gang crime was suppressed to a significant degree.

The Case of East Los Angeles

Another example of how cooperation between agencies and communities can help in gang suppression and intervention is the case of East Los Angeles. In 1990 the number of gang-related crimes rose dramatically in the East Los Angeles area after having been under control for a long time. A local political action group requested law enforcement assistance. The Probation Department, the Los Angeles County Sheriff's Department, and the Los Angeles County District Attorney's Office brought their particular expertise to bear on the situation.

Initial discussions between the agencies and the community members revealed the following: Essentially, the local hard-core gang "veteranos" had been put in prison years before—and the gangs had gone dormant. However, now the veteranos were out and active again, urging renewed gang warfare. The result was that over 30 gang murders were committed in that area within less than a year. This crisis was exacerbated by recent large-scale immigration from Mexico and Central America. Some of these new arrivals were contesting the established groups for turf, again resulting in increased violence in the area.

The initial approach involved focusing on the prison returnees. A number of them were rearrested for new crimes. Gang members on probation were monitored more intensely—in fact, it was made clear to them that they were being closely watched because of their gang involvement. Additional gang community workers were brought into the area to monitor disputes. The Los Angeles County Sheriff's Department also brought in additional gang-focused deputies, particularly Gang Enforcement Teams (GETs), which were highly mobile and active in their gang contacts. The Los Angeles County District Attorney's Office contributed an added prosecutor to focus solely on the East Los Angeles arrests and prosecutions and to provide support to the police. Community action by local civilian antigang groups, such as antigraffiti efforts and antigang rallies, was supported. Finally, Street Terrorism Enforcement and Prevention Act procedures were initiated.

The Los Angeles County District Attorney's Office was one of the primary forces behind the passage, in 1989, of the Street Terrorism Enforcement and Prevention Act (STEP; 186.20 *et seq.* of the California Penal Code). Essentially, the statute declared that if (a) an individual actively participated in a criminal street gang, (b) had knowledge that the gang's members had engaged in a pattern of criminal activity (i.e., committed multiple crimes of murder, robbery, felonious assaults, etc.) over a 3-year period, and (c) that individual promoted felonious criminal conduct or assisted members of the gang in such conduct, then he or she was also guilty of a separate felony. There was a limitation on these sections: Prosecutors had to prove that gang members had knowledge that they were participating in a criminal street gang. However, that hurdle was overcome by the district attorney. The district attorney developed a notice that was printed by the District Attorney's Office and served to targeted gang members by police officers. This notice was written in both English and Spanish and informed the gang members that they were in a criminal street gang, why the gang had been designated a criminal street gang, and what the consequences of remaining in a criminal street gang were. After word got out, when gang members saw police officers approaching them they would run, knowing that otherwise they were going to be served. But the result of the measure is clear—gang crime in the targeted area has started to level off.

DEVELOPMENT OF A PROSECUTOR'S OUTREACH PROGRAM FOR GANG SUPPRESSION

Legal Interventions

We have already discussed the STEP Act. Clearly, it was devised to fit a prosecutorial need—gang suppression. Prosecutors' determination to write and enact the law stemmed from the perception that adequate tools were unavailable and had to be created. The perception was acted on by writing the statute, going to the legislature, explaining the need, and arguing for its enactment.

There are other similar examples of prosecutors' aggressive response to gang violence through the development of a law or ordinance. In one community, for example, two rival criminal street gangs were fighting for control of a park. As a result, community residents were afraid to use the park, virtually abandoning it to the gang members. Municipalities have a special interest in controlling their parks, parks being where their children play. It was apparent that this particular community was in an emergency situation. Residents had actually been shot in the crossfire of the two gangs. But the city was a small one with a tax base that made 24-hour patrolling an onerous financial burden. The solution was an ordinance, written to prevent criminal street gang members from entering the park. The ordinance was simple in form but complex in ramification.

The ordinance, like the STEP Act, indicated that it only applied to criminal street gangs, as defined within the statute. A gang member's entering the park was established as an infraction of the ordinance, meaning that the ordinance would be enforced through the serving of citations, much like a traffic ticket. Why just a citation? Because the objective was not to put more people in jail, but to tell gang members that law enforcement had put them under a microscope. The citation served as a warning that they were being watched. That first rung on the enforcement ladder to jail also involved a large chunk out of their pocketbooks. Early indications are that gang members now give the park a wide berth.

Nontraditional Interventions

Occasionally, prosecutorial agencies will have to act in a situation that traditionally falls within the purview of some other agency. For example, children who act out frequently and consistently in elementary or junior high school often become criminal. Truancy is, in fact, present in the history of a great number of criminal street gang members. But truancy is typically an issue for the schools. Although much depends on the particular jurisdiction, the district attorney in California found a way to attack the truancy problem.

California has a system of School Attendance Review Boards (SARBS). SARBS intervene when the school district identifies students with school attendance or school behavior problems. Although SARBS were giving advice and counseling, nothing being done was compelling enough to change students' behavior. The district attorney decided to step in.

In conjunction with the school district, the District Attorney Truancy Mediation Program was established. A hearing officer from the District Attorney's Office meets with the minor, the parent or guardian, and a school representative to try to resolve the truancy problem. If this effort fails, a deputy district attorney prepares a truancy petition and refers it to the probation department. The probation department then takes it to juvenile court. If it is determined that the parent is at fault for the truancy, a criminal complaint is prepared charging that parent. If both parent and child are at fault, a dual filing is made. The schools are now forced to take quick and decisive action on truants. Is this role outside the traditional jurisdiction of the district attorney? Of course, but this was a proactive response to an apparent hole in the system—a solution created to fit the need.

Community Interventions

People in a gang-threatened community become frightened that the justice system is breaking down. Prosecutorial, court, and police agencies may put a record number of defendants in jail, but if the public doesn't realize this fact they can become swept away by newspaper rhetoric or television hyperbole. The prosecutor can assist in controlling the hysteria or despair that this misapprehension causes. One solution is establishing a hot line.

In one such case, gang-trained paralegals operated a 24-hour hot line for giving advice to parents or inhabitants of gang neighborhoods and to gang members who might want out. The hot-line number was disseminated by donations of free, public service air time on television and radio stations. And the public did call in, making the hot line a rumor control network as well as a crime-related information exchange.

In another instance, prosecutors responded to public fears with a poster program. The District Attorney's Office of the community in question realized that information on how they and the police were dealing with the gang issue had to get out to the public. The public needed to know that the system was working. They developed a "Community Partnership" program. As part of the program, posters of gang members serving long sentences were distributed by police and placed on billboards, in post offices, in schools, and in parks. The gang members were pictured behind bars, with a large red-lettered stamp across their faces proclaiming them "convicted."

The poster program served to assure victims, witnesses, and the general community that the system was doing its job for them. It acted as a warning to gang members, particularly those from the convicted members' gangs, that law enforcement was keeping an eye on them. And finally, the poster program was a boost to the morale of the police agencies involved, who could point with pride to the job they were doing.

CONCLUSIONS

It is clear that a large range of options are available for the prosecutor dealing with gang crimes. Options can include providing support for victims of gang crimes and protection for witnesses; utilizing data-tracking systems, vertical prosecution techniques, and vertical prosecution divisions; interceding with the schools and communities; and passing special laws to deal with specific gang problems.

Assisting in the development of long-term, comprehensive, and coordinated strategies that include prevention and early intervention for youth at risk is not outside prosecutors' ambit. Developing fundamental reforms to the system, most particularly the juvenile justice system, is a necessary task. And supporting community mobilization or interacting with the public outside the court system may be prosecutors' new mission. In responding to law enforcement and community needs, prosecutors combining flexibility with a creative imagination can generate solutions to even such troubling criminal issues as those generated by criminal street gangs.

REFERENCES

Ehrensoft, K. (1990). *Prosecutor's model* (National Youth Gang Suppression and Intervention Program). Chicago: School of Social Service Administration.

Fagan, J. (1990). Social processes of delinquency and drug use among urban gangs. In C. R. Huff, *Gangs in America*. Newbury Park, CA: Sage.

Klein, M. W. (1968). *From association to guilt: The group guidance project in juvenile gang intervention*. Los Angeles: Youth Studies Center and the Los Angeles County Probation Department.

CHAPTER 15

Correctional Interventions

Elaine B. Duxbury

Over the last several decades, a great many contributions to the delinquency literature have addressed the problem of gangs. Most of this work has focused on the nature, scope, and development of gangs and on street intervention, primarily from a prevention perspective. Little of the gang literature has focused on interventions specifically targeted toward gangs and gang members in a correctional setting.

Until recently, juvenile correctional organizations typically did not consider gang problems a high priority for specific policies and programs. For example, they generally did not classify incoming juvenile offenders according to gang membership, had no staff charged with coordinating information about gangs, had no programs to address gang issues, and did not establish special field caseloads for the supervision of gang offenders. That situation has changed.

The changing nature of gangs has meant changes in the treatment of gang members in juvenile institutions and in field probation and parole. What has elevated the concern among youth correctional policymakers and practitioners has primarily been the increased amount and severity of gang violence, whose victims are gang members themselves, their families and friends, and others in the community. The role of drugs and the availability of weapons cannot be totally separated from the increase in gang violence.

A fundamental challenge facing youth corrections in formulating responses to gang problems is to individualize interventions according to the needs and the level of risk each offender brings to the correctional setting. This principle is consistent with good youth correctional policies. The 12-year-old wannabe who has committed a minor offense and been referred to probation for the first time clearly needs some other type of intervention than that provided for the late teen who has had several prior serious arrests, was engaged in drug trafficking, and has been committed to the state youth correctional agency for a drive-by shooting that resulted in murder. The challenge for corrections professionals is to provide appropriate supervision and services for youths who are on the periphery of gang membership, for those who are hard-core gang members with chronic violent offense patterns, and for the substantial numbers who are somewhere in between.

In addition to interventions that are individually tailored to the extent possible, good youth correctional policies need to be applied whether or not the program population consists primarily of gang members. In either case, issues of institutional and field supervision and of training and treatment programs must be addressed with vigor.

Most of the policies and programs described in this chapter have not undergone extensive evaluative research. Their merits at this time are based primarily on the experiences of the policymakers and practitioners who have lived with the problems and solutions on a day-to-day basis. This chapter focuses on street gangs—on youth gangs. It does not deal with prison gangs, although the latter are no longer an entirely separate issue in some jurisdictions.

The chapter first considers coordination, cooperation, and communication among various elements of the criminal justice system—primarily between law enforcement and corrections—then looks at the management of detention facilities and longer term institutions. Some examples of institutional programs for gang-involved offenders are presented, and probation and parole alternatives are examined. The chapter concludes with a discussion of prevention issues as they relate to correctional organizations and a set of recommendations for correctional interventions with gang members.

COORDINATION, COOPERATION, AND COMMUNICATION

Although the focus here is on correctional interventions, the problem of gang-related offenses, especially violent ones, must be dealt with from a broader perspective. A comprehensive systems approach is needed and requires close coordination with prevention and law enforcement efforts. Coordination of policies among community organizations, schools, the criminal justice system, and all other groups with an interest in reducing gang problems and promoting healthy, legal youth development are more likely to produce effective results than are efforts that are fragmented and perhaps even contradictory.

A youth correctional agency may have departmental or institutional gang coordinators charged with gathering information inside and outside the facility and communicating regularly with law enforcement about gang activity in the community. These gang coordinators may participate in community gang task forces or networks to exchange information. With their knowledge of the nature and etiology of gangs, and with up-to-date information about gang activity, the coordinators can be valuable resources for policymakers and for institutional and field supervision staff who work directly with gang youths. Gang coordinators may also be responsible for files containing gang information and for automated data systems concerning gangs, if these are separated from the agency's other offender information for security reasons. Possible categories of gang information are discussed in the following section.

MANAGEMENT ISSUES

Aspects of management in youth correctional institutions where gang members are present or gang activity creates problems include intake and classification, orientation, and ongoing institutional management.

Intake and Classification

In intake units at detention facilities and in reception units for longer term incarceration, incoming youths need to be classified for risks and needs, gang identification, and program assignment. Accurate classification can lead to a living and working environment that is safer for staff and youths and is more conducive to the training and treatment of young offenders, whether gang members or not.

Gang offenders, like all youths who enter detention or incarceration, bring with them an array of personal characteristics, including the risks they pose to themselves and others and the skill and behavior deficits that need remediation. Identifying these risks and needs early in the detention process is important in the short run for the safe functioning of the institution and the safety of each youth. Assessing each youth's risks and needs in more detail—and addressing these factors through programs—is important over the course of correctional intervention if the young person is to develop into a contributing, law-abiding young adult. All this requires a system for objectively classifying individual risks and needs at intake and again periodically throughout the youth's institutional stay and period of field supervision.

All incoming youths, gang members or not, need to be assessed and objectively classified for escape risk, suicide risk, and risk of violence. Classification of needs may concern such factors as educational skills and level (both academic and vocational), drug and alcohol abuse, mental health problems, other health problems, and maturity and social skill levels.

When a young offender entering a detention facility or other youth correctional institution has risks or needs related to gang membership, identifying and classifying gang-related characteristics becomes another essential component of intake. In developing a gang identification process, a youth correctional facility or department can benefit from the combined knowledge of gang researchers, practitioners who have developed similar systems, and participants in geographical gang networks, discussed earlier.

An essential early step is to clarify the purpose of the gang information and classification system. A clear purpose will be a good indicator of the types of data that should be gathered, how and where the information should be stored and updated, and who should have access to it. One agency identified the purpose of its classification process thus: "To develop a legally defensible system of identifying, classifying and tracking gang oriented youth in the juvenile justice system, as well as to identify the degree of commitment of youth to the gang ideology" (California Department of the Youth Authority, 1985).

Gang designations or groupings, rivalries, structures, and types of membership may all be important elements in classification. Among gang researchers, for example, Spergel and Curry (1988) note that typologies or classifications of gangs abound in the gang literature and in the operational manuals of law enforcement agencies. They describe how street gangs have been classified as organized vertically along age lines (e.g., within a neighborhood) or horizontally in separate groups with similar names or traditions, transcending geographic boundaries. Elsewhere, Spergel (1990) describes the types of gang members, such as core members (including leaders) and peripheral or fringe members.

To avoid overclassification of gangs and gang members, a facility needs clear criteria for starting an individual gang file on an incoming offender. Criteria for identifying a youth as being affiliated with a gang may include the following:

- Self-admission

- Presence of tattoos

- Gang-related commitment offense

- Prior record of gang-related offenses

- Involvement in gang-related incidents during incarceration, probation, or parole

- Prior law enforcement contact

- Information from legal documents

- Reports from staff or other agencies

- Reports from inmate informants

- Association with known gang members

- Family background

- Status as victim/enemy of another gang

- Possession of identifiable gang paraphernalia

- Possession of photos showing gang insignia or known gang members

- Possession of written material such as enemy lists or organizational plans

Self-report through intake interviews conducted by trained staff has been demonstrated to yield full and fairly accurate responses. A direct question—"Are you a member of a gang?"—may produce a false low affirmative response rate. But staff have found that giving the incoming young offender a questionnaire to complete in a confidential setting usually results in information that can be corroborated elsewhere. Confirming self-admission with information from another source can prevent manipulation of the classification system.

A questionnaire used by the California Department of the Youth Authority (see Figure 15.1) asks the youth to circle the gang affiliation he or she claims (e.g., Northern or Southern Hispanic, Crip, Blood, Supreme White Power, Skinhead, or other—including various Asian gangs). Next the young person is asked to name the group or "set" and specify its location. Gang status, such as leader, associate, member, or potential victim, is also elicited. The youth is asked to identify his or her best friend, as well as rival gangs or groups. The questionnaire asks about victimization of family or friends ("Has anything happened to members of your family or your friends as a result of *your* gang activities?"), although victimization of others is not mentioned at this point. Victimization of all kinds of people is addressed during institutional programming. An item asking the young person to write the gang name in his or her own style and handwriting provides another measure of self-admission. The incoming offender is also asked to note tattoos and their location on the body. The youth is also asked to identify the commitment offense and explain whether it was gang related. Finally, there is an opportunity for the offender to claim that he or she has discontinued gang activity.

Information from the intake interview, accompanied by other measures of gang affiliation and status, may be used in the determination of program assignment and may then be entered in an automated gang information system. An accurate knowledge of current gang affiliations and rivalries is important in making unit and other assignments. When rivalries are active and violent, attention must be paid to the balance of power among groups. In extreme instances, protective custody may be necessary.

Orientation

The first step in educating young offenders about institutional gang policies is providing orientation to the detention or longer term facility. Orientation provides an early opportunity to spell out for new arrivals what kinds of clothing are acceptable and the manner in which they can be worn. (Rapid changes in gang fashions also require information from knowledgeable gang coordinators.) Staff must make clear what constitutes contraband. For example, items created in woodworking shop or in arts and crafts classes may be prohibited from bearing gang symbols.

Another important concern in orientation is behavior that identifies an incarcerated youth as a gang member or that rival gang members perceive as a threat. Using hand signals or gang language, walking in a gang-identified manner, and defacing public property with graffiti are all matters to be addressed during orientation. Rules about gang-related visitors and mail must be laid out as well.

Although the foregoing elements of orientation concern behavior that is prohibited for the young offender, the underlying purpose of the prohibitions is to create an institutional climate that is safe and in which new, nongang behaviors can be learned and practiced.

Figure 15.1 California Department of the Youth Authority Confidential Gang Data Sheet

Name: _____ YA # or M #:_____

Birthday: _____ Race:_____ Court: Juvenile _____
                                                          Superior _____

Home Address: _____ City: _____

Have you been in the Youth Authority before? _____ If so, where? _____

Have you been on parole before? _____ If so, where? _____

Circle which you claim: North South Crip Blood SWP Skins Other _____

Name of group/gang/set/clique: _____

Where is your group/gang located? (Street and city) _____

Circle gang status: Leader Associate Member Potential victim

Name of your best friend/road dog: _____

Rival gangs/groups/enemies: _____

Has anything happened to members of your family or your friends as a result of *your* gang activities? _____ Yes _____ No

Write your gang name/placa/hit up your set and nickname:

Write down your tattoos and location on your body: _____

Commitment offense: _____

Was your commitment offense gang related? *(Explain)* _____

_____ Ward claims he or she discontinued gang activity.

Sign your name

Signature of interviewer   Date

Ongoing Institutional Management

The degree to which gang members provocatively demonstrate gang membership while in the institution depends on the institution's policies and how well they are administered. Permitted and prohibited behaviors are determined not only by the institution's formal policies, manuals, and standards. It is also crucial that managers provide effective leadership in this area and that staff be trained and motivated to implement the policies in ways that promote both institutional safety and individual dignity and self-respect among young offenders. A positive environment for learning and growth requires consistent, respectful application of institutional policies.

Institutional gang coordinators, thorough their specialized knowledge, can help to maintain a prosocial environment. Their contributions may include analyzing patterns of contraband, providing ongoing staff training, and maintaining systematic records of gang incidents (threats, fights, etc.).

POSITIVE PROGRAMMING FOR YOUNG OFFENDERS

Fundamental to effective intervention with gang members is a sound program for all young offenders detained or incarcerated—one that develops skills and self-esteem while addressing mental and physical health problems. Building on this foundation, an institution can introduce preventive and remedial gang programs.

An example of effective programming is a gang awareness curriculum used throughout the California Department of the Youth Authority with variations from institution to institution to adapt for age and other characteristics of the offenders. One of the institutional gang awareness programs is that developed and taught by John Berge at the Youth Training School in Chino. His GANGS Program (Gang Awareness Necessary for Growth in Society) is a voluntary, 2-week program youths may join toward the end of the institutional stay. Incarcerated offenders are recruited by word of mouth and an occasional newsletter. The first newsletter to prospective students, as Berge prefers to call them, begins, "You have worth!!!" Briefly and clearly, it tells the prospective students about self-esteem, dreams, and resources available to them and describes the GANGS class.

The purpose of the program is identified this way:

> During a two-week period the student will gain an overview of
> gangs and how gangs negatively impact the community. The stu-
> dent will learn the negative impact of gang involvement in his own
> life, and the effects on his family. The student will learn to identify
> and seek out alternatives to involvement in the gang-active sub-
> culture. (Heman G. Stark Youth Training School, n.d.)

In the program application, prospective students are told that nobody is "fronted off" (confronted or humiliated) in the GANGS class and urged to turn the negative experience of being locked up into a positive start for a successful future.

Specifically, the program includes 10 elements:

1. Orientation and expectations of participants

2. Overview of the GANGS program

3. Parole and the gang-active person

4. Effects of gang violence

5. Legal aspects of gang involvement

6. Coping, responsibility, accountability

7. Family, community expectations

8. Peer expectations

9. Cultural expectations

10. Individual/personal expectations

Students admitted to the program sign a contract to respect their peers and guests and to participate fully in assignments and classroom interaction. They take a pretest on their knowledge of gangs. During the 2 weeks of the program students keep a journal, responding to such questions as these:

- Who has more control over your life: family, yourself, homies? Explain why.

- I know my family cares for me because . . .

- List two positive results of gang involvement.

- Innocent victims are being assaulted almost daily by gang activity. The general response is: "Hey, they got in the way." Describe how you would feel if a family member were a victim of gang activity.

Documentary films and videos portraying gang activity are shown and discussed. Students develop a personal resource guide for use when they are paroled; in developing the guide, they look up and record the names and addresses of persons or organizations to turn to for job referrals or community services assistance on their release. These resources supplement other job and survival skills that they learn throughout their institutional stay. At the end of the program, students receive a certificate of completion and take with them the resource guide they have developed.

Other gang awareness programs in the California Department of the Youth Authority have similar curricula. Often, role-playing exercises are used to teach young offenders about the feelings of grief, the value of trust, the impact of gangs on the family unit, and other realities. One exercise, focusing on the costs of gang involvement, asks participants to identify the costs for them, their families, and the community. They estimate costs in these areas:

* Me (time, injuries, loss of homeboys, jobs, fear, etc.)
* My family (pain, influence on younger siblings, financial cost)
* Community (victimization of innocent people, graffiti, loss of jobs, higher insurance rates, lower property values)

Finally, participants ask themselves, "What did I get out of being in a gang?"

Another exercise, entitled "If I had six months to live," is designed to increase awareness of the reality of death and to help prioritize personal values. The leader encourages participants to be explicit, accepts their statements, refrains from judging, and discusses what the choices are. An additional exercise invites participants to compose their own obituaries.

The merits of these programs have been assessed by observation and by the evaluations of the participants. Empirical evidence of their effectiveness is limited because they have not been evaluated objectively. Nevertheless, they attempt to meet the real and immediate need to address the gang issues faced by many young offenders of all ethnicities.

PROBATION AND PAROLE ALTERNATIVES

Gang issues related to field supervision include caseload designations, conditions of probation or parole, and placement. Like other correctional matters, classification of young offenders according to their risks and needs—including classification by gang affiliation and status—is a fundamental part of managing resources, enhancing public safety, and fostering positive outcomes.

Some youth correctional departments have addressed field supervision of gang members by creating separate or special caseloads. This practice enables field staff to apply specialized knowledge to their case supervision. Special caseloads, entailing, for instance, fewer cases and intensive supervision, allow for a concentration of service and surveillance resources on gang members who can benefit most from it.

Gang-related conditions of probation or parole may include special restrictions on gang-affiliated contraband or on association with gang members. Because many youthful offenders return to their former neighborhoods, a prohibition against association with "homeboys" may not be realistic for offenders living in areas where most neighborhood youths participate in gang activities. One alternative may be out-of-home placement in another area. Although some practitioners advocate out-of-home placement as a method of disengaging some youthful offenders from local gang activities, others express concern that it may merely encourage the spread of gang activity. On a limited basis, residential programs such as the CASA program, operated by the California Department of the Youth Authority in San Diego, have provided opportunities for a small number of youthful offenders who have expressed a desire to abandon gang activity to do so away from their former neighborhoods.

Electronic monitoring has been anecdotally reported as useful to some youths attempting to discontinue their gang activities. Some young people on field supervision have expressed a wish to begin or continue electronic monitoring so that they have an excuse when their friends urge them to join in gangbanging. As yet, researchers have evaluated few of these methods empirically to determine what constitutes effective field supervision for gang-involved offenders.

PREVENTION ISSUES

Although the main tasks of correctional intervention are the supervision, training, and treatment of young offenders, correctional organizations also have a responsibility to ensure that gang prevention policies and programs are in place. They may do so through policy coordination with other organizations, through provision of seed money, or through direct operation of prevention programs.

One example of the latter is the Gang Violence Reduction Project, operated since the mid-1970s in East Los Angeles by the California Department of the Youth Authority (Torres, 1985). This prevention program employs gang members to mediate between gangs whose rivalries may result in violence. The gang member–workers also develop and supervise a variety of preventive recreational and other activities for younger siblings and current gang members.

Correctional practitioners may also be catalytic in bringing together community representatives to provide information and a forum for action when the community is in denial about an emerging gang problem. Correctional representatives may offer their leadership in sharing information, dispelling rumors, and planning a strategy for preventing additional violence in a crisis situation. Their skills and experience in working with young people in trouble, gang members or not, can help a community orient its gang members and other youths in constructive directions.

RECOMMENDATIONS

The following are recommendations for intervention with gang members in correctional settings:

1. Correctional policies and program directed toward youth gangs and gang members should be coordinated with those of organizations engaged in prevention and suppression within a community or governmental jurisdiction. Curry and Spergel (1988) note that community organization and provision of social opportunity in conjunction with suppression may be more effective responses to youth gang problems than suppression and incapacitation alone.

Coordinated interventions by youth correctional organizations and other service providers offer the most promise of a consistent approach to gang problems and the related social problems that give rise to gangs and that gang crimes in turn exacerbate.

2. More systematic research should be conducted on correctional interventions with youth gang members.

3. Individual correctional interventions should be based on objective classification of the gang member's risks and needs, including those related to gang participation.

4. Institutional policies should create a climate in which youths may relinquish gang membership if they choose and in which nonmembers feel no need to join for protection.

5. Institutional programs should offer young people opportunities to develop their skills and knowledge so that, upon release, they will have the tools and self-esteem to choose activities other than participation in illegal gang activities.

6. Field supervision programs should provide transitional services and, when appropriate, adequate surveillance to increase the likelihood that the released youthful offender can make socially responsible choices.

REFERENCES

California Department of the Youth Authority. (1985). *Classification of youthful gang members in local detention facilities* (Proceedings of the Transfer of Knowledge Workshop, September 1–12, 1985, Fresno). Sacramento: Author.

Curry, G. D., and Spergel, I. A. (1988). Gang homicide, delinquency and community. *Criminology, 26,* 381-405.

Heman G. Stark Youth Training School. (n.d.). *Gang awareness necessary for growth in society.* Chino: California Department of the Youth Authority.

Spergel, I. A. (1990). Youth gangs: Continuity and change. In M. Tonry & N. Morris (Eds.), *Crime and justice: A review of research* (Vol. 12). University of Chicago Press.

Spergel, I. A., & Curry, G. D. (1988). *Socialization to gangs: Baseline preliminary report.* Unpublished manuscript, University of Chicago.

Torres, D. M. (1985). *Gang violence reduction project: Update.* Sacramento: California Department of the Youth Authority.

PART V

Special Intervention Parameters

CHAPTER 16

Cultural Sensitivity
and Gang Intervention

Fernando I. Soriano

Although gangs have existed for decades, there is increasing concern over their proliferation and their involvement in violence (Huff, 1990; Goldstein, 1991). For example, in 1988 Los Angeles County recorded 452 gang-related homicides, which represented a 16.8 % increase over the previous year's figure (Genelin & Coplen, 1989). Gangs are not a regional problem nor even strictly an urban phenomenon, a fact made most evident in a recent national survey by Spergel et al. (1990). This survey showed gangs to be present in almost all 50 states, including Alaska and Hawaii, as well as in Puerto Rico and in other U. S. territories. This same survey produced estimates of well over 1,439 gangs and 120,636 gang members in the cities surveyed. What this survey and earlier surveys (Miller, 1974; Needle & Stapleton, 1982) have consistently found is a disproportionate number of ethnic minorities in gangs. In this chapter, the term *minority groups* is used; traditionally, the term has referred to numerical presence. However, in many regions of the United States, those we call ethnic minorities will soon become majorities owing to their numerical increases, concomitant with decreases in the Anglo-Saxon population.

Estimates are that well over two-thirds of gang members represent ethnic minorities (Spergel & Curry, 1990). Numerically, the majority of gangs are either African American or Hispanic, although white non-Hispanic gangs, such as skinhead and neo-Nazi gangs, are believed to be increasing significantly. According to Spergel et al. (1990), over half (approximately 55 %) of gang members are African American and another third, or 33 %, are Hispanic. Although these figures may in fact reflect law enforcement's disproportionate focus on and adjudication of ethnic minority youths (Mirande, 1987) along with an undercount of white non-Hispanic youth, they nevertheless point to undeniable gang problems facing ethnic communities throughout the United States.

The assistance of Ms. Karen Seratti and Ms. Sandy Soriano in the preparation of this manuscript is gratefully acknowledged. Ms. Seratti assisted in gathering much of the literature, while Ms. Soriano reviewed earlier drafts of this manuscript.

Accompanying the growing concern over youth participation in gangs has been increased interest in the development of effective prevention and intervention efforts to curtail both the numerical increases and the violence associated with youth gangs. Several chapters in this book describe promising gang intervention efforts; however, little is written anywhere about the need to take cultural context into account in the development of gang or substance abuse programs. Many social scientists would agree that for any gang prevention or intervention project to be successful, it must be culturally sensitive and relevant to the ethnic groups it seeks to address (Soriano & De La Rosa, 1990).

But what does it mean for an intervention or prevention effort to be culturally sensitive or relevant? Some would argue that it means the presence of program staff who can communicate linguistically with targeted ethnic groups, such as Hispanic or Asian youths. Others would hold that cultural sensitivity entails an effort to staff programs with minorities, either exclusively or at least substantially. Still others would suggest that, to be culturally sensitive, project staff must acquire considerable knowledge of and familiarity with a particular cultural group or groups. Many community-based programs are making efforts to become culturally sensitive in one or more of these ways.

Generally, however, much of the literature on cultural sensitivity is found in counseling fields. Literature proposing programmatic accommodation to the uniqueness of cultural groups reached its apex in the later 1960s and continued through the 1970s (Glick & Moore, 1990). Before that era, ethnic groups were, by and large, viewed as "culturally deprived" or "culturally disadvantaged." Social, educational, and economic problems facing minorities were believed to be tied to specific cultural values or traits that hampered upward mobility and success. An early statement by Heller (1966) illustrates this type of thinking as applied to Mexican Americans:

> The kind of socialization that Mexican American children
> generally receive at home is not conducive to the development
> of the capacities needed for advancement . . . by stressing values
> that hinder mobility—family ties, honor, masculinity, and living
> in the present—and by neglecting the values that are conducive
> to it—achievement, independence, and deferred gratification.
> (pp. 34–35)

Unlike their predecessors, however, contemporary social scientists acknowledge the need to appreciate and incorporate salient cultural values and worldviews in community and individual interventions that involve ethnic minorities. Efforts to meet this need and make interventions culturally sensitive have focused on a variety of factors believed to foster cultural sensitivity in program personnel, such as language, cultural background, experience, training, and knowledge.

All too often, representatives of intervention programs believe they can meet cultural sensitivity requirements through very simple program accommodations, such as the hiring of street workers who are bilingual or who share the ethnicity or race of gang members. However, cultural sensitivity is a very complex issue requiring more serious examination and treatment. Although most program representatives acknowledge the importance of cultural sensitivity in intervention or prevention efforts, few understand the numerous factors that make a program culturally sensitive.

The objectives of this chapter are threefold: first, to offer a critical review of commonly accepted operational approaches to cultural sensitivity; second, to propose a definition of cultural sensitivity based on an existing tridimensional approach that focuses on building self-awareness, cultural knowledge, and interpersonal skill; and, finally, to advocate that individual youths' multiple social roles and identities be understood and taken into consideration in community intervention efforts targeting ethnic minority gangs.

COMMON INDICATORS OF CULTURAL SENSITIVITY

The following definition of *cultural sensitivity* emerges from the literature reviewed in this chapter:

> Cultural sensitivity refers to a person's or a program's objective understanding, appraisal, appreciation, and knowledge of a particular cultural group that is used equitably in behavioral dispositions toward members of that group. Cultural sensitivity is developed through self-awareness, elimination of stereotypes and unfounded views, and acquisition of objective knowledge about and actual interaction with members of a particular cultural group in question.

This definition encompasses many commonly used indicators of cultural sensitivity, such as linguistic capability, ethnic background, social science training, cultural knowledge, and background experience of program staff members. Ethnic minority community prevention and intervention programs have often relied on these characteristics, singly or in combination, to develop cultural sensitivity. Following is a discussion of the value and role of each major factor in the development of cultural sensitivity.

Linguistic and Behavioral Communication

Like all community-based programs, gang intervention efforts require clear and effective communication with their potential clients. Communication is accomplished both verbally, through language, and behaviorally, through gestures and body movements. Both verbal and behavioral communication are extremely important in conveying clear programmatic expectations and in developing trust and rapport with gang members.

Verbal communication is an obvious yet often overlooked barrier to the development of culturally sensitive intervention programs. Program personnel must understand the targeted group's language if they are to develop the kinds of interpersonal relationships necessary for effective gang intervention. This necessity has led many social scientists to agree with Grove (1976) that "language barriers may be the most easily surmounted of the many impediments blocking communications across cultures" (p. 10).

The benefits of effective communication are clear. In a recent study concerning communication and common understanding between physicians and monolingual, Spanish-speaking elderly patients, Seijo, Gomez, and Freidenberg (1991) found that Hispanic patients had better recall of medical information and asked more questions with bilingual doctors than they did with monolingual, English-speaking doctors. Similarly, when staff members lack appropriate language capability, gang intervention projects unwittingly but systematically exclude from meaningful participation such minority subgroups as monolingual, non-English-speaking Asians, Caribbeans, and Hispanics. Moreover, even relationships with African Americans are affected by communication problems (e.g., when "Black English" is used; Blake, 1987).

It is important to keep in mind, however, that a staff member's ability to speak a targeted group's language or a gang member's ability to speak English does not necessarily preclude the emergence of communication problems that can lead to misunderstandings and distrust. Effective communication entails more than just sharing the same language. It involves applying the same meaning to either verbal or nonverbal behavior. Thus, two Hispanics fluent in Spanish can misunderstand each other because they attach different meanings to the same words or actions. A comical but daunting incident illustrates this problem. A man from Puerto Rico once asked his Cuban girlfriend for her "pepita" in a bus crowded with the girlfriend's relatives. A physical attack on the man was averted by a knowledgeable and understanding rider, who quickly explained to the angry crowd that a "pepita" in Puerto Rico refers to a fruit seed and not to the woman's vagina, as Cubans commonly understand it! The hapless man simply wanted to help his girlfriend discard her litter.

Grove (1976) has reported that speech is responsible for only about 35% of all communication in face-to-face interactions. This percentage shrinks even further when one considers communication across cultures and, particularly, communication with gang members who often use their own slang. Vigil (1988) and others suggest that gang members develop their own language—called "Spanglish" or "Caló" for Hispanics, and "Black English" for African Americans (Blake, 1987). These variants of mainstream languages, in this case of English and Spanish, are often compared to a particular middle-class linguistic standard, leading to misunderstandings and mistrust.

Sue and Sue (1977) have called attention to problems that arise when human service providers, such as counselors, expect clients from lower income groups to use standard English. According to these observers, the use and expectation of standard English in human service programs can lead to discrimination against ethnic minorities and create an inaccurate impression that "minorities are inferior, lack awareness, or lack conceptual thinking powers" (p. 422). The authors point to key differences between the standard English of the middle class and the languages of major ethnic groups. Middle-class standard English tends to center on verbal expressions of feelings and behaviors, whereas communication among lower class minorities relies more on nonverbal communication.

According to Sue and Sue (1977), the lower class African American tends to use black street language, which stresses nonverbal communication involving "a great deal of implicitness in communication, such as shorter sentences and less grammatical elaboration" (p. 422). Similarly, lower class Chicanos and Hispanics tend to employ nonverbal communication along with Spanish. Like Hispanics, Asians rely on their native languages, and they often use silence as an expression of respect and deference. Hispanics and Asians share a preference for one-way communication, from an authority figure to the individual in question. Many Native Americans share these characteristics, but in addition tend to be creative, experiential, intuitive, and nonverbal (Sue & Sue, 1977).

In general, effective communication requires that gang intervention workers and researchers not only understand the dominant language and the linguistic preferences and nuances of a particular cultural subgroup, but also pay particular attention to nonverbal behaviors and cues. Because most communication is nonverbal, gang workers need to become versed in the meaning and appropriate use of such nonverbal communication forms as eye contact, physical distance, and the like. The combination of effective verbal and nonverbal communication will result in interpersonal communication that engenders respect, confidence, and trust.

Ethnic Background of Program Staff

Community programs are frequently believed to be culturally relevant and sensitive if they include staff who are of the same cultural background, ethnicity, or race as those being targeted. Unfortunately, this tenuous assumption is perhaps one of the least challenged. I call it the "ethnic homogeneity assumption" because it is based on the notion that all members of an ethnic group come from the same background and have common experiences, attitudes, values, norms, beliefs, and expectations.

Undeniably, there is a somewhat higher probability of shared cultural values and norms among people of similar ethnicity. Likewise, it is probable that many members of an ethnic minority group will be particularly sensitive to and understanding of the feelings associated with discrimination and the sense of helplessness and frustration. At one level, common ethnicity or race does facilitate quick establishment of rapport (Gim, Atkinson, & Kim, 1991). However, the initial rapport due to commonality of background can quickly turn to mistrust if a program worker lacks the sensitivity and understanding that come from knowledge and experience. The mere presence of minority members within an intervention program does not in itself result in a program that is culturally sensitive.

There are other reasons why the presence of minority group members does not guarantee cultural sensitivity of a program. First, even assuming that a program does have workers who represent the targeted ethnic group and are culturally sensitive as well, there is no assurance that the program itself, including objectives and materials, is culturally sensitive or relevant. Further, those workers may not have the decision-making power to steer the program's efforts in a culturally sensitive and relevant direction.

Assuming that both ethnic minority and nonminority staff members possess cultural sensitivity, the question remains: Is it still important that program staff be of the same ethnicity or race as members of the targeted group? The accumulating literature on psychotherapeutic outcomes based on culture pairing suggests that there are negligible differences, whether the therapist is white or is of the same minority ethnicity as the client (see Sue, 1988, for a comprehensive review of this literature). Instead, the research suggests that treatment success depends on the therapist's communication skills (verbal and otherwise), sensitivity, and understanding of the client's values, life-style, and background (Casas, 1985; Jenkins, 1985; Leong, 1986; Sue, 1988; Sue, Wagner, Ja, Margullis, & Lew, 1976; Trimble & LaFromboise, 1985). Furthermore, a recent study by Wade and Bernstein (1991) suggests that ethnic minorities themselves, such as African Americans, can benefit from cultural sensitivity training. This study revealed that experienced African American counselors completing cultural sensitivity training gained credibility, returned for more follow-up sessions, and experienced more satisfaction when compared with equally experienced African American counselors not undertaking the training.

According to Miller (1990), overemphasis on the cultural background of gang community workers excludes from consideration an existing pool of culturally sensitive non-ethnic-minority individuals, who can be just as effective as minorities. This view has much empirical support. However, there is a critical caveat: Workers from the majority culture need appropriate communication and linguistic skills, knowledge of the minority culture, and skill and experience in serving members of the ethnic group in question. Moreover, in working with ethnic gangs, members of ethnic minorities have an initial advantage in that similarity in physical characteristics leads gang members to assume greater commonality in background than may be the case. This assumed commonality can facilitate quick establishment of rapport. In addition, members of minorities are more likely than nonminorities to have past experiences (e.g., of poverty and discrimination) that would foster critical empathy with the target population.

In summary, ethnicity in common with gang members facilitates rapport but is not essential to an intervention program worker's effectiveness. Hence, paired ethnicity does not ensure cultural sensitivity. More important than cultural background are understanding, appreciation, and respect toward the culture and the individual. Nevertheless, paired ethnicity does confer up-front advantages, which facilitate the establishment of credibility and rapport (Jankowski, 1991).

Although a shared ethnic background may not be essential for developing cultural sensitivity, cultural training is widely acknowledged as important. There are varied perceptions of what constitutes appropriate cultural sensitivity training, ranging from general preparation in the social sciences to more specialized training. Let us consider more closely and critically this range of cultural training, including assumptions and implications. We will start with an infrequently mentioned assumption that training in the social sciences is sufficient for developing cultural sensitivity.

Social Science Training

Directors of community-based programs can believe they are satisfying the cultural sensitivity requirement simply by hiring staff with training in the social sciences. They assume that social science training prepares a person to respond to the full range of social and cultural diversity found in society. This assumption is similar to the misconception common among laypersons that all psychologists are equally trained in therapy and psychopathology.

Most social scientists would agree that traditional social science training in and of itself does not automatically impart cultural knowledge or sensitivity vis-à-vis minority groups. In fact, it is the admitted potential lack of sensitivity that has led editors of many professional social science journals to provide for "blind" peer review of manuscripts. Blind reviews keep authors' names confidential, thereby reducing the likelihood of bias or disparity triggered by names associated with particular ethnic groups.

Currently, there is growing recognition in the social sciences that traditional academic training falls seriously short in preparing students to study, understand, and work with culturally diverse populations (Leong & Kim, 1991; Parker, Valley, & Geary, 1986; Ponterotto & Casas, 1987; Rogler, 1989). Nevertheless, despite the acknowledgment that general social science training cannot be assumed to instill cultural sensitivity or knowledge regarding important ethnic minority groups, the need for programs to develop such sensitivity and knowledge has yet to be met.

It is clear that human service professionals must improve their understanding of ethnic minority groups, given the numerical growth of minority populations in this country. It is not clear, however, what constitutes appropriate cultural sensitivity training for human service workers interacting with members of ethnic minorities. Some important questions remain unanswered: What type of information leads to adequate understanding of ethnic minorities? Is cultural knowledge sufficient to instill cultural sensitivity? The following section shows that cultural knowledge is important but cannot be assumed automatically to produce cultural sensitivity.

Cultural Knowledge

Many community programs have considered whether imparting cultural knowledge is the way to develop cultural sensitivity. The question frequently asked is, Does a person automatically become culturally sensitive to a particular ethnic group when he or she has acquired significant knowledge about that group? Many cultural sensitivity training programs have, in fact, traditionally emphasized cultural knowledge. Here we rely on the social psychology literature on attitude change to highlight both beneficial and negligible effects of providing cultural knowledge to those in whom we wish to develop cultural sensitivity.

Research in social psychology on attitude formation and change clearly suggests that the simple introduction of information does not automatically lead to the
adoption or incorporation of the new information into a receiver's belief system
(McGuire, 1985). Resistance to new information (for example, information reflecting favorably on an ethnic group) is likely if the new information is inconsistent
with a well-established existing belief system. This may occur, for instance, when
new, favorable information about an ethnic group confronts a strong, prejudicial
belief system (McGuire, 1960).

The negligible impact of new information on an existing belief system is
illustrated by a number of studies. In a study of 51 desegregated high schools, Slavin
and Madden (1979) found that the use of multiethnic readers, which acquainted
students with the values, norms, and perceptions of African Americans and other
cultural groups, did not diminish the prejudice of either white or black students.
Stephan (1985) reported on other studies suggesting that informational interventions
produced no changes. One of those studies, by Greenberg, Pierson, and Sherman
(1957), showed that single lectures, debates, or discussions designed to reduce
prejudice did not have that effect. Best, Smith, Graves, and Williams (1975) similarly found that a 12-hour race-related curriculum for white elementary children
had no effect on racial attitudes. Lessing and Clarke (1976) found that even the
introduction to junior high school students of a comprehensive 8-week curriculum
in which students read and prepared reports about different ethnic groups and used
supplementary materials in a variety of media had no effect on prejudice.

Even in the face of the negligible results documented by some researchers,
many cultural sensitivity training programs, including those implicit in college
textbooks, continue to emphasize cultural knowledge in the development of cultural
sensitivity (Atkinson, Morten, & Sue, 1989; Leong & Kim, 1991; Rogler, Malgady,
Costantino, & Blumenthal, 1987; Sue, 1981). In their review of the literature on
effective cultural sensitivity training programs, Parker, Valley, and Geary (1986)
concluded that cultural knowledge has been one of the most heavily emphasized
factors in cultural sensitivity training programs.

Unfortunately, the answer to the question about the importance of cultural
knowledge to cultural sensitivity is not as straightforward as we would wish. What
is clear, however, is that merely providing knowledge does not necessarily produce
cultural sensitivity. Rather, the research evidence suggests that various social-
psychological conditions affecting the learner or trainee determine whether or not
the transmission of information about a culture results in heightened sensitivity.
There is evidence that ethnic and racial attitudes can and do change with the introduction of new information, particularly if the new information capitalizes on preexisting information that is compatible with it (McGuire, 1985).

Research on attitude change suggests that information provided in training is
most likely to be assimilated when it is compatible with preexisting knowledge
(Cialdini, Petty, & Cacioppo, 1981; McGuire, 1985). In the context of our concerns,
the knowledge conveyed through cultural sensitivity training is most likely to be
adopted and utilized by trainees whose preexisting attitudes toward the targeted
group are compatible with the information provided in training. Stephan (1985),
reviewing empirical studies of intergroup relations, reached this conclusion:

"Considered in the aggregate, these [attitude change] studies indicate that [pre-existing] evaluative inferences about ethnic group members increasingly override factual information across time" (p. 623).

Applied to the matter of gang intervention and cultural sensitivity, research on intergroup relations suggests that the goal of sensitizing program personnel is more easily accomplished through knowledge-based programs, provided that the trainees' initial attitudes are at least neutral, if not positive, toward the ethnic group in question (even if the positive appraisal lacks a firm knowledge base).

Pedersen's (1991) broader understanding of culture leads to the consideration of ethnic gangs as living in their own unique cultures. In this context, it is recommended that cultural sensitivity training for professionals and paraprofessionals include a focus on the positive aspects of gangs, such as their role in the protection and socialization of adolescents (Miller, 1990). Learning about the positive functions of gangs in the lives of their members fosters sensitivity toward the gang and toward the broader ethnic culture as well. If preexisting negative attitudes are not countered, the cultural knowledge imparted in sensitivity training will more than likely soon be forgotten or dismissed (Higgins & King, 1981; Stephan, 1985).

For this reason, Pedersen (1988) recommends assessing the nature and strength of existing attitudes before delivering cultural knowledge training. Those with preexisting negative views toward a cultural group would benefit particularly from awareness (preknowledge) training that is designed to increase self-awareness of beliefs and attitudes toward cultural groups and to reveal their biases. Only by first dealing with pejorative cultural attitudes can a person benefit from knowledge about the unique values, beliefs, and norms that give meaning to a cultural group's behavior and motivations.

In general, cultural information or knowledge is critical for the development of cultural sensitivity, but cultural knowledge cannot be assumed from educational training or ethnic group membership. Moreover, cultural knowledge is not static but rather is dynamic and susceptible to change. Open-mindedness and receptivity to different modes of thinking and behaving are a crucial part of developing cultural sensitivity (Casas, 1986). Gang intervention programs will gain cultural sensitivity as they are staffed with personnel who not only are sensitive to the broader cultural values and norms of ethnic minorities but also are sensitive to, knowledgeable about, and appreciative of the more specific social and cultural contributions of specific gang cultures.

In summary, cultural knowledge, though essential, is not enough to ensure cultural sensitivity. Other important and related considerations are appreciation and acceptance of the gang subculture and the gang member's ethnic culture. We will now address an additional factor that frequently has been considered a viable indicator of an individual's cultural sensitivity: previous experience with ethnic groups or gangs.

The Role of Background Experience

As mentioned earlier, a common misconception in community programs is that ethnic group membership automatically leads to cultural sensitivity. A related question is whether previous experience in interacting with a targeted ethnic group results in cultural sensitivity toward that group. In the context of gang work, a more specific question arises: Does inclusion of ex–gang members in gang intervention programs help facilitate cultural sensitivity? The next two sections address these related yet distinct questions.

Ex–Gang Members and Cultural Sensitivity

Ex–gang members are often employed in gang intervention and prevention programs and have served as outreach workers or researchers (Jankowski, 1991; Moore, 1978; Vigil, 1988). Is it advisable to give preference to individuals who themselves have background and experience in gangs, and does this practice help make a community intervention program culturally sensitive?

According to Spergel (1966) the selection of gang street workers is critical because of the complexity and demands of their tasks. The specific worker's background and characteristics can facilitate or hinder his or her acceptance by gang members. In Spergel's view, there is no single optimal characteristic, but rather a combination of desirable attributes of which ethnicity is but one. Other helpful attributes include lower class origin, similar interests, good training, and relevant skills and experience.

In his ethnographic study of 35 gangs, Jankowski (1991) indicated that gaining access to the various white, African American, and Hispanic gangs required demonstrating several personal qualities, which included confidentiality, respect, and an absence of fear. Jankowski noted that his own Hispanic background facilitated access to Hispanic and African American gangs but proved to be a barrier with white gangs. However, through his forthright interest and persistence, he eventually gained access even to white gangs. His own experience of growing up in Chicago among various cultural gangs had sensitized him to gangs in general and to ethnic gangs in particular. Jankowski's experience suggests that both ethnicity and background experience interacting with gangs stand the gang worker in good stead.

Both Spergel (1966) and Jankowski (1991) have stressed the importance of a worker's individual and background characteristics in gang intervention efforts. Similarly, Moore's (1978) experience in working with gangs suggested the need to highlight values shared by community workers and gang members, and to emphasize the common objectives held by gang members and workers or researchers—for example, reduction of the threat of injury or death from gang violence.

Whereas Spergel and others have focused on street workers and researchers, community program administrators likewise need to develop cultural knowledge and sensitivity. Unlike street workers, administrative staff are responsible for program development, policy guidelines, and the overall implementation and operation of the program. Critical decisions, such as the hiring of personnel, are in the administrators' hands. Their responsibility requires special sensitivity to and knowledge of the targeted population.

I have suggested here that employing ex–gang members in intervention programs can help facilitate the establishment of rapport with gangs. The intimate understanding of the situation can also help ensure the overall program's cultural sensitivity. That is, ex–gang members can potentially train and sensitize other program staff who have no direct contact with gangs to better understand and appreciate gang members and their cultures. Nevertheless, it is clear that non–gang members can conceivably be just as effective as ex–gang members in intervention programs. The essential qualities appear to be understanding, appreciation, and a genuine desire to establish rapport with gang members. We will next consider the role of past experience with gangs or other minority groups in the development of cultural sensitivity.

Previous Experience With Ethnic Groups

Social psychologists have asked whether previous contact or interaction with an ethnic group in itself lessens prejudice or counters negative attitudes toward that group. More directly germane to the purpose of this chapter is to ask whether those who have had experience and contact with ethnic minority groups and with gangs are necessarily more culturally sensitive and therefore more effective in community intervention programs. However, like appreciation and cultural knowledge, past contact and experience with ethnic groups or gangs does not guarantee cultural sensitivity.

Research on intergroup relations (e.g., Allport, 1954; Sherif & Sherif, 1953; Williams, 1947) going back more than half a century suggests that intergroup or interethnic contact is not sufficient for developing or improving cultural sensitivity. More recent studies—for example, those by Aronson and his colleagues (Aronson & Osherow, 1980; Aronson, Stephan, Sikes, Blaney, & Snapp, 1978; Blaney, Stephan, Rosenfield, Aronson, & Sikes, 1977)—have shown that the interdependence among members of small interethnic groups, in which common objectives can be achieved only through cooperative efforts, significantly increases interethnic cordiality and appreciation. Following is an adaptation from Stephan's (1985) list of conditions that are conducive to improvement of interethnic relations or development of cultural sensitivity. It is based on research on intergroup relations but is particularly applicable to intercultural cooperation and sensitivity. Cultural sensitivity is enhanced when the relationship between cultural groups is characterized by these circumstances:

1. Maximized cooperation and minimized competition between groups

2. Equality of social status between groups

3. Similarity of groups on nonstatus dimensions (beliefs, values, etc.)

4. Efforts to avoid pointing out differences in competence between groups

5. Positive intergroup outcomes

6. Strong normative and institutional support for intergroup contact

7. Potential for further intergroup contact beyond the immediate situation

8. Promotion of group members' individuation

9. Nonsuperficial contact (e.g, involving mutual disclosure of information)

10. Voluntary (noncompulsory) contact

11. Positive effects correlated with the duration of the contact

12. Contact occurring in a variety of contexts with a variety of ingroup and outgroup members (or, in our context, gang members and non–gang members)

13. Numerical equality

This list has several implications for gang intervention programs. First, intercultural contact in and of itself is not sufficient to promote cultural sensitivity. This means that both street workers and administrative personnel can have extensive contact with culturally different gang members and still be culturally insensitive. Second, previous contact with gang members is most formative if based on an attitude of respect, appreciation, and social equality. Third, the list identifies interpersonal conditions that foster sensitivity to specific cultural groups and suggests some important requirements for an effective cultural sensitivity training program, such as having commitment to ongoing contact and treating group members as individuals. Finally, the list can provide guidance in assessing the cultural sensitivity of candidates for administrative and staff positions in terms of background experience and training.

Thus far we have considered individual characteristics commonly used as indicators of cultural sensitivity. However, cultural sensitivity is multidimensional, involving all of the various individual characteristics. For a more comprehensive approach, we will now consider a tridimensional perspective, which takes into account the importance of self-awareness, cultural knowledge, and interpersonal skill for those working with culturally diverse populations.

A TRIDIMENSIONAL PERSPECTIVE ON CULTURAL SENSITIVITY

The common indicators of cultural sensitivity all have important elements that collectively contribute to the development of cultural sensitivity: understanding verbal and nonverbal forms of communication, being sensitive to universal human needs and concepts as taught in social science training, gaining cultural knowledge through specialized training, and acquiring experience by interacting with a particular population. The tridimensional perspective is an attempt to synthesize these individual contributors to cultural sensitivity and encompass them within three general and sequential factors or dimensions: self-awareness, cultural knowledge, and skill development.

The definition of cultural sensitivity proposed earlier in this chapter emphasizes objectivity and knowledge in developing fair evaluative judgments and behavioral responses toward cultural groups. But it also suggests that those objective evaluations and appropriate behavioral patterns are developed through a candid and dispassionate introspective assessment of one's current attitudes and one's views toward them. Further, this definition underscores the importance of contact with the cultural group in developing cultural sensitivity. In our definition, cultural sensitivity has three main components: awareness, knowledge, and skill. This conceptualization corresponds to Pedersen's (1988) view of multicultural training, which moves in three stages from awareness to knowledge and then to skill.

For Pedersen (1988), *awareness* means an initial assessment of a person's current attitudes, opinions, and assumptions regarding a particular culture. It concerns assumptions about cultural features, behaviors, attitudes, and values similar to or different from one's own. According to Sue and Sue (1982), as reported by Pedersen, awareness training entails acquiring several competencies. The first is the ability to understand one's own cultural values and biases. The second involves becoming aware of the way one's cultural values and biases affect ethnic minority clients. The third competency involves becoming comfortable with cultural differences between one's own values and norms and those of others who are culturally different. The fourth competency requires learning to recognize and understand situations when it is advisable to refer a culturally different person elsewhere for various possible reasons (e.g., personal bias, preference due to ethnic identity).

Knowledge is considered the starting point for true cultural understanding. Knowledge consists of facts about a culture's history, social position, values, norms, and beliefs. According to Sue and Sue (1982), cultural knowledge training for counselors should develop several specific competencies that are needed for working with persons from other cultures. First, cultural knowledge training should offer a good understanding of the sociopolitical system in the United States and of its past and present treatment of ethnic minorities. Second, this training should impart specific information about the culture itself—its salient cultural values, beliefs, practices, and norms—and should treat the matter of heterogeneity, including the role of assimilation and acculturation in altering cultural characteristics. Third, the training should also develop a keen understanding of potential intervention strategies and their appropriateness in light of knowledge of the culture, including the role of language. Fourth, cultural knowledge training should inform participants about institutional barriers that limit access to services and compromise intervention efforts. Common institutional barriers include language, geographic access, a perceived lack of confidentiality, and mistrust due to cultural ignorance.

Skill refers to the stage at which one has become aware of oneself and knowledgeable about a particular cultural group and can apply this knowledge in effective interpersonal contact with members of that group. Sue and Sue (1982) provide guidance in developing skills that are relevant to gang intervention. First, the acquired cultural knowledge must be used to develop a broad range of verbal and nonverbal responses that are acceptable, appropriate, and sensitive to the values and norms of ethnic minorities. A second aspect of cultural skill concerns receptive communication with culturally different groups: It entails learning to receive both verbal and nonverbal communication appropriately and to interpret it accurately. Third, skill development requires implementing intervention efforts in a respectful manner, with attention to the cultural context.

An additional requirement for intercultural skill development is interaction and meaningful contact with minority group members. Actual contact with culturally different people puts cultural awareness and knowledge to the test, and it allows for the emergence of behavioral and verbal repertoires that are mindful and respectful of the other culture's beliefs, norms, and values.

The tridimensional perspective including cultural awareness, knowledge, and skill is comprehensive and dynamic. One's competency in each element evolves continually because culture is not static but fluid and ever-changing. According to Pedersen (1988), many traditional cultural sensitivity training programs emphasize one component at the expense of the others, thus creating imbalance and distortion. For example, the possession of knowledge about a cultural group does not in itself guarantee a counselor or community worker's ability to apply this knowledge in the work setting. Similarly, overemphasis on awareness, by revealing false assumptions and stereotypes regarding a cultural group, can lead to guilt and self-consciousness. At the same time, a premature emphasis on skill development without the necessary awareness or knowledge of the target cultural group can lead to the blind or inappropriate development of verbal and nonverbal behavioral patterns.

Within the tridimensional perspective, knowledge—whether gained through self-awareness, through a training program, or through interpersonal interaction with cultural group members—is critical to cultural sensitivity. In work with ethnic gang members, this knowledge needs to encompass not only universal concerns, but also the unique social and cultural experiences of gang members.

THE SOCIOCULTURAL CONTEXT OF GANG MEMBERS

Being sensitive to ethnic gang members means recognizing that gang members, like any other individuals, experience universal human needs—physical, psychological, and social. Unfortunately, the current law enforcement approach to gang violence emphasizes the reduction or eradication of gangs altogether (see, for example, California Council on Criminal Justice, 1989, excerpted in chapter 2 of this book). Gang members are viewed as outsiders to society, unfit to participate in a civilized world. This generalization obscures the fact that gangs often serve a benign role in the socialization of adolescent members (Miller, 1990), as well as constitute part of their members' social support systems.

Sensitivity to ethnic gang members requires adopting a more complex view of gang members than that prevalent in law enforcement. Gang members, like others, live in social realms that require them to fulfill multiple social roles, including the role of gang member. But gang members have other roles as well: son or daughter, father or mother, employee, member of a cultural group, and so on. As individuals fulfill their multiple roles, they develop multiple identities. Culturally sensitive and effective intervention efforts take this fact into consideration and view gang members in light of their multiple roles or identities, including those stemming from membership in an ethnic group. Gang intervention workers need to be sensitive to gang members' varied identities and subcultures and not focus on gang membership alone.

To better understand multicultural identities, one can examine identities at three levels: the international level, the ethnic level, and the social role level (Pedersen, 1988). At the international level, which concerns citizenship, gang members and non-gang members alike can identify themselves as being American and/or some other nationality (e.g., Jamaican, Mexican). At the ethnic level, gang members, like others, can identify strongly with particular ethnic groups; thus, for example, a gang member may identify himself as Chicano/Mexican American, African American, Jamaican, Puerto Rican, Vietnamese, Hmong, Chinese, Irish, or Italian (or a combination of two or more). At the social role level, an individual's identity as a gang member often is very concomitant. However, at this level, there can also be concomitant identities associated with one's gender, occupation, role within the family (e.g., son/daughter, father/mother), and the like.

Not only do gang members have multiple identities, but the salience and importance of those identities vary from individual to individual and may be related to centrality and organizational position within the gang (e.g., "inner circle," "fringers"; Thrasher, 1927/1963). Those working with gangs need to be attuned to individual differences among gang members, differences that would reflect diverse roles and identities. Workers should continually check and monitor their awareness of their own preconceived assumptions and stereotypes regarding gang members and regarding the cultural group as a whole.

Finally, intervention programs need to be tied closely to aspects of gang members' identities that are associated with class-related values (Sue, 1989) and with multiple oppression (Reynolds & Pope, 1991). An example of multiple oppression is the combination of being poor, belonging to an ethnic minority group, and being a gang member. The combined results of such circumstances are believed to form individuals' self-concepts and to influence not only their behavior but also the behavior of others toward them.

Goldstein (1991) has proposed a prescriptive approach to gang prevention and intervention efforts, whether at the individual, gang, community, or state level. The prescriptive approach "recognizes that different juveniles will be responsive to different change methods" (p. 156). The critical question posed in this approach is, "Which types of youth meeting with which types of change agents for which types of interventions will yield optimal outcomes?" (p. 156). The prescriptive approach recognizes the social, psychological, and cultural diversity among gang members. Recognizing the important role of culture in gang participation, Goldstein states that gang members bring to their gang participation diverse and often culture-specific motivations, perceptions, behaviors, and beliefs. The meaning of aggression; the perception of gang as family; the gang as an arena for acquiring status, honor, or "rep"; the gang's duration, cohesiveness, and typical and atypical legal and illegal pursuits; its place in the community—these features and many more are substantially shaped by cultural traditions and mores. (p. 244)

A multidimensional effort to ensure cultural sensitivity in gang interventions should adopt a prescriptive approach, which recognizes the multiple identities of gang members and the salience of culture in the development of those identities. Moreover, cultural sensitivity should not simply be seen as a concern of street workers, but its importance should be recognized at all programmatic levels. Cultural sensitivity is as essential for program sponsors, administrators, and evaluators as it is for those on the streets. In other words, all of a program's major stake holders need to develop awareness of their own assumptions, knowledge of other cultural groups, and skill at relating to those cultural groups—whether they interact with gang members directly or indirectly. Table 16.1 shows the main developmental stages of intervention programs and the stake holders involved in each stage.

Achieving cultural sensitivity at each stage helps sponsors promote more culturally responsive programs. Cultural sensitivity helps administrators better appreciate and understand the role of culture in gang member motivation and behavior and thereby be more in tune with the people who work directly with the program's clients. Finally, for those working directly with gang members (e.g., street workers), cultural sensitivity helps situate gang-related activities within a sociocultural context. It helps workers understand that gang activity, disruptive as it may be, only constitutes part of a single level of the gang member's social involvement, which is tied to a single social identity and role.

Developing cultural sensitivity in gang intervention programs requires first a programmatic commitment, then an individual commitment to the development of cultural understanding and intercultural skills. The tridimensional perspective discussed earlier highlights the three main components of cultural sensitivity— self-awareness, cultural knowledge, and intercultural skill—and the sequence of their development. The proposed definition of cultural sensitivity encompasses these three components and stresses their importance in achieving cultural sensitivity. We have also suggested that cultural sensitivity requires a better understanding and appreciation of the many sociocultural and individual characteristics associated with ethnic gang members and their environment. Within this complex framework, gangs cannot be seen as the sole problem responsible for the increased violence and delinquency in American communities. A broader and deeper understanding of the basic but unmet physical, social, and psychological needs of ethnic communities is needed; such an understanding may clarify the true etiological factors underlying the increase in gang participation and violence throughout the United States.

Table 16.1   Gang Intervention Program Stages and Stake Holders

Program stage	Stake holder
Program objectives	Sponsoring organization Administrative staff
Program design	Sponsoring organization Administrative staff
Program implementation	Administrative staff Street workers Support staff
Program evaluation	Administrative staff Evaluators

CONCLUSIONS

Cultural sensitivity has been discussed in the literature but has not been well defined. A review of commonly used indicators or characteristics of cultural sensitivity (language, cultural knowledge, etc.) reveals shortcomings inherent in the use of each alone. That is, each of the characteristics on its own does not automatically result in cultural sensitivity. However, this is not to deny the important role of each characteristic in promoting cultural sensitivity. For example, effective language and communication skills are essential for cultural sensitivity; knowledge about ethnic cultures is also important for developing an objective appreciation of ethnic minorities.

A tridimensional perspective on cultural sensitivity (Pedersen, 1988) views self-awareness, cultural knowledge, and interpersonal skill development as critical in the development of cultural sensitivity within community-based intervention programs. It is essential that cultural sensitivity not be stressed only for outreach or street workers but that its importance be recognized at all organizational levels, including program sponsorship and administration.

Promoting, developing, or maintaining cultural sensitivity against the background of the current conservative, ethnocentric zeitgeist is a formidable challenge for intervention programs. Nevertheless, the success of any prevention or intervention program requires a keen understanding and appreciation of gangs—of their functions for individual members and even for communities—because gangs also are symptomatic of the depressed social and economic conditions prevailing in largely ethnic communities. A culturally sensitive view of ethnic minority gang members requires that they be seen within a psychological and sociocultural context that acknowledges the basic physical, psychological, and social needs common to all, including gang members.

Our definition of cultural sensitivity emphasizes the importance of self-awareness, objective knowledge, and interethnic group skills in developing cultural sensitivity. It is important to note that being culturally sensitive to one ethnic group does not necessarily mean being culturally sensitive to or knowledgeable about any other ethnic group. Although there may be some similarities across cultural groups, clearly there are many differences that must be understood (Atkinson et al., 1989; Sue, 1981; Pedersen, 1988). Failure to understand the unique meaning of language, gesture, and behavior as used by a particular group can easily lead to miscommunication and misunderstandings. For example, an African American counselor may interpret an Asian American client's quiet and shy behavior as a feature of personality, whereas it may actually be a culturally appropriate expression of deference to authority (Sue, 1989).

It is hoped that the views presented in this chapter will spur interest, debate, and research concerning this critical topic and that the result will be an even better understanding of cultural sensitivity and its impact on ethnic group members targeted by community programs.

REFERENCES

Allport, G. W. (1954). *The nature of prejudice.* Cambridge, MA: Addison-Wesley.

Aronson, E., & Osherow, N. (1980). Cooperation, prosocial behavior, and academic performance: Experiments in the desegregated classroom. In L. Bickman (Ed.), *Applied social psychology annual.* Newbury Park, CA: Sage.

Aronson, E., Stephan, C., Sikes, J., Blaney, N., & Snapp, M. (1978). *The jigsaw classroom.* Newbury Park, CA: Sage.

Atkinson, D. R., Morten, G., & Sue, D. W. (1989). *Counseling American minorities: A cross cultural perspective* (3rd ed.). Dubuque, IA: William C. Brown.

Best, D. L., Smith, S. C., Graves, D. J., & Williams, J. E. (1975). The modification of racial bias in preschool children. *Journal of Experimental Child Psychology, 20,* 193–205.

Blake, T. A. (1987). The meaning of culturally appropriate treatment for the Hispanic adolescent. In M. Singer, L. Davidson, & F. Yalin (Eds.), *Alcohol use and abuse among Hispanic adolescents.* Hartford, CT: Hispanic Health Council.

Blaney, N., Stephan, C., Rosenfield, D., Aronson, E., & Sikes, J. (1977). Interdependence in the classroom: A field study. *Journal of Educational Psychology, 69,* 121–128.

California Council on Criminal Justice. (1989). *State Task Force on Gangs and Drugs: Final report.* Sacramento, CA: Author.

Casas, J. M. (1985). The status of racial- and ethnic-minority counseling: A training perspective. In P. Pedersen (Ed.), *Handbook of cross-cultural counseling and therapy.* Westport, CT: Greenwood.

Casas, J. M. (1986). Making effective use of research to impact the training of culturally sensitive mental health workers. In M. R. Miranda & H. H. L. Kitano (Eds.), *Mental health research and practice in minority communities: Development of culturally sensitive training programs.* Rockville, MD: National Institute of Mental Health.

Cialdini, R. B., Petty, R. E., & Cacioppo, J. T. (1981). Attitude and attitude change. *Annual Review of Psychology, 32,* 357–404.

Genelin, M., & Coplen, B. (1989). *Los Angeles street gangs.* Los Angeles: Criminal Justice Coordination Committee Interagency Gang Task Force.

Gim, R. H., Atkinson, D. R., & Kim, S. J. (1991). Asian-American acculturation, counselor ethnicity and cultural sensitivity, and ratings of counselors. *Journal of Counseling Psychology, 38,* 57–62.

Glick, R., & Moore, J. (1990). *Drugs in Hispanic communities.* New Brunswick, NJ: Rutgers University Press.

Goldstein, A. P. (1991). *Delinquent gangs: A psychological perspective.* Champaign, IL: Research Press.

Greenberg, H., Pierson, J., & Sherman, S. (1957). The effects of single-session education techniques on prejudice attitudes. *Journal of Educational Sociology, 31,* 82–86.

Grove, C. L. (1976). *Communications across cultures.* Washington, DC: National Education Association.

Heller, C. S. (1966). *Mexican American youth at the crossroads.* New York: Random House.

Higgins, E. T., & King, G. (1981). Accessibility of social constructs: Information processing consequences of individual and contextual variability. In N. Cantor & J. F. Kihlstrom (Eds.), *Personality, cognition and social interaction.* Hillsdale, NJ: Erlbaum.

Huff, C. R. (1990). Introduction: Two generations of gang research. In C. R. Huff (Ed.), *Gangs in America.* Newbury Park, CA: Sage.

Jankowski, M. S. (1991). *Islands in the street: Gangs and American urban society.* Berkeley: University of California Press.

Jenkins, A. H. (1985). Attending to self-activity in the Afro-American client. *Psychotherapy, 22,* 335–341.

Leong, F. T. L. (1986). Counseling and psychotherapy with Asian-Americans: Review of the literature. *Journal of Counseling Psychology, 33,* 196–206.

Leong, F. T. L., & Kim, H. H. W. (1991). Going beyond cultural sensitivity on the road to multiculturalism: Using the intercultural sensitizer as a counselor training tool. *Journal of Counseling and Development, 70,* 112–118.

Lessing, E. E., & Clarke, C. C. (1976). An attempt to reduce ethnic prejudice and assess its correlates in a junior high school sample. *Educational Research Quarterly, 1,* 3–16.

McGuire, W. J. (1960). Direct and indirect persuasive effects of dissonance-producing messages. *Journal of Abnormal Social Psychology, 60,* 354–358.

McGuire, W. J. (1985). Attitudes and attitude change. In G. Lindsey & E. Aronson (Eds.), *Handbook of social psychology* (Vol. 2). New York: Random House.

Miller, W. B. (1974). American youth gangs: Past and present. In A. Blumberg (Ed.), *Current perspectives on criminal behavior.* New York: Knopf.

Miller, W. B. (1990). Why the United States has failed to solve its youth gang problem. In C. R. Huff (Ed.), *Gangs in America.* Newbury Park, CA: Sage.

Mirande, A. (1987). *Gringo justice.* Notre Dame, IN: University of Notre Dame Press.

Moore, J. (1978). *Homeboys: Gangs, drugs and prison in the barrios of Los Angeles.* Philadelphia: Temple University Press.

Needle, J. A., & Stapleton, W. V. (1982). *Police handling of youth gangs.* Washington, DC: National Juvenile Justice Assessment Center.

Parker, W. M., Valley, M. M., & Geary, C. A. (1986). Acquiring cultural knowledge for counselors in training: A multifaceted approach. *Counselor Education Supervision, 26*(1), 61–71.

Pedersen, P. (1988). *A handbook for developing multicultural awareness.* Alexandria, VA: American Association for Counseling and Development.

Pedersen, P. (1991). Multiculturalism as a generic approach to counseling. *Journal of Counseling and Development, 70*, 6–12.

Ponterotto, J. G., & Casas, J. M. (1987). In search of multicultural competence within counselor education programs. *Journal of Counseling and Development, 65*, 430–434.

Reynolds, A. L., & Pope, R. L. (1991). The complexities of diversity: exploring multiple oppressions. *Journal of Counseling and Development, 70*, 174–180.

Rogler, L. H. (1989). The meaning of culturally sensitive research in mental health. *American Journal of Psychiatry, 146*, 296–303.

Rogler, L. H., Malgady, R. G., Costantino, G., & Blumenthal, R. (1987). What do culturally sensitive mental health services mean? The case of Hispanics. *American Psychologist, 42*, 565–570.

Seijo, R., Gomez, H., & Freidenberg, J. (1991). Language as a communication barrier in medical care for Hispanic patients. *Hispanic Journal of Behavioral Science, 13*(4), 363–376.

Sherif, M., & Sherif, C. W. (1953). *Groups in harmony and tension*. New York: Harper & Row.

Slavin, R., & Madden, N. A. (1979). School practices that improve race relations. *American Educational Research Journal, 16*, 169–180.

Soriano, F. I., & De La Rosa, M. R. (1990). Cocaine use and criminal activities among Hispanic juvenile delinquents in Florida. In R. Glick & J. Moore (Eds.), *Drugs in Hispanic communities*. New Brunswick, NJ: Rutgers University Press.

Spergel, I. A. (1966). *Street gang work: Theory and practice*. Reading, MA: Addison-Wesley.

Spergel, I. A., & Curry, G. D. (1990). *Survey of youth gang problems and programs in 45 cities and 6 sites* (National Youth Gang Suppression and Intervention Program). Washington, DC: U. S. Department of Justice, Office of Juvenile Justice and Delinquency Prevention.

Spergel, I. A., Curry, G. D., Chance, R. L., Kane, C., Ross, R. E., Lexander, A., Simmons, E., & Oh, S. (1990). *Youth gangs: Problem and response: Stage 1. Assessment*. Washington, DC: U. S. Department of Justice, Office of Juvenile Justice and Delinquency Prevention.

Stephan, W. G. (1985). Intergroup relations. In G. Lindzey & E. Aronson (Eds.), *Handbook of social psychology* (Vol. 2). New York: Random House.

Sue, D. W. (1981). *Counseling the culturally different: Theory and practice*. New York: Wiley.

Sue, D. W. (1989). Ethnic identity: The impact of two cultures on the psychological development of Asians in America. In D. R. Atkinson, G. Morten, & D. W. Sue (Eds.), *Counseling American minorities: A cross cultural perspective* (3rd ed.). Dubuque, IA: William C. Brown.

Sue, D. W., & Sue, D. (1977). Barriers to effective cross cultural counseling. *Journal of Counseling Psychology, 24*, 420–429.

Sue, D. W., & Sue, S. (1982). Cross-cultural counseling competencies. *The Counseling Psychologist, 19*(2), 45–52.

Sue, S. (1988). Psychotherapeutic services for ethnic minorities: Two decades of research findings. *American Psychologist, 43*, 301–308.

Sue, S., Wagner, N. N., Ja, D., Margullis, C., & Lew, L. (1976). Conceptions of mental illness among Asian and Caucasian American students. *Psychological Reports, 38*, 703–708.

Thrasher, F. M. (1963). *The gang: A study of 1,313 gangs in Chicago*. University of Chicago Press. (Original work published 1927)

Trimble, J. E., & LaFromboise, T. (1985). American Indian and the counseling process: Culture, adaptation, and style. In P. Pedersen (Ed.), *Handbook of cross-cultural counseling and therapy*. Westport, CT: Greenwood.

Vigil, J. D. (1988). *Barrio gangs: Street life and identity in southern California*. Austin: University of Texas Press.

Wade, P., & Bernstein, B. L. (1991). Culture sensitivity training and counselor's race: Effects on Black female clients' perceptions and attrition. *Journal of Counseling Psychology, 38,* 9–15.

Williams, R. M. (1947). *The reduction of intergroup tensions: A survey of research on problems of ethnic, racial and religious group relations* (Bulletin 57). New York: Social Science Research Council.

CHAPTER 17

Gangs and Public Policy: Macrolevel Interventions

C. Ronald Huff

Gangs are not a new phenomenon in the United States. Thrasher's (1963) classic study of 1,313 gangs appeared in 1927. By the 1950s, gangs were generally regarded as a serious problem in the nation's major cities. However, in the past decade, the problem has grown worse. Walter Miller, who has written about gangs in each of the last five decades, recently observed that "youth gangs of the 1980s and 1990s are more numerous, more prevalent, and more violent than in the 1950s, probably more so than at any time in the country's history" (1990, p. 263). Miller went on to ask why the nation has failed to solve its youth gang problem, identifying the following major reasons for this failure: (a) failure to develop a comprehensive gang control strategy; (b) failure to take a national, rather than a local, perspective on the problem; (c) failure to insist on a close linkage between solid theoretical rationales and program design; (d) failure to insist on rigorous program evaluation; (e) failure to provide resources commensurate with the severity of the gang problem; (f) failure to establish a central clearinghouse or organization with primary responsibility for gang prevention and control; and (g) failure to recognize the implications of the social context of gang life.

This volume has focused primarily on Miller's seventh point, the failure to recognize the implications of the social (and, we would add, economic and psychological) context of gang life. Various chapters have discussed interventions at the level of the individual, the group, the community, and the criminal justice system. In addition to considering these types of intervention, it is important that we understand the *macrolevel* context of gangs and gang behavior and ask what public policy interventions may be useful in preventing and controlling gang-related crime in the United States. From a macrolevel perspective, gangs are not "the problem." Rather, they are a symptom of underlying socioeconomic problems—problems such as structural unemployment and children living in poverty—that have associated microlevel implications, such as racism and its daily social and psychological effects. The view that youth gangs and their members are "the problem" and that the answer lies in simply suppressing these gangs and arresting, convicting, and incarcerating their members is a futile assumption that has now been rejected even by most law enforcement leaders. Los Angeles is the prime example: In part because of the futility of a policy based solely on suppression, the Los Angeles Police Department created the DARE (Drug Abuse Resistance Education) program and has begun to emphasize prevention as its key strategy. Some of the more enlightened law enforcement organizations, such as the Honolulu Police Department, work actively with community agencies to ensure that prevention receives sufficient emphasis in local and state responses to gangs and crime.

The aggressive enforcement and deterrence approach, as indicated by Spergel and Curry in chapter 12, can at best supply only one piece of the puzzle. As the Los Angeles experience has shown, we cannot depend solely on aggressive enforcement, prosecution, and incarceration to solve the gang problem. In fact, if the studies showing that gangs simply reproduce themselves in prison are correct, the incarceration/incapacitation strategy may even contribute somewhat to gang persistence (see, for example, Jankowski, 1991). We need both sticks and carrots. Most youths will respond to carrots (properly structured incentives and rewards), but all except the most naive will concede that not every youth will respond favorably to such positive approaches. For those who won't respond to carrots, we do need sticks (sanctions), including incapacitation for those who pose a clear and present danger to public safety or who, despite repeated (and progressively restrictive) community-based interventions, have demonstrated that they are chronic recidivists. It is perhaps especially unlikely, though by no means impossible, that those who have reaped substantial profit from criminal behavior (e.g., drug sales, auto theft) will respond favorably to anything less than big money.

The fundamental socioeconomic problems of our society have both macrolevel and microlevel components. But from the macrolevel perspective, most of the microlevel components—such as the daily impact of racism in producing a feeling of rage—are directly related to macrolevel variables like structural unemployment. A glance at a wide array of data comparing blacks and whites shows that to be true. Everyone knows that life expectancy is lower for African Americans as a group than for whites as a group. But what happens if we control for socioeconomic class? Middle-class African Americans are comparable to middle-class whites on most important outcome measures, such as life expectancy, precisely because education and income make an important difference in the quality of one's life and in one's ability to avoid criminality as well as in other social and medical pathologies.

The fact that we have not been plagued by middle-class gangs should be instructive. Middle-class youths do sometimes join gangs, and they also commit some violent crimes (in fact, some of the more dysfunctional American families are middle-class or wealthier families, in which children receive plenty of money and Nintendo games but little of their parents' love or time). In the aggregate, however, our nation's gang problem overwhelmingly involves members of the urban underclass. Whether one looks at the Crips, the Bloods, and the barrio gangs of Los Angeles; the Black Gangster Disciples and the Vice Lords of Chicago; or the Filipino and Samoan gangs of Hawaii, gangs in the United States consist overwhelmingly of poor youths, mostly minorities, with some recent immigrants thrown into the mix. These are the dispossessed members of our society. Cloward and Ohlin (1960) would point out that they are, by and large, pursuing "success" via illegal means because they believe that the legal routes to success are not open to them.

And why shouldn't they believe that? Because it's un-American? Horatio Alger stories notwithstanding, the realities of contemporary life suggest that underclass America often questions whether it makes any sense to complete high school (or even college) if the graduate still cannot find a job owing to racial discrimination or qualitatively inadequate education. This poses a real dilemma, especially because young people from the underclass want the same symbols of material success—150-dollar sneakers, expensive cars, the latest designer clothing, and other conspicuous consumer goods—all of us have been conditioned to want. And if their futures do not include IBM, the NBA, the NFL, major league baseball, or even a respectable modestly paying career, they might still believe they can buy nice "wheels" and nice "threads" if they can earn enough selling drugs, standing lookout for a crack house, pimping, prostituting, stealing cars, or exercising any of dozens of other illegal ways of making money. And with children constituting the largest and fastest growing impoverished group in the United States, the implications for the pool of potential gang members are clear.

If we as a society do not provide better social support and better access to the legitimate routes to success, we are ultimately guilty of blaming the victim, at least in part, when some of these young people turn to gangs and crime to fulfill their needs. This does not excuse or condone their illegal behavior, but it certainly helps explain it. The question is, What public policy responses might be useful?

The failures named by Miller as accounting for the magnitude of the youth gang problem are parallel to failures in other important areas of our society, ranging from health care to homelessness. These failures are reflective of ineffective and inefficient social policy. Problems such as crime, gangs, mental illness, homelessness, and inadequate health care require public policy based on long-term planning and effective long-term strategies of prevention and control. But this is virtually unheard of in a society whose values are more accurately mirrored by the prevalence of fast food, microwave ovens, and 15-second sound bites, and whose political system rewards only short-term quick fixes that can be used as ammunition in reelection campaigns—that ultimate triumph of form over substance. With these observations in mind, we'd like to present some longer term strategies to address major social problems at the national, state, and local levels.

Our emphasis on macrolevel policy is not meant to minimize the importance of the individual, group, community, and criminal justice system interventions discussed earlier in this volume. Rather, we believe that it is important to intervene on all of these levels as well as on the societal level if we are to be effective in countering the negative aspects of youth gangs. The incentives to join youth gangs operate on four different levels: the psychological and emotional need for acceptance (individual level); the culturally derived meanings of gangs and the fact of belonging to an extended family (group level); the presence of segregated housing patterns and daily discrimination (community level); and illegitimate economic opportunities, afforded by some gangs, which often compete successfully with the limited legitimate opportunities available to many gang members (societal level). In addition, some of the most policy-relevant variables are those with indirect rather than direct effects on youths, and many of these appear at the societal level of intervention.

POLICY PARTNERSHIPS FOR YOUTH

If we think of gangs, for a moment at least, as a symptom of broader socioeconomic problems (in more formal terms, a dependent rather than an independent variable), we realize that the strategies likely to have a positive impact on gangs are also likely to affect crime, mental illness, homelessness, and other forms of social pathology. We'd like to concentrate on four such strategies, focusing on education, employment, and intervention in high-risk, dysfunctional communities. We term these strategies "policy partnerships" because they require close cooperation among government agencies (federal, state, and local) as well as private sector participation involving for-profit and nonprofit organizations. The four strategies include (a) the development of a full employment economy; (b) the development of a program of targeted youth service and youth employment; (c) nationwide, mandatory preschool Head Start; and (d) targeted, community-based, public/private (nonprofit) intervention projects in high risk urban areas. We support other strategies, such as expanded family assistance programs, but have not included them here because our focus is on federal/state/local partnership initiatives involving education, employment, and intervention in targeted communities.

Development of a Full-Employment Economy

One of the findings from the corpus of recent youth gang studies is that gang members tend to remain in the gangs longer than was formerly the case. Instead of maturing out of the gang, it is relatively common these days for a young person to begin gang activity in his early to mid-teens, perhaps do time for delinquent and/or criminal offenses, then return from the correctional system directly to the gang (see, for example, Hagedorn, 1988). One of the main reasons for this pattern is the shift in our economy from an industrial to a postindustrial, service-oriented system.

Gang members often drop out of high school in rebellion or in reaction to disciplinary measures, academic failure, and/or—occasionally—the numbing effects of sometimes unresponsive teachers who have become mere employees instead of professionals and of a curriculum that seems largely irrelevant to the aspirations and interests of these youths. Formerly, such high school dropouts could find decent jobs if and when they became motivated to do so. A high school diploma was not required. One could work in the steel mills, the auto plants, or other manufacturing facilities, especially in the northeastern and midwestern industrial cities.

Many of the industrial and manufacturing jobs are gone. Either they have disappeared entirely through the shift to a service-oriented economy or they have migrated to domestic sunbelt locations or to international sites as we move toward much more competitive regional (domestic) and global economies. Many of the cities that are currently plagued by gangs lack jobs for which gang members can successfully compete. But even without such jobs, young high school dropouts formerly could join the military. That is not the case today—the military insists on at least the completion of a high school equivalency degree.

What options are left? More and more, these youths are turning to street hustling, robbery, auto theft, participation in a drug distribution network, theft from vending machines, and other illegal means of supporting themselves. Because drug distribution and other illegal enterprises tend to be equal opportunity employers, the youths find a more level playing field on which to compete than they generally would find in the legitimate economic markets, which are more often characterized by emphasis on formal education and higher level job skills and by employment discrimination based on extralegal variables such as race.

Increasingly, these youths are functioning entirely within what is known as the hidden economy of our nation. They do not pay taxes on their earnings. What they earn sometimes comes at great risk—risk to themselves, to their families, and to innocent victims. In a recent study following up on the 37 founding members of Milwaukee's African American gangs, John Hagedorn (1991) discovered that 59% of them had been involved in drug trafficking within 5 years, whereas only 19% had full-time jobs. Similarly, Spergel (1991) found that of 276 gang members on probation in San Diego County, fully 75% had been convicted of drug offenses at one time or another.

Unemployment and underemployment in our society have disproportionate impact on minorities (Wilson, 1987), who are also disproportionately represented in the juvenile and criminal justice systems. The structural problem has visible historical roots. As Moynihan (1973) noted, the United States alone among western nations failed to institute a postwar economic policy that gave top priority to continued full employment. Unlike some European nations, we did not develop systematic apprenticeship programs, job retraining procedures, public job creation, or long-term planning to prepare for the shift to a postindustrial economic system. Instead, we opted to let market forces dictate employment prospects in a form of social Darwinism and malignant neglect from which we have never recovered.

It is imperative that legal economic opportunities for our youth—and their parents or guardians—be able to compete successfully with illegal economic opportunities. Today, in many of our cities, they cannot. In reality, the hidden economy, as an equal opportunity employer, often offers some of our citizens more opportunity than do the national and local legitimate economic systems. Given this deplorable situation, a poor youth must have strong internal values and external support to resist the lure of illegal activities. For far too many of our children, the structural incentives lead in the opposite direction, so it is not surprising that many of them—and many adults—break the law to make money.

We think that the best way to address this problem is to commit ourselves to a full employment economy so that every American of working age who is able to work and who wants a job has one. The necessary commitment is greater than that required by either the Employment Act of 1946 or the Humphrey-Hawkins "Full Employment" Act of 1978. More than 7 of every 10 Americans, in responding to surveys, consistently agree that "government should see that everyone who wants to work has a job" (Currie, 1985, p. 274). To accomplish this will require significant redistribution of both our priorities and our resources, but it is worth doing. It will also require more cooperation (policy partnerships) among federal, state, and local government (including local schools) and the private sector. The private sector has a direct interest in such a policy: It would mean more emphasis on a well-educated, well-prepared labor pool, without which neither our cities nor our employers have much of a future.

One corporation that has recognized this interest is British Petroleum (BP), whose American headquarters is in Cleveland, Ohio. BP has contributed substantially to Cleveland's Scholarship in Escrow Program, a partnership between the Cleveland Public Schools and the local business community. The program was established in recognition of the fact that if Cleveland is to have a viable economic future it must have an educated labor pool and that the public schools bear the brunt of the responsibility for generating that pool. The program essentially creates a trust fund for all students enrolled in grades 7 through 12 and credits each of their accounts with 10 dollars for each grade of C, 20 dollars for each B, and 40 dollars for each A. The money goes into a scholarship fund, where it earns interest. Each student earning money for grades receives a certificate, somewhat like a stock certificate, indicating the amount earned. Students who graduate from Cleveland public high schools have up to 8 years to use their scholarship monies at any Pell Grant–certified college or technical school. The program is based on two rationales: (a) If wealthy families can create trust funds for their children's future, why cannot we as a society create trust funds for *all* children? and (b) Because future income is highly correlated with educational achievement, why not pay children for doing well in school now as an intermediate reinforcement?

Our nation's position as a globally competitive economic power depends on such commitment because our population is aging, and the proportion of workers to retirees is declining now and will decline for quite some time. The schools will have to reassess their curricula in order to prepare a shrinking number of young people to be productive workers. It is both feasible and timely now to propose a full employment economy. Surely this is possible, given the diminishing labor pool. Just as surely, it is imperative if we are to maintain a competitive global economic position and support our own aging citizens. The full employment economy, often advocated as a measure to help the less fortunate and less well educated, is all of that and more—it is also in the self-interest both of our nation's economy and of private sector employers who will need a productive labor force and may have increasing difficulty recruiting one if we fail to invest in our youth now.

Targeted Youth Service and Youth Employment

According to recent gang studies, the population most at risk for gang involvement is 14- to 24-year-old males, especially those living in poor inner-city neighborhoods.

Our second policy goal should be to develop a program to address the specific window of vulnerability of unemployed, disengaged young people. At a time of life when they most desire independence, youths are legally, socially, and economically dependent on adults. Those who drop out of high school (and even many who complete high school) are, as noted earlier, increasingly unable to support themselves legally because they lack marketable job skills. In addition to reassessing school curricula to determine how well we are preparing youths (other than "college prep" kids) for our society, we should also create a targeted national youth service and employment program.

The targets of the proposed program would be youths aged 14 to 21. They would be required to complete a year of national service unless they were (a) enrolled full time in an accredited school, college, university, or vocational training program; (b) engaged in military service; (c) employed full time; (d) required to be at home for valid reasons (e.g., to care for a family member with a significant physical disability); or (e) severely physically or mentally disabled.

Examples of national service projects might be a national youth conservation corps, a job training corps, and a system of premilitary boot camps designed not for a presumed rehabilitative effect, but to prepare youths to enter military service. This latter possibility would require some willingness on the part of the military to experiment by allowing, at least on a trial basis, participating youths to enter the service and prove that they can be both responsible and effective. The procedure should be evaluated and refined as necessary. Dozens of other imaginative and useful programs might be developed to provide service to the nation and prepare youths for productive lives.

Following a year of service (subsidized at a level of subsistence plus the cost of the training being delivered), participating youths would be assured a year of subsidized employment from one of three sources: (a) the private sector (with federal, state, and local tax incentives to encourage firms to hire these youths and give them a chance to prove themselves); (b) federal, state, or local government (with federal funding); or (c) the military (in the case of the boot camp graduates). The 2-year period of training and paid work would give program participants an opportunity to mature, to develop good work habits and marketable job skills, and to offer prospective employers a much more impressive resumé than they could have at the outset.

This program would target only certain youths in the 14-to-21 age range. Youths productively engaged in one of the activities specified earlier (or limited by a physical or mental disability) would not be included. Although a universal national service requirement (similar to Israel's but broader than military service alone) has many appealing aspects, we do not think this is the moment in American history to introduce such a program. The demographics argue against it for some of the reasons just discussed. With an aging population and a declining pool of youths moving into productive positions and preparing to replace the retirees, we simply cannot afford to interrupt the education and training of the very people who soon must be actively engaged in the economy. Moreover, youths between 14 and 21 who are productively engaged in jobs, education, training, or military service are at lower risk for criminal involvement. Finally, targeting the program should limit its cost, as it would by definition be smaller than a universal program.

A Mandatory National Head Start Program

We know that most delinquents and criminals did not get a "head start" toward success in our society. Generally, quite the opposite is true: The early lives of most such individuals contain a litany of handicaps. To address these handicaps, which elevate a child's risk not only of becoming involved in gangs and crime but also of having other social problems, we should adopt a mandatory national Head Start program. Ideally, all children should begin the program at age 3, so that we can take fullest advantage of the important early learning opportunities available at that age. Such a program would help prepare children to succeed in school; would help reduce child abuse in the home by providing much-needed assistance to parents under stress; would improve the children's daily nutrition; and would help children develop cognitive and social skills, including conflict resolution skills, at a critical age.

We know that Head Start works. For example, we have longitudinal evidence concerning the 123 African American youths of low socioeconomic status (and therefore at risk for school failure) who participated in the 1962 Perry Preschool Project in Ypsilanti, Michigan. This project was the forerunner of the national Head Start program. At ages 3 and 4, the participants attended a high-quality preschool program. Researchers tracked them annually from age 3 to 11, then followed up on them at ages 14, 15, and 19. Data were also collected for a control group of 65 children.

The longitudinal data point to the program's effectiveness. Analyzing the involvement of both groups with the legal system, the researchers found that, of the experimental group, 69% had no reported offenses (compared with just 49% of the controls) and only 16% had ever been arrested as juveniles (compared with 25% of the controls). Moreover, by age 19, three-fifths of the Head Start group were employed, versus less than a third of the control group; more than two-thirds of the experimental group (compared with less than half of the controls) had graduated from high school; and two-fifths of the Head Starters were enrolled in college or a postsecondary vocational program, compared with only one-fifth of the control group; only one-fifth of the experimentals (versus one-third of the controls) were on welfare; the teenage pregnancy rate was twice as high for the control group. The benefit/cost ratio was about 7:1, given the reduced welfare dependency and increased earning potential represented by these data (Berrueta-Clement, Schweinhart, Barnett, Epstein, & Weikert, 1984).

Head Start and other sound preschool programs are real bargains for the American taxpayer. According to the Committee for Economic Development, composed of American corporate executives, "It would be hard to imagine that society could find a higher yield for a dollar of investment than that found in preschool programs for its at-risk children. Every $1.00 spent on early prevention and intervention can save $4.75 in the cost of remedial education, welfare, and crime further down the road" (Eisenhower Foundation, 1990, p. 11). We can only add that the program should be both mandatory and universal in the United States, in recognition of the importance of investing in all of our youth for the reasons already mentioned. In a very real sense all of our children are at risk in many ways, given the fast-paced, drug-dependent, high-pressure society in which we live.

Targeted Community-Based Programs

In addition to a full-employment economy, targeted youth service and youth employment, and mandatory, universal Head Start, we should develop programs to assist the urban areas most at risk. We recognize that there are many troubled rural and suburban areas as well, but in terms of population density and maximum return on investment, it makes sense to focus, at least initially, on the large populations in underclass, socially disorganized urban areas. Our proposed approach would entail the following three stages.

Stage 1. The federal government would fund empirical, descriptive studies in all 50 states. These studies would be designed to determine the costliest areas of our cities in terms of crime, commitments to juvenile and adult correctional institutions, commitments to mental hospitals, proportion of the population receiving public assistance, percent unemployed, and other empirical indicators of social pathology. Agencies would routinely collect these data and record them by zip code if not by more precise geographic designation. Using these zip code data, researchers could determine the exact addresses of the individuals involved and organize them by census tract, neighborhood, or any other lowest common denominator available. This idea was prompted by an internal study by the Ohio Department of Youth Services analyzing commitment data according to zip code. The idea seems worthy of broader application across various systems of social control (criminal justice, mental health, welfare, etc.) because zip code information is one of the few common denominators among state and federal government data bases. It is highly probable that a relatively small number of zip codes, or census tracts, account for a relatively large proportion of crime, delinquency, mental illness, homelessness, unemployment, child abuse, and other costly social and economic problems in any given state. Although we may have different theoretical explanations for this, we may at least be able to agree on ecological areas to target for intervention.

Stage 2. The most problematic areas, in terms of cost to the state and the nation, would be targeted for intervention programming. The states would issue requests for proposals to public, private, and nonprofit agencies and organizations, describing the target areas and inviting innovative ideas to address the problems. Programmatic thrusts might include housing rehabilitation; parental effectiveness training; alcohol and drug abuse counseling; improved maternal, prenatal, and neonatal health care; problem pregnancy counseling; improved birth control education; job training; gang mediation; and a host of other worthwhile possibilities. Many of these programmatic emphases reflect our view that some of the most policy-relevant variables are those with *indirect* effects on gangs and gang-related crime. In the course of our individual and group interventions with gang members and at-risk youths, we should be emphasizing preventive programs to alter the social and economic conditions that let gangs flourish. Many of these are "quality of life" programs.

Stage 3. Agencies whose proposals are funded would be required to cooperate in monitoring and in both formative (process) and summative evalua-tion. The purpose would be to learn about programs as they unfold and to improve program design around the nation, thus facilitating the transfer of knowledge from one community to others.

The malignant neglect of urban problems, begun in the 1970s and still continu-ing, must be reversed. Indiscriminate cuts in federally supported urban programs eviscerated promising initiatives along with those that deserved to be cut. Our re-newed commitment to our cities should be centered conceptually on the Eisenhower Foundation's (1990) "community enterprise" development strategy for the inner city. Recognizing that the corporate response to the labor market demographics of the 1990s is likely to be grossly inadequate, the Eisenhower Foundation (1990) warned that the

> "trickle down" approach has been tried; it has had little success,
> especially compared to our "bubble up" approach of directly em-
> powering nonprofit minority community organizations. . . . The
> private market has repeatedly pronounced its judgment on the
> current condition of the inner cities. Without substantial change,
> these communities will remain too volatile, their work forces
> too poorly skilled and unstable, to attract private enterprise
> consistently. (p. 75)

The Eisenhower Foundation's strategies include linking public sector job crea-tion and local community needs via economic development programs led by non-profit sector entrepreneurs. The foundation, like the earlier National Advisory (Kerner) Commission on Civil Disorders (1968) and the National Commission on the Causes and Prevention of Violence (1969), emphasizes the need to improve the quality of urban life and the chances of success for youths living in our cities. The foundation's specific job creation scheme focuses on rebuilding our com-munities' physical infrastructure (e.g., roads and housing) using the labor of young people currently at high risk for joining gangs, abusing or selling drugs, and enter-ing into criminal careers. The foundation's community enterprise development strategy is conceptually sound. Policymakers should consider it carefully along with other important elements of the foundation's Youth Investment and Com-munity Reconstruction strategies (Eisenhower Foundation, 1990).

Why not work toward a public policy response that recognizes the long-range importance of local community development and empowerment? One way to pursue that worthy goal is to rebuild our physical infrastructure and our human infrastructure at the same time, by linking the needs of both and creating public sector jobs, managed by private nonprofits, providing training and employment for at-risk youths. Such an initiative could not only neutralize some important incentives to join gangs and commit crimes, but could broadly address the roots of related social pathologies such as mental illness, homelessness, and drug and alcohol abuse. Equally important, it would give the United States a chance to be globally competitive when those now in childhood assume their roles in our labor force.

A "DOMESTIC MARSHALL PLAN"

Is all of this a massive undertaking? Absolutely! We are at a point in history where, in our judgment, our nation needs a sort of domestic Marshall Plan—in this case to rebuild our human infrastructure by reinvesting in children and families. Is the undertaking too expensive? Compared to what? Children dropping out of school? Unemployment? Youth violence? Given that it was in our national interest to intervene, at great expense, in the Persian Gulf when Iraq invaded Kuwait, is it not also in our national interest to intervene in our own cities, where far more people die each year in gang-related violence alone than died in the Persian Gulf War? Each year, Los Angeles alone has been reporting from 500 to 700 homicides that are considered gang related.

Gangs and gang-related crime are, from the macrolevel perspective, merely symptoms of the fundamental socioeconomic problems we have discussed in this chapter. For too long we have shortchanged ourselves and our young people, mortgaging the nation's future by putting many of our youths at risk of failure. The new youth gangs and other manifestations of social and economic pathology, including the decline in our global economic position, bring a new urgency to the need for reform. For too long, we've isolated problems such as gangs or crime from other, interrelated problems.

We *can* pay for the initiatives outlined here—if we have the political leadership and commitment. Funding would come primarily through reductions in Defense Department spending that is nonessential, especially in light of the dissolution of the Soviet Union and in view of recent improvements in surveillance technology that strengthen our defense. The Eisenhower Foundation (1990) has identified billions of dollars in defense spending that even conservatives agree is unnecessary to our national defense.

Moreover, we already spend a great deal of money attempting to address, in very inefficient ways, the failures of our current system. An example is the billions of dollars spent each year on corrections and on unemployment compensation alone. Compare our national investment strategy with that of the Japanese, whose successes in both education and global economic competition have attracted much notice over the past two decades. We greatly underinvest in the youths whom we must count on to be responsible citizens and become our future labor pool. In our view, a significant increase in that investment is essential, both in addressing the problems posed by youth gangs and in shoring up the nation's declining position in the world's economy.

The fact is, however, that we cannot make much headway against these problems until we address the underlying problems of inequality and social injustice. We can keep the incentives that are the best part of capitalism and still broaden the opportunities for our less fortunate citizens. An affluent nation need not retain in its socioeconomic system the vestiges of social Darwinism to which we cling. In the final analysis, global competition and the aging of our own population put all of us in the United States at risk, at least in economic terms. We will need the productive labor of all of our citizens to meet these challenges.

The problems posed by youth gangs and gang-related crime are, from a macro-level perspective, deeply intertwined with other social and economic problems threatening our society. We have nothing that truly constitutes a national youth policy (perhaps this is not surprising because children under 18 don't vote), but for the reasons discussed, we believe that serious consideration should be given to the development of such a policy. (States should also seriously consider formulating their own comprehensive youth policies.) We agree with Elliott Currie's (1985) observation:

> If we wanted to sketch a hypothetical portrait of an especially violent society, it would surely contain these elements: It would separate large numbers of people, especially the young, from the kind of work that could include them securely in community life. It would encourage policies of economic development and income distribution that sharply increased inequalities between sectors of the population. It would rapidly shift vast amounts of capital from place to place without regard for the impact on local communities, causing massive movements of population away from family and neighborhood supports in search of livelihood. It would avoid providing new mechanisms of care and support for those uprooted. . . . It would promote a culture of intense interpersonal competition and spur its citizens to a level of material consumption many could not lawfully sustain. (p. 278)

If Currie's prescription for violence is accurate, then most readers of this volume will recognize our own nation's face when we gaze into the mirror of violence. The work of rebuilding our human infrastructure must begin. It will be costly. It will be difficult. It will require a significant shift in our national priorities, as reflected in the federal budget. It will require political leadership and courage in the face of narrow special interest lobbies. But we must invest in children and families if we are to reduce the level of violence, both gang-related and non–gang-related, and remain economically productive.

REFERENCES

Berrueta-Clement, J. R., Schweinhart, L. J., Barnett, W. S., Epstein, A. S., & Weikert, D. J. (1984). Preschool's effects on social responsibility. In D. J. Weikert (Ed.), *Changed lives: The effects of the Perry Preschool Program on youths through age 19.* Ypsilanti, MI: High/Scope Press.

Cloward, R. A., & Ohlin, L. E. (1960). *Delinquency and opportunity: A theory of delinquent gangs.* New York: Free Press.

Currie, E. (1985). *Confronting crime: An American challenge.* New York: Pantheon.

Eisenhower Foundation. (1990). *Youth investment and community reconstruction: Street lessons on drugs and crime for the nineties.* Washington, DC: Author.

Hagedorn, J. M. (1988). *People and folks: Gangs, crime and the underclass in a rustbelt city.* Chicago: Lake View.

Hagedorn, J. M. (1991). Gangs, neighborhoods, and public policy. Unpublished paper.

Jankowski, M. (1991). *Islands in the street: Gangs and American urban society.* Berkeley, CA: University of California Press.

Miller, W. B. (1990). Why the United States has failed to solve its youth gang problem. In C. R. Huff (Ed.), *Gangs in America.* Newbury Park, CA: Sage.

Moynihan, D. P. (1973). *The politics of a guaranteed income.* New York: Random House.

National Advisory Commission on Civil Disorders. (1968). *Final report.* Washington, DC: U. S. Government Printing Office.

National Commission on the Causes and Prevention of Violence. (1969). *Final report.* Washington, DC: U. S. Government Printing Office.

Spergel, I. A. (1991). *Youth gangs: Problem and response.* Washington, DC: U. S. Department of Justice, Office of Juvenile Justice and Delinquency Prevention.

Thrasher, F. M. (1963). *The gang: A study of 1,313 gangs in Chicago.* University of Chicago Press. (Original work published 1927)

Wilson, W. J. (1987). *The truly disadvantaged: The inner city, the underclass, and public policy.* University of Chicago Press.

CHAPTER 18

Gang Intervention: Issues and Opportunities

Arnold P. Goldstein

OPTIMAL INTERVENTION CHARACTERISTICS

Whether comprehensive in thrust or single-targeted, and whether oriented toward the individual gang member or the gang as a whole, there are a number of features we wish to recommend for enduring gang intervention effectiveness. Such qualities concern the intervention's goals, underlying strategies, and constituent procedures.

Intervention Goals

Gang intervention efforts will optimally aspire to serve both *preventive* and *rehabilitative* purposes. In fact, we have chosen to define *intervention* as subsuming both preventive and rehabilitative activities. In this we are in accord with Martin, Sechrest, and Redner (1981), who view prevention and rehabilitation as part of a continuum rather than as discrete strategies. The commonly used distinction among primary, secondary, and tertiary prevention (Bolman, 1969) is relevant here. Primary prevention efforts are typically broadly applied interventions designed to reduce the incidence of a particular disorder or class of behaviors. Secondary prevention interventions are usually targeted toward especially at-risk populations showing early signs of the condition in question. Tertiary prevention interventions, equivalent to rehabilitation, are efforts to reduce the reoccurrence of or impairment from conditions that have already taken place. All three levels—primary, secondary, and tertiary (rehabilitation)—are relevant to delinquent gang youths and thus will be our focus. In the terms of Trojanowicz and Morash (1987), our dual concern will be for "pure prevention, which attempts to inhibit delinquency before it takes place, and rehabilitative prevention . . . which treats the youngster who has already come into contact with the formal juvenile justice system" (p. 199).

Both gang youths and societal needs must be served if intervention attempts are to yield both initial and lasting success. Youths join gangs and commit illegal activities therein to satisfy needs no different from those motivating all youths, gang or nongang. Adolescents of all types seek recognition from peers, status, clarification of their identity, pride, tangible resources, self-esteem, excitement, camaraderie. Such needs are age-appropriate, developmentally desirable, and to be encouraged, not thwarted. It is, of course, the *means* by which such need satisfaction is sought that is at issue. Effective gang interventions will provide means for satisfying such needs in prosocial, growth-enhancing, and societally acceptable ways—and not ignore or deny their pressing reality.

The larger community, however, has its needs, and they too are appropriately a primary goal of gang intervention programming. In recent decades, the major expression of this belief has crystallized around societal *protection,* as manifested in a broad array of gang-busting efforts: criminal justice deterrence, suppression, and incarceration. Such interventions are indeed often appropriate, but, we would assert, they have been employed too broadly, too nonprescriptively, and too frequently in isolation rather than in combination with home, school, work, and/or other preventive/rehabilitative programming. Our homes, schools, and streets must be safe, and thus some youths must be incarcerated. But these youths are our future; they too will be out among us again. Certainly, it is helpful to society at large, not only to the youths themselves, that when they return they are better, more prosocial, and more competent community citizens—not better, more antisocial, more competent criminals.

Intervention Strategies

Strategies designed to achieve both preventive and rehabilitative goals, as well as to satisfy appropriate youth and societal aspirations, will optimally be prescriptive, appreciative, and comprehensive.

Prescriptive Programming

Consistently effective rehabilitative and preventive gang interventions are in our view likely to be treatments developed, implemented, and evaluated according to the spirit and methodology of what we have termed *prescriptive programming* (Goldstein & Glick, 1987). Simple to define in general terms but quite difficult to implement effectively, prescriptive programming recognizes that different juveniles will be responsive to different change methods. The central question in prescriptive programming is, *Which types of youths meeting with which types of change agents for which types of interventions will yield optimal outcomes?* This view runs counter to the prevailing one-true-light assumption underlying most intervention efforts directed toward juvenile offenders. The one-true-light assumption, the antithesis of a prescriptive viewpoint, holds that specific interventions are sufficiently powerful to override substantial individual differences and aid heterogeneous groups of people.

The spirit and substance of the alternative many-true-lights, prescriptive programming viewpoint have roots in analogous thinking and programming in change endeavors with populations other than gang youths. In work with emotionally disturbed adults and children, for example, there is Kiesler's (1969) grid model, matching treaters, treatments, and clients; Magaro's (1969) individualization of the psychotherapy offered and the psychotherapist offering it as a function of patient social class and premorbid personality; and our own factorial, tridifferential research schema for enhancing the development of prescriptive matches (Goldstein, 1978; Goldstein & Stein, 1976). In elementary and secondary education contexts, examples of prescriptive programming include Keller's (1966) personalized instruction; Cronbach and Snow's (1977) aptitude-treatment interactions; Hunt's (1972) matching of student conceptual level and teacher instructional style; and Klausmeier, Rossmiller, and Sailey's (1977) individually guided education model.

These ample precedents, however, are not the only beginnings of concern with prescriptive programs relevant to juvenile corrections. Early research specifically targeted to juvenile delinquents also points to the value of prescriptive programming. Individual psychotherapy, for example, has been shown to be effective with highly anxious delinquent adolescents (Adams, 1962), the socially withdrawn (Stein & Bogin, 1978), those displaying at most a moderate level of psychopathic behavior (Carney, 1966; Craft, Stephenson, & Granger, 1964), and those who display a set of characteristics summarized by Adams (1961) as "amenable." Adolescents who are more blatantly psychopathic, who manifest a low level of anxiety, or who are "non-amenable" in Adams' terms are appropriately viewed as poor candidates for individual psychotherapy.

Research demonstrates that a number of group intervention approaches are indeed useful for older, more sociable and person-oriented adolescents (Knight, 1969); for those who tend to be confrontation accepting (Warren, 1974); for the more neurotic-conflicted (Harrison & Mueller, 1964); and for acting-out neurotics (California Department of the Youth Authority, 1967). Juveniles who are younger, less sociable, or more delinquent (Knight, 1969) or who are confrontation avoiding (Warren, 1974) or psychopathic (Craft et al., 1964) are less likely to benefit from group interventions. Other investigations report differentially positive results for such subsamples of delinquents receiving individual or group psychotherapy as the immature-neurotic (Jesness, 1965), those under short-term rather than long-term incarceration (Bernstein & Christiansen, 1965), the conflicted (Glaser, 1973), and those reacting to an adolescent growth crisis (Warren, 1974).

Yet other investigators, studying these and other interventions, continue to succumb to their own one-true-light beliefs and suggest or imply that their non-differentially applied approach is an appropriate blanket prescription, useful with all delinquent subtypes. Keith (1984) writes in this manner as he reviews the past and current use of psychoanalytically oriented individual psychotherapy with juvenile delinquents. Others assume an analogously broad, nonprescriptive stance toward group psychotherapy (Levin, Trabka, & Kahn, 1984). As already noted, we strongly view this stance as nonproductive; evidence favoring prescriptive programming appears substantial.

The exploration of prescriptive programming to this point has focused on two of the three classes of variables that combine to yield optimal prescriptions—the interventions and the types of youths to whom the interventions are directed. But optimal prescriptions should be tridifferential, specifying type of intervention by type of client by type of change agent. This last class of variable merits attention. Interventions as received by the youths to whom they are directed are never identical to the procedures as specified in a textbook or treatment manual. In actual practice, the intervention specified in a manual is interpreted and implemented by the change agent and perceived and experienced by the youths. The change agent looms large in this sequence. Just as it is erroneous to think that all delinquents are equivalent, it is likewise erroneous to view all change agents as the same. Who administers the intervention does make a difference, an assertion for which there already exists supporting, if preliminary, evidence in the context of interventions with juvenile delinquents. Grant and Grant (1959) report finding internally oriented change agents to be highly effective with high-maturity offenders but detrimental to low-maturity offenders. Palmer (1973) found that change agents judged high in relationship/self-expression achieved their best results with communicative-alert, impulsive-anxious, or verbally hostile–defensive youths and did least well with dependent-anxious ones. Change agents characterized by surveillance/self-control did poorly with verbally hostile–defensive or defiant-indifferent delinquents but quite well with dependent-anxious ones.

Agee (1979) reports similar optimal pairings. In her work, delinquents and the change agents responsible for them were each divided into expressive and instrumental subtypes. The expressive group included adolescents who were overtly vulnerable, hurting, and dependent. The instrumental group included youths who were defended against their emotions, independent, and nontrusting. Expressive staff members were defined as open in expressing their feelings and working with the feelings of others. They typically valued therapy and personal growth, which they saw as an ongoing process for themselves and for the youths they treated. Unlike the expressive delinquent youngsters, though, they had resolved significant past problems and were good role models because of their ability to establish warm, rewarding interpersonal relationships. Instrumental staff members were defined as being less comfortable with feelings than were the expressive staff members. They were more likely to be invested in getting the job done than in processing feelings and were more alert to behavioral issues. They appeared self-confident, cool, and somewhat distant—all of which impressed the instrumental delinquents.

Agee thus reports evidence suggesting the outcome superiority of (a) expressive-expressive and (b) instrumental-instrumental youth/change agent pairings, a finding substantially confirmed in our own examination of optimal change agent empathy levels in work with delinquent youths (Edelman & Goldstein, 1984). Clearly, these several studies of youth, treater, and/or treatment differential matching indicate an especially promising path for future planning, implementation, and evaluation.

As described in chapter 2 in our examination of the strengths and weaknesses of detached worker intervention programming, a prescriptive strategy has already been manifested in the gang intervention contributions of Klein (1968), Needle and Stapleton (1982), Spergel (1991), and Yablonsky (1967). Clearly, it is a crucial intervention quality, one to be very much encouraged.

Appreciative Programming

Gang intervention programming is in our view likely to fail unless its strategic planning and tactical implementation involve major, sustained, and seriously acknowledged gang member involvement. An accurate and heuristic understanding of gang structure, motivation, perception, aspiration, and routine and dramatic behavior cannot be obtained from the outside looking in. Such understanding depends on substantial input from gang members themselves. But such input is not easily acquired. Hagedorn (1988) observes in this regard that

> we are in the absurd position of having very few first hand studies of, but numerous theoretical speculations about, juvenile gangs. . . . One reason is that the vast majority of sociologists and researchers are white, and gangs today are overwhelmingly minority. (pp. 26–27)

African American, Hispanic, Asian, and other minority youths do indeed constitute a large portion of contemporary gang membership in the United States. They bring to their gang participation diverse and often culture-specific membership motivations, perceptions, behaviors, and beliefs. The meaning of aggression; the perception of gang as family; the gang as an arena for acquiring status, honor, or "rep"; the gang's duration, cohesiveness, and typical and atypical legal and illegal pursuits; its place in the community; and much, much more about gangs are substantially shaped by cultural traditions and mores. A rich literature exists describing in depth the cultural patterns and perspectives of our country's ethnic and racial subgroups: African American (Beverly & Stanback, 1986; Brown, 1978; Glasgow, 1980; Helmreich, 1973; Keiser, 1969; Kochman, 1981; Meltzer, 1980; Silverstein & Krate, 1975; White, 1984), Hispanic (Horowitz, 1983; Mirande, 1987; Moore, Garcia, Garcia, Cerda, & Valencia, 1978; Quicker, 1983; Ramirez, 1983; Vigil, 1983), Asian (Bloodworth, 1966; Bresler, 1980; Kaplan & Dubro, 1986; Meltzer, 1980; President's Commission on Organized Crime, 1985; Wilson, 1970), and others (Hagedorn, 1988; Howard & Scott, 1981; Schwartz & Disch, 1970). Especially useful in much of this culture-clarifying literature is the opportunity it provides to view the structure, dynamics, and purposes of delinquent gangs through the cultural lenses of their members, as well as the support it implies for the crucial role of gang member input for effective programming.

Such information also helps provide the means for gang interveners to move in their thinking from the typical perception of gang youths as broadly deficient and in need of remediation to what Gonzalez (1981) has described as a more appreciative perspective. The latter view recognizes the appropriateness, survival value, and self-esteem enhancement potency of many gang member qualities and behaviors that are more typically seen by mainstream perspectives as weaknesses, deficiencies, or maladaptive. As Mirande (1987) notes, "Whereas the correctional perspective viewed those being studied as objects, the new [appreciative] perspective treats them as subjects and assumes their definition of the situation" (p. 198).

Youth input must be energetically and sensitively sought but employed with caution when obtained. Hagedorn (1988) urges such caution in the acceptance and processing of information provided by gang members. For a variety of self-protective reasons, some quite realistic and others not, such information may contain exaggerations, minimizations, or other inaccuracies. In a similar vein, Kleiner,

Holger, and Lanahan (1975) describe anticipated distortion of information obtained from gang members as a result of "anxiety over being identified, fear of reprisal, fears for the security of the gang, [and feeling] uncomfortable talking to middle-class Whites" (p. 394).

In spite of hindrances to obtaining accurate and valuable input from delinquent youths—about themselves, their lives, their gangs—successes do exist. There are a small but highly informative number of primarily qualitative research reports on the phenomenology of gang membership, juvenile delinquency, and kindred topics. Included in these are Shaw's (1930/1966) *The Jack-Roller: A Delinquent Boy's Own Story;* Strodtbeck, Short, and Kolegar's (1962) *The Analysis of Self-Descriptions by Members of Delinquent Gangs;* Bennett's (1981) *Oral History and Delinquency: The Rhetoric of Criminology;* Brown's (1983) *The Other Side of Delinquency;* Hanson, Beschner, Walters, and Bovelle's (1985) *Life With Heroin: Voices From the Inner City;* Roberts's (1987) *The Inner World of the Black Juvenile Delinquent;* Williams's (1989) *The Cocaine Kids;* and our own recent effort, *Delinquents on Delinquency* (Goldstein, 1990). In the same vein, there also exist several informative interview studies of unreported delinquent behavior (Gold, 1970; Kratcoski & Kratcoski, 1975; Kulik, Stein, & Sarbin, 1968; Short & Nye, 1957) and of the employment of delinquents as paid experts on delinquency in studies of experimenter-subject psychotherapy (Schwitzgebel & Kolb, 1964; Slack, 1960).

We would also suggest that valuable phenomenological insights regarding juvenile gangs may also be obtained from ex-delinquents and ex–gang members whose criminal careers ceased in the absence of outside intervention (Jenkins & Brown, 1988; Mulvey & LaRosa, 1986; Shannon, 1988), as well as from youths growing up in areas characterized by poverty, crime, serious school dropout, major drug use, or gang activity who do not become gang members. Williams and Kornblum's (1985) *Growing Up Poor;* Ross and Glasser's (1973) *Making It Out of the Ghetto;* Monroe and Goldman's (1988) *Brothers Black and Poor—A True Story of Courage and Survival;* Kotlowitz's (1991) *There Are No Children Here;* and recent research on youths described as vulnerable but invincible (Werner & Smith, 1982), resilient (Goldstein, 1988), superkids (Pines, 1979), or as simply nondelinquent though growing up in high-delinquency environments (Fagan, Piper, & Moore, 1986) are examples of some of the resources describing such youths. These examples of successful entrance into the phenomenology of gang-involved and other delinquent youths underscore the value of obtaining gang youth input and the desirability of processing such input in a culturally sensitive, empathic, and appreciative manner.

Comprehensive Programming

We have described, illustrated, and commented upon this strategic view at length in chapter 2. The New York State Division for Youth (1990) and the California Council on Criminal Justice (1989) reports described there exemplify and concretize this perspective especially well. It is, we hope, the perspective that will increasingly come to guide gang intervention policy, procedures, implementation, and evaluation in the years ahead.

Intervention Procedures

Intervention Integrity

As noted in chapter 2 with regard to its characteristic absence in implementations of detached worker programming, intervention integrity is the degree to which the intervention as conducted follows the intervention as planned. It is not only detached worker interventions, however, that chronically suffer from such plan-implementation discrepancy, but most gang interventions of whatever type. Even in those rather exceptional instances in which the intervention strategy is concretized in a systematic manner and in which the intervener is well trained in its implementation, the actual application of intervention procedures will often depart substantially from the underlying plan. A wide and usually unpredictable variety of "emergencies," "exigencies," "realities," and the like may arise. Caseloads may expand. Workers may grow tired, lazy, or overburdened. Planned supervision and tracking may only partially materialize. Even if appropriately described, detailed, and exemplified in an intervention procedures manual, the intervention plan may fail to anticipate an array of crucial circumstances. Whatever the bases for diminished intervention integrity, program efficacy is likely to suffer. Gang interventions cannot, nor should they be, automated or implemented unswervingly and unresponsively in a manner dictated by program manuals, and we are not championing such literalness of application here. But well-thought-out gang interventions, adequately reflected in detailed intervention procedures, deserve implementation in a manner consistent with the intervention as planned.

Intervention Intensity

Inadequacy of amount, level, or dosage of the intervention provided characterizes not only the detached worker approach to gang intervention (recall the 5 minutes per youth per week of the Group Guidance Project, described in chapter 2), but all categories of gang intervention programming. The various individual and group counseling or therapy-like interventions often provided (especially incarcerated) gang youths typically take place once or at most twice weekly—hardly a potent dosage level when viewed against the youths' past (preincarceration) and present (during incarceration) exposure to powerful antisocial influences.

Opportunities provision similarly suffers from grossly insufficient intervention intensity. Surely it is valid to assert that youths at risk and in gangs have been offered inadequate levels of intervention services relevant to family life, schooling, employment, health, recreation, and other domains of the opportunities provision intervention approach.

Depending upon one's political stance, one may or may not assert that the accusation of insufficient intervention intensity also fits the deterrence/incarceration gang intervention approach. Such a view is in fact often heard on the political right, with the political left claiming in the opposite that such "get tough," "just deserts" approaches are employed at too high, not too low, a level of frequency or intensity. As suggested in chapter 2, our view is that the major shortcoming of the deterrence/incarceration intervention approach is not so much its intensity— its overuse or underuse—but its characteristic use in isolation (i.e., the failure to employ it in equal partnership with family, school, employment, and other preventive/rehabilitative programming).

Finally, and most clearly, what we have termed a comprehensive approach to gang intervention seemingly suffers most from a failure of intervention intensity. When offered, it is often offered weakly, sometimes with major emphasis (high intensity) on deterrence/incarceration and only token provision (low intensity) of social or psychological programming.

Intervention Coordination

Society's agents often work in splendid isolation from one another. Their efforts are sometimes conflicting or at cross purposes, often quite independent, and infrequently additive. Not unlike the far too specialized physician who has not a "whole patient" but "an interesting liver" on his ward, agency personnel often fail to see and respond to the gang youth as a gestalt. Instead, they concern themselves exclusively with their own segmented, limited-domain, or mandated agency focus. When this occurs, the potential for uncoordinated, nonadditive, and conflicting interventions is high. Major attention to intervention coordination is crucial, especially in the context of comprehensive intervention programming, in which a number of diversely targeted agencies may be simultaneously involved with the same youth. As we have commented elsewhere:

> The diverse youth care, educational, employment market, criminal justice and other agency personnel responsible to initiate and implement comprehensive programming for youth at risk of gang involvement must function as a coordinated body. In-place networking systems for the sharing of appropriate information, willingness to put youth concerns ahead of turf concerns, and creative use of time and energy, in order to combine and build upon one another's professional efforts, are each requisites of successful coordination. (New York State Division for Youth, 1990, p. 42)

Thus far in the present chapter we have urged a gang youth and societally oriented perspective toward preventive and rehabilitative intervention that rests upon a three-pronged strategic base. Specifically, this base is concerned with (a) individualizing the interventions provided, (b) being heavily responsive to the gang youth's view of the world in determining what to provide and how to provide it, and (c) offering interventions that are broadly comprehensive in both their goals and their procedures. In seeking to reach these strategic objectives, the interventions provided must carefully follow the intervention as operationally planned, be offered at high levels of dosage or intensity, and reflect both the spirit and reality of high-quality interagency coordination. Once offered in this manner, intervention efficacy must then be systematically evaluated in order that data-based, not impression-based, decisions can be made regarding the intervention's continuance and possible dissemination. We wish to turn now, therefore, to a fuller consideration of intervention evaluation.

INTERVENTION EVALUATION

It is not our goal here to provide either a primer or a complete discussion of guidelines for conducting rigorous intervention evaluations. For such guidelines, the reader is referred to Barlow, Hayes, and Nelson (1984); Bellack and Hersen (1984); and Krathwohl (1985). Our purpose here, in a manner complementary to such basic material, is to highlight those aspects of the intervention evaluation process that appear especially central to gang-oriented intervention evaluation attempts.

Rigor-Relevance Balance

Ogden Lindsley (personal communication, June 6, 1965) spoke of three orientations to experimentation on intervention effectiveness. The Rigorless Magician orientation is reflected in the "shoot from the hip," "impressions-count-for-everything" stance held by the individual who eschews objective measurement of effect and relies totally on clinical judgment. At the opposite extreme is the Rigor Mortician, so fixated on objective measurement that he or she sacrifices the richness, uniqueness, and individuality of the very phenomena being studied in the effort to obtain standardized measurement information. At an intermediate position, and to be recommended, is the Rigorous Clinician. Here, the balance of rigor of experimental design and measurement and relevance to the real world of those being studied is the goal. Rigor of the evaluation conducted is facilitated by use of the several design and measurement characteristics recommended in the sources already cited. Relevance of the intervention and its evaluation to the real world of gang youths—that is, its external, ecological, or social validity—is promoted by obtaining gang youth input at all stages of the evaluation process (planning, implementation, analysis, conclusions, dissemination) and by assuming an appreciative perspective regarding the cultural context and goals of such youths.

Evaluation Design

A wide variety of evaluation designs have been employed in the study of intervention effectiveness, broadly defined. Some are experimental designs, examining efficacy via between-group, within-group, or intrasubject comparisons. In carrying out such examinations, evaluators may compare the full intervention with the full intervention minus one or more of its components in order to determine which components are active (the dismantling evaluation strategy). Or the evaluator, building incrementally, may begin with a narrow or circumscribed intervention and add components, making stepwise comparison with each addition (the constructive evaluation strategy). Alternatively, two or more different full interventions or intervention packages may be compared (the comparative evaluation strategy). The ability or inability of the evaluator to control nonintervention aspects of the intervention context and to employ randomization of selection of participants and their assignment to intervention conditions, along with related operational considerations, will determine whether the evaluation conducted is an experiment, a quasi-experiment, a correlational evaluation, or a case study. By far the greatest percentage of gang intervention evaluations are case studies. An ethnographically oriented social or behavioral scientist or scientific team interact with a youth gang or in a community with more than one gang over an extended period of time. Eventually, they report their perceptions, impressions, conclusions, and generalizations. Examples include Campbell (1984), Fishman (1988), Gonzalez (1981), Hagedorn (1988), Hanson (1964), Jankowski (1991), Keiser (1969), Moore et al. (1978), Taylor (1990), and Vigil (1988).

With regard to evaluation of gang intervention, such case studies can serve as valuable sources of new interventions and provide useful clues (but not conclusions) about how, when, and with whom such interventions are likely to be effective. However, case history–based impressions of intervention effectiveness may be seriously biased. Kazdin (1980) observes the following in a context concerning therapists and clients, but, we would hold, one equally relevant to gang workers, gang youths, and their perceptions of intervention effectiveness:

> The information available in therapy is filtered through the eyes of the therapist and is highly subject to biases and impressions. In the absence of objective records, the therapist's conclusions cannot be accorded scientific status. Many inferences are based upon reports of the clients, these reports being the "data" upon which interpretations are made. Yet the reports themselves may be highly distorted and have little bearing upon what actually happened. . . . Unless subjective accounts are independently corroborated, they could be completely unreliable. (p. 27)

Descriptive case studies of juvenile gang intervention attempts, therefore, may serve as excellent sources for hypothesis generating but poor sources for hypothesis testing. The intervention methods pioneered in and reported by such case studies must be evaluated for their efficacy in a less impressionistic, more objective manner —usually requiring an evaluation experiment. Stated more broadly, in furthering attempts to better understand the gang intervention process and improve the effectiveness of such interventions, a combination of diverse qualitative and quantitative evaluation designs will be required.

Measurement of effect in such evaluations will optimally be similarly diverse. First, it will be multisource. No one concerned with the impact of an intervention— evaluator, youth, peers, family—perceives the "truth." All report their own, idiosyncratic, subjective perspectives. Truth can best be construed as information conjointly reflecting diverse subjective viewpoints, whether they converge or diverge.

Such measurement will also ideally be multimethod. It has been demonstrated that responses to a measuring instrument are in part a function of the form of that measure and thus can contribute to error variance. Utilization of diverse types of measures (self-report, other-report, behavioral, archival, etc.) may largely compensate for this source of error variance.

Both proximal and distal effectiveness criteria will optimally be included in the evaluation's dependent variable measurement. Proximal measures seek to reflect changes in youths' behaviors and attitudes that are the direct target of the intervention. Distal measures seek to capture derivative changes (i.e., changes that in turn are potentiated if direct target changes first occur). Thus, if such proximal changes as enhanced social skills, anger control, and problem-solving ability first occur, then such distal outcomes as better school performance, employment, and reduction in delinquent behaviors become more possible.

Both proximal and distal effectiveness criterion measurement will optimally take place on both an immediate postintervention and extended follow-up basis. Interventions rarely if ever serve as inoculations. Even when immediately effective, durability of gain seldom occurs. Nor should we expect it to, both because existing interventions are seldom that potent and because the real-life environment of the gang is often pushing youths in a direction quite opposite from that targeted by the intervention. Thus, in order to discern whether and to what degree the intervention(s) being employed is powerful enough to reverse this common failure of generalization and yield proximal and/or distal effects that do endure, long-term follow-up measurement of intervention outcome is crucial.

We have highlighted in this section the major features of high-quality research designed to rigorously evaluate the efficacy of gang intervention efforts. As the chapters in this book make abundantly clear, interventions exist. The task of determining their effectiveness looms large before us.

FUTURE PERSPECTIVES

We have called for growth in the design, implementation, and systematic evaluation of gang intervention programming that is prescriptive, appreciative, comprehensive in substance, and offered with integrity to plan, intensity of dosage, and coordination of effort. We also believe that great potential exists for enhancing the efficacy of such interventions to the degree that gang interveners and researchers rely increasingly in their efforts on theory and research in diverse fields of psychology. To date, the major contributions to our understanding of gang formation, functioning, and intervention have come from sociology and criminology. The value of such contributions notwithstanding, we would assert that gangs are also psychological phenomena and, as such, psychology has a great deal to offer. In a recent text (Goldstein, 1991), we proposed a series of substantive ways in which clinical, developmental, social, and community psychology might profitably be drawn upon or extrapolated from to serve such gang clarification and intervention goals. Clinical psychology provides a theoretical understanding of gang member delinquency in its personality, social learning, neurohormonal, and multicomponent theories. Developmental psychology examines and elucidates qualities of typical adolescents that appear to exist in exaggerated form in many gang youths: marginality, striving for independence, search for identity, challenge of authority, need for self-esteem enhancement, and focus on peer relationships. Social psychology offers the gang intervention professional both theory and data concerned with group development, leadership, cohesiveness, communication, conflict and conflict resolution, norm and role development, influence processes, utilization of power, deindividuation, and groupthink. Community psychology adds to the pool of information from which gang-relevant extrapolations may be drawn via its findings regarding natural communities, neighborhoods, social networks, and social support. All of these bodies of psychological knowledge hold potential value for adding to our understanding of why gangs form, why they behave as they do, and how to alter much of their behavior. Very few such extrapolatory efforts have yet been made or tested, either in practice or research. We feel their likely value is especially great and thus enthusiastically encourage such attempts.

Given a diverse array of creatively developed gang interventions and systematic research rigorously evaluating their effectiveness, what is our view of the future of ganging in the United States? We believe there is much to be pessimistic about. Gangs are currently an American growth industry (Goldstein, 1991; Huff, 1990). There are more gangs, more gang members, more older gang members, more financial rewards for maintaining one's gang membership, fewer economic reasons for leaving one's gang, and, most important, more youths in the 10- to 20-year age range prone to gang membership. We believe there are and will be in the current decade more gangs and gang youths, as well as more violence perpetrated by such youths. The levels, forms, and causes of aggression by such youths appear to parallel and reflect the levels, forms, and causes of aggression in general in the United States. The street, home, school, and mass media have clearly displayed ever higher levels of aggression in recent years, and thus much the same has been evidenced by gang youths. There is little reason to expect such a pattern to change in the near future. Broad and deep cuts in social service programming, the continuing influx of and demand for illegal drugs, the country's continuing love affair with private gun ownership, ever-higher rates of violence in the mass media, and related phenomena provide fertile soil for the continued growth of gang violence.

Are there any bases for optimism, any factors suggestive of more benevolent countertrends? Miller (1990) believes so. Gang problems in the United States, he asserts, do wax and wane. We may not fully understand why—perhaps as a result of gang intervention programs or community development, or due to economic reasons. But wax and wane they do, and perhaps fuller insight into why such ebb and flow occurs will, as Miller suggests, enable us to capture and utilize the causative factors to gang-reduction advantage. The century-long awareness that delinquent youth gangs typically spring from socially and economically underserved and depressed, often minority and/or immigrant, communities points clearly to the value of ameliorative social/economic infusion programming, although perhaps Miller (1990) is more hopeful than we are that such programming will in fact be forthcoming in the current fiscally and politically conservative climate.

Miller (1990) also optimistically suggests that a further positive indicator for the future of gang reduction

> is the relatively young age of [many] gang members—particularly of the "midgets," "peewees," or "wanna-bes" in their early teens. Despite the appeal of the gang and the influence of older adolescents and gang adults as role models, most gang members simply have not made the degree of commitment to crime found in older career criminals. . . . For many, gang membership is a passing phase, and youths "mature out" to become law-abiding adults.
>
> A final characteristic of youth gangs affecting prospects for gang control is the degree of visibility of gang activities. . . . Youth gangs . . . are for the most part highly visible, often ostentatiously so. . . . Both criminal justice and social service personnel throughout the years have had relatively little difficulty in identifying members of local youth gangs and tracking their activities. This characteristic greatly facilitates the task of locating and dealing with gang crime. (pp. 265–266)

Whether the prospect for the 1990s is pessimistic, optimistic, or realistic, youth gangs are with us today and, to a greater or lesser degree, will continue to be a serious societal problem in the United States for decades to come. It is our hope that the interventions reviewed and recommended in this book will help an optimistic perspective prevail.

REFERENCES

Adams, S. (1961). *Assessment of the psychiatric treatment program, Phase I* (Research Report No. 21). Sacramento: California Department of the Youth Authority.

Adams, S. (1962). The PICO project. In N. Johnston, L. Savitz, & M. E. Wolfgang (Eds.), *The sociology of punishment and correction.* New York: Wiley.

Agee, V. L. (1979). *Treatment of the violent incorrigible adolescent.* Lexington, MA: Lexington.

Barlow, D., Hayes, S. C., & Nelson, R. O. (1984). *The scientist practitioner.* Elmsford, NY: Pergamon.

Bellack, A. S., & Hersen, M. (1984). *Research methods in clinical psychology.* Elmsford, NY: Pergamon.

Bennett, J. (1981). *Oral history and delinquency: The rhetoric of criminology.* University of Chicago Press.

Bernstein, K., & Christiansen, K. (1965). A resocialization experiment with short-term offenders. *Scandinavian Studies in Criminology, 1,* 35–44.

Beverly, C. C., & Stanback, H. J. (1986). The Black underclass: Theory and reality. *The Black Scholar, 17,* 24–31.

Bloodworth, D. (1966). *The Chinese looking glass.* New York: Dell.

Bolman, W. M. (1969). Toward realizing the prevention of mental illness. In L. Bellack & H. Barten (Eds.), *Progress in community mental health* (Vol. 1). New York: Grune & Stratton.

Bresler, F. (1980). *The Chinese mafia.* New York: Stein & Day.

Brown, W. (1983). *The other side of delinquency.* New Brunswick, NJ: Rutgers University Press.

Brown, W. K. (1978). Black gangs as family extensions. *International Journal of Offender Therapy and Comparative Criminology, 22,* 39–48.

California Council on Criminal Justice. (1989). *State Task Force on Gangs and Drugs: Final report.* Sacramento, CA: Author.

California Department of the Youth Authority. (1967). *James Marshall Treatment Program.* Unpublished manuscript.

Campbell, A. (1984). *The girls in the gang.* Oxford, England: Basil Blackwell.

Carney, F. J. (1966). *Summary of studies on the derivation of base expectancy categories for predicting recidivism of subjects released from institutions of the Massachusetts Department of Corrections.* Boston: Massachusetts Department of Corrections.

Craft, M., Stephenson, G., & Granger, C. (1964). A controlled trial of authoritarian and self-governing regimes with adolescent psychopaths. *American Journal of Orthopsychiatry, 34,* 543–554.

Cronbach, L. J., & Snow, R. E. (1977). *Aptitudes and instructional methods.* New York: Irvington.

Edelman, E. M., & Goldstein, A. P. (1984). Prescriptive relationship levels for juvenile delinquents in a psychotherapy analog. *Aggressive Behavior, 10,* 269–278.

Fagan, J. A., Piper, E., & Moore, E. (1986). Violent delinquents and urban youths. *Criminology, 24,* 439–471.

Fishman, L. (1988, November). *The Vice Queens: An ethnographic study of black female gang behavior.* Paper presented at the meeting of the American Society of Criminology, Chicago.

Glaser, D. (1973, November). *The state of the art of criminal justice evaluation.* Paper presented at the meeting of the Association for Criminal Justice Research, Los Angeles.

Glasgow, D. G. (1980). *The Black underclass: Poverty, unemployment, and entrapment of ghetto youth.* San Francisco: Jossey-Bass.

Gold, M. (1970). *Delinquent behavior in an American city.* Pacific Grove, CA: Brooks/Cole.

Goldstein, A. P. (Ed.). (1978). *Prescriptions for child mental health and education.* Elmsford, NY: Pergamon.

Goldstein, A. P. (1988). *The Prepare Curriculum: Teaching prosocial competencies.* Champaign, IL: Research Press.

Goldstein, A. P. (1990). *Delinquents on delinquency.* Champaign, IL: Research Press.

Goldstein, A. P. (1991). *Delinquent gangs: A psychological perspective.* Champaign, IL: Research Press.

Goldstein, A. P., & Glick, B. (1987). *Aggression Replacement Training: A comprehensive intervention for aggressive youth.* Champaign, IL: Research Press.

Goldstein, A. P., & Stein, N. (1976). *Prescriptive psychotherapies.* Elmsford, NY: Pergamon.

Gonzalez, A. (1981). *Mexican/Chicano gangs in Los Angeles: A socio-historical case study.* Unpublished doctoral dissertation, University of California, Berkeley.

Grant, J., & Grant, M. Q. (1959). A group dynamics approach to the treatment of nonconformists in the navy. *Annals of the American Academy of Political and Social Sciences, 322,* 126–135.

Hagedorn, J. (1988). *People and folks: Gangs, crime and the underclass in a rustbelt city.* Chicago: Lake View.

Hanson, B., Beschner, G., Walters, J. M., & Bovelle, E. (1985). *Life with heroin: Voices from the inner city.* Lexington MA: Lexington.

Hanson, K. (1964). *Rebels in the streets: The story of New York's girl gangs.* Englewood Cliffs, NJ: Prentice-Hall.

Harrison, R. M., & Mueller, P. (1964). *Clue hunting about group counseling and parole outcome.* Sacramento: California Department of Corrections.

Helmreich, W. B. (1973). Race, sex and gangs. *Society, 11,* 44–50.

Horowitz, R. (1983). *Honor and the American dream.* New Brunswick, NJ: Rutgers University Press.

Howard, A., & Scott, R. A. (1981). The study of minority groups in complex societies. In R. H. Monroe, R. L. Monroe, & B. B. Whiting (Eds.), *Handbook of cross-cultural human development.* New York: Garland.

Huff, C. R. (1990). *Gangs in America.* Newbury Park, CA: Sage.

Hunt, D. E. (1972). Matching models for teacher training. In B. R. Joyce & M. Weil (Eds.), *Perspectives for reform in teacher education.* Englewood Cliffs, NJ: Prentice-Hall.

Jankowski, M. S. (1991). *Islands in the street: Gangs and American urban society.* Berkeley: University of California Press.

Jenkins, R. L., & Brown, W. K. (1988). *The abandonment of delinquent behavior.* New York: Praeger.

Jesness, C. (1965). *The Fricot Ranch Study.* Sacramento: California Department of the Youth Authority.

Kaplan, D. E., & Dubro, A. (1986). *Yakuza: The explosive account of Japan's criminal underworld.* Reading, MA: Addison-Wesley.

Kazdin, A. (1980). *Research designs in clinical psychology.* New York: Harper & Row.

Keiser, R. L. (1969). *The Vice Lords: Warriors of the streets.* New York: Holt, Rinehart & Winston.

Keith, C. R. (1984). Individual psychotherapy and psychoanalysis with the aggressive adolescent: A historical review. In C. R. Keith (Ed.), *The aggressive adolescent.* New York: Free Press.

Keller, F. S. (1966). A personal course in psychology. In R. Ulrich, T. Stachnik, & J. Mabry (Eds.), *Control of human behavior.* Glenview, IL: Scott, Foresman.

Kiesler, D. J. (1969). A grid model for theory and research. In L. D. Eron & R. Callahan (Eds.), *The relation of theory to practice in psychotherapy.* Chicago: Aldine.

Klausmeier, H. J., Rossmiller, R. A., & Sailey, M. (1977). *Individually guided elementary education.* New York: Academic.

Klein, M. W. (1968). Impressions of juvenile gang members. *Adolescence, 3,* 53–78.

Kleiner, R. J., Holger, R. S., & Lanahan, J. (1975). A study of Black youth groups: Implications for research, action, and the role of the investigator. *Human Organization, 34,* 391–394.

Knight, D. (1969). *The Marshall Program—Assessment of a short-term institutional treatment program* (Research Report No. 56). Sacramento: California Department of the Youth Authority.

Kochman, T. (1981). *Black and White styles in conflict.* University of Chicago Press.

Kotlowitz, A. (1991). *There are no children here.* New York: Doubleday.

Kratcoski, P. C., & Kratcoski, M. A. (1975). Changing patterns in the delinquent activities of boys and girls: A self-reported delinquency analysis. *Adolescence, 10,* 83–91.

Krathwohl, D. R. (1985). *Social and behavioral science research.* San Francisco: Jossey-Bass.

Kulik, J. A., Stein, K. B., & Sarbin, T. R. (1968). Disclosure of delinquent behavior under conditions of anonymity and nonanonymity. *Journal of Consulting and Clinical Psychology, 32,* 506–509.

Levin, G. K., Trabka, S., & Kahn, E. M. (1984). Group therapy with aggressive and delinquent adolescents. In C. R. Keith (Ed.), *The aggressive adolescent.* New York: Free Press.

Magaro, P. A. (1969). A prescriptive treatment model based upon social class and premorbid adjustment. *Psychotherapy: Theory, Research and Practice, 6,* 57–70.

Martin, S. E., Sechrest, L., & Redner, R. (1981). *New directions in the rehabilitation of criminal offenders.* Washington, DC: National Academy Press.

Meltzer, M. (1980). *The Chinese Americans.* New York: Crowell.

Miller, W. B. (1990). Why the United States has failed to solve its youth gang problem. In C. R. Huff (Ed.), *Gangs in America.* Newbury Park, CA: Sage.

Mirande, A. (1987). *Gringo justice.* Notre Dame, IN: University of Notre Dame Press.

Monroe, S., & Goldman, P. (1988). *Brothers: Black and poor—A true story of courage and survival.* New York: William Morrow.

Moore, J. W., Garcia, R., Garcia, C., Cerda, L., & Valencia, F. (1978). *Homeboys, gangs, drugs, and prison in the barrios of Los Angeles.* Philadelphia: Temple University Press.

Mulvey, E. P., & LaRosa, J. F. (1986). Delinquency cessation and adolescent development: Preliminary data. *American Journal of Orthopsychiatry, 56,* 212–224.

Needle, J. A., & Stapleton, W. V. (1982). *Police handling of youth gangs.* Washington, DC: National Juvenile Justice Assessment Center.

New York State Division for Youth. (1990). *Reaffirming prevention: Report of the Task Force on Juvenile Gangs.* Albany, NY: Author.

Palmer, T. B. (1973). Matching worker and client in corrections. *Social Work, 18,* 95–103.

Pines, M. (1979, March). Superkids. *Psychology Today,* pp. 53–63.

President's Commission on Organized Crime. (1985). *Organized crime of Asian origin.* Washington, DC: U. S. Government Printing Office.

Quicker, J. C. (1983). *Homegirls: Characterizing Chicana gangs.* San Pedro, CA: International Universities Press.

Ramirez, M. (1983). *Psychology of the Americas.* Elmsford, NY: Pergamon.

Roberts, H. B. (1987). *The inner world of the Black juvenile delinquent.* Hillsdale, NJ: Erlbaum.

Ross, H. L., & Glasser, E. M. (1973). Making it out of the ghetto. *Professional Psychology, 4,* 347–356.

Schwartz, B. N., & Disch, R. (1970). *White racism.* New York: Dell.

Schwitzgebel, R. L., & Kolb, D. A. (1964). Inducing behavior change in adolescent delinquents. *Behavior Research and Therapy, 1,* 297–304.

Shannon, L. W. (1988). *Criminal career continuity.* New York: Human Sciences Press.

Shaw, C. R. (1966). *The jack-roller: A delinquent boy's own story.* University of Chicago Press. (Original work published 1930)

Short, J. F., & Nye, F. I. (1957). Reported behavior as a criterion of deviant behavior. *Social Problems, 5,* 207–213.

Silverstein, B., & Krate, R. (1975). *Children of the dark ghetto.* New York: Praeger.

Slack, C. W. (1960). Experimenter-subject psychotherapy: A new method of introducing intensive office treatment for unreachable cases. *Mental Hygiene, 44,* 238–256.

Spergel, I. A. (1991). *Youth gangs: Problems and response.* Washington, DC: U. S. Department of Justice, Office of Juvenile Justice and Delinquency Prevention.

Stein, N., & Bogin, D. (1978). Individual child psychotherapy. In A. P. Goldstein (Ed.), *Prescriptions for child mental health and education.* Elmsford, NY: Pergamon.

Strodtbeck, F. L., Short, J. F., & Kolegar, E. (1962). The analysis of self-descriptions by members of delinquent gangs. *Sociological Quarterly, 3,* 331–356.

Taylor, C. S. (1990). *Dangerous society.* East Lansing: Michigan State University Press.

Trojanowicz, R. C., & Morash, M. (1987). *Juvenile delinquency: Concepts and control.* Englewood Cliffs, NJ: Prentice-Hall.

Vigil, J. D. (1983). Chicano gangs: One response to Mexican urban adaptation in the Los Angeles area. *Urban Anthropology, 12,* 45–75.

Vigil, J. D. (1988). *Barrio gangs: Street life and identity in southern California.* Austin: University of Texas Press.

Warren, M. Q. (1974, April). *Classification for treatment.* Paper presented at the Seminar on the Classification of Criminal Behavior, National Institute of Law Enforcement and Criminal Justice, Washington, DC.

Werner, E. E., & Smith, R. S. (1982). *Vulnerable but invincible: A study of resilient children.* New York: McGraw-Hill.

White, J. L. (1984). *The psychology of Blacks.* Englewood Cliffs, NJ: Prentice-Hall.

Williams, T. (1989). *The cocaine kids.* Reading, MA: Addison-Wesley.

Williams, T., & Kornblum, W. (1985). *Growing up poor.* Lexington, MA: Lexington.

Wilson, R. W. (1970). *Learning to be Chinese.* Cambridge, MA: MIT Press.

Yablonsky, L. (1967). *The violent gang.* New York: Penguin.

Author Index

Subject Index

About the Editors

Arnold P. Goldstein joined the clinical psychology section of Syracuse University's Psychology Department in 1963 and both taught there and directed its Psychotherapy Center until 1980. In 1981, he founded the Center for Research on Aggression, which he currently directs. He joined Syracuse University's Division of Special Education in 1985 and in 1990 helped organize and codirect the New York State Task Force on Juvenile Gangs. Dr. Goldstein has a career-long interest, as both researcher and practitioner, in difficult-to-reach clients. Since 1980, his main research and psychoeducational focus has been juvenile offenders. He is the developer of psychoeducational programs and curricula designed to teach prosocial behaviors to chronically antisocial persons. Dr. Goldstein's many books include, among others, *Aggression Replacement Training: A Comprehensive Intervention for Aggressive Youth; Changing the Abusive Parent; The Prepare Curriculum: Teaching Prosocial Competencies; Refusal Skills: Preventing Drug Use in Adolescents; Skillstreaming the Adolescent: A Structured Learning Approach to Teaching Prosocial Skills; Delinquents on Delinquency;* and *Delinquent Gangs: A Psychological Perspective.*

C. Ronald Huff is Director of the Criminal Justice Research Center and a professor of public policy and management at The Ohio State University, Columbus. Dr. Huff taught at the University of California at Irvine and at Purdue University before joining the Ohio State faculty in 1979. Prior to his academic career, he held professional positions in corrections, mental health, and children's services. He frequently serves as a consultant to governmental and private sector organizations, including recent consulting on gangs with the U. S. Department of Justice, the FBI National Academy, the U. S. Senate Judiciary Committee, the U. S. Department of Health and Human Services, the State of Hawaii, and Price Waterhouse. His publications include more than 40 journal articles and book chapters and seven books, including the present volume and *Gangs in America* (Sage, 1990). Dr. Huff is currently completing additional research on gangs with grants awarded by the National Institute of Justice and the Ohio Governor's Office of Criminal Justice Services. He is the 1992 recipient of the Donald R. Cressey Award for distinguished contributions to criminology and justice, presented by the National Council on Crime and Delinquency.

About the Contributors

Joanne Y. Corsica is a postdoctoral research fellow with the Alcohol Research Group/Prevention Research Center, School of Public Health, University of California at Berkeley.

G. David Curry is an associate professor of sociology at West Virginia University.

William S. Davidson II is a professor of ecological-community psychology and Director of the Adolescent Diversion Project at Michigan State University.

Elaine B. Duxbury is Chief of Research for the California Department of the Youth Authority.

Loren A. Evenrud is a Police Sergeant with the Minneapolis Park Police, Minneapolis, Minnesota.

Michael Genelin is the Head Deputy of the Hardcore Gang Division in the Los Angeles District Attorney's Office and Chairperson of the California District Attorney's Association Gang Violence Committee.

John C. Gibbs is a professor of developmental psychology at The Ohio State University, Columbus.

Clive R. Hollin is a Senior Lecturer in Psychology at the University of Birmingham, United Kingdom, and Research Psychologist with the Youth Treatment Service.

Arthur M. Horne is Head of the Department of Counseling and Human Services and Director of Training in Counseling Psychology at the University of Georgia, Athens.

Donald W. Kodluboy is a psychologist with the Minneapolis Public School System.

Rick Lovell is an associate professor of criminal justice in the School of Social Welfare, University of Wisconsin at Milwaukee.

Wesley D. McBride is a member of the Los Angeles County Sheriff's Department. He is the operations sergeant for Operation Safe Streets, the Sheriff's Department's gang detail, and the president of the California Gang Investigators Association.

Carl E. Pope is a professor of criminal justice at the University of Wisconsin at Milwaukee.

Kurt M. Ribisl is a doctoral candidate in ecological-community psychology at Michigan State University.

Fernando I. Soriano is currently a visiting professor in psychology and education at Stanford University. He holds an appointment in the Department of Behavioral Science in the School of Dentistry at the University of Missouri at Kansas City.

Irving A. Spergel is George Herbert Jones Professor in the School of Social Service Administration and an associate member of the Department of Sociology, University of Chicago.

Ronald D. Stephens is Executive Director of the National School Safety Center and serves as professor of education at Pepperdine University's Graduate School of Education and Psychology.